Data Algorithms

Mahmoud Parsian

Beijing · Boston · Farnham · Sebastopol · Tokyo

Data Algorithms

by Mahmoud Parsian

Copyright © 2015 Mahmoud Parsian. All rights reserved.

Printed in the United States of America.

Published by O'Reilly Media, Inc., 1005 Gravenstein Highway North, Sebastopol, CA 95472.

O'Reilly books may be purchased for educational, business, or sales promotional use. Online editions are also available for most titles (*http://safaribooksonline.com*). For more information, contact our corporate/institutional sales department: 800-998-9938 or *corporate@oreilly.com*.

Editors: Ann Spencer and Marie Beaugureau
Production Editor: Matthew Hacker
Copyeditor: Rachel Monaghan
Proofreader: Rachel Head

Indexer: Judith McConville
Interior Designer: David Futato
Cover Designer: Ellie Volckhausen
Illustrator: Rebecca Demarest

July 2015:   First Edition

Revision History for the First Edition
2015-07-10:   First Release

See *http://oreilly.com/catalog/errata.csp?isbn=9781491906187* for release details.

978-1-491-90618-7

[LSI]

This book is dedicated to my dear family:
wife, Behnaz,
daughter, Maral,
son, Yaseen

Table of Contents

Foreword. xix

Preface. xxi

1. Secondary Sort: Introduction. 1
   Solutions to the Secondary Sort Problem   3
      Implementation Details   3
      Data Flow Using Plug-in Classes   6
   MapReduce/Hadoop Solution to Secondary Sort   7
      Input   7
      Expected Output   7
      map() Function   8
      reduce() Function   8
      Hadoop Implementation Classes   9
      Sample Run of Hadoop Implementation   10
      How to Sort in Ascending or Descending Order   12
   Spark Solution to Secondary Sort   12
      Time Series as Input   12
      Expected Output   13
      Option 1: Secondary Sorting in Memory   13
      Spark Sample Run   20
      Option #2: Secondary Sorting Using the Spark Framework   24
      Further Reading on Secondary Sorting   25

2. Secondary Sort: A Detailed Example. 27
   Secondary Sorting Technique   28
   Complete Example of Secondary Sorting   32
      Input Format   32

Output Format   33
Composite Key   33
Sample Run—Old Hadoop API   36
Input   36
Running the MapReduce Job   37
Output   37
Sample Run—New Hadoop API   37
Input   38
Running the MapReduce Job   38
Output   39

3. Top 10 List **41**
Top N, Formalized   42
MapReduce/Hadoop Implementation: Unique Keys   43
Implementation Classes in MapReduce/Hadoop   47
Top 10 Sample Run   47
Finding the Top 5   49
Finding the Bottom 10   49
Spark Implementation: Unique Keys   50
RDD Refresher   50
Spark's Function Classes   51
Review of the Top N Pattern for Spark   52
Complete Spark Top 10 Solution   53
Sample Run: Finding the Top 10   58
Parameterizing Top N   59
Finding the Bottom N   61
Spark Implementation: Nonunique Keys   62
Complete Spark Top 10 Solution   64
Sample Run   72
Spark Top 10 Solution Using takeOrdered()   73
Complete Spark Implementation   74
Finding the Bottom N   79
Alternative to Using takeOrdered()   80
MapReduce/Hadoop Top 10 Solution: Nonunique Keys   81
Sample Run   82

4. Left Outer Join **85**
Left Outer Join Example   85
Example Queries   87
Implementation of Left Outer Join in MapReduce   88
MapReduce Phase 1: Finding Product Locations   88
MapReduce Phase 2: Counting Unique Locations   92

Implementation Classes in Hadoop   93
Sample Run   93
Spark Implementation of Left Outer Join   95
Spark Program   97
Running the Spark Solution   104
Running Spark on YARN   106
Spark Implementation with leftOuterJoin()   107
Spark Program   109
Sample Run on YARN   116

5. Order Inversion. 119
Example of the Order Inversion Pattern   120
MapReduce/Hadoop Implementation of the Order Inversion Pattern   122
Custom Partitioner   123
Relative Frequency Mapper   124
Relative Frequency Reducer   126
Implementation Classes in Hadoop   127
Sample Run   127
Input   127
Running the MapReduce Job   127
Generated Output   128

6. Moving Average. 131
Example 1: Time Series Data (Stock Prices)   131
Example 2: Time Series Data (URL Visits)   132
Formal Definition   133
POJO Moving Average Solutions   134
Solution 1: Using a Queue   134
Solution 2: Using an Array   135
Testing the Moving Average   136
Sample Run   136
MapReduce/Hadoop Moving Average Solution   137
Input   137
Output   137
Option #1: Sorting in Memory   138
Sample Run   141
Option #2: Sorting Using the MapReduce Framework   143
Sample Run   147

7. Market Basket Analysis. 151
MBA Goals   151
Application Areas for MBA   153

Market Basket Analysis Using MapReduce 153
    Input 154
    Expected Output for Tuple2 (Order of 2) 155
    Expected Output for Tuple3 (Order of 3) 155
    Informal Mapper 155
    Formal Mapper 156
    Reducer 157
    MapReduce/Hadoop Implementation Classes 158
    Sample Run 162
Spark Solution 163
    MapReduce Algorithm Workflow 165
    Input 166
    Spark Implementation 166
    YARN Script for Spark 178
    Creating Item Sets from Transactions 178

8. Common Friends. **181**
Input 182
POJO Common Friends Solution 182
MapReduce Algorithm 183
    The MapReduce Algorithm in Action 184
Solution 1: Hadoop Implementation Using Text 187
    Sample Run for Solution 1 187
Solution 2: Hadoop Implementation Using ArrayListOfLongsWritable 189
    Sample Run for Solution 2 189
Spark Solution 190
    Spark Program 191
    Sample Run of Spark Program 197

9. Recommendation Engines Using MapReduce. **201**
Customers Who Bought This Item Also Bought 202
    Input 202
    Expected Output 202
    MapReduce Solution 203
Frequently Bought Together 206
    Input and Expected Output 207
    MapReduce Solution 208
Recommend Connection 211
    Input 213
    Output 214
    MapReduce Solution 214
    Spark Implementation 216

Sample Run of Spark Program   222

10. Content-Based Recommendation: Movies. 227
   Input   228
   MapReduce Phase 1   229
   MapReduce Phases 2 and 3   229
      MapReduce Phase 2: Mapper   230
      MapReduce Phase 2: Reducer   231
      MapReduce Phase 3: Mapper   233
      MapReduce Phase 3: Reducer   234
      Similarity Measures   236
   Movie Recommendation Implementation in Spark   236
      High-Level Solution in Spark   237
      Sample Run of Spark Program   250

11. Smarter Email Marketing with the Markov Model. 257
   Markov Chains in a Nutshell   258
   Markov Model Using MapReduce   261
      Generating Time-Ordered Transactions with MapReduce   262
      Hadoop Solution 1: Time-Ordered Transactions   263
      Hadoop Solution 2: Time-Ordered Transactions   264
      Generating State Sequences   268
      Generating a Markov State Transition Matrix with MapReduce 271
      Using the Markov Model to Predict the Next Smart Email Marketing Date 274
   Spark Solution   275
      Input Format   275
      High-Level Steps   276
      Spark Program   277
      Script to Run the Spark Program   286
      Sample Run   287

12. K-Means Clustering. 289
   What Is K-Means Clustering?   292
   Application Areas for Clustering   292
   Informal K-Means Clustering Method: Partitioning Approach   293
   K-Means Distance Function   294
   K-Means Clustering Formalized   295
   MapReduce Solution for K-Means Clustering   295
      MapReduce Solution: map()   297
      MapReduce Solution: combine()   298
      MapReduce Solution: reduce()   299
   K-Means Implementation by Spark   300

Sample Run of Spark K-Means Implementation   302

13. k-Nearest Neighbors. **305**
kNN Classification   306
Distance Functions   307
kNN Example   308
An Informal kNN Algorithm   308
Formal kNN Algorithm   309
Java-like Non-MapReduce Solution for kNN   309
kNN Implementation in Spark   311
    Formalizing kNN for the Spark Implementation   312
    Input Data Set Formats   313
    Spark Implementation   313
    YARN shell script   325

14. Naive Bayes. **327**
Training and Learning Examples   328
    Numeric Training Data   328
    Symbolic Training Data   329
Conditional Probability   331
The Naive Bayes Classifier in Depth   331
    Naive Bayes Classifier Example   332
The Naive Bayes Classifier: MapReduce Solution for Symbolic Data   334
    Stage 1: Building a Classifier Using Symbolic Training Data   335
    Stage 2: Using the Classifier to Classify New Symbolic Data   341
The Naive Bayes Classifier: MapReduce Solution for Numeric Data   343
Naive Bayes Classifier Implementation in Spark   345
    Stage 1: Building a Classifier Using Training Data   346
    Stage 2: Using the Classifier to Classify New Data   355
Using Spark and Mahout   361
    Apache Spark   361
    Apache Mahout   362

15. Sentiment Analysis. **363**
Sentiment Examples   364
Sentiment Scores: Positive or Negative   364
A Simple MapReduce Sentiment Analysis Example   365
    map() Function for Sentiment Analysis   366
    reduce() Function for Sentiment Analysis   367
Sentiment Analysis in the Real World   367

16. Finding, Counting, and Listing All Triangles in Large Graphs. **369**

Basic Graph Concepts   370
Importance of Counting Triangles   372
MapReduce/Hadoop Solution   372
  Step 1: MapReduce in Action   373
  Step 2: Identify Triangles   375
  Step 3: Remove Duplicate Triangles   376
  Hadoop Implementation Classes   377
  Sample Run   377
Spark Solution   380
  High-Level Steps   380
  Sample Run   387

17. K-mer Counting. **391**

Input Data for K-mer Counting   392
  Sample Data for K-mer Counting   392
Applications of K-mer Counting   392
K-mer Counting Solution in MapReduce/Hadoop   393
  The map() Function   393
  The reduce() Function   394
  Hadoop Implementation Classes   394
K-mer Counting Solution in Spark   395
  Spark Solution   396
  Sample Run   405

18. DNA Sequencing. **407**

Input Data for DNA Sequencing   409
Input Data Validation   410
DNA Sequence Alignment   411
MapReduce Algorithms for DNA Sequencing   412
  Step 1: Alignment   415
  Step 2: Recalibration   423
  Step 3: Variant Detection   428

19. Cox Regression. **433**

The Cox Model in a Nutshell   434
  Cox Regression Basic Terminology   435
Cox Regression Using R   436
  Expression Data   436
Cox Regression Application   437
Cox Regression POJO Solution   437
Input for MapReduce   439

Input Format   440
Cox Regression Using MapReduce   440
  Cox Regression Phase 1: map()   440
  Cox Regression Phase 1: reduce()   441
  Cox Regression Phase 2: map()   442
  Sample Output Generated by Phase 1 reduce() Function   444
  Sample Output Generated by the Phase 2 map() Function   445
  Cox Regression Script for MapReduce   445

20. Cochran-Armitage Test for Trend. **447**
Cochran-Armitage Algorithm   448
Application of Cochran-Armitage   454
MapReduce Solution   456
  Input   456
  Expected Output   457
  Mapper   458
  Reducer   459
  MapReduce/Hadoop Implementation Classes   463
  Sample Run   463

21. Allelic Frequency. **465**
Basic Definitions   466
  Chromosome   466
  Bioset   467
  Allele and Allelic Frequency   467
  Source of Data for Allelic Frequency   467
  Allelic Frequency Analysis Using Fisher's Exact Test   469
  Fisher's Exact Test   469
Formal Problem Statement   471
MapReduce Solution for Allelic Frequency   471
MapReduce Solution, Phase 1   472
  Input   472
  Output/Result   473
  Phase 1 Mapper   474
  Phase 1 Reducer   475
  Sample Run of Phase 1 MapReduce/Hadoop Implementation   479
  Sample Plot of P-Values   481
MapReduce Solution, Phase 2   482
  Phase 2 Mapper for Bottom 100 P-Values   482
  Phase 2 Reducer for Bottom 100 P-Values   484
  Is Our Bottom 100 List a Monoid?   485
  Hadoop Implementation Classes for Bottom 100 List   486

MapReduce Solution, Phase 3 486
    Phase 3 Mapper for Bottom 100 P-Values 487
    Phase 3 Reducer for Bottom 100 P-Values 489
    Hadoop Implementation Classes for Bottom 100 List for Each
      Chromosome 490
Special Handling of Chromosomes X and Y 490

22. The T-Test. 491
Performing the T-Test on Biosets 492
MapReduce Problem Statement 495
Input 496
Expected Output 496
MapReduce Solution 496
    Hadoop Implementation Classes 499
Spark Implementation 499
    High-Level Steps 500
    T-Test Algorithm 507
    Sample Run 509

23. Pearson Correlation. 513
Pearson Correlation Formula 514
Pearson Correlation Example 516
Data Set for Pearson Correlation 517
POJO Solution for Pearson Correlation 517
POJO Solution Test Drive 518
MapReduce Solution for Pearson Correlation 519
    map() Function for Pearson Correlation 519
    reduce() Function for Pearson Correlation 520
Hadoop Implementation Classes 521
Spark Solution for Pearson Correlation 522
    Input 523
    Output 523
    Spark Solution 524
    High-Level Steps 525
    Step 1: Import required classes and interfaces 527
    smaller() method 528
    MutableDouble class 529
    toMap() method 530
    toListOfString() method 530
    readBiosets() method 531
    Step 2: Handle input parameters 532
    Step 3: Create a Spark context object 533

Step 4: Create list of input files/biomarkers 534
Step 5: Broadcast reference as global shared object 534
Step 6: Read all biomarkers from HDFS and create the first RDD 534
Step 7: Filter biomarkers by reference 535
Step 8: Create (Gene-ID, (Patient-ID, Gene-Value)) pairs 536
Step 9: Group by gene 537
Step 10: Create Cartesian product of all genes 538
Step 11: Filter redundant pairs of genes 538
Step 12: Calculate Pearson correlation and p-value 539
Pearson Correlation Wrapper Class 542
Testing the Pearson Class 543
Pearson Correlation Using R 543
YARN Script to Run Spark Program 544
Spearman Correlation Using Spark 544
Spearman Correlation Wrapper Class 544
Testing the Spearman Correlation Wrapper Class 545

24. DNA Base Count... 547
FASTA Format 548
FASTA Format Example 549
FASTQ Format 549
FASTQ Format Example 549
MapReduce Solution: FASTA Format 550
Reading FASTA Files 550
MapReduce FASTA Solution: map() 550
MapReduce FASTA Solution: reduce() 551
Sample Run 552
Log of sample run 552
Generated output 552
Custom Sorting 553
Custom Partitioning 554
MapReduce Solution: FASTQ Format 556
Reading FASTQ Files 557
MapReduce FASTQ Solution: map() 558
MapReduce FASTQ Solution: reduce() 559
Hadoop Implementation Classes: FASTQ Format 560
Sample Run 560
Spark Solution: FASTA Format 561
High-Level Steps 561
Sample Run 564
Spark Solution: FASTQ Format 566
High-Level Steps 566

Step 1: Import required classes and interfaces   567
Step 2: Handle input parameters   567
Step 3: Create a JavaPairRDD from FASTQ input   568
Step 4: Map partitions   568
Step 5: Collect all DNA base counts   569
Step 6: Emit Final Counts   570
Sample Run   570

25. RNA Sequencing. **573**
Data Size and Format   574
MapReduce Workflow   574
  Input Data Validation   574
RNA Sequencing Analysis Overview   575
MapReduce Algorithms for RNA Sequencing   578
  Step 1: MapReduce TopHat Mapping   579
  Step 2: MapReduce Calling Cuffdiff   582

26. Gene Aggregation. **585**
Input   586
Output   586
MapReduce Solutions (Filter by Individual and by Average)   587
  Mapper: Filter by Individual   588
  Reducer: Filter by Individual   590
  Mapper: Filter by Average   590
  Reducer: Filter by Average   592
  Computing Gene Aggregation   592
  Hadoop Implementation Classes   594
  Analysis of Output   597
Gene Aggregation in Spark   600
Spark Solution: Filter by Individual   601
  Sharing Data Between Cluster Nodes   601
  High-Level Steps   602
  Utility Functions   607
  Sample Run   609
Spark Solution: Filter by Average   610
  High-Level Steps   611
  Utility Functions   616
  Sample Run   619

27. Linear Regression. **621**
Basic Definitions   622
Simple Example   622

Problem Statement   624
Input Data   625
Expected Output   625
MapReduce Solution Using SimpleRegression   626
Hadoop Implementation Classes   628
MapReduce Solution Using R's Linear Model   629
Phase 1   630
Phase 2   633
Hadoop Implementation Using Classes   635

28. MapReduce and Monoids. 637
Introduction   637
Definition of Monoid   639
How to Form a Monoid   640
Monoidic and Non-Monoidic Examples   640
Maximum over a Set of Integers   641
Subtraction over a Set of Integers   641
Addition over a Set of Integers   641
Multiplication over a Set of Integers   641
Mean over a Set of Integers   642
Non-Commutative Example   642
Median over a Set of Integers   642
Concatenation over Lists   642
Union/Intersection over Integers   643
Functional Example   643
Matrix Example   644
MapReduce Example: Not a Monoid   644
MapReduce Example: Monoid   646
Hadoop Implementation Classes   647
Sample Run   648
View Hadoop output   650
Spark Example Using Monoids   650
High-Level Steps   652
Sample Run   656
Conclusion on Using Monoids   657
Functors and Monoids   658

29. The Small Files Problem. 661
Solution 1: Merging Small Files Client-Side   662
Input Data   665
Solution with SmallFilesConsolidator   665
Solution Without SmallFilesConsolidator   667

  Solution 2: Solving the Small Files Problem with CombineFileInputFormat   668
    Custom CombineFileInputFormat   672
    Sample Run Using CustomCFIF   672
  Alternative Solutions   674

30. Huge Cache for MapReduce. **675**
  Implementation Options   676
  Formalizing the Cache Problem   677
  An Elegant, Scalable Solution   678
  Implementing the LRUMap Cache   681
    Extending the LRUMap Class   681
    Testing the Custom Class   682
    The MapDBEntry Class   683
    Using MapDB   684
    Testing MapDB: put()   686
    Testing MapDB: get()   687
  MapReduce Using the LRUMap Cache   687
    CacheManager Definition   688
    Initializing the Cache   689
    Using the Cache   690
    Closing the Cache   691

31. The Bloom Filter. **693**
  Bloom Filter Properties   693
  A Simple Bloom Filter Example   696
  Bloom Filters in Guava Library   696
  Using Bloom Filters in MapReduce   698

A. Bioset. **699**

B. Spark RDDs. **701**

Bibliography. **721**

Index. **725**

Foreword

Unlocking the power of the genome is a powerful notion—one that intimates knowledge, understanding, and the ability of science and technology to be transformative. But transformation requires alignment and synergy, and synergy almost always requires deep collaboration. From scientists to software engineers, and from academia into the clinic, we will need to work together to pave the way for our genetically empowered future.

The creation of data algorithms that analyze the information generated from large-scale genetic sequencing studies is key. Genetic variations are diverse; they can be complex and novel, compounded by a need to connect them to an individual's physical presentation in a meaningful way for clinical insights to be gained and applied. Accelerating our ability to do this at scale, across populations of individuals, is critical. The methods in this book serve as a compass for the road ahead.

MapReduce, Hadoop, and Spark are key technologies that will help us scale the use of genetic sequencing, enabling us to store, process, and analyze the "big data" of genomics. Mahmoud's book covers these topics in a simple and practical manner. *Data Algorithms* illuminates the way for data scientists, software engineers, and ultimately clinicians to unlock the power of the genome, helping to move human health into an era of precision, personalization, and transformation.

> —*Jay Flatley*
> *CEO, Illumina Inc.*

Preface

With the development of massive search engines (such as Google and Yahoo!), genomic analysis (in DNA sequencing, RNA sequencing, and biomarker analysis), and social networks (such as Facebook and Twitter), the volumes of data being generated and processed have crossed the petabytes threshold. To satisfy these massive computational requirements, we need efficient, scalable, and parallel algorithms. One framework to tackle these problems is the MapReduce paradigm.

MapReduce is a software framework for processing large (giga-, tera-, or petabytes) data sets in a parallel and distributed fashion, and an execution framework for large-scale data processing on clusters of commodity servers. There are many ways to implement MapReduce, but in this book our primary focus will be Apache Spark and MapReduce/Hadoop. You will learn how to implement MapReduce in Spark and Hadoop through simple and concrete examples.

This book provides essential distributed algorithms (implemented in MapReduce, Hadoop, and Spark) in the following areas, and the chapters are organized accordingly:

- Basic design patterns
- Data mining and machine learning
- Bioinformatics, genomics, and statistics
- Optimization techniques

What Is MapReduce?

MapReduce is a programming paradigm that allows for massive scalability across hundreds or thousands of servers in a cluster environment. The term *MapReduce* originated from functional programming and was introduced by Google in a paper called "MapReduce: Simplified Data Processing on Large Clusters." Google's

MapReduce[8] implementation is a proprietary solution and has not yet been released to the public.

A simple view of the MapReduce process is illustrated in Figure P-1. Simply put, MapReduce is about scalability. Using the MapReduce paradigm, you focus on writing two functions:

map()
   Filters and aggregates data

reduce()
   Reduces, groups, and summarizes by keys generated by map()

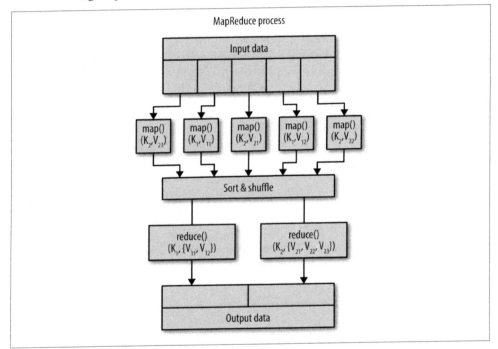

Figure P-1. The simple view of the MapReduce process

These two functions can be defined as follows:

map() *function*
   The master node takes the input, partitions it into smaller data chunks, and distributes them to worker (slave) nodes. The worker nodes apply the same transformation function to each data chunk, then pass the results back to the master node. In MapReduce, the programmer defines a mapper with the following signature:

```
map(): (Key₁, Value₁) → [(Key₂, Value₂)]
```

reduce() *function*

The master node shuffles and clusters the received results based on unique key-value pairs; then, through another redistribution to the workers/slaves, these values are combined via another type of transformation function. In MapReduce, the programmer defines a reducer with the following signature:

```
reduce(): (Key₂, [Value₂]) → [(Key₃, Value₃)]
```

 In informal presentations of the map() and reduce() functions throughout this book, I've used square brackets, [], to denote a list.

In Figure P-1, input data is partitioned into small chunks (here we have five input partitions), and each chunk is sent to a mapper. Each mapper may generate any number of key-value pairs. The mappers' output is illustrated by Table P-1.

Table P-1. Mappers' output

Key	Value
K_1	V_{11}
K_2	V_{21}
K_1	V_{12}
K_2	V_{22}
K_2	V_{23}

In this example, all mappers generate only two unique keys: $\{K_1, K_2\}$. When all mappers are completed, the keys are sorted, shuffled, grouped, and sent to reducers. Finally, the reducers generate the desired outputs. For this example, we have two reducers identified by $\{K_1, K_2\}$ keys (illustrated by Table P-2).

Table P-2. Reducers' input

Key	Value
K_1	$\{V_{11}, V_{12}\}$
K_2	$\{V_{21}, V_{22}, V_{23}\}$

Once all mappers are completed, the reducers start their execution process. Each reducer may create as an output any number—zero or more—of new key-value pairs.

When writing your map() and reduce() functions, you need to make sure that your solution is scalable. For example, if you are utilizing any data structure (such as List, Array, or HashMap) that will not easily fit into the memory of a commodity server, then your solution is not scalable. Note that your map() and reduce() functions will be executing in basic commodity servers, which might have 32 GB or 64 GB of RAM at most (note that this is just an example; today's servers have 256 GB or 512 GB of RAM, and in the next few years basic servers might have even 1 TB of RAM). Scalability is therefore the heart of MapReduce. If your MapReduce solution does not scale well, you should not call it a MapReduce solution. Here, when we talk about scalability, we mean scaling out (the term *scale out* means to add more commodity nodes to a system). MapReduce is mainly about scaling out (as opposed to *scaling up*, which means adding resources such as memory and CPUs to a single node). For example, if DNA sequencing takes 60 hours with 3 servers, then scaling out to 50 similar servers might accomplish the same DNA sequencing in less than 2 hours.

The core concept behind MapReduce is mapping your input data set into a collection of key-value pairs, and then reducing over all pairs with the same key. Even though the overall concept is simple, it is actually quite expressive and powerful when you consider that:

- Almost all data can be mapped into key-value pairs.
- Your keys and values may be of any type: Strings, Integers, FASTQ (for DNA sequencing), user-defined custom types, and, of course, key-value pairs themselves.

How does MapReduce scale over a set of servers? The key to how MapReduce works is to take input as, conceptually, a list of records (each single record can be one or more lines of data). Then the input records are split and passed to the many servers in the cluster to be consumed by the map() function. The result of the map() computation is a list of key-value pairs. Then the reduce() function takes each set of values that have the same key and combines them into a single value (or set of values). In other words, the map() function takes a set of data chunks and produces key-value pairs, and reduce() merges the output of the data generated by map(), so that instead of a set of key-value pairs, you get your desired result.

One of the major benefits of MapReduce is its "shared-nothing" data-processing platform. This means that all mappers can work independently, and when mappers complete their tasks, reducers start to work independently (no data or critical region is shared among mappers or reducers; having a critical region will slow distributed computing). This shared-nothing paradigm enables us to write map() and reduce() functions easily and improves parallelism effectively and effortlessly.

Simple Explanation of MapReduce

What is a very simple explanation of MapReduce? Let's say that we want to count the number of books in a library that has 1,000 shelves and report the final result to the librarian. Here are two possible MapReduce solutions:

- Solution #1 (using `map()` and `reduce()`):

  — `map()`: Hire 1,000 workers; each worker counts one shelf.

  — `reduce()`: All workers get together and add up their individual counts (by reporting the results to the librarian).

- Solution #2 (using `map()`, `combine()`, and `reduce()`):

  — `map()`: Hire 1,110 workers (1,000 workers, 100 managers, 10 supervisors—each supervisor manages 10 managers, and each manager manages 10 workers); each worker counts one shelf, and reports its count to its manager.

  — `combine()`: Every 10 managers add up their individual counts and report the total to a supervisor.

  — `reduce()`: All supervisors get together and add up their individual counts (by reporting the results to the librarian).

When to Use MapReduce

Is MapReduce good for everything? The simple answer is no. When we have big data, if we can partition it and each partition can be processed independently, then we can start to think about MapReduce algorithms. For example, graph algorithms do not work very well with MapReduce due to their iterative approach. But if you are grouping or aggregating a lot of data, the MapReduce paradigm works pretty well. To process graphs using MapReduce, you should take a look at the Apache Giraph (*http:// giraph.apache.org/*) and Apache Spark GraphX (*https://spark.apache.org/graphx/*) projects.

Here are other scenarios where MapReduce should not be used:

- If the computation of a value depends on previously computed values. One good example is the Fibonacci series, where each value is a summation of the previous two values:

      F(k + 2) = F(k + 1) + F(k)

- If the data set is small enough to be computed on a single machine. It is better to do this as a single `reduce(map(data))` operation rather than going through the entire MapReduce process.

- If synchronization is required to access shared data.

- If all of your input data fits in memory.
- If one operation depends on other operations.
- If basic computations are processor-intensive.

However, there are many cases where MapReduce is appropriate, such as:

- When you have to handle lots of input data (e.g., aggregate or compute statistics over large amounts of data).
- When you need to take advantage of parallel and distributed computing, data storage, and data locality.
- When you can do many tasks independently without synchronization.
- When you can take advantage of sorting and shuffling.
- When you need fault tolerance and you cannot afford job failures.

What MapReduce Isn't

MapReduce is a groundbreaking technology for distributed computing, but there are a lot of myths about it, some of which are debunked here:

- MapReduce is not a programming language, but rather a framework to develop distributed applications using Java, Scala, and other programming languages.
- MapReduce's distributed filesystem is not a replacement for a relational database management system (such as MySQL or Oracle). Typically, the input to MapReduce is plain-text files (a mapper input record can be one or many lines).
- The MapReduce framework is designed mainly for batch processing, so we should not expect to get the results in under two seconds; however, with proper use of clusters you may achieve near-real-time response.
- MapReduce is not a solution for all software problems.

Why Use MapReduce?

As we've discussed, MapReduce works on the premise of "scaling out" by adding more commodity servers. This is in contrast to "scaling up," by adding more resources, such as memory and CPUs, to a single node in a system); this can be very costly, and at some point you won't be able to add more resources due to cost and software or hardware limits. Many times, there are promising main memory–based algorithms available for solving data problems, but they lack scalability because the main memory is a bottleneck. For example, in DNA sequencing analysis, you might need over 512 GB of RAM, which is very costly and not scalable.

If you need to increase your computational power, you'll need to distribute it across more than one machine. For example, to do DNA sequencing of 500 GB of sample data, it would take one server over four days to complete just the alignment phase; using 60 servers with MapReduce can cut this time to less than two hours. To process large volumes of data, you must be able to split up the data into chunks for processing, which are then recombined later. MapReduce/Hadoop and Spark/Hadoop enable you to increase your computational power by writing just two functions: map() and reduce(). So it's clear that data analytics has a powerful new tool with the MapReduce paradigm, which has recently surged in popularity thanks to open source solutions such as Hadoop.

In a nutshell, MapReduce provides the following benefits:

- Programming model + infrastructure
- The ability to write programs that run on hundreds/thousands of machines
- Automatic parallelization and distribution
- Fault tolerance (if a server dies, the job will be completed by other servers)
- Program/job scheduling, status checking, and monitoring

Hadoop and Spark

Hadoop (*http://hadoop.apache.org/*) is the de facto standard for implementation of MapReduce applications. It is composed of one or more master nodes and any number of slave nodes. Hadoop simplifies distributed applications by saying that "the data center is the computer," and by providing map() and reduce() functions (defined by the programmer) that allow application developers or programmers to utilize those data centers. Hadoop implements the MapReduce paradigm efficiently and is quite simple to learn; it is a powerful tool for processing large amounts of data in the range of terabytes and petabytes.

In this book, most of the MapReduce algorithms are presented in a cookbook format (compiled, complete, and working solutions) and implemented in Java/MapReduce/Hadoop and/or Java/Spark/Hadoop. Both the Hadoop and Spark (*http://spark.apache.org/*) frameworks are open source and enable us to perform a huge volume of computations and data processing in distributed environments.

These frameworks enable scaling by providing "scale-out" methodology. They can be set up to run intensive computations in the MapReduce paradigm on thousands of servers. Spark's API has a higher-level abstraction than Hadoop's API; for this reason, we are able to express Spark solutions in a single Java driver class.

Hadoop and Spark are two different distributed software frameworks. Hadoop is a MapReduce framework on which you may run jobs supporting the `map()`, `combine()`, and `reduce()` functions. The MapReduce paradigm works well at one-pass computation (first `map()`, then `reduce()`), but is inefficient for multipass algorithms. Spark is not a MapReduce framework, but can be easily used to support a MapReduce framework's functionality; it has the proper API to handle `map()` and `reduce()` functionality. Spark is not tied to a map phase and then a reduce phase. A Spark job can be an arbitrary *DAG* (directed acyclic graph) of map and/or reduce/shuffle phases. Spark programs may run with or without Hadoop, and Spark may use *HDFS* (Hadoop Distributed File System) or other persistent storage for input/output. In a nutshell, for a given Spark program or job, the Spark engine creates a DAG of task stages to be performed on the cluster, while Hadoop/MapReduce, on the other hand, creates a DAG with two predefined stages, map and reduce. Note that DAGs created by Spark can contain any number of stages. This allows most Spark jobs to complete faster than they would in Hadoop/MapReduce, with simple jobs completing after just one stage and more complex tasks completing in a single run of many stages, rather than having to be split into multiple jobs. As mentioned, Spark's API is a higher-level abstraction than MapReduce/Hadoop. For example, a few lines of code in Spark might be equivalent to 30–40 lines of code in MapReduce/Hadoop.

Even though frameworks such as Hadoop and Spark are built on a "shared-nothing" paradigm, they do support sharing immutable data structures among all cluster nodes. In Hadoop, you may pass these values to mappers and reducers via Hadoop's `Configuration` object; in Spark, you may share data structures among mappers and reducers by using `Broadcast` objects. In addition to `Broadcast` read-only objects, Spark supports write-only accumulators. Hadoop and Spark provide the following benefits for big data processing:

Reliability
Hadoop and Spark are fault-tolerant (any node can go down without losing the result of the desired computation).

Scalability
Hadoop and Spark support large clusters of servers.

Distributed processing
In Spark and Hadoop, input data and processing are distributed (they support big data from the ground up).

Parallelism
Computations are executed on a cluster of nodes in parallel.

Hadoop is designed mainly for batch processing, while with enough memory/RAM, Spark may be used for near real-time processing. To understand basic usage of Spark RDDs (resilient distributed data sets), see Appendix B.

So what are the core components of MapReduce/Hadoop?

- Input/output data consists of key-value pairs. Typically, keys are integers, longs, and strings, while values can be almost any data type (string, integer, long, sentence, special-format data, etc.).
- Data is partitioned over commodity nodes, filling racks in a data center.
- The software handles failures, restarts, and other interruptions. Known as *fault tolerance*, this is an important feature of Hadoop.

Hadoop and Spark provide more than `map()` and `reduce()` functionality: they provide plug-in model for custom record reading, secondary data sorting, and much more.

A high-level view of the relationship between Spark, YARN, and Hadoop's HDFS is illustrated in Figure P-2.

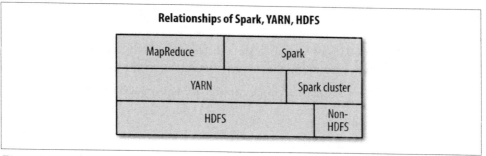

Figure P-2. Relationship between MapReduce, Spark, and HDFS

This relationship shows that there are many ways to run MapReduce and Spark using HDFS (and non-HDFS filesystems). In this book, I will use the following keywords and terminology:

- *MapReduce* refers to the general MapReduce framework paradigm.
- *MapReduce/Hadoop* refers to a specific implementation of the MapReduce framework using Hadoop.
- *Spark* refers to a specific implementation of Spark using HDFS as a persistent storage or a compute engine (note that Spark can run against any data store, but here we focus mostly on Hadoop's):
  — Spark can run without Hadoop using standalone cluster mode (which may use HDFS, NFS, or another medium as a persistent data store).
  — Spark can run with Hadoop using Hadoop's YARN or MapReduce framework.

Using this book, you will learn step by step the algorithms and tools you need to build MapReduce applications with Hadoop. MapReduce/Hadoop has become the programming model of choice for processing large data sets (such as log data, genome sequences, statistical applications, and social graphs). MapReduce can be used for any application that does not require tightly coupled parallel processing. Keep in mind that Hadoop is designed for MapReduce batch processing and is not an ideal solution for real-time processing. Do not expect to get your answers from Hadoop in 2 to 5 seconds; the smallest jobs might take 20+ seconds. Spark is a top-level Apache project that is well suited for near real-time processing, and will perform better with more RAM. With Spark, it is very possible to run a job (such as biomarker analysis or Cox regression) that processes 200 million records in 25 to 35 seconds by just using a cluster of 100 nodes. Typically, Hadoop jobs have a latency of 15 to 20 seconds, but this depends on the size and configuration of the Hadoop cluster.

An implementation of MapReduce (such as Hadoop) runs on a large cluster of commodity machines and is highly scalable. For example, a typical MapReduce computation processes many petabytes or terabytes of data on hundreds or thousands of machines. Programmers find MapReduce easy to use because it hides the messy details of parallelization, fault tolerance, data distribution, and load balancing, letting the programmers focus on writing the two key functions, `map()` and `reduce()`.

The following are some of the major applications of MapReduce/Hadoop/Spark:

- Query log processing
- Crawling, indexing, and search
- Analytics, text processing, and sentiment analysis
- Machine learning (such as Markov chains and the Naive Bayes classifier)
- Recommendation systems
- Document clustering and classification
- Bioinformatics (alignment, recalibration, germline ingestion, and DNA/RNA sequencing)
- Genome analysis (biomarker analysis, and regression algorithms such as linear and Cox)

What Is in This Book?

Each chapter of this book presents a problem and solves it through a set of MapReduce algorithms. MapReduce algorithms/solutions are complete recipes (including the MapReduce driver, mapper, combiner, and reducer programs). You can use the code directly in your projects (although sometimes you may need to cut and paste the sections you need). This book does not cover the theory behind the MapReduce framework, but rather offers practical algorithms and examples using MapReduce/ Hadoop and Spark to solve tough big data problems. Topics covered include:

- Market Basket Analysis for a large set of transactions
- Data mining algorithms (K-Means, kNN, and Naive Bayes)
- DNA sequencing and RNA sequencing using huge genomic data
- Naive Bayes classification and Markov chains for data and market prediction
- Recommendation algorithms and pairwise document similarity
- Linear regression, Cox regression, and Pearson correlation
- Allelic frequency and mining DNA
- Social network analysis (recommendation systems, counting triangles, sentiment analysis)

You may cut and paste the provided solutions from this book to build your own Map-Reduce applications and solutions using Hadoop and Spark. All the solutions have been compiled and tested. This book is ideal for anyone who knows some Java (i.e., can read and write basic Java programs) and wants to write and deploy MapReduce algorithms using Java/Hadoop/Spark. The general topic of MapReduce has been discussed in detail in an excellent book by Jimmy Lin and Chris Dyer[16]; again, the goal of this book is to provide concrete MapReduce algorithms and solutions using Hadoop and Spark. Likewise, this book will not discuss Hadoop itself in detail; Tom White's excellent book[31] does that very well.

This book will not cover how to install Hadoop or Spark; I am going to assume you already have these installed. Also, any Hadoop commands are executed relative to the directory where Hadoop is installed (the $HADOOP_HOME environment variable). This book is explicitly about presenting distributed algorithms using MapReduce/Hadoop and Spark. For example, I discuss APIs, cover command-line invocations for running jobs, and provide complete working programs (including the driver, mapper, combiner, and reducer).

What Is the Focus of This Book?

The focus of this book is to embrace the MapReduce paradigm and provide concrete problems that can be solved using MapReduce/Hadoop algorithms. For each problem presented, we will detail the map(), combine(), and reduce() functions and provide a complete solution, which has:

- A client, which calls the driver with proper input and output parameters.
- A driver, which identifies `map()` and `reduce()` functions, and identifies input and output.
- A mapper class, which implements the `map()` function.
- A combiner class (when possible), which implements the `combine()` function. We will discuss when it is possible to use a combiner.
- A reducer class, which implements the `reduce()` function.

One goal of this book is to provide step-by-step instructions for using Spark and Hadoop as a solution for MapReduce algorithms. Another is to show how an output of one MapReduce job can be used as an input to another (this is called *chaining* or *pipelining* MapReduce jobs).

Who Is This Book For?

This book is for software engineers, software architects, data scientists, and application developers who know the basics of Java and want to develop MapReduce algorithms (in data mining, machine learning, bioinformatics, genomics, and statistics) and solutions using Hadoop and Spark. As I've noted, I assume you know the basics of the Java programming language (e.g., writing a class, defining a new class from an existing class, and using basic control structures such as the `while` loop and `if-then-else`).

More specifically, this book is targeted to the following readers:

- Data science engineers and professionals who want to do analytics (classification, regression algorithms) on big data. The book shows the basic steps, in the format of a cookbook, to apply classification and regression algorithms using big data. The book details the `map()` and `reduce()` functions by demonstrating how they are applied to real data, and shows where to apply basic design patterns to solve MapReduce problems. These MapReduce algorithms can be easily adapted across professions with some minor changes (for example, by changing the input format). All solutions have been implemented in Apache Hadoop/Spark so that these examples can be adapted in real-world situations.

- Software engineers and software architects who want to design machine learning algorithms such as Naive Bayes and Markov chain algorithms. The book shows how to build the model and then apply it to a new data set using MapReduce design patterns.

- Software engineers and software architects who want to use data mining algorithms (such as K-Means clustering and k-Nearest Neighbors) with MapReduce.

Detailed examples are given to guide professionals in implementing similar algorithms.

- Data science engineers who want to apply MapReduce algorithms to clinical and biological data (such as DNA sequencing and RNA sequencing). This book clearly explains practical algorithms suitable for bioinformaticians and clinicians. It presents the most relevant regression/analytical algorithms used for different biological data types. The majority of these algorithms have been deployed in real-world production systems.

- Software architects who want to apply the most important optimizations in a MapReduce/distributed environment.

This book assumes you have a basic understanding of Java and Hadoop's HDFS. If you need to become familiar with Hadoop and Spark, the following books will offer you the background information you will need:

- *Hadoop: The Definitive Guide* by Tom White (O'Reilly)
- *Hadoop in Action* by Chuck Lam (Manning Publications)
- *Hadoop in Practice* by Alex Holmes (Manning Publications)
- *Learning Spark* by Holden Karau, Andy Konwinski, Patrick Wendell, and Matei Zaharia (O'Reilly)

Online Resources

Two websites accompany this book:

https://github.com/mahmoudparsian/data-algorithms-book/
  At this GitHub site, you will find links to the source code (organized by chapter), shell scripts (for running MapReduce/Hadoop and Spark programs), sample input files for testing, and some extra content that isn't in the book, including a couple of bonus chapters.

http://mapreduce4hackers.com
  At this site, you will find links to extra source files (not mentioned in the book) plus some additional content that is not in the book. Expect more coverage of MapReduce/Hadoop/Spark topics in the future.

What Software Is Used in This Book?

When developing solutions and examples for this book, I used the software and programming environments listed in Table P-3.

Table P-3. Software/programming environments used in this book

Software	Version
Java programming language (JDK7)	1.7.0_67
Operating system: Linux CentOS	6.3
Operating system: Mac OS X	10.9
Apache Hadoop	2.5.0, 2.6.0
Apache Spark	1.1.0, 1.3.0, 1.4.0
Eclipse IDE	Luna

All programs in this book were tested with Java/JDK7, Hadoop 2.5.0, and Spark (1.1.0, 1.3.0, 1.4.0). Examples are given in mixed operating system environments (Linux and OS X). For all examples and solutions, I engaged basic text editors (such as vi, vim, and TextWrangler) and compiled them using the Java command-line compiler (`javac`).

In this book, shell scripts (such as bash scripts) are used to run sample MapReduce/Hadoop and Spark programs. Lines that begin with a $ or # character indicate that the commands must be entered at a terminal prompt (such as bash).

Conventions Used in This Book

The following typographical conventions are used in this book:

Italic
> Indicates new terms, URLs, email addresses, filenames, and file extensions.

`Constant width`
> Used for program listings, as well as within paragraphs to refer to program elements such as variable or function names, databases, data types, environment variables, statements, and keywords.

 This element signifies a general note.

Using Code Examples

As mentioned previously, supplemental material (code examples, exercises, etc.) is available for download at *https://github.com/mahmoudparsian/data-algorithms-book/* and *http://www.mapreduce4hackers.com*.

This book is here to help you get your job done. In general, if example code is offered with this book, you may use it in your programs and documentation. You do not need to contact us for permission unless you're reproducing a significant portion of the code. For example, writing a program that uses several chunks of code from this book does not require permission. Selling or distributing a CD-ROM of examples from O'Reilly books does require permission. Answering a question by citing this book and quoting example code does not require permission. Incorporating a significant amount of example code from this book into your product's documentation does require permission.

We appreciate, but do not require, attribution. An attribution usually includes the title, author, publisher, and ISBN. For example: *"Data Algorithms* by Mahmoud Parsian (O'Reilly). Copyright 2015 Mahmoud Parsian, 978-1-491-90618-7."

If you feel your use of code examples falls outside fair use or the permission given above, feel free to contact us at *permissions@oreilly.com*.

Safari® Books Online

 *Safari Books Online* is an on-demand digital library that delivers expert content in both book and video form from the world's leading authors in technology and business.

Technology professionals, software developers, web designers, and business and creative professionals use Safari Books Online as their primary resource for research, problem solving, learning, and certification training.

Safari Books Online offers a range of plans and pricing for enterprise, government, education, and individuals.

Members have access to thousands of books, training videos, and prepublication manuscripts in one fully searchable database from publishers like O'Reilly Media, Prentice Hall Professional, Addison-Wesley Professional, Microsoft Press, Sams, Que, Peachpit Press, Focal Press, Cisco Press, John Wiley & Sons, Syngress, Morgan Kaufmann, IBM Redbooks, Packt, Adobe Press, FT Press, Apress, Manning, New Riders, McGraw-Hill, Jones & Bartlett, Course Technology, and hundreds more. For more information about Safari Books Online, please visit us online.

How to Contact Us

Please address comments and questions concerning this book to the publisher:

O'Reilly Media, Inc.
1005 Gravenstein Highway North
Sebastopol, CA 95472
800-998-9938 (in the United States or Canada)
707-829-0515 (international or local)
707-829-0104 (fax)

We have a web page for this book, where we list errata, examples, and any additional information. You can access this page at *http://bit.ly/data_algorithms*.

To comment or ask technical questions about this book, send email to *bookquestions@oreilly.com*.

For more information about our books, courses, conferences, and news, see our website at *http://www.oreilly.com*.

Find us on Facebook: *http://facebook.com/oreilly*

Follow us on Twitter: *http://twitter.com/oreillymedia*

Watch us on YouTube: *http://www.youtube.com/oreillymedia*

Acknowledgments

To each reader: a big thank you for reading my book. I hope that this book is useful and serves you well.

Thank you to my editor at O'Reilly, Ann Spencer, for believing in my book project, supporting me in reorganizing the chapters, and suggesting a new title (originally, I proposed a title of *MapReduce for Hackers*). Also, I want to thank Mike Loukides (VP of Content Strategy for O'Reilly Media) for believing in and supporting my book project.

Thank you so much to my editor, Marie Beaugureau, data and development editor at O'Reilly, who has worked with me patiently for a long time and supported me during every phase of this project. Marie's comments and suggestions have been very useful and helpful.

A big thank you to Rachel Monaghan, copyeditor, for her superb knowledge of book editing and her valuable comments and suggestions. This book is more readable because of her. Also, I want to say a big thank you to Matthew Hacker, production editor, who has done a great job in getting this book through production. Thanks to

Rebecca Demarest (O'Reilly's illustrator) and Dan Fauxsmith (Director of Publishing Services for O'Reilly) for polishing the artwork. Also, I want to say thank you to Rachel Head (as proofreader), Judith McConville (as indexer), David Futato (as interior designer), and Ellie Volckhausen (as cover designer).

Thanks to my technical reviewers, Cody Koeninger, Kun Lu, Neera Vats, Dr. Phanendra Babu, Willy Bruns, and Mohan Reddy. Your comments were useful, and I have incorporated your suggestions as much as possible. Special thanks to Cody for providing detailed feedback.

A big thank you to Jay Flatley (CEO of Illumina), who has provided a tremendous opportunity and environment in which to unlock the power of the genome. Thank you to my dear friends Saeid Akhtari (CEO, NextBio) and Dr. Satnam Alag (VP of Engineering at Illumina) for believing in me and supporting me for the past five years.

Thanks to my longtime dear friend, Dr. Ramachandran Krishnaswamy (my Ph.D. advisor), for his excellent guidance and for providing me with the environment to work on computer science.

Thanks to my dear parents (mother Monireh Azemoun and father Bagher Parsian) for making education their number one priority. They have supported me tremendously. Thanks to my brother, Dr. Ahmad Parsian, for helping me to understand mathematics. Thanks to my sister, Nayer Azam Parsian, for helping me to understand compassion.

Last, but not least, thanks to my dear family—Behnaz, Maral, and Yaseen—whose encouragement and support throughout the writing process means more than I can say.

Comments and Questions for This Book

I am always interested in your feedback and comments regarding the problems and solutions described in this book. Please email comments and questions for this book to *mahmoud.parsian@yahoo.com*. You can also find me at *http://www.mapreduce4hackers.com*.

—*Mahmoud Parsian*
Sunnyvale, California
March 26, 2015

## CHAPTER 1

Secondary Sort: Introduction

A *secondary sort problem* relates to sorting values associated with a key in the reduce phase. Sometimes, it is called *value-to-key conversion*. The secondary sorting technique will enable us to sort the values (in ascending or descending order) passed to each reducer. I will provide concrete examples of how to achieve secondary sorting in ascending or descending order.

The goal of this chapter is to implement the Secondary Sort design pattern in MapReduce/Hadoop and Spark. In software design and programming, a *design pattern* is a reusable algorithm that is used to solve a commonly occurring problem. Typically, a design pattern is not presented in a specific programming language but instead can be implemented by many programming languages.

The MapReduce framework automatically sorts the keys generated by mappers. This means that, before starting reducers, all intermediate key-value pairs generated by mappers must be sorted by key (and not by value). Values passed to each reducer are not sorted at all; they can be in any order. What if you also want to sort a reducer's values? MapReduce/Hadoop and Spark do not sort values for a reducer. So, for those applications (such as time series data) in which you want to sort your reducer data, the Secondary Sort design pattern enables you to do so.

First we'll focus on the MapReduce/Hadoop solution. Let's look at the MapReduce paradigm and then unpack the concept of the secondary sort:

$$\text{map}(\text{key}_1, \text{value}_1) \rightarrow \text{list}(\text{key}_2, \text{value}_2)$$

$$\text{reduce}(\text{key}_2, \text{list}(\text{value}_2)) \rightarrow \text{list}(\text{key}_3, \text{value}_3)$$

First, the map() function receives a key-value pair input, (key$_1$, value$_1$). Then it outputs any number of key-value pairs, (key$_2$, value$_2$). Next, the reduce() function receives as input another key-value pair, $(key_2, list(value_2))$, and outputs any number of $(key_3, value_3)$ pairs.

Now consider the following key-value pair, $(key_2, list(value_2))$, as an input for a reducer:

$$list(value_2) = (V_1, V_2, ..., V_n)$$

where there is no ordering between reducer values $(V_1, V_2, ..., V_n)$.

The goal of the Secondary Sort pattern is to give *some ordering* to the values received by a reducer. So, once we apply the pattern to our MapReduce paradigm, then we will have:

$$SORT(V_1, V_2, ..., V_n) = (S_1, S_2, ..., S_n)$$
$$list(value_2) = (S_1, S_2, ..., S_n)$$

where:

- $S_1 < S_2 < ... < S_n$ (ascending order), or
- $S_1 > S_2 > ... > S_n$ (descending order)

Here is an example of a secondary sorting problem: consider the temperature data from a scientific experiment. A dump of the temperature data might look something like the following (columns are year, month, day, and daily temperature, respectively):

```
2012, 01, 01, 5
2012, 01, 02, 45
2012, 01, 03, 35
2012, 01, 04, 10
...
2001, 11, 01, 46
2001, 11, 02, 47
2001, 11, 03, 48
2001, 11, 04, 40
...
2005, 08, 20, 50
2005, 08, 21, 52
2005, 08, 22, 38
2005, 08, 23, 70
```

Suppose we want to output the temperature for every year-month with the values sorted in ascending order. Essentially, we want the reducer values iterator to be sorted. Therefore, we want to generate something like this output (the first column is year-month and the second column is the sorted temperatures):

```
2012-01:  5, 10, 35, 45, ...
2001-11: 40, 46, 47, 48, ...
2005-08: 38, 50, 52, 70, ...
```

Solutions to the Secondary Sort Problem

There are at least two possible approaches for sorting the reducer values. These solutions may be applied to both the MapReduce/Hadoop and Spark frameworks:

- The first approach involves having the reducer read and buffer all of the values for a given *key* (in an array data structure, for example), then doing an in-reducer sort on the values. This approach will not scale: since the reducer will be receiving all values for a given *key*, this approach might cause the reducer to run out of memory (`java.lang.OutOfMemoryError`). On the other hand, this approach can work well if the number of values is small enough that it will not cause an out-of-memory error.

- The second approach involves using the MapReduce framework for sorting the reducer values (this does not require in-reducer sorting of values passed to the reducer). This approach consists of "creating a composite key by adding a part of, or the entire value to, the natural key to achieve your sorting objectives." For the details on this approach, see Java Code Geeks (*http://bit.ly/secondary_sorting*). This option is scalable and will not generate out-of-memory errors. Here, we basically offload the sorting to the MapReduce framework (sorting is a paramount feature of the MapReduce/Hadoop framework).

  This is a summary of the second approach:

  1. Use the *Value-to-Key Conversion* design pattern: form a composite intermediate key, (K, V_1), where V_1 is the secondary key. Here, K is called a *natural key*. To inject a value (i.e., V_1) into a reducer key, simply create a composite key (for details, see the `DateTemperaturePair` class). In our example, V_1 is the `tempera ture` data.
  2. Let the MapReduce execution framework do the sorting (rather than sorting in memory, let the framework sort by using the cluster nodes).
  3. Preserve state across multiple key-value pairs to handle processing; you can achieve this by having proper mapper output partitioners (for example, we partition the mapper's output by the natural key).

Implementation Details

To implement the secondary sort feature, we need additional plug-in Java classes. We have to tell the MapReduce/Hadoop framework:

- How to sort reducer keys
- How to partition keys passed to reducers (custom partitioner)
- How to group data that has arrived at each reducer

Sort order of intermediate keys

To accomplish secondary sorting, we need to take control of the sort order of inter-mediate keys and the control order in which reducers process keys. First, we inject a value (`temperature` data) into the composite key, and then we take control of the sort order of intermediate keys. The relationships between the natural key, composite key, and key-value pairs are depicted in Figure 1-1.

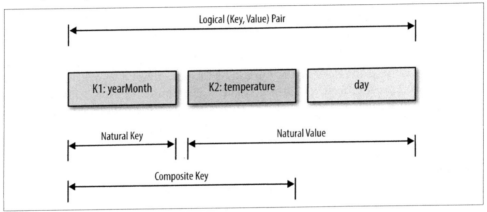

Figure 1-1. Secondary sorting keys

The main question is what value we should add to the natural key to accomplish the secondary sort. The answer is the `temperature` data field (because we want the reducers' values to be sorted by `temperature`). So, we have to indicate how `DateTempera turePair` objects should be sorted using the `compareTo()` method. We need to define a proper data structure for holding our key and value, while also providing the sort order of intermediate keys. In Hadoop, for custom data types (such as `DateTempera turePair`) to be persisted, they have to implement the `Writable` interface; and if we are going to compare custom data types, then they have to implement an additional interface called `WritableComparable` (see Example 1-1).

Example 1-1. DateTemperaturePair class

```
1 import org.apache.hadoop.io.Writable;
2 import org.apache.hadoop.io.WritableComparable;
3 ...
4 public class DateTemperaturePair
```

```
 5    implements Writable, WritableComparable<DateTemperaturePair> {
 6
 7      private Text yearMonth = new Text();                    // natural key
 8      private Text day = new Text();
 9      private IntWritable temperature = new IntWritable(); // secondary key
10
11      ...
12
13      @Override
14      /**
15       * This comparator controls the sort order of the keys.
16       */
17      public int compareTo(DateTemperaturePair pair) {
18          int compareValue = this.yearMonth.compareTo(pair.getYearMonth());
19          if (compareValue == 0) {
20              compareValue = temperature.compareTo(pair.getTemperature());
21          }
22          //return compareValue;    // sort ascending
23          return -1*compareValue;   // sort descending
24      }
25      ...
26 }
```

Custom partitioner

In a nutshell, the partitioner decides which mapper's output goes to which reducer based on the mapper's output key. For this, we need two plug-in classes: a custom partitioner to control which reducer processes which keys, and a custom Comparator to sort reducer values. The custom partitioner ensures that all data with the same key (the natural key, not including the composite key with the temperature value) is sent to the same reducer. The custom Comparator does sorting so that the natural key (year-month) groups the data once it arrives at the reducer.

Example 1-2. DateTemperaturePartitioner class

```
 1 import org.apache.hadoop.io.Text;
 2 import org.apache.hadoop.mapreduce.Partitioner;
 3
 4 public class DateTemperaturePartitioner
 5      extends Partitioner<DateTemperaturePair, Text> {
 6
 7      @Override
 8      public int getPartition(DateTemperaturePair pair,
 9                              Text text,
10                              int numberOfPartitions) {
11          // make sure that partitions are non-negative
12          return Math.abs(pair.getYearMonth().hashCode() % numberOfPartitions);
13      }
14 }
```

Hadoop provides a plug-in architecture for injecting the custom partitioner code into the framework. This is how we do so inside the driver class (which submits the Map-Reduce job to Hadoop):

```
import org.apache.hadoop.mapreduce.Job;
...
Job job = ...;
...
job.setPartitionerClass(TemperaturePartitioner.class);
```

Grouping comparator

In Example 1-3, we define the comparator (DateTemperatureGroupingComparator class) that controls which keys are grouped together for a single call to the Reducer.reduce() function.

Example 1-3. DateTemperatureGroupingComparator class

```
1  import org.apache.hadoop.io.WritableComparable;
2  import org.apache.hadoop.io.WritableComparator;
3
4  public class DateTemperatureGroupingComparator
5      extends WritableComparator {
6
7      public DateTemperatureGroupingComparator() {
8          super(DateTemperaturePair.class, true);
9      }
10
11     @Override
12     /**
13      * This comparator controls which keys are grouped
14      * together into a single call to the reduce() method
15      */
16     public int compare(WritableComparable wc1, WritableComparable wc2) {
17         DateTemperaturePair pair = (DateTemperaturePair) wc1;
18         DateTemperaturePair pair2 = (DateTemperaturePair) wc2;
19         return pair.getYearMonth().compareTo(pair2.getYearMonth());
20     }
21 }
```

Hadoop provides a plug-in architecture for injecting the grouping comparator code into the framework. This is how we do so inside the driver class (which submits the MapReduce job to Hadoop):

```
job.setGroupingComparatorClass(YearMonthGroupingComparator.class);
```

Data Flow Using Plug-in Classes

To help you understand the map() and reduce() functions and custom plug-in classes, Figure 1-2 illustrates the data flow for a portion of input.

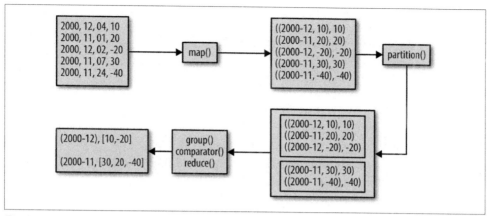

Figure 1-2. Secondary sorting data flow

The mappers create (K, V) pairs, where K is a composite key of (year,month,tempera ture) and V is temperature. The (year,month) part of the composite key is the natural key. The partitioner plug-in class enables us to send all natural keys to the same reducer and the grouping comparator plug-in class enables temperatures to arrive sorted at reducers. The Secondary Sort design pattern uses MapReduce's framework for sorting the reducers' values rather than collecting them all and then sorting them in memory. The Secondary Sort design pattern enables us to "scale out" no matter how many reducer values we want to sort.

MapReduce/Hadoop Solution to Secondary Sort

This section provides a complete MapReduce implementation of the secondary sort problem using the Hadoop framework.

Input

The input will be a set of files, where each record (line) will have the following format:

```
Format:
        <year><,><month><,><day><,><temperature>

Example:
        2012, 01, 01, 35
        2011, 12, 23, -4
```

Expected Output

The expected output will have the following format:

```
Format:
        <year><-><month>: <temperature1><,><temperature2><,> ...
        where temperature1 <= temperature2 <= ...

Example:
        2012-01:  5, 10, 35, 45, ...
        2001-11: 40, 46, 47, 48, ...
        2005-08: 38, 50, 52, 70, ...
```

map() Function

The map() function parses and tokenizes the input and then injects the value (temper
ature) into the reducer key, as shown in Example 1-4.

Example 1-4. map() for secondary sorting

```
 1 /**
 2  * @param key is generated by Hadoop (ignored here)
 3  * @param value has this format: "YYYY,MM,DD,temperature"
 4  */
 5 map(key, value) {
 6     String[] tokens = value.split(",");
 7     // YYYY = tokens[0]
 8     // MM = tokens[1]
 9     // DD = tokens[2]
10     // temperature = tokens[3]
11     String yearMonth = tokens[0] + tokens[1];
12     String day = tokens[2];
13     int temperature = Integer.parseInt(tokens[3]);
14     // prepare reducer key
15     DateTemperaturePair reducerKey = new DateTemperaturePair();
16     reducerKey.setYearMonth(yearMonth);
17     reducerKey.setDay(day);
18     reducerKey.setTemperature(temperature); // inject value into key
19     // send it to reducer
20     emit(reducerKey, temperature);
21 }
```

reduce() Function

The reducer's primary function is to concatenate the values (which are already sorted
through the Secondary Sort design pattern) and emit them as output. The reduce()
function is given in Example 1-5.

Example 1-5. reduce() for secondary sorting

```
 1 /**
 2  * @param key is a DateTemperaturePair object
 3  * @param value is a list of temperatures
 4  */
```

```
 5 reduce(key, value) {
 6     StringBuilder sortedTemperatureList = new StringBuilder();
 7     for (Integer temperature : value) {
 8         sortedTemperatureList.append(temperature);
 9         sortedTemperatureList.append(",");
10     }
11     emit(key, sortedTemperatureList);
12 }
```

Hadoop Implementation Classes

The classes shown in Table 1-1 are used to solve the problem.

Table 1-1. Classes used in MapReduce/Hadoop solution

Class name	Class description
SecondarySortDriver	The driver class; defines input/output and registers plug-in classes
SecondarySortMapper	Defines the map() function
SecondarySortReducer	Defines the reduce() function
DateTemperatureGroupingComparator	Defines how keys will be grouped together
DateTemperaturePair	Defines paired date and temperature as a Java object
DateTemperaturePartitioner	Defines custom partitioner

How is the value injected into the key? The first comparator (the DateTemperature
Pair.compareTo() method) controls the sort order of the keys, while the second
comparator (the DateTemperatureGroupingComparator.compare() method) controls which keys are grouped together into a single call to the reduce() method. The
combination of these two comparators allows you to set up jobs that act like you've
defined an order for the values.

The SecondarySortDriver is the driver class, which registers the custom plug-in
classes (DateTemperaturePartitioner and DateTemperatureGroupingComparator)
with the MapReduce/Hadoop framework. This driver class is presented in
Example 1-6.

Example 1-6. SecondarySortDriver class

```
 1 public class SecondarySortDriver extends Configured implements Tool {
 2     public int run(String[] args) throws Exception {
 3         Configuration conf = getConf();
 4         Job job = new Job(conf);
 5         job.setJarByClass(SecondarySortDriver.class);
 6         job.setJobName("SecondarySortDriver");
 7
 8         Path inputPath = new Path(args[0]);
 9         Path outputPath = new Path(args[1]);
```

```
10          FileInputFormat.setInputPaths(job, inputPath);
11          FileOutputFormat.setOutputPath(job, outputPath);
12
13          job.setOutputKeyClass(TemperaturePair.class);
14          job.setOutputValueClass(NullWritable.class);
15
16          job.setMapperClass(SecondarySortingTemperatureMapper.class);
17          job.setReducerClass(SecondarySortingTemperatureReducer.class);
18          job.setPartitionerClass(TemperaturePartitioner.class);
19          job.setGroupingComparatorClass(YearMonthGroupingComparator.class);
20
21          boolean status = job.waitForCompletion(true);
22          theLogger.info("run(): status="+status);
23          return status ? 0 : 1;
24      }
25
26      /**
27       * The main driver for the secondary sort MapReduce program.
28       * Invoke this method to submit the MapReduce job.
29       * @throws Exception when there are communication
30       * problems with the job tracker.
31       */
32      public static void main(String[] args) throws Exception {
33          // Make sure there are exactly 2 parameters
34          if (args.length != 2) {
35              throw new IllegalArgumentException("Usage: SecondarySortDriver" +
36                                      " <input-path> <output-path>");
37          }
38
39          //String inputPath = args[0];
40          //String outputPath = args[1];
41          int returnStatus = ToolRunner.run(new SecondarySortDriver(), args);
42          System.exit(returnStatus);
43      }
44
45 }
```

Sample Run of Hadoop Implementation

Input

```
# cat sample_input.txt
2000,12,04, 10
2000,11,01,20
2000,12,02,-20
2000,11,07,30
2000,11,24,-40
2012,12,21,30
2012,12,22,-20
2012,12,23,60
2012,12,24,70
2012,12,25,10
```

```
2013,01,22,80
2013,01,23,90
2013,01,24,70
2013,01,20,-10
```

HDFS input

```
# hadoop fs -mkdir /secondary_sort
# hadoop fs -mkdir /secondary_sort/input
# hadoop fs -mkdir /secondary_sort/output
# hadoop fs -put sample_input.txt /secondary_sort/input/
# hadoop fs -ls /secondary_sort/input/
Found 1 items
-rw-r--r-- 1 ... 128  ...  /secondary_sort/input/sample_input.txt
```

The script

```
# cat run.sh
export JAVA_HOME=/usr/java/jdk7
export BOOK_HOME=/home/mp/data-algorithms-book
export APP_JAR=$BOOK_HOME/dist/data_algorithms_book.jar
INPUT=/secondary_sort/input
OUTPUT=/secondary_sort/output
$HADOOP_HOME/bin/hadoop fs -rmr $OUTPUT
PROG=org.dataalgorithms.chap01.mapreduce.SecondarySortDriver
$HADOOP_HOME/bin/hadoop jar $APP_JAR $PROG $INPUT $OUTPUT
```

Log of sample run

```
# ./run.sh
...
Deleted hdfs://localhost:9000/secondary_sort/output
13/02/27 19:39:54 INFO input.FileInputFormat: Total input paths to process : 1
...
13/02/27 19:39:54 INFO mapred.JobClient: Running job: job_201302271939_0001
13/02/27 19:39:55 INFO mapred.JobClient:  map 0% reduce 0%
13/02/27 19:40:10 INFO mapred.JobClient:  map 100% reduce 0%
13/02/27 19:40:22 INFO mapred.JobClient:  map 100% reduce 10%
...
13/02/27 19:41:10 INFO mapred.JobClient:  map 100% reduce 90%
13/02/27 19:41:16 INFO mapred.JobClient:  map 100% reduce 100%
13/02/27 19:41:21 INFO mapred.JobClient: Job complete: job_201302271939_0001
...
13/02/27 19:41:21 INFO mapred.JobClient:    Map-Reduce Framework
...
13/02/27 19:41:21 INFO mapred.JobClient:       Reduce input records=14
13/02/27 19:41:21 INFO mapred.JobClient:       Reduce input groups=4
13/02/27 19:41:21 INFO mapred.JobClient:       Combine output records=0
13/02/27 19:41:21 INFO mapred.JobClient:       Reduce output records=4
13/02/27 19:41:21 INFO mapred.JobClient:       Map output records=14
13/02/27 19:41:21 INFO SecondarySortDriver: run(): status=true
13/02/27 19:41:21 INFO SecondarySortDriver: returnStatus=0
```

Inspecting the output

```
# hadoop fs -cat /secondary_sort/output/p*
2013-01  90,80,70,-10
2000-12  10,-20
2000-11  30,20,-40
2012-12  70,60,30,10,-20
```

How to Sort in Ascending or Descending Order

You can easily control the sorting order of the values (ascending or descending) by using the DateTemperaturePair.compareTo() method as follows:

```
1 public int compareTo(DateTemperaturePair pair) {
2     int compareValue = this.yearMonth.compareTo(pair.getYearMonth());
3     if (compareValue == 0) {
4         compareValue = temperature.compareTo(pair.getTemperature());
5     }
6     //return compareValue; // sort ascending
7     return -1*compareValue; // sort descending
8 }
```

Spark Solution to Secondary Sort

To solve a secondary sorting problem in Spark, we have at least two options:

Option #1

Read and buffer all of the values for a given *key* in an Array or List data structure and then do an in-reducer sort on the values. This solution works if you have a small set of values (which will fit in memory) per reducer key.

Option #2

Use the Spark framework for sorting the reducer values (this option does not require in-reducer sorting of values passed to the reducer). This approach involves "creating a composite key by adding a part of, or the entire value to, the natural key to achieve your sorting objectives." This option always scales (because you are not limited by the memory of a commodity server).

Time Series as Input

To demonstrate secondary sorting, let's use time series data:

```
name time value
  x    2    9
  y    2    5
  x    1    3
  y    1    7
  y    3    1
  x    3    6
  z    1    4
```

```
z    2    8
z    3    7
z    4    0
p    2    6
p    4    7
p    1    9
p    6    0
p    7    3
```

Expected Output

Our expected output is as follows. Note that the values of reducers are grouped by name and sorted by time:

```
name   t1   t2  t3   t4    t5 ...
x =>   [3,   9,   6]
y =>   [7,   5,   1]
z =>   [4,   8,   7,   0]
p =>   [9,   6,   7,   0,   3]
```

Option 1: Secondary Sorting in Memory

Since Spark has a very powerful and high-level API, I will present the entire solution in a single Java class. The Spark API is built upon the basic abstraction concept of the RDD (resilient distributed data set). To fully utilize Spark's API, we have to understand RDDs. An RDD<T> (i.e., an RDD of type T) *object* represents an immutable, partitioned collection of elements (of type T) that can be operated on in parallel. The RDD<T> *class* contains the basic MapReduce operations available on all RDDs, such as map(), filter(), and persist(), while the JavaPairRDD<K,V> class contains MapReduce operations such as mapToPair(), flatMapToPair(), and groupByKey(). In addition, Spark's PairRDDFunctions contains operations available only on RDDs of key-value pairs, such as reduce(), groupByKey(), and join(). (For details on RDDs, see Spark's API (*http://bit.ly/spark_rdd*) and Appendix B of this book.) Therefore, JavaRDD<T> is a list of objects of type T, and JavaPairRDD<K,V> is a list of objects of type Tuple2<K,V> (where each tuple represents a key-value pair).

The Spark-based algorithm is listed next. Although there are 10 steps, most of them are trivial and some are provided for debugging purposes only:

1. We import the required Java/Spark classes. The main Java classes for MapReduce are given in the org.apache.spark.api.java package. This package includes the following classes and interfaces:

   - JavaRDDLike (interface)

   - JavaDoubleRDD

   - JavaPairRDD

- JavaRDD

- JavaSparkContext

- StorageLevels

2. We pass input data as arguments and validate.
3. We connect to the Spark master by creating a JavaSparkContext object, which is used to create new RDDs.
4. Using the context object (created in step 3), we create an RDD for the input file; the resulting RDD will be a JavaRDD<String>. Each element of this RDD will be a record of time series data: <name><,><time><,><value>.
5. Next we want to create key-value pairs from a JavaRDD<String>, where the key is the name and the value is a pair of (time, value). The resulting RDD will be a JavaPairRDD<String, Tuple2<Integer, Integer>>.
6. To validate step 5, we collect all values from the JavaPairRDD<> and print them.
7. We group JavaPairRDD<> elements by the key (name). To accomplish this, we use the groupByKey() method.

   The result will be the RDD:

   ```
   JavaPairRDD<String, Iterable<Tuple2<Integer, Integer>>>
   ```

   Note that the resulting list (Iterable<Tuple2<Integer, Integer>>) is unsorted. In general, Spark's reduceByKey() is preferred over groupByKey() for performance reasons, but here we have no other option than groupByKey() (since reduceByKey() does not allow us to sort the values in place for a given key).

8. To validate step 7, we collect all values from the JavaPairRDD<String, Iterable<Tuple2<Integer, Integer>>> and print them.
9. We sort the reducer's values to get the final output. We accomplish this by writing a custom mapValues() method. We just sort the values (the key remains the same).
10. To validate the final result, we collect all values from the sorted JavaPairRDD<> and print them.

A solution for option #1 is implemented by a single driver class: SecondarySorting (see Example 1-7). All steps, 1–10, are listed inside the class definition, which will be presented in the following sections. Typically, a Spark application consists of a driver program that runs the user's main() function and executes various parallel operations on a cluster. Parallel operations will be achieved through the extensive use of RDDs. For further details on RDDs, see Appendix B.

Example 1-7. SecondarySort class overall structure

```
 1 // Step 1: import required Java/Spark classes
 2 public class SecondarySort {
 3   public static void main(String[] args) throws Exception {
 4     // Step 2: read input parameters and validate them
 5     // Step 3: connect to the Spark master by creating a JavaSparkContext
 6     // object (ctx)
 6     // Step 4: use ctx to create JavaRDD<String>
 7     // Step 5: create key-value pairs from JavaRDD<String>, where
 8     // key is the {name} and value is a pair of (time, value)
 9     // Step 6: validate step 5-collect all values from JavaPairRDD<>
10     // and print them
11     // Step 7: group JavaPairRDD<> elements by the key ({name})
12     // Step 8: validate step 7-collect all values from JavaPairRDD<>
13     // and print them
14     // Step 9: sort the reducer's values; this will give us the final output
15     // Step 10: validate step 9-collect all values from JavaPairRDD<>
16     // and print them
17
18     // done
19     ctx.close();
20     System.exit(0);
21   }
22 }
```

Step 1: Import required classes

As shown in Example 1-8, the main Spark package for the Java API is
`org.apache.spark.api.java`, which includes the JavaRDD, JavaPairRDD, and JavaS
parkContext classes. JavaSparkContext is a factory class for creating new RDDs
(such as JavaRDD and JavaPairRDD objects).

Example 1-8. Step 1: Import required classes

```
 1 // Step 1: import required Java/Spark classes
 2 import scala.Tuple2;
 3 import org.apache.spark.api.java.JavaRDD;
 4 import org.apache.spark.api.java.JavaPairRDD;
 5 import org.apache.spark.api.java.JavaSparkContext;
 6 import org.apache.spark.api.java.function.Function;
 7 import org.apache.spark.api.java.function.Function2;
 8 import org.apache.spark.api.java.function.PairFunction;
 9
10 import java.util.List;
11 import java.util.ArrayList;
12 import java.util.Map;
13 import java.util.Collections;
14 import java.util.Comparator;
```

Step 2: Read input parameters

This step, demonstrated in Example 1-9, reads the HDFS input file (Spark may read data from HDFS and other persistent stores, such as a Linux filesystem), which might look like */dir1/dir2/myfile.txt.*

Example 1-9. Step 2: Read input parameters

```
1    // Step 2: read input parameters and validate them
2    if (args.length < 1) {
3       System.err.println("Usage: SecondarySort <file>");
4       System.exit(1);
5    }
6    String inputPath = args[0];
7    System.out.println("args[0]: <file>="+args[0]);
```

Step 3: Connect to the Spark master

To work with RDDs, first you need to create a JavaSparkContext object (as shown in Example 1-10), which is a factory for creating JavaRDD and JavaPairRDD objects. It is also possible to create a JavaSparkContext object by injecting a SparkConf object into the JavaSparkContext's class constructor. This approach is useful when you read your cluster configurations from an XML file. In a nutshell, the JavaSparkContext object has the following responsibilities:

- Initializes the application driver.
- Registers the application driver to the cluster manager. (If you are using the Spark cluster, then this will be the Spark master; if you are using YARN, then it will be YARN's resource manager.)
- Obtains a list of executors for executing your application driver.

Example 1-10. Step 3: Connect to the Spark master

```
1    // Step 3: connect to the Spark master by creating a JavaSparkContext object
2    final JavaSparkContext ctx = new JavaSparkContext();
```

Step 4: Use the JavaSparkContext to create a JavaRDD

This step, illustrated in Example 1-11, reads an HDFS file and creates a Jav aRDD<String> (which represents a set of records where each record is a String object). By definition, Spark's RDDs are *immutable* (i.e., they cannot be altered or modified). Note that Spark's RDDs are the basic abstraction for parallel execution. Note also that you may use textFile() to read HDFS or non-HDFS files.

Example 1-11. Step 4: Create JavaRDD

```
1    // Step 4: use ctx to create JavaRDD<String>
2    // input record format: <name><,><time><,><value>
3    JavaRDD<String> lines = ctx.textFile(inputPath, 1);
```

Step 5: Create key-value pairs from the JavaRDD

This step, shown in Example 1-12, implements a mapper. Each record (from the Jav
aRDD<String> and consisting of <name><,><time><,><value>) is converted to a key-
value pair, where the key is a name and the value is a Tuple2(time, value).

Example 1-12. Step 5: Create key-value pairs from JavaRDD

```
1    // Step 5: create key-value pairs from JavaRDD<String>, where
2    // key is the {name} and value is a pair of (time, value).
3    // The resulting RDD will be a JavaPairRDD<String, Tuple2<Integer, Integer>>.
4    // Convert each record into Tuple2(name, time, value).
5    // PairFunction<T, K, V>
6    //      T => Tuple2(K, V) where T is input (as String),
7    //      K=String
8    //      V=Tuple2<Integer, Integer>
9    JavaPairRDD<String, Tuple2<Integer, Integer>> pairs =
10        lines.mapToPair(new PairFunction<
                                           String,             // T
                                           String,             // K
                                           Tuple2<Integer, Integer> // V
                                           >() {
15     public Tuple2<String, Tuple2<Integer, Integer>> call(String s) {
16        String[] tokens = s.split(","); // x,2,5
17        System.out.println(tokens[0] + "," + tokens[1] + "," + tokens[2]);
18        Integer time = new Integer(tokens[1]);
19        Integer value = new Integer(tokens[2]);
20        Tuple2<Integer, Integer> timevalue =
              new Tuple2<Integer, Integer>(time, value);
21        return new Tuple2<String, Tuple2<Integer, Integer>>(tokens[0], timevalue);
22     }
23    });
```

Step 6: Validate step 5

To debug and validate your steps in Spark (as shown in Example 1-13), you may use
JavaRDD.collect() and JavaPairRDD.collect(). Note that collect() is used for
debugging and educational purposes (but avoid using collect() for debugging purposes in production clusters; doing so will impact performance). Also, you may use
JavaRDD.saveAsTextFile() for debugging as well as creating your desired outputs.

Example 1-13. Step 6: Validate step 5

```
1    // Step 6: validate step 5-collect all values from JavaPairRDD<>
2    // and print them
3    List<Tuple2<String, Tuple2<Integer, Integer>>> output = pairs.collect();
4    for (Tuple2 t : output) {
5        Tuple2<Integer, Integer> timevalue = (Tuple2<Integer, Integer>) t._2;
6        System.out.println(t._1 + "," + timevalue._1 + "," + timevalue._1);
7    }
```

Step 7: Group JavaPairRDD elements by the key (name)

We implement the reducer operation using groupByKey(). As you can see in Example 1-14, it is much easier to implement the reducer through Spark than Map-Reduce/Hadoop. Note that in Spark, in general, reduceByKey() is more efficient than groupByKey(). Here, however, we cannot use reduceByKey().

Example 1-14. Step 7: Group JavaPairRDD elements

```
1    // Step 7: group JavaPairRDD<> elements by the key ({name})
2    JavaPairRDD<String, Iterable<Tuple2<Integer, Integer>>> groups =
3            pairs.groupByKey();
```

Step 8: Validate step 7

This step, shown in Example 1-15, validates the previous step by using the collect() function, which gets all values from the groups RDD.

Example 1-15. Step 8: Validate step 7

```
1    // Step 8: validate step 7-we collect all values from JavaPairRDD<>
2    // and print them
2    System.out.println("===DEBUG1===");
3    List<Tuple2<String, Iterable<Tuple2<Integer, Integer>>>> output2 =
4            groups.collect();
5    for (Tuple2<String, Iterable<Tuple2<Integer, Integer>>> t : output2) {
6        Iterable<Tuple2<Integer, Integer>> list = t._2;
7        System.out.println(t._1);
8        for (Tuple2<Integer, Integer> t2 : list) {
9            System.out.println(t2._1 + "," + t2._2);
10       }
11       System.out.println("=====");
12   }
```

The following shows the output of this step. As you can see, the reducer values are not sorted:

```
y
2,5
1,7
```

```
3,1
=====
x
2,9
1,3
3,6
=====
z
1,4
2,8
3,7
4,0
=====
p
2,6
4,7
6,0
7,3
1,9
=====
```

Step 9: Sort the reducer's values in memory

This step, shown in Example 1-16, uses another powerful Spark method, mapVal
ues(), to just sort the values generated by reducers. The mapValues() method enables us to convert (K, V_1) into (K, V_2), where V_2 is a sorted V_1. One important note
about Spark's RDD is that it is immutable and cannot be altered/updated by any
means. For example, in this step, to sort our values, we have to copy them into
another list first. Immutability applies to the RDD itself and its elements.

Example 1-16. Step 9: sort the reducer's values in memory

```
1    // Step 9: sort the reducer's values; this will give us the final output.
2    // Option #1: worked
3    // mapValues[U](f: (V) => U): JavaPairRDD[K, U]
4    // Pass each value in the key-value pair RDD through a map function
5    // without changing the keys;
6    // this also retains the original RDD's partitioning.
7    JavaPairRDD<String, Iterable<Tuple2<Integer, Integer>>> sorted =
8        groups.mapValues(
9          new Function<Iterable<Tuple2<Integer, Integer>>,  // input
10                    Iterable<Tuple2<Integer, Integer>>   // output
11                    >() {
12      public Iterable<Tuple2<Integer, Integer>> call(Iterable<Tuple2<Integer,
13                                                      Integer>> s) {
14       List<Tuple2<Integer, Integer>> newList = new ArrayList<Tuple2<Integer,
15                                                      Integer>>(s);
16       Collections.sort(newList, new TupleComparator());
17       return newList;
```

```
18      }
19   });
```

Step 10: output final result

The `collect()` method collects all of the RDD's elements into a `java.util.List` object. Then we iterate through the `List` to get all the final elements (see Example 1-17).

Example 1-17. Step 10: Output final result

```
1    // Step 10: validate step 9-collect all values from JavaPairRDD<>
2    // and print them
3    System.out.println("===DEBUG2=");
4    List<Tuple2<String, Iterable<Tuple2<Integer, Integer>>>> output3 =
5        sorted.collect();
6    for (Tuple2<String, Iterable<Tuple2<Integer, Integer>>> t : output3) {
7       Iterable<Tuple2<Integer, Integer>> list = t._2;
8       System.out.println(t._1);
9       for (Tuple2<Integer, Integer> t2 : list) {
10          System.out.println(t2._1 + "," + t2._2);
11      }
12      System.out.println("=====");
13   }
```

Spark Sample Run

As far as Spark/Hadoop is concerned, you can run a Spark application in three different modes:[1]

Standalone mode
  This is the default setup. You start the Spark master on a master node and a "worker" on every slave node, and submit your Spark application to the Spark master.

YARN client mode
  In this mode, you do not start a Spark master or worker nodes. Instead, you submit the Spark application to YARN, which runs the Spark driver in the client Spark process that submits the application.

YARN cluster mode
  In this mode, you do not start a Spark master or worker nodes. Instead, you submit the Spark application to YARN, which runs the Spark driver in the ApplicationMaster in YARN.

---

[1] For details, see the Spark documentation (*http://bit.ly/spark_on_yarn*).

Next, we will cover how to submit the secondary sort application in the standalone and YARN cluster modes.

Running Spark in standalone mode

The following subsections provide the input, script, and log output of a sample run of our secondary sort application in Spark's standalone mode.

HDFS input.

```
# hadoop fs -cat /mp/timeseries.txt
x,2,9
y,2,5
x,1,3
y,1,7
y,3,1
x,3,6
z,1,4
z,2,8
z,3,7
z,4,0
p,2,6
p,4,7
p,1,9
p,6,0
p,7,3
```

The script.

```
# cat run_secondarysorting.sh
#!/bin/bash
export JAVA_HOME=/usr/java/jdk7
export SPARK_HOME=/home/hadoop/spark-1.1.0
export SPARK_MASTER=spark://myserver100:7077
BOOK_HOME=/home/mp/data-algorithms-book
APP_JAR=$BOOK_HOME/dist/data_algorithms_book.jar
INPUT=/home/hadoop/testspark/timeseries.txt
# Run on a Spark standalone cluster
prog=org.dataalgorithms.chap01.spark.SparkSecondarySort
$SPARK_HOME/bin/spark-submit \
  --class $prog \
  --master $SPARK_MASTER \
  --executor-memory 2G \
  --total-executor-cores 20 \
  $APP_JAR \
  $INPUT
```

Log of the run.

```
# ./run_secondarysorting.sh
args[0]: <file>=/mp/timeseries.txt
...
===  DEBUG STEP 5 ===
```

```
...
x,2,2
y,2,2
x,1,1
y,1,1
y,3,3
x,3,3
z,1,1
z,2,2
z,3,3
z,4,4
p,2,2
p,4,4
p,1,1
p,6,6
p,7,7
=== DEBUG STEP 7 ===
14/06/04 08:42:54 INFO spark.SparkContext: Starting job: collect
  at SecondarySort.java:96
14/06/04 08:42:54 INFO scheduler.DAGScheduler: Registering RDD 2
  (mapToPair at SecondarySort.java:75)
...
14/06/04 08:42:55 INFO scheduler.DAGScheduler: Stage 1
  (collect at SecondarySort.java:96) finished in 0.273 s
14/06/04 08:42:55 INFO spark.SparkContext: Job finished:
  collect at SecondarySort.java:96, took 1.587001929 s
z
1,4
2,8
3,7
4,0
=====
p
2,6
4,7
1,9
6,0
7,3
=====
x
2,9
1,3
3,6
=====
y
2,5
1,7
3,1
=====
=== DEBUG STEP 9 ===
14/06/04 08:42:55 INFO spark.SparkContext: Starting job: collect
  at SecondarySort.java:158
```

```
...
14/06/04 08:42:55 INFO scheduler.TaskSchedulerImpl: Removed TaskSet 3.0,
  whose tasks have all completed, from pool
14/06/04 08:42:55 INFO spark.SparkContext: Job finished: collect at
  SecondarySort.java:158, took 0.074271723 s
z
1,4
2,8
3,7
4,0
=====
p
1,9
2,6
4,7
6,0
7,3
=====
x
1,3
2,9
3,6
=====
y
1,7
2,5
3,1
=====
```

Typically, you save the final result to HDFS. You can accomplish this by adding the following line of code after creating your "sorted" RDD:

```
sorted.saveAsTextFile("/mp/output");
```

Then you may view the output as follows:

```
# hadoop fs -ls /mp/output/
Found 2 items
-rw-r--r--   3 hadoop root,hadoop      0 2014-06-04 10:49 /mp/output/_SUCCESS
-rw-r--r--   3 hadoop root,hadoop    125 2014-06-04 10:49 /mp/output/part-00000

# hadoop fs -cat /mp/output/part-00000
(z,[(1,4), (2,8), (3,7), (4,0)])
(p,[(1,9), (2,6), (4,7), (6,0), (7,3)])
(x,[(1,3), (2,9), (3,6)])
(y,[(1,7), (2,5), (3,1)])
```

Running Spark in YARN cluster mode.   The script to submit our Spark application in YARN cluster mode is as follows:

```
# cat run_secondarysorting_yarn.sh
#!/bin/bash
export JAVA_HOME=/usr/java/jdk7
```

```
export HADOOP_HOME=/usr/local/hadoop-2.5.0
export HADOOP_CONF_DIR=$HADOOP_HOME/etc/hadoop
export YARN_CONF_DIR=$HADOOP_HOME/etc/hadoop
export SPARK_HOME=/home/hadoop/spark-1.1.0
BOOK_HOME=/home/mp/data-algorithms-book
APP_JAR=$BOOK_HOME/dist/data_algorithms_book.jar
INPUT=/mp/timeseries.txt
prog=org.dataalgorithms.chap01.spark.SparkSecondarySort
$SPARK_HOME/bin/spark-submit \
  --class $prog \
  --master yarn-cluster \
  --executor-memory 2G \
  --num-executors 10 \
  $APP_JAR \
  $INPUT
```

Option #2: Secondary Sorting Using the Spark Framework

In the solution for option #1, we sorted reducer values in memory (using Java's Col
lections.sort() method), which might not scale if the reducer values will not fit in
a commodity server's memory. Next we will implement option #2 for the MapRe-
duce/Hadoop framework. We cannot achieve this in the current Spark (Spark-1.1.0)
framework, because currently Spark's shuffle is based on a hash, which is different
from MapReduce's sort-based shuffle. So, you should implement sorting explicitly
using an RDD operator. If we had a partitioner by a natural key (name) that preserved
the order of the RDD, that would be a viable solution—for example, if we sorted by
(name, time), we would get:

```
(p,1),(1,9)
(p,4),(4,7)
(p,6),(6,0)
(p,7),(7,3)

(x,1),(1,3)
(x,2),(2,9)
(x,3),(3,6)

(y,1),(1,7)
(y,2),(2,5)
(y,3),(3,1)

(z,1),(1,4)
(z,2),(2,8)
(z,3),(3,7)
(z,4),(4,0)
```

There is a partitioner (represented as an abstract class, org.apache.spark.Parti
tioner), but it does not preserve the order of the original RDD elements. Therefore,
option #2 cannot be implemented by the current version of Spark (1.1.0).

Further Reading on Secondary Sorting

To support secondary sorting in Spark, you may extend the `JavaPairRDD` class and add additional methods such as `groupByKeyAndSortValues()`. For further work on this topic, you may refer to the following:

- Support sorting of values in addition to keys (i.e., secondary sort) (*http://bit.ly/ secondary_sort_ticket*)
- *https://github.com/tresata/spark-sorted*

Chapter 2 provides a detailed implementation of the Secondary Sort design pattern using the MapReduce and Spark frameworks.

Secondary Sort: A Detailed Example

The MapReduce framework sorts input to reducers by key, but values of reducers are arbitrarily ordered. This means that if all mappers generate the following key-value pairs for key = K:

$$(K, V_1), (K, V_2), ..., (K, V_n)$$

then all these values $\{V_1, V_2, ..., V_n\}$ will be processed by a single reducer (for key = K), but there will be no order (ascending or descending) between instances of V_i. As you learned in Chapter 1, Secondary Sort is a design pattern we can use to apply an order (such as "ascending sort" or "descending sort") to the values. How do we accomplish this? Say we want to apply some order to the reducer values:

$$S_1 \leq S_2 \leq ... \leq S_n$$

or:

$$S_1 \geq S_2 \geq ... \geq S_n$$

where $S_i \in \{V_1, V_2, ..., V_n\}$ for i = {1, 2, ..., n}. Note that each V_i might be a simple data type, such as String or Integer, or a tuple (more than a single value—that is, a composite object).

There are two ways to sort reducer values:

Solution #1

> Buffer reducer values in memory, then sort. If the number of reducer values is small enough to fit in memory (per reducer), then this solution will work. But if the number of reducer values is high, then they might not fit in memory (not a

preferable solution). Implementation of this solution is simple; it is presented in Chapter 1 and will not be discussed in this chapter.

Solution #2

Use the Secondary Sort design pattern of the MapReduce framework, and reducer values will arrive sorted (i.e., there's no need to sort values in memory). This technique uses the shuffle and sort technique of the MapReduce framework to sort reducer values. This solution is preferable to solution #1 because you do not depend on the memory for sorting (again, if you have too many values, solution #1 might not be a viable option). The rest of this chapter will focus on presenting solution #2.

We implement solution #2 in Hadoop by using:

- The old Hadoop API (using `org.apache.hadoop.mapred.JobConf` and `org.apache.hadoop.mapred.*`); I have intentionally included this API in case you have not migrated to the new Hadoop API.

- The new Hadoop API (using `org.apache.hadoop.mapreduce.Job` and `org.apache.hadoop.mapreduce.lib.*`).

Secondary Sorting Technique

Say we have the following values for key = K:

$$(K, V_1), (K, V_2), \ldots, (K, V_n)$$

and further assume that each V_i is a tuple of m attributes as follows:

$$(a_{i1}, a_{i2}, \ldots, a_{im})$$

where we want to sort the reducer's tuple values by a_{i1}. We will denote $(a_{i2}, \ldots, a_{im})$ (the remaining attributes) with r. Therefore, we can express reducer values as:

$$(K, (a_1, r_1)), (K, (a_2, r_2)), \ldots, (K, (a_n, r_n))$$

To sort the reducer values by a_i, we create a composite key: (K, a_i). Our new mappers will emit the key-value pairs for key = K shown in Table 2-1.

Table 2-1. Key-value pairs emitted by mappers

Key	Value
(K, a_1)	(a_1, r_1)
(K, a_2)	(a_2, r_2)
...	...
(K, a_n)	(a_n, r_n)

So, the composite key is (K, a_i), and the natural key is K. Defining the composite key (by adding the attribute a_i to the natural key) enables us to sort the reducer values using the MapReduce framework, but when we want to partition keys, we will partition them by the natural key (K). The composite key and the natural key are illustrated in Figure 2-1.

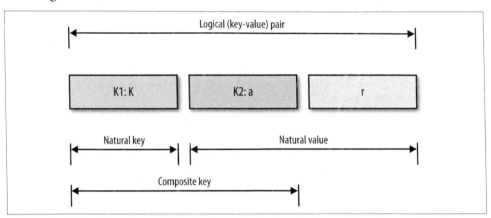

Figure 2-1. Secondary sorting keys

We have to tell the MapReduce framework how to sort the keys by using a composite key composed of two fields, K and a_i. For this we need to define a plug-in sort class, `CompositeKeyComparator`, which will be sorting the composite keys. Example 2-1 shows how you plug this comparator class into a MapReduce framework.

Example 2-1. Plugging in the comparator class

```
1 import org.apache.hadoop.mapred.JobConf;
2 ...
3 JobConf conf = new JobConf(getConf(), <your-mapreduce-driver-class>.class);
4 ...
5 // map() creates key-value pairs of
6 // (CompositeKey, NaturalValue)
7 conf.setMapOutputKeyClass(CompositeKey.class);
```

```
 8 conf.setMapOutputValueClass(NaturalValue.class);
 9 ...
10 // Plug-in Comparator class:
11 // how CompositeKey objects will be sorted
12 conf.setOutputKeyComparatorClass(CompositeKeyComparator.class);
```

The CompositeKeyComparator class tells the MapReduce framework how to sort the composite keys. The implementation in Example 2-2 compares two WritableComparable objects (representing a CompositeKey object).

Example 2-2. Comparator class: CompositeKeyComparator

```
 1 import org.apache.hadoop.io.WritableComparable;
 2 import org.apache.hadoop.io.WritableComparator;
 3
 4 public class CompositeKeyComparator extends WritableComparator {
 5
 6     protected CompositeKeyComparator() {
 7         super(CompositeKey.class, true);
 8     }
 9
10     @Override
11     public int compare(WritableComparable k1, WritableComparable k2) {
12         CompositeKey ck1 = (CompositeKey) k1;
13         CompositeKey ck2 = (CompositeKey) k2;
14
15         // compare ck1 with ck2 and return
16         //  0,  if ck1 and ck2 are identical
17         //  1,  if ck1 > ck2
18         // -1,  if ck1 < ck2
19
20         // detail of implementation is provided in subsections
21     }
22 }
```

The next class to plug in is a "natural key partitioner" class (let's call it NaturalKeyPartitioner) that will implement the Partitioner[1] interface. Example 2-3 shows how we plug this class into the MapReduce framework.

Example 2-3. Plugging in NaturalKeyPartitioner

```
1 import org.apache.hadoop.mapred.JobConf;
2 ...
3 JobConf conf = new JobConf(getConf(), <your-mapreduce-driver-class>.class);
4 ...
5 conf.setPartitionerClass(NaturalKeyPartitioner.class);
```

---

[1] org.apache.hadoop.mapred.Partitioner

Next, we define the `NaturalKeyPartitioner` class, as shown in Example 2-4.

Example 2-4. Defining the NaturalKeyPartitioner class

```
1 import org.apache.hadoop.mapred.JobConf;
2 import org.apache.hadoop.mapred.Partitioner;
3
4 /**
5  * NaturalKeyPartitioner partitions the data output from the
6  * map phase before it is sent through the shuffle phase.
7  *
8  * getPartition() partitions data generated by mappers.
9  * This function should partition data by the natural key.
10  *
11  */
12 public class NaturalKeyPartitioner implements
13      Partitioner<CompositeKey, NaturalValue> {
14
15      @Override
16      public int getPartition(CompositeKey key,
17                              NaturalValue value,
18                              int numberOfPartitions) {
19          return <number-based-on-composite-key>  % numberOfPartitions;
20      }
21
22      @Override
23      public void configure(JobConf arg) {
24      }
25 }
```

The last piece to plug in is `NaturalKeyGroupingComparator`, which just compares two natural keys. Example 2-5 shows how you plug this class into the MapReduce framework.

Example 2-5. Plugging in NaturalKeyGroupingComparator

```
1 import org.apache.hadoop.mapred.JobConf;
2 ...
3 JobConf conf = new JobConf(getConf(), <your-mapreduce-driver-class>.class);
4 ...
5 conf.setOutputValueGroupingComparator(NaturalKeyGroupingComparator.class);
```

Next, as shown in Example 2-6, we define the `NaturalKeyGroupingComparator` class.

Example 2-6. Defining the NaturalKeyGroupingComparator class

```
1 import org.apache.hadoop.io.WritableComparable;
2 import org.apache.hadoop.io.WritableComparator;
3
4 /**
```

```
 5   *
 6   * NaturalKeyGroupingComparator
 7   *
 8   * This class is used during Hadoop's shuffle phase to group
 9   * composite keys by the first part (natural) of their key.
10   */
11  public class NaturalKeyGroupingComparator extends WritableComparator {
12
13      protected NaturalKeyGroupingComparator() {
14          super(NaturalKey.class, true);
15      }
16
17      @Override
18      public int compare(WritableComparable o1, WritableComparable o2) {
19          NaturalKey nk1 = (NaturalKey) o1;
20          NaturalKey nk2 = (NaturalKey) o2;
21          return nk1.getNaturalKey().compareTo(nk2.getNaturalKey());
22      }
23  }
```

Complete Example of Secondary Sorting

Consider the following data:

```
Stock-Symbol    Date    Closed-Price
```

and assume that we want to generate the following output data per stock symbol:

```
Stock-Symbol: (Date₁, Price₁)(Date₂, Price₂)...(Dateₙ, Priceₙ)
```

where:

$$Date_1 \leq Date_2 \leq \ldots \leq Date_n$$

We want the reducer values to be sorted by the date of the closed price. We can accomplish this by secondary sorting.

Input Format

We assume that our input data is in CSV format:

```
Stock-Symbol,Date,Closed-Price
```

For example:

```
ILMN,2013-12-05,97.65
GOOG,2013-12-09,1078.14
IBM,2013-12-09,177.46
ILMN,2013-12-09,101.33
ILMN,2013-12-06,99.25
GOOG,2013-12-06,1069.87
IBM,2013-12-06,177.67
GOOG,2013-12-05,1057.34
```

Output Format

We want our output to be sorted by date of closed price, so for our sample input, our desired output is listed as follows:

```
ILMN: (2013-12-05,97.65)(2013-12-06,99.25)(2013-12-09,101.33)
GOOG: (2013-12-05,1057.34)(2013-12-06,1069.87)(2013-12-09,1078.14)
IBM: (2013-12-06,177.67)(2013-12-09,177.46)
```

Composite Key

The natural key is the stock symbol, and the composite key is a pair of (Stock-Symbol,Date). The Date field has to be part of our composite key because we want reducer values to be sorted by Date. The natural key and composite key are illustrated in Figure 2-2.

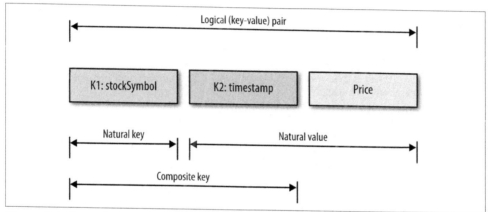

Figure 2-2. Secondary sorting: composite and natural keys

We can define the composite key class as CompositeKey and its associated comparator class as CompositeKeyComparator (this class tells MapReduce how to sort objects of CompositeKey).

Composite key definition

In Example 2-7, the composite key is defined as the CompositeKey class, which implements the WritableComparable<CompositeKey> interface.[2]

---

[2] WritableComparable(s) can be compared to each other, typically via Comparator(s). Any type that is to be used as a key in the Hadoop/MapReduce framework should implement this interface.

Example 2-7. Defining the composite key

```
 1 import java.io.DataInput;
 2 import java.io.DataOutput;
 3 import java.io.IOException;
 4 import org.apache.hadoop.io.WritableComparable;
 5 import org.apache.hadoop.io.WritableComparator;
 6
 7 /**
 8  *
 9  * CompositeKey: represents a pair of (String stockSymbol, long timestamp).
10  * Note that timestamp represents the Date.
11  *
12  * We do a primary grouping pass on the stockSymbol field to get all of
13  * the data of one type together, and then our secondary sort during
14  * the shuffle phase uses the timestamp long member to sort the data points
15  * so that they arrive at the reducer partitioned and in sorted order (by date).
16  *
17  */
18 public class CompositeKey implements WritableComparable<CompositeKey> {
19     // natural key is (stockSymbol)
20     // composite key is a pair (stockSymbol, timestamp)
21     private String stockSymbol;  // stock symbol
22     private long timestamp;       // date
23
24     public CompositeKey(String stockSymbol, long timestamp) {
25         set(stockSymbol, timestamp);
26     }
27
28     public CompositeKey() {
29     }
30
31     public void set(String stockSymbol, long timestamp) {
32         this.stockSymbol = stockSymbol;
33         this.timestamp = timestamp;
34     }
35
36     public String getStockSymbol() {
37         return this.stockSymbol;
38     }
39
40     public long getTimestamp() {
41         return this.timestamp;
42     }
43
44     @Override
45     public void readFields(DataInput in) throws IOException {
46         this.stockSymbol = in.readUTF();
47         this.timestamp = in.readLong();
48     }
49
50     @Override
```

```
51    public void write(DataOutput out) throws IOException {
52        out.writeUTF(this.stockSymbol);
53        out.writeLong(this.timestamp);
54    }
55
56    @Override
57    public int compareTo(CompositeKey other) {
58        if (this.stockSymbol.compareTo(other.stockSymbol) != 0) {
59            return this.stockSymbol.compareTo(other.stockSymbol);
60        }
61        else if (this.timestamp != other.timestamp) {
62            return timestamp < other.timestamp ? -1 : 1;
63        }
64        else {
65            return 0;
66        }
67    }
68
69 }
```

Composite key comparator definition

Example 2-8 defines the composite key comparator as the CompositeKeyComparator class, which compares two CompositeKey objects by implementing the compare() method. The compare() method returns 0 if they are identical, -1 if the first composite key is smaller than the second one, and +1 otherwise.

Example 2-8. Defining the composite key comparator

```
1 import org.apache.hadoop.io.WritableComparable;
2 import org.apache.hadoop.io.WritableComparator;
3
4 /**
5  * CompositeKeyComparator
6  *
7  * The purpose of this class is to enable comparison of two CompositeKeys.
8  *
9  */
10 public class CompositeKeyComparator extends WritableComparator {
11
12     protected CompositeKeyComparator() {
13         super(CompositeKey.class, true);
14     }
15
16     @Override
17     public int compare(WritableComparable wc1, WritableComparable wc2) {
18         CompositeKey ck1 = (CompositeKey) wc1;
19         CompositeKey ck2 = (CompositeKey) wc2;
20
21         int comparison = ck1.getStockSymbol().compareTo(ck2.getStockSymbol());
22         if (comparison == 0) {
```

```
23              // stock symbols are equal here
24              if (ck1.getTimestamp() == ck2.getTimestamp()) {
25                  return 0;
26              }
27              else if (ck1.getTimestamp() < ck2.getTimestamp()) {
28                  return -1;
29              }
30              else {
31                  return 1;
32              }
33          }
34          else {
35              return comparison;
36          }
37      }
38 }
```

Sample Run—Old Hadoop API

The classes shown in Table 2-2 use the old Hadoop API to implement the Secondary Sort design pattern.

Table 2-2. Implementation classes using the old Hadoop API

Class name	Description
CompositeKey	Defines a composite key
CompositeKeyComparator	Implements sorting composite keys
DateUtil	Defines some useful date handling methods
HadoopUtil	Defines some utility functions
NaturalKeyGroupingComparator	Defines how natural keys will be grouped together
NaturalKeyPartitioner	Implements how natural keys will be partitioned
NaturalValue	Defines a natural value
SecondarySortDriver	Submits a job to Hadoop
SecondarySortMapper	Defines map()
SecondarySortReducer	Defines reduce()

Input

```
# hadoop fs -ls  /secondary_sort_chapter/input/
Found 1 items
-rw-r--r--   ...  /secondary_sort_chapter/input/sample_input.txt

# hadoop fs -cat /secondary_sort_chapter/input/sample_input.txt
ILMN,2013-12-05,97.65
GOOG,2013-12-09,1078.14
IBM,2013-12-09,177.46
```

```
ILMN,2013-12-09,101.33
ILMN,2013-12-06,99.25
GOOG,2013-12-06,1069.87
IBM,2013-12-06,177.67
GOOG,2013-12-05,1057.34
```

Running the MapReduce Job

```
# ./run.sh
...
13/12/12 21:13:20 INFO mapred.FileInputFormat: Total input paths to process : 1
13/12/12 21:13:21 INFO mapred.JobClient: Running job: job_201312122109_0002
13/12/12 21:13:22 INFO mapred.JobClient: map 0% reduce 0%
...
13/12/12 21:14:25 INFO mapred.JobClient: map 100% reduce 100%
...
13/12/12 21:14:26 INFO mapred.JobClient: Map-Reduce Framework
13/12/12 21:14:26 INFO mapred.JobClient: Map input records=8
13/12/12 21:14:26 INFO mapred.JobClient: Combine input records=0
13/12/12 21:14:26 INFO mapred.JobClient: Reduce input records=8
13/12/12 21:14:26 INFO mapred.JobClient: Reduce input groups=3
13/12/12 21:14:26 INFO mapred.JobClient: Combine output records=0
13/12/12 21:14:26 INFO mapred.JobClient: Reduce output records=3
13/12/12 21:14:26 INFO mapred.JobClient: Map output records=8
```

Output

```
# hadoop fs -ls /secondary_sort_chapter/output/
-rw-r--r-- 1 ... 0 2013-12-12 21:14 /secondary_sort_chapter/output/_SUCCESS
drwxr-xr-x - ... 0 2013-12-12 21:13 /secondary_sort_chapter/output/_logs
-rw-r--r-- 1 ... 0 2013-12-12 21:13 /secondary_sort_chapter/output/part-00000
-rw-r--r-- 1 ... 66 2013-12-12 21:13 /secondary_sort_chapter/output/part-00001
...
-rw-r--r-- 1 ... 0 2013-12-12 21:14 /secondary_sort_chapter/output/part-00008
-rw-r--r-- 1 ... 43 2013-12-12 21:14 /secondary_sort_chapter/output/part-00009

# hadoop fs -cat /secondary_sort_chapter/output/part*
GOOG (2013-12-05,1057.34)(2013-12-06,1069.87)(2013-12-09,1078.14)
ILMN (2013-12-05,97.65)(2013-12-06,99.25)(2013-12-09,101.33)
IBM (2013-12-06,177.67)(2013-12-09,177.46)
```

Sample Run—New Hadoop API

The classes shown in Table 2-3 use the new Hadoop API to implement the Secondary
Sort design pattern.

Table 2-3. Implementation classes using the new Hadoop API

Class name	Description
CompositeKey	Defines a composite key
CompositeKeyComparator	Implements sorting composite keys
DateUtil	Defines some useful date handling methods
HadoopUtil	Defines some utility functions
NaturalKeyGroupingComparator	Defines how natural keys will be grouped together
NaturalKeyPartitioner	Implements how natural keys will be partitioned
NaturalValue	Defines a natural value
SecondarySortDriver	Submits a job to Hadoop
SecondarySortMapper	Defines map()
SecondarySortReducer	Defines reduce()

Input

```
# hadoop fs -ls /secondary_sort_chapter_new_api/input/
Found 1 items
-rw-r--r--   ... /secondary_sort_chapter_new_api/input/sample_input.txt
# hadoop fs -cat /secondary_sort_chapter_new_api/input/sample_input.txt
ILMN,2013-12-05,97.65
GOOG,2013-12-09,1078.14
IBM,2013-12-09,177.46
ILMN,2013-12-09,101.33
ILMN,2013-12-06,99.25
GOOG,2013-12-06,1069.87
IBM,2013-12-06,177.67
GOOG,2013-12-05,1057.34
```

Running the MapReduce Job

```
 # ./run.sh
...
13/12/14 21:18:25 INFO ... Total input paths to process : 1
...
13/12/14 21:18:25 INFO mapred.JobClient: Running job: job_201312142112_0002
13/12/14 21:18:26 INFO mapred.JobClient: map 0% reduce 0%

13/12/14 21:19:15 INFO mapred.JobClient: map 100% reduce 100%
13/12/14 21:19:16 INFO mapred.JobClient: Job complete: job_201312142112_0002
...
13/12/14 21:19:16 INFO mapred.JobClient: Map-Reduce Framework
13/12/14 21:19:16 INFO mapred.JobClient: Map input records=8
13/12/14 21:19:16 INFO mapred.JobClient: Spilled Records=16
13/12/14 21:19:16 INFO mapred.JobClient: Combine input records=0
13/12/14 21:19:16 INFO mapred.JobClient: Reduce input records=8
```

```
13/12/14 21:19:16 INFO mapred.JobClient: Reduce input groups=3
13/12/14 21:19:16 INFO mapred.JobClient: Combine output records=0
13/12/14 21:19:16 INFO mapred.JobClient: Reduce output records=3
13/12/14 21:19:16 INFO mapred.JobClient: Map output records=8
```

Output

```
# hadoop fs -cat /secondary_sort_chapter_new_api/output/part*
GOOG    (2013-12-05,1057.34)(2013-12-06,1069.87)(2013-12-09,1078.14)
ILMN    (2013-12-05,97.65)(2013-12-06,99.25)(2013-12-09,101.33)
IBM     (2013-12-06,177.67)(2013-12-09,177.46)
```

This chapter and the preceding one presented concrete solutions implementing the Secondary Sort design pattern. The next chapter shows how to implement the Top N design pattern through MapReduce/Hadoop and Spark.

## CHAPTER 3

Top 10 List

Given a set of (`key-as-string, value-as-integer`) pairs, say we want to create a *top N* (where $N > 0$) list. Top N is a design pattern (recall from Chapter 1 that a design pattern is a language-independent reusable solution to a common problem that enables us to produce reusable code). For example, if `key-as-string` is a URL and `value-as-integer` is the number of times that URL is visited, then you might ask: what are the top 10 URLs for last week? This kind of question is common for these types of key-value pairs. Finding a top 10 list is categorized as a filtering pattern (i.e., you filter out data and find the top 10 list). For details on the Top N design pattern, refer to the book *MapReduce Design Patterns* by Donald Miner and Adam Shook[18].

This chapter provides five complete MapReduce solutions for the Top N design pattern and its associated implementations with Apache Hadoop (using classic MapReduce's `map()` and `reduce()` functions) and Apache Spark (using resilient distributed data sets):

- Top 10 solution in MapReduce/Hadoop. We assume that all input keys are unique. That is, for a given input set $\{(K, V)\}$, all Ks are unique.

- Top 10 solution in Spark. We assume that all input keys are unique. That is, for a given input set $\{(K, V)\}$, all Ks are unique. For this solution, we do not use Spark's sorting functions, such as `top()` or `takeOrdered()`.

- Top 10 solution in Spark. We assume that all input keys are not unique. That is, for a given input set $\{(K, V)\}$, all Ks are not unique. For this solution, we do not use Spark's sorting functions, such as `top()` or `takeOrdered()`.

- Top 10 solution in Spark. We assume that all input keys are not unique. That is, for a given input set $\{(K, V)\}$, all Ks are not unique. For this solution, we use Spark's powerful sorting function `takeOrdered()`.

- Top 10 solution in MapReduce/Hadoop. We assume that all input keys are non-unique. That is, for a given input set {(K, V)}, all Ks are nonunique.

Our MapReduce solutions will generalize the top 10 list and will be able to find the top N list (for N > 0). For example, we will be able to find the "top 10 cats," "top 50 most visited websites," or "top 100 search queries of a search engine."

Top N, Formalized

Let N be an integer number and N > 0. Let L be a List<Tuple2<T,Integer>>, where T can be any type (such as a string or URL); L.size() = S; S > N; and elements of L be:

$$\{(K_i, V_i), 1 \le i \le S\}$$

where K_i has a type of T and V_i is an Integer type (this is the frequency of K_i). Let sort(L) return the sorted values of L by using the frequency as a key, as follows:

$$\{(A_j, B_j), 1 \le j \le S, B_1 \ge B_2 \ge ... \ge B_S\}$$

where $(A_j, B_j) \in L$. Then the top N of L is defined as:

$$\mathsf{topN}(L) = \{(A_j, B_j), 1 \le j \le N, B_1 \ge B_2 \ge ... \ge B_N \ge B_{N+1} \ge ... \ge B_S\}$$

To implement Top N, we need a hash table data structure such that we can have a total order on its keys (keys represent frequencies). The easy way to implement Top N in Java is to use SortedMap<K,V>[1] (as an interface) and TreeMap<K,V> (as an implementation class for SortedMap) and then keep adding all elements of L to topN, making sure to remove the first element (the element with the smallest frequency) of topN if topN.size() > N (i.e., keep only N entries at all times). Example 3-1 illustrates the Top N algorithm for list L.

Example 3-1. Top N algorithm

```
1 import scala.Tuple2;
2 import java.util.List;
3 import java.util.TreeMap;     // class, implements SortedMap
4 import java.util.SortedMap;   // interface, maintains sorted map
5 import <your-package>.T;      // your desired type T
6 ...
```

---

1 This is a map that further provides a total ordering on its keys. The map is ordered according to the natural ordering of its keys, or by a comparator typically provided when the sorted map is created. (Source: Java SE 7 documentation (http://bit.ly/sortedmap).)

```
 7 static SortedMap<Integer, T> topN(List<Tuple2<T, Integer>> L, int N) {
 8     if ( (L == null) || (L.isEmpty()) ) {
 9         return null;
10     }
11     SortedMap<Integer, T> topN = new TreeMap<Integer, T>();
12     for (Tuple2<T,Integer> element : L) {
13         // element._1 is a type T
14         // element._2 is the frequency, of type Integer
15         topN.put(element._2, element._1);
16         // keep only top N
17         if (topN.size() > N) {
18             // remove element with the smallest frequency
19             topN.remove(topN.firstKey());
20         }
21     }
22     return topN;
23 }
```

MapReduce/Hadoop Implementation: Unique Keys

For our first MapReduce solution, let cats be a relation of three attributes: cat_id, cat_name, and cat_weight, as shown in Table 3-1. Assume we have billions of cats (big data).

Table 3-1. Cat attributes

Attribute name	Attribute type
cat_id	String
cat_name	String
cat_weight	Double

Let N be an integer number, $N > 0$, and suppose we want to find the top N list of cats (based on cat_weight). Before we delve into this MapReduce solution, let's see how we can express a top 10 list of cats in SQL:

```
SELECT cat_id, cat_name, cat_weight
    FROM cats
        ORDER BY cat_weight DESC LIMIT 10;
```

The solution in SQL is very straightforward and will simply require sorting the whole cats table. So, you might be wondering why we don't just use a relational database and SQL for this. The short answer is that most often our big data is not as structured as relational databases and tables, and quite often we need to parse semistructured data such as logfiles or other types of data to sort it. And when the size of the data is huge, relational databases become nonresponsive and do not scale well.

The MapReduce solution is pretty straightforward: each mapper will find a local top N list (for $N > 0$) and then will pass it to a *single* reducer. Then the single reducer will find the final top *N* list from all the local top *N* lists passed from the mappers. In general, in most of the MapReduce algorithms, having a single reducer is problematic and will cause a performance bottleneck (because one reducer in one server receives all the data—which can be a large volume—and all the other cluster nodes do nothing, so all of the pressure and load is on that single node). Here, our single reducer will not cause a performance problem. Why? Let's assume that we have 1,000 mappers, so each mapper will generate only 10 key-value pairs. Therefore, our single reducer will get only 10,000 (10 × 1,000) records—which is not nearly enough data to cause a performance bottleneck!

The Top N algorithm is presented in Figure 3-1. Input is partitioned into smaller chunks, and each chunk is sent to a mapper. As just explained, each mapper creates a local top 10 list and then emits the local top 10 to be sent to the reducer. In emitting the mappers' output, we use a single reducer key so that all the mappers' output will be consumed by a single reducer.

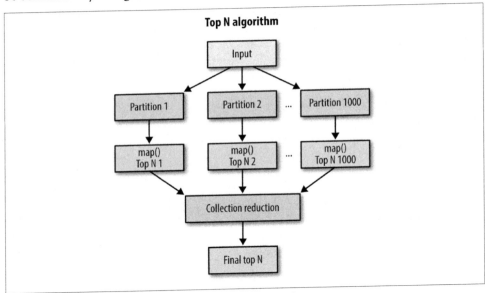

Figure 3-1. Top N MapReduce algorithm: for unique keys

To parameterize the top *N* list, we just need to pass the *N* from the driver (which launched the MapReduce job) to the map() and reduce() functions by using the MapReduce Configuration object.[2] The driver sets the "top.n" parameter and map() and reduce() read that parameter, in their setup() functions.

---

2 org.apache.hadoop.conf.Configuration

Here we will focus on finding the top N list of cats. The mapper class will have the structure shown in Example 3-2.

Example 3-2. Mapper class outline for top N cats

```
1  // imports ...
2  public class TopN_Mapper {
3     // define data structures needed for finding local top 10
4     private SortedMap<Double, Text> top10cats = new TreeMap<Double, Text>();
5     private int N = 10; // default is top 10
6
7     // setup() function will be executed once per mapper
8     setup(Context context) {
9        ...
10    }
11
12    map(key, value) {
13       ... process (key, value) pair
14    }
15
16    // cleanup() function will be executed once per mapper
17    cleanup(Context context) {
18       ...
19    }
20 }
```

Next, we define the `setup()` function, which will be executed once per mapper (Example 3-3).

Example 3-3. setup() for top N list

```
1  public class TopN_Mapper {
2     ...
3     private SortedMap<Double, Text> top10cats = new TreeMap<Double, Text>();
4     private int N = 10; // default is top 10
5
6  /**
7   * setup() function will be executed once per mapper
8   * Here we set up the "cats top N list" as top10cats
9   */
10 setup(Context context) {
11    // "top.n" has to be set up by the driver of our job
12    Configuration conf = context.getConfiguration();
13    N = conf.get("top.n");
14 }
```

The `map()` function accepts a chunk of input and generates a local top 10 list (Example 3-4). We are using different delimiters to optimize parsing input by mappers and reducers (to avoid unnecessary string concatenations).

Example 3-4. map() for top N list

```
1 /**
2  * @param key is generated by MapReduce framework, ignored here
3  * @param value as a String has the format:
4  *    <cat_weight><,><cat_id><;><cat_name>
5  */
6 map(key, value) {
7    String[] tokens = value.split(",");
8    // cat_weight = tokens[0];
9    // <cat_id><;><cat_name> = tokens[1]
10   Double weight = Double.parseDouble(tokens[0]);
11   top10cats.put(weight, value);
12
13   // keep only top N
14   if (top10cats.size() > N) {
15       // remove the element with the smallest frequency
16       top10cats.remove(top10cats.firstKey());
17   }
18 }
```

Each mapper accepts a partition of cats. After the mapper finishes creating a top 10 list as a `SortedMap<Double, Text>`, the `cleanup()` method emits that list (Example 3-5). Note that we use a single key, retrieved by calling `NullWrita ble.get()`, which guarantees that all the mappers' output will be consumed by a single reducer.

Example 3-5. cleanup() for top N list

```
1 /**
2  * cleanup() function will be executed once at the end of each mapper
3  * Here we set up the "cats top N list" as top10cats
4  */
5 cleanup(Context context) {
6    // now we emit top N from this mapper
7    for (String catAttributes : top10cats.values() ) {
8        context.write(NullWritable.get(), catAttributes);
9    }
10 }
```

The single reducer gets all local top 10 lists and creates a single, final top 10 list, as shown in Example 3-6.

Example 3-6. reduce() for top N list

```
1 /**
2  * @param key is null (single reducer)
3  * @param values is a List of Strings, and each element
4  *      of the list has the format <cat_weight>,<cat_id>;<cat_name>
5  */
```

```
 6 reduce(key, values) {
 7    SortedMap<Double, Text> finaltop10 = new TreeMap< Double, Text>();
 8
 9    // aggregate all local top 10 lists
10    for (Text catRecord : values) {
11       String[] tokens = catRecord.split(",");
12       Double weight = Double.parseDouble(tokens[0]);
13       finaltop10.put(weight, value);
14
15       if (finaltop10.size() > N) {
16          // remove the element with the smallest frequency
17          finaltop10.remove(finaltop10.firstKey());
18       }
19    }
20
21    // emit final top 10 list
22    for (Text text : finaltop10.values()) {
23       context.write(NullWritable.get(), text);
24    }
25 }
```

Implementation Classes in MapReduce/Hadoop

The MapReduce/Hadoop implementation is composed of the classes shown in Table 3-2. Note that this solution assumes that all cats (i.e., keys) are unique, which means that there will not be an aggregation on the input.

Table 3-2. Implementation classes in Hadoop

Class name	Class description
TopN_Driver	Driver to submit job
TopN_Mapper	Defines map()
TopN_Reducer	Defines reduce()

The TopN_Driver class reads N from a command line and sets it in the Hadoop Con figuration object to be read by the map() function.

Top 10 Sample Run

Input

```
# hadoop fs -cat /top10list/input/sample_input.txt
12,cat1,cat1
13,cat2,cat2
14,cat3,cat3
15,cat4,cat4
10,cat5,cat5
100,cat100,cat100
200,cat200,cat200
```

```
300,cat300,cat300
1,cat001,cat001
67,cat67,cat67
22,cat22,cat22
23,cat23,cat23
1000,cat1000,cat1000
2000,cat2000,cat2000
```

Script

```
# cat run.sh
#/bin/bash
export JAVA_HOME=/usr/java/jdk6
export HADOOP_HOME=/usr/local/hadoop-1.0.3
export HADOOP_HOME_WARN_SUPPRESS=true
export BOOK_HOME=/mp/data-algorithms-book
export APP_JAR=$BOOK_HOME/dist/data_algorithms_book.jar
export PATH=$PATH:$JAVA_HOME/bin:$HADOOP_HOME/bin
#
INPUT="/top10list/input"
OUTPUT="/top10list/output"
HADOOP_HOME/bin/hadoop  fs  -rmr  $OUTPUT
HADOOP_HOME/bin/hadoop  jar  $APP_JAR  TopN_Driver  $INPUT  $OUTPUT
```

Log of sample run

```
# ./run.sh
...
added manifest
adding: TopN_Driver.class(in = 3481) (out= 1660)(deflated 52%)
adding: TopN_Mapper.class(in = 3537) (out= 1505)(deflated 57%)
adding: TopN_Reducer.class(in = 3693) (out= 1599)(deflated 56%)
rmr: cannot remove /top10list/output: No such file or directory.
13/03/06 15:17:54 INFO TopN_Driver: inputDir=/top10list/input
13/03/06 15:17:54 INFO TopN_Driver: outputDir=/top10list/output
13/03/06 15:17:54 INFO TopN_Driver: top.n=10
13/03/06 15:17:54 INFO input.FileInputFormat: Total input paths to process : 1
...
13/03/06 15:17:55 INFO mapred.JobClient: Running job: job_201303061200_0022
13/03/06 15:17:56 INFO mapred.JobClient:  map 0% reduce 0%
13/03/06 15:18:10 INFO mapred.JobClient:  map 100% reduce 0%
13/03/06 15:18:22 INFO mapred.JobClient:  map 100% reduce 100%
13/03/06 15:18:27 INFO mapred.JobClient: Job complete: job_201303061200_0022
...
13/03/06 15:18:27 INFO mapred.JobClient:  Map-Reduce Framework
13/03/06 15:18:27 INFO mapred.JobClient:    Map output materialized bytes=193
13/03/06 15:18:27 INFO mapred.JobClient:    Map input records=14
13/03/06 15:18:27 INFO mapred.JobClient:    Reduce shuffle bytes=0
...
13/03/06 15:18:27 INFO mapred.JobClient:    Reduce input records=10
13/03/06 15:18:27 INFO mapred.JobClient:    Reduce input groups=1
13/03/06 15:18:27 INFO mapred.JobClient:    Combine output records=0
13/03/06 15:18:27 INFO mapred.JobClient:    Reduce output records=10
```

```
13/03/06 15:18:27 INFO mapred.JobClient:    Map output records=10
13/03/06 15:18:27 INFO TopN_Driver: run(): status=true
13/03/06 15:18:27 INFO TopN_Driver: returnStatus=0
```

Output

```
# hadoop fs -cat /top10list/output/part*
14.0     14,cat3,cat3
15.0     15,cat4,cat4
22.0     22,cat22,cat22
23.0     23,cat23,cat23
67.0     67,cat67,cat67
100.0    100,cat100,cat100
200.0    200,cat200,cat200
300.0    300,cat300,cat300
1000.0   1000,cat1000,cat1000
2000.0   2000,cat2000,cat2000
```

Finding the Top 5

The default returns a top 10 list, but if we want to get a top 5 list instead we just need to pass another parameter:

```
$  INPUT="/top10list/input"
$  OUTPUT="/top10list/output"
$  $HADOOP_HOME/bin/hadoop jar  $APP_JAR TopN_Driver  $INPUT  $OUTPUT  5
$  hadoop fs -cat /top10list/output/*
100.0    100,cat100,cat100
200.0    200,cat200,cat200
300.0    300,cat300,cat300
1000.0   1000,cat1000,cat1000
2000.0   2000,cat2000,cat2000
```

Finding the Bottom 10

To find the bottom 10 instead of the top 10, we just need to change one line of code.

Replace the following:

```
// find top 10
if (top10cats.size() > N) {
    // remove the element with the smallest frequency
    top10cats.remove(top10cats.firstKey());
}
```

with:

```
// find bottom 10
if (top10cats.size() > N) {
    // remove the element with the largest frequency
    top10cats.remove(top10cats.lastKey());
}
```

Spark Implementation: Unique Keys

For this Spark implementation, we assume that for all given input, (K, V) pairs, Ks are unique. Spark has a higher level of abstraction than classic MapReduce/Hadoop. Spark provides a rich set of functional programming APIs, which makes MapReduce programming easy. Spark can read/write data from the local filesystem as well as Hadoop's HDFS. It uses the Hadoop client library to read from and write to HDFS and other Hadoop-supported storage systems.

Here, I am assuming that you have a Spark cluster running on top of Hadoop (or you may run Spark on YARN without starting a Spark cluster). To learn how to install Spark/Hadoop, check out:

- The Apache Spark website (*http://spark.apache.org/*)
- *Fast Data Processing with Spark* by Holden Karau (Packt Publishing)

RDD Refresher

To understand Spark, we need to revisit the concept of RDDs (resilient distributed data sets). As you learned in Chapter 1, an RDD is the basic abstraction in Spark: it represents an immutable, partitioned collection of elements that you can operate on in parallel. Rather than working with different types of input/output, you work with an RDD, which can represent typed input/output. For example, the following code snippet presents two RDDs (lines and words):

```
1  JavaSparkContext ctx = new JavaSparkContext();
2  JavaRDD<String> lines = ctx.textFile(args[1], 1);
3  JavaRDD<String> words = lines.flatMap(new FlatMapFunction<String, String>() {
4     public Iterable<String> call(String s) {
5        return Arrays.asList(s.split(" "));
6     }
7  });
```

Table 3-3 explains the code.

Table 3-3. Spark RDD explanation

Line(s)	Description
1	Creates a Java Spark context object(JavaSparkContext). This represents the connection to a Spark cluster and can be used to create RDDs, accumulators, and broadcast variables on that cluster.
2	Creates a new RDD as JavaRDD<String>, which represents a text file as a set of lines (each line/record is a String object).
3–7	Create a new RDD (from an existing RDD) as JavaRDD<String>, which represents a tokenized set of words. FlatMapFunction<T, R> has a function type of T => Iterable<R>.

Spark is very powerful for creating new RDDs from existing ones. For example, next we use `lines` to create a new RDD, `JavaPairRDD<String, Integer>`, from `pairs`:

```
1 JavaPairRDD<String,Integer> pairs =
2    lines.map(new PairFunction<String, String, Integer>() {
3    public Tuple2<String,Integer> call(String s) {
4       String[] tokens = s.split(",");
5       return new Tuple2<String,Integer>(tokens[0],
6                                         Integer.parseInt(tokens[1])
7                                        );
8    }
9 });
```

Each item in the `JavaPairRDD<String,Integer>` represents a `Tuple2<String,Integer>`. Here we assume that each input record has two tokens: `<String><,><Integer>`.

Spark's Function Classes

Java does not support anonymous or first-class functions (some of these are implemented in JDK8), so we must implement functions by extending the classes `Function`,[3] `Function2`,[4] and so on. Spark's RDD methods, like `collect()` and `countByKey()`, return Java collection data types, such as `java.util.List` and `java.util.Map`. To represent key-value pairs, you may use `scala.Tuple2`, which is a Scala class, and you can create a new key-value pair by using `new Tuple2<K, V>(key, value)`.

The main power of Spark is in the function classes (see Table 3-4) used by the Java API, where each class has a single abstract method, `call()`, that must be implemented by a programmer.

Table 3-4. Spark function classes used by the Java API

Spark Java class	Function type
`Function<T, R>`	`T => R`
`DoubleFunction<T>`	`T => Double`
`PairFunction<T, K, V>`	`T => Tuple2<K, V>`
`FlatMapFunction<T, R>`	`T => Iterable<R>`
`DoubleFlatMapFunction<T>`	`T => Iterable<Double>`
`PairFlatMapFunction<T, K, V>`	`T => Iterable<Tuple2<K, V>>`
`Function2<T1, T2, R>`	`T1, T2 => R` (function of two arguments)

---

3 `org.apache.spark.api.java.function.Function`

4 `org.apache.spark.api.java.function.Function2`

Review of the Top N Pattern for Spark

In Spark, you can write your whole big data processing job in a single driver, thanks to Spark's rich high-level abstraction of the MapReduce paradigm. Before presenting the complete top 10 solution in Spark, let's review the Top 10 algorithm. We'll assume that our input records have the following format:

```
<Integer><,><String>
```

and our goal is to find the top 10 list for a given input. First, we will partition our input into segments (let's say we partition our input into 1,000 mappers, and each mapper will work on one segment of the partition independently):

```
 1 class mapper :
 2     setup(): initialize top10 SortedMap<Integer, String>
 3
 4     map(key, inputRecord):
 5         key is system generated and ignored here
 6         insert inputRecord into top10 SortedMap
 7         if (length of top10 is greater than 10) {
 8             truncate list to a length of 10
 9         }
10
11     cleanup(): emit top10 as SortedMap<Integer, String>
```

Since Spark does not support the classic MapReduce/Hadoop `setup()` and `cleanup()` functions in the mapper or reducer, we will use the `JavaPairRDD.mapPartitions()` method to achieve the same functionality.

But how do we implement Spark's equivalent of the `setup()` and `cleanup()` functions? In the classic MapReduce/Hadoop framework, we use `setup()` and `cleanup()` as follows:

```
 1 public class ClassicMapper extends Mapper<K,V,K2,V2> {
 2    private ExpensiveConnection expensiveConn;
 3    @Override
 4    protected void setup(Context context) {
 5      expensiveConn = ...;
 6    }
 7    ...
 8    @Override
 9    protected void cleanup(Context context) {
10      expensiveConn.close();
11    }
12    ...
13    // map() functionality: use expensiveConn
14 }
```

In Spark, here's how the same functionality is achieved with `mapPartitions()`:

```
1 JavaRDD<Tuple2<K2,V2>> partitions = pairRDD.mapPartitions(
2     new FlatMapFunction<Iterator<Tuple2<K,V>>, Tuple2<K2,V2>>() {
3     @Override
4     public Iterable<Tuple2<K2,V2>> call(Iterator<Tuple2<K,V>> iter) {
5         setup();
6         while (iter.hasNext()) {
7             // map() functionality
8         }
9         cleanup();
10        return <the-result>;
11    }
12 });
```

The reducer's job is similar to the mapper's: it finds the final top 10 from a given set of all the top 10 lists generated by mappers. The reducer will get a collection of Sorted Map<Integer, String> objects as an input and will create a single final Sorted Map<Integer, String> as an output:

```
1 class reducer:
2     setup(): initialize finaltop10 SortedMap<Integer, String>
3
4     reduce(key, List<SortedMap<Integer, String>>):
5         build finaltop10 from List<SortedMap<Integer, String>>
6         emit finaltop10
```

Complete Spark Top 10 Solution

First, I will present all the main steps (Example 3-7), and then I will describe each step in detail. We use a single Java class (represented as Top10.java) for finding the top 10 in Spark.

Example 3-7. The top 10 program in Spark

```
1 // Step 1: import required classes
2 public class Top10 {
3     public static void main(String[] args) throws Exception {
4         // Step 2: make sure we have proper input parameters
5         // Step 3: create a connection to the Spark master
6         // Step 4: read input file from HDFS and create first RDD
7         // Step 5: create a set of Tuple2<Integer, String>
8         // Step 6: create a local top 10 for each input partition
9         // Step 7: collect all local top 10s and create a final top 10 list
10        // Step 8: output the final top 10 list
11        System.exit(0);
12    }
13 }
```

Step 1: Import required classes

Example 3-8 shows the classes that need to be imported as the first step.

Example 3-8. Step 1: import required classes

```
1 // Step 1: import required classes
2 import scala.Tuple2;
3 import org.apache.spark.api.java.JavaRDD;
4 import org.apache.spark.api.java.JavaPairRDD;
5 import org.apache.spark.api.java.JavaSparkContext;
6 import org.apache.spark.api.java.function.FlatMapFunction;
7 import org.apache.spark.api.java.function.Function2;
8 import org.apache.spark.api.java.function.PairFunction;
9
10 import java.util.Arrays;
11 import java.util.List;
12 import java.util.Map;
13 import java.util.TreeMap;
14 import java.util.SortedMap;
15 import java.util.Iterator;
16 import java.util.Collections;
```

Step 2: Handle input parameters

In this step (shown in Example 3-9), we make sure we have one input parameter: the HDFS input file. For example:

```
args[0]: /top10/input/top10data.txt
```

Example 3-9. Step 2: handle input parameters

```
1    // Step 2: make sure we have proper input parameters
2    if (args.length < 1) {
3        System.err.println("Usage: Top10 <hdfs-file>");
4        System.exit(1);
5    }
6    String inputPath = args[0];
7    System.out.println("inputPath: <hdfs-file>="+inputPath);
```

Step 3: Connect to Spark master

In this step (shown in Example 3-10), we create a connection object (JavaSparkCon text) to a Sparkmaster. We will use the ctx object to create RDDs.

Example 3-10. Step 3: connect to Spark master

```
1    // Step 3: create a connection to the Spark master
2    JavaSparkContext ctx = new JavaSparkContext();
```

Step 4: Read input file from HDFS and create RDD

In this step, shown in Example 3-11, we read a file from HDFS and create an RDD (JavaRDD<String>).

Example 3-11. Step 4: read input file from HDFS

```
1    // Step 4: read input file from HDFS and create first RDD
2    // input record format: <string-key><,><integer-value>
3    JavaRDD<String> lines = ctx.textFile(inputPath, 1);
```

Top10 class: Step 5

In this step (shown in Example 3-12), we create a new RDD (JavaPairRDD<Integer, String>) from an existing RDD (JavaRDD<String>). The PairFunction class has three arguments—the first argument (T) is an input, and the last two (K, V) are output:

- Spark Java class: PairFunction<T, K, V>

- Function type: T => Tuple2<K, V>

Example 3-12. Step 5: create a set of Tuple2

```
1    // Step 5: create a set of Tuple2<String,Integer>
2    // PairFunction<T, K, V>
3    // T => Tuple2<K, V>
4    JavaPairRDD<String,Integer> pairs =
5        lines.mapToPair(new PairFunction<
6                                    String,   // input (T)
7                                    String,   // K
8                                    Integer   // V
9                                    >() {
10      public Tuple2<String,Integer> call(String s) {
11        String[] tokens = s.split(","); // cat24,123
12        return new Tuple2<String,Integer>(tokens[0], Integer.parseInt(tokens[1]));
13      }
14   });
```

Step 6: Create a local top 10 list for each input partition

In this step, again, we create a new RDD (JavaRDD<SortedMap<Integer, String>>) from an existing RDD (JavaPairRDD<String,Integer>). As we've discussed, mapPartitions() is a very powerful method that enables us to reproduce the functionality of the classic MapReduce/Hadoop methods setup(), map(), and cleanup(). As you can see in Example 3-13, we create a local top 10 list from each partition.

Example 3-13. Step 6: create a local top 10 list for each input partition

```
1    // Step 6: create a local top 10 for each input partition
2    JavaRDD<SortedMap<Integer, String>> partitions = pairs.mapPartitions(
3        new FlatMapFunction<
4                        Iterator<Tuple2<String,Integer>>,
```

```
  5                         SortedMap<Integer, String>
  6                 >() {
  7       @Override
  8       public Iterable<SortedMap<Integer, String>>
  9          call(Iterator<Tuple2<String,Integer>> iter) {
 10          SortedMap<Integer, String> top10 = new TreeMap<Integer, String>();
 11          while (iter.hasNext()) {
 12             Tuple2<String,Integer> tuple = iter.next();
 13             // tuple._1 : unique key such as cat_id
 14             // tuple._2 : frequency of the item (cat_weight)
 15             top10.put(tuple._2, tuple._1);
 16             // keep only top N
 17             if (top10.size() > 10) {
 18                // remove the element with the smallest frequency
 19                top10.remove(top10.firstKey());
 20             }
 21          }
 22          return Collections.singletonList(top10);
 23       }
 24    });
```

Line 10 accomplishes the MapReduce/Hadoop `setup()` equivalent functionality (i.e., it creates and initializes a local top 10 list as a `SortedMap<Integer, String>`). Lines 11–20 mimic the `map()` function. Finally, the `cleanup()` method is reproduced by line 22 (which returns the result of a local top 10 list).

Step 7: Create the final top 10 list using collect()

This step iterates over all local top 10 lists created per partition and creates a single, final top 10 list. To get all local top 10 lists, we use the `collect()` method, as shown in Example 3-14.

Example 3-14. Step 7: create the final top 10 list using collect()

```
  1    // Step 7: collect all local top 10 lists and create a final top 10 list
  2    SortedMap<Integer, String> finaltop10 = new TreeMap<Integer, String>();
  3    List<SortedMap<Integer, String>> alltop10 = partitions.collect();
  4    for (SortedMap<Integer, String> localtop10 : alltop10) {
  5       // weight = tuple._1 (frequency)
  6       // catname = tuple._2
  7       for (Map.Entry<Integer, String> entry : localtop10.entrySet()) {
  8          //    System.out.println(entry.getKey() + "--" + entry.getValue());
  9          finaltop10.put(entry.getKey(), entry.getValue());
 10          // keep only top 10
 11          if (finaltop10.size() > 10) {
 12             // remove the element with the smallest frequency
 13             finaltop10.remove(finaltop10.firstKey());
 14          }
 15       }
 16    }
```

There is an alternative solution for this step: use `JavaRDD.reduce()`. The alternative solution is presented in Example 3-15. Before you review that solution, let's look at its signature:

```
T reduce(Function2<T,T,T> f)
// Reduces the elements of this RDD using the
// specified commutative and associative binary operator.
```

Example 3-15. Step 7: create the final top 10 list using reduce()

```
1     // Step 7: collect all local top 10s and create a final top 10 list
2     SortedMap<Integer, String> finaltop10 = partitions.reduce(
3         new Function2<
4                     SortedMap<Integer, String>, // m1 (as input)
5                     SortedMap<Integer, String>, // m2 (as input)
6                     SortedMap<Integer, String>  // output: merge of m1 and m2
7                 >() {
8         @Override
9         public SortedMap<Integer, String> call(SortedMap<Integer, String> m1,
10                                    SortedMap<Integer, String> m2) {
11            // merge m1 and m2 into a single top 10
12            SortedMap<Integer, String> top10 = new TreeMap<Integer, String>();
13
14            // process m1
15            for (Map.Entry<Integer, String> entry : m1.entrySet()) {
16                top10.put(entry.getKey(), entry.getValue());
17                if (top10.size() > 10) {
18                    // keep only top 10, remove element with smallest frequency
19                    top10.remove(top10.firstKey());
20                }
21            }
22
23            // process m2
24            for (Map.Entry<Integer, String> entry : m2.entrySet()) {
25                top10.put(entry.getKey(), entry.getValue());
26                if (top10.size() > 10) {
27                    // keep only top 10, remove element with smallest frequency
28                    top10.remove(top10.firstKey());
29                }
30            }
31
32            return top10;
33        }
34    });
```

Step 8: Emit the final top 10 list

This step, shown in Example 3-16, emits the final top 10 list by iterating over the `SortedMap<Integer, String>`.

Example 3-16. Step 8: emit the final top-10 list

```
1    // Step 8: output the final top 10 list
2    System.out.println("=== top-10 list ===");
3    for (Map.Entry<Integer, String> entry : finaltop10.entrySet()) {
4        System.out.println(entry.getKey() + "--" + entry.getValue());
5    }
```

Sample Run: Finding the Top 10

This sample run is done on a three-node cluster—sparkserver100, sparkserver200, and sparkserver300—where sparkserver100 is the master Spark node.

Input

For our sample run, I have created the following sample input file:

```
# hadoop fs -ls /top10/input/top10data.txt
Found 1 items
-rw-r--r--   ... 161 2014-04-28 14:22 /top10/input/top10data.txt

# hadoop fs -cat /top10/input/top10data.txt
cat1,12
cat2,13
cat3,14
cat4,15
cat5,10
cat100,100
cat200,200
cat300,300
cat1001,1001
cat67,67
cat22,22
cat23,23
cat1000,1000
cat2000,2000
cat400,400
cat500,500
```

The script

```
# cat run_top10.sh
export JAVA_HOME=/usr/java/jdk7
export SPARK_HOME=/usr/local/spark-1.1.0
export SPARK_MASTER=spark://myserver100:7077
BOOK_HOME=/mp/data-algorithms-book
APP_JAR=$BOOK_HOME/data_algorithms_book.jar
INPUT=/top10/top10data.txt
prog=org.dataalgorithms.chap03.spark.Top10
# Run on a Spark standalone cluster
$SPARK_HOME/bin/spark-submit \
  --class $prog \
```

```
  --master $SPARK_MASTER \
  --executor-memory 2G \
  --total-executor-cores 20 \
    $APP_JAR $INPUT
```

Top 10 run with Spark cluster

The log output of a sample run is shown here, formatted to fit the page:

```
# ./run_top10.sh
inputPath: <file>=/top10/top10data.txt
...
14/06/03 22:42:24 INFO spark.SparkContext: Job finished:
collect at Top10.java:69, took 4.521464436 s
key= cat10 value= 10
key= cat1 value= 1
key= cat10000 value= 10000
key= cat400 value= 400
key= cat500 value= 500
key= cat2 value= 2
key= cat4 value= 4
key= cat6 value= 6
key= cat1200 value= 1200
key= cat10 value= 10
key= cat11 value= 11
key= cat12 value= 12
key= cat13 value= 13
key= cat50 value= 50
key= cat51 value= 51
key= cat45 value= 45
key= cat46 value= 46
key= cat200 value= 200
key= cat234 value= 234
...
collect at Top10.java:116, took 1.15125893 s
45--cat45
46--cat46
50--cat50
51--cat51
200--cat200
234--cat234
400--cat400
500--cat500
1200--cat1200
10000--cat10000
```

Parameterizing Top N

In the MapReduce/Hadoop implementation we were able to parameterize N, so we could find the top 10, top 20, or top 100. But how do we parameterize N in Spark? By using the `Broadcast` object. `Broadcast` allows us to make *N* available as globally shared data so we'll be able to access it from any cluster node. This is how we do that:

```
 1 import org.apache.spark.broadcast.Broadcast;
 2 import org.apache.spark.api.java.JavaSparkContext;
 3 ...
 4 int topN = <any-integer-number-greater-than-zero>;
 5 ...
 6 JavaSparkContext context = new JavaSparkContext();
 7 ...
 8 // broadcastTopN can be accessed from any cluster node
 9 final Broadcast<Integer> broadcastTopN = context.broadcast(topN);
10
11 RDD.map() {
12     ...
13     final int topN = broadcastTopN.value();
14     // use topN
15     ...
16 }
17
18 RDD.groupBy() {
19     ...
20     final int topN = broadcastTopN.value();
21     // use topN
22     ...
23 }
```

The breakdown of this code is as follows:

- Lines 1–2 import the required classes. The `Broadcast` class enables us to define globally shared data structures and then read them from any cluster node. The general format to define a shared data structure of type `T` is:

```
JavaSparkContext context = <an-instance-of-JavaSparkContext>;
...
T t = <create-data-structure-of-type-T>;
Broadcast<T> broadcastT = context.broadcast(t);
```

After the data structure, `broadcastT`, is broadcasted, it may be read from any cluster node within mappers, reducers, and transformers. Note that in this example we just broadcasted a single integer value (for top *N*), but you may broadcast any data structure you wish to share.

- Line 4 defines our `topN` as top 10, top 20, or top 100.

- Line 6 creates an instance of `JavaSparkContext`.

- Line 9 defines a global shared data structure for `topN` (which can be any value).

- Lines 13 and 20 read and use a globally shared data structure for topN (from any cluster node). The general format to read a shared data structure of type T is:

```
T t = broadcastT.value();
```

Finding the Bottom N

What if you want to find the bottom *N* instead of the top *N*? You can achieve this with another parameter, which will be shared among all cluster nodes. The value of this shared variable, called direction, can be either {"top" or "bottom"}:

```
 1 import org.apache.spark.broadcast.Broadcast;
 2 import org.apache.spark.api.java.JavaSparkContext;
 3 ...
 4 final int N = <any-integer-number-greater-than-zero>;
 5 ...
 6 JavaSparkContext context = <create-a-context-object>;
 7 ...
 8 String direction = "top"; // or "bottom"
 9 ...
10 final Broadcast<Integer> broadcastN = context.broadcast(N);
11 final Broadcast<String> broadcastDirection = context.broadcast(direction);
```

Now, based on the value of broadcastDirection, we will either remove the first entry (when direction is equal to "top") or the last entry (when direction is equal to "bottom"). This has to be done consistently to all code:

```
 1 final int N = broadcastN.value();
 2 final String direction = broadcastDirection.value();
 3 SortedMap<Integer, String> finalN = new TreeMap<Integer, String>();
 4 ...
 5 if (finalN.size() > N) {
 6     if (direction.equals("top")) {
 7         // remove element with the smallest frequency
 8         finalN.remove(finalN.firstKey());
 9     }
10     else {
11         // direction.equals("bottom")
12         // remove element with the largest frequency
13         finalN.remove(finalN.lastKey());
14     }
15 }
```

Spark Implementation: Nonunique Keys

For this implementation, we assume that for all given (K, V) pairs, Ks are not unique. Since our Ks are not unique, we have to do some extra steps to make sure that our keys are unique before applying the top 10 (or bottom 10) algorithm. To help you understand the solution for nonunique keys, I've provided a simple example. Let's assume that we want to find the 10 most visited URLs for a website. Further, assume that we have three web servers (web server 1, web server 2, and web server 3), and each web server has collected URLs in this form:

    (URL, count)

Let's also assume that we have only seven URLs, labeled *A*, *B*, *C*, *D*, *E*, *F*, and *G*. Table 3-5 lists the tallies of URLs generated for each web server.

Table 3-5. (URL, count) for each web server

Web server 1	Web server 2	Web server 3
(A, 2)	(A, 1)	(A, 2)
(B, 2)	(B, 1)	(B, 2)
(C, 3)	(C, 3)	(C, 1)
(D, 2)	(E, 1)	(D, 2)
(E, 1)	(F, 1)	(E, 1)
(G, 2)	(G, 2)	(F, 1)
		(G, 2)

Say we want to get the 2 most visited URLs. If we get the local top 2 for each web server and then get the top 2 of all three local top 2 lists, the result will not be correct. The reason is that URLs are not unique among all web servers. To get the correct result, first we must create a set of unique URLs from all the input and then partition those unique URLs into $M > 0$ partitions. Next we get the local top 2 for each partition, and finally we determine the final top 2 among all local top 2 lists. For our example, the generated unique URLs are listed in Table 3-6.

Table 3-6. Aggregated (URL, count) pairs

Aggregated/reduced (URL, count) pairs
(A, 5)
(B, 5)
(C, 7)
(D, 4)
(E, 3)

Aggregated/reduced (URL, count) pairs
(F, 2)
(G, 6)

Now assume that we partition all unique URLs into two partitions, as shown in Table 3-7.

Table 3-7. (URL, count) per partition

Partition 1	Partition 2
(A, 5)	(D, 4)
(B, 4)	(E, 3)
(C, 7)	(F, 2)
	(G, 6)

Here is how we find the top 2 of all data:

```
top-2(Partition-1) = { (C, 7), (A, 5) }
top-2(Partition-2) = { (G, 6), (D, 4) }
top-2(Partition-1, Partition-2) = { (C, 7), (G, 6) }
```

So, the main point is that before finding the top N of any set of (K, V) pairs, we have to make sure that all Ks are unique.

This section presents a Spark/Hadoop implementation of the Top N design pattern with the assumption that all Ks are nonunique. The main steps of our Top 10 algorithm are as follows:

1. Make all Ks unique. To make Ks unique, we will map our input into `Java PairRDD<K, V>` pairs and then `reduceByKey()`.
2. Partition all unique (K, V) pairs into M partitions.
3. Find the top N for each partition (we'll call this a *local* top N).
4. Find the top N from all local top Ns.

The Top 10 algorithm for nonunique keys is presented in Figure 3-2.

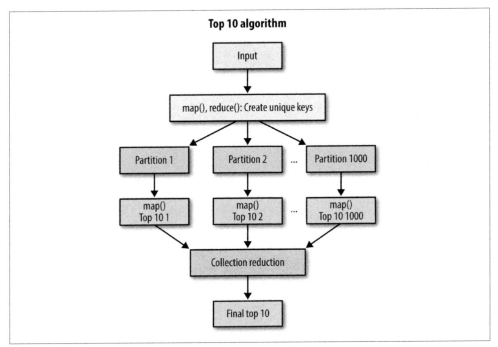

Figure 3-2. Top 10 MapReduce algorithm: for nonunique keys

Complete Spark Top 10 Solution

For the top 10 Spark solution, I will present all the high-level steps in Example 3-17 and then will expand upon each step. We use a single Java class (represented as Top10NonUnique.java) for finding the top 10 in Spark. Note that this solution is general, and despite the fact that one of the steps is to make sure all the keys are unique, in practice it really does not matter if they are or not.

Example 3-17. Top 10 nonunique program in Spark

```
1 package org.dataalgorithms.chap03;
2 // Step 1: import required classes and interfaces
3 /**
4  * Assumption: for all input (K, V), Ks are nonunique.
5  * This class implements the Top N design pattern for N > 0.
6  * The main assumption is that for all input (K, V) pairs, Ks
7  * are nonunique. This means that we may find entries like
8  * (A, 2), ..., (A, 5),.... If we find duplicate Ks, then
9  * we will sum up the values for them and then create a unique
10  * K. If we have (A, 2) and (A, 5), then a unique entry will
11  * be created as (A, 7) where (7=2+5).
12  *
```

```
13   * This class may be used to find the bottom N as well (by
14   * just keeping the N smallest elements in the set).
15   *
16   *  Top 10 Design Pattern: Top 10 Structure
17   *
18   *  1. map(input) => (K, V)
19   *  2. reduce(K, List<V1, V2, ..., Vn>) => (K, V),
20   *     where V = V1+V2+...+Vn; now all Ks are unique
21   *  3. partition (K,V) pairs into P partitions
22   *  4. Find top N for each partition (we call this a local top N)
23   *  5. Find top N from all local top Ns
24   *
25   * @author Mahmoud Parsian
26   *
27   */
28 public class Top10NonUnique {
29     public static void main(String[] args) throws Exception {
30         // Step 2:  handle input parameters
31         // Step 3:  create a Java Spark context object
32         // Step 4:  broadcast the topN to all cluster nodes
33         // Step 5:  create an RDD from input
34         // Step 6:  partition the RDD
35         // Step 7:  map input (T) into (K,V) pairs
36         // Step 8:  reduce frequent Ks
37         // Step 9:  create a local top N
38         // Step 10:  find a final top N
39         // Step 11: emit final top N
40         System.exit(0);
41     }
42 }
```

Input

Sample input is provided. We use this HDFS input to print out output for each step. As you can observe, the keys are nonunique. Before applying the Top 10 algorithm, unique keys will be generated:

```
# hadoop fs -ls /top10/top10input/
Found 3 items
-rw-r--r--   3 hadoop hadoop     24 2014-08-31 12:50 /top10/top10input/file1.txt
-rw-r--r--   3 hadoop hadoop     24 2014-08-31 12:50 /top10/top10input/file2.txt
-rw-r--r--   3 hadoop hadoop     28 2014-08-31 12:50 /top10/top10input/file3.txt

# hadoop fs -cat /top10/top10input/file1.txt
A,2
B,2
C,3
D,2
E,1
G,2

# hadoop fs -cat /top10/top10input/file2.txt
```

```
A,1
B,1
C,3
E,1
F,1
G,2

# hadoop fs -cat /top10/top10input/file3.txt
A,2
B,2
C,1
D,2
E,1
F,1
G,2
```

Step 1: Import required classes and interfaces

Example 3-18 imports all required Java classes and interfaces.

Example 3-18. Step 1: import required classes and interfaces

```
 1 // Step 1: import required classes and interfaces
 2 import org.dataalgorithms.util.SparkUtil;
 3
 4 import scala.Tuple2;
 5 import org.apache.spark.api.java.JavaRDD;
 6 import org.apache.spark.api.java.JavaPairRDD;
 7 import org.apache.spark.api.java.JavaSparkContext;
 8 import org.apache.spark.api.java.function.FlatMapFunction;
 9 import org.apache.spark.api.java.function.PairFunction;
10 import org.apache.spark.api.java.function.Function2;
11 import org.apache.spark.broadcast.Broadcast;
12
13 import java.util.List;
14 import java.util.Map;
15 import java.util.TreeMap;
16 import java.util.SortedMap;
17 import java.util.Iterator;
18 import java.util.Collections;
```

Step 2: Handle input parameters

Example 3-19 demonstrates step 2, in which we handle the input parameters.

Example 3-19. Step 2: Handle input parameters

```
1     // Step 2: handle input parameters
2     if (args.length < 2) {
3         System.err.println("Usage: Top10NonUnique <input-path> <topN>");
4         System.exit(1);
```

```
5     }
6     System.out.println("args[0]: <input-path>="+args[0]);
7     System.out.println("args[1]: <topN>="+args[1]);
8     final String inputPath = args[0];
9     final int N = Integer.parseInt(args[1]);
```

Step 3: Create a Java Spark context object

In this step, shown in Example 3-20, we create our Java Spark context object.

Example 3-20. Step 3: Create a Java Spark context object

```
1 // Step 3: Create a Java Spark context object
2 JavaSparkContext ctx = SparkUtil.createJavaSparkContext("Top10NonUnique");
```

Step 4: Broadcast the topN to all cluster nodes

To broadcast or share objects and data structures among all cluster nodes, you can use Spark's `Broadcast` class (Example 3-21).

Example 3-21. Step 4: broadcast the topN to all cluster nodes

```
1 // Step 4: broadcast the topN to all cluster nodes
2 final Broadcast<Integer> topN = ctx.broadcast(N);
3 // now topN is available to be read from all cluster nodes
```

Step 5: Create an RDD from input

In Example 3-22, input data is read from HDFS and the first RDD is created.

Example 3-22. Step 5: Create an RDD from input

```
1 // Step 5: create an RDD from input
2 //    input record format:
3 //        <string-key><,><integer-value-count>
4 JavaRDD<String> lines = ctx.textFile(inputPath, 1);
5 lines.saveAsTextFile("/output/1");
```

To debug step 5, the first RDD is printed out:

```
# hadoop fs -cat /output/1/part*
A,2
B,2
C,3
D,2
E,1
G,2
A,1
B,1
C,3
```

```
E,1
F,1
G,2
A,2
B,2
C,1
D,2
E,1
F,1
G,2
```

Step 6: Partition the RDD

Partitioning the RDD, demonstrated in Example 3-23, is a combination of art and science. What is the right number of partitions? There is no magic bullet for calculating the number of partitions. It depends on the number of cluster nodes, the number of cores per server, and the size of RAM available. My experience indicates that you need to set this through trial and error. The general rule of thumb is to use (2 × num_executors × cores_per_executor) per executor.

Example 3-23. Step 6: partition the RDD

```
1    // Step 6: partition the RDD
2    // public JavaRDD<T> coalesce(int numPartitions)
3    // Return a new RDD that is reduced into numPartitions partitions.
4    JavaRDD<String> rdd = lines.coalesce(9);
```

Step 7: Map input (T) into (K,V) pairs

This step, shown in Example 3-24, does basic mapping: it converts every input record into a (*K*, *V*) pair, where *K* is a key such as URL and *V* is a value such as count. This step will generate duplicate keys.

Example 3-24. Step 7: Map input (T) into (K,V) pairs

```
1    // Step 7: map input(T) into (K,V) pairs
2    // PairFunction<T, K, V>
3    // T => Tuple2<K, V>
4    JavaPairRDD<String,Integer> kv =
5      rdd.mapToPair(new PairFunction<String,String,Integer>() {
6      public Tuple2<String,Integer> call(String s) {
7        String[] tokens = s.split(","); // url,789
8        return new Tuple2<String,Integer>(tokens[0],
9                                    Integer.parseInt(tokens[1]));
10     }
11   });
12   kv.saveAsTextFile("/output/2");
```

This step produces the following output:

```
# hadoop fs -cat /output/2/part*
(A,2)
(B,2)
(C,3)
(D,2)
(E,1)
(G,2)
(A,1)
(B,1)
(C,3)
(E,1)
(F,1)
(G,2)
(A,2)
(B,2)
(C,1)
(D,2)
(E,1)
(F,1)
(G,2)
```

Step 8: Reduce frequent keys

Step 7 generated duplicate keys, whereas this step creates unique keys and aggregates the associated values. For example, if for a key K we have:

$$\{(K, V_1), (K, V_2), ..., (K, V_n)\}$$

then these will be aggregated/reduced into a (K, V) where:

$$V = (V_1 + V_2 + ... + V_n)$$

In Example 3-25, the reducer is implemented by `JavaPairRDD.reduceByKey()`.

Example 3-25. Step 8: Reduce frequent keys

```
1    // Step 8: reduce frequent Ks
2    JavaPairRDD<String, Integer> uniqueKeys =
3        kv.reduceByKey(new Function2<Integer, Integer, Integer>() {
4        public Integer call(Integer i1, Integer i2) {
5            return i1 + i2;
6        }
7    });
8    uniqueKeys.saveAsTextFile("/output/3");
```

This step creates the following output:

```
# hadoop fs -cat /output/3/part*
(B,5)
(E,3)
```

```
(C,7)
(F,2)
(G,6)
(A,5)
(D,4)
```

Step 9: Create a local top N

The goal of this step, demonstrated in Example 3-26, is to create a local top 10 for each partition.

Example 3-26. Step 9: Create a local top N

```
1    // Step 9: create a local top N
2    JavaRDD<SortedMap<Integer, String>> partitions = uniqueKeys.mapPartitions(
3      new FlatMapFunction<
4                          Iterator<Tuple2<String,Integer>>,
5                          SortedMap<Integer, String>
6                        >() {
7      @Override
8      public Iterable<SortedMap<Integer, String>>
9        call(Iterator<Tuple2<String,Integer>> iter) {
10       final int N = topN.value();
11       SortedMap<Integer, String> localTopN = new TreeMap<Integer, String>();
12       while (iter.hasNext()) {
13         Tuple2<String,Integer> tuple = iter.next();
14         localTopN.put(tuple._2, tuple._1);
15         // keep only top N
16         if (localTopN.size() > N) {
17           // remove element with the smallest frequency
18           localTopN.remove(localTopN.firstKey());
19         }
20       }
21       return Collections.singletonList(localTopN);
22     }
23   });
24   partitions.saveAsTextFile("/output/4");
```

This step produces the following output:

```
# hadoop fs -ls /output/4/
Found 4 items
-rw-r--r--   3 hadoop hadoop       0 2014-08-31 13:11 /output/4/_SUCCESS
-rw-r--r--   3 hadoop hadoop      11 2014-08-31 13:11 /output/4/part-00000
-rw-r--r--   3 hadoop hadoop      11 2014-08-31 13:11 /output/4/part-00001
-rw-r--r--   3 hadoop hadoop      11 2014-08-31 13:11 /output/4/part-00002

# hadoop fs -cat /output/4/part-00000
{3=E, 5=B}

# hadoop fs -cat /output/4/part-00001
{2=F, 7=C}
```

```
# hadoop fs -cat /output/4/part-00002
{5=A, 6=G}

# hadoop fs -cat /output/4/part*
{3=E, 5=B}
{2=F, 7=C}
{5=A, 6=G}
```

Step 10: Find a final top N

This step, shown in Example 3-27, accepts all local top 10 lists and generates the final one.

Example 3-27. Step 10: Find a final top N

```
1    // Step 10: find a final top N
2    SortedMap<Integer, String> finalTopN = new TreeMap<Integer, String>();
3    List<SortedMap<Integer, String>> allTopN = partitions.collect();
4    for (SortedMap<Integer, String> localTopN : allTopN) {
5        for (Map.Entry<Integer, String> entry : localTopN.entrySet()) {
6            // count = entry.getKey()
7            // url = entry.getValue()
8            finalTopN.put(entry.getKey(), entry.getValue());
9            // keep only top N
10           if (finalTopN.size() > N) {
11               finalTopN.remove(finalTopN.firstKey());
12           }
13       }
14   }
```

You can also implement step 10 by using the `JavaRDD.reduce()` operation (for a complete solution, refer to previous sections in this chapter).

Step 11: Emit the final top N

This step emits the final output on the standard output device; see Example 3-28.

Example 3-28. Step 11: Emit final top N

```
1 // Step 11: emit final top N
2 System.out.println("--- Top-N List ---");
3 System.out.println("------------------");
4 for (Map.Entry<Integer, String> entry : finalTopN.entrySet()) {
5     System.out.println("key="+ entry.getValue()+ " value = " +entry.getKey());
6 }
```

The resulting final top *N* list looks like this:

```
--- Top-N List ---
------------------
key=G   value=6
key=C   value=7
```

Sample Run

The script

```
 1 # cat ./run_top10_nonunique.sh
 2 export JAVA_HOME=/usr/java/jdk7
 3 export SPARK_HOME=/usr/local/spark-1.1.0
 4 export SPARK_MASTER=spark://myserver100:7077
 5 BOOK_HOME=/mp/data-algorithms-book
 6 APP_JAR=$BOOK_HOME/dist/data_algorithms_book.jar
 7 INPUT=/top10/top10input
 8 TOPN=4
 9 prog=org.dataalgorithms.chap03.spark.Top10NonUnique
10 # Run on a Spark standalone cluster
11 $SPARK_HOME/bin/spark-submit \
12    --class $prog \
13    --master $SPARK_MASTER \
14    --executor-memory 2G \
15    --total-executor-cores 20 \
16       $APP_JAR $INPUT $TOPN
```

Top 10 run with Spark cluster

The output of our sample run, shown here, has been trimmed and edited to fit the page. For this run, the Spark cluster had three server nodes: `myserver100`, `myserver200`, and `myserver300`.

```
 1 # ./run_top10_nonunique.sh
 2 args[0]: <input-path>=/top10/top10input
 3 args[1]: <topN>=2
 4 ...
 5 INFO : Total input paths to process : 3
 6 INFO : Starting job: saveAsTextFile at Top10NonUnique.java:73
 7 INFO : Got job 0 (saveAsTextFile at Top10NonUnique.java:73) with
 8 ...
 9 INFO : Completed ResultTask(4, 0)
10 INFO : Finished TID 12 in 244 ms on myserver100 (progress: 1/3)
11 INFO : Completed ResultTask(4, 2)
12 INFO : Finished TID 14 in 304 ms on myserver200 (progress: 2/3)
13 INFO : Completed ResultTask(4, 1)
14 INFO : Finished TID 13 in 362 ms on myserver300 (progress: 3/3)
15 ...
16 INFO : Adding task set 6.0 with 3 tasks
17 ...
18 INFO : Job finished: collect at Top10NonUnique.java:121, took 0.076470196 s
```

```
19 --- Top-N List ---
19 -----------------
20 key=G value=6
21 key=C value=7
```

Spark Top 10 Solution Using takeOrdered()

This solution is an alteration of Top10NonUnique.java that uses a very powerful feature of Spark: a function called takeOrdered(). The signature of this function is as follows:

```
java.util.List<T> takeOrdered(int N,
                              java.util.Comparator<T> comp)
Description:
    Returns the first N elements from this RDD as defined
    by the specified Comparator[T] and maintains the order.

Parameters:
    N - the number of top elements to return
    comp - the comparator that defines the order

Returns:
    an array of top N elements
```

After we find all unique keys (let's call this RDD uniqueKeys), we find the top N by executing:

```
JavaPairRDD<String, Integer> uniqueKeys = kv.reduceByKey(...);
List<JavaPairRDD<String, Integer>>
    uniqueKeys.takeOrdered(N, MyTupleComparator.INSTANCE);
```

where MyTupleComparator.INSTANCE is the comparator that defines the order of (K, V) pairs. The MyTupleComparator class is defined as follows:

```
static class MyTupleComparator implements
    Comparator<Tuple2<String, Integer>> ,java.io.Serializable {
    final static MyTupleComparator INSTANCE = new MyTupleComparator();
    // note that the comparison is performed on the key's frequency
    public int compare(Tuple2<String, Integer> t1,
                       Tuple2<String, Integer> t2) {
        return -t1._2.compareTo(t2._2);    // return top N
        // return -t1._2.compareTo(t2._2); // return bottom N
    }
}
```

Note that the comparator class, MyTupleComparator, has to implement the java.io.Serializable interface; otherwise, Spark will throw this exception:

```
Caused by: org.apache.spark.SparkException: Task not serializable
at org.apache.spark.util.ClosureCleaner$.ensureSerializable
(ClosureCleaner.scala:166)
```

Complete Spark Implementation

Example 3-29 gives the complete top 10 solution in Spark.

Example 3-29. Complete top 10 nonunique program in Spark

```
1 package org.dataalgorithms.chap03;
2 // Step 1: import required classes and interfaces
3 /**
4  * Assumption: for all input (K, V), Ks are nonunique.
5  * This class implements the Top N design pattern for N > 0.
6  * The main assumption is that for all input (K, V) pairs, Ks
7  * are nonunique. This means that you will find entries like
8  * (A, 2), ..., (A, 5),...
9  *
10  * This is a general Top N algorithm that will work with unique
11  * and nonunique keys.
12  *
13  * This class may be used to find the bottom N as well (by
14  * just keeping the N smallest elements in the set).
15  *
16  *   Top 10 Design Pattern: Top 10 Structure
17  *
18  *   1. map(input) => (K, V)
19  *
20  *   2. reduce(K, List<V1, V2, ..., Vn>) => (K, V),
21  *                 where V = V1+V2+...+Vn
22  *      Now all Ks are unique.
23  *
24  *   3. Find top N using the following high-level Spark API:
25  *      java.util.List<T> takeOrdered(int N, java.util.Comparator<T> comp)
26  *      Returns the first N elements from this RDD as defined by the specified
27  *      Comparator[T] and maintains the order.
28  *
29  * @author Mahmoud Parsian
30  *
31  */
32 public class Top10UsingTakeOrdered implements Serializable {
33    public static void main(String[] args) throws Exception {
34       // Step 2:  handle input parameters
35       // Step 3:  create a Java Spark context object
36       // Step 4:  create an RDD from input
37       // Step 5:  partition the RDD
38       // Step 6:  map input (T) into (K,V) pairs
39       // Step 7:  reduce frequent Ks
40       // Step 8:  find final top N by calling takeOrdered()
41       // Step 9:  emit final top N
42       System.exit(0);
43    }
44 }
```

Input

The input for this example is identical to that of the previous section (see "Input" on page 65).

Step 1: Import required classes and interfaces

Our first step, shown in Example 3-30, is to import the required classes and interfaces for our solution.

Example 3-30. Step 1: Import required classes and interfaces

```
 1 // Step 1: import required classes and interfaces
 2 import org.dataalgorithms.util.SparkUtil;
 3
 4 import scala.Tuple2;
 5 import org.apache.spark.api.java.JavaRDD;
 6 import org.apache.spark.api.java.JavaPairRDD;
 7 import org.apache.spark.api.java.JavaSparkContext;
 8 import org.apache.spark.api.java.function.FlatMapFunction;
 9 import org.apache.spark.api.java.function.PairFunction;
10 import org.apache.spark.api.java.function.Function2;
11
12 import java.util.List;
13 import java.util.Map;
14 import java.util.TreeMap;
15 import java.util.SortedMap;
16 import java.util.Iterator;
17 import java.util.Collections;
18 import java.util.Comparator;
19 import java.io.Serializable;
```

Step 2: Handle input parameters

Example 3-31 handles input parameters for the Spark driver program.

Example 3-31. Step 2: Handle input parameters

```
1    // Step 2: handle input parameters
2    if (args.length < 2) {
3       System.err.println("Usage: Top10UsingTakeOrdered <input-path> <topN>");
4       System.exit(1);
5    }
6    System.out.println("args[0]: <input-path>="+args[0]);
7    System.out.println("args[1]: <topN>="+args[1]);
8    final String inputPath = args[0];
9    final int N = Integer.parseInt(args[1]);
```

Step 3: Create a Java Spark Context object

In the next step (Example 3-32), we create a Java Spark context object.

Example 3-32. Step 3: Create a Java Spark context object

```
1    // Step 3: create a Java Spark context object
2    JavaSparkContext ctx = SparkUtil.createJavaSparkContext("top-10");
```

Step 4: Create an RDD from input

In Example 3-33, input data is read from HDFS (or other persistent filesystems, such as the Linux NFS filesystem) and the first RDD is created.

Example 3-33. Step 4: Create an RDD from input

```
1    // Step 4: create an RDD from input
2    //    input record format:
3    //       <string-key><,><integer-value-count>
4 JavaRDD<String> lines = ctx.textFile(inputPath, 1);
5 lines.saveAsTextFile("/output/1");
```

To debug step 4, print out the first RDD:

```
# hadoop fs -cat /output/1/part*
A,2
B,2
C,3
D,2
E,1
G,2
A,1
B,1
C,3
E,1
F,1
G,2
A,2
B,2
C,1
D,2
E,1
F,1
G,2
```

Step 5: Partition the RDD

Partitioning RDDs, shown in Example 3-34, is an art and a science. What is the right number of partitions? As noted earlier in the chapter, there is no magic bullet for calculating the number of partitions. It depends on the number of cluster nodes, the number of cores per server, and the size of RAM available. My experience indicates that you need to determine this through trial and error.

Example 3-34. Step 5: Partition the RDD

```
1    // Step 5: partition the RDD
2    // public JavaRDD<T> coalesce(int numPartitions)
3    // Return a new RDD that is reduced into numPartitions partitions.
4    JavaRDD<String> rdd = lines.coalesce(9);
```

Step 6: Map input (T) into (K,V) pairs

This step, shown in Example 3-35, does basic mapping: it converts every input record into a (*K*, *V*) pair, where *K* is a key such as URL and *V* is a value such as count. This step will generate duplicate keys.

Example 3-35. Step 6: Map input (T) into (K,V) pairs

```
1    // Step 6: map input (T) into (K,V) pairs
2    // PairFunction<T, K, V>
3    // T => Tuple2<K, V>
4    JavaPairRDD<String,Integer> kv =
5        rdd.mapToPair(new PairFunction<String,String,Integer>() {
6          public Tuple2<String,Integer> call(String s) {
7              String[] tokens = s.split(","); // url,789
8              return new Tuple2<String,Integer>(tokens[0],
9                                        Integer.parseInt(tokens[1]));
10         }
11   });
12   kv.saveAsTextFile("/output/2");
```

This step creates the output shown here:

```
# hadoop fs -cat /output/2/part*
(A,2)
(B,2)
(C,3)
(D,2)
(E,1)
(G,2)
(A,1)
(B,1)
(C,3)
(E,1)
(F,1)
(G,2)
(A,2)
(B,2)
(C,1)
(D,2)
(E,1)
(F,1)
(G,2)
```

Step 7: Reduce frequent keys

Step 6 generated duplicate keys, whereas this step creates unique keys and aggregates the associated values. For example, if for a key K we have:

$$\{(K, V_1), (K, V_2), ..., (K, V_n)\}$$

then these will be aggregated/reduced into a (K,V) where:

$$V = (V_1 + V_2 + ... + V_n)$$

The reducer is implemented by `JavaPairRDD.reduceByKey()`, as shown in Example 3-36.

Example 3-36. Step 7: Reduce frequent keys

```
1   // Step 7: reduce frequent Ks
2   JavaPairRDD<String, Integer> uniqueKeys =
3       kv.reduceByKey(new Function2<Integer, Integer, Integer>() {
4       public Integer call(Integer i1, Integer i2) {
5           return i1 + i2;
6       }
7   });
8 uniqueKeys.saveAsTextFile("/output/3");
```

This step produces the following output:

```
# hadoop fs -cat /output/3/part*
(B,5)
(E,3)
(C,7)
(F,2)
(G,6)
(A,5)
(D,4)
```

Step 8: Find final top N by calling takeOrdered()

This step uses a very powerful function of Spark, `takeOrdered()`, to find the top N for a given list of (K,V) pairs. The `takeOrdered()` function sorts the given RDD and returns the top N elements, as you can see in Example 3-37.

Example 3-37. Step 8: Find final top N by calling takeOrdered()

```
1   // Step 8: find final top N by calling takeOrdered()
2   List<Tuple2<String, Integer>> topNResult =
3       uniqueKeys.takeOrdered(N, MyTupleComparator.INSTANCE);
```

Step 9: Emit final top N

This step, demonstrated in Example 3-38, emits the final output.

Example 3-38. Step 9: Emit final top N

```
1    // Step 9: emit final top N
2    for (Tuple2<String, Integer> entry : topNResult) {
3        System.out.println(entry._2 + "--" + entry._1);
4 }
```

The output from this step is as follows:

```
7--C
6--G
5--A
5--B
```

Shell script to run Spark program

Here is the shell script to run our Spark program:

```
 1 # cat run_top10usingtakeordered_yarn.sh
 2 #!/bin/bash
 3 export MP=/home/hadoop/testspark
 4 export THE_SPARK_JAR=$MP/spark-assembly-1.1.0-hadoop2.5.0.jar
 5 export JAVA_HOME=/usr/java/jdk7
 6 export APP_JAR=$MP/mp.jar
 7 export SPARK_HOME=/home/hadoop/spark-1.1.0
 8 #
 9 export HADOOP_HOME=/usr/local/hadoop/hadoop-2.5.0
10 export HADOOP_CONF_DIR=$HADOOP_HOME/etc/hadoop
11 INPUT=/top10/top10input
12 TOPN=4
13 DRIVER=org.dataalgorithms.chap03.spark.Top10UsingTakeOrdered
14 $SPARK_HOME/bin/spark-submit --class $DRIVER \
15     --master yarn-cluster \
16     --num-executors 12 \
17     --driver-memory 3g \
18     --executor-memory 7g \
19     --executor-cores 12 \
20     --conf "spark.yarn.jar=$THE_SPARK_JAR" \
21     $APP_JAR $INPUT $TOPN
```

Finding the Bottom N

If you want to generate the bottom *N* instead of the top *N*, you may do so in your comparator class: just negate the result of the compare() function.

Example 3-39 uses MyTupleComparatorAscending to find the bottom *N* elements.

Example 3-39. Tuple comparator: ascending

```
1   static class MyTupleComparatorAscending implements
2       Comparator<Tuple2<String, Integer>> ,java.io.Serializable {
3       final static MyTupleComparatorAscending INSTANCE =
4           new MyTupleComparatorAscending();
5       // note that the comparison is performed on the key's frequency
6       public int compare(Tuple2<String, Integer> t1,
7                           Tuple2<String, Integer> t2) {
8       // sorts ascending and returns bottom N
9       return t1._2.compareTo(t2._2);
10      }
11  }
```

Example 3-40 uses `MyTupleComparatorDescending` to find the top *N* elements.

Example 3-40. Tuple comparator: descending

```
1   static class MyTupleComparatorDescending implements
2       Comparator<Tuple2<String, Integer>> ,java.io.Serializable {
3       final static MyTupleComparatorDescending INSTANCE =
4           new MyTupleComparatorDescending();
5       // note that the comparison is performed on the key's frequency
6       public int compare(Tuple2<String, Integer> t1,
7                           Tuple2<String, Integer> t2) {
8       // sorts descending and returns top N
9       return -t1._2.compareTo(t2._2);
10      }
11  }
```

Then the final output will be:

```
2--F
3--E
4--D
5--A
```

Alternative to Using takeOrdered()

An alternative to using the `takeOrdered()` function is to use Spark's `top()` function, defined as shown in Example 3-41.

Example 3-41. Alternative to using takeOrdered()

```
1 import java.util.List;
2 import java.util.Comparator;
3 ...
4 List<T> top(int N, Comparator<T> comp)
5 // Returns the top N elements from this RDD as
6 // defined by the specified Comparator[T].
7 // Parameters:
```

```
8 //    N - the number of top elements to return
9 //    comp - the comparator that defines the order of sorting
```

MapReduce/Hadoop Top 10 Solution: Nonunique Keys

This is the last solution for the Top N design pattern. The assumption is that all input keys are nonunique—that is, for a given input (K, V), all Ks are nonunique. For example, our input may have entries like $(K, 2)$, $(K, 3)$, and $(K, 36)$.

This MapReduce/Hadoop solution for the top N is presented in two phases. N is parameterized so that you can find the top 5, top 20, or top 100.

 All Java classes for this section are provided on GitHub (*http://bit.ly/da_book*).

The phases are as follows:

Phase 1

Convert nonunique keys into unique keys. For example, if our input contains key-value pairs of $(K, 2)$, $(K, 3)$, and $(K, 36)$, then we aggregate all Ks into a single one: $(K, 41)$, where $41 = 2+3+36$. This phase is implemented by three classes:

- AggregateByKeyDriver
- AggregateByKeyMapper
- AggregateByKeyReducer

For this phase, since the output of mappers over aggregation (i.e., summing up frequency values) forms a monoid, we utilize combiners as well. We achieve this inside the run() method of the driver class (AggregateByKeyDriver):

```
...
job.setMapperClass(AggregateByKeyMapper.class);
job.setReducerClass(AggregateByKeyReducer.class);
job.setCombinerClass(AggregateByKeyReducer.class);
...
```

Phase 2

The input to this phase consists of unique key-value pairs generated by phase 1. In this phase, each mapper creates a local top N list, all of which are passed to a single reducer. The single reducer in this case is not a bottleneck because each mapper produces such a small amount of data (its local top N). For example, if we have 1,000 mappers and each produces a local top N, then the single reducer will process only (1,000 × N), which is not much considering that N will be 5, 20, or 100. This phase is implemented by three classes:

- TopNDriver
- TopNMapper
- TopNReducer

Sample Run

The following subsections outline a sample run using TopNDriver as a driver. The log output has been trimmed and formatted to fit the page.

Input

```
$ hadoop fs -ls /kv/input/
Found 3 items
-rw-r--r--   3 hadoop haoop  42 2014-11-30 15:18 /kv/input/file1.txt
-rw-r--r--   3 hadoop haoop  33 2014-11-30 15:18 /kv/input/file2.txt
-rw-r--r--   3 hadoop haoop  28 2014-11-30 15:18 /kv/input/file3.txt

$ hadoop fs -cat /kv/input/file1.txt
A,2
B,2
C,3
D,2
E,1
G,2
A,3
B,4
Z,100
Z,1

$ hadoop fs -cat /kv/input/file2.txt
A,1
B,1
C,3
E,1
F,1
G,2
A,65
A,3

$ hadoop fs -cat /kv/input/file3.txt
A,2
B,2
C,1
D,2
E,1
```

```
F,1
G,2
```

Script

```
$ cat ./run_top_N_mapreduce.sh
#!/bin/bash
export HADOOP_HOME=/usr/local/hadoop-2.5.0
export PATH=$HADOOP_HOME/bin:$PATH
export BOOK_HOME=/mp/data-algorithms-book
export APP_JAR=$BOOK_HOME/dist/data_algorithms_book.jar
#
# Generate unique (K,V) pairs
#
INPUT=/kv/input
OUTPUT=/kv/output
hadoop fs -rmr $OUTPUT
AGGREGATOR=org.dataalgorithms.chap03.mapreduce.AggregateByKeyDriver
hadoop jar $APP_JAR  $AGGREGATOR $INPUT $OUTPUT
#
# Find Top N
#
N=5
TopN_INPUT=/kv/output
TopN_OUTPUT=/kv/final
hadoop fs -rmr $TopN_OUTPUT
TopN=org.dataalgorithms.chap03.mapreduce.TopNDriver
hadoop jar $APP_JAR $TopN $N $TopN_INPUT $TopN_OUTPUT
```

Log of sample run

```
$ ./run_top_N_mapreduce.sh
...
14/11/30 16:08:04 INFO mapreduce.AggregateByKeyDriver: inputDir=/kv/input
14/11/30 16:08:04 INFO mapreduce.AggregateByKeyDriver: outputDir=/kv/output
...
14/11/30 16:08:07 INFO mapreduce.Job: Running job: job_1416535300416_0017
14/11/30 16:08:14 INFO mapreduce.Job: map 0% reduce 0%
...
14/11/30 16:08:31 INFO mapreduce.Job: map 100% reduce 100%
14/11/30 16:08:32 INFO mapreduce.Job: Job job_1416535300416_0017
   completed successfully
...
14/11/30 16:08:32 INFO mapreduce.AggregateByKeyDriver: run(): status=true
...
14/11/30 16:08:35 INFO mapreduce.TopNDriver: N=5
14/11/30 16:08:35 INFO mapreduce.TopNDriver: inputDir=/kv/output
14/11/30 16:08:35 INFO mapreduce.TopNDriver: outputDir=/kv/final
...
14/11/30 16:08:39 INFO mapreduce.Job: Running job: job_1416535300416_0018
14/11/30 16:08:45 INFO mapreduce.Job: map 0% reduce 0%
...
14/11/30 16:09:28 INFO mapreduce.Job: map 100% reduce 100%
```

```
14/11/30 16:09:28 INFO mapreduce.Job: Job job_1416535300416_0018
  completed successfully
...
14/11/30 16:09:29 INFO mapreduce.TopNDriver: run(): status=true
```

Intermediate output

```
$ hadoop fs -text /kv/output/part*
A 76
B 9
Z 101
C 7
D 4
E 3
F 2
G 6
```

Final top N output

```
$ hadoop fs -text /kv/final/part*
101 Z
76 A
9 B
7 C
6 G
```

This chapter implemented a very important filtering classification design pattern, Top N, by utilizing MapReduce/Hadoop and Spark. The next chapter provides several MapReduce solutions to another important design pattern, called Left Outer Join, which is often used to analyze business transactions.

## CHAPTER 4

Left Outer Join

This chapter shows you how to implement a left outer join in the MapReduce environment. I provide three distinct implementations in MapReduce/Hadoop and Spark:

- MapReduce/Hadoop solution using the classic `map()` and `reduce()` functions
- Spark solution without using the built-in `JavaPairRDD.leftOuterJoin()`
- Spark solution using the built-in `JavaPairRDD.leftOuterJoin()`

Left Outer Join Example

Consider a company such as Amazon, which has over 200 million users and can do hundreds of millions of transactions per day. To understand the concept of a left outer join, assume we have two types of data: users and transactions. The users data consists of users' location information (say, `location_id`) and the transactions data includes user identity information (say, `user_id`), but no direct information about a user's location. Given `users` and `transactions`, then:

```
users(user_id, location_id)
transactions(transaction_id, product_id, user_id, quantity, amount)
```

our goal is to find the number of unique locations in which each product has been sold.

But what exactly *is* a left outer join? Let T_1 (a left table) and T_2 (a right table) be two relations defined as follows (where t_1 is attributes of T_1 and t_2 is attributes of T_2):

$$T_1 = (K, t_1)$$
$$T_2 = (K, t_2)$$

The result of a left outer join for relations T_1 and T_2 on the join key of K contains all records of the left table (T_1), even if the join condition does not find any matching record in the right table (T_2). If the ON clause with key K matches zero records in T_2 (for a given record in T_1), the join will still return a row in the result (for that record), but with NULL in each column from T_2. A left outer join returns all the values from an inner join plus all values in the left table that do not match to those of the right table. Formally, we can express this as:

$$\text{LeftOuterJoin}(T_1, T_2, K) \quad = \quad \{(k, t_1, t_2) \text{ where } k \in T_1.K \text{ and } k \in T_2.K\}$$
$$\cup$$
$$\{(k, t_1, null) \text{ where } k \in T_1.K \text{ and } k \notin T_2.K\}$$

In SQL, we can express a left outer join as (where K is the column on which T_1 and T_2 are joined):

```
SELECT field_1, field_2, ...
    FROM T1 LEFT OUTER JOIN T2
        ON T1.K = T2.K;
```

A left outer join is visually expressed in Figure 4-1 (the colored part is included and the white part is excluded).

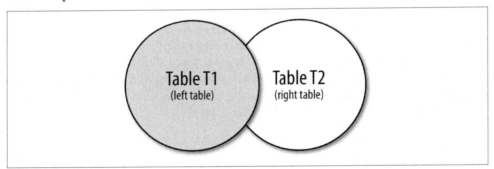

Figure 4-1. Left outer join

Consider the values in Tables 4-1 and 4-2 for our users and transactions (note that these values are just examples to demonstrate the concept of a left outer join in the MapReduce environment).

Table 4-1. Users in our left outer join

user_id	location_id
u1	UT
u2	GA
u3	CA
u4	CA
u5	GA

Table 4-2. Transactions in our left outer join

transaction_id	product_id	user_id	quantity	amount
t1	p3	u1	1	300
t2	p1	u2	1	100
t3	p1	u1	1	100
t4	p2	u2	1	10
t5	p4	u4	1	9
t6	p1	u1	1	100
t7	p4	u1	1	9
t8	p4	u5	2	40

Example Queries

Here are some example SQL queries relating to our left outer join:

- Query 1: find all products sold (and their associated locations):

```
mysql> SELECT product_id, location_id
    -> FROM transactions LEFT OUTER JOIN users
    ->   ON transactions.user_id = users.user_id;
+------------+-------------+
| product_id | location_id |
+------------+-------------+
| p3         | UT          |
| p1         | GA          |
| p1         | UT          |
| p2         | GA          |
| p4         | CA          |
| p1         | UT          |
| p4         | UT          |
| p4         | GA          |
+------------+-------------+
8 rows in set (0.00 sec)
```

- Query 2: find all products sold (and their associated location counts):

```
mysql> SELECT product_id, count(location_id)
    -> FROM transactions LEFT OUTER JOIN users
    ->    ON transactions.user_id = users.user_id
    ->    group by product_id;
+------------+--------------------+
| product_id | count(location_id) |
+------------+--------------------+
| p1         |                  3 |
| p2         |                  1 |
| p3         |                  1 |
| p4         |                  3 |
+------------+--------------------+
4 rows in set (0.00 sec)
```

- Query 3: find all products sold (and their unique location counts):

```
mysql> SELECT product_id, count(distinct location_id)
    -> FROM transactions LEFT OUTER JOIN users
    ->    ON transactions.user_id = users.user_id
    ->    group by product_id;
+------------+-----------------------------+
| product_id | count(distinct location_id) |
+------------+-----------------------------+
| p1         |                           2 |
| p2         |                           1 |
| p3         |                           1 |
| p4         |                           3 |
+------------+-----------------------------+
4 rows in set (0.00 sec)
```

Implementation of Left Outer Join in MapReduce

Our desired output is provided in the preceding section by SQL query 3, which finds all distinct (unique) locations in which each product has been sold given all transactions. We present our solution for the left outer join problem in two phases:

- MapReduce phase 1: find all products sold (and their associated locations). We accomplish this using SQL query 1 from the previous section.

- MapReduce phase 2: find all products sold (and their associated unique location counts). We accomplish this using SQL query 3 from the previous section.

MapReduce Phase 1: Finding Product Locations

This phase will perform the left outer join operation with a MapReduce job, which will utilize two mappers (one for users and the other for transactions) and whose reducer will emit a key-value pair with the key being `product_id`, and the value being `location_id`. Using multiple mappers is enabled by the `MultipleInputs` class (note that if we had a single mapper, we would have used `Job.setMapperClass()` instead):

```
import org.apache.hadoop.mapreduce.lib.input.MultipleInputs;
...
Job job = new Job(...);
...
Path transactions = <hdfs-path-to-transactions-data>;
Path users = <hdfs-path-to-users-data>;

MultipleInputs.addInputPath(job,
                            transactions,
                            TextInputFormat.class,
                            TransactionMapper.class);
MultipleInputs.addInputPath(job,
                            users,
                            TextInputFormat.class,
                            UserMapper.class);
```

Figures 4-2 and 4-3 illustrate the working MapReduce flow of the Left Outer Join algorithm, consisting of the two MapReduce jobs (phases 1 and 2).

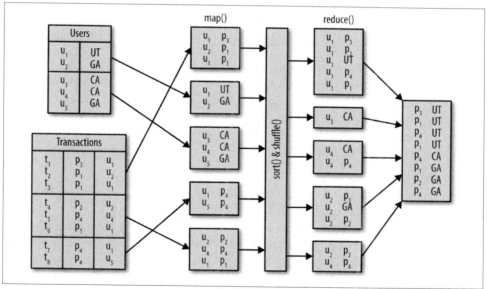

Figure 4-2. Left outer join data flow, phase 1

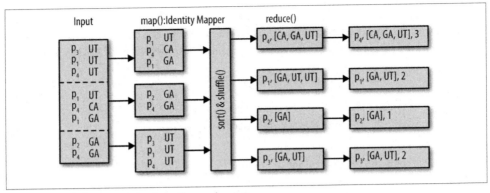

Figure 4-3. Left outer join data flow, phase 2

The core pieces of the left outer join data flow are as follows:

Transaction mapper

> The transaction `map()` reads (`transaction_id, product_id, user_id, quan tity, amount`) and emits a key-value pair composed of (`user_id, product_id`).

User mapper

> The user `map()` reads (`user_id, location_id`) and emits a key-value pair composed of (`user_id, location_id`).

The reducer for phase 1 gets both the user's `location_id` and `product_id` and emits (`product_id, location_id`). Now, the question is how the reducer will distinguish `location_id` from `product_id`. In Hadoop, the order of reducer values is undefined. Therefore, the reducer for a specific key (`user_id`) has no clue how to process the values. To remedy this problem we modify the transaction and user mappers/reducers (which we will call version 2):

Transaction mapper (version 2)

> As shown in Example 4-1, the transaction `map()` reads (`transaction_id, prod uct_id, user_id, quantity, amount`) and emits the key pair (`user_id, 2`) and the value pair (`"P", product_id`). By adding a "2" to the reducer key, we guarantee that `product_id(s)` arrive at the end. This will be accomplished through the secondary sorting technique described in Chapters 1 and 2. We added "P" to the value to identify products. In Hadoop, to implement `Pair(String, String)`, we will use the `PairOfStrings` class.[1]

---

1 `edu.umd.cloud9.io.pair.PairOfStrings` (which implements `WritableComparable<PairOfStrings>`)

Example 4-1. Transaction mapper (version 2)

```
1 /**
2  * @param key is framework generated, ignored here
3  * @param value is the
4  *     transaction_id<TAB>product_id<TAB>user_id<TAB>quantity<TAB>amount
5  */
6 map(key, value) {
7    String[] tokens = StringUtil.split(value, "\t");
8    String productID = tokens[1];
9    String userID = tokens[2];
10   outputKey = Pair(userID, 2);
11   outputValue = Pair("P", productID);
12   emit(outputKey, outputValue);
13 }
```

User mapper (version 2)

As shown in Example 4-2, the user map() reads (user_id, location_id) and emits the key pair (user_id, 1) and the value pair ("L", location_id). By adding a "1" to the reducer key, we guarantee that location_id(s) arrive first. This will be accomplished through the secondary sorting technique described in Chapters 1 and 2. We added "L" to the value to identify locations.

Example 4-2. User mapper (version 2)

```
1 /**
2  * @param key is framework generated, ignored here
3  * @param value is the user_id<TAB>location_id
4  */
5 map(key, value) {
6    String[] tokens = StringUtil.split(value, "\t");
7    String userID = tokens[0];
8    String locationID = tokens[1];
9    outputKey = Pair(userID, 1); // make sure location shows before products
10   outputValue = Pair("L", locationID);
11   emit(outputKey, outputValue);
12 }
```

As shown in Example 4-3, the reducer for phase 1 (version 2) gets both the ("L", location_id) and ("P", product_id) pairs and emits a key-value pair of (prod uct_id, location_id). Note that since 1 < 2, this means that the user's location_id arrives first.

Example 4-3. The reducer for phase 1 (version 2)

```
1 /**
2  * @param key is user_id
3  * @param values is List<Pair<left, right>>, where
4  * values = List<{
```

```
5  *                   Pair<"L", locationID>,
6  *                   Pair<"P", productID1>,
7  *                   Pair<"P", productID2>,
8  *                   ...
9  *                   }
10 * NOTE that the Pair<"L", locationID> arrives
11 * before all product pairs. The first value is location;
12 * if it's not, then we don't have a user record, so we'll
13 * set the locationID as "undefined".
14 */
15 reduce(key, values) {
16    locationID = "undefined";
17    for (Pair<left, right> value: values) {
18        // the following if-stmt will be true
19        // once at the first iteration
20        if (value.left.equals("L")) {
21            locationID = value.right;
22            continue;
23        }
24
25        // here we have a product: value.left.equals("P")
26        productID = value.right;
27        emit(productID, locationID);
28    }
29 }
```

MapReduce Phase 2: Counting Unique Locations

This phase will use the output of phase 1 (which is a sequence of pairs of (product_id, location_id) and generate pairs of (product_id, number_of_unique_locations). The mapper for this phase is an identity mapper (Example 4-4), and the reducer will count the number of unique locations (by using a Set data structure) per product (Example 4-5).

Example 4-4. Mapper phase 2: counting unique locations

```
1 /**
2  * @param key is product_id
3  * @param value is location_id
4  */
5 map(key, value) {
6    emit(key, value);
7 }
```

Example 4-5. Reducer phase 2: counting unique locations

```
1 /**
2  * @param key is product_id
3  * @param value is List<location_id>
4  */
```

```
 5 reduce(key, values) {
 6    Set<String> set = new HashSet<String>();
 7    for (String locationID : values) {
 8        set.add(locationID);
 9    }
10
11    int uniqueLocationsCount = set.size();
12    emit(key, uniqueLocationsCount);
13 }
```

Implementation Classes in Hadoop

The classes shown in Table 4-3 implement both phases of the Left Outer Join design pattern using the MapReduce/Hadoop framework.

Table 4-3. Implementation classes in Hadoop

Phase	Class name	Class description
Phase 1	LeftJoinDriver	Driver to submit job for phase 1
	LeftJoinReducer	Left join reducer
	LeftJoinTransactionMapper	Left join transaction mapper
	LeftJoinUserMapper	Left join user mapper
	SecondarySortPartitioner	How to partition natural keys
	SecondarySortGroupComparator	How to group by natural key
Phase 2	LocationCountDriver	Driver to submit job for phase 2
	LocationCountMapper	Define map() for location count
	LocationCountReducer	Define reduce() for location count

Sample Run

Input for phase 1

```
# hadoop fs -cat /left_join/zbook/users/users.txt
u1 UT
u2 GA
u3 CA
u4 CA
u5 GA

# hadoop fs -cat /left_join/zbook/transactions/transactions.txt
t1 p3 u1 3 330
t2 p1 u2 1 400
t3 p1 u1 3 600
t4 p2 u2 10 1000
t5 p4 u4 9 90
t6 p1 u1 4 120
t7 p4 u1 8 160
t8 p4 u5 2 40
```

Running phase 1

```
# ./run_phase1_left_join.sh
...
13/12/29 21:17:48 INFO input.FileInputFormat: Total input paths to process : 1
...
13/12/29 21:17:48 INFO input.FileInputFormat: Total input paths to process : 1
13/12/29 21:17:49 INFO mapred.JobClient: Running job: job_201312291929_0004
13/12/29 21:17:50 INFO mapred.JobClient:  map 0% reduce 0%
...
13/12/29 21:18:41 INFO mapred.JobClient:  map 100% reduce 100%
13/12/29 21:18:41 INFO mapred.JobClient: Job complete: job_201312291929_0004
...
13/12/29 21:18:41 INFO mapred.JobClient: Map-Reduce Framework
13/12/29 21:18:41 INFO mapred.JobClient:   Map input records=13
...
13/12/29 21:18:41 INFO mapred.JobClient:   Reduce input records=13
13/12/29 21:18:41 INFO mapred.JobClient:   Reduce input groups=5
13/12/29 21:18:41 INFO mapred.JobClient:   Combine output records=0
13/12/29 21:18:41 INFO mapred.JobClient:   Reduce output records=8
13/12/29 21:18:41 INFO mapred.JobClient:   Map output records=13
```

Output of phase 1 (input for phase 2)

```
# hadoop fs -text /left_join/zbook/output/part*
p4 GA
p3 UT
p1 UT
p1 UT
p4 UT
p1 GA
p2 GA
p4 CA
```

Running phase 2

```
# ./run_phase2_location_count.sh
...
13/12/29 21:19:28 INFO input.FileInputFormat: Total input paths to process : 10
13/12/29 21:19:28 INFO mapred.JobClient: Running job: job_201312291929_0005
13/12/29 21:19:29 INFO mapred.JobClient:  map 0% reduce 0%
...
13/12/29 21:20:24 INFO mapred.JobClient:  map 100% reduce 100%
13/12/29 21:20:25 INFO mapred.JobClient: Job complete: job_201312291929_0005
...
13/12/29 21:20:25 INFO mapred.JobClient: Map-Reduce Framework
13/12/29 21:20:25 INFO mapred.JobClient:   Map input records=8
...
13/12/29 21:20:25 INFO mapred.JobClient:   Reduce input records=8
13/12/29 21:20:25 INFO mapred.JobClient:   Reduce input groups=4
13/12/29 21:20:25 INFO mapred.JobClient:   Combine output records=0
13/12/29 21:20:25 INFO mapred.JobClient:   Reduce output records=4
13/12/29 21:20:25 INFO mapred.JobClient:   Map output records=8
```

Output of phase 2

```
# hadoop fs -cat /left_join/zbook/output2/part*
p1 2
p2 1
p3 1
p4 3
```

Spark Implementation of Left Outer Join

Since Spark provides a higher-level Java API than the MapReduce/Hadoop API, I will present the whole solution in a single Java class (called LeftOuterJoin), which will include a series of map(), groupByKey(), and reduce() functions. In the MapReduce/Hadoop implementation we used the MultipleInputs class to process two different types of input by two different mappers. As you've learned, Spark provides a much richer API for mappers and reducers. Without needing special plug-in classes, you can have many different types of mappers (by using the map(), flatMap(), and flatMapToPair() functions). In Spark, instead of using Hadoop's MultipleInputs class, we will use the JavaRDD.union() function to return the union of two JavaRDDs (a users RDD and a transactions RDD), which will be merged to create a new RDD. The JavaRDD.union() function is defined as:

```
JavaRDD<T> union(JavaRDD<T> other)
JavaPairRDD<T> union(JavaPairRDD<T> other)

Description: Return the union of this JavaRDD and another one.
             Any identical elements will appear multiple
             times (use .distinct() to eliminate them).
```

You can only apply the union() function to JavaRDDs of the same type (T). Therefore, we will create the same RDD type for users and transactions. This is how we do so:

```
JavaPairRDD<String,Tuple2<String,String>> usersRDD = users.map(...);
JavaPairRDD<String,Tuple2<String,String>> transactionsRDD =
    transactions.map(...);

// here we perform a union() on usersRDD and transactionsRDD
JavaPairRDD<String,Tuple2<String,String>> allRDD =
    transactionsRDD.union(usersRDD);
```

The union() workflow is illustrated in Figure 4-4.

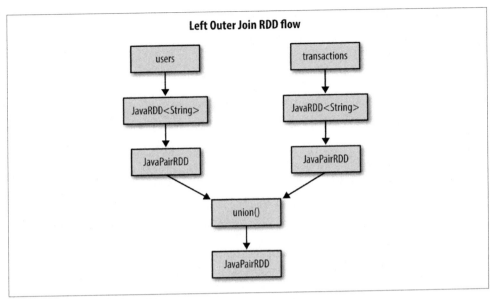

Figure 4-4. union() data flow

To refresh your memory, here is the data for users and transactions (this data will be used as input files for our sample run at the end of this chapter):

```
# hadoop fs -cat /data/leftouterjoins/users.txt
u1 UT
u2 GA
u3 CA
u4 CA
u5 GA

# hadoop fs -cat /data/leftouterjoins/transactions.txt
t1 p3 u1 3 330

t2 p1 u2 1 400
t3 p1 u1 3 600
t4 p2 u2 10 1000
t5 p4 u4 9 90
t6 p1 u1 4 120
t7 p4 u1 8 160
t8 p4 u5 2 40
```

Let's see how the algorithm works. For the users and transactions data, we generate:

```
users => (userID, T2("L", location))
transactions => (userID, T2("P", product))
```

(Here, T2 stands for Tuple2.)

Next, we create a union of these two sets of data:

```
all = transactions.union(users);
    = { (userID1, T2("L", location)),
        (userID1, T2("P", P11)),

        (userID1, T2("P", P12)),
        ...
        (userID1, T2("P", P1n)),
        ...
    }
```

where P_{ij} is a product ID.

The next step is to group the data by userID. This will generate:

```
{
    (userID1, List<T2("L", L1), T2("P", P11), T2("P", P12), T2("P", P13), ...>),
    (userID2, List<T2("L", L2), T2("P", P21), T2("P", P22), T2("P", P23), ...>),
    ...
}
```

where L_i is a locationID, and P_{ij} is a product ID.

Spark Program

First, I will provide a high-level solution in 11 steps (shown in Example 4-6), and then we will dissect each step with a proper working Spark code example.

Example 4-6. LeftOuterJoin high-level solution

```
 1 // Step 1: import required classes and interfaces
 2 public class LeftOuterJoin {
 3   public static void main(String[] args) throws Exception {
 4     // Step 2: read input parameters
 5     // Step 3: create a JavaSparkContext object
 6     // Step 4: create a JavaRDD for users
 7     // Step 5: create a JavaRDD for transactions
 8     // Step 6: create a union of the RDDs created in step 4 and step 5
 9     // Step 7: create a JavaPairRDD(userID, List<T2>) by calling groupByKey()
10     // Step 8: create a productLocationsRDD as JavaPairRDD<String,String>
11     // Step 9: find all locations for a product;
12     // result will be JavaPairRDD<String, List<String>>
13     // Step 10: finalize output by changing "value" from List<String>
14     // to Tuple2<Set<String>, Integer>, where you have a unique
15     // set of locations and their count
16     // Step 11: print the final result RDD
17     System.exit(0);
18   }
19 }
```

Step 1: Import required classes

We first import the required classes and interfaces from the JAR files provided by the binary distributions of the Spark framework. Spark provides two Java packages (`org.apache.spark.api.java` and `org.apache.spark.api.java.function`) for creating and manipulating RDDs. Example 4-7 demonstrates this step.

Example 4-7. Step 1: import required classes and interfaces

```
1 // Step 1: import required classes and interfaces
2 import scala.Tuple2;
3 import org.apache.spark.api.java.JavaRDD;
4 import org.apache.spark.api.java.JavaPairRDD;
5 import org.apache.spark.api.java.JavaSparkContext;
6 import org.apache.spark.api.java.function.Function;
7 import org.apache.spark.api.java.function.PairFlatMapFunction;
8 import org.apache.spark.api.java.function.FlatMapFunction;
9 import org.apache.spark.api.java.function.PairFunction;
10
11 import java.util.Set;
12 import java.util.HashSet;
13 import java.util.Arrays;
14 import java.util.List;
15 import java.util.ArrayList;
16 import java.util.Collections;
```

Step 2: Read input parameters

As shown in Example 4-8, next we read two input parameters: users data and the transactions data. The users and transactions data are provided as HDFS text files.

Example 4-8. Step 2: read input parameters

```
1    // Step 2: read input parameters
2    if (args.length < 2) {
3      System.err.println("Usage: LeftOuterJoin <users> <transactions>");
4      System.exit(1);
5    }
6    String usersInputFile = args[0]; // HDFS text file
7    String transactionsInputFile = args[1]; // HDFS text file
8    System.out.println("users="+ usersInputFile);
9    System.out.println("transactions="+ transactionsInputFile);
```

The output of this step is:

```
users=/data/leftouterjoins/users.txt
transactions=/data/leftouterjoins/transactions.txt
```

Step 3: Create a JavaSparkContext object

As shown in Example 4-9, next we create a `JavaSparkContext` object. This object is used to create the first RDD.

Example 4-9. Step 3: create a JavaSparkContext object

```
1   // Step 3: create a JavaSparkContext object
2   JavaSparkContext ctx = new JavaSparkContext();
```

Step 4: Create a JavaRDD for users

In this step, shown in Example 4-10, we create a users `JavaRDD<String>`, where the RDD element is a single record of the text file (representing `userID` and `locationID`). Next, we use the `JavaRDD<String>.mapToPair()` function to create a new Java `PairRDD<String,Tuple2<String,String>>`, where the key is a `userID` and the value is a `Tuple2("L", location)`. Later we will create `Tuple2("P", product)` pairs for our transactions data. The tags `"L"` and `"P"` identify locations and products, respectively.

Example 4-10. Step 4: create a JavaRDD for users

```
1   // Step 4: create a JavaRDD for users
2   JavaRDD<String> users = ctx.textFile(usersInputFile, 1);
3   // <K2,V2> JavaPairRDD<K2,V2> mapToPair(PairFunction<T,K2,V2> f)
4   // Return a new RDD by applying a function to all elements of this RDD.
5   // PairFunction<T, K, V>  where T => Tuple2<K, V>
6   JavaPairRDD<String,Tuple2<String,String>> usersRDD =
7     users.mapToPair(new PairFunction<
8                                   String, // T
9                                   String, // K
10                                  Tuple2<String,String> // V
11                    >() {
12   public Tuple2<String,Tuple2<String,String>> call(Strings) {
13       String[] userRecord = s.split("\t");
14       Tuple2<String,String> location =
15         new Tuple2<String,String>("L", userRecord[1]);
16       return new Tuple2<String,Tuple2<String,String>>(userRecord[0], location);
17   }
18 });
```

Step 5: Create a JavaRDD for transactions

In this step, shown in Example 4-11, we create a transactions `JavaRDD<String>`, where the RDD element is a single record of the text file (representing a transaction record). Next, we use the `JavaRDD<String>.mapToPair()` function to create a new `JavaPairRDD<String,Tuple2<String,String>>`, where the key is a `userID` and the value is a `Tuple2("P", product)`. In the previous step, we created `Tuple2("L",` location) pairs for users. The tags "L" and "P" identify locations and products, respectively.

Example 4-11. Step 5: create a JavaRDD for transactions

```
1   // Step 5: create a JavaRDD for transactions
2   JavaRDD<String> transactions = ctx.textFile(transactionsInputFile, 1);
3
4   // mapToPair
5   // <K2,V2> JavaPairRDD<K2,V2> mapToPair(PairFunction<T,K2,V2> f)
6   // Return a new RDD by applying a function to all elements of this RDD.
7   // PairFunction<T, K, V>
8   // T => Tuple2<K, V>
9   JavaPairRDD<String,Tuple2<String,String>> transactionsRDD =
10      transactions.mapToPair(new PairFunction<
11                                     String,              // T
12                                     String,              // K
13                                     Tuple2<String,String> // V
14                                 >() {
15   public Tuple2<String,Tuple2<String,String>> call(String s) {
16     String[] transactionRecord = s.split("\t");
17     Tuple2<String,String> product =
18         new Tuple2<String,String>("P", transactionRecord[1]);
19     return new Tuple2<String,Tuple2<String,String>>(transactionRecord[2],
20                                                product);
21   }
22  });
```

Step 6: Create a union of the RDDs created in steps 4 and 5

This step, shown in Example 4-12, creates a union of two instances of Java PairRDD<String,Tuple2<String,String>>. The JavaPairRDD.union() method requires both RDDs to have the same exact types.

Example 4-12. Step 6: create a union of RDDs

```
1   // Step 6: create a union of the RDDs created in step 4 and step 5
2   JavaPairRDD<String,Tuple2<String,String>> allRDD =
3       transactionsRDD.union(usersRDD);
```

Example 4-13 shows a semantically equivalent implementation of this step; we've simply changed the order of the union parameters.

Example 4-13. Step 6: Create a union of RDDs (alternative implementation)

```
1   // Here we perform a union() on usersRDD and transactionsRDD.
2   JavaPairRDD<String,Tuple2<String,String>> allRDD =
3       usersRDD.union(transactionsRDD);
```

The result of the union of the two JavaPairRDDs is the following key-value pairs:

```
{
    (userID, Tuple2("L", location)),
    ...
    (userID, Tuple2("P", product))
    ...
}
```

Step 7: Create a JavaPairRDD(userID, List(T2)) by calling groupByKey()

Next, we group our data (created in step 6) by userID. As you can see in Example 4-14, this step is accomplished by JavaPairRDD.groupByKey().

Example 4-14. Step 7: create a JavaPairRDD

```
1   // Step 7: create a JavaPairRDD (userID, List<T2>) by calling groupBy()
1   // group allRDD by userID
2   JavaPairRDD<String, Iterable<Tuple2<String,String>>> groupedRDD =
3       allRDD.groupByKey();
4   // now the groupedRDD entries will be as follows:
5   // <userIDi, List[T2("L", location),
6   //              T2("P", Pi1),
7   //              T2("P", Pi2),
8   //              T2("P", Pi3), ...
9   //          ]
10  // >
```

The result of this step is:

```
(userID1, List[T2("L", location1),
            T2("P", P11),
            T2("P", P12),
            T2("P", P13), ...]),
(userID2, List[T2("L", location2),
            T2("P", P21),
            T2("P", P22),
            T2("P", P23), ...]),
...
```

where P_{ij} is a productID.

Step 8: Create a productLocationsRDD as a JavaPairRDD(String,String)

In this step, the userIDs are dropped from the RDDs. For a given RDD element:

```
(userID, List[T2("L", location),
            T2("P", p1),
            T2("P", p2),
            T2("P", p3), ...])
```

we create a JavaPairRDD<String,String> as:

```
(p1, location)
(p2, location)
(p3, location)
...
```

This step is accomplished by the `JavaPairRDD.flatMapToPair()` function, which we implement as a `PairFlatMapFunction.call()` method. `PairFlatMapFunction` works as follows:

```
PairFlatMapFunction<T, K, V>
T => Iterable<Tuple2<K, V>>

where in our example: T is an input and
we create (K, V) pairs as output:

    T = Tuple2<String, Iterable<Tuple2<String,String>>>
    K = String
    V = String
```

Example 4-15 shows the complete implementation of the `PairFlatMapFunction.call()` method.

Example 4-15. Step 8: create a productLocationsRDD

```
1    // Step 8: create a productLocationsRDD as JavaPairRDD<String,String>
2    // PairFlatMapFunction<T, K, V>
3    // T => Iterable<Tuple2<K, V>>
4    JavaPairRDD<String,String> productLocationsRDD =
5        groupedRDD.flatMapToPair(new PairFlatMapFunction<
6            Tuple2<String, Iterable<Tuple2<String,String>>>, // T
7            String,                                          // K
8            String>() {                                      // V
9      public Iterable<Tuple2<String,String>>
10        call(Tuple2<String, Iterable<Tuple2<String,String>>> s) {
11            // String userID = s._1; // NOT Needed
12            Iterable<Tuple2<String,String>> pairs = s._2;
13             String location = "UNKNOWN";
14            List<String> products = new ArrayList<String>();
15            for (Tuple2<String,String> t2 : pairs) {
16                if (t2._1.equals("L")) {
17                    location = t2._2;
18                }
19                else {
20                    // t2._1.equals("P")
21                    products.add(t2._2);
22                }
23            }
24
25            // now emit (K, V) pairs
26            List<Tuple2<String,String>> kvList =
27                new ArrayList<Tuple2<String,String>>();
28            for (String product : products) {
```

```
29              kvList.add(new Tuple2<String, String>(product, location));
30          }
31          // Note that edges must be reciprocal; that
32          // is, every {source, destination} edge must have
33          // a corresponding {destination, source}.
34      return kvList;
35    }
36  });
```

Step 9: Find all locations for a product

In this step, RDD pairs of (product, location) are grouped by product. We use
JavaPairRDD.groupByKey() to accomplish this, as shown in Example 4-16. This step
does some basic debugging too, by calling the JavaPairRDD.collect() function.

Example 4-16. Step 9: find all locations for a product

```
1   // Step 9: find all locations for a product;
2   // result will be JavaPairRDD <String, List<String>>
3   JavaPairRDD<String, Iterable<String>> productByLocations =
4       productLocationsRDD.groupByKey();
5
6   // debug3
7   List<Tuple2<String, List<String>>> debug3 = productByLocations.collect();
8   System.out.println("--- debug3 begin ---");
9   for (Tuple2<String, Iterable<String>> t2 : debug3) {
10    System.out.println("debug3 t2._1="+t2._1);
11    System.out.println("debug3 t2._2="+t2._2);
12  }
13  System.out.println("--- debug3 end ---");
```

Step 10: Finalize output by changing value

Step 9 produced a JavaPairRDD<String, List<String>> object, where the key is the
product (as a string) and the value is a List<String>, which is a list of locations and
might have duplicates. To remove duplicate elements from a value, we use the Java
PairRDD.mapValues() function. We implement this function by converting a
List<String> to a Set<String>. Note that the keys are not altered. Mapping values is
implemented by Function(T, R).call(), where T is an input (as List<String>) and
R is an output (as Tuple2<Set<String>, Integer>). See Example 4-17.

Example 4-17. Step 10: finalize output

```
1   // Step 10: finalize output by changing "value" from List<String>
2   // to Tuple2<Set<String>, Integer>, where you have a unique
3   // set of locations and their count
4   JavaPairRDD<String, Tuple2<Set<String>, Integer>> productByUniqueLocations =
5       productByLocations.mapValues(
6           new Function<Iterable<String>,       // input
```

```
7            Tuple2<Set<String>, Integer>            // output
8    >() {
9      public Tuple2<Set<String>, Integer> call(Iterable<String> s) {
10        Set<String> uniqueLocations = new HashSet<String>();
11        for (String location : s) {
12            uniqueLocations.add(location);
13        }
14        return new Tuple2<Set<String>, Integer>(uniqueLocations,
15                                      uniqueLocations.size());
16      }
17   });
```

Step 11: Print the final result RDD

The final step, shown in Example 4-18, emits the results using the `JavaPairRDD.col
lect()` method.

Example 4-18. Step 11: print the final result RDD

```
1    // Step 11: print the final result RDD
2    // debug4
3    System.out.println("=== Unique Locations and Counts ===");
4    List<Tuple2<String, Tuple2<Set<String>, Integer>>> debug4 =
5        productByUniqueLocations.collect();
6    System.out.println("--- debug4 begin ---");
7    for (Tuple2<String, Tuple2<Set<String>, Integer>> t2 : debug4) {
8      System.out.println("debug4 t2._1="+t2._1);
9      System.out.println("debug4 t2._2="+t2._2);
10   }
11   System.out.println("--- debug4 end ---");
```

Running the Spark Solution

The shell script

```
# cat run_left_outer_join.sh
#!/bin/bash
export JAVA_HOME=/usr/java/jdk7
export SPARK_HOME=/usr/local/spark-1.1.0
export SPARK_MASTER=spark://myserver100:7077
export BOOK_HOME=/home/data-algorithms-book
export APP_JAR=$BOOK_HOME/dist/data_algorithms_book.jar
USERS=/data/leftouterjoins/users.txt
TRANSACTIONS=/data/leftouterjoins/transactions.txt
# Run on a Spark cluster
prog=org.dataalgorithms.chap04.spark.SparkLeftOuterJoin
$SPARK_HOME/bin/spark-submit \
  --class $prog \
  --master $SPARK_MASTER \
  --executor-memory 2G \
```

```
    --total-executor-cores 20 \
      $APP_JAR $USERS $TRANSACTIONS
```

Running the shell script

The log output from a sample run is shown here; it has been trimmed and formatted to fit the page:

```
# ./run_left_outer_join.sh
users=/data/leftouterjoins/users.txt
transactions=/data/leftouterjoins/transactions.txt
...
14/06/03 17:52:01 INFO scheduler.DAGScheduler: Stage 0
  (collect at LeftOuterJoin2.java:112) finished in 0.163 s
14/06/03 17:52:01 INFO spark.SparkContext: Job finished:
  collect at LeftOuterJoin2.java:112, took 6.365762312 s
--- debug3 begin ---
debug3 t2._1=p2
debug3 t2._2=[GA]
debug3 t2._1=p4
debug3 t2._2=[GA, UT, CA]
debug3 t2._1=p1
debug3 t2._2=[GA, UT, UT]
debug3 t2._1=p3
debug3 t2._2=[UT]
--- debug3 end ---
=== Unique Locations and Counts ===
14/06/03 17:52:01 INFO spark.SparkContext: Starting job:
  collect at LeftOuterJoin2.java:137
14/06/03 17:52:01 INFO spark.MapOutputTrackerMaster: Size
  of output statuses for shuffle 1 is 156 bytes
...
14/06/03 17:52:01 INFO scheduler.DAGScheduler: Stage 3
  (collect at LeftOuterJoin2.java:137) finished in 0.058 s
14/06/03 17:52:01 INFO spark.SparkContext: Job finished:
  collect at LeftOuterJoin2.java:137, took 0.081830132 s
--- debug4 begin ---
debug4 t2._1=p2
debug4 t2._2=([GA],1)
debug4 t2._1=p4
debug4 t2._2=([UT, GA, CA],3)
debug4 t2._1=p1
debug4 t2._2=([UT, GA],2)
debug4 t2._1=p3
debug4 t2._2=([UT],1)
--- debug4 end ---
...
14/06/03 17:52:02 INFO scheduler.DAGScheduler: Stage 6
  (saveAsTextFile at LeftOuterJoin2.java:144) finished in 1.060 s
14/06/03 17:52:02 INFO spark.SparkContext: Job finished: saveAsTextFile
  at LeftOuterJoin2.java:144, took 1.169724354 s
```

Running Spark on YARN

In this section, we cover how to submit Spark's ApplicationMaster to Hadoop YARN's ResourceManager, and instruct Spark to run the left outer join program. Further, we will instruct our Spark program to save our final result into an HDFS file. We save a file to HDFS by adding the following line after creating the `productByUniqueLoca` `tions` RDD (*/left/output* is an HDFS output directory):

```
productByUniqueLocations.saveAsTextFile("/left/output");
```

Script to run Spark on YARN

The script to run Spark on YARN is as follows:

```
# cat leftjoin.sh
export SPARK_HOME=/usr/local/spark-1.0.0
export SPARK_JAR=spark-assembly-1.0.0-hadoop2.3.0.jar
export SPARK_ASSEMBLY_JAR=$SPARK_HOME/assembly/target/scala-2.10/$SPARK_JAR
export JAVA_HOME=/usr/java/jdk6
export HADOOP_HOME=/usr/local/hadoop-2.3.0
export HADOOP_CONF_DIR=$HADOOP_HOME/conf
export YARN_CONF_DIR=$HADOOP_HOME/conf
export BOOK_HOME=/mp/data-algorithms-book
export APP_JAR=$BOOK_HOME/dist/data_algorithms_book.jar
# Submit Spark's ApplicationMaster to YARN's ResourceManager,
# and instruct Spark to run the LeftOuterJoin2 example
prog=org.dataalgorithms.chap04.spark.SparkLeftOuterJoin
SPARK_JAR=$SPARK_ASSEMBLY_JAR \
     $SPARK_HOME/bin/spark-class org.apache.spark.deploy.yarn.Client \
     --jar $APP_JAR \
     --class $prog \
     --args yarn-standalone \
     --args /left/users.txt \
     --args /left/transactions.txt \
     --num-workers 3 \
     --master-memory 4g \
     --worker-memory 2g \
     --worker-cores 1
```

For details on Spark parameters (such as `num-workers` and `worker-memory`) and environment variables, refer to the Spark Summit slides (*http://bit.ly/spark_summit*). Most of these parameters depend on the number of worker nodes, number of cores per cluster node, and amount of RAM available. Finding the optimal settings will require some trial and error and experimentation with different sizes of input data.

Running the script

The log output from a sample run is shown here. It has been trimmed and formatted to fit the page:

```
# ./leftjoin.sh
14/05/28 16:49:31 INFO RMProxy: Connecting to
.. ResourceManager at myserver100:8032
14/05/28 16:49:31 INFO Client:
  Got Cluster metric info from ApplicationsManager (ASM),
number of NodeManagers: 13
...
14/05/28 16:49:33 INFO Client: Command for starting
.. the Spark ApplicationMaster:
$JAVA_HOME/bin/java -server -Xmx4096m -Djava.io.tmpdir=$PWD/tmp
org.apache.spark.deploy.yarn.ApplicationMaster
--class LeftOuterJoin2 --jar /usr/local/spark/tmp/data_algorithms_book.jar
--args 'yarn-standalone' --args '/left/users.txt'
--args '/left/transactions.txt' --worker-memory 2048 --worker-cores 1
--num-workers 3 1> <LOG_DIR>/stdout 2> <LOG_DIR>/stderr
14/05/28 16:49:33 INFO Client: Submitting application to ASM
...
yarnAppState: FINISHED
distributedFinalState: SUCCEEDED
appTrackingUrl: http://myserver100:50030/proxy/application_1401319796895_0008/A
appUser: hadoop
```

Checking the expected output

Here we examine the generated HDFS output:

```
# hadoop fs -ls /left/output
Found 3 items
-rw-r--r--   2 hadoop supergroup          0 2014-05-28 16:49 /left/output/_SUCCESS
-rw-r--r--   2 hadoop supergroup         36 2014-05-28 16:49 /left/output/part-00000
-rw-r--r--   2 hadoop supergroup         32 2014-05-28 16:49 /left/output/part-00001

# hadoop fs -cat /left/output/part*
(p2,([GA],1))
(p4,([UT, GA, CA],3))
(p1,([UT, GA],2))
(p3,([UT],1))
```

Spark Implementation with leftOuterJoin()

This section implements a left outer join by using Spark's built-in `JavaPairRDD.left`
`OuterJoin()` method (note that MapReduce/Hadoop does not offer higher-level API
functionality such as a `leftOuterJoin()` method):

```
import scala.Tuple2;
import com.google.common.base.Optional;
import org.apache.spark.api.java.JavaPairRDD;

JavaPairRDD<K,Tuple2<V,Optional<W>>> leftOuterJoin(JavaPairRDD<K,W> other)
   // Perform a left outer join of this and other. For each
   // element (k, v) in this, the resulting RDD will either
```

```
// contain all pairs (k, (v, Some(w))) for w in other, or
// the pair (k, (v, None)) if no elements in other have key k.
```

Using Sparks's `JavaPairRDD.leftOuterJoin()` method helps us avoid:

- Using the `JavaPairRDD.union()` operation between `users` and `transactions`, which is costly
- Introducing custom flags such as `"L"` for location and `"P"` for products
- Using extra RDD transformations to separate custom flags from each other

Using the `JavaPairRDD.leftOuterJoin()` method enables us to produce the result efficiently. `transactionsRDD` is the left table and `usersRDD` is the right table:

```
JavaPairRDD<String,String> usersRDD = ...;          // (K=userID, V=location)
JavaPairRDD<String,String> transactionsRDD = ...; // (K=userID, V=product)
// perform left outer join by built-in leftOuterJoin()
JavaPairRDD<String, Tuple2<String,Optional<String>>> joined =
    transactionsRDD.leftOuterJoin(usersRDD);
```

Now, the `joined` RDD contains:

```
(u4,(p4,Optional.of(CA)))
(u5,(p4,Optional.of(GA)))
(u2,(p1,Optional.of(GA)))
(u2,(p2,Optional.of(GA)))
(u1,(p3,Optional.of(UT)))
(u1,(p1,Optional.of(UT)))
(u1,(p1,Optional.of(UT)))
(u1,(p4,Optional.of(UT)))
```

Since we are interested only in the products and unique locations, in the next step, we ignore `userID`s (the key). We accomplish this through another `JavaPairRDD.mapToPair()` function. After ignoring `userID`s, we generate:

```
(p4,CA)
(p4,GA)
(p1,GA)
(p2,GA)
(p3,UT)
(p1,UT)
(p1,UT)
(p4,UT)
```

which has the desired information to generate the list of products and unique locations.

Spark Program

In Example 4-19, I present the high-level steps to show you how to use Spark's built-in JavaPairRDD.leftOuterJoin() method. Each step is discussed in detail after the example.

Example 4-19. High-level steps

```
1 // Step 1: import required classes and interfaces
2 public class SparkLeftOuterJoin {
3   public static void main(String[] args) throws Exception {
4     // Step 2: read input parameters
5     // Step 3: create Spark's context object
6     // Step 4: create RDD for users data
7     // Step 5: create (userID,location) pairs for users (the right table)
8     // Step 6: create RDD for transactions data
9     // Step 7: create (userID,product) pairs for transactions (the left table)
10    // Step 8: use Spark's built-in JavaPairRDD.leftOuterJoin() method
11    // Step 9: create (product, location) pairs
12    // Step 10: group (product, location) pairs by key
13    // Step 11: create final output (product, Set<location>) pairs by key
14    System.exit(0);
15  }
16 }
```

Step 1: Import required classes and interfaces

We begin with the necessary imports (Example 4-20).Optional[2] represents an immutable object that may contain a non-null reference to another object (useful for the left outer join, since the joined values may contain nulls if the key is in the left table, but not in the right table). The factory class JavaSparkContext is used to create new RDDs.

Example 4-20. Step 1: import required classes and interfaces

```
1 // Step 1: import required classes and interfaces
2 import scala.Tuple2;
3 import org.apache.spark.api.java.JavaRDD;
4 import org.apache.spark.api.java.JavaPairRDD;
5 import org.apache.spark.api.java.JavaSparkContext;
6 import org.apache.spark.api.java.function.Function;
7 import org.apache.spark.api.java.function.PairFunction;
8 import com.google.common.base.Optional;
9 import java.util.Set;
10 import java.util.HashSet;
```

---

2 com.google.common.base.Optional<T> (*http://bit.ly/optional_t*) is an abstract class.

Step 2: Read input parameters

This step, shown in Example 4-21, reads the locations of the HDFS input files containing our users and transactions data. These input files will be used to create the left table (transactionsRDD) and the right table (usersRDD).

Example 4-21. Step 2: read input parameters

```
1   // Step 2: read input parameters
2   if (args.length < 2) {
3     System.err.println("Usage: LeftOuterJoin <users> <transactions>");
4     System.exit(1);
5   }
6
7   String usersInputFile = args[0];
8   String transactionsInputFile = args[1];
9   System.out.println("users="+ usersInputFile);
10  System.out.println("transactions="+ transactionsInputFile);
```

Step 3: Create Spark's context object

This step, shown in Example 4-22, creates a JavaSparkContext object, which will be used to create new RDDs.

Example 4-22. Step 3: create Spark's context object

```
1   // Step 3: create Spark's context object
2   JavaSparkContext ctx = new JavaSparkContext();
```

Step 4: Create an RDD for the users data

This step, demonstrated in Example 4-23, creates usersRDD, which is a set of (userID, location) pairs. usersRDD represents the "right" table for the left outer join operation.

Example 4-23. Step 4: create RDD for users data

```
1   // Step 4: create RDD for users data
2   JavaRDD<String> users = ctx.textFile(usersInputFile, 1);
```

Step 5: Create usersRDD (the right table)

As you can see in Example 4-24, this step creates the right table, usersRDD, which contains (userID, location) pairs from the users input data.

Example 4-24. Step 5: create (userID,location) pairs for users

```
1   // Step 5: create (userID,location) pairs for users
2   // <K2,V2> JavaPairRDD<K2,V2> mapToPair(PairFunction<T,K2,V2> f)
3   // Return a new RDD by applying a function to all elements of this RDD.
4   // PairFunction<T, K, V>
5   // T => Tuple2<K, V>
6   JavaPairRDD<String,String> usersRDD =
7       //                           T       K       V
8        users.mapToPair(new PairFunction<String, String, String>() {
9     public Tuple2<String,String> call(String s) {
10       String[] userRecord = s.split("\t");
11       String userID = userRecord[0];
12       String location = userRecord[1];
13       return new Tuple2<String,String>(userID, location);
14    }
15  });
```

Step 6: Create an RDD for the transactions data

This step, shown in Example 4-25, creates transactionsRDD, which is a set of (userID, product) pairs. transactionsRDD represents the left table for the left outer join operation.

Example 4-25. Step 6: create RDD for transactions data

```
1   // Step 6: create RDD for the transactions data
2   JavaRDD<String> transactions = ctx.textFile(transactionsInputFile, 1);
```

Step 7: Create transactionsRDD (the left table)

This step, shown in Example 4-26, creates the left table, transactionsRDD, which contains (userID,product) pairs from the transactions input data.

Example 4-26. Step 7: create (userID,product) pairs for transactions

```
1   // Step 7: create (userID,product) pairs for transactions
2   // PairFunction<T, K, V>
3   // T => Tuple2<K, V>
4   // sample transaction input: t1   p3   u1   3   330
5   JavaPairRDD<String,String> transactionsRDD =
6       //                                 T       K       V
7        transactions.mapToPair(new PairFunction<String, String, String>() {
8     public Tuple2<String,String> call(String s) {
9       String[] transactionRecord = s.split("\t");
10       String userID = transactionRecord[2];
11       String product = transactionRecord[1];
12       return new Tuple2<String,String>(userID, product);
13    }
14  });
```

Step 8: Use Spark's built-in JavaPairRDD.leftOuterJoin() method

This is the core step for performing the left outer join operation, using Spark's `Java PairRDD.leftOuterJoin()` method (see Example 4-27).

Example 4-27. Step 8: use Spark's built-in JavaPairRDD.leftOuterJoin() method

```
1    // Step 8: use Spark's built-in JavaPairRDD.leftOuterJoin() method.
2    // JavaPairRDD<K,Tuple2<V,Optional<W>>> leftOuterJoin(JavaPairRDD<K,W> other)
3    // Perform a left outer join of this and other. For each element (k, v) in this,
4    // the resulting RDD will either contain all pairs (k, (v, Some(w))) for w in
5    // other, or the pair (k, (v, None)) if no elements in other have key k.
6    //
7    // Here we perform a transactionsRDD.leftOuterJoin(usersRDD).
8    JavaPairRDD<String, Tuple2<String,Optional<String>>> joined =
9        transactionsRDD.leftOuterJoin(usersRDD);
10   joined.saveAsTextFile("/output/1");
```

This step creates the following output (the result of the left outer join operation):

```
# hadoop fs -cat /output/1/part*
(u4,(p4,Optional.of(CA)))
(u5,(p4,Optional.of(GA)))
(u2,(p1,Optional.of(GA)))
(u2,(p2,Optional.of(GA)))
(u1,(p3,Optional.of(UT)))
(u1,(p1,Optional.of(UT)))
(u1,(p1,Optional.of(UT)))
(u1,(p4,Optional.of(UT)))
```

Step 9: Create (product, location) pairs

This step builds another `JavaPairRDD`, which contains (product, location) pairs. Note in Example 4-28 that we completely ignore the `userIDs`, since we are interested only in products and their unique user locations.

Example 4-28. Step 9: create (product, location) pairs

```
1    // Step 9: create (product, location) pairs
2    JavaPairRDD<String,String> products =
3        joined.mapToPair(new PairFunction<
4            Tuple2<String, Tuple2<String,Optional<String>>>, // T
5            String, // K
6            String> // V
7        () {
8        public Tuple2<String,String> call(Tuple2<String,
9                                    Tuple2<String,Optional<String>>> t) {
10           Tuple2<String,Optional<String>> value = t._2;
11           return new Tuple2<String,String>(value._1, value._2.get());
12       }
```

```
13 });
14 products.saveAsTextFile("/output/2");
```

This step creates the following output:

```
# hadoop fs -cat /output/2/part*
(p4,CA)
(p4,GA)
(p1,GA)
(p2,GA)
(p3,UT)
(p1,UT)
(p1,UT)
(p4,UT)
```

Step 10: Group (K=product, V=location) pairs by key

This step groups (K=product, V=location) pairs by key. The result will be (K, V2), where V2 is a list of locations (which will include duplicate locations).

Example 4-29. Step 10: group (K=product, V=location) pairs by key

```
1   // Step 10: group (K=product, V=location) pairs by key
2   JavaPairRDD<String, Iterable<String>> productByLocations = products.groupByKey();
3   productByLocations.saveAsTextFile("/output/3");
```

This step creates the following output:

```
# hadoop fs -cat /output/3/p*
(p1,[GA, UT, UT])
(p2,[GA])
(p3,[UT])
(p4,[CA, GA, UT])
```

Step 11: Create final output (K=product, V=Set(location))

This final step, shown in Example 4-30, removes duplicate locations and creates (K, V2), where V2 is a Tuple2<Set<location>, size>.

Example 4-30. Step 11: create final output (K=product, V=Set<location>) pairs by key

```
1    // Step 11: create final output (K=product, V=Set<location>) pairs by K
2    JavaPairRDD<String, Tuple2<Set<String>, Integer>> productByUniqueLocations =
3       productByLocations.mapValues(
4         new Function< Iterable<String>,              // input
5                       Tuple2<Set<String>, Integer> // output
6         >() {
7        public Tuple2<Set<String>, Integer> call(Iterable<String>s) {
8          Set<String> uniqueLocations = new HashSet<String>();
9          for (String location : s) {
10             uniqueLocations.add(location);
```

```
11          }
12          return new Tuple2<Set<String>, Integer>(uniqueLocations,
13                                          uniqueLocations.size());
14      }
15  });
16
17  productByUniqueLocations.saveAsTextFile("/output/4");
```

This step creates the following final output:

```
# hadoop fs -cat /output/4/p*
(p1,([UT, GA],2))
(p2,([GA],1))
(p3,([UT],1))
(p4,([UT, GA, CA],3))
```

Combining steps 10 and 11

It is possible to combine steps 10 and 11 into a single Spark operation. We accomplish this with Spark's combineByKey(), the most general of the per-key aggregation functions, which enables us to combine values with the same key in a flexible manner. What is the main difference between reduceByKey() and combineByKey()? reduceBy Key() reduces values of type V into V (the same data type—for example, adding or multiplying integer values). combineByKey(), however, can combine/transform values of type V into another type, C—for example, we may want to combine/transform integer (V) values into a set of integers (Set<Integer>). In a nutshell, combineBy Key() allows us to return values that are not the same type as our input data. To use combineByKey() we need to provide a number of functions. The simplest form of the combineByKey() signature is shown here:

```
public <C> JavaPairRDD<K,C> combineByKey(
                                Function<V,C> createCombiner,
                                Function2<C,V,C> mergeValue,
                                Function2<C,C,C> mergeCombiners
                                )

Description: Generic function to combine the elements for each key
using a custom set of aggregation functions. Turns a JavaPairRDD[(K, V)]
into a result of type JavaPairRDD[(K, C)], for a "combined type" C. Note
that V and C can be different -- for example, one might group an RDD of
type (Int, Int) into an RDD of type (Int, List[Int]).
Users provide three functions:
- createCombiner, which turns a V into a C (e.g., creates a one-element list)
- mergeValue, to merge a V into a C (e.g., adds it to the end of a list)
- mergeCombiners, to combine two Cs into a single one.
```

Our goal is to create a Set<String> for each key (each key has a list of values, and each value is a string). To accomplish this, we need to implement three basic functions, as shown in Example 4-31.

Example 4-31. Basic functions to be used by combineByKey()

```
 1 Function<String, Set<String>> createCombiner =
 2   new Function<String, Set<String>>() {
 3   @Override
 4   public Set<String> call(String x) {
 5     Set<String> set = new HashSet<String>();
 6     set.add(x);
 7     return set;
 8   }
 9 };
10 Function2<Set<String>, String, Set<String>> mergeValue =
11   new Function2<Set<String>, String, Set<String>>() {
12   @Override
13   public Set<String> call(Set<String> set, String x) {
14     set.add(x);
15     return set;
16   }
17 };
18  Function2<Set<String>, Set<String>, Set<String>> mergeCombiners =
19   new Function2<Set<String>, Set<String>, Set<String>>() {
20   @Override
21   public Set<String> call(Set<String> a, Set<String> b) {
22     a.addAll(b);
23     return a;
24   }
25 };
```

After implementing these three basic functions, we are ready to combine steps 10 and 11 by using `combineByKey()`. Before we do so, let's identify the input and output in Table 4-4.

Table 4-4. Input, output, and transformer

Input	products(K:String, V:String)
Output	productUniqueLocations(K: String, V: Set<String>)
Transformer	combineByKey()

Example 4-32 shows you how to use the `combineByKey()` transformer.

Example 4-32. Using combineByKey()

```
1 JavaPairRDD<String, Set<String>> productUniqueLocations =
2     products.combineByKey(createCombiner, mergeValue, mergeCombiners);
3 // emit the final output
4 Map<String, Set<String>> productMap = productLocations.collectAsMap();
5 for (Entry<String, Set<String>> entry : productMap.entrySet()) {
6   System.out.println(entry.getKey() + ":" + entry.getValue());
7 }
```

Sample Run on YARN

Input (right table)

```
# hadoop fs -cat /data/leftouterjoins/users.txt
u1    UT
u2    GA
u3    CA
u4    CA
u5    GA
```

Input (left table)

```
# hadoop fs -cat /data/leftouterjoins/transactions.txt
t1    p3    u1    3     330
t2    p1    u2    1     400
t3    p1    u1    3     600
t4    p2    u2    10    1000
t5    p4    u4    9      90
t6    p1    u1    4     120
t7    p4    u1    8     160
t8    p4    u5    2      40
```

Script

```
# cat ./run_left_outer_join_spark.sh
#!/bin/bash
export JAVA_HOME=/usr/java/jdk7
export SPARK_HOME=/usr/local/spark-1.0.0
export HADOOP_HOME=/usr/local/hadoop-2.5.0
export HADOOP_CONF_DIR=$HADOOP_HOME/etc/hadoop
export YARN_CONF_DIR=$HADOOP_HOME/etc/hadoop
BOOK_HOME=/mp/data-algorithms-book
APP_JAR=$BOOK_HOME/dist/data_algorithms_book.jar
USERS=/data/leftouterjoins/users.txt
TRANSACTIONS=/data/leftouterjoins/transactions.txt
prog=org.dataalgorithms.chap04.spark.SparkLeftOuterJoin
$SPARK_HOME/bin/spark-submit
    --class $prog \
    --master yarn-cluster \
    --num-executors 3 \
    --driver-memory 1g \
    --executor-memory 1g \
    --executor-cores 10 \
    $APP_JAR $USERS $TRANSACTIONS
```

Generated HDFS output

```
# hadoop fs -cat /output/1/p*
(u5,(p4,Optional.of(GA)))
(u2,(p1,Optional.of(GA)))
(u2,(p2,Optional.of(GA)))
```

```
(u1,(p3,Optional.of(UT)))
(u1,(p1,Optional.of(UT)))
(u1,(p1,Optional.of(UT)))
(u1,(p4,Optional.of(UT)))

# hadoop fs -cat /output/2/p*
(p4,CA)
(p4,GA)
(p1,GA)
(p2,GA)
(p3,UT)
(p1,UT)
(p1,UT)
(p4,UT)

# hadoop fs -cat /output/3/p*
(p1,[GA, UT, UT])
(p2,[GA])
(p3,[UT])
(p4,[CA, GA, UT])

# hadoop fs -cat /output/4/p*
(p1,([UT, GA],2))
(p2,([GA],1))
(p3,([UT],1))
(p4,([UT, GA, CA],3))
```

This chapter implemented the Left Outer Join design pattern, which is often used in analyzing business transactions in a distributed programming environment. The next chapter introduces another design pattern, Order Inversion, which will be implemented in the MapReduce paradigm.

## CHAPTER 5

Order Inversion

The main focus of this chapter is the Order Inversion (OI) design pattern, which can be used to control the order of reducer values in the MapReduce framework (which is useful because some computations require ordered data). Typically, the OI pattern is applied during the data analysis phase. In Hadoop and Spark, the order of values arriving at a reducer is undefined (there is no order unless we exploit the sorting phase of MapReduce to push the data needed for calculations to the reducer). The OI pattern works for pair patterns, which use simpler data structures and require less reducer memory, due to the fact that there is no additional sorting and ordering of reducer values in the reducer phase.

To help you understand the OI pattern, we'll start with a simple example. Consider a reducer with a composite key of (K_1, K_2) and assume that K_1 is the natural key component of the composite key. Say this reducer receives the following values (there is no ordering between these values):

$$V_1, V_2, ..., V_n$$

By implementing the OI pattern, we can sort and classify the values arriving at the reducer with a key of (K_1, K_2). The sole purpose of using the OI pattern is to properly sequence data presented to the reducer. To demonstrate the OI design pattern, we'll assume that K_1 is a fixed part of the composite key and that K_2 has only three (this can be any number) distinct values, $\{K_{2a}, K_{2b}, K_{2c}\}$, which generate the values shown in Table 5-1. (Note that we have to send the keys $\{(K_1, K_{2a}), (K_1, K_{2b}), (K_1, K_{2c})\}$ to the same reducer.)

Table 5-1. Keys and values for natural key K_1

Composite key	Values
(K_1, K_{2a})	$\{A_1, A_2, ..., A_m\}$
(K_1, K_{2b})	$\{B_1, B_2, ..., B_p\}$
(K_1, K_{2c})	$\{C_1, C_2, ..., C_q\}$

In this table:

- $m + p + q = n$
- The sort order is as follows:

    $K_{2a} < K_{2b} < K_{2c}$ (ascending order)

    or:

    $K_{2a} > K_{2b} > K_{2c}$ (descending order)

- $A_i, B_j, C_k \in \{V_1, V_2, ..., V_n\}$

With proper implementation of the OI pattern, we will order the reducer values as follows:

$$A_1, A_2, ..., A_m, B_1, B_2, ..., B_p, C_1, C_2, ..., C_q$$

This ordering and sequencing of reducer values will enable us to do some calculations and computations first on A_i, then on B_j, and finally on C_k. Note that buffering values are not needed in memory. The main question is how to produce the desired behavior. The answer lies in defining a *custom partitioner*, which pays attention only to the left component (K_1, which is the natural reducer key) of the composite key (K_1, K_2). That is, the custom partitioner must partition based on the hash of the left key (K_1) only.

Example of the Order Inversion Pattern

In this section, we'll explore a simple example that demonstrates the OI pattern by computing the relative frequencies of words for a given set of documents. The goal is to build an $N \times N$ matrix (we'll call this matrix M), where $N = |V|$ (the vocabulary size of all given documents) and each cell M_{ij} contains the number of times the word W_i co-occurs with the word W_j within a specific context. For simplicity, we define this context as the neighbors of W_i. For example, given the following specific words:

$$W_1, W_2, W_3, W_4, W_5, W_6$$

if we define the *neighborhood* of a word as two words before and two words after that word, then a *neighborhood table* of these six words would look like Table 5-2.

Table 5-2. Neighborhood table

Word	Neighbors ±2
W_1	W_2, W_3
W_2	W_1, W_3, W_4
W_3	W_1, W_2, W_4, W_5
W_4	W_2, W_3, W_5, W_6
W_5	W_3, W_4, W_6
W_6	W_4, W_5

For our example, computing relative frequencies requires *marginal counts*—that is, row and column totals. But we cannot compute marginal counts until we see *all* counts. Therefore, we need to make the marginal counts arrive at the reducer before the joint counts. It is possible to buffer these values in memory, but this approach might not scale up if these values cannot fit in memory. Note that for computing relative frequencies, we will not use an absolute count of words. According to Jimmy Lin and Chris Dyer[17]: "the drawback of absolute counts is that it doesn't take into account the fact that some words appear more frequently than others. Word W_i may co-occur frequently with W_j simply because one of the words is very common. A simple remedy is to convert absolute counts into relative frequencies, $f(W_j|W_i)$. That is, what proportion of the time does W_j appear in the context of W_i?" We can compute this using the following equation:

$$f\left(W_j \mid W_i\right) = \frac{N\left(W_i, W_j\right)}{\displaystyle\sum_w N\left(W_i, w\right)}$$

Here, $N(a, b)$ indicates the number of times a particular co-occurring word pair is observed in the *corpus* (a given set of all documents as input). Therefore, we need the count of the *joint event* (word co-occurrence), divided by the marginal (the sum of the counts of the conditioning variable co-occurring with anything else).

MapReduce/Hadoop Implementation of the Order Inversion Pattern

Continuing our example of computing relative frequencies for a given set of documents, we need to generate two sequences of data. The first sequence will be total neighborhood counts (the total number of co-occurrences of a word) for the word; let's denote this by the composite key $(W, *)$ where W denotes the word. The second sequence will be the counts of that word against other specific words; let's denote this by the composite key (W, W_2). Therefore, a reducer will receive the set of key-value pairs in Table 5-3 in order.

Table 5-3. Reducer key-value pairs, in order

Key	Values as integer numbers
$(W, *)$	$A_1, A_2, ..., A_m$
(W, W_1)	$B_1, B_2, ..., B_p$
(W, W_2)	$C_1, C_2, ..., C_q$
...	...

Table 5-4 shows a concrete example.

Table 5-4. Reducer key-value pairs, in order (concrete example)

Key	Values
(dog, *)	100, 129, 500, ...
(dog, bite)	2, 1, 1, 1
(dog, best)	1, 1, 1, 1, 1
...	...

Now, we want to discuss the relative term co-occurrence and the OI design pattern. For this, we need to compute the co-occurrence matrix by using the relative frequencies of each pair, instead of the absolute value. Therefore, we need to count the number of times each pair (W_i, W_j) occurs divided by the number of total pairs with W_i (marginal). To complete our MapReduce solution, we will provide a map() function, a reduce() function, and a custom partitioner (OrderInversionPartitioner class), which together apply the partitioner only according to the first element in the

`PairOfWords,`[1] sending all data about the same word to the same reducer. Also, we use `PairOfWords` to represent a composite key (composed of two words).

Custom Partitioner

Hadoop provides a plug-in architecture for the custom partitioner, as you can see in Example 5-1.

Example 5-1. Custom partitioner: OrderInversionPartitioner

```
 1 ...
 2 import org.apache.hadoop.mapreduce.Job;
 3 import org.apache.hadoop.conf.Configuration;
 4 ...
 5
 6 public class RelativeFrequencyDriver {
 7
 8     public static void main(String[] args) throws Exception {
 9         Job job = Job.getInstance(new Configuration());
10         ...
11         job.setPartitionerClass(OrderInversionPartitioner.class);
12         ...
13     }
14 }
```

Hadoop also provides a proper API to plug in a custom partitioner:

```
    job.setPartitionerClass(OrderInversionPartitioner.class);
```

Custom partitioner implementation in Hadoop

The custom partitioner must ensure that all pairs with the same left word (i.e., the natural key) are sent to the same reducer. For example, the composite keys {(man, tall), (man, strong), (man, moon), ...} should all be assigned to the same reducer. To send these keys to the same reducer, we must define a custom partitioner that pays attention only to the left word (in our example, the left word is man). That is, the partitioner should partition based only on the hash of the left word. See Example 5-2.

Example 5-2. Custom partitioner implementation: OrderInversionPartitioner

```
1 import org.apache.hadoop.io.IntWritable;
2 import org.apache.hadoop.mapreduce.Partitioner;
```

---

1 We will use the PairOfWords class for representing a pair of words (W_i, W_j). The method PairOfWords.get LeftElement((W_i, W_j)) returns W_i and the method PairOfWords.getRightElement((W_i, W_j)) returns W_j.

```
3
4  public class OrderInversionPartitioner
5      extends Partitioner<PairOfWords, IntWritable> {
6
7      @Override
8      public int getPartition(PairOfWords key,
9                              IntWritable value,
10                             int numberOfPartitions) {
11         // key = (leftWord, rightWord)
12         String leftWord = key.getLeftElement();
13         return Math.abs(hash(leftWord) % numberOfPartitions);
14     }
15
16     // adapted from String.hashCode()
17     private static long hash(String str) {
18         long h = 1125899906842597L; // prime
19         int length = str.length();
20         for (int i = 0; i < length; i++) {
21             h = 31*h + str.charAt(i);
22         }
23         return h;
24     }
25 }
```

Relative Frequency Mapper

The mapper class emits the relative frequencies of a word's neighbors (that is, two words before and two words after). For example, if a mapper receives the following:

```
w1 w2 w3 w4 w5 w6
```

then it will emit the key-value pairs shown in Table 5-5.

Table 5-5. Mapper-generated key-value pairs

Key	Value
(w1, w2)	1
(w1, w3)	1
(w1, *)	2
(w2, w1)	1
(w2, w3)	1
(w2, w4)	1
(w2, *)	3
(w3, w1)	1
(w3, w2)	1
(w3, w4)	1
(w3, w5)	1
(w3, *)	4

Key	Value
(w4, w2)	1
(w4, w3)	1
(w4, w5)	1
(w4, w6)	1
(w4, *)	4
(w5, w3)	1
(w5, w4)	1
(w5, w6)	1
(w5, *)	3
(w6, w4)	1
(w6, w5)	1
(w6, *)	2

The mapper algorithm is presented in Example 5-3.

Example 5-3. Mapper class: RelativeFrequencyMapper

```
1 public class RelativeFrequencyMapper ... {
2
3      private int neighborWindow = 2;
4      private PairOfWords pair = new PairOfWords();
5
6      public void setup(Context context) {
7          // driver will set "neighbor.window"
8          neighborWindow = context.getConfiguration().getInt("neighbor.window", 2);
9      }
10
11     // key is system generated, ignored here
12     // value is a String (set of words)
13     public void map(Object key, String value) {
14         String[] tokens = StringUtils.split(value, " " );
15         if (tokens.length < 2) {
16             return;
17         }
18
19         for (int i = 0; i < tokens.length; i++) {
20             String word = tokens[i];
21             pair.setWord(word);
22             int start = (i - neighborWindow < 0) ? 0 : i - neighborWindow;
23             int end = (i + neighborWindow >= tokens.length) ?
24                 tokens.length - 1 : i + neighborWindow;
25             for (int j = start; j <= end; j++) {
26                 if (i == j) {
27                     continue;
28                 }
29                 pair.setNeighbor(tokens[j]);
30                 emit(pair, 1);
31             }
```

```
32          pair.setNeighbor("*");
33          int totalCount = end - start;
34          emit(pair, totalCount);
35       }
36    }
37 }
```

Relative Frequency Reducer

Since we now have a custom partitioner and implementation of the OI pattern, the values received by a reducer will be based on the natural key of the keys generated by all mappers. For the example presented for the mapper phase, we will have six reducers with the key-value input pairs listed in Table 5-6.

Table 5-6. Input to reducers

Key	Value
(w1, *),(w1, w2),(w1, w3)	2,1,1
(w2, *),(w2, w1),(w2, w3),(w2, w4)	3,1,1,1
(w3, *),(w3, w1),(w3, w2),(w3, w4),(w3, w5)	4,1,1,1,1
(w4, *),(w4, w2),(w4, w3),(w4, w5),(w4, w6)	4,1,1,1,1
(w5, *),(w5, w3),(w5, w4),(w5, w6)	3,1,1,1
(w6, *),(w6, w4),(w6, w5)	2,1,1

The reducer algorithm is presented in Example 5-4.

Example 5-4. Reducer class: RelativeFrequencyReducer

```
1 public class RelativeFrequencyReducer ... {
2     private double totalCount = 0;
3     private String currentWord = "NOT_DEFINED";
4
5     protected void reduce(PairOfWords key, Iterable<Integer> values) {
6         if (key.getRight().equals("*")) {
7             if (key.getLeft().equals(currentWord)) {
8                 totalCount += getTotalCount(values);
9             }
10            else {
11                currentWord = key.getLeft();
12                totalCount = getTotalCount(values);
13            }
14        }
15        else {
16            int count = getTotalCount(values);
17            double relativeCount = count / totalCount;
18            emit(key, relativeCount);
19        }
```

```
20
21     }
22
23     private int getTotalCount(Iterable<Integer> values) {
24         int count = 0;
25         for (Integer value : values) {
26             count += value.get();
27         }
28         return count;
29     }
30 }
```

Implementation Classes in Hadoop

The classes in Table 5-7 implement the OI design pattern for the relative frequency problem in MapReduce/Hadoop.

Table 5-7. Implementation classes in Hadoop

Class name	Class description
RelativeFrequencyDriver	Driver to submit job
RelativeFrequencyMapper	Defines map()
RelativeFrequencyReducer	Defines reduce()
RelativeFrequencyCombiner	Defines combine()
OrderInversionPartitioner	Custom partitioner: how to partition natural keys
PairOfWords	Represents pair of words (*Word1*, *Word2*)

Sample Run

Input

```
# hadoop fs -cat /order_inversion/input/sample_input.txt
java is a great language
java is a programming language
java is green fun language
java is great
programming with java is fun
```

Running the MapReduce Job

The log output from a sample run is shown here, formatted and edited to fit the page:

```
# ./run.sh
...
Deleted hdfs://localhost:9000/lib/order_inversion.jar
Deleted hdfs://localhost:9000/order_inversion/output
...
14/01/04 14:56:56 INFO input.FileInputFormat:
```

```
    Total input paths to process : 1
...
14/01/04 14:56:57 INFO mapred.JobClient:
  Running job: job_201401041453_0002
14/01/04 14:56:58 INFO mapred.JobClient: map 0% reduce 0%
...
14/01/04 14:57:21 INFO mapred.JobClient: map 100% reduce 100%
14/01/04 14:57:21 INFO mapred.JobClient:
  Job complete: job_201401041453_0002
...
14/01/04 14:57:21 INFO mapred.JobClient: Map-Reduce Framework
14/01/04 14:57:21 INFO mapred.JobClient: Map input records=5
14/01/04 14:57:21 INFO mapred.JobClient: Combine input records=85
14/01/04 14:57:21 INFO mapred.JobClient: Reduce input records=53
14/01/04 14:57:21 INFO mapred.JobClient: Reduce input groups=53
14/01/04 14:57:21 INFO mapred.JobClient: Combine output records=53
14/01/04 14:57:21 INFO mapred.JobClient: Reduce output records=44
14/01/04 14:57:21 INFO mapred.JobClient: Map output records=85
14/01/04 14:57:21 INFO RelativeFrequencyDriver:
  Job Finished in milliseconds: 24869
```

Generated Output

```
# hadoop fs -cat /order_inversion/output/part*
(great, a)          0.2
(great, is)          0.4
(great, java)          0.2
(great, language)          0.2
(with, is)          0.3333333333333333
(with, java)          0.3333333333333333
(with, programming)          0.3333333333333333
(fun, green)          0.2
(fun, is)          0.4
(fun, java)          0.2
(fun, language)          0.2
(programming, a)          0.2
(programming, is)          0.2
(programming, java)          0.2
(programming, language)          0.2
(programming, with)          0.2
(a, great)          0.125
(a, is)          0.25
(a, java)          0.25
(a, language)          0.25
(a, programming)          0.125
(green, fun)          0.25
(green, is)          0.25
(green, java)          0.25
(green, language)          0.25
(is, a)          0.14285714285714285
(is, fun)          0.14285714285714285
(is, great)          0.14285714285714285
```

```
(is, green)           0.07142857142857142
(is, java)            0.35714285714285715
(is, programming)          0.07142857142857142
(is, with)            0.07142857142857142
(java, a)             0.16666666666666666
(java, fun)             0.08333333333333333
(java, great)              0.08333333333333333
(java, green)              0.08333333333333333
(java, is)            0.4166666666666667
(java, programming)           0.08333333333333333
(java, with)            0.08333333333333333
(language, a)              0.3333333333333333
(language, fun)             0.16666666666666666
(language, great)             0.16666666666666666
(language, green)             0.16666666666666666
(language, programming)            0.1666666666666666
```

This chapter introduced the Order Inversion design pattern (used to control the order of reducer values) and implemented it using MapReduce/Hadoop. The next chapter implements the Moving Average algorithm (used in time series data analysis) in the MapReduce paradigm.

## CHAPTER 6

Moving Average

The purpose of this chapter is to present a moving average solution in MapReduce/ Hadoop. Before presenting a MapReduce solution, we will look at the basic concepts of a moving average. First, though, we need to understand *time series* data. Time series data represents the values of a variable over a period of time, such as a second, minute, hour, day, week, month, quarter, or year. Semiformally, we can represent time series data as a sequence of triplets:

(k, t, v)

where k is a key (such as a stock symbol), t is a time (in hours, minutes, or seconds), and v is the associated value (such as, value of a stock at point t). Typically, time series data occurs whenever the same measurements are recorded over a period of time. For example, the closing price of a company stock is time series data over minutes, hours, or days. The mean (or average) of time series data (observations equally spaced in time, such as per hour or per day) from several consecutive periods is called the *moving average*. It is called *moving* because the average is continually recomputed as new time series data becomes available, and it progresses by dropping the earliest value and adding the most recent.

Example 1: Time Series Data (Stock Prices)

Consider the data shown in Table 6-1 for the closing stock price of a company called MY-STOCK (note that this is a fake stock symbol).

Table 6-1. Time series data for MY-STOCK closing price

Time series	Date	Closing price
1	2013-10-01	10
2	2013-10-02	18
3	2013-10-03	20
4	2013-10-04	30
5	2013-10-07	24
6	2013-10-08	33
7	2013-10-09	27
...	...	...

For moving averages of three days, we'll get the output shown in Table 6-2.

Table 6-2. Moving averages for MY-STOCK closing price over three days

Time series	Date	Moving average	How calculated
1	2013-10-01	10.00	= (10)/(1)
2	2013-10-02	14.00	= (10+18)/(2)
3	2013-10-03	16.00	= (10+18+20)/(3)
4	2013-10-04	22.66	= (18+20+30)/(3)
5	2013-10-07	24.66	= (20+30+24)/(3)
6	2013-10-08	29.00	= (30+24+33)/(3)
7	2013-10-09	28.00	= (24+33+27)/(3)

Example 2: Time Series Data (URL Visits)

Our second example calculates the moving average of unique visitors to different URLs for each date in a specific time frame. We will use the input shown in Table 6-3.

Table 6-3. Time series data for URL visitors

URL	Date	Unique visitors
URL1	2013-10-01	400
URL1	2013-10-02	200
URL1	2013-10-03	300
URL1	2013-10-04	700
URL1	2013-10-05	800
URL2	2013-10-01	10
URL2	2013-10-02	20

URL	Date	Unique visitors
URL2	2013-10-03	30
URL2	2013-10-04	70

For moving averages of three days, we'll get the output shown in Table 6-4.

Table 6-4. Moving average for URL visitors over three days

URL	Date	Moving average
URL1	2013-10-01	400
URL1	2013-10-02	300
URL1	2013-10-03	300
URL1	2013-10-04	400
URL1	2013-10-05	600
URL2	2013-10-01	10
URL2	2013-10-02	15
URL2	2013-10-03	20
URL2	2013-10-04	40

Formal Definition

Let A be a sequence of an ordered set of objects:

$$A = (a_1, a_2, a_3, ..., a_N)$$

We may express A as:

$$\{a_i\}_{i=1}^{N}$$

Then an n moving average is a new sequence $\{s_i\}_{i=1}^{N-n+1}$ we define from a_i by taking the arithmetic mean of subsequences of n terms:

$$s_i = \frac{1}{n} \sum_{j=i}^{i+n-1} a_j$$

So the sequences S_n giving n moving averages are:

$$S_2 = \frac{1}{2}\big((a_1 + a_2), (a_2 + a_3), \ldots, (a_{n-1} + a_n)\big)$$
$$S_3 = \frac{1}{3}\big((a_1 + a_2 + a_3), (a_2 + a_3 + a_4), \ldots, (a_{n-2} + a_{n-1} + a_n)\big)$$
$$S_4 = \frac{1}{4}\big((a_1 + a_2 + a_3 + a_4), (a_2 + a_3 + a_4 + a_5), \ldots, (a_{n-3} + a_{n-2} + a_{n-1} + a_n)\big) \ldots$$

POJO Moving Average Solutions

For solving moving average problems, I provide two POJO (plain old Java object) solutions:

- Solution 1: using `java.util.Queue`
- Solution 2: using an array and simulating a queue

In both solutions, we take a window as a queue data structure and fill it in a first-in-first-out (FIFO) manner with time series data points until we have N points in it (the average/mean of these N points will be the moving average).

Solution 1: Using a Queue

This solution, shown in Example 6-1, uses a queue data structure implemented by `java.util.Queue`. At any time, we make sure that we keep only the required items (the size of the moving average window) in the queue.

Example 6-1. SimpleMovingAverage class

```
1 import java.util.Queue;
2 import java.util.LinkedList;
3 public class SimpleMovingAverage {
4
5     private double sum = 0.0;
6     private final int period;
7     private final Queue<Double> window = new LinkedList<Double>();
8
9     public SimpleMovingAverage(int period) {
10        if (period < 1) {
11            throw new IllegalArgumentException("period must be > 0");
12        }
13        this.period = period;
14    }
15
16    public void addNewNumber(double number) {
17        sum += number;
18        window.add(number);
19        if (window.size() > period) {
20            sum -= window.remove();
21        }
22    }
```

```
23
24    public double getMovingAverage() {
25        if (window.isEmpty()) {
26            throw new IllegalArgumentException("average is undefined");
27        }
28        return sum / window.size();
29    }
30 }
```

Solution 2: Using an Array

This solution, shown in Example 6-2, uses a simple array (called window) and simulates enqueue and dequeue operations. This solution is more efficient but less intuitive.

Example 6-2. SimpleMovingAverageUsingArray class

```
1 public class SimpleMovingAverageUsingArray {
2
3     private double sum = 0.0;
4     private final int period;
5     private double[] window = null;
6     private int pointer = 0;
7     private int size = 0;
8
9     public SimpleMovingAverageUsingArray(int period) {
10        if (period < 1) {
11            throw new IllegalArgumentException("period must be > 0");
12        }
13        this.period = period;
14        window = new double[period];
15    }
16
17    public void addNewNumber(double number) {
18        sum += number;
19        if (size < period) {
20            window[pointer++] = number;
21            size++;
22        }
23        else {
24            // size = period (size cannot be > period)
25            pointer = pointer % period;
26            sum -= window[pointer];
27            window[pointer++] = number;
28        }
29    }
30
31    public double getMovingAverage() {
32        if (size == 0) {
33            throw new IllegalArgumentException("average is undefined");
34        }
```

```
35          return sum / size;
36      }
37 }
```

Testing the Moving Average

Example 6-3 is a program for testing the moving average using the `SimpleMovingA`verage class. The program is tested by two window sizes, {3, 4}.

Example 6-3. Testing SimpleMovingAverage

```
 1 import org.apache.log4j.Logger;
 2 public class TestSimpleMovingAverage {
 3     private static final Logger THE_LOGGER =
 4         Logger.getLogger(TestSimpleMovingAverage.class);
 5     public static void main(String[] args) {
 6         // time series 1 2 3 4 5 6 7
 7         double[] testData = {10, 18, 20, 30, 24, 33, 27};
 8         int[] allWindowSizes = {3, 4};
 9         for (int windowSize : allWindowSizes) {
10             SimpleMovingAverage sma = new SimpleMovingAverage(windowSize);
11             THE_LOGGER.info("windowSize = " + windowSize);
12             for (double x : testData) {
13                 sma.addNewNumber(x);
14                 THE_LOGGER.info("Next number = " + x + ", SMA = " +
15                                 sma.getMovingAverage());
16             }
17             THE_LOGGER.info("---");
18         }
19     }
20 }
```

Sample Run

```
# javac SimpleMovingAverage.java
# javac TestSimpleMovingAverage.java
# java TestSimpleMovingAverage
13/10/10 22:24:08 INFO TestSimpleMovingAverage: windowSize = 3
13/10/10 22:24:08 INFO TestSimpleMovingAverage: Next number = 10.0, SMA = 10.00
13/10/10 22:24:08 INFO TestSimpleMovingAverage: Next number = 18.0, SMA = 14.00
13/10/10 22:24:08 INFO TestSimpleMovingAverage: Next number = 20.0, SMA = 16.00
13/10/10 22:24:08 INFO TestSimpleMovingAverage: Next number = 30.0, SMA = 22.66
13/10/10 22:24:08 INFO TestSimpleMovingAverage: Next number = 24.0, SMA = 24.66
13/10/10 22:24:08 INFO TestSimpleMovingAverage: Next number = 33.0, SMA = 29.00
13/10/10 22:24:08 INFO TestSimpleMovingAverage: Next number = 27.0, SMA = 28.00
13/10/10 22:24:08 INFO TestSimpleMovingAverage: ------
13/10/10 22:24:08 INFO TestSimpleMovingAverage: windowSize = 4
13/10/10 22:24:08 INFO TestSimpleMovingAverage: Next number = 10.0, SMA = 10.00
13/10/10 22:24:08 INFO TestSimpleMovingAverage: Next number = 18.0, SMA = 14.00
13/10/10 22:24:08 INFO TestSimpleMovingAverage: Next number = 20.0, SMA = 16.00
13/10/10 22:24:08 INFO TestSimpleMovingAverage: Next number = 30.0, SMA = 19.50
```

```
13/10/10 22:24:08 INFO TestSimpleMovingAverage: Next number = 24.0, SMA = 23.00
13/10/10 22:24:08 INFO TestSimpleMovingAverage: Next number = 33.0, SMA = 26.75
13/10/10 22:24:08 INFO TestSimpleMovingAverage: Next number = 27.0, SMA = 28.50
13/10/10 22:24:08 INFO TestSimpleMovingAverage: ------
```

MapReduce/Hadoop Moving Average Solution

Now that we understand the concept of a moving average for time series data, we will focus on the MapReduce solution for a moving average problem. Implementation will be provided through Apache Hadoop. We will see that MapReduce is a very powerful framework for solving moving average problems for a lot of time series data (such as stock prices over a long period of time). Calculation of the moving average will be handled by the reduce() function, where we have all the required data for a specific time series.

Input

The input to our MapReduce solution will have the following format:

```
<name-as-string><,><date-as-timestamp><,><value-as-double>
```

In this simple example, I've provided stock prices for three companies/stock symbols: GOOG, AAPL, and IBM. The first column is the stock symbol, the second is the timestamp, and the third is the adjusted closing price of the stock on that day:

```
GOOG,2004-11-04,184.70
GOOG,2004-11-03,191.67
GOOG,2004-11-02,194.87
AAPL,2013-10-09,486.59
AAPL,2013-10-08,480.94
AAPL,2013-10-07,487.75
AAPL,2013-10-04,483.03
AAPL,2013-10-03,483.41
IBM,2013-09-30,185.18
IBM,2013-09-27,186.92
IBM,2013-09-26,190.22
IBM,2013-09-25,189.47
GOOG,2013-07-19,896.60
GOOG,2013-07-18,910.68
GOOG,2013-07-17,918.55
```

Output

The output from our MapReduce solution will have the following format:

```
<name-as-string><,><date-as-timestamp><,><moving-average-as-double>
```

And here is a sample:

```
Name: GOOG, Date: 2013-07-17    Moving Average: 912.52
Name: GOOG, Date: 2013-07-18    Moving Average: 912.01
Name: GOOG, Date: 2013-07-19    Moving Average: 916.39
```

Now that you understand the Moving Average algorithm, you just need to group data based on the stock symbol, then sort the values based on the timestamp, and finally apply the Moving Average algorithm. There are at least two ways to sort our time series data:

Option #1

Sort the time series data in memory (RAM) for each reducer key. This option has one problem: if you do not have enough RAM for your reducer's sort operation, it will not work.

Option #2

Let the MapReduce framework do the sorting of the time series data (one of the main features of a MapReduce framework is sorting and grouping by key values, and Hadoop does a pretty good job of this). This option is much more scalable than option #1, and sorting is performed by the sort() and shuffle() functions of the MapReduce framework. With this option, we will need to alter key-value pairs and write some plug-in custom classes to perform secondary sorting.

I will provide solutions for both options.

Option #1: Sorting in Memory

The mapper accepts a row of input as:

```
<name-as-string><,><timestamp><,><value-as-double>
```

and emits key-value pairs, where the key is the <name-as-string> and the value is <timestamp><,><value-as-double>. The reducer will receive key-value pairs, where the key is the <name-as-string> and the values will be an unordered list of <timestamp><,><value-as-double>.

Time series data

Time series data is represented as a TimeSeriesData object, which is illustrated in Example 6-4. This class implements Writable (since these objects will persist in Hadoop) and Comparable<TimeSeriesData> (since we will do in-memory sorting on these objects).

Example 6-4. TimeSeriesData class

```
 1 import org.apache.hadoop.io.Writable;
 2 ...
 3 /**
 4  *
 5  * TimeSeriesData represents a pair of
 6  * (time-series-timestamp, time-series-value).
 7  *
 8  */
 9 public class TimeSeriesData
10     implements Writable, Comparable<TimeSeriesData> {
11
12     private long timestamp;
13     private double value;
14
15     public static TimeSeriesData copy(TimeSeriesData tsd) {
16         return new TimeSeriesData(tsd.timestamp, tsd.value);
17     }
18
19     public TimeSeriesData(long timestamp, double value) {
20         set(timestamp, value);
21     }
22     ...
23 }
```

The mapper function

The map() function, which just emits time series data, is defined in Example 6-5.

Example 6-5. The mapper function

```
1 /**
2  * @param key is the <name-as-string>
3  * @param value is the <timestamp><,><value-as-double>
4  */
5 map(key, value) {
6   TimeSeriesData timeseries =
7       new TimeSeriesData(value.timestamp, value.value-as-double);
8   emit(key, timeseries);
9 }
```

The reducer function

The reduce() function, which aggregates time series data and emits moving averages per key, is defined in Example 6-6.

Example 6-6. The reducer function

```
 1 public class MovingAverageSortInRAM_Reducer {
 2
 3     private int windowSize = 4; // default
 4
 5     /**
 6      * called once at the start of the reducer task
 7      */
 8     setup() {
 9         // "moving.average.window.size" will be set at the driver
10         // configuration is MRF's configuration object
11         windowSize = configuration.get("moving.average.window.size");
12     }
13
14     /**
15      * @param key is the <name-as-string>
16      * @param value is a List<TimeSeriesData>
17      * where TimeSeriesData represents a pair of (timestamp, value)
18      */
19     reduce(key, values) {
20         List<TimeSeriesData> sortedTimeSeries = sort(values);
21         // call movingAverage(sortedTimeSeries, windowSize) and emit output(s)
22         // apply Moving Average algorithm to sortedTimeSeries
23         double sum = 0.0;
24         // calculate prefix sum
25         for (int i=0; i < windowSize-1; i++) {
26             sum += sortedTimeSeries.get(i).getValue();
27         }
28
29         // now we have enough time series data to calculate moving average
30         for (int i = windowSize-1; i < sortedTimeSeries.size(); i++) {
31             sum += sortedTimeSeries.get(i).getValue();
32             double movingAverage = sum / windowSize;
33             long timestamp = sortedTimeSeries.get(i).getTimestamp();
34             Text outputValue = timestamp+ "," + movingAverage;
35             // send output to distributed filesystem
36             emit(key, outputValue);
37
38             // prepare for next iteration
39             sum -= sortedTimeSeries.get(i-windowSize+1).getValue();
40         }
41
42     }
43 }
```

Hadoop implementation classes

Our Hadoop implementation is composed of the classes shown in Table 6-5.

Table 6-5. Classes in the Hadoop moving average implementation

Class name	Description
SortInMemory_MovingAverageDriver	A driver program to submit Hadoop jobs
SortInMemory_MovingAverageMapper	Defines map()
SortInMemory_MovingAverageReducer	Defines reduce()
TimeSeriesData	Represents a time series data point expressed as a pair of (timestamp, double)
DateUtil	Provides basic date conversion utilities
HadoopUtil	Provides basic Hadoop utilities

Sample Run

The sample run outlined in the following subsections illustrates the input, the script, and the expected output.

Input

```
# hadoop fs -cat /moving_average/sort_in_memory/input/*
GOOG,2004-11-04,184.70
GOOG,2004-11-03,191.67
GOOG,2004-11-02,194.87
AAPL,2013-10-09,486.59
AAPL,2013-10-08,480.94
AAPL,2013-10-07,487.75
AAPL,2013-10-04,483.03
AAPL,2013-10-03,483.41
IBM,2013-09-30,185.18
IBM,2013-09-27,186.92
IBM,2013-09-26,190.22
IBM,2013-09-25,189.47
GOOG,2013-07-19,896.60
GOOG,2013-07-18,910.68
GOOG,2013-07-17,918.55
```

Script

```
# cat ./run.sh
#/bin/bash
export HADOOP_HOME=/usr/local/hadoop-2.3.0
export HADOOP_HOME_WARN_SUPPRESS=true
export JAVA_HOME=/usr/java/jdk6
export PATH=$PATH:$HADOOP_HOME/bin:$JAVA_HOME/bin
BOOK_HOME=/mp/data-algorithms-book
APP_JAR=$BOOK_HOME/dist/data_algorithms_book.jar
CLASSPATH=.:$HADOOP_HOME/conf:$APP_JAR
export INPUT=/moving_average/sort_in_memory/input
export OUTPUT=/moving_average/sort_in_memory/output
$HADOOP_HOME/bin/hadoop fs -put $APP_JAR /lib/
```

```
$HADOOP_HOME/bin/hadoop fs -rmr $OUTPUT
driver=org.dataalgorithms.chap06.memorysort.SortInMemory_MovingAverageDriver
export WINDOW_SIZE=2
$HADOOP_HOME/bin/hadoop jar $JAR $driver $WINDOW_SIZE $INPUT $OUTPUT
```

Log of a sample run

The output shown here has been edited and formatted to fit the page:

```
# ./run.sh
...
Deleted hdfs://localhost:9000/moving_average/sort_in_memory/output
args[0]: <window_size>=2
args[1]: <input>=/moving_average/sort_in_memory/input
args[2]: <output>=/moving_average/sort_in_memory/output
...
14/05/12 15:07:03 INFO mapred.JobClient: Running job: job_201405121349_0009
14/05/12 15:07:04 INFO mapred.JobClient: map 0% reduce 0%
...
14/05/12 15:07:54 INFO mapred.JobClient: map 100% reduce 100%
14/05/12 15:07:55 INFO mapred.JobClient: Job complete: job_201405121349_0009
...
14/05/12 15:07:55 INFO mapred.JobClient: Map-Reduce Framework
14/05/12 15:07:55 INFO mapred.JobClient: Map input records=15
14/05/12 15:07:55 INFO mapred.JobClient: Spilled Records=30
14/05/12 15:07:55 INFO mapred.JobClient: Map output bytes=311
14/05/12 15:07:55 INFO mapred.JobClient: Combine input records=0
14/05/12 15:07:55 INFO mapred.JobClient: Reduce input records=15
14/05/12 15:07:55 INFO mapred.JobClient: Reduce input groups=3
14/05/12 15:07:55 INFO mapred.JobClient: Combine output records=0
14/05/12 15:07:55 INFO mapred.JobClient: Reduce output records=12
14/05/12 15:07:55 INFO mapred.JobClient: Map output records=15
```

Inspecting the output

```
# hadoop fs -cat /moving_average/sort_in_memory/output/part*
GOOG 2004-11-03,193.26999999999998
GOOG 2004-11-04,188.18499999999997
GOOG 2013-07-17,551.625
GOOG 2013-07-18,914.615
GOOG 2013-07-19,903.6400000000001
AAPL 2013-10-04,483.22
AAPL 2013-10-07,485.39
AAPL 2013-10-08,484.345
AAPL 2013-10-09,483.765
IBM 2013-09-26,189.845
IBM 2013-09-27,188.57
IBM 2013-09-30,186.05
```

Option #2: Sorting Using the MapReduce Framework

In the previous section, you saw how to solve a moving average problem using the MapReduce framework by grouping lots of time series data by name and then sorting (by timestamp) time series values in memory. There is a problem with sorting data in memory, though: if you have a lot of data, then it might not all fit in memory (unless you have a lot of RAM in all cluster nodes, which is not the case to date, since memory is not as cheap as hard disks). In this section, I will show how to use the MapReduce framework (MRF) to sort data without sorting in memory. For example, in Hadoop, we can sort the data during the *shuffle phase* of the MRF. When the MRF does sorting by shuffling, it is called "secondary sorting" (which you learned about in Chapters 1 and 2). The question is how we will accomplish this secondary sorting. We need to write some additional custom Java classes, which we will then plug into the MRF.

How do we plug in the custom Java classes to accomplish sorting with the MRF? First we set the classes shown in Example 6-7 in the driver class.

Example 6-7. The SortByMRF_MovingAverageDriver class

```
1 import ...
2 /**
3  * MapReduce job for calculating moving averages of time series data by
4  * using MapReduce's secondary sort (sort by shuffle function).
5  */
6 public class SortByMRF_MovingAverageDriver {
7    public static void main(String[] args) throws Exception {
8        Configuration conf = new Configuration();
9        JobConf jobconf = new JobConf(conf, SortByMRF_MovingAverageDriver.class);
10       ...
11       // The following three settings are needed for secondary sorting.
12       // The Partitioner decides which mapper output goes to which reducer
13       // based on the mapper output key. In general, a different key is in
14       // a different group (iterator at the reducer side). But sometimes,
15       // we want a different key in the same group. This is the time for the
16       // Output Value Grouping Comparator, which is used to group mapper
17       // output (similar to the group by condition in SQL). The Output Key
18       // Comparator is used during the sort stage for the mapper output key.
19       jobconf.setPartitionerClass(NaturalKeyPartitioner.class);
20       jobconf.setOutputKeyComparatorClass(CompositeKeyComparator.class);
21       jobconf.setOutputValueGroupingComparator(
22           NaturalKeyGroupingComparator.class);
23
24       JobClient.runJob(jobconf);
25    }
26 }
```

To implement secondary sort for a moving average, we need to make the mapper's output key a composite of the natural key (`name-as-string`) and the natural value (`timeseries-timestamp`). Figure 6-1 illustrates the natural and composite keys needed.

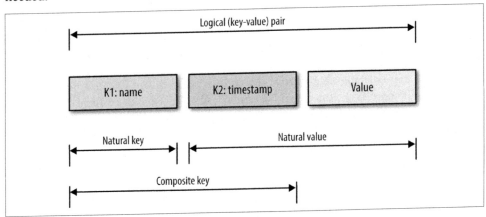

Figure 6-1. Composite and natural keys

The custom `CompositeKey` (composed of `"name"` and `"timestamp"`) is defined in Example 6-8.

Example 6-8. CompositeKey class definition

```
1 import org.apache.hadoop.io.WritableComparable;
2 ...
3 public class CompositeKey
4     implements WritableComparable<CompositeKey> {
5     // composite key is a pair of (name, timestamp)
6     private String name;
7     private long timestamp;
8     ...
9 }
```

The `CompositeKey` class has to implement the `WritableComparable` interface, since these objects will persist in HDFS. Therefore, the custom `CompositeKey` class gives Hadoop the needed information during the shuffle to perform a sort on two fields, `"name"` and `"timestamp"`, rather than `"name"` only. But how will the `CompositeKey` objects be sorted? We need to provide a class that compares composite key objects. This comparison is accomplished by the `CompositeKeyComparator` class (whose main function is to provide the `compare()` method), as shown in Example 6-9.

Example 6-9. CompositeKeyComparator class definition

```
1  import org.apache.hadoop.io.WritableComparable;
2  import org.apache.hadoop.io.WritableComparator;
3  public class CompositeKeyComparator extends WritableComparator {
4      protected CompositeKeyComparator() {
5          super(CompositeKey.class, true);
6      }
7
8      @Override
9      public int compare(WritableComparable w1, WritableComparable w2) {
10         CompositeKey key1 = (CompositeKey) w1;
11         CompositeKey key2 = (CompositeKey) w2;
12
13         int comparison = key1.getName().compareTo(key2.getName());
14         if (comparison == 0) {
15             // names are equal here
16             if (key1.getTimestamp() == key2.getTimestamp()) {
17                 return 0;
18             }
19             else if (key1.getTimestamp() < key2.getTimestamp()) {
20                 return -1;
21             }
22             else {
23                 return 1;
24             }
25         }
26         else {
27             return comparison;
28         }
29     }
30 }
```

`WritableComparator` is a `Comparator` for `WritableComparable`(s). This base implementation uses the natural ordering. To define alternate orderings, we had to override the `compare(WritableComparable,WritableComparable)` method. So, again, sorting of `CompositeKey` objects is handled by the custom `CompositeKeyComparator` class.

Now that you know how the composite keys will be sorted, the next question is how data will arrive at reducers. This will be handled by another custom class, `NaturalKey Partitioner`, which implements the `Partitioner`[1] interface, which in turn partitions the key space generated by all mappers. Even though all keys are sorted by the whole `CompositeKey` (composed of `name` and `timestamp`), in partitioning we will use only

---

[1] `org.apache.hadoop.mapred.Partitioner`. The `Partitioner` controls the partitioning of the keys of the intermediate map outputs. The key (or a subset of the key) is used to derive the partition, typically by a hash function. The total number of partitions is the same as the number of reduce tasks for the job. The custom partitioner divides the data based on the number of reducers so that all the data in a single partition gets executed by a single reducer. (Source: *http://hadoop.apache.org/docs.*)

the name because we want all the sorted values with the same name to go to a single reducer.

Example 6-10 shows the code for our custom partitioner, called NaturalKeyParti tioner.

Example 6-10. NaturalKeyPartitioner class definition

```
1 import org.apache.hadoop.mapred.JobConf;
2 import org.apache.hadoop.mapred.Partitioner;
3 public class NaturalKeyPartitioner implements
4     Partitioner<CompositeKey, TimeSeriesData> {
5
6     @Override
7     public int getPartition(CompositeKey key,
8                             TimeSeriesData value,
9                             int numberOfPartitions) {
10        return Math.abs((int) (hash(key.getName()) % numberOfPartitions));
11    }
12
13    @Override
14    public void configure(JobConf jobconf) {
15    }
16
17    /**
18     * adapted from String.hashCode()
19     */
20    static long hash(String str) {
21        long h = 1125899906842597L; // prime
22        int length = str.length();
23        for (int i = 0; i < length; i++) {
24            h = 31*h + str.charAt(i);
25        }
26        return h;
27    }
28 }
```

Example 6-11 shows the final plug-in class we need, NaturalKeyGroupingCompara tor, which is used during Hadoop's shuffle phase to group composite keys by the natural part of their key (in our example, the name component).

Example 6-11. NaturalKeyGroupingComparator class definition

```
1 import org.apache.hadoop.io.WritableComparable;
2 import org.apache.hadoop.io.WritableComparator;
3 /**
4  *
5  * NaturalKeyGroupingComparator
6  *
7  * This class is used during Hadoop's shuffle phase to
```

```
 8  * group composite keys by the natural part of their key.
 9  * The natural key for time series data is the name.
10  *
11  */
12 public class NaturalKeyGroupingComparator extends WritableComparator {
13     protected NaturalKeyGroupingComparator() {
14         super(CompositeKey.class, true);
15     }
16
17     @Override
18     public int compare(WritableComparable w1, WritableComparable w2) {
19         CompositeKey key1 = (CompositeKey) w1;
20         CompositeKey key2 = (CompositeKey) w2;
21         // natural keys are: key1.getName() and key2.getName()
22         return key1.getName().compareTo(key2.getName());
23     }
24 }
```

Hadoop implementation classes

The classes shown in Table 6-6 are used to implement the Moving Average algorithm
by sorting the reducer's values using the MRF.

Table 6-6. Classes used to implement the Moving Average algorithm in the MRF

Class name	Description
MovingAverage	A simple Moving Average algorithm
SortByMRF_MovingAverageDriver	A driver program to submit Hadoop jobs
SortByMRF_MovingAverageMapper	Defines map()
SortByMRF_MovingAverageReducer	Defines reduce()
TimeSeriesData	Represents a time series data point expressed as a pair of (timestamp, double)
CompositeKey	Defines a custom composite key of (string, timestamp)
CompositeKeyComparator	Defines sorting order for CompositeKey
NaturalKeyPartitioner	Partitions the data output from the map phase before it is sent through the shuffle phase
NaturalKeyGroupingComparator	Used during Hadoop's shuffle phase to group composite keys by the first (natural) part of their key
DateUtil	Provides basic date conversion utilities
HadoopUtil	Provides basic Hadoop utilities

Sample Run

A sample run is provided in the following subsections, which include the input,
script, and expected output.

HDFS input

```
# hadoop fs -cat /moving_average/sort_by_mrf/input/*
GOOG,2004-11-04,184.70
GOOG,2004-11-03,191.67
GOOG,2004-11-02,194.87
AAPL,2013-10-09,486.59
AAPL,2013-10-08,480.94
AAPL,2013-10-07,487.75
AAPL,2013-10-04,483.03
AAPL,2013-10-03,483.41
IBM,2013-09-30,185.18
IBM,2013-09-27,186.92
IBM,2013-09-26,190.22
IBM,2013-09-25,189.47
GOOG,2013-07-19,896.60
GOOG,2013-07-18,910.68
GOOG,2013-07-17,918.55
```

Script

```
# cat ./run.sh
#/bin/bash
export HADOOP_HOME=/usr/local/hadoop-2.3.0
export HADOOP_HOME_WARN_SUPPRESS=true
export JAVA_HOME=/usr/java/jdk6
export PATH=$PATH:$HADOOP_HOME/bin:$JAVA_HOME/bin
BOOK_HOME=/mp/data-algorithms-book
APP_JAR=$BOOK_HOME/dist/data_algorithms_book.jar
CLASSPATH=.:$HADOOP_HOME/conf:$APP_JAR
$HADOOP_HOME/bin/hadoop fs -put $APP_JAR /lib/
export input=/moving_average/sort_by_mrf/input
export output=/moving_average/sort_by_mrf/output
$HADOOP_HOME/bin/hadoop fs -rmr $output
driver=org.dataalgorithms.chap06.secondarysort.SortByMRF_MovingAverageDriver
export window_size=2
$HADOOP_HOME/bin/hadoop jar $APP_JAR $driver $window_size $input $output
```

Log of a sample run

The output has been edited and formatted to fit the page:

```
1 # ./run.sh
2 ...
3 Deleted hdfs://localhost:9000/moving_average/sort_by_mrf/output
4 ...
5 14/05/12 16:15:29 INFO mapred.JobClient: Running job: job_201405121612_0002
6 14/05/12 16:15:30 INFO mapred.JobClient: map 0% reduce 0%
7 ...
8 14/05/12 16:16:32 INFO mapred.JobClient: map 100% reduce 100%
9 14/05/12 16:16:33 INFO mapred.JobClient: Job complete: job_201405121612_0002
10 ...
11 14/05/12 16:16:33 INFO mapred.JobClient: Map-Reduce Framework
```

```
12 14/05/12 16:16:33 INFO mapred.JobClient:  Map input records=15
13 14/05/12 16:16:33 INFO mapred.JobClient:  Spilled Records=30
14 ...
15 14/05/12 16:16:33 INFO mapred.JobClient:  Reduce input records=15
16 14/05/12 16:16:33 INFO mapred.JobClient:  Reduce input groups=3
17 14/05/12 16:16:33 INFO mapred.JobClient:  Combine output records=0
18 14/05/12 16:16:33 INFO mapred.JobClient:  Reduce output records=15
19 14/05/12 16:16:33 INFO mapred.JobClient:  Map output records=15
```

Generated output

```
 1 # hadoop fs -cat /moving_average/sort_by_mrf/output/part*
 2 GOOG        2004-11-02,194.87
 3 GOOG        2004-11-03,193.26999999999998
 4 GOOG        2004-11-04,188.185
 5 GOOG        2013-07-17,551.625
 6 GOOG        2013-07-18,914.6149999999999
 7 GOOG        2013-07-19,903.64
 8 AAPL        2013-10-03,483.41
 9 AAPL        2013-10-04,483.22
10 AAPL        2013-10-07,485.39
11 AAPL        2013-10-08,484.345
12 AAPL        2013-10-09,483.765
13 IBM    2013-09-25,189.47
14 IBM    2013-09-26,189.845
15 IBM    2013-09-27,188.57
16 IBM    2013-09-30,186.04999999999995
```

This chapter provided a basic implementation of the Moving Average algorithm using the MapReduce framework. We also revisited the Secondary Sort design pattern from Chapters 1 and 2 in our implementation. The next chapter implements Market Basket Analysis (a data mining algorithm) using MapReduce/Hadoop and Spark.

## CHAPTER 7

Market Basket Analysis

Market Basket Analysis (MBA) is a popular data mining technique, frequently used by marketing and ecommerce professionals to reveal affinities between individual products or product groupings. The general goal of data mining is to extract interesting correlated information from a large collection of data–for example, millions of supermarket or credit card sales transactions. Market Basket Analysis helps us identify items likely to be purchased together, and association rule mining finds correlations between items in a set of transactions. Marketers may then use these association rules to place correlated products next to each other on store shelves or online so that customers buy more items. Finding *frequent sets* in mining association rules for Market Basket Analysis is a computationally intensive problem, making it an ideal case for MapReduce.

This chapter provides two Market Basket Analysis solutions:

- A MapReduce/Hadoop solution for tuples of order N (where $N = 1, 2, 3, ...$). This solution just finds the frequent patterns.

- A Spark solution, which not only finds frequent patterns, but also generates association rules for them.

MBA Goals

This chapter presents a MapReduce solution for data mining analysis to find the most frequently occurring pair of products (order of 1, 2, ...) in baskets at a given supermarket or ecommerce store. Our MapReduce solution is expandable to find the most frequently occurring TupleN (where N = 1, 2, 3, ...) of products (order of N) in baskets. The "order of N" (as an integer) will be passed as an argument to the MapReduce driver, which will then set it in Hadoop's Configuration object. Finally, the map()

method will read that parameter from Hadoop's `Configuration` object in the `setup()` method. Once we have the most frequent item sets F_i (where $i = 1, 2, ...$), we can use them to produce an association rule of the transaction. For example, if we have five items {A, B, C, D, E} with the following six transactions:

```
Transaction 1: A, C
Transaction 2: B, D
Transaction 3: A, C, E
Transaction 4: C, E
Transaction 5: A, B, E
Transaction 6: B, E
```

then our goal is to build frequent item sets F_1 (size = 1) and F_2 (size = 2) as:

- $F_1 = \{[C, 3], [A, 3], [B, 3], [E, 4]\}$
- $F_2 = \{[<A,C>, 2], [<C,E>, 2], [<A,E>, 2], [<B,E>, 2]\}$

Note that in this example, we applied a minimum *support* of 2, which is a count of how many times a pattern occurs in the entire transaction set. Thus, [D, 1] is eliminated in F_1. The item sets F_1 and F_2 can be used to produce an association rule of the transaction. An association rule is something like:

```
LHS => RHS
coke => chips
if customers purchase coke (called LHDS - lefthand side),
they also buy chips (called RHS - righthand side).
```

In data mining, an association rule has two metrics:

Support
> Frequency of occurrence of an item set. For example, `Support({A,C}) = 2` means that items A and C appear together only in two transactions.

Confidence
> How often the lefthand side of the rule appears with the righthand side.

Market Basket Analysis enables us to understand shoppers' behavior by answering these questions:

- What items are bought together?
- What is in each shopping basket?
- What items should be put on sale?
- How should items be placed next to each other for maximum profit? For example, if a supermarket has 10,000 or more unique items, then there are 50 million two-item combinations and 100 billion three-item combinations.

- How should the catalog of an ecommerce site be determined?

To understand the main ideas of MBA, imagine a shopping cart at a checkout counter in a supermarket filled with various products purchased by a customer. This basket contains a set of products: tuna, milk, orange juice, bananas, eggs, toothpaste, window cleaner, and detergent. This single basket tells us about what one customer purchased at one time. A complete list of purchases made by all customers (all transactions in a supermarket), however, provides much more information; it describes the most important part of a retailing business—what merchandise customers are buying and when. Therefore, one purpose of MBA is to help marketers improve sales by determining which products should be placed next to each other on the shelves, and by carefully designing the layout of products in the catalog of an ecommerce site. The final goal of MBA is the automatic generation of association rules.

Application Areas for MBA

Market Basket Analysis can be applied to supermarket shoppers, but there are many other areas in which it can be applied as well. These include:

- Analysis of credit card purchases
- Analysis of telephone calling patterns
- Identification of fraudulent medical insurance claims (consider cases where common rules are broken)
- Analysis of telecom service purchases
- Analysis of daily/weekly purchases at major online retailers like Amazon.com

Market Basket Analysis Using MapReduce

Since there will be a lot of big data, MapReduce is an ideal framework to do Market Basket Analysis. We will follow the Market Basket Analysis algorithm presented by Jongwook Woo and Yuhang Xu[33]. Given a set of transactions (where each transaction is a set of items), we want to answer this question: what is a pair of items that people frequently buy at the store? The high-level MapReduce solution for Market Basket Analysis is illustrated in Figure 7-1.

What are the `map()` and `reduce()` functions for MBA? Each `map()` function accepts a transaction, which is a set of items $\{I_1, I_2, \ldots, I_n\}$ purchased by a customer. A mapper first sorts items (in either ascending or descending order), which generates $\{S_1, S_2, \ldots, S_n\}$, and then emits (`key`, `1`) pairs, where `key` = `Tuple2(`S_i`, `S_j`)` and

$S_i \leq S_j$, and value is 1 (meaning that the key has been seen once). The job of combiners and reducers is to aggregate and count the frequencies.

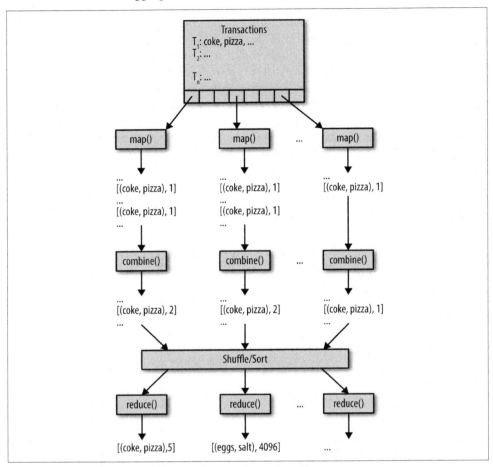

Figure 7-1. MapReduce Market Basket Analysis algorithm

Before we discuss the MapReduce algorithm in detail, let's look at the input and expected output.

Input

We assume that input is given as a sequence of transactions (one transaction per line). Transaction items are separated by spaces. Sample input will be as follows (actual transaction data is provided after ":"):

```
Transaction 1: crackers, icecream, coke, apple
Transaction 2: chicken, pizza, coke, bread
```

```
Transaction 3: baguette, soda, shampoo, crackers, pepsi
Transaction 4: baguette, cream cheese, diapers, milk
...
```

Expected Output for Tuple2 (Order of 2)

For an order of 2, we want to find the frequency of items for all unique pairs of ($Item_1$, $Item_2$). Sample expected output is presented in Table 7-1.

Table 7-1. Expected output for Tuple2 (order of 2)

Pair of items	Frequency
...	...
(bread, crackers)	8,709
(baguette, eggs)	7,524
(crackers, coke)	4,300
...	...

Expected Output for Tuple3 (Order of 3)

For an order of 3, we want to find the frequency of items for all unique sets of ($Item_1$, $Item_2$, $Item_3$). Sample expected output is presented in Table 7-1.

Table 7-2. Expected output for Tuple3 (order of 3)

Triplet of items	Frequency
...	...
(bread, crackers, eggs)	1,940
(baguette, diapers, eggs)	1,900
(crackers, coke, meat)	1,843
...	...

Informal Mapper

The map() function will take a single transaction and generate a set of key-value pairs to be consumed by reduce(). The mapper pairs the transaction items as a key and the number of key occurrences in the basket as its value (for all transactions and without the transaction numbers).

For example, map() for transaction 1 will emit the following key-value pairs:

```
[<crackers, icecream>, 1]
[<crackers, coke>, 1]
[<crackers, apple>, 1]
[<icecream, coke>, 1]
```

```
[<icecream, apple>, 1]
[<coke, apple>, 1]
```

Note that if we select the two items in a basket as a key, the count for those items' occurrence in the pairs will be incorrect. For example, if transactions T_1 and T_2 have the following items (the same items but in a different order):

```
T₁: crackers, icecream, coke
T₂: icecream, coke, crackers
```

then for transaction T_1, map() will generate:

```
[(crackers, icecream), 1]
[(crackers, coke), 1]
[(icecream, coke), 1]
```

and for transaction T_2, map() will generate:

```
[(icecream, coke), 1]
[(icecream, crackers), 1]
[(coke, crackers), 1]
```

As you can see from the map() outputs for transactions T_1 and T_2, we get a total of six different pairs of items that occur only once each, when they should actually amount to only three different pairs. That is, the keys (crackers, icecream) and (ice cream, crackers) are not being counted as the same even though they are, which is not correct. We can avoid this problem if we sort the transaction items in alphabetical order before generating key-value pairs. After sorting the items in the transactions we get:

```
Sorted T₁: coke, crackers, icecream
Sorted T₂: coke, crackers, icecream
```

Now each transaction (T_1 and T_2) has the following three key-value pairs:

```
[(coke, crackers), 1]
[(coke, icecream), 1]
[(crackers, icecream), 1)
```

Sorting items in transactions enables us to get the correct counts for key-value pairs generated by mappers. Here, for transactions T_1 and T_2, the combiner() function will generate the correct output:

```
[(coke, crackers), 2],
[(coke, icecream), 2],
[(crackers, icecream),2]
```

Formal Mapper

The MBA algorithm for the mapper is illustrated in Example 7-1. The mapper reads the input data and creates a list of items for each transaction. For each transaction, its time complexity is $O(n)$, where n is the number of items for a transaction. Then, the items in the transaction list are sorted to avoid duplicate keys like (crackers, coke) and (coke, crackers). The time complexity of Quicksort is $O(n \log n)$. Then, the sorted transaction items are converted to pairs of items as keys, which is a cross-operation in order to generate cross-pairs of the items in the list.

Example 7-1. MBA map() function

```
1 // key is transaction ID and ignored here
2 // value = transaction items (I1, I2, ...,In).
3 map(key, value) {
4     (S1, S2, ..., Sn) = sort(I1, I2, ...,In);
5     // now, we have: S1 < S2 < ... < Sn
6     List<Tuple2<Si, Sj>> listOfPairs =
7         Combinations.generateCombinations(S1, S2, ..., Sn);
8     for ( Tuple2<Si, Sj> pair : listOfPairs) {
9         // reducer key is: Tuple2<Si, Sj>
10        // reducer value is: integer 1
11        emit([Tuple2<Si, Sj>, 1]);
12    }
13 }
```

Combinations is a simple Java utility class that generates combinations of basket items for a given "list of items" and "number of pairs" (as 2, 3, 4, ...). Assume that $(S_1, S_2, ..., S_n)$ is sorted (i.e., $S_1 \le S_2 \le ... \le S_n$). Then the Combinations.generateCombina tions$(S_1, S_2, ..., S_n)$ method generates all combinations of any two items in a given transaction. For example, generateCombinations(S_1, S_2, S_3, S_4) will return the following pairs:

```
(S1, S2)
(S1, S3)
(S1, S4)
(S2, S3)
(S2, S4)
(S3, S4)
```

Reducer

The MBA algorithm for the reducer is illustrated in Example 7-2. The reducer sums up the number of values for each reducer key. Thus, its time complexity is $O(n)$, where n is the number of values per key.

Example 7-2. MBA reduce() function

```
1 // key is in form of Tuple2(Si, Sj)
2 // value = List<integer>, where each element is an integer number
3 reduce(Tuple2(Si, Sj) key, List<integer> values) {
4     integer sum = 0;
```

```
5      for (integer i : values) {
6          sum += i;
7      }
8
9      emit(key, sum);
10 }
```

MapReduce/Hadoop Implementation Classes

The Hadoop implementation is composed of the Java classes listed in Table 7-3.

Table 7-3. Implementation classes in MapReduce/Hadoop

Class name	Class description
Combination	A utility class to create a combination of items
MBADriver	Submits the job to Hadoop
MBAMapper	Defines map()
MBAReducer	Defines reduce()

Find sorted combinations

`Combination.findSortedCombinations()` is a recursive function that will create a unique combination for any order of N (where N = 2, 3, ...), as shown in Example 7-3.

Example 7-3. Find sorted combinations

```
1 /**
2  * If elements = { a, b, c, d },
3  * then findCollections(elements, 2) will return:
4  *     { [a, b], [a, c], [a, d], [b, c], [b, d], [c, d] }
5  *
6  * and findCollections(elements, 3) will return:
7  *     { [a, b, c], [a, b, d], [a, c, d], [b, c, d] }
8  *
9  */
10 public static <T extends Comparable<? super T>> List<List<T>>
11        findSortedCombinations(Collection<T> elements, int n) {
12    List<List<T>> result = new ArrayList<List<T>>();
13
14    // handle initial step for recursion
15    if (n == 0) {
16        result.add(new ArrayList<T>());
17        return result;
18    }
19
20    // handle recursion for n-1
21    List<List<T>> combinations = findSortedCombinations(elements, n - 1);
22    for (List<T> combination: combinations) {
23        for (T element: elements) {
```

```
24              if (combination.contains(element)) {
25                  continue;
26              }
27
28              List<T> list = new ArrayList<T>();
29              list.addAll(combination);
30
31              if (list.contains(element)) {
32                  continue;
33              }
34
35              list.add(element);
36              // sort items to avoid duplicate items
37              // example: (a, b, c) and (a, c, b) might be counted as
38              // different items if not sorted
39              Collections.sort(list);
40
41              if (result.contains(list)) {
42                  continue;
43              }
44              result.add(list);
45          }
46      }
47      return result;
48 }
```

Market Basket Analysis driver: MBADriver

In Example 7-4, the driver class accepts three parameters and submits the job to the MapReduce/Hadoop framework. The driver also sets the "number.of.pairs" configuration parameter to be read by mappers.

Example 7-4. MBADriver

```
1 public class MBADriver extends Configured implements Tool {
2      ...
3      public int run(String args[]) throws Exception {
4          String inputPath = args[0];
5          String outputPath = args[1];
6          int numberOfPairs = Integer.parseInt(args[2]);
7          ...
8          // job configuration
9          Job job = new Job(getConf());
10         ...
11         job.getConfiguration().setInt("number.of.pairs", numberOfPairs);
12
13         // set input/output path
14         FileInputFormat.setInputPaths(job, new Path(inputPath));
15         FileOutputFormat.setOutputPath(job, new Path(outputPath));
16
17         // mapper K, V output
```

```
18        job.setMapOutputKeyClass(Text.class);
19        job.setMapOutputValueClass(IntWritable.class);
20        // output format
21        job.setOutputFormatClass(TextOutputFormat.class);
22
23        // reducer K, V output
24        job.setOutputKeyClass(Text.class);
25        job.setOutputValueClass(IntWritable.class);
26
27        // set mapper/reducer/combiner
28        job.setMapperClass(MBAMapper.class);
29        job.setCombinerClass(MBAReducer.class);
30        job.setReducerClass(MBAReducer.class);
31
32        //delete the output path if it exists to avoid "existing dir/file" error
33        Path outputDir = new Path(outputPath);
34        FileSystem.get(getConf()).delete(outputDir, true);
35
36        // submit job
37        boolean status = job.waitForCompletion(true);
38        ...
39    }
```

Market Basket Analysis mapper: MBAMapper

The map() function reads one transaction at a time and generates a set of key-value pairs, where the key is an order of N combination of items in a given transaction and the value is an integer, 1 (to indicate this combination has been seen once). The mapper's setup() method reads "number.of.pairs" from Hadoop's Configuration object. See Examples 7-5 through 7-7.

Example 7-5. MBAMapper

```
1 public class MBAMapper extends Mapper<LongWritable, Text, Text, IntWritable> {
2
3    public static final int DEFAULT_NUMBER_OF_PAIRS = 2;
4
5    // output key2: list of items paired; can be 2 or 3 ...
6    private static final Text reducerKey = new Text();
7
8    // output value2: number of the paired items in the item list
9    private static final IntWritable NUMBER_ONE = new IntWritable(1);
10
11    int numberOfPairs; // will be read by setup(), set by driver
12
13    protected void setup(Context context)
14        throws IOException, InterruptedException {
15        this.numberOfPairs = context.getConfiguration()
16            .getInt("number.of.pairs", DEFAULT_NUMBER_OF_PAIRS);
17    }
18
```

```
19    public void map(LongWritable key, Text value, Context context)
20        throws IOException, InterruptedException {
21        String line = value.toString().trim();
22        List<String> items = convertItemsToList(line);
23        if ((items == null) || ( items.isEmpty())) {
24           // no mapper output will be generated
25             return;
26        }
27        generateMapperOutput(numberOfPairs, items, context);
28    }
29
30    private static List<String> convertItemsToList(String line) {
31        // see Example 7-6
32    }
33
34    private void generateMapperOutput(...) {
35        // see Example 7-7
36    }
37 }
```

Example 7-6. MBAMapper helper methods: convertItemsToList

```
1    private static List<String> convertItemsToList(String line) {
2        if ((line == null) || ( line.length() == 0)) {
3           // no mapper output will be generated
4           return null;
5        }
6        String[] tokens = StringUtils.split(line, ",");
7        if (( tokens == null) || ( tokens.length == 0) ) {
8           return null;
9        }
10       List<String> items = new ArrayList<String>();
11       for (String token : tokens) {
12           if (token != null) {
13               items.add(token.trim());
14           }
15       }
16       return items;
17    }
```

Example 7-7. MBAMapper helper methods: generateMapperOutput

```
1    /**
2     *
3     * This method builds a set of key-value pairs by sorting the input list.
4     * key is a combination of items in a transaction, and value = 1.
5     * Sorting is required to make sure that (a, b) and (b, a)
6     * represent the same key.
7     * @param numberOfPairs is the number of pairs associated
8     * @param items is a list of items (from input line)
9     * @param context is the Hadoop job context
```

```
10      * @throws IOException
11      * @throws InterruptedException
12      */
13     private void generateMapperOutput(int numberOfPairs,
14                                       List<String> items,
15                                       Context context)
16         throws IOException, InterruptedException {
17         List<List<String>> sortedCombinations =
18             Combination.findSortedCombinations(items, numberOfPairs);
19         for (List<String> itemList: sortedCombinations) {
20             reducerKey.set(itemList.toString());
21             context.write(reducerKey, NUMBER_ONE);
22         }
23     }
24 }
```

Sample Run

Input

```
# hadoop fs -cat /market_basket_analysis/input/input.txt
crackers,bread,banana
crackers,coke,butter,coffee
crackers,bread
crackers,bread
crackers,bread,coffee
butter,coke
butter,coke,bread,crackers
```

Log of sample run

```
# INPUT=/market_basket_analysis/input
# OUTPUT=/market_basket_analysis/output
# $HADOOP_HOME/bin/hadoop fs -rmr $OUTPUT
# $HADOOP_HOME/bin/hadoop jar $JAR MBADriver  $INPUT $OUTPUT 2
...
Deleted hdfs://localhost:9000/market_basket_analysis/output
14/05/02 13:36:36 INFO MBADriver: inputPath: /market_basket_analysis/input
14/05/02 13:36:36 INFO MBADriver: outputPath: /market_basket_analysis/output
14/05/02 13:36:36 INFO MBADriver: numberOfPairs: 2
...
14/05/02 13:36:37 INFO mapred.JobClient: Running job: job_201405021309_0003
14/05/02 13:36:38 INFO mapred.JobClient:  map 0% reduce 0%
...
14/05/02 13:37:29 INFO mapred.JobClient:  map 100% reduce 100%
14/05/02 13:37:30 INFO mapred.JobClient: Job complete: job_201405021309_0003
...
14/05/02 13:37:30 INFO mapred.JobClient:   Map-Reduce Framework
14/05/02 13:37:30 INFO mapred.JobClient:     Map input records=7
...
14/05/02 13:37:30 INFO mapred.JobClient:     Combine input records=21
14/05/02 13:37:30 INFO mapred.JobClient:     Reduce input records=12
```

```
14/05/02 13:37:30 INFO mapred.JobClient:     Reduce input groups=12
14/05/02 13:37:30 INFO mapred.JobClient:     Combine output records=12
14/05/02 13:37:30 INFO mapred.JobClient:     Reduce output records=12
14/05/02 13:37:30 INFO mapred.JobClient:     Map output records=21
14/05/02 13:37:30 INFO MBADriver: job status=true
14/05/02 13:37:30 INFO MBADriver: Elapsed time: 52737 milliseconds
14/05/02 13:37:30 INFO MBADriver: exitStatus=0
```

Output

```
# hadoop fs -cat /market_basket_analysis/output/part*
[bread, coffee]      1
[butter, coffee]     1
[banana, crackers]   1
[butter, coke]       3
[coffee, crackers]   2
[bread, butter]      1
[banana, bread]      1
[bread, crackers]    5
[coke, crackers]     2
[bread, coke]        1
[coffee, coke]       1
[butter, crackers]   2
```

Spark Solution

This section presents the Spark solution for generating all of the association rules for a set of transactions. Association rules are statements of the if-then form $X \rightarrow Y$, which means that if we find all of X items in the market basket (denoted by a transaction), then we have a good chance of finding Y. Before we delve into the generation of association rules, we need some basic definitions. Let $I = \{I_1, I_2, ..., I_n\}$: a set of items. Transaction t is defined as $t = \{S_1, S_2, ..., S_m\}$, where $\{S_i \in I\}$ and $m \leq n$. Then transaction database T is defined to be a set of transactions $T = \{T_1, T_2, ..., T_k\}$. Therefore, each transaction $\{T_i\}$ contains a set of items in I. Given these definitions, now we can define an association rule as:

$X \rightarrow Y$, where $X, Y \in I$, and $X \cap Y = \emptyset$

For example, we might have: $X=\{\text{milk, bread}\}$ and $Y=\{\text{cereal, sugar, butter}\}$. X (item set of two elements) and Y (item set of three elements) are called the *lefthand side* and *righthand side* of an association rule, respectively. Therefore, in a nutshell, we can say that an association rule is a pattern that states when X occurs, then Y occurs with a certain probability. We need a few more definitions before revisiting the two important metrics (support and confidence, as we discussed earlier in the chapter) for an association rule. An *item set* is a collection of one or more items. For example, an item set of $Y=\{\text{cereal, sugar, butter}\}$ contains three elements. A *support count* (denoted by θ) is the frequency of occurrence of an item set in all transactions. For example:

$$\theta(\{I_1, I_2\}) = 3$$

means that among all transactions, items I_1 and I_2 appear together in only three transactions.

Now, we can reiterate the support and confidence metrics for an association rule:

- *Support* is the fraction of transactions that contain an item set. So, for a given association rule $X \to Y$, support is the fraction of transactions that contain both X and Y. We may write this as:

$$\text{support} = \frac{\theta(\{I_1, I_2\})}{\#\text{ of transactions}}$$

For example, if $\theta(\{I_1, I_2\}) = 3$ and the total number of transactions is 24, then support of $\{I_1, I_2\}$ is defined as $\frac{3}{24}$. In frequent item set generation, a *support threshold* is used.

- *Confidence* measures, for a given association rule $X \to Y$, how often items in Y appear in transactions that contain X. In association rule generation, a *confidence threshold* is used. Confidence can be expressed as:

$$\text{confidence} = \frac{\theta(Y)}{\theta(X)}$$

Our goal is to find all association rules that satisfy the user-specified minimum support (`minimum-support`) and minimum confidence (`minimum-confidence`). These two parameters may be passed to limit the number of frequent sets generated and consequently the number of association rules. In summary, we can say that an association rule (denoted by $X \to Y$) is about relationships between two disjoint item sets X and Y, and it presents the pattern "when X occurs, Y also occurs" in transactions.

In our solution, we will not limit frequent sets by `minimum-support`, but our algorithm will calculate the confidence of every association rule generated. Our Spark solution finds all frequent item sets, generates all proper association rules, and finally calculates the confidence of those generated association rules. Calculating support is pretty straightforward: divide the frequency of an item set by the total number of all transactions.

MapReduce Algorithm Workflow

The MapReduce algorithm workflow is presented in Figure 7-2. It comprises two phases:

- MapReduce phase 1: mappers convert transactions to patterns, and reducers find frequent patterns.
- MapReduce phase 2: mappers convert frequent patterns into subpatterns, and finally reducers generate association rules and their associated confidences.

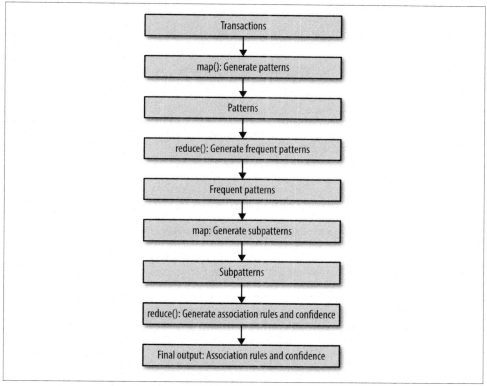

Figure 7-2. MapReduce algorithm workflow

Input

Our input is a set of transactions (one transaction per line). For example, for testing, we will use the following input (composed of four transactions):

```
transaction-1: a,b,c
transaction-2: a,b,d
transaction-3: b,c
transaction-4: b,c
```

Spark Implementation

The Spark implementation follows the two-phase MapReduce algorithm presented. First, I present all high-level steps, and then each step is covered in detail.

Example 7-8 presents the Spark solution in a single Java driver class. This is possible thanks to the Spark API's high level of abstraction, which you've learned about in previous chapters.

Example 7-8. High-level steps

```
 1 // Step 1: import required classes and interfaces
 2 public class FindAssociationRules {
 3
 4     static JavaSparkContext createJavaSparkContext() {...}
 5     static List<String> toList(String transaction) {...}
 6     static List<String> removeOneItem(List<String> list, int i) {...}
 7
 8     public static void main(String[] args) throws Exception {
 9         // Step 2: handle input parameters
10         // Step 3: create a Spark context object
11         // Step 4: read all transactions from HDFS and create the first RDD
12         // Step 5: generate frequent patterns (map() phase 1)
13         // Step 6: combine/reduce frequent patterns (reduce() phase 1)
14         // Step 7: generate all subpatterns (map() phase 2)
15         // Step 8: combine subpatterns
16         // Step 9: generate association rules (reduce() phase 2)
17         System.exit(0);
18     }
19 }
```

Steps 5 and 6 solve the first phase of the MapReduce process and are illustrated in Figure 7-3. Steps 7 through 9 solve the second phase and are illustrated in Figure 7-4. We'll go over each step in more detail in the subsections that follow.

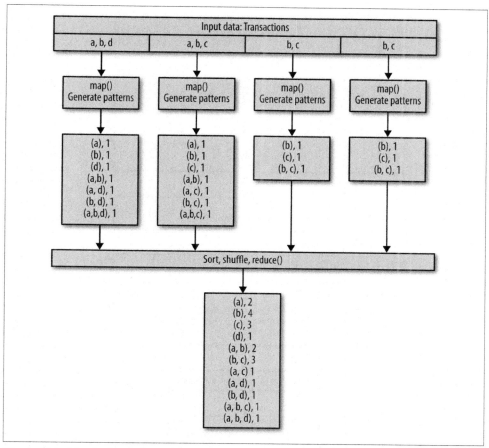

Figure 7-3. MapReduce phase 1: converting transactions to patterns and finding frequent patterns

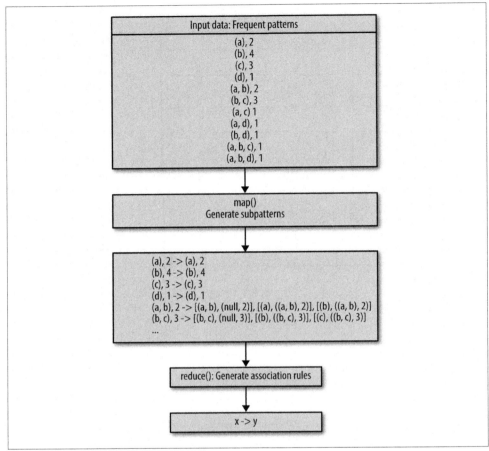

Figure 7-4. MapReduce phase 2: generating association rules

Step 1: Import required classes and interfaces

Example 7-9 imports the required Java classes an interfaces used in the driver Spark program.

Example 7-9. Step 1: import required classes and interfaces

```
1 // Step 1: import required classes and interfaces
2 import java.util.List;
3 import java.util.ArrayList;
4 import scala.Tuple2;
5 import scala.Tuple3;
6 import org.apache.spark.api.java.JavaRDD;
7 import org.apache.spark.api.java.JavaPairRDD;
8 import org.apache.spark.api.java.JavaSparkContext;
```

```
 9 import org.apache.spark.api.java.function.PairFlatMapFunction;
10 import org.apache.spark.api.java.function.FlatMapFunction;
11 import org.apache.spark.api.java.function.Function;
12 import org.apache.spark.api.java.function.Function2;
13 import org.apache.spark.SparkConf;
```

Create a Spark context object

To create RDDs, you need to create a JavaSparkContext object. This is done using the createJavaSparkContext() method, as shown in Example 7-10. JavaSparkCon text is a factory class for creating new RDDs.

Example 7-10. Create a Spark context object

```
 1 static JavaSparkContext createJavaSparkContext() throws Exception {
 2    SparkConf conf = new SparkConf();
 3    conf.setAppName("market-basket-analysis");
 4    // set up a fast serializer
 5    conf.set("spark.serializer", "org.apache.spark.serializer.KryoSerializer");
 6    // Now it's 32 MB of buffer by default instead of 0.064 MB
 7    // See: https://github.com/cloudera/spark/blob/master/docs/configuration.md
 8    conf.set("spark.kryoserializer.buffer.mb","32");
 9    JavaSparkContext ctx = new JavaSparkContext(conf);
10    return ctx;
11 }
```

Utility functions

Example 7-11 presents two utility functions used in our solution. The toList() function accepts a transaction (items separated by commas) and returns a list of items. The removeOneItem() function removes a single item from a given list and returns a new list with that item removed (used for generating the lefthand side of the association rules).

Example 7-11. Utility list functions

```
 1 static List<String> toList(String transaction) {
 2    String[] items = transaction.trim().split(",");
 3    List<String> list = new ArrayList<String>();
 4    for (String item : items) {
 5      list.add(item);
 6    }
 7    return list;
 8 }
 9
10 static List<String> removeOneItem(List<String> list, int i) {
11    if (( list == null) || ( list.isEmpty()) ) {
12      return list;
13    }
```

```
14    if (( i < 0) || ( i > (list.size()-1)) ) {
15        return list;
16    }
17    List<String> cloned = new ArrayList<String>(list);
18    cloned.remove(i);
19    return cloned;
20 }
```

Step 2: Handle input parameters

This step, shown in Example 7-12, reads the transactions file parameter supplied by the command line.

Example 7-12. Step 2: handle input parameters

```
1        // Step 2: handle input parameters
2        if (args.length < 1) {
3            System.err.println("Usage: FindAssociationRules <transactions>");
4            System.exit(1);
5        }
6        String transactionsFileName = args[0];
```

Step 3: Create a Spark context object

This step, shown in Example 7-13, creates a `JavaSparkContext` object, which (as you saw in Example 7-10) is a factory for creating new RDDs.

Example 7-13. Step 3: create a Spark context object

```
1        // Step 3: create a Spark context object
2        JavaSparkContext ctx = createJavaSparkContext();
```

Step 4: Read transactions from HDFS and create an RDD

As shown in Example 7-14, this step reads all transactions from an HDFS file and creates the first RDD (`JavaRDD<String>`), where each item is a transaction.

Example 7-14. Step 4: read all transactions from HDFS and create RDD

```
1        // Step 4: read all transactions from HDFS and create the first RDD
2        JavaRDD<String> transactions = ctx.textFile(transactionsFileName, 1);
3        transactions.saveAsTextFile("/rules/output/1");
```

For debugging purposes, we write the intermediate data to HDFS. Here, we just emit all raw transactions:

```
# hadoop fs -cat /rules/output/1/part*
a,b,c
a,b,d
```

```
b,c
b,c
```

Step 5: Generate frequent patterns

Our mapper generates all patterns for a given transaction. For example, given a transaction with three items, {a, b, c}, the mapper emits the key-value pairs shown in
Table 7-4.

Table 7-4. Key-value pairs emitted by mapper

Key	Value
a	1
b	1
c	1
a,b	1
a,c	1
b,c	1
a,b,c	1

Typically, in MBA, you might select patterns of length two or three. Selecting *all* patterns could be a very time-consuming process. Here, to generate all patterns, we use a
recursive function:

```
List<List<String>> Combination.findSortedCombinations(List<String>)
```

For example, `findSortedCombinations(List<a, b, c, d>)` generates:

```
[
  [],
  [a],
  [b],
  [c],
  [d],
  [a, b],
  [a, c],
  [a, d],
  [b, c],
  [b, d],
  [c, d],
  [a, b, c],
  [a, b, d],
  [a, c, d],
  [b, c, d],
  [a, b, c, d]
]
```

Note that combinations are always sorted; for example, for a list of two items {a, b}, we always create [a, b] and never [b, a]. Having sorted item sets enables us to avoid duplicates. The Combination class is defined at the end of this chapter.

Example 7-15 illustrates this step, where we generate the patterns.

Example 7-15. Step 5: generate frequent patterns

```
1    // Step 5: generate frequent patterns
2    // PairFlatMapFunction<T, K, V>
3    // T => Iterable<Tuple2<K, V>>
4    JavaPairRDD<List<String>,Integer> patterns =
5        transactions.flatMapToPair(new PairFlatMapFunction<
6                                                    String,       // T
7                                                    List<String>, // K
8                                                    Integer       // V
9                                                    >() {
10       public Iterable<Tuple2<List<String>,Integer>> call(String transaction) {
11           List<String> list = toList(transaction);
12           List<List<String>> combinations =
13                   Combination.findSortedCombinations(list);
14           List<Tuple2<List<String>,Integer>> result =
15                   new ArrayList<Tuple2<List<String>,Integer>>();
16           for (List<String> combList : combinations) {
17               if (combList.size() > 0) {
18                   result.add(new Tuple2<List<String>,Integer>(combList, 1));
19               }
20           }
21           return result;
22       }
23    });
24    patterns.saveAsTextFile("/rules/output/2");
```

Here is the output of this step:

```
# hadoop fs -cat /rules/output/2/part*
([a],1)
([b],1)
([c],1)
([a, b],1)
([a, c],1)
([b, c],1)
([a, b, c],1)
([a],1)
([b],1)
([d],1)
([a, b],1)
([a, d],1)
([b, d],1)
([a, b, d],1)
([b],1)
```

```
([c],1)
([b, c],1)
([b],1)
([c],1)
([b, c],1)
```

Step 6: Combine/reduce frequent patterns

This step, shown in Example 7-16, implements the reduceByKey() function for phase 1 of the MapReduce algorithm. It finds all unique frequent patterns and their associated frequencies among all transactions.

Example 7-16. Step 6: combine/reduce frequent patterns

```
1     // Step 6: combine/reduce frequent patterns
2     JavaPairRDD<List<String>, Integer> combined =
3         patterns.reduceByKey(new Function2<
4                                         Integer, // input i1
5                                         Integer, // input i2
6                                         Integer // result of i1+i2
7                                     >() {
8         public Integer call(Integer i1, Integer i2) {
9             return i1 + i2;
10        }
11    });
12    combined.saveAsTextFile("/rules/output/3");
13
14    // Now we have: patterns(K,V)
15    //      K = pattern as List<String>
16    //      V = frequency of pattern
17    // Now, given (K,V) as (List<a,b,c>, 2) we will
18    // generate the following (K2,V2) pairs:
19    //
20    //   (List<a,b,c>, T2(null, 2))
21    //   (List<a,b>,   T2(List<a,b,c>, 2))
22    //   (List<a,c>,   T2(List<a,b,c>, 2))
23    //   (List<b,c>,   T2(List<a,b,c>, 2))
```

Here is the ouput of this step:

```
# hadoop fs -cat /rules/output/3/part*
([a, b],2)
([a, b, d],1)
([c],3)
([b, d],1)
([d],1)
([a],2)
([b, c],3)
([a, b, c],1)
([a, c],1)
```

```
([a, d],1)
([b],4)
```

Step 7: Generate all subpatterns

This step creates all subpatterns, which are needed for the creation of association rules. Given a frequent pattern of:

$$(K = List < A_1, A_2, .., A_n >, V = Frequency)$$

we create the following subpatterns (K_2, V_2) as:

$$(K_2 = List < A_1, A_2, .., A_n >, V_2 = Tuple2(null, Frequency))$$

$$(K_2 = List < A_1, A_2, .., A_{n-1} >, V_2 = Tuple2(K, Frequency))$$

$$(K_2 = List < A_1, A_2, .., A_{n-2}, A_n >, V_2 = Tuple2(K, Frequency))$$

...

For example, given (K, V) as (List(a,b,c), 2), we will generate the (K_2, V_2) pairs shown in Table 7-5.

Table 7-5. Subpatterns (K_2, V_2)

K_2	V_2
List(a,b,c)	Tuple2(null, 2)
List(a,b)	Tuple2(List(a,b,c), 2)
List(a,c)	Tuple2(List(a,b,c), 2)
List(b,c)	Tuple2(List(a,b,c), 2)

This step is illustrated in Example 7-17.

Example 7-17. Step 7: generate all subpatterns

```
1  // Step 7: generate all subpatterns
2  // PairFlatMapFunction<T, K, V>>
3  // T => Iterable<Tuple2<K, V>>
4  JavaPairRDD<List<String>,Tuple2<List<String>,Integer>> subpatterns =
5      combined.flatMapToPair(new PairFlatMapFunction<
6              Tuple2<List<String>, Integer>, // T
7              List<String>,                  // K
8              Tuple2<List<String>,Integer>   // V
```

```
 9                                                  >() {
10      public Iterable<Tuple2<List<String>,Tuple2<List<String>,Integer>>>
11         call(Tuple2<List<String>, Integer> pattern) {
12         List<Tuple2<List<String>,Tuple2<List<String>,Integer>>> result =
13            new ArrayList<Tuple2<List<String>,Tuple2<List<String>,Integer>>>();
14         List<String> list = pattern._1;
15         Integer frequency = pattern._2;
16         result.add(new Tuple2(list, new Tuple2(null,frequency)));
17         if (list.size() == 1) {
18            return result;
19         }
20
21         // pattern has more than one item
22         // result.add(new Tuple2(list, new Tuple2(null,size)));
23         for (int i=0; i < list.size(); i++) {
24            List<String> sublist = removeOneItem(list, i);
25            result.add(new Tuple2(sublist, new Tuple2(list, frequency)));
26         }
27         return result;
28      }
29 });
30 subpatterns.saveAsTextFile("/rules/output/4");
```

Here is the output of this step:

```
# hadoop fs -cat /rules/output/4/part*
([a, b],(null,2))
([b],([a, b],2))
([a],([a, b],2))
([a, b, d],(null,1))
([b, d],([a, b, d],1))
([a, d],([a, b, d],1))
([a, b],([a, b, d],1))
([c],(null,3))
([b, d],(null,1))
([d],([b, d],1))
([b],([b, d],1))
([d],(null,1))
([a],(null,2))
([b, c],(null,3))
([c],([b, c],3))
([b],([b, c],3))
([a, b, c],(null,1))
([b, c],([a, b, c],1))
([a, c],([a, b, c],1))
([a, b],([a, b, c],1))
([a, c],(null,1))
([c],([a, c],1))
([a],([a, c],1))
([a, d],(null,1))
([d],([a, d],1))
([a],([a, d],1))
([b],(null,4))
```

Step 8: Combine subpatterns

As demonstrated in Example 7-18, this step groups subpatterns by key using Spark's groupByKey() method.

Example 7-18. Step 8: combine subpatterns

```
1    // Step 8: combine subpatterns
2    JavaPairRDD<List<String>,Iterable<Tuple2<List<String>,Integer>>> rules =
3        subpatterns.groupByKey();
4    rules.saveAsTextFile("/rules/output/5");
```

Here is the output of this step:

```
# hadoop fs -cat /rules/output/5/part*
([a, b],[(null,2), ([a, b, d],1), ([a, b, c],1)])
([a, b, d],[(null,1)])
([c],[(null,3), ([b, c],3), ([a, c],1)])
([b, d],[([a, b, d],1), (null,1)])
([d],[([b, d],1), (null,1), ([a, d],1)])
([a],[([a, b],2), (null,2), ([a, c],1), ([a, d],1)])
([b, c],[(null,3), ([a, b, c],1)])
([a, b, c],[(null,1)])
([a, c],[([a, b, c],1), (null,1)])
([a, d],[([a, b, d],1), (null,1)])
([b],[([a, b],2), ([b, d],1), ([b, c],3), (null,4)])
```

Step 9: Generate association rules

Now, given a frequent pattern and all subpatterns, we will be able to generate all association rules and their corresponding confidence values. This step is implemented by the JavaPairRDD.map() function, as shown in Example 7-19.

Example 7-19. Step 9: generate association rules

```
1    // Step 9: generate association rules
2    // Now, use (K=List<String>, V=Iterable<Tuple2<List<String>,Integer>>)
3    // to generate association rules
4    // JavaRDD<R> map(Function<T,R> f)
5    // Return a new RDD by applying a function to all elements of this RDD.
6    JavaRDD<List<Tuple3<List<String>,List<String>,Double>>> assocRules =
7        rules.map(new Function<
8            Tuple2<List<String>,Iterable<Tuple2<List<String>,Integer>>>,
9            List<Tuple3<List<String>,List<String>,Double>>
10            // T: input
11            // R: ( ac => b, 1/3): T3(List(a,c), List(b), 0.33)
12            //    ( ad => c, 1/3): T3(List(a,d), List(c), 0.33)
13            >() {
14        public List<Tuple3<List<String>,List<String>,Double>>
15            call(Tuple2<List<String>,Iterable<Tuple2<List<String>,Integer>>> in) {
16            List<Tuple3<List<String>,List<String>,Double>> result =
```

```
17              new ArrayList<Tuple3<List<String>,List<String>,Double>>();
18          List<String> fromList = in._1;
19          Iterable<Tuple2<List<String>,Integer>> to = in._2;
20          List<Tuple2<List<String>,Integer>> toList =
21              new ArrayList<Tuple2<List<String>,Integer>>();
22          Tuple2<List<String>,Integer> fromCount = null;
23          for (Tuple2<List<String>,Integer> t2 : to) {
24              // find the "count" object
25              if (t2._1 == null) {
26                  fromCount = t2;
27              }
28              else {
29                  toList.add(t2);
30              }
31          }
32
33          // now, we have the required objects for generating association rules:
34          // "fromList", "fromCount", and "toList"
35          if (toList.isEmpty()) {
36              // no output generated, but since Spark does not
37              // like null objects, we will fake a null object
38              return result; // an empty list
39          }
40
41          // now using 3 objects, "from", "fromCount", and "toList",
42          // create association rules:
43          for (Tuple2<List<String>,Integer> t2 : toList) {
44              double confidence = (double) t2._2 / (double) fromCount._2;
45              List<String> t2List = new ArrayList<String>(t2._1);
46              t2List.removeAll(fromList);
47              result.add(new Tuple3(fromList, t2List, confidence));
48          }
49          return result;
50      }
51  });
52  assocRules.saveAsTextFile("/rules/output/6");
```

Here is the output of this step (i.e., the final output). Each output entry depicts a list of Tuple3(X, Y, confidence), where X → Y and confidence (as a double value):

```
# hadoop fs -cat /rules/output/6/part*
[([a, b],[d],0.5), ([a, b],[c],0.5)]
[]
[([c],[b],1.0), ([c],[a],0.3333333333333333)]
[([b, d],[a],1.0)]
[([d],[b],1.0), ([d],[a],1.0)]
[([a],[b],1.0), ([a],[c],0.5), ([a],[d],0.5)]
[([b, c],[a],0.3333333333333333)]
[]
[([a, c],[b],1.0)]
[([a, d],[b],1.0)]
[([b],[a],0.5), ([b],[d],0.25), ([b],[c],0.75)]
```

YARN Script for Spark

The following is the script to run our Spark implementation in the YARN environment:

```
 1 # cat run_assoc_rules.sh
 2 #!/bin/bash
 3 export JAVA_HOME=/usr/java/jdk7
 4 export HADOOP_HOME=/usr/local/hadoop2.5.0
 5 export SPARK_HOME=/usr/local/spark-1.1.0
 6 export CLASSPATH=$CLASSPATH:$HADOOP_HOME/etc/hadoop
 7 export HADOOP_CONF_DIR=$HADOOP_HOME/etc/hadoop
 8 export YARN_CONF_DIR=$HADOOP_HOME/etc/hadoop
 9 export BOOK_HOME=/mp/data-algorithms-book
10 export APP_JAR=$BOOK_HOME/dist/data_algorithms_book.jar
11 export SPARK_JAR=$BOOK_HOME/lib/spark-assembly-1.1.0-hadoop2.5.0.jar
12 INPUT=/data/data_mining_transactions.txt
13 prog=org.dataalgorithms.chap07.spark.FindAssociationRules
14 $SPARK_HOME/bin/spark-submit --class $prog \
15     --master yarn-cluster \
16     --num-executors 12 \
17     --driver-memory 3g \
18     --executor-memory 7g \
19     --executor-cores 12 \
20     $APP_JAR $INPUT
```

Creating Item Sets from Transactions

Given a transaction $T = \{I_1, I_2, ..., I_n\}$ (composed of a set of items), we use a simple POJO class (Combination) to generate all combinations of sorted item sets. The Combination class is defined in Example 7-20.

Example 7-20. Combination class

```
 1 import java.util.List;
 2 import java.util.ArrayList;
 3 import java.util.Arrays;
 4 import java.util.Collection;
 5 import java.util.Collections;
 6
 7 public class Combination {
 8
 9     public static <T extends Comparable<? super T>> List<List<T>>
10         findSortedCombinations(Collection<T> elements) {...}
11
12     public static <T extends Comparable<? super T>> List<List<T>>
13         findSortedCombinations(Collection<T> elements, int n) {...}
14
15     public static void main(String[] args) throws Exception {
16         test();
17     }
```

```
18
19      public static void test() throws Exception {
20          List<String> list = Arrays.asList("a", "b", "c", "d");
21          System.out.println("list="+list);
22          List<List<String>> comb = findSortedCombinations(list);
23          System.out.println(comb.size());
24          System.out.println(comb);
25      }
26  }
```

Method definitions are listed in Examples 7-22 and 7-23.

Example 7-21. Combination class: findSortedCombinations(List)

```
1       /**
2        * Will return combinations of all sizes...
3        * If elements = { a, b, c }, then findCollections(elements) will return:
4        * { [], [a], [b], [c], [a, b], [a, c], [b, c], [a, b, c] }
5        *
6        */
7       public static <T extends Comparable<? super T>> List<List<T>>
8           findSortedCombinations(Collection<T> elements) {
9           List<List<T>> result = new ArrayList<List<T>>();
10          for (int i = 0; i <= elements.size(); i++) {
11              result.addAll(findSortedCombinations(elements, i));
12          }
13          return result;
14      }
```

Example 7-22. Combination class: findSortedCombinations(List, n)

```
1       /**
2        * If elements = { a, b, c }, then findCollections(elements, 2) will return:
3        * { [a, b], [a, c], [b, c] }
4        *
5        */
6       public static <T extends Comparable<? super T>> List<List<T>>
7           findSortedCombinations(Collection<T> elements, int n) {
8           List<List<T>> result = new ArrayList<List<T>>();
9           if (n == 0) {
10              result.add(new ArrayList<T>());
11              return result;
12          }
13
14          List<List<T>> combinations = findSortedCombinations(elements, n - 1);
15          for (List<T> combination: combinations) {
16              for (T element: elements) {
17                  if (combination.contains(element)) {
18                      continue;
19                  }
20
```

```
21              List<T> list = new ArrayList<T>();
22              list.addAll(combination);
23              if (list.contains(element)) {
24                  continue;
25              }
26
27              list.add(element);
28              // sort items to avoid duplicate items; for example (a, b, c) and
29              // (a, c, b) might be counted as different items if not sorted
30              Collections.sort(list);
31              if (result.contains(list)) {
32                  continue;
33              }
34              result.add(list);
35          }
36      }
37      return result;
38  }
```

This chapter touched on a well-known data mining algorithm, Market Basket Analysis. I presented several distributed algorithms (using MapReduce/Hadoop and Spark) for finding frequent patterns and their corresponding association rules. The next chapter presents a simple MapReduce algorithm for finding common friends in a social network environment.

## CHAPTER 8

Common Friends

Given a social network with tens of millions of users, in this chapter we'll implement a MapReduce program to identify "common friends" among all pairs of users. Let U be a set of all users: $\{U_1, U_2, ..., U_n\}$. Our goal is to find common friends for every pair of (U_i, U_j) where $i \neq j$.

For finding common friends, I provide three solutions:

- MapReduce/Hadoop using primitive data types
- MapReduce/Hadoop using custom data types
- Spark using RDDs

These days most social network sites (such as Facebook, hi5, and LinkedIn) offer services to help you share messages, pictures, and videos among friends. Some sites even offer video chat services to help you connect with friends. By definition, a friend is a person whom one knows, likes, and trusts. For example, Facebook has your list of friends, and friend relationships are bidirectional on the site; if I'm your friend, you're mine too. Typically social networks precompute calculations when they can to reduce the processing time of requests, and one common processing request involves the "You and Mary (your friend) have 185 friends in common" feature. When you visit someone's profile, you see a list of friends that you have in common. This list doesn't change frequently, so it is wasteful for the site to recalculate it every time you visit that person's profile.

There are many ways to find the common friends between users of a social network. Here are two possible solutions:

- Use a caching strategy and save the common friends in a cache (such as Redis or memcached).
- Use MapReduce to calculate everyone's common friends once a day and store those results.

We will begin with a MapReduce solution for finding common friends, after taking a quick look at the sample input and a POJO solution.

Input

We prepare input as a set of records, where each record has the following format:

```
<person><,><friend₁ ><friend₂ >...<friendN>
```

where `<friend₁><friend₂>` ... `<friendN>` are friends of the `<person>`. Note that in real projects/applications, each person/friend will be identified as a unique user ID. A very simple and complete example of input is as follows:

```
100, 200 300 400 500 600
200, 100 300 400
300, 100 200 400 500
400, 100 200 300
500, 100 300
600, 100
```

In this example, user 500 has two friends identified by the user IDs 100 and 300, and user 600 has only one friend: user 100.

POJO Common Friends Solution

Let $\{A_1, A_2, ..., A_m\}$ be a set of friends for $User_1$ and $\{B_1, B_2, ..., B_n\}$ be a set of friends for $User_2$. Thus, common friends of $User_1$ and $User_2$ can be defined as the intersection (common elements) of these two sets. The POJO (plain old Java object) solution is given in Example 8-1.

Example 8-1. CommonFriends class

```
1 import java.util.Set;
2 import java.util.TreeSet;
3
4 public class CommonFriends {
5   // user1friends = {A1, A2, ..., Am}
6   // user2friends = {B1, B2, ..., Bn}
7   public static Set<Integer> intersection(Set<Integer> user1friends,
8                                           Set<Integer> user2friends) {
9     if ((user1friends == null) || (user1friends.isEmpty())) {
```

```
10        return null;
11    }
12
13    if ((user2friends == null) || (user2friends.isEmpty())) {
14        return null;
15    }
16
17    // both sets are non-null
18    if (user1friends.size() < user2friends.size()) {
19        return intersect(user1friends, user2friends);
20    }
21    else {
22        return intersect(user2friends, user1friends);
23    }
24  }
25
26  private static Set<Integer> intersect(Set<Integer> smallSet,
27                                        Set<Integer> largeSet) {
28    Set<Integer> result = new TreeSet<Integer>();
29    // iterate on small set to improve performance
30    for (Integer x : smallSet) {
31        if (largeSet.contains(x)) {
32            result.add(x);
33        }
34    }
35    return result;
36  }
37 }
```

MapReduce Algorithm

Our MapReduce solution to find "common friends" has both map() and reduce() functions. As Example 8-1 shows, the mapper accepts a (key_1, $value_1$) pair, where key_1 is a person and $value_1$ is a list of associated friends of that person. The mapper emits a set of new (key_2, $value_2$) pairs; key_2 is a Tuple2(key_1, $friend_i$), where $friend_i \in value_1$, and $value_2$ is the same as $value_1$ (a list of all friends for key_1). The reducer's key is a pair of two users ($User_j$, $User_k$) and value is a list of sets of friends. The reduce() function will intersect all sets of friends to find common and mutual friends for the ($User_j$, $User_k$) pair.

Example 8-2. Finding common friends: map() function

```
1 // key is the person
2 // value is a list of friends for this key=person
3 // value = (<friend_1> <friend_2> ... <friend_N>)
4 map(key, value) {
5    reducerValue = (<friend_1>< friend_2> ...< friend_N>);
6    foreach friend in (<friend_1>< friend_2> ... <friend_N>) {
7        reducerKey = buildSortedKey(person, friend);
```

```
 8        emit(reducerKey, reducerValue);
 9    }
10 }
```

The mapper's output keys are sorted via the `buildSortedKey()` function to prevent duplicate keys (see Example 8-3). Note that we assume that friendship is bidirectional: if Alex is a friend of Bob, then Bob is a friend of Alex.

Example 8-3. Finding common friends: buildSortedKey() function

```
1 Tuple2 buildSortedKey(person1, person2) {
2    if (person1 < person2) {
3       return new Tuple2(person1, person2);
4    }
5    else {
6       return new Tuple2(person2, person1);
7    }
8 }
```

The `reduce()` function finds the common friends for every pair of users by intersecting their sets of friends; see Example 8-4.

Example 8-4. Finding common friends: reduce() function

```
1 // key = Tuple2(person1, person2)
2 // value = List {List_1, List_2, ..., List_M}
3 //    where each List_i = { set of unique user IDs }
4 reduce(key, value) {
5    outputKey = key;
6    outputValue = intersection (List_1, List_1, ..., List_M);
7    emit (outputKey, outputValue);
8 }
```

The MapReduce Algorithm in Action

To help you understand our MapReduce algorithm, I will show all the key-value pairs generated by mappers and reducers. Let's apply `map()` to our sample input first.

`map(100, (200 300 400 500 600))` will generate:

```
([100, 200], [200 300 400 500 600])
([100, 300], [200 300 400 500 600])
([100, 400], [200 300 400 500 600])
([100, 500], [200 300 400 500 600])
([100, 600], [200 300 400 500 600])
```

`map(200, (100 300 400))` will generate:

```
([100, 200], [100 300 400])
([200, 300], [100 300 400])
([200, 400], [100 300 400])
```

map(300, (100 200 400 500)) will generate:

```
([100, 300], [100 200 400 500])
([200, 300], [100 200 400 500])
([300, 400], [100 200 400 500])
([300, 500], [100 200 400 500])
```

map(400, (100 200 300)) will generate:

```
([100, 400], [100 200 300])
([200, 400], [100 200 300])
([300, 400], [100 200 300])
```

map(500, (100 300)) will generate:

```
([100, 500], [100 300])
([300, 500], [100 300])
```

map(600, (100)) will generate:

```
([100, 600], [100])
```

So, the mappers generate the following key-value pairs:

```
([100, 200], [200 300 400 500 600])
([100, 300], [200 300 400 500 600])
([100, 400], [200 300 400 500 600])
([100, 500], [200 300 400 500 600])
([100, 600], [200 300 400 500 600])
([100, 200], [100 300 400])
([200, 300], [100 300 400])
([200, 400], [100 300 400])
([100, 300], [100 200 400 500])
([200, 300], [100 200 400 500])
([300, 400], [100 200 400 500])
([300, 500], [100 200 400 500])
([100, 400], [100 200 300])
([200, 400], [100 200 300])
([300, 400], [100 200 300])
([100, 500], [100 300])
([300, 500], [100 300])
([100, 600], [100])
```

Before these key-value pairs are sent to the reducers, they are grouped by keys:

```
([100, 200], [200 300 400 500 600])
([100, 200], [100 300 400])
=> ([100, 200], ([200 300 400 500 600], [100 300 400]))

([100, 300], [200 300 400 500 600])
([100, 300], [100 200 400 500])
=> ([100, 300], ([200 300 400 500 600],[100 200 400 500]))
```

```
([100, 400], [200 300 400 500 600])
([100, 400], [100 200 300])
=> ([100, 400], ([200 300 400 500 600], [100 200 300]))

([100, 500], [200 300 400 500 600])
([100, 500], [100 300])
=> ([100, 500], ([200 300 400 500 600], [100 300]))

([200, 300], [100 300 400])
([200, 300], [100 200 400 500])
=> ([200, 300], ([100 300 400],[100 200 400 500]))

([200, 400], [100 300 400])
([200, 400], [100 200 300])
=> ([200, 400], ([100 300 400],[100 200 300]))

([300, 400], [100 200 400 500])
([300, 400], [100 200 300])
=> ([300, 400], ([100 200 400 500][100 200 300]))

([300, 500], [100 200 400 500])
([300, 500], [100 300])
=> ([300, 500], ([100 200 400 500],[100 300]))

([100, 600], [200 300 400 500 600])
([100, 600], [100])
=> ([100, 600], ([200 300 400 500 600]), [100])
```

So, the reducers will receive the following set of key-value pairs:

```
([100, 200], ([200 300 400 500 600], [100 300 400]))
([100, 300], ([200 300 400 500 600],[100 200 400 500]))
([100, 400], ([200 300 400 500 600], [100 200 300]))
([100, 500], ([200 300 400 500 600], [100 300]))
([200, 300], ([100 300 400],[100 200 400 500]))
([200, 400], ([100 300 400],[100 200 300]))
([300, 400], ([100 200 400 500][100 200 300]))
([300, 500], ([100 200 400 500],[100 300]))
([100, 600], ([200 300 400 500 600], [100]))
```

Finally, the reducers will generate:

```
([100, 200], [300, 400])
([100, 300], [200, 400, 500])
([100, 400], [200, 300])
([100, 500], [300])
([200, 300], [100, 400])
([200, 400], [100, 300])
([300, 400], [100, 200])
([300, 500], [100])
([100, 600], [])
```

Following the generated output, we can see that users 100 and 600 have no common friends. The business case is that when user 100 visits user 200's profile, we can now quickly look up the [100, 200] key and see that they have two friends in common: [300, 400]. Meanwhile, the users identified by 100 and 500 have one friend (identified by user ID 300) in common.

Solution 1: Hadoop Implementation Using Text

Assuming that each user ID is a long data type, in this implementation we represent a "list of friends" as a string object. For example, a list of three user IDs—100, 200, 300 —can be represented as the string object "100,200,300". To traverse this kind of list, we need to tokenize the string object and then retrieve items from it.

Table 8-1 lists the Hadoop implementation classes for finding common friends using primitive data types.

Table 8-1. Implementation classes for finding common friends

Class name	Description
CommonFriendsDriver	A driver program to submit Hadoop jobs
CommonFriendsMapper	Defines map()
CommonFriendsReducer	Defines reduce()
HadoopUtil	Utility methods for Hadoop

Sample Run for Solution 1

Script

The following shell script launches the driver for our MapReduce program to find common friends:

```
$ cat run.sh
export JAVA_HOME=/usr/java/jdk7
export BOOK_HOME=/mp/data-algorithms-book
export APP_JAR=$BOOK_HOME/dist/data_algorithms_book.jar
INPUT=/common_friends/input
OUTPUT=/common_friends/output
$HADOOP_HOME/bin/hadoop fs -rmr $OUTPUT
PROG=org.dataalgorithms.chap08.mapreduce.CommonFriendsDriver
$HADOOP_HOME/bin/hadoop jar $APP_JAR $PROG $INPUT $OUTPUT
```

Preparing input/output

```
$ hadoop fs -mkdir /common_friends
$ hadoop fs -mkdir /common_friends/input
$ hadoop fs -mkdir /common_friends/output
```

```
$ cat input/file1.txt
100 200 300 400 500
200 100 300 400
300 100 200 400 500
400 100 200 300

$ cat input/file2.txt
500 100 300
600 100

$ hadoop fs -copyFromLocal input/file1.txt /common_friends/input/
$ hadoop fs -copyFromLocal input/file2.txt /common_friends/input/

$ hadoop fs -ls /common_friends/input/
Found 2 items
-rw-r--r--   ...   74 ... /common_friends/input/file1.txt
-rw-r--r--   ...   20 ... /common_friends/input/file2.txt
```

Running the script

```
$ ./run.sh
...
Deleted hdfs://localhost:9000/lib/common_friends.jar
Deleted hdfs://localhost:9000/common_friends/output
13/09/21 17:17:25 INFO CommonFriendsDriver: inputDir=/common_friends/input
13/09/21 17:17:25 INFO CommonFriendsDriver: outputDir=/common_friends/output
...
13/09/21 17:17:26 INFO mapred.JobClient: Running job: job_201309211704_0003
13/09/21 17:17:27 INFO mapred.JobClient:  map 0% reduce 0%
...
13/09/21 17:18:20 INFO mapred.JobClient:  map 100% reduce 100%
13/09/21 17:18:21 INFO mapred.JobClient: Job complete: job_201309211704_0003
13/09/21 17:18:21 INFO mapred.JobClient: Counters: 26
13/09/21 17:18:21 INFO mapred.JobClient:   Job Counters
...
13/09/21 17:18:21 INFO mapred.JobClient:     Map-Reduce Framework
13/09/21 17:18:21 INFO mapred.JobClient:       Map input records=6
13/09/21 17:18:21 INFO mapred.JobClient:       Reduce shuffle bytes=510
13/09/21 17:18:21 INFO mapred.JobClient:       Spilled Records=34
...
13/09/21 17:18:21 INFO mapred.JobClient:       Map output records=17
13/09/21 17:18:21 INFO CommonFriendsDriver: run(): status=true
13/09/21 17:18:21 INFO CommonFriendsDriver: jobStatus=0
```

Checking the output

```
$ hadoop fs -cat /common_friends/output/part*
100,200 [300, 400]
100,300 [200, 400, 500]
100,400 [300, 200]
100,500 [300]
100,600 []
200,300 [400, 100]
```

```
200,400 [300, 100]
300,400 [200, 100]
300,500 [100]
```

Solution 2: Hadoop Implementation Using ArrayListOfLongsWritable

This implementation represents a "list of longs" using the `ArrayListOfLongsWrita ble`[1] class (a customized class), which extends `ArrayListOfLongs` and implements the `WritableComparable<ArrayListOfLongsWritable>` object. As long as your object (`ArrayListOfLongsWritable`) implements the `Writable`[2] interface, it can be used as a key or value by mappers and reducers. The rule of thumb is that, in Hadoop, you can have a customized object as a key or value as long as it implements the `Writable` interface. This is how Hadoop persists objects on HDFS.

The Hadoop classes listed in Table 8-2 provide a MapReduce solution for finding common friends using custom data types.

Table 8-2. Classes for finding common friends using custom data types

Class name	Description
`CommonFriendsDriverUsingList`	A driver program to submit Hadoop jobs
`CommonFriendsMapperUsingList`	Defines `map()`
`CommonFriendsReducerUsingList`	Defines `reduce()`
`HadoopUtil`	Utility methods for Hadoop

Sample Run for Solution 2

Script

The following shell script launches the driver for our MapReduce program using custom data types:

```
$ cat run.sh
export JAVA_HOME=/usr/java/jdk7
export BOOK_HOME=/home/mp/data-algorithms-book
export APP_JAR=$BOOK_HOME/dist/data_algorithms_book.jar
input=/common_friends_using_lists/input
output=/common_friends_using_lists/output
```

---

1 `edu.umd.cloud9.io.array.ArrayListOfLongsWritable`

2 `org.apache.hadoop.io.Writable` (a serializable object that implements a simple, efficient serialization protocol, based on `DataInput` and `DataOutput`). Note that any key or value type in the Hadoop MapReduce framework implements this interface.

```
prog=CommonFriendsDriverUsingList
$HADOOP_HOME/bin/hadoop fs -rmr $output
$HADOOP_HOME/bin/hadoop jar $APP_JAR $prog $input $output
```

Running the script

```
$ ./run.sh
...
Deleted hdfs://localhost:9000/lib/common_friends_using_lists.jar
Deleted hdfs://localhost:9000/common_friends_using_lists/output
13/09/23 15:13:33 INFO ... inputDir=/common_friends_using_lists/input
13/09/23 15:13:33 INFO ... outputDir=/common_friends_using_lists/output
...
13/09/23 15:13:33 INFO mapred.JobClient: Running job: job_201309231108_0007
13/09/23 15:13:34 INFO mapred.JobClient:  map 0% reduce 0%
...
13/09/23 15:14:24 INFO mapred.JobClient:  map 100% reduce 100%
13/09/23 15:14:25 INFO mapred.JobClient: Job complete: job_201309231108_0007
13/09/23 15:14:25 INFO mapred.JobClient: Counters: 26
...
13/09/23 15:14:25 INFO mapred.JobClient:      Map output bytes=636
...
13/09/23 15:14:25 INFO mapred.JobClient:      Reduce output records=9
13/09/23 15:14:25 INFO mapred.JobClient:      Map output records=17
13/09/23 15:14:25 INFO CommonFriendsDriverUsingList: run(): status=true
13/09/23 15:14:25 INFO CommonFriendsDriverUsingList: jobStatus=0
```

Examining the output

```
$ hadoop fs -cat /common_friends_using_lists/output/part*
100,200 [400, 300]
100,300 [200, 500, 400]
100,400 [200, 300]
100,500 [300]
100,600 []
200,300 [100, 400]
200,400 [100, 300]
300,400 [100, 200]
300,500 [100]
```

Spark Solution

Next, I present a Spark solution by writing the map() and reduce() functions using
Spark's RDDs. Our users' data is represented as HDFS text files, and each record line
has the following format (P is the person and $\{F_1, F_2, ..., F_n\}$ are direct friends of P):

$$P, F_1, F_2, ..., F_n$$

Our Spark solution will be based on the following `map()` and `reduce()` functions. Here is the mapper function:

```
map(P, {F_1, F_2, ..., F_n}) {
    friends = {F_1, F_2, ..., F_n};
    for (f : friends) {
        key = buildSortedTuple(P, f);
        emit(key, friends);
    }

}
```

And here is the reducer function:

```
// key = Tuple2<user1,user2>
// values = List<List<user>>
reduce(key, values) {
    commonFriends = intersection(values);
    emit(key, friends);
}
```

Spark Program

Because Spark provides a much higher-level API than classic MapReduce/Hadoop, the entire solution is presented in a single Java driver class. First, I present all the steps, and then we will go over the details of each. The high-level solution is shown in Example 8-5.

Example 8-5. High-level steps

```
1 // Step 1: import required classes and interfaces
2 public class FindCommonFriends {
3    public static void main(String[] args) throws Exception {
4
5       // Step 2: check input parameters
6       // Step 3: create a JavaSparkContext object
7       // Step 4: read input text file from HDFS and create
8       //         the first JavaRDD to represent input file
9       // Step 5: map JavaRDD<String> into key-value pairs,
10      //         where key=Tuple<user1,user2>, value=List of friends
11      // Step 6: reduce (key=Tuple2<u1,u2>, value=List<friends>) pairs
12      //         into (key=Tuple2<u1,u2>, value=List<List<friends>>)
13      // Step 7: find common friends by intersection of all List<List<Long>>
14
15      System.exit(0);
16   }
17
18   // build a sorted Tuple to avoid duplicates
19   static Tuple2<Long,Long> buildSortedTuple(long a, long b) {...}
20 }
```

Next, we will explore each step in detail.

Step 1: Import required classes

Spark's main Java classes and interfaces are defined in the `org.apache.spark.api.java` package. Example 8-6 shows how to import them.

Example 8-6. Step 1: import required classes and interfaces

```
 1 // Step 1: import required classes and interfaces
 2 import scala.Tuple2;
 3 import org.apache.spark.api.java.JavaRDD;
 4 import org.apache.spark.api.java.JavaPairRDD;
 5 import org.apache.spark.api.java.JavaSparkContext;
 6 import org.apache.spark.api.java.function.PairFlatMapFunction;
 7 import org.apache.spark.api.java.function.FlatMapFunction;
 8 import org.apache.spark.api.java.function.Function;
 9
10 import java.util.Arrays;
11 import java.util.List;
12 import java.util.ArrayList;
13 import java.util.Map;
14 import java.util.HashMap;
```

Step 2: Check input parameters

For our program, we need one input parameter: the input text file stored in HDFS (represented as `args[0]`, as shown in Example 8-7).

Example 8-7. Step 2: check input parameters

```
1      // Step 2: check input parameters
2      if (args.length < 1) {
3        System.err.println("Usage: FindCommonFriends <file>");
4        System.exit(1);
5      }
6      System.out.println("HDFS input file ="+args[0]);
```

Step 3: Create a JavaSparkContext object

The next step, shown in Example 8-8, is to create a `JavaSparkContext` object. This is a factory object to create new RDDs.

Example 8-8. Step 3: create a JavaSparkContext object

```
1      // Step 3: create a JavaSparkContext object
2      JavaSparkContext ctx = new JavaSparkContext();
```

Step 4: Read input file and create RDD

In Example 8-9, we create the first RDD from an input file by using the context object (JavaSparkContext) we created in step 3. The new RDD (JavaRDD<String>) represents all records of the input file. Each input record is represented as a Java string object.

Example 8-9. Step 4: read input and create RDD

```
1    // Step 4: Read input text file from HDFS and create
2    //         the first JavaRDD to represent input file
3    JavaRDD<String> records = ctx.textFile(args[0], 1);
```

To debug step 4, we use the JavaRDD.collect() function:

```
// debug0
List<String> debug0 = records.collect();
for (String t : debug0) {
    System.out.println("debug0 record="+t);
}
```

Step 5: Apply a mapper

This step maps every record of [P, F_1, F_2, ..., F_n] into a set of key-value pairs where the key is a Tuple2(P, F_i) and the value is a list [F_1, F_2, ..., F_n]. If the size of the friends list is 1, then no friends list will be created (in this case, there cannot be any friends in common). To implement the mapper, we use the JavaRDD.flatMapTo Pair() function. We accomplish this using PairFlatMapFunction as follows (where T is input and (K, V) is generated as an output):

```
PairFlatMapFunction<T, K, V>
T => Iterable<Tuple2<K, V>>
```

Example 8-10 shows the complete implementation of step 5.

Example 8-10. Step 5: apply a mapper

```
1    // Step 5: map JavaRDD<String> into (key, value) pairs,
2    //         where key=Tuple<user1,user2>, value=List of friends
3    //
4    // PairFlatMapFunction<T, K, V>
5    // T => Iterable<Tuple2<K, V>>
6    JavaPairRDD<Tuple2<Long,Long>,Iterable<Long>> pairs =
7        records.flatMapToPair(new PairFlatMapFunction<
8                                    String,                 // T
9                                    Tuple2<Long,Long>,  // K
10                                   Iterable<Long>      // V
11                                  >() {
12       public Iterable<Tuple2<Tuple2<Long,Long>,Iterable<Long>>> call(String s) {
13           String[] tokens = s.split(",");
```

```
14          long person = Long.parseLong(tokens[0]);
15          String friendsAsString = tokens[1];
16          String[] friendsTokenized = friendsAsString.split(" " );
17          if (friendsTokenized.length == 1) {
18             Tuple2<Long,Long> key = buildSortedTuple(person,
19                                       Long.parseLong(friendsTokenized[0]));
20             return Arrays.asList(new Tuple2<Tuple2<Long,Long>,
21                                      Iterable<Long>>(key, new ArrayList<Long>()));
22          }
23          List<Long> friends = new ArrayList<Long>();
24          for (String f : friendsTokenized) {
25             friends.add(Long.parseLong(f));
26          }
27
28          List<Tuple2<Tuple2<Long, Long>,Iterable<Long>>> result =
29             new ArrayList<Tuple2<Tuple2<Long, Long>, Iterable<Long>>>();
30          for (Long f : friends) {
31             Tuple2<Long,Long> key = buildSortedTuple(person, f);
32             result.add(new Tuple2<Tuple2<Long,Long>, Iterable<Long>>(key,
33                        friends));
34          }
35          return result;
36       }
37    });
```

To debug step 5, we use the `JavaRDD.collect()` function:

```
// debug1
List<Tuple2<Tuple2<Long, Long> ,Iterable<Long>>> debug1 = pairs.collect();
for (Tuple2<Tuple2<Long,Long>,Iterable<Long>> t2 : debug1) {
    System.out.println("debug1 key="+t2._1+"\t value="+t2._2);
}
```

Step 6: Apply a reducer

We apply the reducer by calling the `JavaPairRDD.groupByKey()` method, as shown in
Example 8-11.

Example 8-11. Step 6: apply a reducer

```
1    // Step 6: reduce (key=Tuple2<u1,u2>, value=Iterable<friends>) pairs
2    //         into (key=Tuple2<u1,u2>, value=Iterable<Iterable<friends>>)
3    JavaPairRDD<Tuple2<Long, Long>, Iterable<Iterable<Long>>> grouped =
4    pairs.groupByKey();
```

To debug this step, we use the following code:

```
// debug2
List<Tuple2<Tuple2<Long, Long> ,Iterable<Iterable<Long>>>> debug2 =
    grouped.collect();
for (Tuple2<Tuple2<Long,Long>, Iterable<Iterable<Long>>> t2 : debug2) {
```

```
        System.out.println("debug2 key="+t2._1+"\t value="+t2._2);
    }
```

Step 7: Find common friends

To find common friends, we intersect all friends for two users by just altering the values. We accomplish this by using the JavaPairRDD.mapValues() method without changing the keys (see Example 8-12).

Example 8-12. Step 7: find intersection of all

```
1    // Step 7: find intersection of all List<List<Long>>
2    // mapValues[U](f: (V) => U): JavaPairRDD[K, U]
3    // Pass each value in the key-value pair RDD through a map
4    // function without changing the keys;
5    // this also retains the original RDD's partitioning.
6    JavaPairRDD<Tuple2<Long, Long>, Iterable<Long>> commonFriends =
7        grouped.mapValues(new Function< Iterable<Iterable<Long>>, // input
8                                        Iterable<Long>            // output
9                                      >() {
10       public Iterable<Long> call(Iterable<Iterable<Long>> s) {
11         Map<Long, Integer> countCommon = new HashMap<Long, Integer>();
12         int size = 0;
13         for (Iterable<Long> iter : s) {
14           size++;
15           List<Long> list = iterableToList(iter);
16           if ((list == null) || (list.isEmpty())) {
17             continue;
18           }
19           for (Long f : list) {
20             Integer count = countCommon.get(f);
21             if (count == null) {
22               countCommon.put(f, 1);
23             }
24             else {
25               countCommon.put(f, ++count);
26             }
27           }
28         }
29
30         // if countCommon.Entry<f, count> == countCommon.Entry<f, s.size()>
31         // then that is a common friend
32         List<Long> finalCommonFriends = new ArrayList<Long>();
33         for (Map.Entry<Long, Integer> entry : countCommon.entrySet()) {
34           if (entry.getValue() == size) {
35             finalCommonFriends.add(entry.getKey());
36           }
37         }
38         return finalCommonFriends;
39     }
40   });
```

To debug step 7, we use the following code:

```
// debug3
List<Tuple2<Tuple2<Long, Long>, Iterable<Long>>> debug3 =
    commonFriends.collect();
for (Tuple2<Tuple2<Long, Long>, Iterable<Long>> t2 : debug3) {
  System.out.println("debug3 key="+t2._1+ "\t value="+t2._2);
}
```

Finally, we use the following function to make sure that we will not have duplicate `Tuple2<user1,user2>` objects:

```
static Tuple2<Long,Long> buildSortedTuple(long a, long b) {
    if (a < b) {
        return new Tuple2<Long, Long>(a,b);
    }
    else {
        return new Tuple2<Long, Long>(b,a);
    }
}
```

Combining steps 6 and 7

It is possible to combine steps 6 and 7 into a single Spark step/operation. We can accomplish this through Spark's `combineByKey()` or `reduceByKey()` function (both of these transformers combine values with the same key together). Here we will use `reduceByKey()`, which is a simple version of `combineByKey()`. `reduceByKey()` reduces values of type V into V (the same data type)—for example, to add or multiply integer values. `combineByKey()`, on the other hand, can combine/transform values of type V into another type, C—for example, to combine/transform integer (V) values into a set of integers (`Set<Integer>`). The simplest form of the `reduceByKey()` signature is as follows:

```
public JavaPairRDD<K,V> reduceByKey(Function2<V,V,V> func)
// Merge the values for each key using an associative reduce
// function. This will also perform the merging locally on
// each mapper before sending results to a reducer, similarly
// to a "combiner" in MapReduce. Output will be hash-partitioned
// with the existing partitioner/parallelism level.
```

We are ready to combine steps 6 and 7 by using `reduceByKey()`. First, let's identify the input and output, which are listed in Table 8-3.

Table 8-3. Input, output, and transformer

Input	pairs (K: <Tuple2<Long,Long>, V: Iterable<Long>)
Output	commonFriends (K: String, V: Iterable<Long>)
Transformer	reduceByKey()

Example 8-13 shows how to utilize the reduceByKey() transformer, which finds the intersection of friends, represented as an Iterable<Long>.

Example 8-13. Using combineByKey()

```
1 import com.google.common.collect.Sets;
2 ...
3 JavaPairRDD<Tuple2<Long,Long>, Iterable<Long>>
4    commonFriends = pairs.reduceByKey(new Function2<
5                                              Iterable<Long>,
6                                              Iterable<Long>
7                                              >() {
8    // return the intersection of a and b
9    public Iterable<Long> call(Iterable<Long> a, Iterable<Long> b) {
10       Set<Long> x = Sets.newHashSet(a);
11       Set<Long> intersection = new HashSet<Long>();
12       for (Long item : b) {
13          if (x.contains(item)) {
14             intersection.add(item);
15          }
16       }
17       return intersection;
18    }
19 });
20
21 // emit the final output
22 Map<String, Set<String>> commonFriendsMap = commonFriends.collectAsMap();
23 for (Entry<Tuple2<Long,Long>, Iterable<Long>> entry :
24    commonFriendsMap.entrySet()) {
25    System.out.println(entry.getKey() + ":" + entry.getValue());
26 }
```

Sample Run of Spark Program

The following subsections present the sample input, script, and expected output for our Spark program.

HDFS input

This is the HDFS input for our Spark solution:

```
# hadoop fs -cat /data/users_and_friends.txt
100,200 300 400 500
200,100 300 400
300,100 200 400 500
400,100 200 300
500,100 300
600,100
```

Script

The script to run our Spark program is as follows:

```
$ cat run_find_common_friends.sh
#!/bin/bash
export JAVA_HOME=/usr/java/jdk7
export SPARK_HOME=/home/hadoop/spark-1.1.0
export SPARK_MASTER=spark://myserver100:7077
BOOK_HOME=/mp/data-algorithms-book
APP_JAR=$BOOK_HOME/dist/data_algorithms_book.jar
USERS=/data/users_and_friends.txt
# Run on a Spark cluster
prog=org.dataalgorithms.chap08.spark.FindCommonFriends
$SPARK_HOME/bin/spark-submit \
--class $prog \
--master $SPARK_MASTER \
--executor-memory 2G \
--total-executor-cores 20 \
$APP_JAR \
$USERS
```

Log of the sample run

We ran this program in a cluster environment using three servers identified by myserver100 (a Spark master), myserver200, and myserver300. The actual output log has been trimmed and formatted to fit the page:

```
# ./run_find_common_friends.sh
HDFS input file =/data/users_and_friends.txt
...
14/05/31 21:33:40 INFO Remoting: Starting remoting
14/05/31 21:33:40 INFO Remoting: Remoting started; listening on addresses :
  [akka.tcp://spark@myserver100    :33722]
14/05/31 21:33:40 INFO Remoting: Remoting now listens on addresses:
  [akka.tcp://spark@myserver100    :33722]
...
14/05/31 21:33:46 INFO scheduler.TaskSchedulerImpl: Removed TaskSet 0.0,
  whose tasks have all completed, from pool
14/05/31 21:33:46 INFO spark.SparkContext: Job finished: collect at
  FindCommonFriends.java:33, took 3.76636011 s
debug0 record=100,200 300 400 500
debug0 record=200,100 300 400
debug0 record=300,100 200 400 500
debug0 record=400,100 200 300
debug0 record=500,100 300
debug0 record=600,100
14/05/31 21:33:46 INFO spark.SparkContext: Starting job: collect at
  FindCommonFriends.java:69
14/05/31 21:33:46 INFO scheduler.DAGScheduler: Got job 1 (collect at
  FindCommonFriends.java:69) with 1 output partitions (allowLocal=false)
...
14/05/31 21:33:46 INFO scheduler.DAGScheduler: Stage 1 (collect at
```

```
      FindCommonFriends.java:69) finished in 0.043 s
14/05/31 21:33:46 INFO spark.SparkContext: Job finished: collect at
      FindCommonFriends.java:69, took 0.051576509 s
debug1 key=(100,200)  value=[200, 300, 400, 500]
debug1 key=(100,300)  value=[200, 300, 400, 500]
debug1 key=(100,400)  value=[200, 300, 400, 500]
debug1 key=(100,500)  value=[200, 300, 400, 500]
debug1 key=(100,200)  value=[100, 300, 400]
debug1 key=(200,300)  value=[100, 300, 400]
debug1 key=(200,400)  value=[100, 300, 400]
debug1 key=(100,300)  value=[100, 200, 400, 500]
debug1 key=(200,300)  value=[100, 200, 400, 500]
debug1 key=(300,400)  value=[100, 200, 400, 500]
debug1 key=(300,500)  value=[100, 200, 400, 500]
debug1 key=(100,400)  value=[100, 200, 300]
debug1 key=(200,400)  value=[100, 200, 300]
debug1 key=(300,400)  value=[100, 200, 300]
debug1 key=(100,500)  value=[100, 300]
debug1 key=(300,500)  value=[100, 300]
debug1 key=(100,600)  value=[]
14/05/31 21:33:46 INFO spark.SparkContext: Starting job: collect at
      FindCommonFriends.java:78
14/05/31 21:33:46 INFO scheduler.DAGScheduler: Registering RDD 2 (flatMap
      at FindCommonFriends.java:41)
14/05/31 21:33:46 INFO scheduler.DAGScheduler: Got job 2 (collect at
      FindCommonFriends.java:78) with 1 output partitions (allowLocal=false)
...
14/05/31 21:33:46 INFO scheduler.DAGScheduler: Stage 2 (collect at
      FindCommonFriends.java:78) finished in 0.212 s
14/05/31 21:33:46 INFO spark.SparkContext: Job finished: collect at
      FindCommonFriends.java:78, took 0.335984028 s
debug2 key=(200,300)  value=[[100, 300, 400], [100, 200, 400, 500]]
debug2 key=(100,300)  value=[[200, 300, 400, 500], [100, 200, 400, 500]]
debug2 key=(100,200)  value=[[200, 300, 400, 500], [100, 300, 400]]
debug2 key=(300,400)  value=[[100, 200, 400, 500], [100, 200, 300]]
debug2 key=(100,500)  value=[[200, 300, 400, 500], [100, 300]]
debug2 key=(200,400)  value=[[100, 300, 400], [100, 200, 300]]
debug2 key=(100,400)  value=[[200, 300, 400, 500], [100, 200, 300]]
debug2 key=(100,600)  value=[[]]
debug2 key=(300,500)  value=[[100, 200, 400, 500], [100, 300]]
14/05/31 21:33:46 INFO spark.SparkContext: Starting job: collect at
      FindCommonFriends.java:122
14/05/31 21:33:46 INFO scheduler.DAGScheduler: Got job 3 (collect at
      FindCommonFriends.java:122) with 1 output partitions (allowLocal=false)
...
14/05/31 21:33:47 INFO scheduler.DAGScheduler: Stage 4 (collect at
      FindCommonFriends.java:122) finished in 0.068 s
14/05/31 21:33:47 INFO scheduler.TaskSchedulerImpl: Removed TaskSet 4.0,
      whose tasks have all completed, from pool
14/05/31 21:33:47 INFO spark.SparkContext: Job finished: collect at
      FindCommonFriends.java:122, took 0.084085412 s
debug3 key=(200,300)  value=[100, 400]
```

```
debug3 key=(100,300)  value=[200, 500, 400]
debug3 key=(100,200)  value=[400, 300]
debug3 key=(300,400)  value=[100, 200]
debug3 key=(100,500)  value=[300]
debug3 key=(200,400)  value=[100, 300]
debug3 key=(100,400)  value=[200, 300]
debug3 key=(100,600)  value=[]
debug3 key=(300,500)  value=[100]
```

This chapter presented a simple MapReduce solution for finding common friends among all social network users. The next chapter shows how to implement basic recommendation engines using MapReduce frameworks.

## CHAPTER 9

Recommendation Engines Using MapReduce

This chapter deals with implementing recommendation engines using MapReduce algorithms.

If you are a frequent user of Amazon.com, you are probably familiar with the lists of related products (books, CDs, etc.) the site features to help customers find what they are looking for. Amazon.com presents several such lists on every page, including "Frequently Bought Together" and "Customers Who Bought This Item Also Bought." These features have roots and solutions in recommendation engines and systems. Typically, recommendation engines and systems enhance the user experience in the following ways:

- They assist users in finding information.
- They reduce search and navigation time.
- They increase user satisfaction and encourage users to return to the site frequently.

The purpose of a recommendation engine or system is to predict or recommend:

- Items that the user has not rated, bought, or navigated to yet
- Movies or books that a user has not yet considered
- Restaurants or locations that a user has not visited

Recommendation systems have become extremely common in recent years. A few examples of such systems are:

- Amazon.com and MyBuys.com, which provide recommendation systems for similar items that a user might purchase—in other words, when a user views what other shoppers bought along with the currently selected item
- Tripbase.com, a travel website that recommends travel/vacation packages based on a user's input or preferences
- Netflix, which predicts movies that a user might enjoy based on the user's previous ratings and watching habits (as compared to the behavior of other users)

In this chapter we will address the following areas, which have roots in recommendation engines and systems:

- Customers Who Bought This Item Also Bought
- Frequently Bought Together
- Recommend Connection

For details on recommendation systems, refer to [1], [26], and [11].

Customers Who Bought This Item Also Bought

Most ecommerce vendors, including Amazon.com, use the feature "Customers Who Bought This Item Also Bought" (CWBTIAB) on their websites for recommending books, CDs, and other items. Here we will build a simple recommendation system to implement the CWBTIAB feature.

Suppose that the Amazon.com store log contains a `user-id` and `bought-item` for each sale. We are going to implement CWBTIAB functionality using the MapReduce paradigm. Whenever an item is shown, the store will suggest five other items most often bought by buyers of that item.

Input

We assume that the input is a set of large transactions (a transaction log contains a lot of data, including transaction ID, date, price, etc.), which have the following fields:

```
<user-id><,><bought-item>
```

Expected Output

The recommendation engine should emit key-value pairs in which the key is the item and the value is a list of the five items most commonly purchased by customers who also bought the original item.

MapReduce Solution

We implement CWBTIAB with two iterations of MapReduce:

- Phase 1: generate lists of all items bought by the same user. Grouping is handled by the Hadoop framework, where both the mapper and the reducer perform an identity function.
- Phase 2: solve the co-occurrences problem on list items. We use the Stripes design pattern and emit only the five most common co-occurrences.

Before we discuss these two phases, I will explain the concept of Stripes with a simple example.

Stripes design pattern

Stripes is a design pattern, and the main idea behind it is to group together pairs into an associative array. Consider the classic case shown in Table 9-1 of key-value pairs emitted by a mapper (note that in this example, the mapper's output key is a composite key, Tuple2).

Table 9-1. Mapper output: classic approach

Key	Value
(k, k_1)	3
(k, k_2)	2
(k, k_3)	4
(k, k_4)	6
(z, z_1)	7
(z, z_2)	8
(z, z_3)	5

The idea behind the Stripes approach is that rather than emitting many key-value pairs, we just emit one per stripe, as shown in Table 9-2 (note that in this example, k and z are natural keys).

Table 9-2. Mapper output: Stripes approach

Key	Value
k	$\{ (k_1, 3), (k_2, 2), (k_3, 4), (k_4, 6) \}$
z	$\{ (z_1, 7), (z_2, 8), (z_3, 5) \}$

The Stripes approach creates an associative array (or a hash table) for each natural key and reduces the number of key-value pairs emitted by each mapper. While the emitted value of each mapper becomes a complex object (an associative array), with the Stripes approach there will be less sorting and shuffling of key-value pairs.

How does a reducer work in the Stripes approach? Reducers perform an element-wise sum of associative arrays. Consider the following three key-value examples for a reducer (as input):

```
K -> { (a, 1), (b, 2), (c, 4), (d, 3) }
K -> { (a, 2),         (c, 2)         }
K -> { (a, 3), (b, 5),         (d, 5) }
```

The generated output will be:

```
K -> { (a, 1+2+3), (b, 2+5), (c, 4+2), (d, 3+5) }
```

or:

```
K -> { (a, 6), (b, 7), (c, 6), (d, 8) }
```

The advantages of the Stripes approach are as follows:

- Since mappers generate fewer key-value pairs than with the classic approach, there will be less sorting and shuffling required.

- Stripes enables us to make effective use of combiners (as a local per-node optimization).

- Stripes offers us better performance[14].

Some disadvantages of the Stripes approach are:

- It's more difficult to implement (since the value emitted by each mapper is an associative array and we have to write a serializer and deserializer for that associative array).

- The underlying objects (i.e., values generated by mappers as associative arrays) are more heavyweight.

- Stripes has a fundamental limitation in terms of the size of event space (since we are creating an associate array for each natural key, we need to make sure that the mappers have enough RAM to hold these hash tables).

MapReduce phase 1

The first MapReduce phase generates lists of all items bought by the same user. Grouping is done by the MapReduce framework on the userID (as a key). Both the mapper and the reducer perform an identity function. The goal of phase 1 is to find all items purchased by all users.

The mapper is an identity function that emits key-value pairs as received (see Example 9-1).

Example 9-1. Mapper: phase 1

```
1 // key = userID
2 // value = item bought by userID
3 map(userID, item) {
4     emit(userID, item);
5 }
```

The reducer is an identity function that groups all items for a single user (see Example 9-2).

Example 9-2. Reducer: phase 1

```
1 // key = userID
2 // value = list of items bought by userID
3 reduce(userID, items[I1, I2, ..., In])  {
4     emit(userID, items);
5 }
```

MapReduce phase 2

The second MapReduce phase solves the co-occurrences problem on list items. With the Stripes approach, the mappers do most of the work, aggregating data and then passing it to the combiners and reducers. The reducers then emit the expected output (an item followed by a list of the five most common co-occurrences).

Since we might be creating many hash tables (associative arrays) for each mapper/reducer, we need to make sure that we have enough memory to hold these data structures. If the number of users or items were large enough, it might not fit in memory. If your memory/RAM is limited, you might consider creating these hash tables on disk (such a solution is available in MapDB).[1]

As you can see in Example 9-3, the mapper in this phase includes combiner functionality. (Using the Stripes approach, the mappers do most of the work, which has to be done by map() and combine() functions.) As noted earlier, the Stripes approach minimizes the number of keys generated, and therefore the MapReduce execution framework has less shuffling and sorting to perform. However, since we are using a nonprimitive type for our values (an associative array), more serialization and deserialization will be required.

---

1 MapDB (*http://www.mapdb.org*) (developed by Jan Kotek) provides concurrent maps, sets, and queues backed by disk storage or off-heap memory. It is a fast and easy-to-use embedded Java database engine.

Example 9-3. Mapper: phase 2

```
1  // key = userID
2  // value = list of items bought by userID
3  map(userID, items[I1, I2, ..., In]) {
4      for (Item item : items) {
5          Map<Item, Integer> map = new HashMap<Item, Integer>();
6          for (Item j : items) {
7              map(j) = map(j) + 1;
8          }
9          emit(item, map);
10     }
11 }
```

As Example 9-4 shows, in this phase the reducer generates the "top 5" items most commonly purchased along with every item in all transactions. The reducer performs an item-wise sum of all stripes (represented as an associative array) for a given item.

Example 9-4. Reducer: phase 2

```
1  // key = item
2  // value = list of stripes[M1, M2, ..., Mm]
3  reduce(item, stripes[M1, M2, ..., Mm]) {
4      Map<Item, Integer> final = new HashMap<Item, Integer>();
5      for (Map<Item, Integer> map : stripes) {
6          for (all (k, v) in map) {
7              final(k) = final(k) + v;
8          }
9      }
10     emit(key, top(5, final))
11 }
```

`top(N, Map<Item, Integer>)` will return N items, representing the top/maximum frequencies for a given associative array.

Frequently Bought Together

The purpose of this section is to implement the "Frequently Bought Together" (FBT) feature using MapReduce/Hadoop. FBT is a behavioral targeting technique that leverages users' previous purchasing history in order to select and display other relevant products that a user may want to buy. Suppose you are searching for Donald Knuth's *The Art of Computer Programming* (*http://bit.ly/knuth_art_of*) on Amazon.com. On the product detail page, you will see a section called "Frequently Bought Together" that lists the original item you searched for, and books often bought along with it (see Figure 9-1).

Figure 9-1. Frequently Bought Together feature

How does Amazon come up with this list for most of its items? It basically does a search for relationships between items (such as books and CDs). Typically, ecommerce sites like Amazon.com gather data on their customers' purchasing habits. Using association rule learning, these sites can determine which products are frequently bought together and use that information for marketing purposes. This is sometimes referred to as a variation on Market Basket Analysis, a well-known topic in data mining covered in Chapter 7 of this book.

Input and Expected Output

Let's assume that we have an input of product sales transactions for all customers. Let's also assume that we have n transactions (labeled as T_1, ..., T_n) and m products (labeled as P_1, ..., P_m), and that we have compiled the input as shown in Table 9-3.

Table 9-3. Product sales transactions for all customers

Transaction	Purchased items
T_1	$\{P_{1,1}, P_{1,2}, ..., P_{1,k1}\}$
T_2	$\{P_{2,1}, P_{2,2}, ..., P_{2,k2}\}$
...	...
T_n	$\{P_{n,1}, P_{n,2}, ..., P_{n,kn}\}$

In this table:

- $P_{i,j} \in \{P_1, ..., P_m\}$.

- k_i is the number of items purchased in transaction T_i.

- Each line of input is a transaction ID, followed by a list of products purchased.

Our goal is to build a hash table for which the key will be P_i for $i = 1, 2, ..., m$, and the value will be the list of products purchased together.

For example, say we have the input shown in Table 9-4.

Table 9-4. Input for FBT example

Transaction	Purchased items
T_1	$\{P_1, P_2, P_3\}$
T_2	$\{P_2, P_3\}$
T_3	$\{P_2, P_3, P_4\}$
T_4	$\{P_5, P_6\}$
T_5	$\{P_3, P_4\}$

Then our desired output will look like Table 9-5.

Table 9-5. Desired output for FBT example

Item	Frequently bought together
P_1	$\{P_2, P_3\}$
P_2	$\{P_1, P_3, P_4\}$
P_3	$\{P_1, P_2, P_4\}$
P_4	$\{P_2, P_3\}$
P_5	$\{P_6\}$
P_6	$\{P_5\}$

Therefore, if a customer is browsing product P_3, we can say the frequently bought together products are P_1, P_2, and P_4.

MapReduce Solution

The map() function will take a single transaction and generate a set of key-value pairs to be consumed by reduce(). The mapper pairs the transaction items (i.e., products) as a key and the number of occurrences of that key in the transaction as its value (for all transactions and without the transaction ID; the transaction ID is ignored).

For example, map() for transaction 1 (T_1) will emit the following key-value pairs:

```
[<P1, P2>, 1]
[<P1, P3>, 1]
[<P2, P3>, 1]
```

Note that if we select the two products in a transaction as a key, the counts for the occurrences of the products in the pairs will be incorrect. For example, if transactions T_1 and T_2 have the following products (the same items but in a different order):

```
T1: (P1, P2, P3)
T2: (P1, P3, P2)
```

then for transaction T_1, map() will generate:

```
[<P1, P2>, 1]
[<P1, P3>, 1]
[<P2, P3>, 1]
```

and for transaction T_2, map() will generate:

```
[<P1, P3>, 1]
[<P1, P2>, 1]
[<P3, P2>, 1]
```

As you can see from the map() outputs for transactions T_1 and T_2, we get a total of six different pairs of products that occur only once each, when there should actually be only three different pairs. That is, the keys (P2, P3) and (P3, P2) are not being identified as the same even though they are. We know that this is not correct. We can avoid this problem if we sort the transaction products in alphabetical order before generating the key-value pairs. After sorting the items in the transactions we will get:

```
sorted T₁: (P1, P2, P3)
sorted T₂: (P1, P2, P3)
```

Now each transaction (T_1 and T_2) will have the following three key-value pairs:

```
[<P1, P2>, 1]
[<P1, P3>, 1]
[<P2, P3>, 1)
```

We accumulate the values of the occurrences for these two transactions as follows: [<P1, P2>, 2], [<P1, P3>, 2], [<P2, P3>, 2]. This gives us the correct counts for the total number of occurrences.

Mapper

The mapper, shown in Example 9-5, reads the input data and creates a list of items for each transaction. For each transaction, its time complexity is O(n), where n is the number of items for a transaction. Then, the items in the transaction list are sorted to avoid duplicate keys like (P2, P3) and (P3, P2). The time complexity of Quicksort is O(n log n). Then, the sorted transaction items are converted to pairs of items as keys, which is a cross-operation that allows us to generate cross-pairs of the items in the list.

Example 9-5. Frequently Bought Together: map() function

```
1 // key is transaction ID and ignored here
2 // value = transaction items (P1, P2, ...,Pm)
3 map(key, value) {
4     (S1, S2, ..., Sm) = sort(P1, P2, ...,Pm);
5     // now, we have: S1 < S2 < ... < Sm
```

```
6      ListOfPair<Si, Sj> = generateCombinations(S1, S2, ..., Sm)
7      for ( (Si, Sj) pair : ListOfPair<Si, Sj>) {
8          // reducer key is: (Si, Sj)
9          // reducer value is: integer 1
10         emit([(Si, Sj), 1]);
11     }
12 }
```

generateCombinations(S1, S2, ..., Sm) generates all combinations between any two items in a given transaction. For example, generateCombinations(S1, S2, S3, S4) will return the following pairs:

```
(S1, S2)
(S1, S3)
(S1, S4)
(S2, S3)
(S2, S4)
(S3, S4)
```

Finally, map() will output the following key-value pairs:

```
<P1, P2> 1
<P1, P3> 1
<P2, P3> 1
<P2, P3> 1
<P2, P3> 1
<P3, P4> 1
<P5, P6> 1
<P1, P5> 1
<P3, P4> 1
```

Reducer

The FBT algorithm for the reducer is illustrated in Example 9-6. The reducer sums up the number of values for each reducer key. Thus, its time complexity is $O(v)$, where v is the number of values per key.

Example 9-6. Frequently Bought Together: reduce() function

```
1 // key is in form of (Si, Sj)
2 // value = List<integer>, where each element is an integer number
3 reduce(key, value) {
4    int sum = 0;
5    for (int i : List<integer>) {
6       sum += i;
7    }
8    emit(key, sum);
9 }
```

Reducer output

The reducer will create the following output format:

```
<Pᵢ, Pⱼ>, N
```

where N is the number of transactions, and products P_i and P_j have been purchased together. The higher N is, the closer the relationship between these two products is. Now, with this output, we can create the desired hash table, where the keys are $\{P_1, P_2, ..., P_m\}$.

For our input, the reducer will generate the following output:

```
<P1, P2> 1
<P1, P3> 1
<P2, P3> 3
<P2, P4> 1
<P3, P4> 2
<P5, P6> 1
```

Recommend Connection

In this section, I provide a complete Spark-based MapReduce algorithm to recommend that people connect with each other. Spark provides an API for graphs and graph-parallel computation called GraphX (*http://spark.apache.org/graphx/*), but we won't be using that here; we'll only use the Spark API.

These days, there are lots of social network sites (Facebook, Instagram, LinkedIn, Pinterest, etc.). One feature they all have in common is recommending that people connect. For example, the "People You May Know" feature from LinkedIn allows members to see others they might want to link with. The basic idea is this: if Alex is a friend of Bob and Alex is a friend of Barbara (i.e., Alex is a common friend of Bob and Barbara, but Bob and Barbara do not know each other), then the social network system should recommend that Bob connect with Barbara and vice versa. In other words, if two people have a set of mutual friends, but they are not friends, then the MapReduce solution should recommend that they be connected to each other.

Friendship among all users can be expressed as a graph. For our simple example, we can use the graph shown in Figure 9-2.

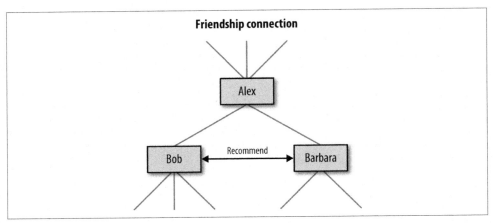

Figure 9-2. Friendship connection

In mathematics, a graph is an ordered pair $G = (V, E)$ comprising a set V of vertices or nodes together with a set E of edges or lines, which are two-element subsets of V (i.e., an edge is related with two vertices, and the relation is represented as an unordered pair of the vertices with respect to the particular edge). This type of graph may be described precisely as undirected and simple. Our assumption for our MapReduce solutions is that a friendship between people can be represented in an undirected graph (if person A is a friend of person B, then B is a friend of A). Most social networks (such as Facebook and LinkedIn) use bidirectional friendships, while friendship on Twitter is directional.

In our case, the graph is an ordered pair $G = (V, E)$ where:

- V is a finite set of people (users of the social network).

- E is a binary relation on V called the *edge set*, whose elements are called a *friendship*.

From a graph theory perspective, for each person or member of a specific social network who is within two degrees of person A, we count how many distinct paths (with two connecting edges) exist between this person and person A. We then rank this list in terms of the number of paths and show the top 10 people that person A should connect with. I will show how we can use a MapReduce solution to compute this top 10 connection list for every person. Therefore, our goal is to precompute (as a batch job) the top 10 recommended people for every member of a social network.

The friendship recommendation problem can be stated as: for every person P, we determine a list $P_1, P_2, ..., P_{10}$ composed of the 10 people with whom person P has the most friends in common.

Input

The social network graph is generally very sparse. Here we assume the input record is an *adjacency list*[2] sorted by name. Therefore, every line of input will be a member ID (such as a user ID, denoted by *P*) followed by a list of immediate friends identified by $F_1, F_2, ..., F_n$:

P F$_1$ F$_2$ ... F$_n$

where $F_1 < F_2 < \ldots < F_n$.

Consider a social network of eight people identified by numbers from 1 to 8. Further assume that their friendship relationships are illustrated by Figure 9-3 (a friendship graph).

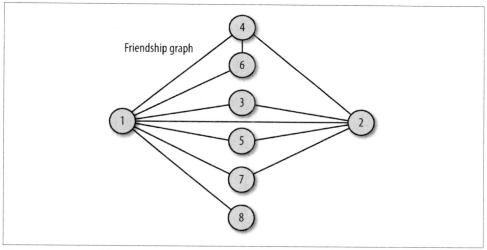

Figure 9-3. Friendship graph for eight friends

Then an *adjacency list* for this graph (sorted by IDs) can be represented by the following (we will read our input from HDFS):

```
# hadoop fs -cat /data/friends2.txt
1 2,3,4,5,6,7,8
2 1,3,4,5,7
3 1,2
4 1,2,6
```

---

2 In graph theory and computer science, an adjacency list representation of a graph is a collection of unordered lists, one for each vertex in the graph. Each list describes the set of neighbors of its vertex. (Source: *http://en.wikipedia.org/wiki/Adjacency_list.*)

```
5 1,2
6 1,4
7 1,2
8 1
```

User 1 is friends with everyone, so we should not make any recommendations for this user. On the other hand, User 3 is friends with Users 1 and 2; we can recommend Users 4, 5, 6, 7, and 8 to User 3 since they are mutual friends of either or both Users 1 and 2.

Output

The output of our Spark program is provided in the following format:

```
<USER><:><F(M: [I1, I2, I3, ...]), ...>
```

where:

- F is a friend recommended to USER.
- M is the number of mutual friends.
- I1, I2, I3, ... are the IDs of mutual friends.

For our sample input, the expected output is:

```
4: 3 (2: [1, 2]),5 (2: [1, 2]),7 (2: [1, 2]),8 (1: [1]),
2: 6 (2: [1, 4]),8 (1: [1]),
6: 2 (2: [1, 4]),3 (1: [1]),5 (1: [1]),7 (1: [1]),8 (1: [1]),
8: 2 (1: [1]),3 (1: [1]),4 (1: [1]),5 (1: [1]),6 (1: [1]),7 (1: [1]),
3: 4 (2: [1, 2]),5 (2: [1, 2]),6 (1: [1]),7 (2: [1, 2]),8 (1: [1]),
1:
7: 3 (2: [1, 2]),4 (2: [1, 2]),5 (2: [1, 2]),6 (1: [1]),8 (1: [1]),
5: 3 (2: [1, 2]),4 (2: [1, 2]),6 (1: [1]),7 (2: [1, 2]),8 (1: [1]),
```

Note again that User 1 does not get any friend recommendations, since this user is already friends with everyone. The output can be verified from the graph.

MapReduce Solution

This section provides a general MapReduce solution without using any specific framework implementations. To implement the friend recommendation feature, we just need a mapper and a reducer. The mapper, outlined in Example 9-7, identifies direct friends and possible future friends (i.e., recommended friends).

Example 9-7. Recommend Connection: mapper

```
1 // key = person (as Long for userID)
2 // value = friends = List<userID> = direct friends of person as {F1, F2, F3, ...}
3 map(key, friends) {
4     // emit all direct friendships
5     for (friend : friends) {
6         // -1 denotes direct friendship
```

```
 7        directFriend = Tuple2(friend, -1);
 8        emit(key, directFriend);
 9    }
10
11    // emit all possible friendships, where
12    // they have mutual friend, person (as a key)
13    for (int i = 0; i < friends.size(); i++) {
14        for (int j = i + 1; j < friends.size(); j++) {
15            // possible friend 1
16            possibleFriend1 = Tuple2(friends.get(j), person);
17            emit(friends.get(i), possibleFriend1);
18            // possible friend 2
19            possibleFriend2 = Tuple2(friends.get(i), person);
20            emit(friends.get(j), possibleFriend2);
21        }
22    }
23 }
```

The reducer, presented in Example 9-8, finds mutual friends between the key (a specific person) and the value (a list of Tuple2<Long, Long>). If any values have a mutual friend (denoted by the special long value -1), then we do not make the recommendation since they are already friends. Finally, we prepare a formatted output, which might be read by other programs for further processing.

Example 9-8. Recommend Connection: reducer

```
 1 // key = person
 2 // values = possible recommendations as List<Tuple2<userID1, userID2>>
 3 reduce(key, values) {
 4
 5    // mutualFriends.key is the recommended friend
 6    // mutualFriends.value is the list of mutual friends
 7    Map<Long, List> mutualFriends = new HashMap<Long, List>();
 8
 9    for (Tuple2<toUser, mutualFriend> t2 : values) {
10        Long toUser = t2.toUser; // t2._1
11        Long mutualFriend = t2.mutualFriend; // t2._2
12        boolean alreadyFriend = (mutualFriend == -1);
13
14        if (mutualFriends.containsKey(toUser)) {
15            if (alreadyFriend) {
16                mutualFriends.put(toUser, null);
17            }
18            else if (mutualFriends.get(toUser) != null) {
19                mutualFriends.get(toUser).add(mutualFriend);
20            }
21        }
22        else {
23            if (alreadyFriend) {
24                mutualFriends.put(toUser, null);
25            }
```

```
26              else {
27                  mutualFriends.put(toUser, List<mutualFriend>)
28              }
29          }
30      }
31
32      String reducerOutput = buildOutput(mutualFriends);
33      emit(key, reducerOutput);
34 }
```

The buildOutput() method is defined in Example 9-9.

Example 9-9. Recommend Connection: buildOutput() method

```
1 String buildOutput(Map<Long, List> map) {
2     String output = "";
3     for (Map.Entry<Long, List> entry : map.entrySet()) {
4         String K = entry.getKey();
5         List V = entry.getValue();
6         output += K + " (" + V.size() + ": " + V + "),";
7     }
8     return output;
9 }
```

Spark Implementation

Our implementation of the MapReduce solution uses the Spark-1.1.0 Java API. Since Spark provides a higher-level Java API than the MapReduce/Hadoop API, we will present the entire solution in a single Java driver class (called SparkFriendRecommen dation), which will include a series of flatMapToPair() and groupBy() functions. Spark's MapReduce abstraction is based on RDDs. We use JavaRDD<T> to represent a set of objects of type T, and JavaPairRDD<K,V> to represent a set of key-value pairs.

First, I will provide a high-level solution in six basic steps (Example 9-10), and then we will dissect each step with the proper working Spark code. Note that some of these steps can be merged (to create somewhat complex steps), but for simplicity's sake I did not do so here.

Example 9-10. SparkFriendRecommendation: high-level steps

```
1 // Step 1: import required classes and interfaces
2 public class SparkFriendRecommendation {
3     public static void main(String[] args) throws Exception {
4         // Step 2: handle input parameters
5         // Step 3: create a Spark context object (as ctx)
6         // Step 4: read HDFS input text and create the first RDD
7         // Step 5: implement map() function
8         // Step 6: implement reduce() function
9         // Step 7: generate desired final output
```

```
10
11      // done
12      ctx.close();
13      System.exit(0);
14    }
15 }
```

Example 9-11 shows some basic utility functions used in our Spark solution.

Example 9-11. Convenience methods

```
1    static String buildRecommendations(Map<Long, List<Long>> mutualFriends) {
2        StringBuilder recommendations = new StringBuilder();
3        for (Map.Entry<Long, List<Long>> entry : mutualFriends.entrySet()) {
4            if (entry.getValue() == null) {
5                // already a friend, no need to recommend again!
6                continue;
7            }
8            recommendations.append(entry.getKey());
9            recommendations.append(" (");
10           recommendations.append(entry.getValue().size());
11           recommendations.append(":" );
12           recommendations.append(entry.getValue());
13           recommendations.append("),");
14       }
15       return recommendations.toString();
16   }
17
18   static Tuple2<Long,Long> T2(long a, long b) {
19       return new Tuple2<Long,Long>(a, b);
20   }
21
22   static Tuple2<Long,Tuple2<Long,Long>> T2(long a, Tuple2<Long,Long> b) {
23       return new Tuple2<Long,Tuple2<Long,Long>>(a, b);
24   }
```

Step 1: Import required classes

This step, shown in Example 9-12, imports the required classes and interfaces. We utilize two important packages from Spark:

org.apache.spark.api.java
   This package defines RDDs (JavaRDD, JavaPairRDD, and JavaSpark-Context).

org.apache.spark.api.java.function
   This package defines transformation functions (Function and PairFlatMapFunction).

Example 9-12. Step 1: import required classes

```
1  // Step 1: import required classes and interfaces
2  import scala.Tuple2;
3  import org.apache.spark.api.java.JavaRDD;
4  import org.apache.spark.api.java.JavaPairRDD;
5  import org.apache.spark.api.java.JavaSparkContext;
6  import org.apache.spark.api.java.function.Function;
7  import org.apache.spark.api.java.function.PairFlatMapFunction;
8  import java.util.Arrays;
9  import java.util.List;
10 import java.util.ArrayList;
11 import java.util.Map;
12 import java.util.HashMap;
```

Step 2: Handle input parameters

As shown in Example 9-13, we read one input parameter: the input path to the HDFS text file, which contains users and their associated friends.

Example 9-13. Step 2: handle input parameters

```
1    // Step 2: handle input parameters
2    if (args.length < 1) {
3      System.err.println("Usage: SparkFriendRecommendation <users-and-friends>");
4      System.exit(1);
5    }
6    String hdfsInputFile = args[0];
```

Step 3: Create a Spark context object

In Example 9-14, a JavaSparkContext[3] object is created; this object is a factory for creating new RDDs. There are several ways to create a JavaSparkContext object; for details, refer to Spark's Java API.

Example 9-14. Step 3: create a Spark context object

```
1    // Step 3: create a Spark context object
2    JavaSparkContext ctx = new JavaSparkContext();
```

Step 4: Read the HDFS input file and create an RDD

In Example 9-15, JavaSparkContext returns the first JavaRDD<String> object, which represents all records from the HDFS input file. I use JavaRDD.collect() for debugging purposes to make sure we have the correct input data.

---

3 org.apache.spark.api.java.JavaSparkContext

Example 9-15. Step 4: read HDFS input file and create RDD

```
1    // Step 4: read HDFS text and create the first RDD
2    JavaRDD<String> records = ctx.textFile(hdfsInputFile, 1);
```

To debug step 4, we use the following code:

```
// debug0
List<String> debug1 = records.collect();
for (String t : debug1) {
  System.out.println("debug1 record="+t);
}
```

Step 5: Implement the map() function

This step implements the `map()` function presented earlier as part of the MapReduce algorithm. The mapper converts each record of:

```
<person><TAB><friend1><,><friend2><,><friend3><,>...
```

into a set of key-value pairs, where the key is the `<person>` and the value is a `Tuple2<friend1,friend2>` signifying direct friendship or possible future friendship. The mapper is implemented by the `JavaRDD.flatMapToPair()` function. We accomplish this implementation by providing the `call()` method as follows:

```
JavaPairRDD<K2,V2> flatMapToPair(PairFlatMapFunction<T,K2,V2> f)
// Return a new RDD by first applying a function to all
// elements of this RDD, and then flattening the results.

PairFlatMapFunction<T, K, V>
T => Iterable<Tuple2<K, V>>
```

where:

- `T` is an input parameter/record.
- Key-value pairs are generated from `T`.

Example 9-16 shows the detailed mapper implementation.

Example 9-16. Step 5: implement map() function

```
1    // Step 5: implement map() function
2    // flatMapToPair
3    //    <K2,V2> JavaPairRDD<K2,V2> flatMapToPair(PairFlatMapFunction<T,K2,V2> f)
4    //    Return a new RDD by first applying a function to all elements of this
5    //    RDD, and then flattening the results.
6    //
7    // PairFlatMapFunction<T, K, V>
8    // T => Iterable<Tuple2<K, V>>
9    JavaPairRDD<Long, Tuple2<Long,Long>> pairs =
10         records.flatMapToPair(new PairFlatMapFunction<
```

```
11                                                   String,              // T
12                                                   Long,                // K
13                                                   Tuple2<Long,Long>    // V
14                                                   >() {
15       public Iterable<Tuple2<Long,Tuple2<Long,Long>>> call(String record) {
16          // record=<person><TAB><friend1><,><friend2><,><friend3><,>...
17          String[] tokens = record.split("\t");
18          long person = Long.parseLong(tokens[0]);
19          String friendsAsString = tokens[1];
20          String[] friendsTokenized = friendsAsString.split(",");
21
22          List<Long> friends = new ArrayList<Long>();
23          List<Tuple2<Long,Tuple2<Long, Long>>> mapperOutput =
24              new ArrayList<Tuple2<Long,Tuple2<Long, Long>>>();
25          for (String friendAsString : friendsTokenized) {
26             long toUser = Long.parseLong(friendAsString);
27             friends.add(toUser);
28             Tuple2<Long,Long> directFriend = T2(toUser, -1L);
29             mapperOutput.add(T2(person, directFriend));
30          }
31
32          for (int i = 0; i < friends.size(); i++) {
33             for (int j = i + 1; j < friends.size(); j++) {
34                // possible friend 1
35                Tuple2<Long,Long> possibleFriend1 = T2(friends.get(j), person);
36                mapperOutput.add(T2(friends.get(i), possibleFriend1));
37                // possible friend 2
38                Tuple2<Long,Long> possibleFriend2 = T2(friends.get(i), person);
39                mapperOutput.add(T2(friends.get(j), possibleFriend2));
40             }
41          }
42          return mapperOutput;
43       }
44    });
```

To debug step 5, we use the following code:

```
// debug2
List<Tuple2<Long,Tuple2<Long,Long>>> debug2 = pairs.collect();
for (Tuple2<Long,Tuple2<Long,Long>> t2 : debug2) {
  System.out.println("debug2 key="+t2._1+"\t value="+t2._2);
}
```

Step 6: Implement the reduce() function

We apply the reduce() function by calling the groupByKey() and collect() methods, as shown in Example 9-17.

Example 9-17. Step 6: implement reduce() function

```
1    // Step 6: implement reduce() function
2    JavaPairRDD<Long, Iterable<Tuple2<Long, Long>>> grouped = pairs.groupByKey();
```

To debug this step, we use the following code:

```
// debug3
List<Tuple2<Long, Iterable<Tuple2<Long, Long>>>> debug3 = grouped.collect();
for (Tuple2<Long, Iterable<Tuple2<Long, Long>>> t2 : debug3) {
  System.out.println("debug3 key="+t2._1+"\t value="+t2._2);
}
```

Step 7: Generate final output

We create the final output by aggregating all values grouped in step 6. This step generates the final recommendations for possible future friendships. It uses the `Java PairRDD.mapValues()` method:

```
public <U> JavaPairRDD<K,U> mapValues(Function<V,U> f)
// Description: Pass each value in the key-value pair
// RDD through a map function without changing the keys;
// this also retains the original RDD's partitioning.
```

This step converts the `Iterable<Tuple2<Long, Long>>` (as input) into a string object (as output). The implementation details are shown in Example 9-18.

Example 9-18. Step 7: generate desired final output

```
1    // Step 7: generate desired final output
2    // Find intersection of all List<List<Long>>
3    // mapValues[U](f: (V) => U): JavaPairRDD[K, U]
4    // Pass each value in the key-value pair RDD through a map
5    // function without changing the keys;
6    // this also retains the original RDD's partitioning.
7    JavaPairRDD<Long, String> recommendations =
8        grouped.mapValues(new Function<
9            Iterable<Tuple2<Long, Long>>, // input
10           String                        // final output
11                               >() {
12        public String call(Iterable<Tuple2<Long, Long>> values) {
13            // mutualFriends.key = the recommended friend
14            // mutualFriends.value = the list of mutual friends
15            final Map<Long, List<Long>> mutualFriends =
16                new HashMap<Long, List<Long>>();
17            for (Tuple2<Long, Long> t2 : values) {
18                final Long toUser = t2._1;
19                final Long mutualFriend = t2._2;
20                final boolean alreadyFriend = (mutualFriend == -1);
21
22                if (mutualFriends.containsKey(toUser)) {
23                    if (alreadyFriend) {
24                        mutualFriends.put(toUser, null);
25                    }
26                    else if (mutualFriends.get(toUser) != null) {
27                        mutualFriends.get(toUser).add(mutualFriend);
28                    }
```

```
29          }
30      else {
31          if (alreadyFriend) {
32              mutualFriends.put(toUser, null);
33          }
34          else {
35              List<Long> list1 =
36                  new ArrayList<Long>(Arrays.asList(mutualFriend));
37              mutualFriends.put(toUser, list1);
38          }
39      }
40  }
41  return buildRecommendations(mutualFriends);
42  }
43 });
```

To debug step 7, we use the following code:

```
// debug4
List<Tuple2<Long,String>> debug4 = recommendations.collect();
for (Tuple2<Long,String> t2 : debug4) {
  System.out.println("debug4 key="+t2._1+ "\t value="+t2._2);
}
```

Combining steps 6 and 7

Steps 6 and 7 can be combined into a single step via Spark's combineByKey() trans-former. In general, groupByKey() followed immediately by mapValues() can be replaced by the reduceByKey() or combineByKey() step.

Sample Run of Spark Program

HDFS input

```
# hadoop fs -cat /data/friends2.txt
1 2,3,4,5,6,7,8
2 1,3,4,5,7
3 1,2
4 1,2,6
5 1,2
6 1,4
7 1,2
8 1
```

Script to run Spark program

```
# cat run_friends_recommendations2.sh
#!/bin/bash
export JAVA_HOME=/usr/java/jdk7
export SPARK_HOME=/home/hadoop/spark-1.1.0
export SPARK_MASTER=spark://myserver100:7077
```

```
BOOK_HOME=/mp/data-algorithms-book
APP_JAR=$BOOK_HOME/dist/data_algorithms_book.jar
USERS=/data/friends2.txt
# Run on a Spark standalone cluster
prog=org.dataalgorithms.chap09.spark.SparkFriendRecommendation
$SPARK_HOME/bin/spark-submit \
  --class $prog \
  --master $SPARK_MASTER \
  --executor-memory 2G \
  --total-executor-cores 20 \
  $APP_JAR $USERS
```

Program run log

The following log has been trimmed and edited to fit the page:

```
# ./run_friends_recommendations2.sh
...
14/06/02 12:46:51 INFO Remoting: Starting remoting
14/06/02 12:46:51 INFO Remoting: Remoting started; listening on addresses :
  [akka.tcp://spark@myserver100:38397]
14/06/02 12:46:51 INFO Remoting: Remoting now listens on addresses:
  [akka.tcp://spark@myserver100:38397]
...
14/06/02 12:46:51 INFO server.AbstractConnector:
  Started SocketConnector@0.0.0.0:43523
14/06/02 12:46:51 INFO broadcast.HttpBroadcast:
  Broadcast server started at http://myserver100:43523
...
14/06/02 12:46:52 INFO client.AppClient$ClientActor:
  Connecting to master spark://myserver100:7077...
...
14/06/02 12:46:57 INFO scheduler.DAGScheduler: Stage 0
  (collect at SparkFriendRecommendation.java:34) finished in 3.446 s
14/06/02 12:46:57 INFO spark.SparkContext: Job finished:
  collect at SparkFriendRecommendation.java:34, took 3.543265173 s
debug1 record=1 2,3,4,5,6,7,8
debug1 record=2 1,3,4,5,7
debug1 record=3 1,2
debug1 record=4 1,2,6
debug1 record=5 1,2
debug1 record=6 1,4
debug1 record=7 1,2
debug1 record=8 1
14/06/02 12:46:57 INFO spark.SparkContext: Starting job:
  collect at SparkFriendRecommendation.java:79
...
14/06/02 12:46:58 INFO scheduler.DAGScheduler: Stage 1
  (collect at SparkFriendRecommendation.java:79) finished in 1.643 s
14/06/02 12:46:58 INFO spark.SparkContext: Job finished:
  collect at SparkFriendRecommendation.java:79, took 1.654938027 s
debug2 key=1  value=(2,-1)
debug2 key=1  value=(3,-1)
```

```
debug2 key=1  value=(4,-1)
debug2 key=1  value=(5,-1)
debug2 key=1  value=(6,-1)
debug2 key=1  value=(7,-1)
debug2 key=1  value=(8,-1)
debug2 key=2  value=(3,1)
debug2 key=3  value=(2,1)
debug2 key=2  value=(4,1)
debug2 key=4  value=(2,1)
debug2 key=2  value=(5,1)
debug2 key=5  value=(2,1)
debug2 key=2  value=(6,1)
debug2 key=6  value=(2,1)
debug2 key=2  value=(7,1)
debug2 key=7  value=(2,1)
debug2 key=2  value=(8,1)
debug2 key=8  value=(2,1)
debug2 key=3  value=(4,1)
debug2 key=4  value=(3,1)
debug2 key=3  value=(5,1)
debug2 key=5  value=(3,1)
debug2 key=3  value=(6,1)
debug2 key=6  value=(3,1)
debug2 key=3  value=(7,1)
debug2 key=7  value=(3,1)
debug2 key=3  value=(8,1)
debug2 key=8  value=(3,1)
debug2 key=4  value=(5,1)
debug2 key=5  value=(4,1)
debug2 key=4  value=(6,1)
debug2 key=6  value=(4,1)
debug2 key=4  value=(7,1)
debug2 key=7  value=(4,1)
debug2 key=4  value=(8,1)
debug2 key=8  value=(4,1)
debug2 key=5  value=(6,1)
debug2 key=6  value=(5,1)
debug2 key=5  value=(7,1)
debug2 key=7  value=(5,1)
debug2 key=5  value=(8,1)
debug2 key=8  value=(5,1)
debug2 key=6  value=(7,1)
debug2 key=7  value=(6,1)
debug2 key=6  value=(8,1)
debug2 key=8  value=(6,1)
debug2 key=7  value=(8,1)
debug2 key=8  value=(7,1)
debug2 key=2  value=(1,-1)
debug2 key=2  value=(3,-1)
debug2 key=2  value=(4,-1)
debug2 key=2  value=(5,-1)
debug2 key=2  value=(7,-1)
```

```
debug2 key=1   value=(3,2)
debug2 key=3   value=(1,2)
debug2 key=1   value=(4,2)
debug2 key=4   value=(1,2)
debug2 key=1   value=(5,2)
debug2 key=5   value=(1,2)
debug2 key=1   value=(7,2)
debug2 key=7   value=(1,2)
debug2 key=3   value=(4,2)
debug2 key=4   value=(3,2)
debug2 key=3   value=(5,2)
debug2 key=5   value=(3,2)
debug2 key=3   value=(7,2)
debug2 key=7   value=(3,2)
debug2 key=4   value=(5,2)
debug2 key=5   value=(4,2)
debug2 key=4   value=(7,2)
debug2 key=7   value=(4,2)
debug2 key=5   value=(7,2)
debug2 key=7   value=(5,2)
debug2 key=3   value=(1,-1)
debug2 key=3   value=(2,-1)
debug2 key=1   value=(2,3)
debug2 key=2   value=(1,3)
debug2 key=4   value=(1,-1)
debug2 key=4   value=(2,-1)
debug2 key=4   value=(6,-1)
debug2 key=1   value=(2,4)
debug2 key=2   value=(1,4)
debug2 key=1   value=(6,4)
debug2 key=6   value=(1,4)
debug2 key=2   value=(6,4)
debug2 key=6   value=(2,4)
debug2 key=5   value=(1,-1)
debug2 key=5   value=(2,-1)
debug2 key=1   value=(2,5)
debug2 key=2   value=(1,5)
debug2 key=6   value=(1,-1)
debug2 key=6   value=(4,-1)
debug2 key=1   value=(4,6)
debug2 key=4   value=(1,6)
debug2 key=7   value=(1,-1)
debug2 key=7   value=(2,-1)
debug2 key=1   value=(2,7)
debug2 key=2   value=(1,7)
debug2 key=8   value=(1,-1)
14/06/02 12:46:58 INFO spark.SparkContext: Starting job:
  collect at SparkFriendRecommendation.java:88
14/06/02 12:46:58 INFO scheduler.DAGScheduler:
  Registering RDD 2 (flatMapToPair at SparkFriendRecommendation.java:42)
...
14/06/02 12:46:59 INFO scheduler.DAGScheduler: Stage 2
```

```
    (collect at SparkFriendRecommendation.java:88) finished in 0.319 s
14/06/02 12:46:59 INFO spark.SparkContext: Job finished:
    collect at SparkFriendRecommendation.java:88, took 0.408234901 s
debug3 key=4  value=[(2,1), (3,1), (5,1), (6,1), (7,1), (8,1),
                     (1,2), (3,2), (5,2), (7,2), (1,-1), (2,-1),
                     (6,-1), (1,6)]
debug3 key=2  value=[(3,1), (4,1), (5,1), (6,1), (7,1), (8,1),
                     (1,-1), (3,-1), (4,-1), (5,-1), (7,-1),
                     (1,3), (1,4), (6,4), (1,5), (1,7)]
debug3 key=6  value=[(2,1), (3,1), (4,1), (5,1), (7,1), (8,1),
                     (1,4), (2,4), (1,-1), (4,-1)]
debug3 key=8  value=[(2,1), (3,1), (4,1), (5,1), (6,1), (7,1), (1,-1)]
debug3 key=3  value=[(2,1), (4,1), (5,1), (6,1), (7,1), (8,1), (1,2),
                     (4,2), (5,2), (7,2), (1,-1), (2,-1)]
debug3 key=1  value=[(2,-1), (3,-1), (4,-1), (5,-1), (6,-1), (7,-1),
                     (8,-1), (3,2), (4,2), (5,2), (7,2), (2,3), (2,4),
                     (6,4), (2,5), (4,6), (2,7)]
debug3 key=7  value=[(2,1), (3,1), (4,1), (5,1), (6,1), (8,1), (1,2),
                     (3,2), (4,2), (5,2), (1,-1), (2,-1)]
debug3 key=5  value=[(2,1), (3,1), (4,1), (6,1), (7,1), (8,1), (1,2),
                     (3,2), (4,2), (7,2), (1,-1), (2,-1)]
14/06/02 12:46:59 INFO spark.SparkContext: Starting job:
    collect at SparkFriendRecommendation.java:135
14/06/02 12:46:59 INFO scheduler.DAGScheduler: Got job 3 (collect at
    SparkFriendRecommendation.java:135) with 1 output partitions (allowLocal=false)
...
14/06/02 12:46:59 INFO scheduler.DAGScheduler: Stage 4 (collect at
    SparkFriendRecommendation.java:135) finished in 0.109 s
14/06/02 12:46:59 INFO spark.SparkContext: Job finished: collect
    at SparkFriendRecommendation.java:135, took 0.124233834 s
debug4 key=4  value=3 (2: [1, 2]),5 (2: [1, 2]),7 (2: [1, 2]),8 (1: [1]),
debug4 key=2  value=6 (2: [1, 4]),8 (1: [1]),
debug4 key=6  value=2 (2: [1, 4]),3 (1: [1]),5 (1: [1]),7 (1: [1]),
                     8 (1: [1]),
debug4 key=8  value=2 (1: [1]),3 (1: [1]),4 (1: [1]),5 (1: [1]),
                     6 (1: [1]),7 (1: [1]),
debug4 key=3  value=4 (2: [1, 2]),5 (2: [1, 2]),6 (1: [1]),
                     7 (2: [1, 2]),8 (1: [1]),
debug4 key=1  value=
debug4 key=7  value=3 (2: [1, 2]),4 (2: [1, 2]),5 (2: [1, 2]),
                     6 (1: [1]),8 (1: [1]),
debug4 key=5  value=3 (2: [1, 2]),4 (2: [1, 2]),6 (1: [1]),
                     7 (2: [1, 2]),8 (1: [1]),
```

This chapter touched on recommendation engines, which are a very important concept in data mining. Through some simple examples, you learned how to implement a basic recommendation engine using the MapReduce paradigm. The next chapter continues our coverage of recommendation engines through the use case of movie recommendations.

## CHAPTER 10

Content-Based Recommendation: Movies

Have you ever wondered how Netflix creates movie recommendations for its users? Or how Amazon creates book recommendations for its users? There must be some kind of magic algorithm to generate this kind of recommendation, right? Netflix even offered a $1 million prize for finding the optimal solution for movie recommendations[20]. Content-based recommendation systems, such as those used by Netflix and Amazon, examine properties of items (such as movies) in order to make recommendations to users. For example, if a user has watched a lot of action movies, then the recommendation system will suggest movies in that category.

This chapter presents a basic MapReduce content-based recommendation solution, based on Edwin Chen's blog[6]. Suppose you run an online movie business, and you want to generate movie recommendations. You have a rating system (people can rate movies from 1 to 5 stars), and we'll assume for simplicity's sake that all of the ratings are stored in a TSV (tab-separated value) files in the HDFS. After presenting a generic MapReduce solution, I'll provide a concrete Spark implementation for movie recommendations.

Note that in content-based recommendation systems, the more information (such as domain knowledge and metadata) we have about the content, the more complex the algorithms become (as more variables are involved), but the recommendations become more accurate and reasonable. For example, for movie recommendations the system should have metadata such as actors, directors, and producers. For our examples here, we will limit our algorithms only to movie ratings. Typically, in a recommendation system application there are two classes of entities: users and items. In our example, the users are the people who watched and rated movies, and the items are the movies. The input data in the following section will show the relationship between users and movies.

The purpose of this chapter is to present a three-phase MapReduce solution for implementing movie recommendations:

- Phase 1: find the total number of raters for each movie.
- Phase 2: for every pair of movies *A* and *B*, find all the people who rated both *A* and *B*.
- Phase 3: find the correlation between every two related movies. For this phase, I will show you how to apply three different correlation algorithms (Pearson, Cosine, and Jaccard). In general, you should select a correlation algorithm based on your data requirements, but in this phase, you may plug in any correlation algorithm you wish.

Input

We assume that the raw input data is in the following format (let's call this Format 1):

```
<user> <movie> <rating>
```

where user is the user ID of the person who rated the movie, and rating is a an integer from 1 to 5. An example is given in Table 10-1.

Table 10-1. Users and movies

User	Movie	Rating
User1	Movie1	1
User1	Movie2	2
User1	Movie3	3
User2	Movie1	1
User2	Movie2	2
User2	Movie3	3
User2	Movie5	5
...	...	...

Using Format 1, we will generate another input, which has the following format (let's call this Format 2)—we add a new column, numberOfRaters, which refers to the number of people who rated that specific movie, and we group by movie:

```
<user> <movie> <rating> <numberOfRaters>
```

MapReduce Phase 1

The goal of this phase is to read data in Format 1 and generate data in Format 2. To find the `numberOfRaters`, we write a simple MapReduce job composed of a mapper and a reducer. Given an input record `<user> <movie> <rating>`, the mapper emits a (K_2, V_2) pair, where K_2 is `<movie>` and V_2 is a `Tuple2(user, rating)`. The reducer determines the number of times a movie has been rated and then generates our desired output (as previously defined).

The mapper for phase 1 is shown in Example 10-1.

Example 10-1. Mapper phase 1

```
1 map( <user>   <movie>   <rating>) {
2    K2 = <movie>;
3    V2 = Tuple2(user, rating);
4    emit(K2, V2);
5 }
```

The reducer for phase 2 is shown in Example 10-2.

Example 10-2. Reducer phase 1

```
 1  //key = <movie>
 2  //values = List<Tuple2<user,rating>>
 3 reduce(key, values) {
 4    numberOfRaters = values.size();
 5    for (Tuple2<user,rating> t2 : values) {
 6        K3 = t2.user;
 7        V3 = Tuple3(key, t2.rating, numberOfRaters);
 8        emit(K3, V3);
 9    }
10 }
```

The output of phase 1 will be used as input to phase 2.

MapReduce Phases 2 and 3

Our MapReduce solution will calculate how similar two movies are, so that if someone watches *The Lion King*, we can recommend films like *Toy Story*. So how should we define the similarity between two movies? One way is to use their *correlation*[32]:

1. For every pair of movies A and B, find all the people who rated both A and B.

2. Use these ratings to form a *Movie A* vector and a *Movie B* vector.

3. Calculate the correlation (mutual relation of two or more items; here, the correlation is a way to measure how associated or related two movies are) between these two vectors.

4. Whenever someone watches a movie, we can then recommend the movies most correlated with it.

The first two steps will be done in MapReduce phase 2 (in which we will generate a *Movie A* vector and a *Movie B* vector). The last two steps will be done in MapReduce phase 3 (to calculate the correlation between every pair of related movies).

To get all pairs of co-rated movies, we'll join our input (all movie ratings) against itself (similar to SQL's joining a table against itself). To join the ratings input against itself, the mapper will collect all movies for each user, and the reducer will generate unique combinations of all movies rated by a user.

To help you understand this better, let's create a sample input for two users (note that this input is generated by phase 1; each record contains <user>, <movie>, <rating>, and <numberOfRaters>), as shown in Table 10-2.

Table 10-2. Users and movies: sample input

User	Movie	Rating	Number of raters
User1	Movie1	1	10
User1	Movie2	2	20
User1	Movie3	3	30
User2	Movie1	1	10
User2	Movie2	2	20
User2	Movie3	3	30
User2	Movie5	5	50
...	...	...	...

MapReduce Phase 2: Mapper

The map() function will accept one line of input:

```
<user> <movie> <rating> <numberOfRaters>
```

and emit a key-value pair:

```
key: <user>
value: <movie> <rating> <numberOfRaters>
```

Example 10-3 defines the map() function.

Example 10-3. Mapper: phase 2

```
1   // key = <user>
2   // value = <movie> <rating> <NumOfRaters>
3   map(key, value) {
4       String[] tokens = value.split("\t");
5       movie = tokens[0];
6       rating = tokens[1];
7       numberOfRaters = tokens[2];
8       Tuple3<String, Integer, Integer> t3 =
9           new Tuple3(movie, rating, numberOfRaters);
10      emit(key, t3);
11  }
```

The mapper will generate the output shown in Table 10-3 for our sample input (to be consumed by reducers).

Table 10-3. Mapper output

Key	Value
User1	<Movie1, 1, 10>
User1	<Movie2, 2, 20>
User1	<Movie3, 3, 30>
User2	<Movie1, 1, 10>
User2	<Movie2, 2, 20>
User2	<Movie3, 3, 30>
User2	<Movie5, 5, 50>
...	...

MapReduce Phase 2: Reducer

The reduce() function will accept a user (as a key) and a list of Tuple3(movie, rating, numOfRaters) (as a value) and will emit unique combinations of all movies rated by each user.

Therefore, the input for the reducer will look like Table 10-4.

Table 10-4. Output of sort and shuffle

Key	Value(s)
User1	[<Movie1, 1, 10>,
	<Movie2, 2, 20>,
	<Movie3, 3, 30>]
User2	[<Movie1, 1, 10>,
	<Movie2, 2, 20>,

Key	Value(s)
	<Movie3, 3, 30>,
	<Movie5, 5, 50>]
...	...

Example 10-4 defines the reduce() function, which will join the output of the "sort and shuffle" phase against itself (the join will be on the "user" key).

Example 10-4. Reducer: phase 2

```
1  // key = user (generated by map())
2  // value = List{ Tuple3(<movie> <rating> <numOfRaters>) }
3  reduce(key, value) {
4      // Generate unique combinations of all movies against each other.
5      // Make sure not to create duplicate entries like (movie1, movie2) and
6      // (movie2, movie1).
7      // To avoid this, we will create (movie1, movie2)
8      // where movie1 < movie2.
9      List[ Tuple2( Tuple3(<movie1> <rating1> <numOfRaters1>),
10                   Tuple3(<movie2> <rating2> <numOfRaters2>) ]
11               list = generateUniqueCombinations(value);
12
13     for (Tuple2( Tuple3(<movie1> <rating1> <numOfRaters1>),
14               Tuple3(<movie2> <rating2> <numOfRaters2>) pair : list) {
15       m1 = pair._1;  // = Tuple3(<movie1> <rating1> <numOfRaters1>)
16       m2 = pair._2;  // = Tuple3(<movie2> <rating2> <numOfRaters2>)
17
18       // define the reducer key
19       reducerKey = Tuple2(m1.movie, m2.movie);
20
21       // calculate additional information, which will be used
22       // by the correlation function
23       int ratingProduct = m1.rating * m2.rating;
24       int rating1Squared = m1.rating * m1.rating;
25       int rating2Squared = m2.rating * m2.rating;
26
27       // define the reducer value
28       reducerValue = Tuple7(m1.rating,
29                             m1.NumOfRaters,
30                             m2.rating,
31                             m2.NumOfRaters,
32                             ratingProduct,
33                             rating1Squared,
34                             rating2Squared);
35       emit(reducerKey, reducerValue);
36   } // end for-loop
37 }
```

The reducer will generate the key-value pairs shown in Tables 10-5 and 10-6.

Table 10-5. Reducer output generated from key=User1

Key	Value
<Movie1, Movie2>	<1 10 2 20 2 1 4>
<Movie1, Movie3>	<1 10 3 30 3 1 9>
<Movie2, Movie3>	<2 20 3 30 6 4 9>

Table 10-6. Reducer output generated from key=User2

Key	Value
<Movie1, Movie2>	<2 10 3 20 6 4 9>
<Movie1, Movie3>	<2 10 4 30 8 4 16>
<Movie1, Movie5>	<2 10 5 50 10 4 25>
<Movie2, Movie3>	<3 20 4 30 12 9 16>
<Movie2, Movie5>	<3 20 5 50 15 9 25>
<Movie3, Movie5>	<4 30 5 50 20 16 25>

MapReduce Phase 3: Mapper

The phase 3 mapper is an identity mapper. The `map()` function will accept key-value input pairs as follows:

```
    key: Tuple2(<movie1>, <movie2>)
  value: Tuple7(<rating1>,
               <numOfRaters1>,
               <rating2>,
               <numOfRaters2>,
               <ratingProduct>,
               <rating1Squared>,
               <rating2Squared>
               )
```

The mapper just emits key-value pairs as received. The `map()` function is defined in Example 10-5.

Example 10-5. Mapper: phase 3

```
1 // key = Tuple2(<movie1>, <movie2>) and generated by reducer of phase 2
2 // value = Tuple7(<rating1> <numOfRaters1> <rating2> <numOfRaters2>
3 //                <ratingProduct> <rating1Squared> <rating2Squared>)
4 map(key, value) {
5    emit(key, value);
6 }
```

The mapper will generate the output shown in Table 10-7 from our sample input (this will be used as an input to the reducer of phase 3).

Table 10-7. Mapper output to be used as input to the reducer in phase 3

Key	Value
<Movie1, Movie2>	<1 10 2 20 2 1 4>
<Movie1, Movie3>	<1 10 3 30 3 1 9>
<Movie2, Movie3>	<2 20 3 30 6 4 9>
<Movie1, Movie2>	<2 10 3 20 6 4 9>
<Movie1, Movie3>	<2 10 4 30 8 4 16>
<Movie1, Movie5>	<2 10 5 50 10 4 25>
<Movie2, Movie3>	<3 20 4 30 12 9 16>
<Movie2, Movie5>	<3 20 5 50 15 9 25>
<Movie3, Movie5>	<4 30 5 50 20 16 25>

MapReduce Phase 3: Reducer

The reduce() function will accept (<movie1>, <movie2>) as a key and a list of:

```
Tuple7(<rating1>
       <numOfRaters1>,
       <rating2>
       <numOfRaters2>
       <ratingProduct>
       <rating1Squared>
       <rating2Squared>)
```

as a value, and will emit the correlation of every two related movies.

So, the input for the reducer will be the key-value pairs shown in Table 10-8.

Table 10-8. Reducer input for phase 3

Key	Value
<Movie1, Movie2>	[<1 10 2 20 2 1 4>, <2 10 3 20 6 4 9>]
<Movie1, Movie3>	[<1 10 3 30 3 1 9>, <2 10 4 30 8 4 16>]
<Movie2, Movie3>	[<2 20 3 30 6 4 9>, <3 20 4 30 12 9 16>]
<Movie1, Movie5>	<2 10 5 50 10 4 25>
<Movie2, Movie5>	<3 20 5 50 15 9 25>
<Movie3, Movie5>	<4 30 5 50 20 16 25>

Example 10-6 shows the definition of reduce( ).

Example 10-6. Reducer: phase 3

```
 1 // key = Tuple2(<movie1, movie2>)
 2 // values = List { Tuple7(<rating1>,
 3 //                        <numOfRaters1>,
 4 //                        <rating2>,
 5 //                        <numOfRaters2>,
 6 //                        <ratingProduct>,
 7 //                        <rating1Squared>,
 8 //                        <rating2Squared>)
 9 // }
10 reduce(key, value) {
11     // calculate additional information, which will be
12     // used by the correlation function
13     int groupSize = value.size();  // length of each vector
14     int dotProduct = 0;   // sum of ratingProd
15     int rating1Sum = 0;   // sum of rating1
16     int rating2Sum = 0;   // sum of rating2
17     int rating1NormSq = 0;  // sum of rating1Squared
18     int rating2NormSq = 0;  // sum of rating2Squared
19     int maxNumOfumRaters1 = 0;  // max of numOfRaters1
20     int maxNumOfumRaters2 = 0;  // max of numOfRaters2
21     for (Tuple7(<rating1>
22                 <numOfRaters1>
23                 <rating2>
24                 <numOfRaters2>
25                 <ratingProduct>
26                 <rating1Squared>
27                 <rating2Squared>) : values) {
28         dotProduct += ratingProd;
29         rating1Sum += rating1;
30         rating2Sum += rating2;
31         rating1NormSq += rating1Squared;
32         rating2NormSq += rating2Squared;
33         if (numOfRaters1 > maxNumOfumRaters1) {
34             maxNumOfumRaters1 = numOfRaters1;
35         }
36         if (numOfRaters2 > maxNumOfumRaters2) {
37             maxNumOfumRaters2 = numOfRaters2;
38         }
39     }
40
41     double pearson = calculatePearsonCorrelation(
42             groupSize,
43             dotProduct,
44             rating1Sum,
45             rating2Sum,
46             rating1NormSq,
47             rating2NormSq);
48
```

```
49    double cosine = calculateCosineCorrelation(dotProduct,
50                                  Math.sqrt(rating1NormSq),
51                                  Math.sqrt(rating2NormSq));
52    double jaccard = calculateJaccardCorrelation(groupSize,
53                                  maxNumOfumRaters1,
54                                  maxNumOfumRaters2);
55    return Tuple3(pearson, cosine, jaccard);
56 }
```

Finally, the reducer will generate similarities for every two movies:

```
<Movie1, Movie2>  pearson1, cosine1, jaccard1
<Movie1, Movie3>  pearson2, cosine2, jaccard2
<Movie2, Movie3>  pearson3, cosine3, jaccard3
<Movie1, Movie2>  pearson4, cosine4, jaccard4
<Movie1, Movie3>  pearson5, cosine5, jaccard5
<Movie1, Movie5>  pearson6, cosine6, jaccard6
<Movie2, Movie3>  pearson7, cosine7, jaccard7
<Movie2, Movie5>  pearson8, cosine8, jaccard8
<Movie3, Movie5>  pearson9, cosine9, jaccard9
```

Similarity Measures

For the preceding correlation calculations, we used the Pearson product-moment correlation coefficient, the Jaccard similarity coefficient, and the cosine similarity coefficient. The Pearson correlation can be defined as follows:

$$\text{correlation}(X, Y) = \frac{n\Sigma xy - \Sigma x \Sigma y}{\sqrt{n\Sigma x^2 - (\Sigma x)^2}\sqrt{n\Sigma y^2 - (\Sigma y)^2}}$$

Jaccard and cosine similarity are two other common vector-based similarity measures. Of course, there are lots of other that can be used to calculate correlation. Other correlation or similarity measures to consider include:

- Regularized correlation
- Euclidean distance
- Manhattan distance

Selecting a correlation or similarity measure algorithm is domain/problem specific. You need to investigate to determine which algorithm gives you better (pragmatic optimal) answers.

Movie Recommendation Implementation in Spark

This section presents the Spark implementation of the three phases of the MapReduce algorithm provided earlier in this chapter. The entire Spark solution is written in a single Java driver class called `MovieRecommendationsWithJoin`. I'll provide the following for our Spark implementation:

- All high-level steps
- A detailed description of each step with the accompanying complete Spark code in Java
- A sample run using Spark-1.1.0

High-Level Solution in Spark

The solution in Spark is presented in 13 steps, which use RDDs. As you know, Spark's primary data abstraction and programming model is based on RDDs. To refresh your memory, these are immutable data structures that have the following properties. RDDs:

- Are created from HDFS files or "parallelized" arrays
- Can be transformed with `map()` and `filter()`
- Can be cached across parallel operations such as `reduce()`, `collect()`, and `foreach()`.

The driver class `MovieRecommendationsWithJoin` is presented in Example 10-7.

Example 10-7. High-level solution: all steps

```
1  //Step 1: import required classes and interfaces
2  public class MovieRecommendationsWithJoin {
3
4      public static void main(String[] args) throws Exception {
5          //Step 2: handle input parameters
6          //Step 3: create a Spark context object
7          //Step 4: read HDFS file and create the first RDD
8          //Step 5: find who has rated this movie
9          //Step 6: group moviesRDD by movie
10         //Step 7: find number of raters per movie and then create (K,V) pairs as
11         //        usersRDD = <K=user, V=<movie,rating,numberOfRaters>>
12         //Step 8: join usersRDD against itself to find all (movie1, movie2) pairs
13         //        joinedRDD = usersRDD.join(usersRDD);
14         //        joinedRDD = (user, T2((m1,r1,n1), (m2,r2,n2)))
15         //Step 9: remove duplicate (movie1, movie2) pairs.
16         //        Note that (movie1, movie2) and (movie2, movie1) are the same.
17         //Step 10: generate all (movie1, movie2) combinations.
18         // The goal of this step is to create (K,V) pairs of
19         //     K: Tuple2(movie1, movie2)
20         //     V: Tuple7(movie1.rating,
21         //              movie1.numOfRaters,
```

```
22      //              movie2.rating,
23      //              movie2.numOfRaters,
24      //              ratingProduct,
25      //              rating1Squared, = movie1.rating * movie1.rating
26      //              rating2Squared  = movie2.rating * movie2.rating
27      //              )
28      //Step 11: group moviePairs by key(movie1,movie2)
29      //Step 12: calculate correlation/similarities between every (movie1,movie2)
30      //Step 13: print final results
31      System.exit(0);
32    }
33
34    static Tuple3<Double,Double,Double> calculateCorrelations(...);
35    static double calculatePearsonCorrelation(...);
36    static double calculateCosineCorrelation(...);
37    static double calculateJaccardCorrelation(...);
38 }
```

Step 1: Import required classes

Most of the classes and interfaces we need are included in the following two packages: `org.apache.spark.api.java` and `org.apache.spark.api.java.function`. Example 10-8 shows how to import them.

Example 10-8. Step 1: import required classes

```
1  //Step 1: import required classes and interfaces
2 import scala.Tuple2;
3 import java.util.List;
4 import java.util.ArrayList;
5 import org.apache.spark.api.java.JavaRDD;
6 import org.apache.spark.api.java.JavaPairRDD;
7 import org.apache.spark.api.java.JavaSparkContext;
8 import org.apache.spark.api.java.function.Function;
9 import org.apache.spark.api.java.function.PairFlatMapFunction;
10 import org.apache.spark.api.java.function.FlatMapFunction;
11 import org.apache.spark.api.java.function.PairFunction;
```

Step 2: Handle input parameters

One parameter is needed to run the Spark program: the HDFS input file (representing users and ratings). Example 10-9 shows how we handle this parameter.

Example 10-9. Step 2: handle input parameters

```
1   //Step 2: handle input parameters
2  if (args.length < 1) {
3     System.err.println("Usage: MovieRecommendationsWithJoin <users-ratings>");
4     System.exit(1);
5  }
```

```
6    String usersRatingsInputFile = args[0];
7    System.out.println("usersRatingsInputFile="+ usersRatingsInputFile);
```

Step 3: Create a Spark context object

This step, shown in Example 10-10, creates a JavaSparkContext object that returns JavaRDDs and works with Java collections. JavaSparkContext is a factory class that creates JavaRDD<T> and JavaPairRDD<K,V> objects.

Example 10-10. Step 3: create a Spark context object

```
1    //Step 3: create a Spark context object
2    JavaSparkContext ctx = new JavaSparkContext();
```

Step 4: Read input file and create RDD

In this step (Example 10-xx), using our JavaSparkContext object, we read an HDFS input text file and create the first JavaRDD<String> object (set of String-type records), which represents the input file.

Example 10-11. Step 4: read input file and create RDD

```
1    //Step 4: read HDFS file and create the first RDD
2    JavaRDD<String> usersRatings = ctx.textFile(usersRatingsInputFile, 1);
```

After we've executed step 4, the usersRating RDD is a list of:

```
{
  "user1 movie1 1",
  "user1 movie2 2",
  "user1 movie3 3",
  "user2 movie1 1",
  "user2 movie2 2"
  "user2 movie3 3"
  "user2 movie5 5"
  ...
}
```

Step 5: Find who has rated movies

The usersRating RDD is an input to step 5. Steps 5–7 find the number of raters for every movie. Step 5 implements a mapper; it accepts a single record (composed of user, movie, and rating) and creates a key-value pair of (movie, user,rating). JavaRDD.mapToPair() accepts a single input record and creates a JavaPairRDD<K2,V2>, where K2=movie and V2=Tuple2(user,rating). See Example 10-12.

Example 10-12. Step 5: find who has rated movies

```
1    // Step 5: find who has rated this movie
2    // <K2,V2> JavaPairRDD<K2,V2> mapToPair(PairFunction<T,K2,V2> f)
3    // Return a new RDD by applying a function to all elements of this RDD.
4    // PairFunction<T, K2, V2>
5    //     T => Tuple2<K2, V2>
6    //     T = <user> <movie> <rating>
7    //     K2 = <movie>
8    //     V2 = Tuple2<user, rating>
9    JavaPairRDD<String,Tuple2<String,Integer>> moviesRDD =
10       usersRatings.mapToPair(
11          new PairFunction<
12                           String,              // T
13                           String,              // K
14                           Tuple2<String,Integer> // V
15                           >() {
16       public Tuple2<String,Tuple2<String,Integer>> call(String s) {
17          String[] record = s.split("\t");
18          String user = record[0];
19          String movie = record[1];
20          Integer rating = new Integer(record[2]);
21          Tuple2<String,Integer> userAndRating =
22             new Tuple2<String,Integer>(user, rating);
23             return new Tuple2<String,Tuple2<String,Integer>>
24                (movie, userAndRating);
25       }
26   });
```

To debug step 5, we use the `JavaPairRDD.collect()` method:

```
System.out.println("=== debug1: moviesRDD: K = <movie>, " +
                   "= Tuple2<user, rating> ===");
List<
     Tuple2<String,Tuple2<String,Integer>>
   > debug1 = moviesRDD.collect();
for (Tuple2<String,Tuple2<String,Integer>> t2 : debug1) {
   System.out.println("debug1 key="+t2._1 + "\t value="+t2._2);
}
```

After step 5 is executed, `moviesRDD` is a list of key-value pairs, as shown in Table 10-9.

Table 10-9. moviesRDD key-value pairs

K2: Movie	V2: Tuple2(user, rating)
movie1	(user1, 1)
movie2	(user1, 2)
movie3	(user1, 3)
movie1	(user2, 1)
movie2	(user2, 2)

K2: Movie	V2: Tuple2(user, rating)
movie3	(user2, 3)
movie5	(user2, 5)
...	...

Step 6: Group moviesRDD by movie

Step 5 created a `JavaPairRDD<K2,V2>` where K2=movie and V2=Tuple2(user,rating). This step groups moviesRDD by its key. The result of this step will be:

```
JavaPairRDD<K,V>
    where  K=movie
           V=List(Tuple2(user,rating))
```

This step is implemented by the `JavaPairRDD.groupByKey()` method, as shown in Example 10-13.

Example 10-13. Step 6: group moviesRDD by movie

```
1    // Step 6: group moviesRDD by movie
2    JavaPairRDD<String, Iterable<Tuple2<String,Integer>>> moviesGrouped =
3        moviesRDD.groupByKey();
4
5    System.out.println("=== debug2: moviesGrouped: K = <movie>, " +
6                       "V = Iterable<Tuple2<user, rating>> ===");
7    List<Tuple2<String,Iterable<Tuple2<String,Integer>>> debug2 =
8        moviesGrouped.collect();
8    for (Tuple2<String,Iterable<Tuple2<String,Integer>>> t2 : debug2) {
9        System.out.println("debug2 key="+t2._1 + "\t value="+t2._2);
10   }
```

After we've executed step 6, moviesGrouped is a list of the following key-value pairs. Clearly, we can count the number of raters (which is the size of the list value per movie) for each movie:

```
{
  (movie1, [(user1, 1), (user2, 1), ...]),
  (movie2, [(user1, 2), (user2, 2), ...]),
  (movie3, [(user1, 3), (user2, 3), ...]),
  (movie5, [(user2, 5), ...])
  ...
}
```

Step 7: Find number of raters per movie

This step, shown in Example 10-14, tallies the raters for each movie and generates another `JavaPairRDD<K,V>` where K=user and V=Tuple3(movie, rating, numberOfRaters). This step is implemented by the `JavaPairRDD.flatMapToPair()` method.

Example 10-14. Step 7: find number of raters per movie

```
1    // Step 7: find number of raters per movie and then create (K,V) pairs as
2    //        K = user
3    //        V = Tuple3<movie, rating, numberOfRaters>
4    //
5    // PairFlatMapFunction<T, K, V>
6    // T => Iterable<Tuple2<K, V>>
7    JavaPairRDD<String,Tuple3<String,Integer,Integer>> usersRDD =
8        moviesGrouped.flatMapToPair(new PairFlatMapFunction<
9           Tuple2<String, Iterable<Tuple2<String,Integer>>>,  // T
10          String,                                            // K
11          Tuple3<String,Integer,Integer>>() {                // V
12    public Iterable<Tuple2<String,Tuple3<String,Integer,Integer>>>
13       call(Tuple2<String, Iterable<Tuple2<String,Integer>>> s) {
14       List<Tuple2<String,Integer>> listOfUsersAndRatings =
15         new ArrayList<Tuple2<String,Integer>>();
16       // now read inputs and generate desired (K,V) pairs
17       String movie = s._1;
18       Iterable<Tuple2<String,Integer>> pairsOfUserAndRating = s._2;
19       int numberOfRaters = 0;
20       for (Tuple2<String,Integer> t2 : pairsOfUserAndRating) {
21           numberOfRaters++;
22           listOfUsersAndRatings.add(t2);
23       }
24
25        // now emit (K, V) pairs
26       List<Tuple2<String,Tuple3<String,Integer,Integer>>> results =
27          new ArrayList<Tuple2<String,Tuple3<String,Integer,Integer>>>();
28       for (Tuple2<String,Integer> t2 : listOfUsersAndRatings) {
29           String user = t2._1;
30           Integer rating = t2._2;
31           Tuple3<String,Integer,Integer> t3 =
32             new Tuple3<String,Integer,Integer>(movie, rating, numberOfRaters);
33             results.add(new Tuple2<String, Tuple3<String,Integer,Integer>>
34               (user, t3));
35       }
36       return results;
37    }
38  });
```

To debug step 7, we use the `JavaPairRDD.collect()` method:

```
System.out.println("=== debug3: moviesGrouped: K = user, "+
    "V = Tuple3<movie, rating, numberOfRaters>   ===");
List<
     Tuple2<String,Tuple3<String,Integer,Integer>>
   > debug3 = usersRDD.collect();
for (Tuple2<String,Tuple3<String,Integer,Integer>> t2 : debug3) {
  System.out.println("debug3 key="+t2._1 + "\t value="+t2._2);
}
```

After we've executed step 7, usersRDD is a list of the following key-value pairs, which include the number of raters per movie. Here, K=user and V=(movie, rating, numberOfRaters):

```
{
  (user1, (movie1, 1, 2)),
  (user1, (movie2, 2, 2))
  (user1, (movie3, 3, 2)),
  (user2, (movie1, 1, 2)),
  (user2, (movie2, 2, 2)),
  (user2, (movie3, 3, 2)),
  (user2, (movie5, 5, 1)),
  ...
}
```

Step 8: Perform self-join

This step uses a very powerful feature of the Spark API: the join operation. A self-join is performed on usersRDD as follows (the join will be done on the user key):

```
joinedRDD = usersRDD.join(usersRDD);
```

where both usersRDD and joinedRDD are JavaRDD types. The signature of join() is given as:

```
public <W> JavaPairRDD<K,scala.Tuple2<V,W>> join(JavaPairRDD<K,W> other)
```

```
Description: Return an RDD containing all pairs of elements with matching
             keys in this and other. Each pair of elements will be returned
             as a (k, (v1, v2)) tuple, where (k, v1) is in this and (k, v2)
             is in other. Performs a hash join across the cluster.
```

Example 10-15 shows the self-join (which is needed to find combinations of (movie1, movie2)) implementation by JavaPairRDD.join(JavaPairRDD).

Example 10-15. Step 8: perform self-join

```
1    // Step 8: join usersRDD against itself to find all (movie1, movie2) pairs
2    // usersRDD = <K=user, V=<movie,rating,numberOfRaters>>
3    // The result will be joinedRDD = (user, T2((m1,r1,n1), (m2,r2,n2))).
4    // The join will be done on the "user" key.
5    JavaPairRDD<String,
6              Tuple2<Tuple3<String,Integer,Integer>,
7                     Tuple3<String,Integer,Integer>
8                  >
9            >
10           joinedRDD = usersRDD.join(usersRDD);
11   List<
12       Tuple2<String,
13           Tuple2<Tuple3<String,Integer,Integer>,
14                  Tuple3<String,Integer,Integer>
```

```
15                          >
16              >
17       > debug5 = joinedRDD.collect();
18     for (Tuple2<String, Tuple2<Tuple3<String,Integer,Integer>,
19                          Tuple3<String,Integer,Integer>>
20              > t2 : debug5) {
21       System.out.println("debug5 key="+t2._1 + "\t value="+t2._2);
22     }
```

After we've executed step 8, `joinedRDD` is a list of the following key-value pairs:

```
{
   (user1, [(movie1, 1, 2), (movie2, 2, 2)]),
   (user1, [(movie1, 1, 2), (movie3, 3, 2)]),
   (user1, [(movie2, 2, 2), (movie1, 1, 2)]),
   (user1, [(movie2, 2, 2), (movie3, 3, 2)]),
   (user1, [(movie3, 3, 2), (movie1, 1, 2)]),
   (user1, [(movie3, 3, 2), (movie2, 2, 2)]),
   ...
}
```

As you can see, for each K=user we have duplicate movie pairs; note that (movie1, movie2) is the same as (movie2, movie1). The next step will remove duplicates via the filter() method.

Step 9: Remove duplicate (movie1, movie2) pairs

In the previous step, we generated (movie1, movie2) pairs that have duplicates. This step removes those duplicates by using the JavaPairRDD.filter() method. The filter() method is defined as follows:

```
public JavaPairRDD<K,V> filter(Function<scala.Tuple2<K,V>,Boolean> f)

Description: Return a new RDD containing only the
            elements that satisfy a predicate.
```

Example 10-16 shows the filter implementation. The filter() method keeps (movie1, movie2) pairs only if movie1 < movie2.

Example 10-16. Step 9: remove duplicate (movie1, movie2) pairs

```
1     // Step 9: remove duplicate (movie1, movie2) pairs.
2     // Note that (movie1, movie2) and (movie2, movie1) are the same.
3     // Now we have filteredRDD = (user, T2((m1,r1,n1), (m2,r2,n2))),
4     // where m1 < m2, to guarantee that we will not have duplicate
5     // movie pairs per user.
6     JavaPairRDD<
7             String,
8             Tuple2<Tuple3<String,Integer,Integer>,
9                    Tuple3<String,Integer,Integer>
10            >
```

```
11              >
12              filteredRDD = joinedRDD.filter(new Function<
13          Tuple2<
14                  String,
15                  Tuple2<Tuple3<String,Integer,Integer>,
16                      Tuple3<String,Integer,Integer>
17                  >
18              >, Boolean>() {
19      public Boolean call(Tuple2<String,
20                      Tuple2<Tuple3<String,Integer,Integer>,
21                          Tuple3<String,Integer,Integer>
22                      >
23                  > s){
24          // to remove duplicates, make sure that movie1 < movie2
25          // for all (movie1, movie2) pairs
26          Tuple3<String,Integer,Integer> movie1 = s._2._1;
27          Tuple3<String,Integer,Integer> movie2 = s._2._2;
28          String movieName1 = movie1.first();
29          String movieName2 = movie2.first();
30          if (movieName1.compareTo(movieName2) < 0) {
31              return true;
32          }
33          else {
34              return false;
35          }
36      }
37  });
```

To debug step 9, we use the `JavaPairRDD.collect()` method:

```
List<
    Tuple2<
        String,
        Tuple2<Tuple3<String,Integer,Integer>,
            Tuple3<String,Integer,Integer>>
        >
    > debug55 = filteredRDD.collect();
for (Tuple2<String,
        Tuple2<Tuple3<String,Integer,Integer>,
            Tuple3<String,Integer,Integer>>
        > t2 : debug55) {
    System.out.println("debug55 key="+t2._1 + "\t value="+t2._2);
}
```

After we've executed step 9, `filteredRDD` is a list of the following key-value pairs (without duplicates):

```
{
    (user1, [(movie1, 1, 2), (movie2, 2, 2)]),
    (user1, [(movie1, 1, 2), (movie3, 3, 2)]),
    (user1, [(movie2, 2, 2), (movie3, 3, 2)]),
    ...
}
```

Step 10: Generate all (movie1, movie2) combinations

For each (`movie1`, `movie2`) pair, this step (shown in Example 10-17) creates some derived data, which will be used for calculating three correlations: Pearson, cosine, and Jaccard. We achieve this through another transformation by using `JavaPairRDD.mapToPair()`.

Example 10-17. Step 10: generate all (movie1, movie2) combinations.

```
1    //Step 10: generate all (movie1, movie2) combinations
2    // The goal of this step is to create (K,V) pairs of
3    //    K: Tuple2(movie1, movie2)
4    //    V: Tuple7(movie1.rating,
5    //             movie1.numOfRaters,
6    //             movie2.rating,
7    //             movie2.numOfRaters,
8    //             ratingProduct,
9    //             rating1Squared, = movie1.rating * movie1.rating
10   //             rating2Squared  = movie2.rating * movie2.rating
11   //             )
12   // PairFunction<T, K, V>
13   // T => Tuple2<K, V>
14   // The user attribute will be dropped at this phase.
15   //          K                    V
16   JavaPairRDD<Tuple2<String,String>,
17          Tuple7<Integer,Integer,Integer,Integer,
18                  Integer,Integer,Integer>>
19     moviePairs = filteredRDD.mapToPair(new PairFunction
20        <Tuple2<String,Tuple2<Tuple3<String,Integer,Integer>,
21                          Tuple3<String,Integer,Integer>>>, // T
22        Tuple2<String,String>,                            // K
23        Tuple7<Integer,Integer,Integer,Integer,
24                  Integer,Integer,Integer> // V
25        >() {
26    public  Tuple2<Tuple2<String,String>, Tuple7<Integer,Integer,Integer,
27                  Integer,Integer,Integer,Integer>>
28      call(Tuple2<String,Tuple2<Tuple3<String,Integer,Integer>,
29                          Tuple3<String,Integer,Integer>>> s) {
30        // String user = s._1; // will be dropped
31        Tuple3<String,Integer,Integer> movie1 = s._2._1;
32        Tuple3<String,Integer,Integer> movie2 = s._2._2;
33        Tuple2<String,String> m1m2Key =
34          new Tuple2<String,String>(movie1.first(), movie2.first());
35        // movie1.rating * movie2.rating;
36        int ratingProduct = movie1.second() * movie2.second();
37        // movie1.rating * movie1.rating;
38        int rating1Squared = movie1.second() * movie1.second();
39        // movie2.rating * movie2.rating;
40        int rating2Squared = movie2.second() * movie2.second();
41        Tuple7<Integer,Integer,Integer,Integer,Integer,Integer,Integer> t7 =
42          new Tuple7<Integer,Integer,Integer,Integer,
```

```
43                         Integer,Integer,Integer>(
44               movie1.second(), // movie1.rating,
45               movie1.third(),  // movie1.numberOfRaters,
46               movie2.second(), // movie2.rating,
47               movie2.third(),  // movie2.numberOfRaters,
48               ratingProduct,   // movie1.rating * movie2.rating
49               rating1Squared,  // movie1.rating * movie1.rating
50               rating2Squared   // movie2.rating * movie2.rating
51           );
52       return new Tuple2<Tuple2<String,String>,
53                     Tuple7<Integer,Integer,Integer,Integer,
54                         Integer,Integer,Integer>>(m1m2Key, t7);
55     }
56  });
```

Step 11: Group movie pairs

This step, shown in Example 10-18, groups data by movie pairs, (movie1, movie2), to gather the data needed for computing correlations.

Example 10-18. Step 11: group movie pairs

```
1   //Step 11: group moviePairs by key(movie1,movie2)
2   JavaPairRDD<Tuple2<String,String>,
3           Iterable<Tuple7<Integer,Integer,Integer,Integer,
4                       Integer,Integer,Integer>>
5       > corrRDD = moviePairs.groupByKey();
```

Step 12: Calculate correlations

This step, shown in Example 10-19, uses three different correlation algorithms to find similarities between every pair of movies. There is no golden rule for selecting a correlation algorithm for a specific application. You should select a correlation algorithm that fits your application environment.

Example 10-19. Step 12: calculate correlations

```
1    // Step 12: calculate correlation/similarities between every
2    // two movies: (movie1,movie2)
3    // coor.key = (movie1,movie2)
4    // corr.value = (pearson, cosine, jaccard) correlations
5    JavaPairRDD<Tuple2<String,String>, Tuple3<Double,Double,Double>> corr =
6        corrRDD.mapValues(new Function<
7            Iterable<Tuple7<Integer,Integer,Integer,Integer,
8                         Integer,Integer,Integer>>,    // input
9            Tuple3<Double,Double,Double>               // output
10       >() {
11     public Tuple3<Double,Double,Double> call(
12       Iterable<Tuple7<Integer,Integer,Integer,
13                    Integer,Integer,Integer,Integer>> s) {
```

```
14          return calculateCorrelations(s);
15      }
16  });
```

Step 13: Print final results

As our last step, we print the final results. Example 10-20 illustrates.

Example 10-20. Step 13: print final results

```
1   // Step 13: print final results
2   System.out.println("=== Movie Correlations ===");
3   List<
4       Tuple2< Tuple2<String,String>, Tuple3<Double,Double,Double>>
5       > debug6 = corr.collect();
6   for (Tuple2<Tuple2<String,String>, Tuple3<Double,Double,Double>> t2 : debug6) {
7       System.out.println("debug5 key="+t2._1 + "\t value="+t2._2);
8   }
9
10  corr.saveAsTextFile("/movies/output");
```

Helper methods

Example 10-21 defines the helper method `calculateCorrelations()`.

Example 10-21. Helper method: calculateCorrelations()

```
1   static Tuple3<Double,Double,Double> calculateCorrelations(
2       Iterable<Tuple7<Integer,Integer,Integer,Integer,Integer,Integer,Integer>>
3       values) {
4       int groupSize = 0;   // length of each vector
5       int dotProduct = 0;  // sum of ratingProd
6       int rating1Sum = 0;  // sum of rating1
7       int rating2Sum = 0;  // sum of rating2
8       int rating1NormSq = 0;  // sum of rating1Squared
9       int rating2NormSq = 0;  // sum of rating2Squared
10      int maxNumOfumRaters1 = 0;  // max of numOfRaters1
11      int maxNumOfumRaters2 = 0;  // max of numOfRaters2
12      for (Tuple7<Integer,Integer,Integer,Integer,Integer,Integer,Integer> t7 :
13          values) {
14              //Tuple7(<rating1>:          t7._1
15              //       <numOfRaters1>:      t7._2
16              //       <rating2>:           t7._3
17              //       <numOfRaters2> :     t7._4
18              //       <ratingProduct> :    t7._5
19              //       <rating1Squared> :   t7._6
20              //       <rating2Squared>):   t7._7
21          groupSize++;
22          dotProduct += t7._5;  // ratingProduct;
23          rating1Sum += t7._1;  // rating1;
24          rating2Sum += t7._3;  // rating2;
```

```
25            rating1NormSq += t7._6;   // rating1Squared;
26            rating2NormSq += t7._7;   // rating2Squared;
27            int numOfRaters1 = t7._2;
28            if (numOfRaters1 > maxNumOfumRaters1) {
29                maxNumOfumRaters1 = numOfRaters1;
30            }
31            int numOfRaters2 = t7._4;
32            if (numOfRaters2 > maxNumOfumRaters2) {
33                maxNumOfumRaters2 = numOfRaters2;
34            }
35     }
36
37     double pearson = calculatePearsonCorrelation(
38                groupSize,
39                dotProduct,
40                rating1Sum,
41                rating2Sum,
42                rating1NormSq,
43                rating2NormSq);
44
45     double cosine = calculateCosineCorrelation(dotProduct,
46                                        Math.sqrt(rating1NormSq),
47                                        Math.sqrt(rating2NormSq));
48
49     double jaccard = calculateJaccardCorrelation(groupSize,
50                                        maxNumOfumRaters1,
51                                        maxNumOfumRaters2);
52
53     return new Tuple3<Double,Double,Double>(pearson, cosine, jaccard);
54 }
```

Example 10-22 defines the helper method calculatePearsonCorrelation(), which calculates the Pearson correlation between two movies.

Example 10-22. Helper method: calculatePearsonCorrelation()

```
1   static double calculatePearsonCorrelation(
2                double size,
3                double dotProduct,
4                double rating1Sum,
5                double rating2Sum,
6                double rating1NormSq,
7                double rating2NormSq) {
8
9      double numerator = size * dotProduct - rating1Sum * rating2Sum;
10       double denominator =
11          Math.sqrt(size * rating1NormSq - rating1Sum * rating1Sum) *
12          Math.sqrt(size * rating2NormSq - rating2Sum * rating2Sum);
13       return numerator / denominator;
14    }
```

Example 10-23 defines the helper method `calculateCosineCorrelation()`.

Example 10-23. Helper method: calculateCosineCorrelation()

```
1   /**
2    * The cosine similarity between two vectors A, B is
3    *    dotProduct(A, B) / (norm(A) * norm(B))
4    */
5   static double calculateCosineCorrelation(double dotProduct,
6                                             double rating1Norm,
7                                             double rating2Norm) {
8     return dotProduct / (rating1Norm * rating2Norm);
9   }
```

Example 10-24 defines the helper method `calculateJaccardCorrelation()`, which calculates the Jaccard correlation between two movies.

Example 10-24. Helper method: calculateJaccardCorrelation()

```
1   /**
2    * The Jaccard similarity between two sets A, B is
3    *    |Intersection(A, B)| / |Union(A, B)|
4    */
5   static double calculateJaccardCorrelation(double inCommon,
6                                             double totalA,
7                                             double totalB) {
8     double union = totalA + totalB - inCommon;
9     return inCommon / union;
10  }
```

Sample Run of Spark Program

The following subsections present the input, script, sample run log, and expected output of our Spark program.

HDFS input

To refresh your memory, we assume that our input data is stored in HDFS as a text file:

```
# hadoop fs -cat /movies.txt
User1    Movie1    3
User1    Movie2    4
User1    Movie3    3
User2    Movie1    2
User2    Movie2    5
User2    Movie3    3
User2    Movie5    5
User3    Movie1    2
User3    Movie2    3
```

```
User3    Movie3    2
User4    Movie1    5
User4    Movie2    3
User4    Movie3    3
User4    Movie4    2
User4    Movie5    3
```

Script

Here is the script for our Spark program:

```
# cat run_movies.sh
#!/bin/bash
export JAVA_HOME=/usr/java/jdk7
export SPARK_HOME=/home/hadoop/spark-1.1.0
export SPARK_MASTER=spark://myserver100:7077
BOOK_HOME=/mp/data-algorithms-book
APP_JAR=$BOOK_HOME/dist/data_algorithms_book.jar
MOVIES=/movies.txt
# Run on a Spark standalone cluster
$SPARK_HOME/bin/spark-submit \
  --class org.dataalgorithms.chap10.spark.MovieRecommendationsWithJoin \
  --master $SPARK_MASTER \
  --executor-memory 2G \
  --total-executor-cores 20 \
$APP_JAR \
$MOVIES
```

Log of sample run

The actual output from a sample run is shown here; it has been edited to fit the page:

```
# ./run_movies.sh
usersRatingsInputFile=/movies.txt
...
14/06/07 23:18:13 INFO scheduler.DAGScheduler: Stage 0
  (collect at MovieRecommendationsWithJoin.java:73) finished in 4.199 s
14/06/07 23:18:13 INFO spark.SparkContext: Job finished: collect at
  MovieRecommendationsWithJoin.java:73, took 4.290270699 s
debug1 key=Movie1    value=(User1,3)
debug1 key=Movie2    value=(User1,4)
debug1 key=Movie3    value=(User1,3)
debug1 key=Movie1    value=(User2,2)
debug1 key=Movie2    value=(User2,5)
debug1 key=Movie3    value=(User2,3)
debug1 key=Movie5    value=(User2,5)
debug1 key=Movie1    value=(User3,2)
debug1 key=Movie2    value=(User3,3)
debug1 key=Movie3    value=(User3,2)
debug1 key=Movie1    value=(User4,5)
debug1 key=Movie2    value=(User4,3)
debug1 key=Movie3    value=(User4,3)
debug1 key=Movie4    value=(User4,2)
```

```
debug1 key=Movie5     value=(User4,3)
=== debug2: moviesGrouped: K = <movie>, V = Iterable<Tuple2<user, rating>> ===
14/06/07 23:18:13 INFO spark.SparkContext: Starting job: collect at
  MovieRecommendationsWithJoin.java:85
14/06/07 23:18:13 INFO scheduler.DAGScheduler: Registering RDD 2
  (mapToPair at MovieRecommendationsWithJoin.java:56)
...
14/06/07 23:18:13 INFO scheduler.DAGScheduler: Stage 1

  (collect at MovieRecommendationsWithJoin.java:85) finished in 0.752 s
14/06/07 23:18:13 INFO spark.SparkContext: Job finished: collect at
  MovieRecommendationsWithJoin.java:85, took 0.833602896 s
debug2 key=Movie2     value=[(User1,4), (User2,5), (User3,3), (User4,3)]
debug2 key=Movie5     value=[(User2,5), (User4,3)]
debug2 key=Movie4     value=[(User4,2)]
debug2 key=Movie3     value=[(User1,3), (User2,3), (User3,2), (User4,3)]
debug2 key=Movie1     value=[(User1,3), (User2,2), (User3,2), (User4,5)]
=== debug3: moviesGrouped: K = user,  V = Tuple3<movie, rating, numberOfRaters>
14/06/07 23:18:13 INFO spark.SparkContext: Starting job: collect at
..MovieRecommendationsWithJoin.java:126
...
14/06/07 23:18:14 INFO scheduler.DAGScheduler: Stage 3
  (collect at MovieRecommendationsWithJoin.java:126) finished in 0.141 s
14/06/07 23:18:14 INFO spark.SparkContext: Job finished:
  collect at MovieRecommendationsWithJoin.java:126, took 0.159691236 s
debug3 key=User1     value=Tuple3[Movie2,4,4]
debug3 key=User2     value=Tuple3[Movie2,5,4]
debug3 key=User3     value=Tuple3[Movie2,3,4]
debug3 key=User4     value=Tuple3[Movie2,3,4]
debug3 key=User2     value=Tuple3[Movie5,5,2]
debug3 key=User4     value=Tuple3[Movie5,3,2]
debug3 key=User4     value=Tuple3[Movie4,2,1]
debug3 key=User1     value=Tuple3[Movie3,3,4]
debug3 key=User2     value=Tuple3[Movie3,3,4]
debug3 key=User3     value=Tuple3[Movie3,2,4]
debug3 key=User4     value=Tuple3[Movie3,3,4]
debug3 key=User1     value=Tuple3[Movie1,3,4]
debug3 key=User2     value=Tuple3[Movie1,2,4]
debug3 key=User3     value=Tuple3[Movie1,2,4]
debug3 key=User4     value=Tuple3[Movie1,5,4]
14/06/07 23:18:14 INFO spark.SparkContext: Starting job: collect
  at MovieRecommendationsWithJoin.java:142
...
14/06/07 23:18:15 INFO scheduler.DAGScheduler: Stage 5 (collect at
  MovieRecommendationsWithJoin.java:142) finished in 0.728 s
14/06/07 23:18:15 INFO spark.SparkContext: Job finished: collect at
  MovieRecommendationsWithJoin.java:142, took 0.846712724 s

debug5 key=User3     value=(Tuple3[Movie2,3,4],Tuple3[Movie2,3,4])
debug5 key=User3     value=(Tuple3[Movie2,3,4],Tuple3[Movie3,2,4])
debug5 key=User3     value=(Tuple3[Movie2,3,4],Tuple3[Movie1,2,4])
debug5 key=User3     value=(Tuple3[Movie3,2,4],Tuple3[Movie2,3,4])
```

```
debug5 key=User3    value=(Tuple3[Movie3,2,4],Tuple3[Movie3,2,4])
debug5 key=User3    value=(Tuple3[Movie3,2,4],Tuple3[Movie1,2,4])
debug5 key=User3    value=(Tuple3[Movie1,2,4],Tuple3[Movie2,3,4])
debug5 key=User3    value=(Tuple3[Movie1,2,4],Tuple3[Movie3,2,4])
debug5 key=User3    value=(Tuple3[Movie1,2,4],Tuple3[Movie1,2,4])
debug5 key=User2    value=(Tuple3[Movie2,5,4],Tuple3[Movie2,5,4])
debug5 key=User2    value=(Tuple3[Movie2,5,4],Tuple3[Movie5,5,2])
debug5 key=User2    value=(Tuple3[Movie2,5,4],Tuple3[Movie3,3,4])
debug5 key=User2    value=(Tuple3[Movie2,5,4],Tuple3[Movie1,2,4])
debug5 key=User2    value=(Tuple3[Movie5,5,2],Tuple3[Movie2,5,4])
debug5 key=User2    value=(Tuple3[Movie5,5,2],Tuple3[Movie5,5,2])
debug5 key=User2    value=(Tuple3[Movie5,5,2],Tuple3[Movie3,3,4])
debug5 key=User2    value=(Tuple3[Movie5,5,2],Tuple3[Movie1,2,4])
debug5 key=User2    value=(Tuple3[Movie3,3,4],Tuple3[Movie2,5,4])
debug5 key=User2    value=(Tuple3[Movie3,3,4],Tuple3[Movie5,5,2])
debug5 key=User2    value=(Tuple3[Movie3,3,4],Tuple3[Movie3,3,4])
debug5 key=User2    value=(Tuple3[Movie3,3,4],Tuple3[Movie1,2,4])
debug5 key=User2    value=(Tuple3[Movie1,2,4],Tuple3[Movie2,5,4])
debug5 key=User2    value=(Tuple3[Movie1,2,4],Tuple3[Movie5,5,2])
debug5 key=User2    value=(Tuple3[Movie1,2,4],Tuple3[Movie3,3,4])
debug5 key=User2    value=(Tuple3[Movie1,2,4],Tuple3[Movie1,2,4])
debug5 key=User4    value=(Tuple3[Movie2,3,4],Tuple3[Movie2,3,4])
debug5 key=User4    value=(Tuple3[Movie2,3,4],Tuple3[Movie5,3,2])
debug5 key=User4    value=(Tuple3[Movie2,3,4],Tuple3[Movie4,2,1])
debug5 key=User4    value=(Tuple3[Movie2,3,4],Tuple3[Movie3,3,4])
debug5 key=User4    value=(Tuple3[Movie2,3,4],Tuple3[Movie1,5,4])
debug5 key=User4    value=(Tuple3[Movie5,3,2],Tuple3[Movie2,3,4])
debug5 key=User4    value=(Tuple3[Movie5,3,2],Tuple3[Movie5,3,2])
debug5 key=User4    value=(Tuple3[Movie5,3,2],Tuple3[Movie4,2,1])
debug5 key=User4    value=(Tuple3[Movie5,3,2],Tuple3[Movie3,3,4])
debug5 key=User4    value=(Tuple3[Movie5,3,2],Tuple3[Movie1,5,4])
debug5 key=User4    value=(Tuple3[Movie4,2,1],Tuple3[Movie2,3,4])
debug5 key=User4    value=(Tuple3[Movie4,2,1],Tuple3[Movie5,3,2])
debug5 key=User4    value=(Tuple3[Movie4,2,1],Tuple3[Movie4,2,1])
debug5 key=User4  value=(Tuple3[Movie4,2,1],Tuple3[Movie3,3,4])
debug5 key=User4  value=(Tuple3[Movie4,2,1],Tuple3[Movie1,5,4])
debug5 key=User4  value=(Tuple3[Movie3,3,4],Tuple3[Movie2,3,4])
debug5 key=User4  value=(Tuple3[Movie3,3,4],Tuple3[Movie5,3,2])
debug5 key=User4  value=(Tuple3[Movie3,3,4],Tuple3[Movie4,2,1])
debug5 key=User4  value=(Tuple3[Movie3,3,4],Tuple3[Movie3,3,4])
debug5 key=User4  value=(Tuple3[Movie3,3,4],Tuple3[Movie1,5,4])
debug5 key=User4  value=(Tuple3[Movie1,5,4],Tuple3[Movie2,3,4])
debug5 key=User4  value=(Tuple3[Movie1,5,4],Tuple3[Movie5,3,2])
debug5 key=User4  value=(Tuple3[Movie1,5,4],Tuple3[Movie4,2,1])
debug5 key=User4  value=(Tuple3[Movie1,5,4],Tuple3[Movie3,3,4])
debug5 key=User4  value=(Tuple3[Movie1,5,4],Tuple3[Movie1,5,4])
debug5 key=User1  value=(Tuple3[Movie2,4,4],Tuple3[Movie2,4,4])
debug5 key=User1  value=(Tuple3[Movie2,4,4],Tuple3[Movie3,3,4])
debug5 key=User1  value=(Tuple3[Movie2,4,4],Tuple3[Movie1,3,4])
debug5 key=User1  value=(Tuple3[Movie3,3,4],Tuple3[Movie2,4,4])
debug5 key=User1  value=(Tuple3[Movie3,3,4],Tuple3[Movie3,3,4])
debug5 key=User1  value=(Tuple3[Movie3,3,4],Tuple3[Movie1,3,4])
```

```
debug5 key=User1    value=(Tuple3[Movie1,3,4],Tuple3[Movie2,4,4])
debug5 key=User1    value=(Tuple3[Movie1,3,4],Tuple3[Movie3,3,4])
debug5 key=User1    value=(Tuple3[Movie1,3,4],Tuple3[Movie1,3,4])
14/06/07 23:18:15 INFO spark.SparkContext: Starting job: collect at
  MovieRecommendationsWithJoin.java:171
...
14/06/07 23:18:15 INFO scheduler.DAGScheduler: Stage 9 (collect at
  MovieRecommendationsWithJoin.java:171) finished in 0.109 s
14/06/07 23:18:15 INFO spark.SparkContext: Job finished: collect at
  MovieRecommendationsWithJoin.java:171, took 0.13069563 s
debug55 key=User3    value=(Tuple3[Movie2,3,4],Tuple3[Movie3,2,4])
debug55 key=User3    value=(Tuple3[Movie1,2,4],Tuple3[Movie2,3,4])
debug55 key=User3    value=(Tuple3[Movie1,2,4],Tuple3[Movie3,2,4])
debug55 key=User2    value=(Tuple3[Movie2,5,4],Tuple3[Movie5,5,2])
debug55 key=User2    value=(Tuple3[Movie2,5,4],Tuple3[Movie3,3,4])
debug55 key=User2    value=(Tuple3[Movie3,3,4],Tuple3[Movie5,5,2])
debug55 key=User2    value=(Tuple3[Movie1,2,4],Tuple3[Movie2,5,4])
debug55 key=User2    value=(Tuple3[Movie1,2,4],Tuple3[Movie5,5,2])
debug55 key=User2    value=(Tuple3[Movie1,2,4],Tuple3[Movie3,3,4])
debug55 key=User4    value=(Tuple3[Movie2,3,4],Tuple3[Movie5,3,2])
debug55 key=User4    value=(Tuple3[Movie2,3,4],Tuple3[Movie4,2,1])
debug55 key=User4    value=(Tuple3[Movie2,3,4],Tuple3[Movie3,3,4])
debug55 key=User4    value=(Tuple3[Movie4,2,1],Tuple3[Movie5,3,2])
debug55 key=User4    value=(Tuple3[Movie3,3,4],Tuple3[Movie5,3,2])
debug55 key=User4    value=(Tuple3[Movie3,3,4],Tuple3[Movie4,2,1])
debug55 key=User4    value=(Tuple3[Movie1,5,4],Tuple3[Movie2,3,4])
debug55 key=User4    value=(Tuple3[Movie1,5,4],Tuple3[Movie5,3,2])
debug55 key=User4    value=(Tuple3[Movie1,5,4],Tuple3[Movie4,2,1])
debug55 key=User4    value=(Tuple3[Movie1,5,4],Tuple3[Movie3,3,4])
debug55 key=User1    value=(Tuple3[Movie2,4,4],Tuple3[Movie3,3,4])
debug55 key=User1    value=(Tuple3[Movie1,3,4],Tuple3[Movie2,4,4])
debug55 key=User1    value=(Tuple3[Movie1,3,4],Tuple3[Movie3,3,4])
=== Movie Correlations ===
14/06/07 23:18:15 INFO spark.SparkContext: Starting job: collect at
  MovieRecommendationsWithJoin.java:242
...
14/06/07 23:18:15 INFO scheduler.DAGScheduler: Stage 13 (collect
  at MovieRecommendationsWithJoin.java:242) finished in 0.075 s
14/06/07 23:18:15 INFO spark.SparkContext: Job finished: collect
  at MovieRecommendationsWithJoin.java:242, took 0.216924159 s
debug5 key=(Movie2,Movie3)
      value=Tuple3[0.5222329678670935,0.9820699844444069,1.0]
debug5 key=(Movie1,Movie3)
      value=Tuple3[0.47140452079103173,0.9422657923052785,1.0]
debug5 key=(Movie3,Movie4)
      value=Tuple3[NaN,1.0,0.25]
debug5 key=(Movie3,Movie5)
      value=Tuple3[NaN,0.970142500145332,0.5]
debug5 key=(Movie4,Movie5)
      value=Tuple3[NaN,1.0,0.5]
debug5 key=(Movie1,Movie2)
      value=Tuple3[-0.492365963917331,0.8638091589670809,1.0]
```

```
debug5 key=(Movie2,Movie5)
       value=Tuple3[1.0,1.0,0.5]
debug5 key=(Movie1,Movie5)
       value=Tuple3[-1.0,0.7961621941231025,0.5]
debug5 key=(Movie1,Movie4)
       value=Tuple3[NaN,1.0,0.25]
debug5 key=(Movie2,Movie4)
       value=Tuple3[NaN,1.0,0.25]
...
14/06/07 23:18:16 INFO scheduler.DAGScheduler: Stage 18 (saveAsTextFile at
  MovieRecommendationsWithJoin.java:247) finished in 1.014 s
14/06/07 23:18:16 INFO spark.SparkContext: Job finished: saveAsTextFile at
  MovieRecommendationsWithJoin.java:247, took 1.131578238 s
```

HDFS output

The following is the expected HDFS output of our Spark program:

```
# hadoop fs -ls /movies/output/
Found 2 items
-rw-r--r--   ...           0 2014-06-07 23:18 /movies/output/_SUCCESS
-rw-r--r--   ...         504 2014-06-07 23:18 /movies/output/part-00000
# hadoop fs -cat /movies/output/part-00000
((Movie2,Movie3),Tuple3[0.5222329678670935,0.9820699844444069,1.0])
((Movie1,Movie3),Tuple3[0.47140452079103173,0.9422657923052785,1.0])
((Movie3,Movie4),Tuple3[NaN,1.0,0.25])
((Movie3,Movie5),Tuple3[NaN,0.970142500145332,0.5])
((Movie4,Movie5),Tuple3[NaN,1.0,0.5])
((Movie1,Movie2),Tuple3[-0.492365963917331,0.8638091589670809,1.0])
((Movie2,Movie5),Tuple3[1.0,1.0,0.5])
((Movie1,Movie5),Tuple3[-1.0,0.7961621941231025,0.5])
((Movie1,Movie4),Tuple3[NaN,1.0,0.25])
((Movie2,Movie4),Tuple3[NaN,1.0,0.25])
```

This chapter presented basic distributed recommendation algorithms using similarity measures such as the Pearson correlation coefficient and Jaccard and cosine similarity. Note that to build realistic recommendation engines, you need to consider an additional set of metadata, such as actor/actress names, director, type of movie, and other related attributes.

The next chapter shows you how to use Markov models to predict future events.

## CHAPTER 11

Smarter Email Marketing with the Markov Model

This chapter will show how the Markov model (in its simplest form, known as the *Markov chain*) can be used to predict the "next smart email marketing date" for customers based on their transaction history. Given a set of random variables (such as customers' last purchase dates), the Markov model indicates that the distribution for this variable (i.e., the last purchase date) depends only on the distribution of the previous state (another last purchase date). For this "smarter email marketing" problem, two distinct solutions are provided:

- A MapReduce/Hadoop solution using the classic `map()` and `reduce()` functions
- A Spark solution using a directed acyclic graph (an arbitrary set of transformations and actions)

In writing this chapter, I was inspired by Pranab Ghosh's blog post "Smarter Email Marketing with Markov Model" (*http://bit.ly/ghosh_markov*). For the implementation of the MapReduce phases in this chapter, I developed brand new modular Java classes to demonstrate the core values (such as sorting reduced values through MapReduce's secondary sort technique, defining a custom partitioner class, and defining a grouping comparator class). Therefore, given a customer's transaction history, represented by (`purchase-date, amount-purchased`), our goal here is to use MapReduce and the Markov model to predict the next effective date to send a marketing email to that customer. This is kind of a machine learning algorithm. Typically, machine learning–based solutions consist of two distinct phases:

- Phase 1: build a model by using historical training data.
- Phase 2: make a prediction for the next new data using the model built in phase 1.

Markov Chains in a Nutshell

Let $S = \{S_1, S_2, S_3, ...\}$ be a set of finite states. We want to collect the following probabilities:

$$P\left(S_n | S_{n-1}, S_{n-2}, ..., S_1\right)$$

Markov's first-order assumption is the following:

$$P\left(S_n | S_{n-1}, S_{n-2}, ..., S_1\right) \approx P\left(S_n | S_{n-1}\right)$$

This approximation states the *Markov property*: the state of the system at time $t + 1$ depends only on the state of the system at time t.

The Markov second-order assumption is the following:

$$P\left(S_n | S_{n-1}, S_{n-2}, ..., S_1\right) \approx P\left(S_n | S_{n-1}, S_{n-2}\right)$$

Now, we can express the joint probability using the Markov assumption:

$$P\left(S_1, S_2, ..., S_n\right) = \prod_{i=1}^{n} P\left(S_i, S_{i-1}\right)$$

Markov random processes can be summarized as follows:[1]

- A random sequence has the Markov property if its distribution is determined solely by its current state. Any random process having this property is called a *Markov random process*.
- For observable state sequences (i.e., when the state is known from data), this leads to a *Markov chain model*, which we will use to predict the next effective email marketing date.

---

[1] Based on slides by Mehmet Yunus Dnmez: *http://bit.ly/hidden_markov_mod*.

- For nonobservable states, this leads to a *hidden Markov model* (HMM).

Now, let's formalize the Markov chain that we will use in this chapter. Our Markov chain has three components:

State space
A finite set of states $S = \{S_1, S_2, S_3, ...\}$

Transition probabilities
A function $f: S \times S \to R$ such that:

- $0 \le f(a, b) \le 1$ for all $a, b \in S$
- $\sum_{b \in S} f(a, b) = 1$ for every $a \in S$

Initial distribution
A function $g: S \times R$ such that:

- $0 \le g(a) \le 1$ for every $a \in S$
- $\sum_{a \in S} g(a) = 1$

Then a Markov chain is a random process in S such that:

- At time 0 the state of the chain is distributed according to function g.
- If at time t the state of the chain is a, then at time $t + 1$ it will be at state b with a probability of $f(a, b)$ for every $b \in S$.

Let's consider an example: let a weather pattern for a city consist of four states— sunny, cloudy, rainy, foggy—and further assume that the state does not change for a day. The sum of each row shown in Table 11-1 is 1.00.

Table 11-1. City weather pattern (one state per day)

Today's weather Tomorrow's weather	sunny	rainy	cloudy	foggy
sunny	0.6	0.1	0.2	0.1
rainy	0.5	0.2	0.2	0.1
cloudy	0.1	0.7	0.1	0.1
foggy	0.0	0.3	0.4	0.3

Now, we can answer the following questions:

- Given that today is sunny, what is the probability that tomorrow will be cloudy and the day after will be foggy? We compute this as follows:

$P\left(S_2 = \text{cloudy}, S_3 = \text{foggy} | S_1 = \text{sunny}\right)$

$= P\left(S_3 = \text{foggy} | S_2 = \text{cloudy}, S_1 = \text{sunny}\right) \times$

$P\left(S_2 = \text{cloudy} | S_1 = \text{sunny}\right)$

$= P\left(S_3 = \text{foggy} | S_2 = \text{cloudy}\right) \times$

$P\left(S_2 = \text{cloudy} | S_1 = \text{sunny}\right)$

$= 0.1 \times 0.2$

$= 0.02$

- Given that today is foggy, what is the probability that it will be rainy two days from now? (This means that the second day can be any of sunny, cloudy, rainy, or foggy.)

$P\left(S_3 = \text{foggy} | S_1 = \text{foggy}\right) =$

$P\left(S_3 = \text{foggy}, S_2 = \text{sunny} | S_1 = \text{foggy}\right) +$

$P\left(S_3 = \text{foggy}, S_2 = \text{cloudy} | S_1 = \text{foggy}\right) +$

$P\left(S_3 = \text{foggy}, S_2 = \text{rainy} | S_1 = \text{foggy}\right) +$

$P\left(S_3 = \text{foggy}, S_2 = \text{foggy} | S_1 = \text{foggy}\right) +$

$= P\left(S_3 = \text{foggy} | S_2 = \text{sunny}\right) \times P\left(S_2 = \text{sunny} | S_1 = \text{foggy}\right) +$

$P\left(S_3 = \text{foggy} | S_2 = \text{cloudy}\right) \times P\left(S_2 = \text{cloudy} | S_1 = \text{foggy}\right) +$

$P\left(S_3 = \text{foggy} | S_2 = \text{rainy}\right) \times P\left(S_2 = \text{rainy} | S_1 = \text{foggy}\right) +$

$P\left(S_3 = \text{foggy} | S_2 = \text{foggy}\right) \times P\left(S_2 = \text{foggy} | S_1 = \text{foggy}\right)$

$= 0.1 \times 0.0 +$

$0.1 \times 0.4 +$

$0.1 \times 0.3 +$

0.3×0.3

$= 0.00 + 0.04 + 0.03 + 0.09$

$= 0.16$

One of the main goals of this chapter is to build the model (that is, the probability transition table) that will define $f(a, b)$ for all $a \in S$. Once we have created this model, the rest is easy.

Markov Model Using MapReduce

Assume we have historical customer transaction data that includes transaction-id, customer-id, purchase-date, and amount. Therefore, each input record will have the following format:

```
<customerID><,><transactionID><,><purchaseDate><,><amount>
```

The entire solution involves two MapReduce jobs and a set of Ruby scripts (the Ruby scripts were developed by Pranab Ghosh; I will provide pointers for them as we use them).

The entire workflow is depicted in Figure 11-1, and our solution (the steps shown in Figure 11-1) is outlined here:

1. We use a script to generate fake customer data (1).

2. The MapReduce projection (2) accepts customer data (1) as an input and generates sorted data (3). The sorted data (3) consists of purchase dates in ascending order.

3. The state converter script (4) accepts the sorted data (3) and generates the state sequence (5).

4. The MapReduce Markov state transition model (6) accepts the state sequence (5) as an input and generates a Markov chain model (7). This model enables us to predict the next state.

5. Finally, the next state prediction script (9), which accepts new customer data (8) and the Markov chain model (7), predicts the best date for our next marketing email.

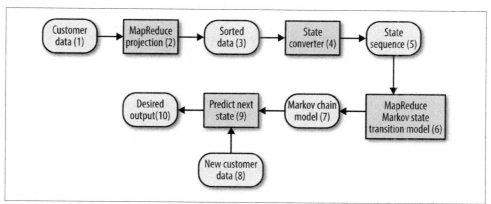

Figure 11-1. Markov workflow

Generating Time-Ordered Transactions with MapReduce

The goal of this MapReduce phase is to accept historical customer transaction data and generate the following output for every `customer-id`:

customerID (Date$_1$, Amount$_1$);(Date$_2$, Amount$_2$);...(Date$_N$, Amount$_N$)

such that:

Date$_1$ ≤ Date$_2$ ≤ ... ≤ Date$_N$

The MapReduce output is sorted by purchase date in ascending order. Generating sorted output can be accomplished in two ways: each reducer can sort its output by the purchase date in ascending order (here you need enough RAM to hold all your data for sorting), or you can use MapReduce's secondary sorting technique to sort data by date (with this option, you do not need much RAM at all). After the output is generated, we will convert (`Date, Amount`) into a two-letter symbol (this step is done by a script) that stands for a Markov chain state. I will present solutions for both cases. The final output generated from this phase will have the following format:

customerID, State$_1$, State$_2$, ..., State$_n$

Example 11-1 defines the `map()` function for our time-ordered transactions.

Example 11-1. Time-ordered transactions: map() function

```
1 /**
2  * @param key is ignored
3  * @param value is transaction-id, customer-id, purchase-date, amount
4  */
5 map(key, value) {
6     pair(Date, Integer) pair = (value.purchase-date, value.amount);
7     emit(value.customer-id, pair);
8 }
```

Example 11-2 defines the `reduce()` function for our time-ordered transactions.

Example 11-2. Time-ordered transactions: reduce() function

```
1 /**
2  * @param key is a customer-id
3  * @param values is a list of pairs of Pair(Date, Integer)
4  */
5 reduce(String key, List<Pair<Date, Integer>> values) {
```

```
6    sortedValues = sortbyDateInAscendingOrder(values);
7    emit(key, sortedValues);
8 }
```

Hadoop Solution 1: Time-Ordered Transactions

In this solution, mappers emit key-value pairs, where the key is a customer-id and the value is a pair of (purchase-date, amount). Data arrives at the reducers unsorted. This solution performs transaction sorting in the reducer. If the number of transactions arriving at the reducers is too big, then this might cause an out-of-memory exception in the reducers. Our second Hadoop solution will not have this restriction: rather than sorting data in memory for each reducer, we will use secondary sorting, which (as you might recall from earlier in this book), is a feature of the MapReduce paradigm for sorting the values of reducers.

Table 11-2 lists the implementation classes we'll need for Hadoop solution 1.

Table 11-2. Hadoop solution 1: implementation classes

Class name	Description
SortInMemoryProjectionDriver	Driver class to submit jobs
SortInMemoryProjectionMapper	Mapper class
SortInMemoryProjectionReducer	Reducer class
DateUtil	Basic date utility class
HadoopUtil	Basic Hadoop utility class

Partial input

Pranab Ghosh has provided a Ruby script (*buy_xaction.rb* (*https://github.com/pranab/avenir/blob/master/resource/buy_xaction.rb*)) that generates fake customer transaction data:

```
$ # create test data by using a ruby script:
$ ./buy_xaction.rb 80000 210 .05 > training.txt

$ # copy test data to Hadoop/HDFS
$ hadoop fs -copyFromLocal training.txt
    /markov/projection_by_sorting_in_ram/input/

$ # inspect data in HDFS
$ hadoop fs -cat
    /markov/projection_by_sorting_in_ram/input/training.txt
...
EY2I3D12PZ,1382705171,2013-07-29,28
VC38QFM2IF,1382705172,2013-07-29,84
1022R2QPWG,1382705173,2013-07-29,27
4G02MW73CK,1382705174,2013-07-29,31
VKV2K1S0D2,1382705175,2013-07-29,28
```

```
LDFK8WZQFH,1382705176,2013-07-29,25
8874144Q11,1382705177,2013-07-29,180
...
```

Log of sample run

The log output is shown here; it has been edited and formatted to fit the page:

```
# ./run.sh
...
Deleted hdfs://localhost:9000/lib/projection_by_sorting_in_ram.jar
Deleted hdfs://localhost:9000/markov/projection_by_sorting_in_ram/output
...
13/11/27 12:03:16 INFO mapred.JobClient: Running job: job_201311271011_0012
13/11/27 12:03:17 INFO mapred.JobClient: map 0% reduce 0%
...
13/11/27 12:04:16 INFO mapred.JobClient: map 100% reduce 100%
13/11/27 12:04:17 INFO mapred.JobClient: Job complete: job_201311271011_0012
...
13/11/27 12:04:17 INFO mapred.JobClient: Map-Reduce Framework
13/11/27 12:04:17 INFO mapred.JobClient: Map input records=832280
13/11/27 12:04:17 INFO mapred.JobClient: Reduce input records=832280
13/11/27 12:04:17 INFO mapred.JobClient: Reduce input groups=79998
13/11/27 12:04:17 INFO mapred.JobClient: Reduce output records=79998
13/11/27 12:04:17 INFO mapred.JobClient: Map output records=832280
13/11/27 12:04:17 INFO SortInMemoryProjectionDriver: jobStatus: true
13/11/27 12:04:17 INFO SortInMemoryProjectionDriver:
  elapsedTime (in milliseconds): 62063
```

Partial output

```
...
ZTOBR28AH2 2013-01-06,190;2013-04-02,109;2013-04-09,26;...
ZV2A56WNI6 2013-01-22,51;2013-01-24,34;2013-02-09,52;...
ZXN7727FBA 2013-02-07,164;2013-02-23,30;2013-03-28,107;...
ZY44ATNBK7 2013-03-27,191;2013-04-27,51;2013-05-06,31;...
...
```

The next step is to build our model's transition probabilities—that is, to define:

$$0.0 \leq P\left(state_1, state_2\right) \leq 1.0$$

where $state_1$ and $state_2 \in \{SL, SE, SG, ML, ME, MG, LL, LE, LG\}$.

Hadoop Solution 2: Time-Ordered Transactions

This implementation provides a solution that sorts reducer values using the secondary sort technique (this approach is an alternative to Hadoop solution 1; by using the Secondary Sort design pattern, we no longer must buffer all reducer values in memory/RAM for sorting). To accomplish this, we need some custom classes, which will be plugged into the MapReduce framework implementation. Mappers emit key-value pairs where the key is a pair of (customer-id, purchase-date) and the value is a pair of (purchase-date, amount). Data arrives to the reducers sorted. As you can see, to generate sorted values for each reducer key, we include the purchase-date (i.e., the first part of the emitted mapper value) as part of the mapper key. So, again, the CompositeKey comprises a pair (customer-id, purchase-date). The value (purchase-date, amount) is represented as the class edu.umd.cloud9.io.pair.PairOfLongInt, where the Long part represents the purchase date and Int represents the purchase amount.

The MapReduce framework states that once the data values reach a reducer, all data is grouped by key. As just noted, we have a CompositeKey, so we need to make sure that records are grouped solely by the natural key (i.e., the customer-id). We accomplish this by writing a custom partitioner class: NaturalKeyPartitioner. We also need to provide more plug-in classes:

```
Configuration conf = new Configuration();
JobConf jobconf = new JobConf(conf, SecondarySortProjectionDriver.class);
...
jobconf.setPartitionerClass(NaturalKeyPartitioner.class);
jobconf.setOutputKeyComparatorClass(CompositeKeyComparator.class);
jobconf.setOutputValueGroupingComparator(NaturalKeyGroupingComparator.class);
```

Now let's refresh your memory of the Secondary Sort pattern covered in Chapters 1 and 2. Mappers generate key-value pairs. The order of the values arriving at a reducer is unspecified and can vary between job runs. For example, let all mappers generate (K, V1), (K, V2), and (K, V3). So, for the key K, we have three values: V1, V2, V3. A reducer that is processing key K, then, might get one (out of six) of the following orders:

```
V1, V2, V3
V1, V3, V2
V2, V1, V3
V2, V3, V1
V3, V1, V2
V3, V2, V1
```

In most situations (depending on your requirements and how you will process reducer values), it really does not matter in what order these values arrive. But if you want the values you're receiving and processing to be sorted in some order (such as ascending or descending), your first option is to get all values V1, V2, V3 and then apply a sort function on them to get your desired order. As we've discussed, this sort technique might not be feasible if you do not have enough RAM in your servers to hold all the values. But there is another, preferable method that scales out very well and eliminates any worry about big RAM requirements: you can use the sort and shuffle feature of the MapReduce framework. As you've learned, this technique is called a secondary sort, and it allows the MapReduce programmer to control the order in which the values appear within a `reduce()` function call. To achieve this, you need to use a composite key that contains the information needed to sort both by key and by value, and then you decouple the grouping and the sorting of the intermediate data. Secondary sorting, then, enables us to define the sorting order of the values generated by mappers. Again, sorting is done on both the keys and the values. Further, grouping enables us to decide which key-value pairs are put together into a single `reduce()` function call. The composite key for our example is illustrated in Figure 11-2.

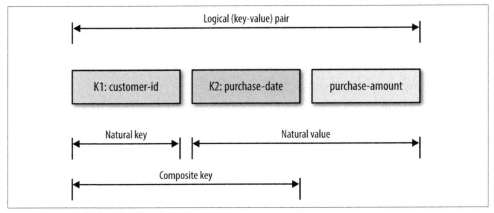

Figure 11-2. Composite key for secondary sorting

In Hadoop, the grouping is controlled in two places: the partitioner, which sends mapper output to reducer tasks, and the grouping comparator, which groups data within a reducer task. Both the partitioner and group comparator functionality can be accomplished through pluggable classes for each MapReduce job. To sort the values for reducers, we have to define a pluggable class, which sets the output key comparator. Therefore, using raw MapReduce, implementing secondary sorting can take a little bit of work: we must define a composite key and specify three functions (by defining pluggable classes for the MapReduce job—details are given in Table 11-3) that each use it in a different way. Note that for our example the natural key is a `customer-id` (as a string object) and there is no need to wrap it in another class, which we might call as a natural key. The natural key is what you would normally use as the key or "group by" operator.

Table 11-3. Hadoop solution 2: implementation classes

Class name	Description
`SecondarySortProjectionDriver`	Driver class to submit jobs
`SecondarySortProjectionMapper`	Mapper class
`SecondarySortProjectionReducer`	Reducer class

Class name	Description
CompositeKey	Custom key to hold a pair of (customer-id, purchase-date), which is a combination of the natural key and the natural value we want to sort by
CompositeKeyComparator	How to sort CompositeKey objects; compares two composite keys for sorting
NaturalKeyGroupingComparator	Considers the natural key; makes sure that a single reducer sees a custom view of the groups (how to group customer-id)
NaturalKeyPartitioner	How to partition by the natural key (customer-id) to reducers; blocks all data into a logical group in which we want the secondary sort to occur on the natural value
DateUtil	Basic date utility class
HadoopUtil	Basic Hadoop utility class

Partial input

```
# hadoop fs -cat /markov/projection_by_secondary_sort/input/training.txt | head
V31E55G4FI,1381872898,2013-01-01,123
301UNH7I2F,1381872899,2013-01-01,148
PP2KVIR4LD,1381872900,2013-01-01,163
AC57MM3WNV,1381872901,2013-01-01,188
BN020INHUM,1381872902,2013-01-01,116
UP8R2SOR77,1381872903,2013-01-01,183
VD91210MGH,1381872904,2013-01-01,204
COI40XHET1,1381872905,2013-01-01,78
76S34ZE89C,1381872906,2013-01-01,105
6K3SNF2EG1,1381872907,2013-01-01,214
```

Log of sample run

The log output is shown here; it has been edited and formatted to fit the page:

```
# ./run.sh
JAVA_HOME=/System/Library/Java/JavaVirtualMachines/1.6.0.jdk/Contents/Home
...
Deleted hdfs://localhost:9000/lib/projection_by_secondary_sort.jar
Deleted hdfs://localhost:9000/markov/projection_by_secondary_sort/output
...
13/11/27 15:14:34 INFO mapred.FileInputFormat: Total input paths to process : 1
13/11/27 15:14:34 INFO mapred.JobClient: Running job: job_201311271459_0003
13/11/27 15:14:35 INFO mapred.JobClient:  map 0% reduce 0%
...
13/11/27 15:16:02 INFO mapred.JobClient:  map 100% reduce 100%
13/11/27 15:16:03 INFO mapred.JobClient: Job complete: job_201311271459_0003
...
13/11/27 15:16:03 INFO mapred.JobClient: Map-Reduce Framework
13/11/27 15:16:03 INFO mapred.JobClient:   Map input records=832280
13/11/27 15:16:03 INFO mapred.JobClient:   Combine input records=0
13/11/27 15:16:03 INFO mapred.JobClient:   Reduce input records=832280
```

```
13/11/27 15:16:03 INFO mapred.JobClient:    Reduce input groups=79998
13/11/27 15:16:03 INFO mapred.JobClient:    Combine output records=0
13/11/27 15:16:03 INFO mapred.JobClient:    Reduce output records=79998
13/11/27 15:16:03 INFO mapred.JobClient:    Map output records=832280
13/11/27 15:16:03 INFO SecondarySortProjectionDriver: elapsedTime
  (in milliseconds): 89809
```

Partial output

```
...
ZSY40NVPS6 2013-01-01,110;2013-01-11,32;2013-03-04,111;2013-04-09,65;...
ZTLNF0O4LN 2013-01-16,55;2013-03-21,164;2013-05-14,66;2013-06-29,81;...
ZV20AIXG8L 2013-01-13,210;2013-02-03,32;2013-02-10,48;2013-02-23,27;...
...
```

Generating State Sequences

The goal of this section is to convert a *transaction sequence* into a *state sequence*. Both of our Hadoop solutions generated the following output (i.e., the transaction sequence):

customer-id (Date$_1$, Amount$_1$);(Date$_2$, Amount$_2$);...(Date$_N$, Amount$_N$)

such that:

Date$_1$ ≤ Date$_2$ ≤ ... ≤ Date$_N$

We need to convert this output ("transaction sequence") into a "state sequence" as:

customer-id, State$_1$, State$_2$, ..., State$_n$

The next task is to convert (using another Ruby script developed by Pranab Ghosh) the sorted sequence of (purchase-date, amount) pairs into a set of Markov chain states. The state is indicated by a two-letter symbol; each letter is defined in Table 11-4.

Table 11-4. Letters indicating a Markov chain state

Time elapsed since last transaction	Amount spent compared to previous transaction
S: Small	L: Significantly less than
M: Medium	E: More or less same
L: Large	G: Significantly greater than

Therefore, we will have nine (3 × 3) states, as shown in Table 11-5.

Table 11-5. Two-letter Markov chain state names and definitions

State name	Time elapsed since last transaction: amount spent compared to previous transaction
SL	Small: significantly less than
SE	Small: more or less same
SG	Small: significantly greater than
ML	Medium: significantly less than
ME	Medium: more or less same
MG	Medium: significantly greater than
LL	Large: significantly less than
LE	Large: more or less same
LG	Large: significantly greater than

As you can see, our Markov chain model has nine states (transition matrix of 9 × 9).

The following set of shell commands shows how to generate the state sequence from the transaction sequence using the Ruby script *xaction_state.rb* (*http://bit.ly/ xaction_state*):

```
$ cat transaction_sequence.txt
00VVD1E210,2012-06-18,87
00W6TWFW4S,2012-03-24,22,2012-05-22,80,2012-06-15,33
00W86Y0GFT,2012-02-15,141,2012-03-10,30,2012-03-25,49,2012-05-17,107
00W92K8A1W,2012-04-19,25
00W9W3Y3XH,2012-03-25,123
00XL1QERUO,2012-01-07,81,2012-05-10,154
00XPR1XW1P,2012-04-26,103
00Y1B0Y4CO,2012-03-10,81
00YR97DWWO,2012-07-15,118
00Z5SOHKED,2012-01-28,43,2012-02-25,27
00ZLLMHKND,2012-02-21,185,2012-04-02,63,2012-04-03,30

$ ./xaction_state.rb transaction_sequence.txt
00W6TWFW4S,ML,SG
00W86Y0GFT,SG,SL,ML
00XL1QERUO,LL
00Z5SOHKED,SG
00ZLLMHKND,MG,SG
```

For such a small amount of data, the Ruby script does the job. For a large volume of data, however, you may need to use a mapper program instead, as shown in Example 11-3.

Example 11-3. Mapper to generate state sequence

```
1 /**
2  * @param key is MapReduce generated, ignored here
3  * @param value is:
4  * <customerID><,><Date1><,><Amount1><,><Date2><,><Amount2>...
5  * where Date1 <= Date2 <= ...
6  */
7 map(key, value) {
8    tokens[] = value.split(",");
9    if (tokens.length < 5) {
10       // not enough data
11       return;
12   }
13   customerID = tokens[0];
14   sequence = [];
15   i = 4;
16   while (i < tokens.length) {
17     amount = tokens[i];
18     priorAmount = tokens[i-2];
19     date = tokens[i-1];
20     priorDate = tokens[i-3];
21     daysDiff = date - priorDate;
22     amountDiff = amount - priorAmount;
23
24     if (daysDiff < 30) {
25         dd = "S";
26     }
27     elsif (daysDiff < 60) {
28         dd = "M";
29     }
30     else {
31         dd = "L";
32     }
33
34     if (priorAmount < 0.9 * amount) {
35         ad = "L";
36     }
37     elsif (priorAmount < 1.1 * amount) {
38         ad = "E";
39     }
40     else {
41       ad = "G";
42     }
43
44     sequence << (dd + ad);
45     i += 2;
46   }
47   emit (customerID, ",", sequence.join(","));
48 }
```

Generating a Markov State Transition Matrix with MapReduce

The goal of this MapReduce phase is to generate a Markov state transition matrix. The input for this phase will be the state sequence and will have the following format:

```
customer-id, State₁, State₂, ..., Stateₙ
```

The output will be a matrix of $N \times N$, where N is the number of states (in our model $N = 9$) for the Markov chain model. The matrix entries will indicate the probability of going from one state to another. This MapReduce phase will count the number of instances of state transitions. Since the number of states for our model is 9, we will have $9 \times 9 = 81$ possible state transitions.

Example 11-4 defines the `map()` function for the Markov state transition.

Example 11-4. Markov state transition: map() function

```
 1 /**
 2  * @param key is the Customer-ID, ignored
 3  * @param value is the sequence of states = {S1, S2, ..., Sn}
 4  * We assume value is an array of n states (indexed from 0 to n-1).
 5  */
 6 map(key, value) {
 7      for (i=0, i < n-1, i++) {
 8          // value[i] denotes "from state"
 9          // value[i+1] denotes "to state"
10          reducerKey = pair(value[i], value[i+1]);
11          emit(reducerKey, 1);
12      }
13 }
```

Example 11-5 defines the `combine()` function for our Markov state transition.

Example 11-5. Markov state transition: combine() function

```
 1 /**
 2  * @param key is a Pair(state1, state2)
 3  * @param value is a list of integers (partial count of "state1" to "state2")
 4  */
 5 combine(Pair(state1, state2) key, List<integer> values) {
 6      int partialSum = 0;
 7      for (int count : values) {
 8          partialSum += count;
 9      }
10      emit(key, partialSum);
11 }
```

Example 11-6 defines the `reduce()` function for our Markov state transition.

Example 11-6. Markov state transition: reduce() function

```
 1 /**
 2  * @param key is a Pair(state1, state2)
 3  * @param value is a list of integers (partial count of "state1" to "state2")
 4  */
 5 reduce(Pair(state1, state2) key, List<integer> value) {
 6     int sum = 0;
 7     for (int count : value) {
 8         sum += count;
 9     }
10     emit(key, sum);
11 }
```

Hadoop implementation of the state transition model

Table 11-6 shows the classes we'll need for our Hadoop implementation of the state transition model.

Table 11-6. State transition model: implementation classes

Class name	Description
MarkovStateTransitionModelDriver	Driver class to submit jobs
MarkovStateTransitionModelMapper	Mapper class
MarkovStateTransitionModelCombiner	Combiner class
MarkovStateTransitionModelReducer	Reducer class
ReadDataFromHDFS	Reads data from HDFS and creates List<TableItem>
StateTransitionTableBuilder	Builds transition table and defines P(state1, state2)
TableItem	Represents a triplet of (fromState, toState, count)
HadoopUtil	Basic Hadoop utility class

Input

```
# hadoop fs -cat /markov/state_transition_model/input/state_seq.txt | head
000IA1PHVZ,SG,SL,SG,SL,ML,MG,SG,SL,SG,SL,ML
000KH3DK15,SG,SL,SG,ML,SG,SL,SG,SL,SG,SL,SG,ML,SG,SL,SG
001KD25DTD,SG,SL,SG,SL,SG,SL,SG
00241F24T4,SG,SL,SG,SL,SG,SL,SG,ML,SG,SL,ML,SG,ML,SG
002C11GB8Y,SG,SL,SG,SL,SG,SL,SG,ML,SG,SL,SG,ML,SG
002SG5SKJT,SG,SL,SG,ML,SG,SL,SG
0030B44HD0,SG,SL,SG,SL,SG,SL,SG,SL,ML,SG
004ADRKOEW,SG,SL,SG,ML,MG,SG,SL,SG,LL
004MT1M5BY,SG,SL,SG,SL,SG,ML,SG,ML,SG,SL,ML
007DI3WJ5B,SL,SL,ML,MG,SG,SE,SL,SG,SG,SL,SG
```

Log of sample run

A shortened version of the log output is shown here:

```
# ./run.sh
...
adding: HadoopUtil.class(in = 1797) (out= 840)(deflated 53%)
...
adding: TableItem.class(in = 375) (out= 263)(deflated 29%)
...
13/11/29 21:16:17 INFO mapred.JobClient: Running job: job_201311291911_0003
13/11/29 21:16:18 INFO mapred.JobClient: map 0% reduce 0%
...
13/11/29 21:17:10 INFO mapred.JobClient: map 100% reduce 100%
13/11/29 21:17:11 INFO mapred.JobClient: Job complete: job_201311291911_0003
...
13/11/29 21:17:11 INFO mapred.JobClient: Map-Reduce Framework
13/11/29 21:17:11 INFO mapred.JobClient: Map input records=79977
13/11/29 21:17:11 INFO mapred.JobClient: Reduce shuffle bytes=844
...
13/11/29 21:17:11 INFO mapred.JobClient: Combine input records=672461
13/11/29 21:17:11 INFO mapred.JobClient: Reduce input records=56
13/11/29 21:17:11 INFO mapred.JobClient: Reduce input groups=56
13/11/29 21:17:11 INFO mapred.JobClient: Combine output records=212
13/11/29 21:17:11 INFO mapred.JobClient: Reduce output records=56
13/11/29 21:17:11 INFO mapred.JobClient: Map output records=672305
```

Output

```
# hadoop fs -ls /markov/state_transition_model/output/part*
-rw-r--r--   ... 58 2013-11-29 21:16 /markov/state_transition_model/output/
  part-r-00000
...
-rw-r--r--   ... 46 2013-11-29 21:17 /markov/state_transition_model/output/
  part-r-00009

# hadoop fs -cat /markov/state_transition_model/output/part*
LL,MG 2990
ME,SG 172
MG,LL 803
...
SL,SE 2099
LE,LG 2
LG,LE 1
MG,SG 19485
ML,SL 268
...
SL,ME 151
LG,SL 510
LL,SG 17062
...
SG,SG 5090
SL,SL 2772
```

```
...
SG,LE 140

# javac ReadDataFromHDFS.java TableItem.java
# java ReadDataFromHDFS /markov/state_transition_model/output
Nov 30 2013 12:24:18 [main] [INFO ] [ReadDataFromHDFS] - path=...
Nov 30 2013 12:24:18 [main] [INFO ] [ReadDataFromHDFS] - line=ME,SG 172
Nov 30 2013 12:24:18 [main] [INFO ] [ReadDataFromHDFS] - line=MG,LL 803
...
Nov 30 2013 12:24:18 [main] [INFO ] [ReadDataFromHDFS] - line=LL,LG 507
Nov 30 2013 12:24:18 [main] [INFO ] [ReadDataFromHDFS] - line=SE,LG 2
Nov 30 2013 12:24:18 [main] [INFO ] [ReadDataFromHDFS] - line=SG,LE 140
Nov 30 2013 12:27:45 [main] [INFO ] [ReadDataFromHDFS] -
  list=[{LL,MG,2990}, ..., {MG,LL,803}]
```

Using the Markov Model to Predict the Next Smart Email Marketing Date

Now that we have built the Markov model from the given training data, we can persist it using the following piece of code:

```
# cat StateTransitionTableBuilder.java
...
public class StateTransitionTableBuilder {
    ...
    public static void main(String[] args) {
        String hdfsDirectory = args[0];
        generateStateTransitionTable(hdfsDirectory);
    }
}

# export hdfsDir="/markov/state_transition_model/output"
# java StateTransitionTableBuilder $hdfsDir > model.txt
```

Now that we have *model.txt* (represented as a two-dimensional table), we can use the Ruby scripts *buy_xaction.rb* and *mark_plan.rb* (*http://bit.ly/mark_plan*) (developed by Pranab Ghosh) to predict the next smart email marketing dates:

```
# Generate validation data
# ----------------------
./buy_xaction.rb 80000 30 .05 > validation.txt
head validation.txt
XURQDBEHME,1385141945,2013-01-01,98
3RT4PONSUP,1385141946,2013-01-01,53
4NYCEUD3YG,1385141947,2013-01-01,164
SF9KAY8F42,1385141948,2013-01-01,204
LKNCID1DRV,1385141949,2013-01-01,83
4EZJDVB4W1,1385141950,2013-01-01,116
ITJ39B3NX3,1385141951,2013-01-01,72
D8VVPAHG8I,1385141952,2013-01-01,124
21XHZJY561,1385141953,2013-01-01,103
F7LS37R08X,1385141954,2013-01-01,211
```

```
# Predict email marketing time
# --------------------------
./mark_plan.rb validation.txt model.txt
XURQDBEHME, 2013-04-27
4NYCEUD3YG, 2013-04-14
SF9KAY8F42, 2013-04-07
LKNCID1DRV, 2013-04-30
4EZJDVB4W1, 2013-02-02
ITJ39B3NX3, 2013-04-27
D8VVPAHG8I, 2013-04-29
21XHZJY561, 2013-01-18
F7LS37R08X, 2013-02-14
...
```

Now we are able to predict the next smart date for sending a marketing email based on a user's transaction history.

Spark Solution

In this section, I present a Spark solution for smarter email marketing using the Markov Chain algorithm. Our Spark solution has a set of transformations, such as mapTo Pair(), groupByKey(), reduceByKey(), and mapValues(). First, I'll present the solution as a set of high-level steps, and then I'll demonstrate each step as a Spark transformation or action. Finally, a sample run and script are provided.

Input Format

Each input record consists of four fields:

```
<customerID><,><transactionID><,><purchaseDate><,><amount>
```

Here is some sample input data:

```
$ ls -l smart_email_training.txt
-rw-r--r-- 1 hadoop hadoop 30089506 Nov 5 16:57 smart_email_training.txt
$ wc -l smart_email_training.txt
832280 smart_email_training.txt
$ hadoop fs -copyFromLocal smart_email_training.txt /home/hadoop/testspark/
$ hadoop fs -cat /home/hadoop/testspark/smart_email_training.txt | head
V31E55G4FI,1381872898,2013-01-01,123
301UNH7I2F,1381872899,2013-01-01,148
PP2KVIR4LD,1381872900,2013-01-01,163
AC57MM3WNV,1381872901,2013-01-01,188
BN020INHUM,1381872902,2013-01-01,116
UP8R2SOR77,1381872903,2013-01-01,183
VD91210MGH,1381872904,2013-01-01,204
COI4OXHET1,1381872905,2013-01-01,78
76S34ZE89C,1381872906,2013-01-01,105
6K3SNF2EG1,1381872907,2013-01-01,214
```

High-Level Steps

Our Spark solution is presented in seven basic steps:

1. Handle input parameters. There is only a single parameter for this program. This step reads the input path for the transaction data, which will be analyzed and processed.

2. Create a context object and convert the input into a `JavaRDD<String>`, where each element is an input record (as defined in the preceding subsection).

3. Convert the `JavaRDD<String>` into a `JavaPairRDD<K,V>`, where K is a `customerID` and V is a `Tuple2<purchaseDate, amount>`.

   Note that the `transactionID` field is ignored (as it's not needed for further processing).

4. Group transactions by `customerID`. We apply `groupByKey()` to the output of step 3, and the result is a `JavaPairRDD<K2,V2>`, where K2 is a `customerID` and V2 is an `Iterable<Tuple2<purchaseDate, Amount>>`.

5. Create a Markov state sequence:

   `State₁, State₂, ..., Stateₙ`

   We apply the `mapValues()` transformation to the `JavaPairRDD<K2,V2>` and generate a `JavaPairRDD<K4, V4>`. First we convert (K2, V2) pairs into (K3, V3) pairs, where K2 = K3 = K4 = `customerID`, V3 is a sorted V2 (order is based on `purchaseDate`)—that is, a sorted transaction sequence. Then, we use V3 to create a Markov state sequence (as V4).

6. Generate a Markov state transition with the following input/output:

   Input
   : `JavaPairRDD<K4, V4>` pairs.

   Output
   : A matrix of states {S1, S2, S3, ...} (see Table 11-7) that defines the probability of going from one state to another. After this matrix is built, we can use the new data to predict the next smart marketing date.

In the following table, P_{ij} is the probability of going from state S_i to state S_j.

Table 11-7. Markov state transition probabilities

States	S_1	S_2	S_3	...
S_1	P_{11}	P_{12}	P_{13}	...
S_2	P_{21}	P_{22}	P_{23}	...
S_3	P_{31}	P_{32}	P_{33}	...
...	...	...	...	...

7. Emit the final output, which defines the probability of going from one state to another.

Spark Program

The entire Spark solution is provided by a single Java driver class, shown in Example 11-7.

Example 11-7. Structure of Spark program

```
1 package org.dataalgorithms.chap11.spark;
2 // Step 0: import required classes and interfaces
3 // source code reference:
4 //     https://github.com/mahmoudparsian/data-algorithms-book/
5 //     .../src/main/java/org/dataalgorithms/chap11/spark/SparkMarkov.java
6 public class SparkMarkov implements Serializable {
7
8    static List<Tuple2<Long,Integer>> toList(Iterable<Tuple2<Long,Integer>>
9 iterable) {...}
10    static List<String> toStateSequence(List<Tuple2<Long,Integer>> list) {...}
11    static class TupleComparatorAscending implements
12        Comparator<Tuple2<Long, Integer>>, Serializable {...}
13
14    public static void main(String[] args) throws Exception {
15        // Step 1: handle input parameters
16        // Step 2: create context object (ctx) and convert input into
17        //         JavaRDD<String>, where each element is an input record
18        // Step 3: convert RDD<String> into JavaPairRDD<K,V>, where
19        //         K: customerID
20        //         V: Tuple2<purchaseDate, Amount> : Tuple2<Long, Integer>
21        // Step 4: group transactions by customerID: apply groupByKey()
22        // Step 5: create Markov state sequence: State1, State2, ..., StateN
23        // Step 6: generate Markov state transition matrix
24        // Step 7: emit final output
25
26        // done
27        ctx.close();
28        System.exit(0);
```

```
29    }
30 }
```

Step 1: Handle input parameters

This step, shown in Example 11-8, reads the input path for the transaction data from a shell script. The input path can be a Linux path or an HDFS path (Spark can read both Linux and HDFS files).

Example 11-8. Step 1: handle input parameters

```
1    // Step 1: handle input parameters
2    if (args.length != 1) {
3        System.err.println("Usage: SparkMarkov <input-path>");
4        System.exit(1);
5    }
6    final String inputPath = args[0];
7    System.out.println("inputPath:args[0]="+args[0]);
```

Step 2: Create Spark context object and convert Input into RDD

This step, shown in Example 11-9, reads in the input file(s) and creates the first RDD for this program (by using the factory class `JavaSparkContext`).

Example 11-9. Step 2: create context object and convert input into RDD

```
1    // Step 2: create Spark context object (ctx) and convert input into
2    //         JavaRDD<String>,
3    // where each element is an input record
4    JavaSparkContext ctx = new JavaSparkContext();
5    JavaRDD<String> records = ctx.textFile(inputPath, 1);
6    records.saveAsTextFile("/output/2");
7
8    // You may optionally partition RDD
9    // public JavaRDD<T> coalesce(int N)
10   // Return a new RDD that is reduced into N partitions.
11   // JavaRDD<String> records = ctx.textFile(inputPath, 1).coalesce(9);
```

To debug this step, we save the RDD elements:

```
$ hadoop fs -cat /output/2/part* | head -3
V31E55G4FI,1381872898,2013-01-01,123
301UNH7I2F,1381872899,2013-01-01,148
PP2KVIR4LD,1381872900,2013-01-01,163
```

Step 3: Convert RDD into JavaPairRDD

As Example 11-10 shows, this step converts a single record into a `JavaPairRDD<K,V>`, where K is a `customerID` and V is a `Tuple2<purchaseDate,Amount>` (purchaseDate is converted into a `Long` data type with the date in milliseconds).

Example 11-10. Step 3: convert RDD into JavaPairRDD

```
1    // Step 3: convert JavaRDD<String> into JavaPairRDD<K,V>, where
2    //    K: customerID
3    //    V: Tuple2<purchaseDate, Amount> : Tuple2<Long, Integer>
4    //    PairFunction<T, K, V>
5    //    T => Tuple2<K, V>
6    JavaPairRDD<String, Tuple2<Long,Integer>> kv = records.mapToPair(
7        new PairFunction<
8                        String,              // T
9                        String,              // K
10                       Tuple2<Long,Integer> // V
11                       >() {
12       public Tuple2<String,Tuple2<Long,Integer>> call(String rec) {
13           String[] tokens = StringUtils.split(rec, ",");
14           if (tokens.length != 4) {
15           // not a proper format
16           return null;
17           }
18           // tokens[0] = customer-id
19           // tokens[1] = transaction-id
20           // tokens[2] = purchase-date
21           // tokens[3] = amount
22           long date = 0;
23           try {
24               date = DateUtil.getDateAsMilliSeconds(tokens[2]);
25           }
26           catch(Exception e) {
27               // ignore for now -- must be handled
28           }
29           int amount = Integer.parseInt(tokens[3]);
30           Tuple2<Long,Integer> V = new Tuple2<Long,Integer>(date, amount);
31           return new Tuple2<String,Tuple2<Long,Integer>>(tokens[0], V);
32       }
33    });
34    kv.saveAsTextFile("/output/3");
```

To debug this step, we save the RDD elements:

```
$ hadoop fs -cat /output/3/part* | head
(V31E55G4FI,(1357027200000,123))
(301UNH7I2F,(1357027200000,148))
(PP2KVIR4LD,(1357027200000,163))
(AC57MM3WNV,(1357027200000,188))
(BN020INHUM,(1357027200000,116))
(UP8R2SOR77,(1357027200000,183))
(VD91210MGH,(1357027200000,204))
(COI4OXHET1,(1357027200000,78))
(76S34ZE89C,(1357027200000,105))
(6K3SNF2EG1,(1357027200000,214))
```

Step 4: Group transactions by customerID

This step, shown in Example 11-11, groups all transactions by `customerID` by using `groupByKey()`.

Example 11-11. Step 4: group transactions by customerID

```
1    // Step 4: group transactions by customerID. Apply groupByKey()
2    //          to the output of step 2; result will be
3    //          JavaPairRDD<K2,V2>, where
4    //             K2: customerID
5    //             V2: Iterable<Tuple2<purchaseDate, Amount>>
6    JavaPairRDD<String, Iterable<Tuple2<Long,Integer>>> customerRDD =
8       kv.groupByKey();
9    customerRDD.saveAsTextFile("/output/4");
```

To debug this step, we save the RDD elements:

```
$ hadoop fs -cat /output/4/part* | head -3
(0IROUCA5O2,[(1361347200000,86), (1362643200000,30), (1362816000000,45),
            (1364886000000,27), (1366009200000,40), (1366182000000,28),
            (1369724400000,115), (1370502000000,32), (1371970800000,42),
            (1372575600000,32), (1374649200000,43)])
(4N0B1U5HVG,[(1358668800000,81), (1359446400000,33), (1363071600000,98),
            (1365750000000,50), (1366614000000,29), (1367218800000,48),
            (1369378800000,30), (1369810800000,41), (1370674800000,28),
            (1373353200000,107)])
(3KJR1907D9,[(1361088000000,105), (1362211200000,26), (1366182000000,103),
            (1366182000000,28), (1370415600000,111), (1373266800000,61),
            (1373439600000,34)])
```

Step 5: Create a Markov state sequence

As Example 11-12 shows, this step converts transaction sequences into state sequences. First, we sort transaction sequences by purchase date, and then we convert those sorted transaction sequences into state sequences.

Example 11-12. Step 5: create Markov state sequence

```
1    // Step 5: Create Markov state sequence: State1, State2, ..., StateN. Apply
2    //          mapValues() to JavaPairRDD<K2,V2> and generate JavaPairRDD<K4, V4>.
3    //          First convert (K2, V2) into (K3, V3) pairs [K2 = K3 = K4].
4    //          V3 is a sorted V2 (order is based on purchaseDate);
5    //          i.e., a sorted transaction sequence.
6    //          Then use V3 to create Markov state sequence (as V4).
7    // mapValues[U](f: (V) => U): JavaPairRDD[K, U]
8    // Pass each value in the key-value pair RDD through a map function without
9    // changing the keys; this also retains the original RDD's partitioning.
10   JavaPairRDD<String, List<String>> stateSequence = customerRDD.mapValues(
11       new Function<
12                   Iterable<Tuple2<Long,Integer>>, // input
```

```
13                    List<String>                              // output ("state sequence")
14                >() {
15        public List<String> call(Iterable<Tuple2<Long,Integer>> dateAndAmount) {
16            List<Tuple2<Long,Integer>> list = toList(dateAndAmount);
17            Collections.sort(list, TupleComparatorAscending.INSTANCE);
18            // now convert sorted list (by date) into a state sequence
19            List<String> stateSequence = toStateSequence(list);
20            return stateSequence;
21        }
22    });
23    stateSequence.saveAsTextFile("/output/5");
```

To debug this step, we save the RDD elements:

```
$ hadoop fs -cat /output/5/part* | head
(0IROUCA5O2,[SG, SL, SG, SL, SG, ML, SG, SL, SG, SL])
(4N0B1U5HVG,[SG, ML, MG, SG, SL, SG, SL, SG, ML])
(3KJR1907D9,[SG, ML, SG, ML, MG, SG])
(8555DQOK14,[SG, ML, LL])
(J6VXOTY7IA,[SG, ML, SG, SL, SG, ML, SG])
(T29M0VFTO4,[SG, SL, SG, SL, ML, SG, SL, SG, SL, SG, SL, SG, SL, SG])
(J0B064093C,[SG, SL, SG, SL, ML, SG, SG, SL, SG, SL, SG, SL, ML, SG, SL])
(NT58RT7KK4,[MG, SG, SL, SG, SL, SG, SL, SG, SL, SG])
(HBD6YAC69Y,[SG, SL, SG, SL, SG, SL, SG, SL, ML, MG])
(1BNFI5D3Z1,[SG, SL, SG, SL, SG, SL, SG, SL])
```

Step 6: Generate a Markov state transition matrix

This step is the mapper phase to generate a Markov state transition table. If in our training data set there has been a transition from fromState to toState, then we emit (K, V) pairs where K is a Tuple2(fromState, toState) and V is 1.

Example 11-13. Step 6: generate Markov state transition matrix

```
1    // Step 6: generate Markov state transition matrix
2    //          Input is JavaPairRDD<K4, V4> pairs
3    //             where K4 = customerID, V4 = List<State>
4    //          Output is a matrix of states {S1, S2, S3, ...}
5    //
6    //              | S1   S2   S3 ...
7    //          ---+----------------------
8    //          S1 |      <probability-value>
9    //             |
10   //          S2 |
11   //             |
12   //          S3 |
13   //             |
14   //          ...|
15   //
16   //          which defines the probability of going from one state to
17   //          another state. After this matrix is built, we can use the new
```

```
18   //          data to predict the next smart marketing date.
19   // For implementation of this step, we use:
20   //     PairFlatMapFunction<T, K, V>
21   //     T => Iterable<Tuple2<K, V>>
22   JavaPairRDD<Tuple2<String,String>, Integer> model = stateSequence.flatMapToPair(
23       new PairFlatMapFunction<
24                           Tuple2<String, List<String>>, // T
25                           Tuple2<String,String>,        // K
26                           Integer                       // V
27                       >() {
28       public Iterable<Tuple2<Tuple2<String,String>, Integer>>
29           call(Tuple2<String, List<String>> s) {
30           List<String> states = s._2;
31           if ( (states == null) || (states.size() < 2) ) {
32               return Collections.emptyList();
33           }
34
35           List<Tuple2<Tuple2<String,String>, Integer>> mapperOutput =
36               new ArrayList<Tuple2<Tuple2<String,String>, Integer>>();
37           for (int i = 0; i < (states.size() -1); i++) {
38               String fromState = states.get(i);
39               String toState = states.get(i+1);
40               Tuple2<String,String> k = new Tuple2<String,String>(fromState,
41                                                               toState);
42               mapperOutput.add(new Tuple2<Tuple2<String,String>, Integer>(k, 1));
43           }
44           return mapperOutput;
45       }
46   });
47   model.saveAsTextFile("/output/6.1");
```

To debug this step, we save the RDD elements:

```
$ hadoop fs -cat /output/6.1/part* | head
((SG,SL),1)
((SL,SG),1)
((SG,SL),1)
((SL,SG),1)
((SG,ML),1)
((ML,SG),1)
((SG,SL),1)
((SL,SG),1)
((SG,SL),1)
((SG,ML),1)
```

Combine/reduce frequent (fromState, toState). The reduceByKey() transformation is used to combine/reduce the frequency count from one state (fromState) to another one (toState), as shown in Example 11-14.

Example 11-14. Combine/reduce frequent (fromState, toState)

```
1   // combine/reduce frequent patterns (fromState, toState)
2   JavaPairRDD<Tuple2<String,String>, Integer> markovModel =
3      model.reduceByKey(new Function2<Integer, Integer, Integer>() {
4      public Integer call(Integer i1, Integer i2) {
5         return i1 + i2;
6      }
7   });
8   markovModel.saveAsTextFile("/output/6.2");
```

To debug this step, we save the RDD elements:

```
$ hadoop fs -cat /output/6.2/part*
((SL,LL),7890)
((SG,LL),11140)
...
((MG,SG),19769)
((LL,MG),2885)
...
((SG,SL),254532)
((SG,ML),50112)
...
((ML,LL),2450)
((ML,SG),66275)
```

This output:

```
((fromState, toState), count)
```

will be used to normalize the data and generate P(fromState, toState) (i.e., a Markov probability table). We do this through the StateTransitionTableBuilder class, as illustrated shortly.

Step 7: Emit final output

In this step (demonstrated in Example 11-15) we emit the final output, formatted as:

```
<fromState><,><toState><TAB><frequency-count>
```

Example 11-15. Step 7: emit final output

```
1    // Step 7: emit final output
2    // convert markovModel into "<fromState><,><toState><TAB><count>"
3    // Use map() to convert JavaPairRDD into JavaRDD:
4    // <R> JavaRDD<R> map(Function<T,R> f)
5    // Return a new RDD by applying a function to all elements of this RDD.
6    JavaRDD<String> markovModelFormatted = markovModel.map(
7       new Function<Tuple2<Tuple2<String,String>, Integer>, String>() {
8       public String call(Tuple2<Tuple2<String,String>, Integer> t) {
9          return t._1._1 + "," + t._1._2 + "\t" + t._2;
10      }
```

```
11  });
12  markovModelFormatted.saveAsTextFile("/output/6.3");
```

To debug this step, we save the RDD elements. The following output is modified to fit the page. The output shows ((fromState, toState), frequency), where frequency indicates the number of times a state has transitioned from fromState to toState:

```
$ export hdfsDir=/output/6.3
$ java org.dataalgorithms.chap11.statemodel.ReadDataFromHDFS $hdfsDir
INFO : path=hdfs://hnode01319.nextbiosystem.net:8020/output/6.3/part-00000
INFO : line=SL,LL 7890
INFO : line=SL,MG 209
INFO : line=SG,LL 11140
...
INFO : line=ML,LL 2450
INFO : line=ML,SG 66275
INFO : list=[{SL,LL,7890},
            {SL,MG,209},
            {SG,LL,11140},

            ...,
            {ML,LL,2450},
            {ML,SG,66275}]
```

Generating the Markov probability model

The StateTransitionTableBuilder class normalizes data and generates a Markov model (which defines the probability of going from one state to another). Since we have nine states, our generated Markov probability model will be a 9×9 matrix:

```
$ export hdfsDir=/output/6.3
$ export prog=org.dataalgorithms.chap11.statemodel.StateTransitionTableBuilder
$ java $prog $hdfsDir > model.txt
$ cat model.txt
0.001882,4.376e-06,0.8060,0.1567,4.376e-06,0.0009190,0.03453,4.376e-06,4.376e-06
0.1000,0.1000,0.2000,0.1000,0.1000,0.1000,0.1000,0.1000,0.1000
0.8056,3.165e-06,0.0004653,0.1586,3.165e-06,3.165e-06,0.03526,3.165e-06,3.165e-06
1.234e-05,1.234e-05,0.8178,0.0004812,1.234e-05,0.1511,0.03024,1.234e-05,0.0003208
0.01075,0.01075,0.7419,0.01075,0.01075,0.1290,0.06452,0.01075,0.01075
0.003234,4.146e-05,0.8197,0.1444,4.146e-05,0.0004561,0.03205,4.146e-05,4.146e-05
4.828e-05,4.828e-05,0.8370,4.828e-05,4.828e-05,0.1393,4.828e-05,9.655e-05,0.02332
0.01852,0.01852,0.6852,0.01852,0.01852,0.1481,0.01852,0.01852,0.05556
0.0005238,0.0005238,0.7973,0.001048,0.0005238,0.1650,0.03353,0.001048,0.0005238
```

Helper methods

The toList() method, illustrated in Example 11-16, converts an Iterable<Tuple2<Long,Integer>> into a List<Tuple2<Long,Integer>>.

Example 11-16. toList() method

```
1 static List<Tuple2<Long,Integer>> toList(Iterable<Tuple2<Long,Integer>> iterable) {
2     List<Tuple2<Long,Integer>> list = new ArrayList<Tuple2<Long,Integer>>();
3     for (Tuple2<Long,Integer> element: iterable) {
4         list.add(element);
5     }
6     return list;
7 }
```

The toStateSequence() method, shown in Example 11-17, converts a sorted transaction sequence (List<Tuple2<Date,Amount>>) into a state sequence (List<String>), where each element represents a Markov state.

Example 11-17. toStateSequence() method

```
1 /**
2  * @param list : List<Tuple2<Date,Amount>>
3  * list = [T2(Date1,Amount1), T2(Date2,Amount2), ..., T2(DateN,AmountN)]
4  * where Date1 <= Date2 <= ... <= DateN
5  */
6 static List<String> toStateSequence(List<Tuple2<Long,Integer>> list) {
7     if (list.size() < 2) {
8       // not enough data
9       return null;
10    }
11    List<String> stateSequence = new ArrayList<String>();
12    Tuple2<Long,Integer> prior = list.get(0);
13    for (int i = 1; i < list.size(); i++) {
14        Tuple2<Long,Integer> current = list.get(i);
15
16        long priorDate = prior._1;
17        long date = current._1;
18        // one day = 24*60*60*1000 = 86400000 milliseconds
19        long daysDiff = (date - priorDate) / 86400000;
20
21        int priorAmount = prior._2;
22        int amount = current._2;
23        int amountDiff = amount - priorAmount;
24
25        String dd = null;
26        if (daysDiff < 30) {
27            dd = "S";
28        }
29        else if (daysDiff < 60) {
30            dd = "M";
31        }
32        else {
33            dd = "L";
34        }
35
```

```
36      String ad = null;
37      if (priorAmount < 0.9 * amount) {
38          ad = "L";
39      }
40      else if (priorAmount < 1.1 * amount) {
41          ad = "E";
42      }
43      else {
44          ad = "G";
45      }
46
47      String element = dd + ad;
48      stateSequence.add(element);
49      prior = current;
50  }
51  return stateSequence;
52 }
```

Comparator class

The Comparator class, shown in Example 11-18, is a plug-in class for sorting a
List<Tuple2<Long, Integer>>. Sorting is based on the "date" field, represented as a
Long data type.

Example 11-18. Comparator class

```
1 static class TupleComparatorAscending implements
2     Comparator<Tuple2<Long, Integer>>, Serializable {
3     final static TupleComparatorAscending INSTANCE = new TupleComparatorAscending();
4     public int compare(Tuple2<Long, Integer> t1, Tuple2<Long, Integer> t2) {
5         // return -t1._1.compareTo(t2._1);    // sorts RDD elements descending
6         return t1._1.compareTo(t2._1);        // sorts RDD elements ascending
7     }
8 }
```

Script to Run the Spark Program

The following shell script submits our Spark program to a Spark cluster composed of
three nodes:

```
$ cat run_build_markov_model.sh
#!/bin/bash
export JAVA_HOME=/usr/java/jdk7
export SPARK_HOME=/usr/local/spark-1.1.0
export SPARK_MASTER=spark://myserver100:7077
export BOOK_HOME=/mp/data-algorithms-book
export APP_JAR=$BOOK_HOME/dist/data_algorithms_book.jar
INPUT=/home/hadoop/testspark/smart_email_training.txt
# Run on a Spark standalone cluster
prog=org.dataalgorithms.chap11.spark.SparkMarkov
$SPARK_HOME/bin/spark-submit \
```

```
--class $prog \
--master $SPARK_MASTER \
--executor-memory 2G \
--total-executor-cores 20 \
$APP_JAR \
$INPUT
```

Sample Run

Here is the output when the Spark program is run in the aforementioned three-node Spark cluster:

```
$ ./run_build_markov_model.sh
inputPath:args[0]=/home/hadoop/testspark/smart_email_training.txt
...
INFO : Executor updated: app-20141106000336-0011/0 is now RUNNING
INFO : Executor updated: app-20141106000336-0011/1 is now RUNNING
INFO : Executor updated: app-20141106000336-0011/2 is now RUNNING
...
INFO : Stage 8 (saveAsTextFile at SparkMarkov.java:277) finished in 0.300 s
INFO : Removed TaskSet 8.0, whose tasks have all completed, from pool
INFO : Job finished: saveAsTextFile at SparkMarkov.java:277, took 3.769665517 s
...
```

This chapter touched on a very important mathematical and statistical concept: the Markov model. We saw how the Markov model can be used in a distributed programming environment to predict the next state from a given prior state.

The next chapter discusses how to implement K-Means clustering in the MapReduce environment.

## CHAPTER 12

K-Means Clustering

This chapter will provide a MapReduce solution for the K-Means clustering algorithm. The K-Means clustering algorithm is interesting and different from other MapReduce algorithms. It is an iterative algorithm (that is, it requires multiple Map-Reduce phases) that you execute many times with different *centroids* until it converges (meaning that K optimal clusters are found after many iterations of the same MapReduce job).

But what is clustering? And what is K-Means? In a nutshell, we can say that, given $K > 0$ (where K is the number of clusters) and a set of N d-dimensional objects to be clustered:

- Clustering is the process of grouping a set of N d-dimensional (2-dimensional, 3-dimensional, etc.) objects into K clusters of similar objects.

- Objects should be similar to one another within the same cluster and dissimilar to those in other clusters.

K-Means is a distance-based clustering algorithm. K-Means clustering has many useful applications. For example, it can be used to find a group of consumers with common behaviors, or to cluster documents based on the similarity of their contents. The first question is: how do we determine the value of K as the number of groups or clusters we want to generate from our input data? Selection of K is specific to the application or problem domain. There is no magic formula to find K.

An example of a K-Means for $K = 3$ is given in Figures 12-1 and 12-2. Figure 12-1 shows the raw data, whereas Figure 12-2 shows an application of K-Means. In Figure 12-2, the red points represent the first cluster, the black points represent the second cluster, and finally the green points represent the third cluster. The goal of K-Means, then, is to convert the raw data into clusters.

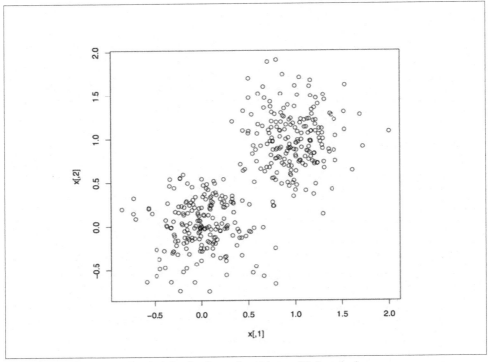

Figure 12-1. Raw data (http://bit.ly/data-algorithms_12-1_color)

This is how K-Means works: the algorithm is given as inputs a set of N d-dimensional points and a number of desired clusters, K. For simplicity's sake, we will consider points in a Euclidean space. However, the K-Means clustering algorithm will work in any space provided a distance metric is given as input as well. Therefore, our input of N (we use n and N interchangeably here) d-dimensional points will be:

$$p_1 = (a_{11}, a_{12}, ..., a_{1d})$$

$$p_2 = (a_{21}, a_{22}, ..., a_{2d})$$

...

$$p_n = (a_{n1}, a_{n2}, ..., a_{nd})$$

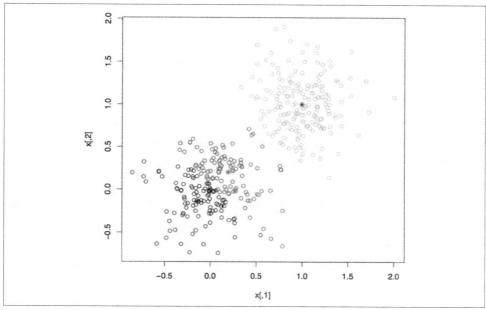

Figure 12-2. Clustered data (http://bit.ly/data-algorithms_12-2_color)

For example, in a 2-dimensional environment, our input data might be as follows, where each row represents a point (x, y):

```
p1 = (1,1)
p2 = (2,1)
p3 = (1,2)
p4 = (5,5)
p5 = (6,5)
p6 = (5,6)
p7 = (7,7)
p8 = (9,6)
```

Initially, K points are chosen as cluster centers; these are called cluster *centroids*. There are many ways to initialize the cluster centroids, one of which is to choose the K points randomly from the sample of n points. Once the K initial cluster centroids are chosen, we calculate the distance from every point in the input set to each of the K centers, and then assign each point to the specific cluster center whose distance is closest. When all objects have been assigned, then we again recalculate the positions of the K centroids. These two steps are repeated until the cluster centroids no longer change (or change very little).

Before I present our MapReduce solution, we will look at the basic definition of K-Means clustering, and then we will briefly focus on informal and formal algorithms for K-Means clustering. The better you understand K-Means clustering, the easier it will be to comprehend the MapReduce solution.

What Is K-Means Clustering?

In a nutshell, K-Means clustering (aka unsupervised learning) is a data mining algorithm to cluster, classify, or group your N objects based on their attributes or features into K number of groups (so-called clusters). K is a positive integer ($K = 2, 3, 4, ...$). If we apply K-Means to a set of N objects, then the result will be K disjoint groups (i.e., adding all objects in K groups will result in N objects). So, how do we group these N objects into K disjoint groups? We do the grouping by minimizing the sum of squares of distances between data and the corresponding cluster centroid. The next two questions, then, are why do we use clustering, and how do we find cluster centroids? The first answer is that we use K-Means clustering to categorize data—for example, to classify student grades into five categories ($K = 5$): A (excellent), B (good), C (average), D (poor), and F (failing). Or, as another example, we could use K-Means to predict students' academic performance[27]. I will return to the second question of how to find cluster centroids in the next sections.

Next, we'll formalize the K-Means clustering. Given n d-dimensional points:

$X_1 = (x_{11}, x_{12}, ..., x_{1d})$

$X_2 = (x_{21}, x_{22}, ..., x_{2d})$

...

$X_n = (x_{n1}, x_{n2}, ..., x_{nd})$

our goal is to partition these $\{X_1, X_2, ..., X_n\}$ into K clusters: $\{C_1, C_2, ..., C_k\}$. K-Means aims to find the positions μ_i ($i = 1, ..., K$) of the clusters that minimize the distance from the data points to the cluster centroids. K-means clustering solves the following cost minimization algorithm:

$$\arg\min_{C} \sum_{i=1}^{k} \sum_{\mathbf{X}_j \in C_i} \| \mathbf{X}_j - \mu_i \|^2$$

where $\boldsymbol{\mu}_i$ is the mean of points in C_i.

Application Areas for Clustering

Clustering algorithms have many possible applications, including the following:

Marketing
> Given a large set of customer transactions, find groups of customers with similar purchasing behaviors.

Document classification

Cluster web log data to discover groups of similar access patterns.

Insurance

Pick out groups of vehicle insurance policy holders with a high average claim cost, identifying potential frauds.

Informal K-Means Clustering Method: Partitioning Approach

As mentioned at the start of this chapter, the K-Means clustering algorithm is iterative. Accordingly, in subsequent sections I will provide a MapReduce implementation that we will continue running until the K-Means clustering algorithm converges by finding a proper optimal solution. Informally, we can summarize the K-Means clustering algorithm as follows: given a set of N objects to be grouped into K clusters, the K-Means algorithm performs the following steps:

1. Partition N objects into K nonempty subsets.
2. Compute the centroids of the clusters in the current partition (the centroid is the center, or mean point, of the cluster). For all $i = 1, 2, ..., K$, compute μ_i as:

$$\mu_i = \frac{1}{|c_i|} \sum_{j \in c_i} x_j, \ \forall i$$

3. Assign each object to the cluster with the nearest centroid. This is simply attributing the closest cluster to each data point:

$$c_i = \{j : d(x_j, \mu_i) \leq d(x_j, \mu_l), l \neq i, j = 1, ..., n\}$$

where $d(a, b)$ is the distance function for two points: a and b.

4. Stop when there are no more new assignments. Otherwise, go back to step 2. Basically, we repeat steps 2 and 3 until convergence.

The algorithm iterates until there are no changes in the centroids, at which point we have found our K clusters. Because the K-Means algorithm is an iterative process, at each step the membership of each object in a cluster is reevaluated based on the current centers of each existing cluster. This process is repeated until the desired number of clusters (or number of objects) is reached.

K-Means Distance Function

The first step of the K-Means clustering algorithm involves exclusive assignment of data points to the closest cluster centroids. For a given data point (of d dimensions), we determine the closest cluster centroid by using a distance function, which calculates how probable it is that the centroid generated the data point. There are many distance functions, some of which are mentioned here:

- Euclidean distance
- Manhattan distance
- Inner product space
- Maximum norm
- Your own custom function (any metric you define over the d-dimensional space)

For example, Euclidean distance has been used in many K-Means algorithms. To find the Euclidean distance between two data point instances, X and Y, which are represented by d continuous attributes (d-dimensional):

Let:

$$X = (X_1, X_2, ..., X_d)$$

$$Y = (Y_1, Y_2, ..., Y_d)$$

then:

$$distance(X, Y) = \sqrt{(X_1 - Y_1)^2 + (X_2 - Y_2)^2 + \ldots + (X_d - Y_d)^2}$$

The Euclidean distance function has some interesting properties:

- $distance(i,j) \geq 0$
- $distance(i,i) = 0$
- $distance(i,j) = distance(j,i)$
- $distance(i,j) \leq distance(i,k) + distance(k,j)$

A Java-like Euclidean distance function can be expressed as follows:

```java
public class EuclideanDistance {
    // Let Vector[i] be the i'th position of the Vector
    public static double calculateDistance(Vector center, Vector data) {
        double sum = 0.0;
```

```
// center.length = data.length
int length = center.length;
for (int i = 0; i < length; i++) {
    sum += Math.pow((center[i] - data[i]), 2.0);
}
return Math.sqrt(sum);
    }
}
```

When implementing K-Means, we have to make sure that our algorithm converges and we can properly calculate the mean and distance functions over the space we have.

K-Means Clustering Formalized

K-Means is a simple learning algorithm for clustering analysis. The goal of the K-Means clustering algorithm is to find the best division of n entities—so-called objects or points—in K groups, so that the total distance between a group's members and its corresponding centroid, representative of the group, is minimized. Formally, the goal is to partition the n entities into K sets $\{S_i, i = 1, 2, ..., K\}$ in order to minimize the within-cluster sum of squares (WCSS), defined as:

$$\min \sum_{j=1}^{k} \sum_{i=1}^{n} \| x_i^j - c_j \|$$

where term $\| x_i^j - c_j \|$ provides the distance between an entity point and the cluster's centroid.

MapReduce Solution for K-Means Clustering

The MapReduce solution for K-Means clustering is an iterative solution, where each iteration is implemented as a MapReduce job. K-Means needs an iterative version of MapReduce, which is not a standard formulation of the MapReduce paradigm. To implement an iterative MapReduce solution, we need a driver or control program on the client side to initialize the K centroid positions, call the iteration of MapReduce jobs, and determine whether the iteration should continue or end. The mapper needs to fetch the data point and all cluster centroids; the cluster centroids have to be shared among all mappers. We can manage this in many different ways by using HDFS or a global data structure server like Redis or memcached. The reducer recomputes new means.

Note that each iteration of the algorithm is structured as a single MapReduce job, which iteratively improves partitioning of data into K clusters. The overall MapReduce pseudocode solution is shown in Example 12-1. The change() function is used to terminate the MapReduce iteration when there is not much change in centroids.

Example 12-1. K-Means clustering algorithm

```
 1 // k = number of desired clusters
 2 // delta = acceptable error for convergence
 3 // data = input data
 4 kmeans(k, delta, data) {
 5    // initialize the cluster centroids
 6    initial_centroids = pick(k, data);
 7
 8    // this is how we broadcast centers to mappers
 9    writeToHDFS(initial_centroids);
10
11    // iterate as long as necessary
12    current_centroids = initial_centroids;
13    while (true) {
14        // theMapReduceJob() does 2 tasks:
15        //     1. uses current_centroids in map()
16        //     2. reduce() creates new_centroids and writes it to HDFS
17        theMapReduceJob();
18        new_centroids = readFromHDFS();
19        if change(new_centroids, current_centroids) <= delta {
20            // we are done, terminate loop-iteration
21            break;
22        }
23        else {
24            current_centroids = new_centroids;
25        }
26    }
27
28    result = readFromHDFS();
29    return result;
30 }
```

The change() method is presented in Example 12-2.

Example 12-2. K-Means clustering algorithm: change() method

```
1 change(new_centroids, current_centroids) {
2    new_distance = [sum of squared distance in the new_centroids];
3    current_distance = [sum of squared distance in the current_centroids];
4    changed = absoulteValue(new_distance - current_distance);
5    return changed;
6 }
```

The next three subsections provide the details of the MapReduce job. It will have three functions: map(), combine(), and reduce().

MapReduce Solution: map()

The map() function classifies data. It uses the cluster centroids and assigns each point $p \in 1, 2, ..., n$ to the nearest center. Note that in the first iteration, the centroids will be the ones selected at random or created manually. map() accepts points in the data set and outputs one (Cluster-ID, Vector) pair for each point, where the Cluster-ID is the integer ID of the cluster that is closest to the point, and the Vector is a d-dimensional vector (an array of the double data type).

The map() function will do the following, as shown in Example 12-3:

- Read the cluster centroids into memory from a SequenceFile[1] (note that we may also use Redis or memcached for persisting cluster centroids). In Hadoop's implementation, this will be done in the setup() method of the mapper class.

- Iterate over each cluster centroid for each input key-value pair. In Hadoop's implementation, for the map() function, the key is generated by Hadoop and ignored (not used).

- Compute the Euclidean distances and save the nearest center with the lowest distance to the input point (as a d-dimensional vector).

- Write the key-value pair to be consumed by reducers, where the key is the nearest cluster center to the input point (and the value is a d-dimensional vector). Both the key and the value are of the Vector data type.

Example 12-3. K-Means MapReduce: map() function

```
 1 public class KmeansMapper ... {
 2
 3     private List<Vector> centers = null;
 4
 5     private List<Vector> readCentersFromSequenceFile() {
 6         // read cluster centroids from a SequenceFile,
 7         // which is a set of key-value pairs
 8         ...
 9     }
10
11     // called once at the beginning of the map task
12     public void setup(Context context) {
13         this.centers = readCentersFromSequenceFile();
14     }
15
16     /**
```

---

[1] org.apache.hadoop.io.SequenceFile

```
17      * @param key is MapReduce generated, ignored here
18      * @param value is the d-dimensional Vector (V1, V2, ..., Vd)
19      */
20    map(Object key, Vector value) {
21       Vector nearest = null;
22       double nearestDistance = Double.MAX_VALUE;
23       for (Vector center : centers) {
24          double distance = EuclideanDistance.calculateDistance(center, value);
25          if (nearest == null) {
26             nearest = center;
27             nearestDistance = distance;
28          }
29          else {
30             if (nearestDistance > distance) {
31                nearest = center;
32                nearestDistance = distance;
33             }
34          }
35       }
36
37       // prepare key-value for reducers
38       emit(nearest, value);
39    }
40
41 } // end of class KmeansMapper
```

MapReduce Solution: combine()

After each map task, a combiner is applied to mix the map task's intermediate data.
The combiner sums up the values—the sum is needed to compute the mean values—
for each dimension of vector objects. In the combine() function, we partially sum the
values of the points (as vectors) assigned to the same cluster. The combine() function
improves the efficiency of our algorithm because it avoids network traffic by transfer-
ring less data between slave (i.e., worker) nodes. See Example 12-4.

Example 12-4. K-Means MapReduce: combine() function

```
1 /**
2  * @param key is the Centroid
3  * @param values is a list of Vectors
4  */
5 combine(Vector key, Iterable<Vector> values) {
6    // all dimensions in sum Vector are initialized to 0.0
7    Vector sum = new Vector();
8    for (Vector value : values) {
9       // note that value.length = d,
10      // where d is the number of dimensions for input objects
11      for (int i = 0; i < value.length; i++) {
12         sum[i] += value[i];
13      }
```

```
14   }
15
16   emit(key, sum);
17 }
```

MapReduce Solution: reduce()

The reducer does recentering: it recreates the centroids for all clusters by recalculating the means for all clusters (see Example 12-5). In the reduce() phase, the outputs of the map() function are grouped by Cluster-ID, and for each Cluster-ID the centroid of the points associated with that Cluster-ID is calculated. Each reduce() function generates (Cluster-ID, Centroid) pairs, which represent the newly calculated cluster centers. The reduce() function can be summarized as follows:

- The main task of the reduce() function is to recenter.

- Each reducer iterates over each value vector and calculates the mean vector. Once you have found the mean, this is the new center; your final step is to save it into a persistent store (such as a SequenceFile).

Example 12-5. K-Means MapReduce: reduce() function

```
 1 /**
 2  * @param key is the Centroid
 3  * @param values is a list of Vectors
 4  */
 5 reduce(Vector key, Iterable<Vector> values) {
 6   // all dimensions in newCenter are initialized to 0.0
 7   Vector newCenter = new Vector();
 8   int count = 0;
 9   for (Vector value : values) {
10     count++;
11     for (int i = 0; i < value.length; i++) {
12       newCenter[i] += value[i];
13     }
14   }
15
16   for (int i = 0; i < key.length; i++) {
17     // set new mean for each dimension
18     newCenter[i] = newCenter[i] / count;
19   }
20
21   emit(key.ID, newCenter);
22 }
```

K-Means Implementation by Spark

The Spark framework provides some common machine learning (ML) functionality in a library called MLlib. MLlib (*http://bit.ly/machine_learning_lib*) supports the following types of machine learning algorithms:

- Binary classification
- Regression
- Clustering (includes K-Means)
- Collaborative filtering
- Gradient descent optimization primitive

MLlib supports K-Means clustering that groups the data points into a predefined number of clusters. The MLlib implementation includes a parallelized variant of the k-means++ method called kmeans|| (i.e., a parallel implementation of K-Means algorithm). Spark's implementation of K-Means has the following parameters:

- K is the number of desired clusters.
- maxIterations is the maximum number of iterations to run.
- initializationMode specifies either random initialization or initialization via kmeans||.
- runs is the number of times to run the K-Means algorithm (note that K-Means is not guaranteed to find a globally optimal solution, and when run multiple times on a given data set, the algorithm returns the best clustering result).
- initializiationSteps determines the number of steps in the kmeans|| algorithm.
- epsilon determines the distance threshold within which we consider K-Means to have converged.

A sample implementation of K-Means is given by Spark as a JavaKMeans[2] class. In Example 12-6, I present the JavaKMeans class, after which I will show a sample run.

Example 12-6. Using MLlib K-Means from Java

```
1 package org.apache.spark.examples.mllib;
2
3 import java.util.regex.Pattern;
4 import org.apache.spark.SparkConf;
```

---

2 org.apache.spark.examples.mllib.JavaKMeans

```
 5 import org.apache.spark.api.java.JavaRDD;
 6 import org.apache.spark.api.java.JavaSparkContext;
 7 import org.apache.spark.api.java.function.Function;
 8 import org.apache.spark.mllib.clustering.KMeans;
 9 import org.apache.spark.mllib.clustering.KMeansModel;
10 import org.apache.spark.mllib.linalg.Vector;
11 import org.apache.spark.mllib.linalg.Vectors;
12
13 /**
14  * Example using MLlib K-Means from Java.
15  */
16 public final class JavaKMeans {
17
18     private static class ParsePoint implements Function<String, Vector> {
19         private static final Pattern SPACE = Pattern.compile(" ");
20         @Override
21         public Vector call(String line) {
22             String[] tok = SPACE.split(line);
23             double[] point = new double[tok.length];
24             for (int i = 0; i < tok.length; ++i) {
25                 point[i] = Double.parseDouble(tok[i]);
26             }
27             return Vectors.dense(point);
28         }
29     }
30
31     public static void main(String[] args) {
32         if (args.length < 3) {
33             System.err.println(
34                 "Usage: JavaKMeans <input_file> <k> <max_iterations> [<runs>]");
35             System.exit(1);
36         }
37         String inputFile = args[0];
38         int k = Integer.parseInt(args[1]);
39         int iterations = Integer.parseInt(args[2]);
40         int runs = 1;
41
42         if (args.length >= 4) {
43             runs = Integer.parseInt(args[3]);
44         }
45
46         SparkConf sparkConf = new SparkConf().setAppName("JavaKMeans");
47         JavaSparkContext sc = new JavaSparkContext(sparkConf);
48         JavaRDD<String> lines = sc.textFile(inputFile);
49         JavaRDD<Vector> points = lines.map(new ParsePoint());
50         KMeansModel model = KMeans.train(points.rdd(), k, iterations, runs,
51                                     KMeans.K_MEANS_PARALLEL());
52
53         System.out.println("Cluster centers:");
54         for (Vector center : model.clusterCenters()) {
55             System.out.println(" " + center);
56         }
```

```
57      double cost = model.computeCost(points.rdd());
58      System.out.println("Cost: " + cost);
59
60      sc.stop();
61    }
62 }
```

Some of the key points of the JavaKMeans class are:

- Line 47: Create the JavaSparkContext object, which is a connection object to a Spark master and an entry point to run jobs in the Spark cluster.

- Line 48: Read the input file (as a record of strings) and create a new JavaRDD<String> (a set of string objects).

- Line 49: Convert each string record in JavaRDD<String> to a Vector of doubles. We accomplish this using the ParsePoint class, which takes a string object and tokenizes it.

- Line 50: The K-Means algorithm is called by the KMeans[3] class, which generates a KMeansModel[4] (a clustering model for K-Means, where each point belongs to the cluster with the closest center).

- Lines 53–55: Print the cluster centers.

- Line 57: Return the K-Means cost (the sum of squared distances of points to their nearest center) for this model on the given data.

Sample Run of Spark K-Means Implementation

This section presents a script, sample input, and a log of a sample run for Spark's K-Means implementation.

Script

This sample shell script runs the K-Means program:

```
1 $ cat run_spark_kmeans_example.sh
2 #!/bin/bash
3 export JAVA_HOME=/usr/java/jdk7
4 export SPARK_HOME=/home/hadoop/spark-1.1.0
5 export SPARK_MASTER=spark://myserver100:7077
6 SPARK_JAR=spark-examples-1.1.0-hadoop2.5.0.jar
export APP_JAR=$SPARK_HOME/examples/target/scala-2.10/$SPARK_JAR
7 # Run on a Spark cluster
```

---

3 org.apache.spark.mllib.clustering.KMeans

4 org.apache.spark.mllib.clustering.KMeansModel

```
 8 prog=org.apache.spark.examples.mllib.JavaKMeans
 9 inputfile=/home/hadoop/testspark/kmeans_input_file.txt
10 K=3
11 iterations=10
12 $SPARK_HOME/bin/spark-submit \
13   --class $prog \
14   --master $SPARK_MASTER \
15   --executor-memory 2G \
16   --total-executor-cores 20 \
17   $APP_JAR \
18   $inputfile $K $iterations
```

Input

```
$hadoop fs -cat /home/hadoop/testspark/kmeans_input_file.txt
1.0 2.0
1.0 3.0
1.0 4.0
2.0 5.0
2.0 6.0
2.0 7.0
2.0 8.0
3.0 100.0
3.0 101.0
3.0 102.0
3.0 103.0
3.0 104.0
```

Log of sample run

```
$ ./run_spark_kmeans_example.sh
...
INFO : Job finished: collectAsMap at KMeans.scala:193, took 0.174752238 s
INFO : Run 0 finished in 1 iterations
INFO : Iterations took 0.193 seconds.
INFO : KMeans converged in 1 iterations.
INFO : The cost for the best run is 17.750000000000007.
INFO : Removing RDD 3 from persistence list
INFO : Removing RDD 3
Cluster centers:
 [3.0, 102.0]
 [1.25, 3.5]
 [2.0, 7.0]
...
INFO : Job finished: sum at KMeansModel.scala:56, took 0.090478143 s
Cost: 17.750000000000007
...
```

This chapter introduced the K-Means clustering technique. I presented an iterative MapReduce algorithm to solve K-Means clustering, and we also examined a Spark solution for K-Means clustering.

The next chapter discusses a machine learning algorithm known as kNN (k-Nearest Neighbors).

k-Nearest Neighbors

This chapter focuses on an important machine learning algorithm called k-Nearest Neighbors (kNN), where k is an integer greater than 0. The kNN classification problem is to find the k nearest data points in a data set to a given query data point. This operation is also known as a *kNN join*, and can be defined as: given two data sets R and S, we want to find the k nearest Neighbor from S for every object in R. In data mining, R and S are called the *query* and *training* data sets, respectively. The training data set (S) refers to data that has already been classified, while the query data set (R) refers to data that is going to be classified using S's classifications.

The objective of this chapter is to present a MapReduce solution using Spark for the kNN join algorithm. The kNN algorithm has been discussed extensively in many machine learning books, such as *Machine Learning for Hackers*[8] and *Machine Learning in Action*[10]. kNN is an important clustering algorithm that has many applications in data mining (such as pattern recognition) and bioinformatics (such as the breast cancer diagnosis problem[23], the weather generating model, and product recommendation systems). The kNN algorithm can be fairly expensive, especially when we have a large training set, which is why MapReduce is well suited for it.

So what exactly is kNN? Nearest Neighbor analysis, or Nearest Neighbor search, is an algorithm for classifying n-dimensional objects[1] based on their similarity to other n-dimensional objects. In machine learning, Nearest Neighbor analysis has been developed as a way to recognize patterns of data without requiring an exact match to any stored patterns or objects. Similar n-dimensional objects are near each other and

---

1 An n-dimensional object x, which has n attributes, will be represented as $(x_1, x_2, ..., x_n)$.

dissimilar *n*-dimensional objects are distant from each other. Thus, the distance between two cases is a measure of their dissimilarity. According to Wikipedia:[2]

> In pattern recognition, the k-Nearest Neighbors algorithm (kNN) is a nonparametric method for classifying objects based on the closest training examples in the feature space. kNN is a type of instance-based learning, or lazy learning where the function is only approximated locally and all computation is deferred until classification. The kNN algorithm is among the simplest of all machine learning algorithms: an object is classified by a majority vote of its neighbors, with the object being assigned to the class most common among its *k* nearest neighbors (*k* is a positive integer, typically small). If *k* = 1, then the object is simply assigned to the class of its nearest neighbor.

kNN Classification

The central idea of kNN is to build a classification method making no assumptions about the form of the "smooth" function *f*:

$$x = (x_1, x_2, ..., x_n)$$

$$y = f(x)$$

that relates *y* (the response variable) to *x* (predictor variables). The function *f* is non-parametric because it does not involve any estimation of parameters in any shape or form. In kNN, given a new point $p = (p_1, p_2, ..., p_n)$, we dynamically identify *k* observations in the training data set that are similar to *p* (the *k* nearest neighbors). Neighbors are defined by a distance or dissimilarity measure that we can compute between observations based on the independent variables. For simplicity, we will use the Euclidean distance.

The Euclidean distance between the points $(x_1, x_2, ..., x_n)$ and $(p_1, p_2, ..., p_n)$ is defined as:

$$\sqrt{(x_1 - p_1)^2 + (x_2 - p_2)^2 + ... + (x_n - p_n)^2}$$

So how do you find the *k* nearest neighbors? For each queried *n*-dimensional object (i.e., an object that has *n* attributes), the Euclidean distances between the queried object and all the training data objects are calculated, and the queried object is assigned the class label that most of the *k* closest training data has. Note that the kNN algorithm assumes that all data corresponds to an *n*-dimensional metric (denoted by R_n) space, which means that the data type of all attributes is `double`. This data type is

---

2 Accessed September 2014.

required since we need to calculate the Euclidean distance between n-dimensional objects.

Distance Functions

As mentioned earlier, the Euclidean distance function has been used in many data mining clustering algorithms. The Euclidean distance between two n-dimensional objects X and Y is given here. Let X and Y be defined as:

$$X = (X_1, X_2, ..., X_n)$$
$$Y = (Y_1, Y_2, ..., Y_n)$$

Then $distance(X, Y)$ is defined as:

$$distance(X, Y) = \sqrt{\sum_{i=1}^{n} (X_i - Y_i)^2}$$

$$distance(X, Y) = \sqrt{(X_1 - Y_1)^2 + (X_2 - Y_2)^2 + \ldots + (X_n - Y_n)^2}$$

Note again that the Euclidean distance function will work only for metric data, where all attributes have the `double` primitive data type. But what if our attributes are non-numeric (e.g., `"big spender"`, `"medium spender"`, `"small spender"`, and `"non spender"`)? In that case, we need to come up with custom distance functions to accommodate different data types; that is, we need to answer `distance("big spender", "small spender")` and so on. Most of the time, in real applications, we will need custom distance functions.

Depending on your application or problem domain, you may also want to consider alternative distance functions for kNN, such as:

- Manhattan:

$$\sum_{i=1}^{n} |X_i - Y_i|$$

- Minkowski:

$$\left(\sqrt{\sum_{i=1}^{n}\left(|X_i - Y_i|\right)^q}\right)^{1/q}$$

kNN Example

To recap, the kNN algorithm is an intuitive method for classifying unclassified data (called an *input query*) based on its similarity to or distance from the data in the training data set. For our example, let our training data set have four classes, $\{C_1, C_2, C_3, C_4\}$, as illustrated in Figure 13-1.

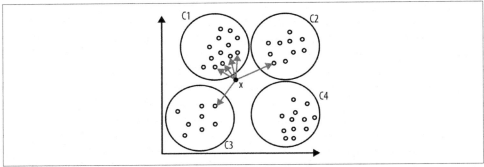

Figure 13-1. kNN classification with four classes, {C1, C2, C3, C4}

Given $k=6$ and $X = (X_1, X_2, ..., X_n)$, our goal is to find a class label from $\{C_1, C_2, C_3, C_4\}$ for the unknown data X. As you can see in Figure 13-1, of the six closest neighbors, four belong to C_1, one belongs to C_2, one belongs to C_3, and zero belong to C_4. Therefore, by a majority vote, X is assigned to C_1, which is a predominant class.

An Informal kNN Algorithm

The kNN algorithm can be summarized in the following simple steps:

1. Determine k (the selection of k depends on your data and project requirements; there is no magic formula for k).

2. Calculate the distances between the new input and all the training data (as with k, the selection of a distance function also depends on the type of data).

3. Sort the distance and determine the k nearest neighbors based on the kth minimum distance.

4. Gather the categories of those neighbors.

5. Determine the category based on majority vote.

Formal kNN Algorithm

To define the kNN algorithm formally, we need to go over some terms:

Distance function
> The distance function depends on your application domain, but most of the time the Euclidean distance function works for most metric data. The distance between two points $(x_1, x_2, ..., x_n)$ and $(y_1, y_2, ..., y_n)$ is defined as $|x, y|$.

k nearest neighbors
> Given an object q (called a *query object*), a training data set S, and an integer k, the k nearest neighbors of q from S, denoted as kNN(q, S), are a set of k objects from S such that:

$$\forall o \in kNN(q, S), \forall s \in \{S - kNN(q, S)\}, |o, q| \le |s, q|$$

kNN join
> Given two data sets R and S (where S is a training data set) and an integer k, the kNN join of R and S is defined as:

$$kNNjoin(R, S) = \{(r, s)|\forall r \in R, \forall s \in kNN(r, S)\}$$

> Basically, this combines each object $r \in R$ with its k nearest neighbors from S.

Java-like Non-MapReduce Solution for kNN

Given $K > 0$, a query set (i.e., the data that we want to classify), and a training set (i.e., the training data whose data objects are already classified), next I provide a Java-like non-MapReduce solution for the kNN algorithm. In Example 13-1, the Point class is used to represent *n*-dimensional data.

Example 13-1. classify() method

```
1 /**
2  * Classify queried data using kNN analysis
3  * @param k is an integer > 0
4  * @param querySet is a set of data objects that we want to classify
5  * @param trainingSet is a set of training data (already classified)
6  */
7 public static void classify(int k,
```

```
 8                         Point[] querySet,
 9                         Point[] trainingSet) {
10      foreach (Point query : querySet) {
11          knn(k, query, trainingSet);
12      }
13 }
```

The kNN algorithm (non-MapReduce version) is illustrated in Example 13-2.

Example 13-2. kNN algorithm

```
 1 /**
 2  * kNN analysis
 3  * @param k is an integer > 0
 4  * @param query is a data object that we want to classify
 5  * @param trainingSet is a set of training data (already classified)
 6  */
 7 public static void knn(int k,
 8                        Point query,
 9                        Point[] trainingSet) {
10      foreach (Point training : trainingSet) {
11          // Create a fixed-size sorted map of length k,
12          // where we map the distance to a training point.
13          SortedMap<Double, Point> map = new TreeMap<Double, Point>(k);
14
15          // Calculate distance of test point to training point.
16          double d = calculateEuclidianDistance(query, training);
17
18          // Insert training point into sorted list, discarding
19          // if training point not within k nearest neighbors
20          // of query point.
21          map.put(d, training);
22      }
23
24      // Do majority vote on k nearest neighbors
25      // and assign the corresponding label to the
26      // query point.
27      query.label = majorityVote(map, k);
28 }
```

Example 13-3 defines the Euclidean distance function.

Example 13-3. Euclidean distance function

```
 1 /**
 2  * @param query is an n-dimensional query data object
 3  * @param reference is an n-dimensional reference data object
 4  * @return the quadratic Euclidean distance
 5  */
 6 public static double calculateEuclidianDistance(Point query,
 7                                                 Point reference) {
```

```
8      double sum = 0.0;
9
10     // n is the number of dimensions in the vector
11     // space. Here n is equal to query.length, which
12     // is equal to reference.length.
13     int n = query.length;
14
15     for (int i = 0; i < n; i++) {
16         double difference = reference.vector[i] - query.vector[i];
17         sum += difference * difference;
18     }
19
20     return Math.sqrt(sum);
21 }
```

kNN Implementation in Spark

Given two data sets R and S, our goal is to find the k nearest neighbors from S for every object in R. As you've learned, in data mining, S is called a training data set. The complexity of this kNN join algorithm is $O(N^2)$, because for every object r in R, you want to calculate $distance(r, s)$ for every s in S. Finding $distance(r, s)$ requires the Cartesian product of R and S. Spark provides a high-level API to calculate the Cartesian product between two data sets. For example, `JavaPairRDD.cartesian(JavaPairRDD)` finds the Cartesian product of two data sets. The signature of the `cartesian()` function is defined as follows:

```
<U> JavaPairRDD<T,U> cartesian(JavaRDDLike<U,?> other)

// Description: Return the Cartesian product of this RDD
//              and another one; that is, the RDD of all pairs of elements
//              (a, b) where a is in this and b is in other.
```

The following example shows how to calculate the Cartesian product of two data sets in Spark:

```
// data set R
List<Tuple2<String,String>> R = new ArrayList<Tuple2<String,String>>();
R.add(new Tuple2<String,String>("r1", "R1"));
R.add(new Tuple2<String,String>("r2", "R2"));
R.add(new Tuple2<String,String>("r3", "R3"));

// data set S
List<Tuple2<String,String>> S = new ArrayList<Tuple2<String,String>>();
S.add(new Tuple2<String,String>("s1", "S1"));
S.add(new Tuple2<String,String>("s2", "S2"));
S.add(new Tuple2<String,String>("s3", "S3"));
S.add(new Tuple2<String,String>("s4", "S4"));

JavaPairRDD<String,String> R_RDD = ctx.parallelizePairs(R);
JavaPairRDD<String,String> S_RDD = ctx.parallelizePairs(S);
```

```
// perform the Cartesian product of this R and S
JavaPairRDD<Tuple2<String,String>, Tuple2<String,String>> cart =
    R_RDD.cartesian(S_RDD);

// save output
cart.saveAsTextFile("/output/z");
```

The output of this calculation for the Cartesian product of *R* and *S* is as follows:

```
# hadoop fs -cat /output/z/part*
((r1,R1),(s1,S1))
((r1,R1),(s2,S2))
((r1,R1),(s3,S3))
((r1,R1),(s4,S4))
((r2,R2),(s1,S1))
((r2,R2),(s2,S2))
((r2,R2),(s3,S3))
((r2,R2),(s4,S4))
((r3,R3),(s1,S1))
((r3,R3),(s2,S2))
((r3,R3),(s3,S3))
((r3,R3),(s4,S4))
```

Formalizing kNN for the Spark Implementation

Let R (the query data set) and S (the training data set) be d-dimensional data sets, for which we want to find kNN(R, S). Further assume that all training data (S) has been classified into $C = \{C_1, C_2, ...\}$, where C denotes all available classifications. We define R, S, and C as:

- $R = \{R_1, R_2, ..., R_m\}$
- $S = \{S_1, S_2, ..., S_n\}$
- $C = \{C_1, C_2, ..., C_p\}$

where:

- $R_i = (r_i, a_1, a_2, ..., a_d)$
- $S_j = (s_j, b_1, b_2, ..., b_d, C_j)$
- r_i is a unique record ID for R_i
- $a_1, a_2, ..., a_d$ are attributes of R_i
- s_j is a unique record ID for S_j
- $b_1, b_2, ..., b_d$ are attributes of S_j
- C_j is a classification identifier for S_j

Our goal is to find *kNN(R, S)*. To do so, we will calculate the Cartesian product of *R* and *S*, and then group the data by r_i (a unique record ID for R_i). After grouping, we will find the *k* nearest data points from *S* (by sorting distances in ascending order and then picking the first *k* elements). Once the *k* nearest data points from *S* are found, we will select the classification by a majority rule. Figure 13-2 illustrates this process.

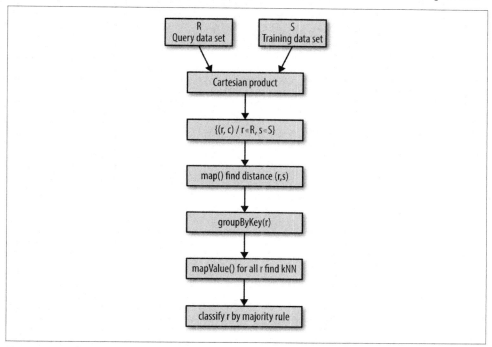

Figure 13-2. kNN implementation in Spark

Input Data Set Formats

We are assuming that *R* and *S* both represent *d*-dimensional data points. The input record for the query data set (*R*) will have the following format:

```
<unique-record-id><;><a-1><,><a-2><,>...<,><a-d>
```

The input record for the training data set (*S*) will have the following format:

```
<unique-record-id><;><classification-id><;><b-1><,><b-2><,>...<,><b-d>
```

Spark Implementation

Example 13-4 demonstrates the high-level steps of our kNN implementation in Spark. In the subsections that follow, we'll go over each step in more detail.

Example 13-4. High-level steps

```
 1 // Step 1: Import required classes and interfaces
 2
 3 public class kNN {
 4     static JavaSparkContext createJavaSparkContext() throws Exception {...}
 5     static List<Double> splitOnToListOfDouble(String str, String delimiter) {...}
 6     static double calculateDistance(String r, String s, int d) {...}
 7     static SortedMap<Double, String> findNearestK(
 8             Iterable<Tuple2<Double,String>> neighbors, int k) {...}
 9     static Map<String, Integer> buildClassificationCount(
10             Map<Double, String> nearestK) {...}
11     static String classifyByMajority(Map<String, Integer> majority) {...}
12
13     public static void main(String[] args) throws Exception {
14         // Step 2: Handle input parameters
15         // Step 3: Create a Spark context object (ctx)
16         // Step 4: Broadcast shared objects
17         // Step 5: Create RDDs for query and training data sets
18         // Step 6: Calculate Cartesian product of (R, S)
19         // Step 7: Find distance(r, s) for r in R and s in S
20         // Step 8: Group distances by r in R
21         // Step 9: Find the k nearest neighbors and classify r
22
23         // done
24         ctx.close();
25         System.exit(0);
26     }
27 }
```

Step 1: Import required classes and interfaces

Most of the Spark classes and interfaces are imported from two packages:
org.apache.spark.api.java and org.apache.spark.api.java.function.
Example 13-5 shows how to import them. The Broadcast class is used to broadcast
shared objects and data structures to all cluster nodes (this is similar to Hadoop's Con
figuration object, in which you can set() and get() objects in mappers and
reducers).

Example 13-5. Step 1: import required classes and interfaces

```
1 // Step 1: Import required classes and interfaces
2 import scala.Tuple2;
3 import org.apache.spark.SparkConf;
4 import org.apache.spark.broadcast.Broadcast;
5 import org.apache.spark.api.java.JavaRDD;
6 import org.apache.spark.api.java.JavaPairRDD;
7 import org.apache.spark.api.java.JavaSparkContext;
8 import org.apache.spark.api.java.function.Function;
9 import org.apache.spark.api.java.function.PairFunction;
```

```
10
11 import java.util.Map;
12 import java.util.HashMap;
13 import java.util.SortedMap;
14 import java.util.TreeMap;
15 import java.util.List;
16 import java.util.ArrayList;
17 import com.google.common.base.Splitter;
```

createJavaSparkContext() method

The `createJavaSparkContext()` method (shown in Example 13-6) creates an instance of a `JavaSparkContext` object, which is a factory for creating RDDs.

Example 13-6. createJavaSparkContext() method

```
1 static JavaSparkContext createJavaSparkContext() throws Exception {
2     SparkConf conf = new SparkConf();
3     // use a fast serializer
4     conf.set("spark.serializer", "org.apache.spark.serializer.KryoSerializer");
5     return ctx;
6 }
```

splitOnToListOfDouble() method

The `splitOnToListOfDouble()` method, shown in Example 13-7, accepts all attributes as a string object and returns a `List<Double>`.

Example 13-7. splitOnToListOfDouble() method

```
 1 /**
 2 * @param str is a comma- or semicolon-separated list of double values
 3 * str is like "1.1,2.2,3.3" or "1.1;2.2;3.3"
 4 *
 5 * @param delimiter is a delimiter such as ",", ";", ...
 6 * @return a List<Double> (all attributes for a data set record)
 7 */
 8 static List<Double> splitOnToListOfDouble(String str, String delimiter) {
 9     Splitter splitter = Splitter.on(delimiter).trimResults();
10     Iterable<String> tokens = splitter.split(str);
11     if (tokens == null) {
12         return null;
13     }
14     List<Double> list = new ArrayList<Double>();
15     for (String token: tokens) {
16         double data = Double.parseDouble(token);
17         list.add(data);
18     }
19     return list;
20 }
```

calculateDistance() method

The `calculateDistance()` method, shown in Example 13-8, accepts two vectors of *R* and *S* and computes the Euclidean distance between them. The Euclidean distance between two points $r = (r_1, r_2, ..., r_d)$ and $s = (s_1, s_2, ..., s_d)$ is defined as:

$$\text{distance}(r, s) = \sqrt{(r_1 - s_1)^2 + (r_2 - s_2)^2 + ... + (r_d - s_d)^2}$$

Based on your project and data requirements, you may select and use other distance functions.[3]

Example 13-8. calculateDistance() method

```
1 /**
2  * @param rAsString = "r.1,r.2,...,r.d"
3  * @param sAsString = "s.1,s.2,...,s.d"
4  * @param d is a dimension of R and S
5  */
6 static double calculateDistance(String rAsString, String sAsString, int d) {
7     List<Double> r = splitOnToListOfDouble(rAsString, ",");
8     List<Double> s = splitOnToListOfDouble(sAsString, ",");
9
10    // d is the number of dimensions in the vector
11    if (r.size() != d) {
12        return Double.NaN;
13    }
14    if (s.size() != d) {
15        return Double.NaN;
16    }
17
18    // here we have (r.size() == s.size() == d)
19    double sum = 0.0;
20    for (int i = 0; i < d; i++) {
21        double difference = r.get(i) - s.get(i);
22        sum += difference * difference;
23    }
24    return Math.sqrt(sum);
25 }
```

findNearestK() method

Given {(distance, classification)}, the `findNearestK()` method (shown in Example 13-9) finds the *k* nearest neighbors based on the distance.

---

3 For details on distance functions, refer to *http://www.saedsayad.com/k_nearest_neighbors.htm* (*http://bit.ly/k_nearest_neighbors*).

Example 13-9. findNearestK() method

```
1 static SortedMap<Double, String> findNearestK(
2   Iterable<Tuple2<Double,String>> neighbors,
3   int k) {
4     // keep only k nearest neighbors
5     SortedMap<Double, String> nearestK = new TreeMap<Double, String>();
6     for (Tuple2<Double,String> neighbor : neighbors) {
7         Double distance = neighbor._1;
8         String classificationID = neighbor._2;
9         nearestK.put(distance, classificationID);
10        // keep only k nearest neighbors
11        if (nearestK.size() > k) {
12            // remove the last-highest-distance neighbor from nearestK
13            nearestK.remove(nearestK.lastKey());
14        }
15    }
16    return nearestK;
17 }
```

buildClassificationCount() method

buildClassificationCount(), shown in Example 13-10, is a simple method that counts the classifications (this will be used to select the classification based on a majority count).

Example 13-10. buildClassificationCount() method

```
1 static Map<String, Integer> buildClassificationCount(Map<Double, String>
2                                                      nearestK) {
3     Map<String, Integer> majority = new HashMap<String, Integer>();
4     for (Map.Entry<Double, String> entry : nearestK.entrySet()) {
5         String classificationID = entry.getValue();
6         Integer count = majority.get(classificationID);
7         if (count == null) {
8             majority.put(classificationID, 1);
9         }
10        else {
11            majority.put(classificationID, count+1);
12        }
13    }
14    return majority;
15 }
```

classifyByMajority() method

The classifyByMajority() method, shown in Example 13-11, selects a classification based on a majority rule. For example, for a given query point r, if $k=6$ and classifications are $\{C_1, C_2, C_3, C_3, C_3, C_4\}$, then C_3 is selected based on a majority rule.

Example 13-11. classifyByMajority() method

```
1 static String classifyByMajority(Map<String, Integer> majority) {
2     int votes = 0;
3     String selectedClassification = null;
4     for (Map.Entry<String, Integer> entry : majority.entrySet()) {
5         if (selectedClassification == null) {
6             selectedClassification = entry.getKey();
7             votes = entry.getValue();
8         }
9         else {
10            int count = entry.getValue();
11            if (count > votes) {
12                selectedClassification = entry.getKey();
13                votes = count;
14            }
15        }
16    }
17    return selectedClassification;
18 }
```

Step 2: Handle input parameters

This step, shown in Example 13-12, reads four input parameters:

- k as an integer for kNN
- d as an integer for the dimension of the R and S vectors
- Query data set R (as an HDFS file)
- Training data set S (as an HDFS file)

Example 13-12. Step 2: handle input parameters

```
1    // Step 2: Handle input parameters
2    if (args.length < 4) {
3        System.err.println("Usage: kNN <k-knn> <d-dimension> <R> <S>");
4        System.exit(1);
5    }
6    Integer k = Integer.valueOf(args[0]); // k for kNN
7    Integer d = Integer.valueOf(args[1]); // d-dimension
8    String datasetR = args[2];
9    String datasetS = args[3];
```

Step 3: Create a Spark context object

This step, demonstrated in Example 13-13, creates a JavaSparkContext object, which is a factory for creating new RDDs.

Example 13-13. Step 3: create a Spark context object

```
1   // Step 3: Create a Spark context object
2   JavaSparkContext ctx = createJavaSparkContext("knn");
```

Step 4: Broadcast shared objects

To enable access to shared objects and data structures from all cluster nodes, Spark offers a Broadcast class with which you can register objects. You can then read them from any node. In Example 13-14, we broadcast two integer values (k and d), which are accessed by all cluster nodes.

Example 13-14. Step 4: broadcast shared objects

```
1   // Step 4: Broadcast shared objects
2   // Broadcast k and d as global shared objects,
3   // which can be accessed from all cluster nodes
4   final Broadcast<Integer> broadcastK = ctx.broadcast(k);
5   final Broadcast<Integer> broadcastD = ctx.broadcast(d);
```

Step 5: Create RDDs for query and training data sets

As shown in Example 13-15, this step creates two RDDs (one for R and another one for S). These RDDs represent raw data as string objects.

Example 13-15. Step 5: create RDDs for query and training data sets

```
1   // Step 5: Create RDDs for query and training data sets
2   JavaRDD<String> R = ctx.textFile(datasetR, 1);
3   R.saveAsTextFile("/output/R");
4   JavaRDD<String> S = ctx.textFile(datasetS, 1);
5   S.saveAsTextFile("/output/S");
```

For debugging/understanding purposes, this step creates the following output for the query data set (R):

```
# hadoop fs -cat /output/R/part*
1000;3.0,3.0
1001;10.1,3.2
1003;2.7,2.7
1004;5.0,5.0
1005;13.1,2.2
1006;12.7,12.7
```

and this output for the training data set (S):

```
# hadoop fs -cat /output/S/part*
100;c1;1.0,1.0
101;c1;1.1,1.2
102;c1;1.2,1.0
```

```
103;c1;1.6,1.5
104;c1;1.3,1.7
105;c1;2.0,2.1
106;c1;2.0,2.2
107;c1;2.3,2.3
208;c2;9.0,9.0
209;c2;9.1,9.2
210;c2;9.2,9.0
211;c2;10.6,10.5
212;c2;10.3,10.7
213;c2;9.6,9.1
214;c2;9.4,10.4
215;c2;10.3,10.3
300;c3;10.0,1.0
301;c3;10.1,1.2
302;c3;10.2,1.0
303;c3;10.6,1.5
304;c3;10.3,1.7
305;c3;10.0,2.1
306;c3;10.0,2.2
307;c3;10.3,2.3
```

Step 6: Calculate the Cartesian product of (R, S)

This step, shown in Example 13-16, finds the Cartesian product of the query data set (R) with the training data set (S). It creates the following RDD:

$$\{(r, s)/r \in R, s \in S\}$$

Example 13-16. Step 6: calculate the Cartesian product of (R, S)

```
1    // Step 6: Perform the Cartesian product of (R, S)
2    //<U> JavaPairRDD<T,U> cartesian(JavaRDDLike<U,?> other)
3    // Return the Cartesian product of this RDD and another
4    // one; that is, the RDD of all pairs of elements (a, b)
5    // where a is in this and b is in other.
6    JavaPairRDD<String,String> cart = R.cartesian(S);
7    cart.saveAsTextFile("/output/cart");
```

For debugging/understanding purposes, this step creates the following output (code has been trimmed to fit the page):

```
# hadoop fs -cat /output/cart/part*
(1000;3.0,3.0,100;c1;1.0,1.0)
(1000;3.0,3.0,101;c1;1.1,1.2)
...
(1000;3.0,3.0,306;c3;10.0,2.2)
(1000;3.0,3.0,307;c3;10.3,2.3)
(1001;10.1,3.2,100;c1;1.0,1.0)
(1001;10.1,3.2,101;c1;1.1,1.2)
...
```

```
(1001;10.1,3.2,306;c3;10.0,2.2)
(1001;10.1,3.2,307;c3;10.3,2.3)
...
...
(1006;12.7,12.7,306;c3;10.0,2.2)
(1006;12.7,12.7,307;c3;10.3,2.3)
```

Step 7: Find distance(r, s) for r in R and s in S

This step, demonstrated in Example 13-17, finds the Euclidian distance between every pair of (R, S). Based on your data and project requirements, you may select and use different distance algorithms (such as Minkowski). Note that the selection of the distance algorithm will influence the bias of the kNN classification. This step creates the following RDD:

$\{(r, \text{(distance, classification)})\}$

Example 13-17. Step 7: find distance(r, s) for r in R and s in S

```
1    // Step 7: Find distance(r, s) for r in R and s in S
2    // (K,V), where K = unique-record-id-of-R, V=Tuple2(distance, classification)
3    // distance = distance(r, s) where r in R and s in S
4    // classification is extracted from s
5    JavaPairRDD<String,Tuple2<Double,String>> knnMapped =
6          cart.mapToPair(new PairFunction<
7                                   Tuple2<String,String>, // input
8                                   String,                 // K
9                                   Tuple2<Double,String>  // V
10                                 >() {
11   public Tuple2<String,Tuple2<Double,String>> call(
12      Tuple2<String,String> cartRecord) {
13          String rRecord = cartRecord._1;
14          String sRecord = cartRecord._2;
15          String[] rTokens = rRecord.split(";");
16          String rRecordID = rTokens[0];
17          String r = rTokens[1]; // r.1, r.2, ..., r.d
18          String[] sTokens = sRecord.split(";");
19          // sTokens[0] = s.recordID
20          String sClassificationID = sTokens[1];
21          String s = sTokens[2]; // s.1, s.2, ..., s.d
22          Integer d = broadcastD.value();
23          double distance = calculateDistance(r, s, d);
24          String K = rRecordID; // r.recordID
25          Tuple2<Double,String> V = new Tuple2<Double,String>(
26                 distance, sClassificationID);
27          return new Tuple2<String,Tuple2<Double,String>>(K, V);
28      }
29   });
30   knnMapped.saveAsTextFile("/output/knnMapped");
```

For debugging/understanding purposes, this step creates the following output:

```
# hadoop fs -cat /output/knnMapped/part*
(1000,(2.8284271247461903,c1))
(1000,(2.6172504656604803,c1))
...
(1000,(7.045565981523415,c3))
(1000,(7.333484846919642,c3))
(1001,(9.362157870918434,c1))
...
(1001,(0.9219544457292893,c3))
...
(1006,(10.84158659975559,c3))
(1006,(10.673331251301065,c3))
```

Step 8: Group distances by r in R

After finding the distances for $\{(r, s)\}$, to find the k nearest neighbors, we group data by r (see Example 13-18). Once data is grouped by r, then we scan the group values and find the k nearest distances (as we'll discuss in step 9).

Example 13-18. Step 8: group distances by r in R

```
1   // Step 8: Group distances by r in R
2   // Now group the results by r.recordID and then find the k nearest neighbors.
3   JavaPairRDD<String, Iterable<Tuple2<Double,String>>> knnGrouped =
4      knnMapped.groupByKey();
```

This step creates the following RDD:

$$\{(r, \{(distance, classification)\}\}$$

Step 9: Find the k nearest neighbors and classify r

This step, shown in Example 13-19, scans the group values to find the k nearest neighbors. To find the k elements that have the smallest distances, we use SortedMap, which keeps only the k nearest neighbors. At every iteration, we make sure that we keep only the k nearest elements. Once the k nearest neighbors are found, we classify the query data by the majority rule.

Example 13-19. Step 9: find the k nearest neighbors and classify r

```
1   // Step 9: find the k nearest neighbors and classify r
2   // mapValues[U](f: (V) => U): JavaPairRDD[K, U]
3   // Pass each value in the key-value pair RDD through a
4   // map() function without changing the keys;
5   // this also retains the original RDD's partitioning.
6   // Generate (K,V) pairs where K=r.recordID, V = classificationID.
```

```
7    JavaPairRDD<String, String> knnOutput =
8      knnGrouped.mapValues(new Function<
9        Iterable<Tuple2<Double,String>>, // input
10       String // output (classification)
11       >() {
12       public String call(Iterable<Tuple2<Double,String>> neighbors) {
13         Integer k = broadcastK.value();
14         SortedMap<Double, String> nearestK = findNearestK(neighbors, k);
15         // now we have the k nearest neighbors in nearestK,
16         // we need to find out the classification by majority
17         // by counting classifications
18         Map<String, Integer> majority = buildClassificationCount(nearestK);
19
20         // find classificationID with majority of vote
21         String selectedClassification = classifyByMajority(majority);
22         return selectedClassification;
23       }
24   });
25   knnOutput.saveAsTextFile("/output/knnOutput");
```

This step creates the final output, which includes classification of the entire query data set:

```
# hadoop fs -cat /output/knnOutput/part*
(1005,c3)
(1001,c3)
(1000,c1)
(1004,c1)
(1006,c2)
(1003,c1)
```

Combining steps 8 and 9

Here I'll show you how the groupByKey() and mapValues() operations can be combined into a single step using reduceByKey() or combineByKey(). We used the following RDDs and transformations in steps 8 and 9:

- RDDs:
  - knnMapped: JavaPairRDD<String,Tuple2<Double,String>>
  - knnGrouped: JavaPairRDD<String, Iterable<Tuple2<Double,String>>>
  - knnOutput: JavaPairRDD<String, String>
- Transformations:
  - knnMapped --> groupBy() --> knnGrouped
  - knnGrouped --> mapValues() --> knnOutput

Based on these RDDs, we cannot use reduceByKey(), since it requires the output type (String in knnOutput.V) to be the same as the type of the input values (Tuple2<Double,String> in knnMapped.V). The combineByKey() transformation is designed for when your return type from the aggregation differs from the type of the values being aggregated. Therefore, we will combine steps 8 and 9 into a single step using `combine` `ByKey()`. The combined step uses the following RDDs and implements one transformation:

- RDDs:
  — `knnMapped: JavaPairRDD<String,Tuple2<Double,String>>`
  — `knnOutput: JavaPairRDD<String, String>`
- Transformation:
  — `knnMapped --> combineByKey() --> knnOutput`

To combine the `groupBy()` and `mapValues()` transformations into a single transformation, `combineByKey()`, we need to write three basic functions. Before we do that, though, let's look at the basic signature of `combineByKey()`:

```
public <C> JavaPairRDD<K,C> combineByKey(
      Function<V,C> createCombiner,
      Function2<C,V,C> mergeValue,
      Function2<C,C,C> mergeCombiners
)

Description: Generic function to combine the elements for each key using a
            custom set of aggregation functions. Turns a JavaPairRDD[(K, V)]
            into a result of type JavaPairRDD[(K, C)], for a "combined type"
            C * Note that V and C can be different -- for example, one might
            group an RDD of type (Int, Int) into an RDD of type (Int, List[Int]).
            Users provide three functions:
            - createCombiner, which turns a V into a C
            (e.g., creates a one-element list)
            - mergeValue, to merge a V into a C (e.g.,
            adds it to the end of a list)
            - mergeCombiners, to combine two C's into
            a single one.
```

And now here are the three functions required for using `combineByKey()`:

```
Function<Tuple2<Double,String>, String> createCombiner =
    new Function<Tuple2<Double,String>, String>() {
    @Override
    public String call(Tuple2<Double,String> x) {
       // left as an exercise to an interested reader
    }
};

Function2<String, Tuple2<Double,String>, String> mergeValue =
new Function2<String, Tuple2<Double,String>, String>() {
    @Override
    public AvgCount call(String a, Tuple2<Double,String> x) {
       // left as an exercise to an interested reader
    }
};
```

```
Function2<String, String, String> mergeCombiners =
   new Function2<String, String, String>() {
   @Override
   public String call(String a, String b) {
      // left as an exercise to an interested reader
   }
};

JavaPairRDD<String, String> knnOutput =
   knnMapped.combineByKey(createCombiner, mergeValue, mergeCombiners);
```

YARN shell script

The following is the script to run our Spark kNN implementation in the YARN environment:

```
 1 $ cat run_knn.sh
 2 #!/bin/bash
 3 export JAVA_HOME=/usr/java/jdk7
 4 export SPARK_HOME=/usr/local/spark-1.0.0
 5 export HADOOP_HOME=/usr/local/hadoop-2.5.0
 6 export HADOOP_CONF_DIR=$HADOOP_HOME/etc/hadoop
 7 export YARN_APPLICATION_CLASSPATH=$HADOOP_CONF_DIR
 8 BOOK_HOME=/mp/data-algorithms-book
 9 APP_JAR=$BOOK_HOME/dist/data_algorithms_book.jar
10 #
11 k=4
12 d=2
13 R=/knn/R.txt
14 S=/knn/S.txt
15 prog=org.dataalgorithms.chap13.spark.kNN
16 $SPARK_HOME/bin/spark-submit
17      --class $prog \
18      --master yarn-cluster \
19      --num-executors 12 \
20      --driver-memory 3g \
21      --executor-memory 7g \
22      --executor-cores 12 \
23      $APP_JAR $k $d $R $S
```

This chapter implemented a distributed algorithm for kNN using Spark. Spark's high-level abstraction enabled us to express the algorithm in a straightforward manner. The next chapter provides a distributed algorithm for Naive Bayes, which is one of the most important classification techniques.

## CHAPTER 14

Naive Bayes

In data mining and machine learning, there are many classification algorithms. One of the simplest but most effective is the Naive Bayes classifier (*http://bit.ly/naive_bayes*) (NBC). The main focus of this chapter is to present a distributed Map-Reduce implementation (using Spark) of the NBC that is a combination of a supervised learning method and probabilistic classifier. Naive Bayes is a linear classifier. To understand it, we need to understand some basic and conditional probabilities. When we are dealing with numeric data, it is better to use clustering techniques (such as K-Means (*http://bit.ly/k-means_clustering*) and k-Nearest Neighbors (*http://bit.ly/k-nearest_algorithm*) methods and algorithms), but for classification of names, symbols, emails, and texts, it may be better to use a probabilistic method such as the NBC. In some cases, the NBC is used to classify numeric data as well. In the following section, you will see examples of both symbolic and numeric data.

The NBC is a probabilistic classifier based on applying Bayes' theorem with strong (naive) independence assumptions. In a nutshell, an NBC assigns inputs into one of the k classes $\{C_1, C_2, ..., C_k\}$ based on some properties (features) of the inputs. NBCs have applications such as email spam filtering and document classification.

For example, a spam filter using a Naive Bayes classifier will assign each email to one of two clusters: *spam mail* or *not a spam mail*. Since Naive Bayes is a supervised learning method, it has two distinct stages:

Stage 1: Training (see Figure 14-1)
  This stage uses training data from a set of finite instances of data samples to build a classifier (which will be used in stage 2). This is the so-called *supervised learning method*—learning from a set of samples and then using this information for the new data classification.

Stage 2: Classification (see Figure 14-2)

In this stage, we use training data and Bayes's theorem to classify new data in one of the categories identified in stage 1.

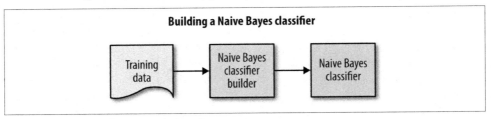

Figure 14-1. Naive Bayes: training phase

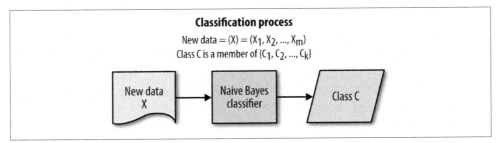

Figure 14-2. Naive Bayes: classification

Training and Learning Examples

Let each data set have m attributes $(X = (x_1, x_2, ..., x_m))$, the size of our training data be n, and our classification have k distinct categories $\{C_1, C_2, ..., C_k\}$, where $k \leq n$. Then we will have:

$(X_{11}, X_{12}, ..., X_{1m})$, (c_1)

$(X_{21}, X_{22}, ..., X_{2m})$, (c_2)

...

$(X_{n1}, X_{n2}, ..., X_{nm})$, (c_n)

where c_i is a member of $\{C_1, C_2, ..., C_k\}$.

Numeric Training Data

Table 14-1 is an example of numeric training data. Note that the first column (Person) is metadata (i.e., it's not part of the actual data).

Table 14-1. Sample numeric training data

Person	Height (feet)	Weight (lbs)	Foot size (inches)	Gender (classification)
1	6.00	180	12	male
2	5.92	190	11	male
3	5.58	170	12	male
4	5.92	165	10	male
5	5.00	100	6	female
6	5.50	150	8	female
7	5.42	130	7	female
8	5.75	150	9	female

Here are the facts about this numeric training data:

- The Gender column is the classification column. There are two ($k = 2$) classification classes, {male, female}, where $C_1 = male$ and $C_2 = female$.

- There are three attributes ($m = 3$) per data set: `height`, `weight`, and `foot size`. We consider each data instance to be an m-dimensional vector of attribute values: $X = (X_1, X_2, ..., X_m)$.

- The training data size is eight ($n = 8$), identified by the first column (numbers 1, 2, ..., 8).

- Our goal is to use this training data to build a classifier system (using Bayes' theorem) that will enable us to determine whether a person is male or female. This classification will be based on the values of the three attributes `height`, `weight`, and `foot size`.

Symbolic Training Data

Table 14-2 is an example of symbolic training data from Tom Mitchell's book *Machine Learning*[19]. Note that the first column is metadata (i.e., it's not part of the actual data).

Table 14-2. Sample symbolic training data

Day	Outlook	Temperature	Humidity	Wind	PlayTennis (classification)
D_1	Sunny	Hot	High	Weak	No
D_2	Sunny	Hot	High	Strong	No
D_3	Overcast	Hot	High	Weak	Yes
D_4	Rain	Mild	High	Weak	Yes
D_5	Rain	Cool	Normal	Weak	Yes

Day	Outlook	Temperature	Humidity	Wind	PlayTennis (classification)
D_6	Rain	Cool	Normal	Strong	No
D_7	Overcast	Cool	Normal	Strong	Yes
D_8	Sunny	Mild	High	Weak	No
D_9	Sunny	Cool	Normal	Weak	Yes
D_{10}	Rain	Mild	Normal	Weak	Yes
D_{11}	Sunny	Mild	Normal	Strong	Yes
D_{12}	Overcast	Mild	High	Strong	Yes
D_{13}	Overcast	Hot	Normal	Weak	Yes
D_{14}	Rain	Mild	High	Strong	No

Here are the facts about this symbolic training data:

- The PlayTennis column is the classification column. There are two ($k = 2$) classification classes: {Yes, No}, where $C_1 =$ Yes and $C_2 =$ No.

- There are four attributes ($m = 4$) per data set: outlook, temperature, humidity, and wind. We consider each data instance to be an m-dimensional vector of attribute values: $X = (X_1, X_2, ..., X_m)$.

- The training data size is 14 ($n = 14$), identified by the first column {$D_1, D_2, ..., D_{14}$}.

- Our goal is to use this training data to build a classifier system (using Bayes' theorem) that will enable us to decide whether to play tennis based on the weather conditions (i.e., we wish to classify the data into two classes, Yes or No, for Play-Tennis). This classification will be based on the values of the four attributes outlook, temperature, humidity, and windy.

Now the real question is, if our input data is the following:

```
X = (X1 = u1, X2=u2, X3=u3, X4=u4)
  = (Outlook = Overcast,
     Temperature = Hot,
     Humidity = High,
     Wind = Strong)
```

then will our classification to PlayTennis be Yes or No? The Naive Bayes classifier (using Bayes' theorem) can answer this question based on the data given in the training/learning phase. Here, *naive* refers to the fact that we assume that all probabilities for our data attributes are independent; that is, for a given data set $X = (X_1, X_2, ..., X_m)$, we will assume that these attributes are independent of each other and therefore that the probabilities for each attribute will also be independent. This is a very strong ("naive") assumption. Some statisticians argue that the use of the NBC is problematic because the "naive" assumption of independence is almost always invalid in the real world. But in fact, the Naive Bayes method has been shown to perform surprisingly well in a wide variety of real-world contexts.

Conditional Probability

Since Naive Bayes is based on probabilistic classification (and especially on conditional probability), I will provide a very short introduction to probability and conditional probability. The conditional probability (denoted by P) of event A given event B is defined as follows:

$$P(A \mid B) = \frac{P(A \cap B)}{P(B)}$$

Furthermore, events A and B are independent if and only if:

$$P(A \cap B) = P(A)P(B)$$

The Naive Bayes Classifier in Depth

As you've learned, the Naive Bayes classifier is a simple and stable method for classification and predictor selection. The general form of Bayes's theorem (from Bayesian statistics), on which this classifier is based, is stated next. Let A be a sequence of mutually exclusive events $\{A_1, A_2, ..., A_n\}$ whose union is the sample space, and let E be any event. It is assumed that all of the events have nonzero probability ($P(E) > 0$ and $P(A_i) > 0$ for all i). Bayes' theorem states:

$$P\left(A_j \mid E\right) = \frac{P\left(A_j\right)P\left(E \mid A_j\right)}{\sum_{i=1}^{n} P(A_i)P(E \mid A_i)}$$

for any $j \in \{1, 2, ..., n\}$

A *simpler* formulation of Bayes' theorem can be stated as: let A and B be two events (with some attribute values in a given statistical space). Then, Bayes' theorem gives the relationship between the probabilities of A and B—that is, $P(A)$ and $P(B)$—and the conditional probabilities of A given B (denoted by $P(A|B)$) and B given A (denoted by $P(B|A)$). Bayes' theorem can be stated as follows (for both events, A and B, we assume nonzero probability):

$$P(A|B) = \frac{P(B|A)P(A)}{P(B)}$$

For more details on Bayes' theorem, see [4].

Next, we formalize Bayes' theorem for classification: let $X = (X_1 = u_1, ..., X_m = u_m)$ be an instance of data that needs to be classified, and let $C = \{C_1, C_2, ..., C_k\}$ be a set of finite distinct classes (generated/deduced by training data). Then, using Bayes' theorem, we can predict a class $C^{predict} \in \{C_1, C_2, ..., C_k\}$ for a given X as:

$$C^{predict} = \arg\max_c P\big(C = c \,\big|\, X_1 = u_1, \ldots, X_m = u_m\big)$$

$$= \arg\max_c \frac{P\big(C = c, X_1 = u_1, \ldots, X_m = u_m\big)}{P\big(X_1 = u_1, \ldots, X_m = u_m\big)}$$

$$= \arg\max_c \frac{P\big(X_1 = u_1, \ldots, X_m = u_m \,\big|\, C = c\big)P(C = c)}{P\big(X_1 = u_1, \ldots, X_m = u_m\big)}$$

$$= \arg\max_c P\big(X_1 = u_1, \ldots, X_m = u_m \,\big|\, C = c\big)P(C = c)$$

$$= \arg\max_c P(C = c) \prod_{j=1}^{m} P\big(X_j = u_j \,\big|\, C = c\big)$$

Note that we dropped the denominator $P(X_1 = u_1, ..., X_m = u_m)$ from our classification algorithm since it is the same constant for all calculations, and it does not change the outcome of the classification algorithm. Therefore, constructing a classifier from the probability model can be expressed as:

$$\text{classify}\big(X_1 = u_1, \ldots, X_m = u_m\big) = C^{predict}$$

$$C^{predict} = \arg\max_c P(C = c) \prod_{j=1}^{m} P\big(X_j = u_j \,\big|\, C = c\big)$$

Naive Bayes Classifier Example

For this NBC example, we want to know how we classify the following input data:

```
X = (Outlook = Overcast,
     Temperature = Hot,
     Humidity = High,
     Wind = Strong)
```

```
X = (Overcast, Hot, High, Strong)
X = (X1, X2, X3, X4)
```

Will the answer be Yes (play tennis) or No (do not play tennis)? For our example, we have two classes:

- $C = (C_1, C_2) = (\text{Yes}, \text{No})$
- $P(C_1) = P(\text{Yes}) = 9/14$
- $P(C_2) = P(\text{No}) = 5/14$

Now, following the Bayes classifier, we will have:

$$C^{\text{predict}} = \arg\max_c P(C = c) \prod_{j=1}^{m} P\left(X_j = u_j \mid C = c\right) = max\{V_1, V_2\}$$

where:

$$V_1 = \{P(C = C_1)P(X_1 \mid C = C_1)P(X_2 \mid C = C_1)P(X_3 \mid C = C_1)P(X_4 \mid C = C_1)\}$$
$$V_2 = \{P(C = C_2)P(X_1 \mid C = C_2)P(X_2 \mid C = C_2)P(X_3 \mid C = C_2)P(X_4 \mid C = C_2)\}$$

If $V_1 > V_2$, then our classification of X will be $C_1 = $ Yes; otherwise, it will be $C_2 = $ No. The following are calculations of conditional probabilities for $C_1 = $ Yes:

$P(X_1 | C = C_1) = P(\text{"Overcast"}|C = \text{Yes}) = ?$
  Of the 9 cases where *PlayTennis* = Yes, there are 4 where *Outlook* = "*Overcast*"; thus, P (*Outlook* = "*Overcast*"|*PlayTennis* = *Yes*) = 4/9. In the notation of this equation, we may write $P(X_1 = Overcast|C_1) = 4/9$.

$P(X_2 | C = C_1) = P(\text{"Hot"}|C = \text{Yes}) = ?$
  Of the 9 cases where *PlayTennis* = Yes, there are 2 where *Temperature* = "*Hot*"; thus, P(*Temperature* = "*Hot*"|*PlayTennis* = *Yes*) = 2/9. In the notation of this equation, we may write $P(X_2 = Hot|C_1) = 2/9$.

$P(X_3 | C = C_1) = P(\text{"High"}|C = \text{Yes}) = ?$
  Of the 9 cases where *PlayTennis* = Yes, there are 3 where *Humidity* = "*High*"; thus, P(*Humidity* = "*High*"|*PlayTennis* = *Yes*) = 3/9. In the notation of this equation, we may write $P(X_3 = High|C_1) = 3/9$.

$P(X_4 | C = C_1) = P(\text{"Strong"}|C = \text{Yes}) = ?$
  Of the 9 cases where *PlayTennis* = Yes, there are 3 where *Wind* = "*Strong*"; thus, P(*Wind* = "*Strong*"|*PlayTennis* = *Yes*) = 3/9. In the notation of this equation, we may write $P(X_4 = Strong|C_1) = 3/9$.

The following are calculations of conditional probabilities for $C_2 = $ No:

$P(X_1|C = C_2) = P(\text{"Overcast"}|C = \text{No}) =?$

Of the 5 cases where *PlayTennis* = No, there are 0 where *Outlook* = "Overcast"; thus, $P(Outlook = \text{"Overcast"}|PlayTennis = No) = 0/5$. In the notation of this equation, we may write $P(X_1 = Overcast|C_2) = 0/5$.

$P(X_2|C = C_2) = P(\text{"Hot"}|C = \text{No}) =?$

Of the 5 cases where *PlayTennis* = No, there are 2 where *Temperature* = "Hot"; thus, $P(Temperature = \text{"Hot"}|PlayTennis = No) = 2/5$. In the notation of this equation, we may write $P(X_2 = Hot|C_2) = 2/5$.

$P(X_3|C = C_2) = P(\text{"High"}|C = \text{No}) =?$

Of the 5 cases where *PlayTennis* = No, there are 4 where *Humidity* = "High"; thus, $P(Humidity = \text{"High"}|PlayTennis = No) = 4/5$. In the notation of this equation, we may write $P(X_3 = High|C_2) = 4/5$.

$P(X_4|C = C_2) = P(\text{"Strong"}|C = \text{No}) =?$

Of the 5 cases where *PlayTennis* = No, there are 3 where *Wind* = "Strong"; thus, $P(Wind = \text{"Strong"}|PlayTennis = No) = 3/5$. In the notation of this equation, we may write $P(X_4 = Strong|C_2) = 3/5$.

Plugging in the values, we will get:

$$V_1 = \left(\frac{9}{14}\right)\left(\frac{4}{9}\right)\left(\frac{2}{9}\right)\left(\frac{3}{9}\right)\left(\frac{3}{9}\right) = \frac{648}{91854}$$

$$V_2 = \left(\frac{5}{14}\right)\left(\frac{0}{5}\right)\left(\frac{2}{5}\right)\left(\frac{4}{5}\right)\left(\frac{3}{5}\right) = 0$$

Since $V_1 > V_2$, we classify X as $C_1 = $ Yes.

The Naive Bayes Classifier: MapReduce Solution for Symbolic Data

This section will present a MapReduce solution for classifying millions or billions of pieces of symbolic (nonnumeric) data. To build a MapReduce solution, we will assume that we have proper training data (which will enable us to use Bayes' theorem for computing probabilities and conditional probabilities). The goal of our MapReduce solution is to classify data into a set of k well-defined classes (defined by training data) identified by $\{C_1, C_2, ..., C_k\}$.

Stage 1: Building a Classifier Using Symbolic Training Data

The goal of this stage is to build a classifier function, using training data, that will accept an instance of data $X = (X_1 = u_1, ..., X_m = u_m)$ and output a class $c \in \{C_1, C_2, ..., C_k\}$ (assuming that all of our training data maps into one of these classes). So, we need to compute $P(X_i = u_i | C = C_j)$ for all distinct X_i and all distinct $C_j (j = 1, 2, ..., k)$ in the training data. When the training data set is small, we can write a non-MapReduce program to build the classifier, but for a large set of training data, we should write a MapReduce job to compute $P(X_i = u_i | C = C_j)$.

Example 14-1 defines the `map()` function for building our classifier.

Example 14-1. map() function for building classifier

```
1 /**
2  * @param key is generated by MapReduce framework, ignored here
3  * @param value is a String with the following format:
4  *     <Data1><,><Data2><,><...><DataM><,><Class>
5  */
6 map(key, value) {
7     String[] tokens = value.split(",");
8     int classIndex = tokens.length -1;
9     String theClass = tokens[classIndex];
10    for(int i=0, i < (classIndex-1); i++) {
11        String reducerKey = tokens[i] + "," + theClass;
12        emit(reducerKey, 1);
13    }
14
15    String reducerKey = "CLASS," + theClass;
16    emit(reducerKey, 1);
17 }
```

To understand the mapper, next we apply the `map()` function to all of our training data, which generates a set of input to be consumed by the `reduce()` function. The `map()` function just wants to count the attributes and their associations with the classification classes.

`map(Sunny, Hot, High, Weak, No)` will generate:

```
<Sunny,No>, <1>
<Hot,No>, <1>
<High,No>, <1>
<Weak,No>, <1>
<CLASS,No>, <1>
```

`map(Sunny, Hot, High, Strong, No)` generates:

```
<Sunny,No>, <1>
<Hot,No>, <1>
<High,No>, <1>
```

```
<Strong,No>, <1>
<CLASS,No>, <1>
```

map(Overcast, Hot, High, Weak, Yes) generates:

```
<Overcast,Yes>, <1>
<Hot,Yes>, <1>
<High,Yes>, <1>
<Weak,Yes>, <1>
<CLASS,Yes>, <1>
```

map(Rain, Mild, High, Weak, Yes) generates:

```
<Rain,Yes>, <1>
<Mild,Yes>, <1>
<High,Yes>, <1>
<Weak,Yes>, <1>
<CLASS,Yes>, <1>
```

map(Rain, Cool, Normal, Weak, Yes) generates:

```
<Rain,Yes>, <1>
<Cool,Yes>, <1>
<Normal,Yes>, <1>
<Weak,Yes>, <1>
<CLASS,Yes>, <1>
```

map(Rain, Cool, Normal, Strong, No) generates:

```
<Rain,No>, <1>
<Cool,No>, <1>
<Normal,No>, <1>
<Strong,No>, <1>
<CLASS,No>, <1>
```

map(Overcast, Cool, Normal, Strong, Yes) generates:

```
<Overcast,Yes>, <1>
<Cool,Yes>, <1>
<Normal,Yes>, <1>
<Strong,Yes>, <1>
<CLASS,Yes>, <1>
```

map(Sunny, Mild, High, Weak, No) generates:

```
<Sunny,No>, <1>
<Mild,No>, <1>
<High,No>, <1>
<Weak,No>, <1>
<CLASS,No>, <1>
```

map(Sunny, Cool, Normal, Weak, Yes) generates:

```
<Sunny,Yes>, <1>
<Cool,Yes>, <1>
<Normal,Yes>, <1>
```

```
<Weak,Yes>, <1>
<CLASS,Yes>, <1>
```

map(Rain, Mild, Normal, Weak, Yes) generates:

```
<Rain,Yes>, <1>
<Mild,Yes>, <1>
<Normal,Yes>, <1>
<Weak,Yes>, <1>
<CLASS,Yes>, <1>
```

map(Sunny, Mild, Normal, Strong, Yes) generates:

```
<Sunny,Yes>, <1>
<Mild,Yes>, <1>
<Normal,Yes>, <1>
<Strong,Yes>, <1>
<CLASS,Yes>, <1>
```

map(Overcast, Mild, High, Strong, Yes) generates:

```
<Overcast,Yes>, <1>
<Mild,Yes>, <1>
<High,Yes>, <1>
<Strong,Yes>, <1>
<CLASS,Yes>, <1>
```

map(Overcast, Hot, Normal, Weak, Yes) generates:

```
<Overcast,Yes>, <1>
<Hot,Yes>, <1>
<Normal,Yes>, <1>
<Weak,Yes>, <1>
<CLASS,Yes>, <1>
```

And finally, map(Rain, Mild, High, Strong, No) generates:

```
<Rain,No>, <1>
<Mild,No>, <1>
<High,No>, <1>
<Strong,No>, <1>
<CLASS,No>, <1>
```

Example 14-2 presents the reducer for building the classifier. Since we are aggregating only values (the counts), the reduce() function can be used as a combiner too. For our example, the reducers will receive the key-value pairs shown in Table 14-3.

Table 14-3. Reducer input

Key	Value
<CLASS,No>	[<1>,<1>,<1>,<1>,<1>]
<CLASS,Yes>	[<1>,<1>,<1>,<1>,<1>,<1>,<1>,<1>,<1>]
<Cool,No>	[<1>]

Key	Value
<Cool,Yes>	[<1>,<1>,<1>]
<High,No>	[<1>,<1>,<1>,<1>]
<High,Yes>	[<1>,<1>,<1>]
<Hot,No>	[<1>,<1>]
<Hot,Yes>	[<1>,<1>]
<Mild,No>	[<1>,<1>]
<Mild,Yes>	[<1>,<1>,<1>,<1>]
<Normal,No>	[<1>]
<Normal,Yes>	[<1>,<1>,<1>,<1>,<1>,<1>]
<Overcast,Yes>	[<1>,<1>,<1>,<1>]
<Rain,No>	[<1>,<1>]
<Rain,Yes>	[<1>,<1>,<1>]
<Strong,No>	[<1>,<1>,<1>]
<Strong,Yes>	[<1>,<1>,<1>]
<Sunny,No>	[<1>,<1>,<1>]
<Sunny,Yes>	[<1>,<1>]
<Weak,No>	[<1>,<1>]
<Weak,Yes>	[<1>,<1>,<1>,<1>,<1>,<1>]

Example 14-2. reduce() function for building classifier

```
1  /**
2   * @param key is <Data, Class> or <CLASS, Class>
3   * @param values is a list of Integers
4   */
5  reduce(key, values) {
6     int total = 0;
7     for(int value : values) {
8          total += value;
9     }
10
11    emit(key, total);
12  }
```

The reduce() function just adds up frequencies (basically, it tallies the counters). The reducers will generate the output shown in Table 14-4.

Table 14-4. Reducer output

Key	Value
<CLASS,No>	5
<CLASS,Yes>	9
<Cool,No>	1
<Cool,Yes>	3
<High,No>	4
<High,Yes>	3
<Hot,No>	2
<Hot,Yes>	2
<Mild,No>	2
<Mild,Yes>	4
<Normal,No>	1
<Normal,Yes>	6
<Overcast,Yes>	4
<Rain,No>	2
<Rain,Yes>	3
<Strong,No>	3
<Strong,Yes>	3
<Sunny,No>	3
<Sunny,Yes>	2
<Weak,No>	2
<Weak,Yes>	6

We will customize our reducers to generate two types of output:

- Class output
- Conditional probabilities output

The class output is presented in Table 14-5.

Table 14-5. Class output

Key	Value
<CLASS,No>	5
<CLASS,Yes>	9

And the conditional probabilities output is presented in Table 14-6.

Table 14-6. Conditional probabilities output

Key	Value
<Cool,No>	1
<Cool,Yes>	3
<High,No>	4
<High,Yes>	3
<Hot,No>	2
<Hot,Yes>	2
<Mild,No>	2
<Mild,Yes>	4
<Normal,No>	1
<Normal,Yes>	6
<Overcast,Yes>	4
<Rain,No>	2
<Rain,Yes>	3
<Strong,No>	3
<Strong,Yes>	3
<Sunny,No>	3
<Sunny,Yes>	2
<Weak,No>	2
<Weak,Yes>	6

From these two types of reducer output (class and conditional probability), we will generate a final probability table, which will be used to classify new data (see Table 14-7).

Table 14-7. Probability table

Key	Probability
<CLASS,No>	5/14
<CLASS,Yes>	9/14
<Cool,No>	1/5
<Cool,Yes>	3/9
<High,No>	4/5
<High,Yes>	3/9
<Hot,No>	2/5
<Hot,Yes>	2/9
<Mild,No>	2/5

Key	Probability
<Mild,Yes>	4/9
<Normal,No>	1/5
<Normal,Yes>	6/9
<Overcast,Yes>	4/9
<Rain,No>	2/5
<Rain,Yes>	3/9
<Strong,No>	3/5
<Strong,Yes>	3/9
<Sunny,No>	3/5
<Sunny,Yes>	2/9
<Weak,No>	2/5
<Weak,Yes>	6/9

If any key is not in our probability table, then its probability is zero. Typically, training data should cover all attributes in such a way that a probability of zero will not happen, but this requirement truly depends on the project and data mining requirements.

Stage 2: Using the Classifier to Classify New Symbolic Data

Now that we have built our classifier (i.e., generated the probability table), we can use it to classify new data. Our goal is to classify $X = \{x_1 = u_1, x_2 = u_2, ..., x_m = u_m\}$ into one of the classes in $\{C_1, C_2, ..., C_k\}$. We will assume that each record of MapReduce input is an instance of data that needs to be classified.

For classification, the `map()` function is an identity mapper, which helps us to avoid classifying the same data more than once. Because classification is an expensive operation, we eliminate duplicate calculations. Now that we have built the probability table from the given training data, all classifications will be done by reducers.

The `map()` function to classify our new symbolic data is shown in Example 14-3.

Example 14-3. map() function for Naive Bayes classifier

```
1 public class NaiveBayesClassifierMapper ... {
2    ...
3    /**
4     * @param key is generated by MapReduce framework, ignored here
5     * @param value is a String with the following format:
6     *    X = (X1, X2, ..., Xm) = <Data1><,><Data2><,><...><,><DataM>
7     */
8    map(key, value) {
```

```
 9          // if desired, we can find out how many
10          // times each input data is duplicated
11          emit(value, 1);
12     }
13     ...
14  }
```

And the `reduce()` function for classifying our new symbolic data is shown in Example 14-4.

Example 14-4. reduce() for Naive Bayes Classifier

```
 1 public class NaiveBayesClassifierReducer ... {
 2
 3    private theProbabilityTable = ...;
 4    // classifications = {C1, C2, ..., Ck}
 5    private List<String> classifications = ...;
 6    public void setup() {
 7        theProbabilityTable = buildTheProbabilityTable();
 8        classifications = buildClassifications();
 9    }
10
11    /**
12     * @param key is X = (X1, X2, ..., Xm)
13     *               = <Data1><,><Data2><,><...><,><DataM>
14     *
15     * @param values is a list of Integers (shows duplicate records)
16     *
17     */
18    reduce(key, values) {
19        // key = (X1, X2, ..., Xm)
20        String[] attributes = key.split(",");
21        String selectedClass = null;
22        double maxPosterior = 0.0;
23        for(String aClass : classifications) {
24            double posterior = theProbabilityTable.getClassProbability(aClass);
25            for (int i=0; i < attributes.length; i++) {
26                posterior *= theProbabilityTable.getConditionalProbability(
27                        attributes[i], aClass);
28            }
29            if (selectedClass == null) {
30                // computing values for the first classification
31                selectedClass = aClass;
32                maxPosterior = posterior;
33            }
34            else {
35                if (posterior > maxPosterior) {
36                    selectedClass = aClass;
37                    maxPosterior = posterior;
38                }
39            }
```

```
40        }
41
42        reducerOutputValue = selectedClass + "," + maxPosterior;
43        emit(key, reducerOutputValue);
44    }
45 }
```

The Naive Bayes Classifier: MapReduce Solution for Numeric Data

This section will present a MapReduce solution for classifying millions or billions of pieces of numeric or so-called *continuous* data. To build our MapReduce solution, we will assume that we have proper training data, which will enable us to use Bayes' theorem for computing probabilities and conditional probabilities. The goal of our MapReduce solution is to classify data into a set of k well-defined classes (defined by training data) and identified by $\{C_1, C_2, ..., C_k\}$.

To work with numeric data, we need to calculate the mean and variance of the training data. Then we will use these values (mean and variance) in the classifier to classify new numeric data. In this numeric example, we have two classes: $\{C_1, C_2\} = \{male, female\}$. The classifier created from the training set using a Gaussian distribution is shown in Table 14-8.

Table 14-8. Training set classifier using a Gaussian distribution

Gender (class)	Mean (height)	Variance (height)	Mean (weight)	Variance (weight)	Mean (foot size)	Variance (foot size)
Male	5.8550	0.035033	176.25	122.92	11.25	0.9167
Female	5.4175	0.097225	132.50	558.33	7.50	1.6667

Since we have four males and four females in our training data, we have equiprobable classes: $P(male) = P(female) = 0.5$.

For numeric data (continuous attributes such as height, weight, and foot size) it is recommended to use a Gaussian normal distribution as outlined here. Let x be a continuous attribute (i.e., numeric value). First, we segment the data by class, and then we compute the mean (μ) and variance (σ^2) of x in each class. The Gaussian normal distribution for conditional probability can be expressed as:

$$P(x = v \mid c) = \frac{1}{\sigma_c \sqrt{2\pi}} e^{-\frac{\left(v - \mu_c\right)^2}{\left(2\sigma_c^2\right)}}$$

where:

- μ_c is the mean of values in x associated with class c.

- σ_c^2 is the variance of values in x associated with class c (σ_c is the standard deviation of values in x associated with class c).

Let's classify our new data as shown in Table 14-9.

Table 14-9. New data classification

Height (feet)	Weight (lbs)	Foot size (inches)	Gender
6.00	130	8	?

In Bayesian statistics, the *posterior probability* is the probability of the parameters T given the evidence X and is written as:

$P(T \mid X)$

Our goal is to classify this data as male/female (that is, we want to determine which posterior probability is greater, male or female). Following Bayes' theorem, we can express this as follows:

```
posterior(male) = evidenceMale / evidence
posterior(female) = evidenceFemale / evidence
```

The evidenceMale, evidenceFemale, and evidence variables (also known as *normalizing constants*) may be calculated as follows since the sum of the posteriors equals 1:

```
evidenceMale = P(male) *
               P(height|male) *
               P(weight|male) *
               P(footsize|male)

evidenceFemale = P(female) *
                 P(height|female) *
                 P(weight|female) *
                 P(footsize|female)

evidence = evidenceMale + evidenceFemale
```

evidence may be ignored since it is a positive constant. We can now determine the gender (classification) of the sample:

```
P(male) = 0.5
P(height|male) = 1.5789 (A probability density greater than
                        1.00 is OK. It is the area under
                        the bell curve that is equal to 1.00)
P(weight|male) = 5.9881e-06
P(footsize|male) = 1.3112e-3
```

```
posterior numerator (male) =
                          P(male) *
                          P(height|male) *
                          P(weight|male) *
                          P(footsize|male)
                    = 6.1984e-09

P(female) = 0.5
P(height|female) = 2.2346e-1
P(weight|female) = 1.6789e-2
P(footsize|female) = 2.8669e-1
posterior numerator (female) =
                          P(female) *
                          P(height|female) *
                          P(weight|female) *
                          P(footsize|female)
                    = 5.3778e-04
```

Since `posterior numerator (female)` > `posterior numerator (male)`, we conclude that the sample is female.

Naive Bayes Classifier Implementation in Spark

The Spark implementation has two stages, illustrated in Figure 14-3:

Stage 1: Build a Naive Bayes classifier using training data

We accomplish this using the `BuildNaiveBayesClassifier` class. This class reads the training data and builds the Naive Bayes classifier. Let $C = \{C_1, C_2, ..., C_k\}$ be a set of classifications and our training data be defined as follows:

- Let $X = \{X_1, X_2, ..., X_n\}$ be raw data.

- Each X_i has m attributes and is classified as:

$$X_1 = \{X_{11}, X_{12}, ..., X_{1m}\} \to c_1 \in C$$
$$X_2 = \{X_{21}, X_{22}, ..., X_{2m}\} \to c_2 \in C$$

...

$$X_n = \{X_{n1}, X_{n2}, ..., X_{nm}\} \to c_n \in C$$

- Our goal is to create the following probability table (`ProbabilityTable`) functions:

  `ProbabilityTable`(C_i) = pValue

  `ProbabilityTable`(A_j, C_i) = pValue

  where A_j is an attribute of X and $0.00 \leq$ pValue ≤ 1.00

Stage 2: Use our newly built NBC to classify new data

Once we've built the Naive Bayes classifier, we will use the `ProbabilityTable()` functions to classify our new data. We accomplish this using the `NaiveBayesClassifier` class. This class reads the classifier (expressed as the `ProbabilityTable()` functions) and new data and classifies the latter using the former.

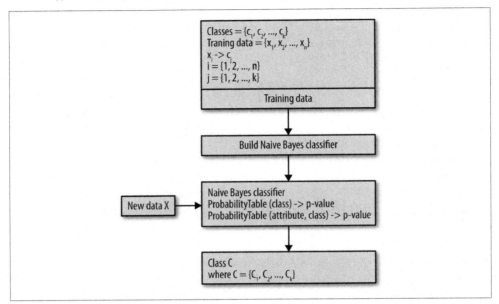

Figure 14-3. Naive Bayes: training phase

Stage 1: Building a Classifier Using Training Data

This stage is implemented by the `BuildNaiveBayesClassifier` class, which accepts training data (which is already classified) and builds a Naive Bayes classifier. The Naive Bayes classifier is a set of probability tables (PT), as discussed in the preceding section. First, Example 14-5 presents the `BuildNaiveBayesClassifier` class as a set of high-level steps, after which I'll explain each step in detail.

Example 14-5. Building a classifier: high-level steps

```
1 // Step 1: import required classes and interfaces
2 /**
3  * Build Naive Bayes classifier. The goal is to build the following
4  * data structures (probabilities and conditional probabilities) to
5  * be used in classifying new data.
6  *   Let C = {C1, C2, ..., Ck} be a set of classifications,
7  *   and let each training data element have m attributes: A = {A1, A2, ..., Am}.
8  *   Then we will build
9  *       ProbabilityTable(c) = p-value where c in C
```

```
10  *      ProbabilityTable(c, a) = p-value where c in C and a in A
11  *   where 1 >= p-value >=0
12  *
13  *   Record example in training data :
14  *     <attribute_1><,><attribute_2><,>...<,><attribute_m><,><classification>
15  *
16  *
17  *   @author Mahmoud Parsian
18  */
19  public class BuildNaiveBayesClassifier implements java.io.Serializable {
20
21     static List<Tuple2<PairOfStrings, DoubleWritable>>
22        toWritableList(Map<Tuple2<Strinwg,String>, Double> PT) {...}
23
24     public static void main(String[] args) throws Exception {
25        // Step 2: handle input parameters
26        // Step 3: create a Spark context object (ctx)
27        // Step 4: read training data
28        // Step 5: implement map() function for all elements of training data
29        // Step 6: implement reduce() function for all elements of training data
30        // Step 7: collect reduced data as Map
31        // Step 8: build the classifier
32        // Step 9: save the classifier
33        //     9.1: the PT (probability table) for classification of new entries
34        //     9.2: the classification list (CLASSIFICATIONS)
35
36        // done
37        ctx.close();
38        System.exit(0);
39     }
40  }
```

toWritableList() method

The toWritableList() method, defined in Example 14-6, prepares the classifier to be saved in HDFS. To be persisted, data types have to implement Hadoop's Writable interface.

Example 14-6. toWritableList() method

```
1     static List<Tuple2<PairOfStrings, DoubleWritable>>
2        toWritableList(Map<Tuple2<String,String>, Double> PT) {
3        List<Tuple2<PairOfStrings, DoubleWritable>> list =
4           new ArrayList<Tuple2<PairOfStrings, DoubleWritable>>();
5        for (Map.Entry<Tuple2<String,String>, Double> entry : PT.entrySet()) {
6           list.add(new Tuple2<PairOfStrings, DoubleWritable>(
7              new PairOfStrings(entry.getKey()._1, entry.getKey()._2),
8              new DoubleWritable(entry.getValue())
9           ));
10       }
```

```
11      return list;
12  }
```

Step 1: import required classes and interfaces

This step imports the required Java classes and interfaces (Example 14-7).

Example 14-7. Step 1: import required classes and interfaces

```
 1 // Step 1: import required classes and interfaces
 2 import java.util.Map;
 3 import java.util.HashMap;
 4 import java.util.List;
 5 import java.util.ArrayList;
 6 import scala.Tuple2;
 7 import org.apache.spark.api.java.JavaRDD;
 8 import org.apache.spark.api.java.JavaPairRDD;
 9 import org.apache.spark.api.java.JavaSparkContext;
10 import org.apache.spark.api.java.function.PairFunction;
11 import org.apache.spark.api.java.function.PairFlatMapFunction;
12 import org.apache.spark.api.java.function.FlatMapFunction;
13 import org.apache.spark.api.java.function.Function;
14 import org.apache.spark.api.java.function.Function2;
15 import org.apache.spark.broadcast.Broadcast;
16 import edu.umd.cloud9.io.pair.PairOfStrings;
17 import org.apache.hadoop.mapred.SequenceFileOutputFormat;
18 import org.apache.hadoop.io.DoubleWritable;
```

Step 2: Handle input parameters

This step, shown in Example 14-8, reads one input parameter, `<training-data-filename>`, which is the HDFS file that represents the training data to be used for building the Naive Bayes classifier.

Example 14-8. Step 2: handle input parameters

```
1      // Step 2: handle input parameters
2      if (args.length < 1) {
3          System.err.println("Usage: BuildNaiveBayesClassifier
4                          <training-data-filename>");
5          System.exit(1);
6      }
7      final String trainingDataFilename = args[0];
```

Step 3: Create a Spark context object

This step, shown in Example 14-9, creates a `SparkContextObject`, which is a factory for creating new RDDs. The `SparkUtil` class has `static` methods for creating instances of `JavaSparkContext` by using YARN's resource manager or by using the Spark master URL.

Example 14-9. Step 3: create a Spark context object

```
1       // Step 3: create a Spark context object
2       JavaSparkContext ctx = SparkUtil.createJavaSparkContext("naive-bayes");
```

Step 4: Read training data

This step, shown in Example 14-10, uses an instance of `JavaSparkContext` to read our training data and create a `JavaRDD<String>`, where each element is a record of the training data set in the following format:

```
<attribute_1><,><attribute_2><,>...<,><attribute_m><,><classification>
```

Example 14-10. Step 4: read training data

```
1       // Step 4: read training data
2       JavaRDD<String> training = ctx.textFile(trainingDataFilename, 1);
3       training.saveAsTextFile("/output/1");
4       // get the training data size, which will be
5       // used in calculating the conditional probabilities
6       long trainingDataSize = training.count();
```

To debug, we can view the created RDD:

```
# hadoop fs -cat /output/1/part*
Sunny,Hot,High,Weak,No
Sunny,Hot,High,Strong,No
Overcast,Hot,High,Weak,Yes
Rain,Mild,High,Weak,Yes
Rain,Cool,Normal,Weak,Yes
Rain,Cool,Normal,Strong,No
Overcast,Cool,Normal,Strong,Yes
Sunny,Mild,High,Weak,No
Sunny,Cool,Normal,Weak,Yes
Rain,Mild,Normal,Weak,Yes
Sunny,Mild,Normal,Strong,Yes
Overcast,Mild,High,Strong,Yes
Overcast,Hot,Normal,Weak,Yes
Rain,Mild,High,Strong,No
```

Step 5: Implement the map() function for all elements of the training data

This step, shown in Example 14-11, maps all elements of our training data so that we can create a count of attributes with respect to classifications. Then we use these counts to calculate conditional probabilities.

Example 14-11. Step 5: implement map() function

```
1    // Step 5: implement map() function for all elements of training data
2    // PairFlatMapFunction<T, K, V>
3    // T => Iterable<Tuple2<K, V>>
4    // K = <CLASS,classification> or <attribute,classification>
5    JavaPairRDD<Tuple2<String,String>,Integer> pairs =
6        training.flatMapToPair(new PairFlatMapFunction<
7        String,                     // A1,A2, ...,An,classification
8        Tuple2<String,String>,      // K = Tuple2(CLASS,classification) or
9                                    //     Tuple2(attribute,classification)
10       Integer                     // V = 1
11       >() {
12       public Iterable<Tuple2<Tuple2<String,String>,Integer>> call(String rec) {
13          List<Tuple2<Tuple2<String,String>,Integer>> result =
14             new ArrayList<Tuple2<Tuple2<String,String>,Integer>>();
15          String[] tokens = rec.split(",");
16          // tokens[0] = A1
17          // tokens[1] = A2
18          // ...
19          // tokens[m-1] = Am
20          // token[m] = classification
21          int classificationIndex = tokens.length -1;
22          String theClassification = tokens[classificationIndex];
23          for(int i=0; i < (classificationIndex-1); i++) {
24             Tuple2<String,String> K = new Tuple2<String,String>("CLASS",
25                            theClassification);
26             result.add(new Tuple2<Tuple2<String,String>,Integer>(K, 1));
27          }
28
29          Tuple2<String,String> K = new Tuple2<String,String>("CLASS",
30                         theClassification);
31          result.add(new Tuple2<Tuple2<String,String>,Integer>(K, 1));
32          return resultt;
33       }
34    });
35    pairs.saveAsTextFile("/output/2");
```

To debug, we can view the created RDD:

```
# hadoop fs -cat /output/2/part*
((Sunny,No),1)
((Hot,No),1)
((High,No),1)
((CLASS,No),1)
((Sunny,No),1)
((Hot,No),1)
((High,No),1)
((CLASS,No),1)
((Overcast,Yes),1)
((Hot,Yes),1)
((High,Yes),1)
((CLASS,Yes),1)
```

```
((Rain,Yes),1)
((Mild,Yes),1)
((High,Yes),1)
((CLASS,Yes),1)
((Rain,Yes),1)
((Cool,Yes),1)
((Normal,Yes),1)
((CLASS,Yes),1)
((Rain,No),1)
((Cool,No),1)
((Normal,No),1)
((CLASS,No),1)
((Overcast,Yes),1)
((Cool,Yes),1)
((Normal,Yes),1)
((CLASS,Yes),1)
((Sunny,No),1)
((Mild,No),1)
((High,No),1)
((CLASS,No),1)
((Sunny,Yes),1)
((Cool,Yes),1)
((Normal,Yes),1)
((CLASS,Yes),1)
((Rain,Yes),1)
((Mild,Yes),1)
((Normal,Yes),1)
((CLASS,Yes),1)
((Sunny,Yes),1)
((Mild,Yes),1)
((Normal,Yes),1)
((CLASS,Yes),1)
((Overcast,Yes),1)
((Mild,Yes),1)
((High,Yes),1)
((CLASS,Yes),1)
((Overcast,Yes),1)
((Hot,Yes),1)
((Normal,Yes),1)
((CLASS,Yes),1)
((Rain,No),1)
((Mild,No),1)
((High,No),1)
((CLASS,No),1)
```

Step 6: Implement reduce() function

This step, shown in Example 14-12, reduces the counts to prepare for calculating the conditional probabilities that will be used by the classifier.

Example 14-12. Step 6: implement reduce() function

```
1        // Step 6: implement reduce() function for all elements of training data
2        JavaPairRDD<Tuple2<String,String>, Integer> counts =
3          pairs.reduceByKey(new Function2<Integer, Integer, Integer>() {
4          public Integer call(Integer i1, Integer i2) {
5            return i1 + i2;
6          }
7        });
8 counts.saveAsTextFile("/output/3");
```

To debug, we can view the created RDD:

```
# hadoop fs -cat /output/3/part*
((Rain,Yes),3)
((Mild,No),2)
((Cool,No),1)
((Mild,Yes),4)
((Sunny,Yes),2)
((High,Yes),3)
((Hot,No),2)
((Sunny,No),3)
((Overcast,Yes),4)
((CLASS,No),5)
((High,No),4)
((Cool,Yes),3)
((Rain,No),2)
((Hot,Yes),2)
((CLASS,Yes),9)
((Normal,Yes),6)
((Normal,No),1)
```

Step 7: Collect reduced data as Map

As shown in Example 14-13, this step uses a powerful feature of the Spark API to collect a JavaPairRDD<K,V> as a Map<K,V>. Next, we'll use the generated Map<K,V> to build the classifier.

Example 14-13. Step 7: collect reduced data as Map

```
1        // Step 7: collect reduced data as Map
2        // java.util.Map<K,V> collectAsMap()
3        // Return the key-value pairs in this RDD to the master as a Map.
4        Map<Tuple2<String,String>, Integer> countsAsMap = counts.collectAsMap();
```

Step 8: Build the classifier data structures

This step, shown in Example 14-14, builds the classifier, which consists of:

- The probability table (PT)

- The classification list (CLASSIFICATIONS)

Example 14-14. Step 8: build the classifier data structures

```
1    // Step 8: build the classifier data structures, which will be used
2    // to classify new data. We need to build the following:
3    //    1. the probability table (PT)
4    //    2. the classification list (CLASSIFICATIONS)
5    Map<Tuple2<String,String>, Double> PT = new HashMap<Tuple2<String,String>,
6                                                          Double>();
7    List<String> CLASSIFICATIONS = new ArrayList<String>();
8    for (Map.Entry<Tuple2<String,String>, Integer> entry :
9                     countsAsMap.entrySet()) {
10       Tuple2<String,String> k = entry.getKey();
11       String classification = k._2;
12       if (k._1.equals("CLASS")) {
13          PT.put(k, ((double) entry.getValue()) /
14                  ((double) trainingDataSize));
12          CLASSIFICATIONS.add(k._2);
13       }
14       else {
15           Tuple2<String,String> k2 = new Tuple2<String,String>("CLASS",
16                                                       classification);
17           Integer count = countsAsMap.get(k2);
18           if (count == null) {
19              PT.put(k, 0.0);
20           }
21           else {
22              PT.put(k, ((double) entry.getValue()) /
23                      ((double) count.intValue()));
24           }
25       }
26    }
27    System.out.println("PT="+PT);
```

To debug, we can view the created PT:

```
PT={
    (Normal,No)=0.2,
    (Mild,Yes)=0.4444444444444444,
    (Normal,Yes)=0.6666666666666666,
    (Overcast,Yes)=0.4444444444444444,
    (CLASS,No)=0.35714285714285715,
    (CLASS,Yes)=0.6428571428571429,
    (Hot,Yes)=0.2222222222222222,
    (Hot,No)=0.4,
    (Cool,No)=0.2,
    (Sunny,No)=0.6,
    (High,No)=0.8,
```

```
        (Rain,No)=0.4,
        (Sunny,Yes)=0.2222222222222222,
        (Cool,Yes)=0.3333333333333333,
        (Rain,Yes)=0.3333333333333333,
        (Mild,No)=0.4,
        (High,Yes)=0.3333333333333333
}
```

Step 9: Save the classifier data structures

This step, shown in Example 14-15, saves the classifier, which consists of:

- The probability table (PT)
- The classification list (CLASSIFICATIONS)

To save any data in Hadoop, your persisting class must implement Hadoop's org.apache.hadoop.io.Writable[1] interface. In the code, I used the PairOfStrings and DoubleWritable classes, which both implement Hadoop's Writable interface.

Example 14-15. Step 9: save the classifier data structures

```
1    // Step 9: save the following, which will be used to classify new data:
2    //    1. the PT (probability table) for classification of new entries
3    //    2. the classification list (CLASSIFICATIONS)
4
5    // Step 9.1: save the PT
6    // public <K,V> JavaPairRDD<K,V>
7    //     parallelizePairs(java.util.List<scala.Tuple2<K,V>> list)
8    // Distribute a local Scala collection to form an RDD.
9    List<Tuple2<PairOfStrings, DoubleWritable>> list = toWritableList(PT);
10   JavaPairRDD<PairOfStrings, DoubleWritable> ptRDD = ctx.parallelizePairs(list);
11   ptRDD.saveAsHadoopFile("/naivebayes/pt",            // name of path
12                   PairOfStrings.class,                 // key class
13                   DoubleWritable.class,                // value class
14                   SequenceFileOutputFormat.class       // output format class
15                   );
16
17   // Step 9.2: save the classification list (CLASSIFICATIONS)
18   // List<Text> writableClassifications = toWritableList(CLASSIFICATIONS);
19   JavaRDD<String> classificationsRDD = ctx.parallelize(CLASSIFICATIONS);
20   classificationsRDD.saveAsTextFile("/naivebayes/classes"); // name of path
```

To debug, we can view the content of the saved classifier:

---

1 A serializable object that implements a simple, efficient serialization protocol, based on DataInput and Data Output.

```
# hadoop fs -text /classifier.seq/part*
(Normal, No)     0.2
(Mild, Yes)      0.4444444444444444
(Normal, Yes)    0.6666666666666666
(Overcast, Yes)  0.4444444444444444
(CLASS, No)      0.35714285714285715
(CLASS, Yes)     0.6428571428571429
(Hot, Yes)       0.2222222222222222
(Hot, No)        0.4
(Cool, No)       0.2
(Sunny, No)      0.6
(High, No)       0.8
(Rain, No)       0.4
(Sunny, Yes)     0.2222222222222222
(Cool, Yes)      0.3333333333333333
(Rain, Yes)      0.3333333333333333
(Mild, No)       0.4
(High, Yes)      0.3333333333333333

# hadoop fs -cat /naivebayes/classes/part*
Yes
No
```

YARN script to build an NBC

The shell script shown here runs our Spark program to build an NBC in the YARN environment:

```
 1 # cat run_build_naive_bayes_classifier.sh
 2 #!/bin/bash
 3 #... set the CLASSPATH(s) accordingly...
 4 BOOK_HOME=/mp/data-algorithms-book
 5 APP_JAR=$BOOK_HOME/dist/data_algorithms_book.jar
 6 THE_JARS=$BOOK_HOME/lib/cloud9-1.3.2.jar
 7 INPUT=/naivebayes/training_data.txt
 8 prog=org.dataalgorithms.chap14.spark.BuildNaiveBayesClassifier
 9 $SPARK_HOME/bin/spark-submit --class $prog \
10     --master yarn-cluster \
11     --num-executors 12 \
12     --driver-memory 3g \
13     --executor-memory 7g \
14     --executor-cores 12 \
15     --jars $THE_JARS \
16     $APP_JAR $INPUT
```

Stage 2: Using the Classifier to Classify New Data

In stage 1, we built a Naive Bayes classifier using the provided training data. The goal of stage 2 is to classify new data using that classifier. In stage 2, we read the classifier from HDFS and then classify our input data accordingly. We will use the following for the Naive Bayes classification of new data:

$$C^{\text{predict}} = \arg\max_{c} P(C = c) \prod_{j=1}^{m} P\left(X_j = u_j \mid C = c\right)$$

The classification is implemented by a single driver class (NaiveBayesClassifier) using the Spark API. Again, I will first present the high-level steps (Example 14-16), then discuss each step in detail.

Example 14-16. High-level steps for Spark NBC solution

```
 1 // Step 1: import required classes and interfaces
 2 /**
 3  * Naive Bayes classifier, which classifies (using the
 4  * classifier built by the BuildNaiveBayesClassifier class)
 5  * new data.
 6  *
 7  * For a given X = (X1, X2, ..., Xm), we will classify it
 8  * by using the following data structures (built by the
 9  * BuildNaiveBayesClassifier class):
10  *
11  *      ProbabilityTable(c) = p-value where c in C
12  *      ProbabilityTable(c, a) = p-value where c in C and a in A
13  *
14  * Therefore, given X, we will classify it as C where C in {C1, C2, ..., Ck}
15  *
16  * @author Mahmoud Parsian
17  */
18 public class NaiveBayesClassifier implements java.io.Serializable {
19    public static void main(String[] args) throws Exception {
20       // Step 2: handle input parameters
21       // Step 3: create a Spark context object (ctx)
22       // Step 4: read new data to be classified
23       // Step 5: read the classifier from Hadoop
24       // Step 6: cache the classifier components,
25       //    which can be used from any node in the cluster
26       // Step 7: classify new data
27
28       // done
29       ctx.close();
30       System.exit(0);
31    }
32 }
```

Step 1: Import required classes and interfaces

For our first step, shown in Example 14-17, we'll import the required classes and interfaces for this solution.

Example 14-17. Step 1: import required classes and interfaces

```
1  // Step 1: import required classes and interfaces
2  import java.util.Map;
3  import java.util.HashMap;
4  import java.util.List;
5  import java.util.ArrayList;
6  import scala.Tuple2;
7  import org.apache.spark.api.java.JavaRDD;
8  import org.apache.spark.api.java.JavaPairRDD;
9  import org.apache.spark.api.java.JavaSparkContext;
10 import org.apache.spark.api.java.function.PairFunction;
11 import org.apache.spark.api.java.function.PairFlatMapFunction;
12 import org.apache.spark.api.java.function.FlatMapFunction;
13 import org.apache.spark.api.java.function.Function;
14 import org.apache.spark.api.java.function.Function2;
15 import org.apache.spark.broadcast.Broadcast;
16 import edu.umd.cloud9.io.pair.PairOfStrings;
17 import org.apache.hadoop.mapred.SequenceFileInputFormat;
18 import org.apache.hadoop.io.DoubleWritable;
```

Step 2: Handle input parameters

The step shown in Example 14-18 handles the input parameters for our solution.

Example 14-18. Step 2: handle input parameters

```
1    // Step 2: handle input parameters
2    if (args.length != 2) {
3       System.err.println("Usage: NaiveBayesClassifier +
4                          <input-data-filename> <NB-PT-path>");
5       System.exit(1);
6    }
7    final String inputDataFilename = args[0];     // data to be classified
8    final String nbProbabilityTablePath = args[1]; // part of classifier
```

Step 3: Create a Spark context object

Using the SparkUtil class, in Example 14-19 we create an instance of JavaSparkCon text, which will be used to create new RDDs.

Example 14-19. Step 3: create a Spark context object

```
1 // Step 3: create a Spark context object
2 JavaSparkContext ctx = SparkUtil.createJavaSparkContext("naive-bayes");
```

Step 4: Read new data to be classified

The raw data to be classified (see Example 14-20) has the following record format:

```
<attribute_1><,><attribute_2><,>...<,><attribute_m>
```

Example 14-20. Step 4: read new data to be classified

```
1 // Step 4: read new data to be classified
2 JavaRDD<String> newdata = ctx.textFile(inputDataFilename, 1);
```

Step 5: Read the classifier from Hadoop

This step, shown in Example 14-21, reads the classifier components and data structures built by the `BuildNaiveBayesClassifier` class (in stage 1). Once the classifier components are read, we are ready to classify new data.

Example 14-21. Step 5: read the classifier from Hadoop

```
1    // Step 5: read the classifier from Hadoop
2    // JavaPairRDD<K,V> hadoopFile(String path,
3    //                           Class<F> inputFormatClass,
4    //                           Class<K> keyClass,
5    //                           Class<V> valueClass)
6    // Get an RDD for a Hadoop file with an arbitrary InputFormat.
7    // '''Note:''' Because Hadoop's RecordReader class reuses the
8    // same Writable object for each record, directly caching the
9    // returned RDD will create many references to the same object.
10   // If you plan to directly cache Hadoop Writable objects, you
11   // should first copy them using a map function.
12   JavaPairRDD<PairOfStrings, DoubleWritable> ptRDD = ctx.hadoopFile(
13                nbProbabilityTablePath,       // "/naivebayes/pt"
14                SequenceFileInputFormat.class,  // input format class
15                PairOfStrings.class,          // key class
16                DoubleWritable.class          // value class
17        );
18
19   // <K2,V2> JavaPairRDD<K2,V2> mapToPair(PairFunction<T,K2,V2> f)
20   // Return a new RDD by applying a function to all elements of this RDD.
21   JavaPairRDD<Tuple2<String,String>, Double> classifierRDD = ptRDD.mapToPair(
22       new PairFunction<
23            Tuple2<PairOfStrings,DoubleWritable>, // T
24            Tuple2<String,String>,              // K2,
25            Double                              // V2
26       >() {
27       public Tuple2<Tuple2<String,String>,Double>
28          call(Tuple2<PairOfStrings,DoubleWritable> rec) {
29          PairOfStrings pair = rec._1;
30          Tuple2<String,String> K2 =
31             new Tuple2<String,String>(pair.getLeftElement(),
32                                   pair.getRightElement());
33          Double V2 = new Double(rec._2.get());
34          return new Tuple2<Tuple2<String,String>,Double>(K2, V2);
35       }
36      });
```

Step 6: Cache the classifier components

This step, shown in Example 14-22, caches the classifier components (using Spark's Broadcast class) so that they can be accessed and used from any cluster nodes.

Example 14-22. Step 6: cache the classifier components

```
1    // Step 6: cache the classifier components,
2    //   which can be used from any node in the cluster.
3    Map<Tuple2<String,String>, Double> classifier = classifierRDD.collectAsMap();
4    final Broadcast<Map<Tuple2<String,String>, Double>> broadcastClassifier =
5        ctx.broadcast(classifier);
6
7    // We need all classification classes, which were created by the
8    // BuildNaiveBayesClassifier class.
9    JavaRDD<String> classesRDD = ctx.textFile("/naivebayes/classes", 1);
10   List<String> CLASSES = classesRDD.collect();
11   final Broadcast<List<String>> broadcastClasses =
12       ctx.broadcast(CLASSEDS);
```

Step 7: Classify new data

This step, shown in Example 14-23, uses the classifier components to classify new data.

Example 14-23. Step 7: classify new data

```
1  // Step 7: classify new data
2  // Now, we have a Naive Bayes classifier and new data.
3  // Use the classifier to classify new data.
4  // PairFlatMapFunction<T, K, V>
5  // T => Iterable<Tuple2<K, V>>
6  // K = <CLASS,classification> or <attribute,classification>
7  JavaPairRDD<String,String> classified = newdata.mapToPair(new PairFunction<
8      String,                    // T = A1,A2,...,Am (data to be classified)
9      String,                    // K = A1,A2,...,Am (data to be classified)
10     String                     // V = classification for T
11     >() {
12     public Tuple2<String,String> call(String rec) {
13         // get the classifer from the Spark cache
14         Map<Tuple2<String,String>, Double> CLASSIFIER =
15             broadcastClassifier.value();
16         // get the classes from the Spark cache
17         List<String> CLASSES = broadcastClasses.value();
18
19         // rec = (A1, A2, ..., Am)
20         String[] attributes = rec.split(",");
21         String selectedClass = null;
22         double maxPosterior = 0.0;
23         for (String aClass : CLASSES) {
24             double posterior = CLASSIFIER.get(new Tuple2<String,String>("CLASS",
```

```
25                                                          aClass));
26              for (int i=0; i < attributes.length; i++) {
27                  Double probability = CLASSIFIER.get(new Tuple2<String,String>(
28                                              attributes[i], aClass));
29                  if (probability == null) {
30                      posterior = 0.0;
31                      break;
32                  }
33                  else {
34                      posterior *= probability.doubleValue();
35                  }
36              }
37              if (selectedClass == null) {
38                  // computing values for the first classification
39                  selectedClass = aClass;
40                  maxPosterior = posterior;
41              }
42              else {
43                  if (posterior > maxPosterior) {
44                      selectedClass = aClass;
45                      maxPosterior = posterior;
46                  }
47              }
48          }
49
50          return new Tuple2<String,String>(rec, selectedClass);
51      }
52 });
53 classified.saveAsTextFile("/output/classified");
```

The input—that is, the data to be classified—is as follows:

```
# hadoop fs -cat /naivebayes/new_data_to_be_classified.txt
Rain,Hot,High,Strong
Overcast,Mild,Normal,Weak
Sunny,Mild,Normal,Week
```

And here is the output (i.e., classified data):

```
# hadoop fs -cat /output/classified/part*
(Rain,Hot,High,Strong,Yes)
(Overcast,Mild,Normal,Weak,Yes)
(Sunny,Mild,Normal,Week,Yes)
```

YARN script for Spark

Here is the YARN script for our Spark NBC solution:

```
1 # cat run_classify_new_data.sh
2 #... set up required CLASSPATH
3 BOOK_HOME=/mp/data-algorithms-book
4 APP_JAR=$BOOK_HOME/dist/data_algorithms_book.jar
5 THE_JARS=$BOOK_HOME/lib/cloud9-1.3.2.jar
```

```
 6 prog=org.dataalgorithms.chap14.spark.NaiveBayesClassifier
 7 NEW_DATA=/naivebayes/new_data_to_be_classified.txt
 8 CLASSIFIER_PT=/naivebayes/pt
 9 CLASSIFIER_CLASSES=/naivebayes/classes
10 $SPARK_HOME/bin/spark-submit --class $prog \
11     --master yarn-cluster \
12     --num-executors 12 \
13     --driver-memory 3g \
14     --executor-memory 7g \
15     --executor-cores 12 \
16     --jars $THE_JARS \
17     $MY_JAR $NEW_DATA $CLASSIFIER_PT $CLASSIFIER_CLASSES
```

Using Spark and Mahout

Apache Spark (*http://spark.apache.org/*) and Apache Mahout (*http://mahout.apache.org/*) provide machine learning algorithms. If you do not want to roll your own machine learning algorithms, you may use one of these options.

Apache Spark

MLlib is Apache Spark's scalable machine learning library. The root Java package for MLlib is `org.apache.spark.mllib`. MLlib offers the following functionality:

- Naive Bayes
- Clustering and K-Means
- Basic and summary statistics
- Correlations
- Hypothesis testing
- Classification and regression
- Linear models (logistic regression, linear regression, etc.)

MLlib offers two important classes for Naive Bayes:

`org.apache.spark.mllib.classification.NaiveBayes`
Trains a Naive Bayes model given an RDD of (`label`, `features`) pairs

`org.apache.spark.mllib.classification.NaiveBayesModel`
Model for Naive Bayes classifiers

The basic usage of these two classes is expressed in Example 14-24 (this code segment is from *http://bit.ly/mllib_naive_bayes*).

Example 14-24. Spark's Naive Bayes classes

```
1    JavaRDD<LabeledPoint> training = ... // training set
2    JavaRDD<LabeledPoint> test = ... // test set
3
4    double theSmoothingParameter = 1.0;
5    // trains a Naive Bayes model given an RDD of (label, features) pairs
6    final NaiveBayesModel model = NaiveBayes.train(training.rdd(),
                                                theSmoothingParameter);
7    JavaPairRDD<Double, Double> predictionAndLabel =
8      test.mapToPair(new PairFunction<LabeledPoint, Double, Double>() {
9      @Override
10     public Tuple2<Double, Double> call(LabeledPoint p) {
11         return new Tuple2<Double, Double>(model.predict(p.features()), p.label());
12     }
13     });
14
15   double accuracy = 1.0 * predictionAndLabel.filter(new Function<
16         Tuple2<Double, Double>,
17         Boolean>() {
18      @Override
19      public Boolean call(Tuple2<Double, Double> pl) {
20        return pl._1() == pl._2();
21      }
22   }).count() / test.count();
```

Apache Mahout

The Apache Mahout project's goal is to build a scalable machine learning library. Here are two blog posts describing how you can classify tweets using Mahout:

- "Using the Mahout Naive Bayes classifier to automatically classify Twitter messages" (*http://bit.ly/mahout_naive_bayes*)
- "Using the Mahout Naive Bayes Classifier to automatically classify Twitter messages (part 2: distribute classification with Hadoop)" (*http://bit.ly/mahout_naive_bayes2*)

## CHAPTER 15

Sentiment Analysis

Sentiment means "a general thought, view, feeling, emotion, opinion, or sense," and Wikipedia (*http://en.wikipedia.org/wiki/Sentiment_analysis*) describes *sentiment analysis* (also known as *opinion mining*) as "the use of natural language processing, text analysis, and computational linguistics to identify and extract subjective information in source materials." Bo Pang and Lillian Lee[21] wrote that "sentiment analysis seeks to identify the viewpoint(s) underlying a text span; an example application is classifying a movie review as *thumbs up* or *thumbs down*." To perform a sentiment analysis about some event, we need to teach computers what a sentiment is (i.e., how to define "positive" or "negative" and "good" or "bad"). This is where machine learning comes in: we must *teach* computers the meaning of positive, negative, and so on. The first step in this process is to build a model from a set of training data. After the model is built, we will use it to analyze new data.

So what is *sentiment data*? Typically, it is unstructured data that represents opinions and emotions contained in sources such as special news bulletins, customer support emails, social media posts (such as tweets and Facebook comments), and online product reviews.

To perform a good sentiment analysis, the sentiment analysis engine has to conduct some level of speech analysis and word-sense disambiguation. Therefore, a sentiment analysis of a text document involves more than tokenizing words and checking them against a list of "positive" and "negative" words. Sometimes, we need to understand the *intensity* of words, and account for factors like negation and diminishers. For example, consider the following sentence:

> The movie was not good.

If you just look at the individual words without considering their relationships, you might decide that the sentiment is "neutral" (since *not* is negative and *good* is positive). But if you look at the semantics of the whole sentence, clearly it is a negative sentiment. Therefore, the objective of sentiment analysis is to understand opinions expressed about some subject and distill them into discrete categories such has *happy*, *sad*, and *angry* or, more simply, *positive*, *negative*, and *neutral*.

Sentiment Examples

The following are some examples of sentiment analysis applications:

- What are bloggers saying about a brand like Toyota after a recall of the braking system in some Toyota cars?

- What is the sentiment of viewers of *Iron Man 3* before and after seeing the movie? (We can answer this by analyzing tweets before and after viewing.) Did people really like the movie?

- What is the sentiment of customers before and after the announcement of a new iPhone?

- What is the sentiment of voters before and after a presidential debate? Is there a certain sentiment toward the Democratic or Republican party?

- What is the sentiment of consumers about a customer service experience (happy or sad)? Here, for sentiment analysis, we need customer service log data and a dictionary of "happy" and "sad" words.

Sentiment Scores: Positive or Negative

Given a short sentence (such as a tweet, which is 140 characters or fewer), how do you determine whether it expresses a positive or negative sentiment? To score syntactically (by ignoring contextual semantics), you can tokenize the sentence into words and then check these words against a list of positive and negative words.[1]

For example, given the following sentences (**bold** words are positive and <u>underlined</u> words are negative):

- Sentence 1: "The movie was **great** and I **loved** it."

- Sentence 2: "The hamburger had a <u>bad</u> taste and was <u>terrible</u>, but I **loved** the fries."

what are the sentiment scores of sentence 1 and sentence 2?

---

1 Hu and Liu have published an "opinion lexicon" that categorizes approximately 6,800 words as positive or negative and can be downloaded from *http://bit.ly/opinion_lexicon*. For example, positive words include *love*, *best*, *cool*, *great*, and *good*, while negative words include *terrible*, *bad*, *hate*, *worst*, and *sucks*.

```
sentimentScore(Sentence-1) = 1 positive +
                             1 positive
                           = 2 positives (Positive sentiment)

sentimentScore(Sentence-2) = 1 negative +
                             1 negative +
                             1 positive
                           = 1 negative (Negative sentiment)
```

In most sentiment analysis situations, checking/examining the individual words against a list of positive and negative words is not enough and might not yield the expected results. In real sentiment analysis, it is better not to rely simply on pure syntax, but rather to understand the semantics—the intensity of words, and factors like negation and diminishers. For example, consider the following sentence:

"The movie was <u>not</u> **great** and I did <u>not</u> **love** it."

In a real-world sentiment analysis, checking pure syntax here will not yield accurate results. As noted earlier, if you just look at individual words without their relationships, your pure syntactical algorithm might indicate that the sentiment is "neutral" (since *not* is negative and *great* and *love* are positive). But when you look at the semantics of the whole sentence, clearly it is a negative sentiment.

So, in a nutshell, we can say that *sentiment analysis* is the task of determining whether the statement/opinion expressed in text is positive, negative, or neutral toward a particular topic or trend.

A Simple MapReduce Sentiment Analysis Example

Now let's go over an example for performing sentiment analysis on a given set of tweets. Let our keywords of interest be *Obama* and *Romney*, and further assume that it is an election year and you want to know the sentiment of people tweeting about these two presidential candidates. Let's assume that you want to find the sentiment trend for each candidate per day. The mapper accepts a tweet, normalizes the text, looks for a keyword of interest (*Obama* or *Romney*), counts the positive and negative keywords, and then subtracts the ratio of negative words from the ratio of positive words. To perform mapping, we need two distinct sets of words:

- A set of positive words (such as *good*, *like*, and *enjoy*)
- A set of negative words (such as *hate*, *bad*, and *terrible*)

These two sets are passed to mappers by the driver program. In Hadoop we can accomplish this by using a distributed cache (the `DistributedCache`[2] class).

map() Function for Sentiment Analysis

We assume that there exists a normalizer and a tokenizer function for a given tweet, as shown in Example 15-1.

Example 15-1. The mapper function

```
1 private static List<String> normalizeAndTokenize(String tweet) {
2    List<String> tokens = <normalize and tokenize all
3                           the words in the tweet text>;
4    return tokens;
5 }
```

Using the `normalizeAndTokenize()` method we can complete the `map()` method, as shown in Example 15-2.

Example 15-2. The mapper function, with a complete map() method

```
 1 private Set<String> positiveWords = null;
 2 private Set<String> negativeWords = null;
 3 // default candidates values
 4 private Set<String> allCandidates = {"obama", "romney"};
 5
 6 setup() {
 7    positiveWords = <load positive words from distributed cache>;
 8    negativeWords = <load negative words from distributed cache>;
 9    allCandidates = <load all candidates from distributed cache>;
10 }
11
12 /**
13  * @param key is the date of a tweet: YYYY-MM-DD:hh:mm:ss
14  * @param value is a single tweet
15  */
16 map(key, value) {
17    date = key; // date of a tweet as YYYY-MM-DD
18    List<String> tweetWords = normalizeAndTokenize(value);
19    int positiveCount = 0;
20    int negativeCount = 0;
21    for (String candidate : allCandidates) {
22        if (candidate is in the tweetWords) {
23            int positiveCount = <count of positive words in tweetWords>;
24            int negativeCount = <count of negative words in tweetWords>;
```

---

2 `DistributedCache` (`org.apache.hadoop.filecache.DistributedCache`) is a facility provided by Hadoop's MapReduce framework to cache text and archive files needed by applications.

```
25          double positiveRatio = positiveCount / tweetWords.size();
26          double negativeRatio = negativeCount / tweetWords.size();
27          outputKey = Pair(date, candidate);
28          outputValue = positiveRatio - negativeRatio;
29          emit (outputKey, outputValue);
30      }
31   }
32 }
```

reduce() Function for Sentiment Analysis

Example 15-3 provides the reduce() function for basic sentiment analysis.

Example 15-3. The reducer function

```
 1 /**
 2 * @param key is the Pair(Date, String)
 3 *     where
 4 *         Date = YYYY-MM-DD
 5 *         String = a candidate ("obama" or "romney")
 6 * @param values is a List<Double> where Double represents a ratio
 7 */
 8 reduce(key, values) {
 9    double sumOfRatio = 0.0;
10    int n = 0; // number ratios
11    for (Double ratio : values) {
12        n++;
13        sumOfRatio += ratio;
14    }
15    emit (key, sumOfRatio / n);
16 }
```

Sentiment Analysis in the Real World

The algorithms described in this chapter are very simplistic and trivial (they can be applied only to the simplest problems). Implementing a realistic context-based sentiment analysis is a very complex process, and understanding the data requires a lot of attention. If you're interested in learning more, Siddharth Batra and Deepak Rao[3] describe a realistic entity-based sentiment analysis on Twitter that can be implemented in a MapReduce paradigm.

## CHAPTER 16

Finding, Counting, and Listing All Triangles in Large Graphs

Graphs and matrices are used by social network analysts to represent and analyze information about patterns of ties among social actors (users, friends, and "friends of friends"). In network analysis, data is usually modeled as a graph or set of graphs. A graph is a data structure that has a finite set of nodes, called *vertices*, together with a finite set of lines, called *edges*, that join some or all of these nodes. Before we define some metrics using the count of triangles, we need to define a triad and a triangle. Let $T = (a,b,c)$ be a set of three distinct nodes in a graph (identified by G). T is a *triad* if two of those nodes are connected ($\{(a,b), (a,c)\}$) and it is a *triangle* if all three nodes are connected ($\{(a,b), (a,c), (b,c)\}$).

In graph analysis, there are three important metrics:

- Global clustering coefficient
- Transitivity ratio, defined as:

$$T(G) = \frac{3 \times (\text{number of triangles on the graph})}{(\text{number of connected triads of vertices})}$$

- Local clustering coefficient

In order to calculate these three metrics in a large graph, we need to know the number of triangles in the graph. For details on these metrics, see [28], [25], and [34].

A graph might have hundreds of millions of nodes (e.g., users in a social network) and edges (the relationships between these users), and counting the number of triangles is very time-consuming. This chapter provides two MapReduce solutions that find, count, and list all triangles for a given graph or set of graphs. The solutions are given in Hadoop and Spark:

- The MapReduce/Hadoop solution is composed of three steps, and each step is a separate MapReduce job.

- The Spark solution is composed of a single Java driver class, which manipulates several `JavaRDD` objects. As you've learned in previous chapters, Spark's API is higher level than the MapReduce/Hadoop API, which is why we can fit all `map()` and `reduce()` functions in a single Java driver class. Spark provides GraphX, which is Apache Spark's API for graphs and graph-parallel computation, but for this chapter we use only the Spark API without using the GraphX library.

Basic Graph Concepts

Let V be a finite set of nodes (again, a node can represent a user, a computer, or a tangible/intangible object) and E be a finite set of edges (an edge represents a relationship and connectivity between two nodes). Then we can define an undirected simple graph as: $G = (V, E)$. We use n for the number of nodes and m for the number of edges. The degree $d(v) = |u \in V: \exists \{v, u\} \in E|$ of node v is defined to be the number of nodes in V that are adjacent to v. A triangle $\Delta = (V_\Delta, E_\Delta)$ of a graph $G = (V, E)$ is a three-node subgraph with $V_\Delta = \{u, v, w\} \subset V$ and $E_\Delta = \{\{u, v\}, \{v, w\}, \{w, u\}\} \subset E$. We use the symbol $T(G)$ to denote the number of triangles in graph G.

For example, the graph shown in Figure 16-1 has these two triangles:

- $\{\{2, 3\}, \{3, 4\}, \{4, 2\}\}$
- $\{\{2, 4\}, \{4, 5\}, \{5, 2\}\}$

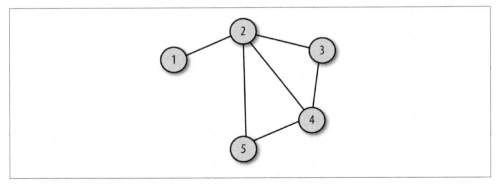

Figure 16-1. Graph triangles

Let's formalize some of these graph metrics. Given an undirected graph $G = (V, E)$, we can define some social metrics for the graph. But first we need some basic definitions:

- The degree of a node v, denoted by $d(v)$, is the number of nodes in V that are adjacent to v.

- The number of triangles of node v is defined as:

$$T(v) = |(u, w) \in E : (v, u) \in E \text{ and } (v, w) \in E|$$

- The number of triangles of graph G is defined as:

$$T(G) = \frac{1}{3} \sum_{v \in V} T(v)$$

- The number of triads of node v is defined as:

$$t(v) = \binom{d(v)}{2}$$

- The number of triads of graph G is defined as:

$$t(G) = \sum_{v \in V} t(v)$$

Using these basic definitions, now we can define our clustering coefficients:

- The clustering coefficient for a node v, is defined as $c(v)$, where $d(v) \geq 2$:

$$c(v) = T(v)/t(v)$$

- The clustering coefficient of a graph G, denoted as $C(G)$, is the average of the clustering coefficients of its nodes:

$$C(G) = \frac{1}{|W|} \sum_{w \in W} c(w)$$

where W is the set of nodes w with $d(w) \geq 2$.

Importance of Counting Triangles

Identifying and counting triangles helps us to measure two important metrics (clustering coefficients and transitive ratios) about large graphs. Counting triangles also helps us to find patterns in social graphs, which is useful for intrusion detection and for identifying communities and spamming. Similarly, triangle detections in biological networks help us to find protein–protein interaction networks.

Triangles and clustering coefficients play important roles in the analysis of complex networks using graph data structures. The existence of triangles and the resulting high clustering coefficient reveals important characteristics of social, biological, web, and other networks.

Given that counting the number of triangles in a graph is very time-consuming (for details, see [24]), we can use MapReduce to distribute graph data and its computation. As mentioned earlier, the goal of this chapter is to provide MapReduce solutions for finding, listing, and counting triangles in large graphs. Schank and Wagner [24] provide a sequential (non-MapReduce) algorithm for finding and counting all triangles in large graphs.

MapReduce/Hadoop Solution

I'll present the MapReduce solution in three steps (each step is a separate MapReduce job):

1. Generate paths through u of length 2 and copy all edges from u as keys—no associated data. From these paths we will generate possible triangles. This step can be solved through the $\mathtt{map()}$ and $\mathtt{reduce()}$ functions as follows:

$$\mathtt{mapper_1: (K, V) \rightarrow \{(K, V),}$$
$$\mathtt{(V, K)\}}$$
$$\mathtt{reducer_1: \{(K, V_1), (K, V_2), \ldots, (K, V_n)\} \rightarrow \{[(V_1, V_2), (K)],}$$
$$\mathtt{[(V_1, V_3), (K)],}$$
$$\mathtt{\ldots,}$$
$$\mathtt{[(V_{n-1}, V_n), (K)],}$$
$$\mathtt{[(K, V_1), (-)],}$$
$$\mathtt{\ldots,}$$
$$\mathtt{[(K, V_n), (-)]\}}$$

2. Identify triangles as $\{\{u, v\}, \{v, w\}, \{w, u\}\}$. This step will generate duplicate triangles and can be implemented through the following $\mathtt{map()}$ and $\mathtt{reduce()}$ functions:

$$\text{mapper}_2\colon\ [(U, V), (W)] \to [(U, V), (W)]$$
$$\text{reducer}_2\colon\ \{[(U, V)(-)], [(U, V)(W_1)], \ldots, [(U, V)(W_n)]\} \to \{[(U, V, W_1)],$$
$$\ldots,$$
$$[(U, V, W_n)]\}$$
$$\text{reducer}_2\colon\ \{[(U, V)(W_1)], \ldots, [(U, V)(W_n)]\} \to \text{NoOutput}$$

3. Remove duplicate triangles ((a, b, c) is the same as (a, c, b)). This step can be solved through the map() and reduce() functions as follows:

$$\text{mapper}_3\colon\ (K_3, V_3) \to (\text{sort}(K_3), V_3)$$
$$\text{reducer}_3\colon\ \{(K_3, V_{31}), (K_3, V_{32}), (K_3, V_{33}), \ldots\} \to \{(K_3, \text{null})$$

Step 1: MapReduce in Action

The input to the first step (i.e., *mapper₁* of step 1) will be the edges in a given undirected graph. Each line of input will be in the (u, v) format, such that $u < v$ ($\{u, v\}$ is an edge of the graph). For our graph in Figure 16-1, we have the records shown in Table 16-1.

Table 16-1. Input to mapper₁ of step 1

Key (startNode)	Value (endNode)
1	2
2	3
2	4
2	5
3	4
4	5

The *mapper₁* of step 1 generates the output shown in Table 16-2 (which will be an input to the *reducer₁* of step 1). Note that edges must be reciprocal; that is, every {startNode, endNode} edge must have a corresponding {endNode, startNode}.

Table 16-2. Output of mapper₁ of step 1

Key (startNode)	Value (endNode)
1	2
2	1
2	3
3	2
2	4
4	2

Key (startNode)	Value (endNode)
2	5
5	2
3	4
4	3
4	5
5	4

After the shuffle and sort phase, the data in Table 16-3 will be ready as an input to the *reducer₁* of step 1.

Table 16-3. Input to reducer₁ of step 1

Key	Value (as list of nodes)
1	[2]
2	[1, 3, 4, 5]
3	[2, 4]
4	[2, 3, 5]
5	[2, 4]

The *reducer₁* of step 1 is defined as:

$$
\text{mapper}_1: (K, V) \rightarrow \{(K, V),
$$
$$
(V, K)\}
$$
$$
\text{reducer}_1: \{(K, V_1), (K, V_2), \ldots, (K, V_n)\} \rightarrow \{[(V_1, V_2), (K)],
$$
$$
[(V_1, V_3), (K)],
$$
$$
\ldots,
$$
$$
[(V_{n-1}, V_n), (K)],
$$
$$
[(K, V_1), (-)],
$$
$$
\ldots,
$$
$$
[(K, V_n), (-)]\}
$$

The *reducer₁* of step 1 will behave as shown in Table 16-4.

Table 16-4. reducer₁ input/output for step 1

Input	Output
[1],[2]	[(1, 2), (-)]
[2],[1, 3, 4, 5]	[(2, 1), (-)] [(2, 3), (-)] [(2, 4), (-)] [(2, 5), (-)] [(1, 3), (2)] [(1, 4), (2)] [(1, 5), (2)] [(3, 4), (2)] [(3, 5), (2)] [(4, 5), (2)]
[3],[2, 4]	[(3, 2), (-)] [(3, 4), (-)] [(2, 4), (3)]
[4],[2, 3, 5]	[(4, 2), (-)] [(4, 3), (-)] [(4, 5), (-)] [(2, 3), (4)] [(2, 5), (4)] [(3, 5), (4)]
[5],[2, 4]	[(5, 2), (-)] [(5, 4), (-)] [(2, 4), (5)]

Step 2: Identify Triangles

The *mapper₂* of step 2 is an identity mapper; it just passes keys and values without any further processing. This enables us to generate proper keys and values for the *reducer₂* of step 2. The *reducer₂* of step 2 will have the input/output shown in Table 16-5.

Table 16-5. reducer₂ input/output of step 2

Input	Output (as triangle(s))
(1, 2) [-]	
(2, 1) [-]	
(2, 3) [-, 4]	(2, 3, 4)
(2, 4) [-, 3, 5]	(2, 4, 3), (2, 4, 5)
(2, 5) [-, 4]	(2, 4, 5)
(1, 3) [2]	
(1, 4) [2]	

Input	Output (as triangle(s))	
(1, 5) [2]		
(3, 4) [2, -]	(3, 4, 2)	
(3, 5) [2, 4]		
(4, 5) [2, -]	(4, 5, 2)	
(3, 2) [-]		
(4, 2) [-]		
(4, 3) [-]		
(5, 4) [-]		
(5, 2) [-]		

As you can see, each triangle is listed three times; this is to highlight the definition of a triangle. For example, a single triangle with three nodes of *u*, *v*, and *w* can be equivalently expressed as:

```
{{u, v},{v, w},{w, u}}
{{v, w},{w, u},{u, v}}
{{w, u},{u, v},{v, w}}
```

Step 3: Remove Duplicate Triangles

This step removes duplicate triangles, resulting in unique triangles. The input for this step will be in the form (a, b, c), where a, b, and c each represent a vertex of the triangle.

Mapper

The mapper will accept a triangle in the form of (a, b, c) and will emit sorted vertices. For example:

(1, 2, 3) will emit (1, 2, 3)
(1, 3, 2) will emit (1, 2, 3)
(2, 1, 3) will emit (1, 2, 3)
(2, 3, 1) will emit (1, 2, 3)
(3, 1, 2) will emit (1, 2, 3)
(3, 2, 1) will emit (1, 2, 3)

Example 16-1 defines the mapper for this step.

Example 16-1. Step 3: the mapper function

```
1 // key is not used
2 // value = (a, b, c)
3 map(key, value) {
```

```
4   triangle = sort(value);
5   // triangle = (x, y, z)
6   // x < y < z
7   // x, y, z in {a, b, c}
8   emit(triangle, null)
9 }
```

Reducer

Since the mapper output will be grouped by the mapper's key, the reducer will just emit the received key (see Example 16-2). This will generate unique triangles. We do not care about the values of this reducer at all (since a key represents a unique triangle).

Example 16-2. Step 3: the reducer function

```
1 // key is a triangle (a, b, c)
2 // where a < b < c
3 // values = list of nulls
4 reduce(key, values) {
5   emit(key, null)
6 }
```

Hadoop Implementation Classes

The Hadoop implementation classes for this solution are given in Table 16-6.

Table 16-6. Implementation classes in Hadoop

Phase	Class name	Class description
Job submitter	TriangleCounterDriver	Driver to submit job for all three phases
1	GraphEdgeMapper GraphEdgeReducer	Generates possible triangle paths Identifies possible triangles
2	TriadsMapper TriadsReducer	Identity mapper Identifies triangles with duplicates
3	UniqueTriadsMapper UniqueTriadsReducer	Identity mapper Generates unique triangles

Sample Run

The next subsections provide the script, HDFS input, sample run log, and expected output for our MapReduce solution.

Script

Here is the script to run our MapReduce/Hadoop solution:

```
 1 $ cat run.sh
 2 #/bin/bash
 3 export JAVA_HOME=/usr/java/jdk7
 4 export BOOK_HOME=/mp/data-algorithms-book
 5 export APP_JAR=$BOOK_HOME/dist/data_algorithms_book.jar
 6 #
 7 export HADOOP_HOME=/usr/local/hadoop-2.3.0
 8 export HADOOP_CONF_DIR=$HADOOP_HOME/etc/hadoop
 9 export PATH=.:$JAVA_HOME/bin:$HADOOP_HOME/bin:$PATH
10 #
11 $HADOOP_HOME/bin/hadoop fs -rm /lib/data_algorithms_book.jar
12 $HADOOP_HOME/bin/hadoop fs -put $APP_JAR /lib/
13 export INPUT=/triangles/input
14 export OUTPUT=/triangles/output
15 $HADOOP_HOME/bin/hadoop fs -rmr $OUTPUT
16 $HADOOP_HOME/bin/hadoop fs -rmr /triangles/tmp1
17 $HADOOP_HOME/bin/hadoop fs -rmr /triangles/tmp2
18 $HADOOP_HOME/bin/hadoop jar $APP_JAR TriangleCounterDriver $INPUT $OUTPUT
```

HDFS input

```
# hadoop fs -ls /triangles/input/
-rw-r--r-- ... 24 2014-05-25 11:06 /triangles/input/sample_graph.txt
# hadoop fs -cat /triangles/input/sample_graph.txt
1 2
2 3
2 4
2 5
3 4
4 5
```

Log of sample run

The log output is shown here; it has been edited and formatted to fit the page:

```
# ./run.sh
...
14/05/25 13:40:17 INFO input.FileInputFormat: Total input paths to process : 1
...
14/05/25 13:40:17 INFO mapred.JobClient: Running job: job_201405251213_0025
14/05/25 13:40:18 INFO mapred.JobClient: map 0% reduce 0%
...
14/05/25 13:41:08 INFO mapred.JobClient: map 100% reduce 100%
14/05/25 13:41:09 INFO mapred.JobClient: Job complete: job_201405251213_0025
...
14/05/25 13:41:09 INFO mapred.JobClient: Map-Reduce Framework
14/05/25 13:41:09 INFO mapred.JobClient: Map input records=6
...
14/05/25 13:41:09 INFO mapred.JobClient: Reduce input records=12
14/05/25 13:41:09 INFO mapred.JobClient: Reduce output records=23
14/05/25 13:41:09 INFO mapred.JobClient: Map output records=12
14/05/25 13:41:10 INFO input.FileInputFormat: Total input paths to process : 10
14/05/25 13:41:10 INFO mapred.JobClient: Running job: job_201405251213_0026
```

```
14/05/25 13:41:11 INFO mapred.JobClient: map 0% reduce 0%
...
14/05/25 13:42:06 INFO mapred.JobClient: map 100% reduce 100%
14/05/25 13:42:06 INFO mapred.JobClient: Job complete: job_201405251213_0026
...
14/05/25 13:42:06 INFO mapred.JobClient: Map-Reduce Framework
14/05/25 13:42:06 INFO mapred.JobClient: Map input records=23
14/05/25 13:42:06 INFO mapred.JobClient: Reduce input records=23
14/05/25 13:42:06 INFO mapred.JobClient: Combine output records=0
14/05/25 13:42:06 INFO mapred.JobClient: Reduce output records=6
14/05/25 13:42:06 INFO mapred.JobClient: Map output records=23
14/05/25 13:42:06 INFO input.FileInputFormat: Total input paths to process : 10
14/05/25 13:42:06 INFO mapred.JobClient: Running job: job_201405251213_0027
14/05/25 13:42:07 INFO mapred.JobClient: map 0% reduce 0%
...
14/05/25 13:43:00 INFO mapred.JobClient: map 100% reduce 100%
14/05/25 13:43:01 INFO mapred.JobClient: Job complete: job_201405251213_0027
...
14/05/25 13:43:01 INFO mapred.JobClient: Map-Reduce Framework
14/05/25 13:43:01 INFO mapred.JobClient: Map input records=6
14/05/25 13:43:01 INFO mapred.JobClient: Reduce input records=6
14/05/25 13:43:01 INFO mapred.JobClient: Combine output records=0
14/05/25 13:43:01 INFO mapred.JobClient: Reduce output records=2
14/05/25 13:43:01 INFO mapred.JobClient: Map output records=6
```

Expected output

```
# hadoop fs -cat /triangles/tmp1/part*
1,2 0
2,1 0
2,3 0
2,4 0
2,5 0
1,3 2
1,4 2
1,5 2
3,4 2
3,5 2
4,5 2
3,2 0
3,4 0
2,4 3
4,2 0
4,3 0
4,5 0
2,3 4
2,5 4
3,5 4
5,2 0
5,4 0
2,4 5
```

```
# hadoop fs -cat /triangles/tmp2/part*
4,5,2
2,3,4
2,4,3
2,4,5
2,5,4
3,4,2

# hadoop fs -cat /triangles/output/part*
2,3,4
2,4,5
```

Spark Solution

Our Hadoop solution for finding all unique triangles comprised three distinct Map-Reduce jobs (each job had its own `map()` and `reduce()` functions). Since Spark offers a high-level API for mappers and reducers, the Spark solution is given in a single Java driver class that has 10 basic steps. First, I present all 10 steps, and then we will dissect each step before I provide the sample run.

High-Level Steps

For our Spark solution, shown in Example 16-3, we closely follow the three-phase MapReduce algorithms presented for the Hadoop implementation.

Example 16-3. Spark's high-level solution

```
 1 // Step 1: import required classes and interfaces
 2 public class CountTriangles {
 3
 4    public static void main(String[] args) throws Exception {
 5      // Step 2: read and validate input parameters
 6      // Step 3: create a JavaSparkContext object (ctx)
 7      // Step 4: read an HDFS input text file representing a graph;
 8      //         records are represented as JavaRDD<String>
 9      // Step 5: create a new JavaPairRDD for all edges, which includes
10      //         (source, destination) and (destination, source)
11      // Step 6: create a new JavaPairRDD, which will generate triads
12      // Step 7: create a new JavaPairRDD, representing all possible triads
13      // Step 8: create a new JavaPairRDD, which will generate triangles
14      // Step 9: create a new JavaPairRDD, representing all triangles
15      // Step 10: eliminate duplicate triangles and create unique triangles
16
17      // done
18      ctx.close();
19      System.exit(0);
20    }
21 }
```

Step 1: Import required classes and interfaces

As shown in Example 16-4, we first import the required classes and interfaces from the JAR files provided with Spark's binary distribution. Most of the classes and interfaces are defined in the `org.apache.spark.api.java` package.

Example 16-4. Step 1: import required classes and interfaces

```
1 // Step 1: import required classes and interfaces
2 import scala.Tuple2;
3 import scala.Tuple3;
4
5 import org.apache.spark.api.java.JavaRDD;
6 import org.apache.spark.api.java.JavaPairRDD;
7 import org.apache.spark.api.java.JavaSparkContext;
8 import org.apache.spark.api.java.function.PairFlatMapFunction;
9 import org.apache.spark.api.java.function.FlatMapFunction;
10
11 import java.util.Arrays;
12 import java.util.List;
13 import java.util.ArrayList;
14 import java.util.Collections;
```

Step 2: Read input parameters

This step, shown in Example 16-5, reads input data (as an HDFS file), which represents our input graph as a set of edges in the form of (`source, destination`) and (`destination, source`).

Example 16-5. Step 2: read and validate input parameters

```
1      // Step 2: read and validate input parameters
2      if (args.length < 1) {
3        System.err.println("Usage: CountTriangles <hdfs-file>");
4        System.exit(1);
5      }
6      String hdfsFile = args[0];
```

Step 3: Create a Spark context object

In Example 16-6 we create a `JavaSparkContext` object that returns `JavaRDDs` and works with Java collections. Once we create a `JavaSparkContext` object, we will be able to create and manipulate our data with RDDs. We use the Spark master node name for this. For example, if our Spark cluster is composed of four servers {`myserver100, myserver200, myserver300, myserver400`} and the Spark master is represented by `myserver100`, the actual Spark master URL will be *spark:// myserver100:7077* (which will be configured from the command-line invocation).

Example 16-6. Step 3: create a Spark context object

```
1     // Step 3: create a JavaSparkContext object
2     // This is the object used for creating the first RDD.
3     JavaSparkContext ctx = new JavaSparkContext();
```

Step 4: Read graph via HDFS input

In this step, shown in Example 16-7, our input graph (represented by hdfsFile) is read by the JavaSparkContext object and the first JavaRDD<String> is created. For example, we used the HDFS file */triangles/sample_graph.txt* as an input file to represent our input graph. As you know, Spark's main abstraction is a distributed collection of items called a resilient distributed data set (RDD). RDDs can be created from Hadoop InputFormats (such as HDFS files) or by transforming other RDDs. To refresh your memory, Spark RDDs have actions (such as reduce() and collect()), which return values, and transformations (such as map(), flatMap(), flatMapTo Pair(), union(), and filter()), which return pointers to new RDDs.

Example 16-7. Step 4: read an HDFS input text file representing a graph

```
1     // Step 4: read an HDFS input text file representing a graph;
2     //         records are represented as JavaRDD<String>
3     // args[1] = HDFS text file: /triangles/sample_graph.txt
4 JavaRDD<String> lines = ctx.textFile(hdfsFile, 1);
```

Step 5: Create all graph edges

This step, as shown in Example 16-8, creates a new JavaPairRDD<Long,Long> from each of a set of edges represented as lines (a JavaRDD<String>). We convert each edge (as nodeA nodeB) into two pairs as follows:

```
(nodeA, nodeB)
(nodeB, nodeA)
```

Note that edges must be reciprocal; that is, every (source, destination) edge must have a corresponding (destination, source). To accomplish our mapping, we use PairFlatMapFunction<T, K, V>, where T is the input and K and V are outputs (creating a (key=K, value=V) pair). We use Spark's JavaRDD.flatMapToPair() method to generate all required key-value pairs (represented as JavaPairRDD<Long,Long>).

Example 16-8. Step 5: create a new JavaPairRDD for all edges

```
1     // Step 5: create a new JavaPairRDD for all edges, which
2     // includes (source, destination) and (destination, source)
3     // PairFlatMapFunction<T, K, V>
4     // T => Iterable<Tuple2<K, V>>
5     JavaPairRDD<Long,Long> edges =
6             lines.flatMapToPair(new PairFlatMapFunction<
```

```
7                                                            String, // T
8                                                            Long,   // K
9                                                            Long    // V
10                                                           >() {
11              public Iterable<Tuple2<Long,Long>> call(String s) {
12                  String[] nodes = s.split(" ");
13                  long start = Long.parseLong(nodes[0]);
14                  long end = Long.parseLong(nodes[1]);
15                  // Note that edges must be reciprocal; that is, every
16                  // (source, destination) edge must have a corresponding
17                  // (destination, source).
18                  return Arrays.asList(new Tuple2<Long, Long>(start, end),
19                                       new Tuple2<Long, Long>(end, start));
20              }
21          });
```

Step 6: Create RDD to generate triads

Now that we have all the edges, we try to form data structures, which eventually will create triangles. For every node, we find all corresponding destinations that might form possible *triads*. To accomplish this task, we use `JavaPairRDD.groupByKey()`, as shown in Example 16-9. The new RDD will be denoted by:

```
JavaPairRDD<Long, Iterable<Long>>
```

Note that values are returned as `Iterable<Long>` instead of `List<Long>`. This is another high-level abstraction by Spark to keep the implementation hidden from users (for possible optimizations by the Spark platform; Spark can implement `Itera ble<Long>` by `ArrayList`, `LinkedList`, or other proper data structures).

Example 16-9. Step 6: create a new JavaPairRDD, which will generate triads

```
1      // Step 6: create a new JavaPairRDD, which will generate triads
2      JavaPairRDD<Long, Iterable<Long>> triads = edges.groupByKey();
```

For debugging step 6, we collect all `triads` objects and display them:

```
// Step 6.1: debug1
List<Tuple2<Long, Iterable<Long>>> debug1 = triads.collect();
for (Tuple2<Long, Iterable<Long>> t2 : debug1) {
    System.out.println("debug1 t2._1="+t2._1);
    System.out.println("debug1 t2._2="+t2._2);
}
```

Step 7: Create all possible triads

This step, shown in Example 16-10, creates all possible triads (candidates for further checking that may form a triangle). To implement this step, we use the `Java PairRDD.flatMapToPair()` function to create proper key-value pairs, where the key is an edge (represented by a `Tuple2<node1,node2>`) and the value is a node (represented as a Long). Note that all RDDs are immutable, meaning they are *read-only*; they cannot be modified, altered, or sorted in any way. If you want to sort your RDDs, clone them and then perform your transformation or action.

Example 16-10. Step 7: create a new JavaPairRDD, which will generate possible triads

```
1  // Step 7: create a new JavaPairRDD, which will generate possible triads
2  JavaPairRDD<Tuple2<Long,Long>, Long> possibleTriads =
3      triads.flatMapToPair(
4          new PairFlatMapFunction<
5                                  Tuple2<Long, Iterable<Long>>, // input
6                                  Tuple2<Long,Long>,            // key (output)
7                                  Long                          // value (output)
8                                  >() {
9      public Iterable<Tuple2<Tuple2<Long,Long>, Long>>
10             call(Tuple2<Long, Iterable<Long>> s) {
11
12         // s._1 = Long (as a key)
13         // s._2 = Iterable<Long> (as values)
14         Iterable<Long> values = s._2;
15         // we assume that no node has an ID of zero
16         List<Tuple2<Tuple2<Long,Long>, Long>> result =
17         new ArrayList<Tuple2<Tuple2<Long,Long>, Long>>();
18
19         // Generate possible triads.
20         for (Long value : values) {
21             Tuple2<Long,Long> k2 = new Tuple2<Long,Long>(s._1, value);
22             Tuple2<Tuple2<Long,Long>, Long> k2v2 =
23                 new Tuple2<Tuple2<Long,Long>, Long>(k2, 0l);
24             result.add(k2v2);
25         }
26
27         // RDDs values are immutable, so we have to copy the values;
28         // copy values to valuesCopy.
29         List<Long> valuesCopy = new ArrayList<Long>();
30         for (Long item : values) {
31             valuesCopy.add(item);
32         }
33         Collections.sort(valuesCopy);
34
35         // Generate possible triads.
36         for (int i=0; i< valuesCopy.size() -1; ++i) {
37             for (int j=i+1; j< valuesCopy.size(); ++j) {
38                 Tuple2<Long,Long> k2 =
39                     new Tuple2<Long,Long>(valuesCopy.get(i), valuesCopy.get(j));
40                 Tuple2<Tuple2<Long,Long>, Long> k2v2 =
41                     new Tuple2<Tuple2<Long,Long>, Long>(k2, s._1);
42                 result.add(k2v2);
43             }
44         }
45         return result;
```

```
46      }
47   });
```

To debug step 7, we collect all possibleTriads objects and display them:

```
// Step 7.1: debug2
List<Tuple2<Tuple2<Long,Long>, Long>> debug2 =
  possibleTriads.collect();
for (Tuple2<Tuple2<Long,Long>, Long> t2 : debug2) {
    System.out.println("debug2 t2._1="+t2._1);
    System.out.println("debug2 t2._2="+t2._2);
}
```

Step 8: Create RDD to generate triangles

This step, shown in Example 16-11, creates an RDD that will be used to generate the actual triangles. The resulting JavaPairRDD will have an edge (represented as a Tuple2<Long,Long>) and a set of nodes (represented as an Iterable<Long>) for possible triangle formation.

Example 16-11. Step 8: create a new JavaPairRDD, which will generate triangles

```
1      // Step 8: create a new JavaPairRDD, which will generate triangles
2      JavaPairRDD<Tuple2<Long,Long>, Iterable<Long>> triadsGrouped =
3              possibleTriads.groupByKey();
```

To debug this step, we use the JavaRDD.collect() method:

```
// Step 8.1: debug3
List<Tuple2<Tuple2<Long,Long>, Iterable<Long>>> debug3 =
  triadsGrouped.collect();
for (Tuple2<Tuple2<Long,Long>, Iterable<Long>> t2 : debug3) {
    System.out.println("debug3 t2._1="+t2._1);
    System.out.println("debug3 t2._2="+t2._2);
}
```

Step 9: Create all triangles

This step generates all possible triangles, but it will include duplicates. We use a Flat MapFunction, which works as follows:

```
FlatMapFunction<T, R>
T => Iterable<R>
```

where T is an input and Iterable<R> is an output. In our case:

```
T = Tuple2<Tuple2<Long,Long>, Iterable<Long>>
  = Tuple2 (Tuple2(nodeA,nodeB), <node1,node2, ...>)

R = Tuple3<Long,Long,Long>
```

```
    = Tuple3(nodeA,nodeB,nodeC>
    = as a triangle where nodeC in {node1, node2, ...}
```

We accomplish this step by calling the `JavaPairRDD.flatMap()` function, as shown in
Example 16-12.

Example 16-12. Step 9: create a new JavaPairRDD, which will generate all triangles

```
1     // Step 9: create a new JavaPairRDD, which will generate all triangles
2     JavaRDD<Tuple3<Long,Long,Long>> trianglesWithDuplicates =
3             triadsGrouped.flatMap(new FlatMapFunction<
4                 Tuple2<Tuple2<Long,Long>, Iterable<Long>>, // input
5                 Tuple3<Long,Long,Long>                     // output
6                                                     >() {
7         public Iterable<Tuple3<Long,Long,Long>>
8             call(Tuple2<Tuple2<Long,Long>, Iterable<Long>> s) {
9
10            // s._1 = Tuple2<Long,Long> (as a key) = "<nodeA><,><nodeB>"
11            // s._2 = Iterable<Long> (as values) = {0, n1, n2, n3, ...} or
12            //                                      {n1, n2, n3, ...}
13            // note that 0 is a fake node, which does not exist
14            Tuple2<Long,Long> key = s._1;
15            Iterable<Long> values = s._2;
16            // we assume that no node has an ID of zero
17
18            List<Long> list = new ArrayList<Long>();
19            boolean haveSeenSpecialNodeZero = false;
20            for (Long node : values) {
21                if (node == 0) {
22                    haveSeenSpecialNodeZero = true;
23                }
24                else {
25                    list.add(node);
26                }
27            }
28
29            List<Tuple3<Long,Long,Long>> result =
30                new ArrayList<Tuple3<Long,Long,Long>>();
31            if (haveSeenSpecialNodeZero) {
32                if (list.isEmpty()) {
33                    // no triangles found
34                    return result;
35                }
36                // emit triangles
37                for (long node : list) {
38                    long[] aTriangle = {key._1, key._2, node};
39                    Arrays.sort(aTriangle);
40                    Tuple3<Long,Long,Long> t3 =
41                        new Tuple3<Long,Long,Long>(aTriangle[0], aTriangle[1],
42                                                   aTriangle[2]);
43                    result.add(t3);
44                }
```

```
45              }
46              else {
47                  // no triangles found
48                  return result;
49              }
50
51              return result;
52          }
53      });
```

To debug this step, we use the `JavaRDD.collect()` method:

```
// Step 9.1: debug4: print all triangles (includes duplicates)
System.out.println("=== Triangles with Duplicates ===");
List<Tuple3<Long,Long,Long>> debug4 = trianglesWithDuplicates.collect();
for (Tuple3<Long,Long,Long> t3 : debug4) {
  //System.out.println(t3._1 + "," + t3._2+ "," + t3._3);
  System.out.println("t3="+t3);
}
```

Step 10: Create unique triangles

Spark provides a very powerful API to find distinct elements for a given RDD. `JavaRDD<Tuple3<Long,Long,Long>>.distinct()` will create a new `JavaRDD<Tuple3<Long,Long,Long>>`, where all elements are distinct (see Example 16-13).

Example 16-13. Step 10: eliminate duplicate triangles and create unique triangles

```
1       // Step 10: eliminate duplicate triangles and create unique triangles
2       JavaRDD<Tuple3<Long,Long,Long>> uniqueTriangles =
3           trianglesWithDuplicates.distinct();
```

To debug this step, we use the `JavaRDD.collect` method:

```
// Step 10.1: print unique triangles
System.out.println("=== Unique Triangles ===");
List<Tuple3<Long,Long,Long>> output = uniqueTriangles.collect();
for (Tuple3<Long,Long,Long> t3 : output) {
  //System.out.println(t3._1 + "," + t3._2+ "," + t3._3);
  System.out.println("t3="+t3);
}
```

Sample Run

Here is a complete run of Spark's program for counting triangles.

Input

We use HDFS as an input medium:

```
# hadoop fs -ls /triangles/
Found 1 items
-rw-r--r--   3 hadoop root,hadoop 24 2014-05-25 17:45 /triangles/sample_graph.txt

# hadoop fs -cat /triangles/sample_graph.txt
1 2
2 3
2 4
2 5
3 4
4 5
```

Script

We use a convenient shell script to run our Spark program:

```
# cat run_count_triangles.sh
#!/bin/bash
export JAVA_HOME=/usr/java/jdk7
export BOOK_HOME=/mp/data-algorithms-book
export APP_JAR=$BOOK_HOME/dist/data_algorithms_book.jar
export SPARK_HOME=/usr/local/spark-1.0.0
export SPARK_MASTER=spark://myserver100:7077
export SPARK_JAR=$DAB/lib/spark-assembly-1.0.0-hadoop2.3.0.jar
export INPUT=/triangles/sample_graph.txt
prog=org.dataalgorithms.chap16.spark.CountTriangles
$SPARK_HOME/bin/spark-submit
    --class $prog \
    --master $SPARK_MASTER \
    --num-executors 12 \
    --driver-memory 3g \
    --executor-memory 7g \
    --executor-cores 12 \
    $APP_JAR $INPUT
```

Running script

The output of a sample run (using the shell script *run_count_triangles.sh*) is shown here; it has been edited, formatted, and trimmed into several debugging sections:

```
Output log for debug1:
=======================
debug1 t2._1=4
debug1 t2._2=[2, 3, 5]
debug1 t2._1=1
debug1 t2._2=[2]
debug1 t2._1=3
debug1 t2._2=[2, 4]
debug1 t2._1=5
debug1 t2._2=[2, 4]
debug1 t2._1=2
debug1 t2._2=[1, 3, 4, 5]
```

```
Output log for debug2:
======================
debug2 t2._1=(4,2)
debug2 t2._2=0
debug2 t2._1=(4,3)
debug2 t2._2=0
debug2 t2._1=(4,5)
debug2 t2._2=0
debug2 t2._1=(2,3)
debug2 t2._2=4
debug2 t2._1=(2,5)
debug2 t2._2=4
debug2 t2._1=(3,5)
debug2 t2._2=4
debug2 t2._1=(1,2)
debug2 t2._2=0
debug2 t2._1=(3,2)
debug2 t2._2=0
debug2 t2._1=(3,4)
debug2 t2._2=0
debug2 t2._1=(2,4)
debug2 t2._2=3
debug2 t2._1=(5,2)
debug2 t2._2=0
debug2 t2._1=(5,4)
debug2 t2._2=0
debug2 t2._1=(2,4)
debug2 t2._2=5
debug2 t2._1=(2,1)
debug2 t2._2=0
debug2 t2._1=(2,3)
debug2 t2._2=0
debug2 t2._1=(2,4)
debug2 t2._2=0
debug2 t2._1=(2,5)
debug2 t2._2=0
debug2 t2._1=(1,3)
debug2 t2._2=2
debug2 t2._1=(1,4)
debug2 t2._2=2
debug2 t2._1=(1,5)
debug2 t2._2=2
debug2 t2._1=(3,4)
debug2 t2._2=2
debug2 t2._1=(3,5)
debug2 t2._2=2
debug2 t2._1=(4,5)
debug2 t2._2=2

Output log for debug3:
======================
debug3 t2._1=(4,5)
```

```
debug3 t2._2=[0, 2]
debug3 t2._1=(1,4)
debug3 t2._2=[2]
debug3 t2._1=(4,2)
debug3 t2._2=[0]
debug3 t2._1=(3,5)
debug3 t2._2=[4, 2]
debug3 t2._1=(2,3)
debug3 t2._2=[4, 0]
debug3 t2._1=(5,4)
debug3 t2._2=[0]
debug3 t2._1=(2,4)
debug3 t2._2=[3, 5, 0]
debug3 t2._1=(1,2)
debug3 t2._2=[0]
debug3 t2._1=(3,2)
debug3 t2._2=[0]
debug3 t2._1=(2,5)
debug3 t2._2=[4, 0]
debug3 t2._1=(1,5)
debug3 t2._2=[2]
debug3 t2._1=(3,4)
debug3 t2._2=[0, 2]
debug3 t2._1=(4,3)
debug3 t2._2=[0]
debug3 t2._1=(2,1)
debug3 t2._2=[0]
debug3 t2._1=(1,3)
debug3 t2._2=[2]
debug3 t2._1=(5,2)
debug3 t2._2=[0]

=== Triangles with Duplicates ===
t3=(2,4,5)
t3=(2,3,4)
t3=(2,3,4)
t3=(2,4,5)
t3=(2,4,5)
t3=(2,3,4)

=== Unique Triangles ===
t3=(2,3,4)
t3=(2,4,5)
```

This chapter provided two distinct MapReduce solutions (Hadoop and Spark) for identifying, listing, and counting triangles in a given set of graphs, which has a sound impact on our understanding of social graphs. The next chapter provides MapReduce solutions for counting K-mers for DNA sequences.

## CHAPTER 17

K-mer Counting

A K-mer is a substring of length K ($K > 0$), and counting the occurrences of all such substrings is a central step in many analyses of DNA sequence data. Counting K-mers for a DNA sequence means finding frequencies of K-mers for the entire sequence. In bioinformatics, K-mer counting is used for genome and transcriptome assembly, metagenomic sequencing, and error correction of sequence reads. Although simple in principle, K-mer counting is a big data challenge, since a single DNA sample can contain several billion DNA sequences. The K-mer counting problem has been defined by the Schatz lab (*http://bit.ly/k-mer_counting*).

This chapter will provide a complete K-mer solution using MapReduce/Hadoop and Spark. Our implementation discovers all K-mers for a given $K > 0$ and finds the top N K-mers for a given $N > 0$. The complete MapReduce/Hadoop and Spark solutions are available on GitHub (*http://bit.ly/da_book*).

A K-mer is a DNA sequence of length K. For example, if a sample DNA sequence is *CACACACAGT*, then the following are 3-mers and 5-mers for that sequence:

```
original sequence: CACACACAGT
3-mers:            CAC
                    ACA
                     CAC
                      ACA
                       CAC
                        ACA
                         CAG
                          AGT

original sequence: CACACACAGT
5-mers:            CACAC
                    ACACA
                     CACAC
                      ACACA
```

CACAG
ACAGT

Given a DNA sequence (we'll call it string *S*) comprising any of {*A*, *C*, *G*, *T*}, which represent the primary nucleobases, we are interested in counting the number of occurrences in *S* of every substring of length *K*.

Input Data for K-mer Counting

For input, we will use FASTQ (*http://maq.sourceforge.net/fastq.shtml*), a concise and compact format that stores DNA sequences in a text file. Each set of four consecutive lines in a FASTQ file represents a single sequence. For example, the following four lines represent a sequence:

```
@EAS54_6_R7_30800
GTTGCTTCCCGCGTGGGTGGGTCGGGG
+EAS54_6_R7
;;;;;;;;33;;;;9;7;;.7;393333
```

To read the FASTQ file format, we need to understand the format specification. Line 1 begins with @, line 3 begins with +, and line 4 represents the quality of the sequence. Line 2 represents the sequence to be analyzed. Therefore, we will discard all lines except the second.

Sample Data for K-mer Counting

You may use the following sample data to test your K-mer counting solution:

- *E. coli* genome from *http://bit.ly/e_coli_genome*.
- Human genome from *http://bit.ly/hum_genome*. Note that *hg19* means human genome, build 19.

And then you may use the K-mer counting solution to answer the following questions:

- What are the top 10 most frequently occurring 9-mers in *E. coli*?
- What are the top 10 most frequently occurring 9-mers in hg19?
- What are the top 10 most frequently occurring 21-mers in hg19?

Applications of K-mer Counting

Counting the K-mers in a DNA sequence is a very important step in many bioinformatics applications. The following are examples of applications of K-mer counting:

- Determining whether a misalignment between reads is a sequencing error or a genuine difference in sequence

- Detecting repeated sequences, such as transposons, which are an important factor for biological role applications

- Correcting short-read assembly errors

- Computing metrics such as *relatedness* and *unique enough* (useful in metagenomic applications)

K-mer Counting Solution in MapReduce/Hadoop

Conceptually, K-mer counting using MapReduce is similar to the "word count" program, but since there are no spaces in the human genome, we will count overlapping K-mers instead of discrete words.

The map() Function

If the genome sequence is CACACACAGT and *K*=3, then we are counting 3-mers, and the map() function (see Example 17-1) will output the following key-value pairs:

```
CAC    1
ACA    1
CAC    1
ACA    1
CAC    1
ACA    1
CAG    1
AGT    1
```

Example 17-1. K-mer counting: map() function

```
 1 /**
 2  * @param key is generated by MapReduce, ignored here
 3  * @param sequence (as value) is one line of input for a given genome sequence
 4  */
 5 map(Long key, String sequence) {
 6     // MapReduce/Hadoop: get the value of K (K-mer) from setup()
 7     // Spark: use broadcast which will be called once
 8     for (int i=0; i < sequence.length()-K+1 ; i++) {
 9         String kmer = sequence.substring(i, K+i);
10         emit(kmer, 1));
11     }
12 }
```

The reduce() Function

The sort and shuffle phase will sort the output of `map()` so that the same keys are grouped together as follows:

```
ACA    1
ACA    1
ACA    1
CAC    1
CAC    1
CAC    1
CAG    1
AGT    1
```

Finally, the `reduce()` function (see Example 17-2) will output:

```
ACA    3
CAC    3
CAG    1
AGT    1
```

Example 17-2. K-mer counting: reduce() function

```
1  /**
2   * @param key is a unique K-mer generated by mappers
3   * @param value is a list of integers (partial count of a K-mer)
4   */
5  reduce(String key, List<integer> value) {
6      int sum = 0;
7      for (int count : value) {
8          sum += count;
9      }
10     emit(key, sum);
11 }
```

Hadoop Implementation Classes

I have provided a complete solution of K-mer counting using the four small classes listed in Table 17-1.

Table 17-1. K-mer counting solution

Class name	Class description
KmerCountDriver	MapReduce/Hadoop job driver
KmerCountMapper	Defines the map() function
KmerCountReduce	Defines the reduce() function
KmerUtil	Generates K-mers for a given *K*

K-mer Counting Solution in Spark

The K-mer MapReduce workflow is illustrated in Figure 17-1. Let's step through it before we go over our Spark solution.

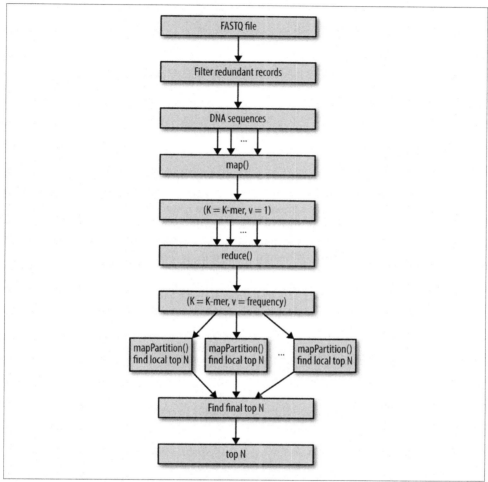

Figure 17-1. K-mer MapReduce workflow

Assume that we want to discover all K-mers (for a given $K > 0$) and the top N (for a given $N > 0$) for a set of FASTQ files. Since the FASTQ file format is very well defined, first we create a `JavaRDD<String>` for the given FASTQ file. Next, we remove the records that are not sequences (those similar to lines 1, 3, and 4 from the aforementioned input data). This filtering is implemented by the `JavaRDD.filter()` function. Once we have only sequences, we create $(K, 1)$ pairs, where K is a K-mer. Then, we find the frequency of K-mers. Finally, we can find the top N K-mers for $N > 0$. Finding the top N is simple: we assume that (K_2, V_2) are partitioned (K_2 is a K-mer and V_2 is the frequency of K_2), and then we map each partition into the top N. Once we have a top N list (comprising one top N from each partition), we can do the final reduction to find the final top N.

We have three inputs to our Spark program:

- The FASTQ file stored in HDFS
- $K > 0$ to find K-mers
- $N > 0$ to find top N K-mers

Spark Solution

Our Spark solution is implemented in a single Java driver class, thanks to the Spark API's high abstraction level. The Spark solution reads FASTQ files as input and converts them to `JavaRDD<String>`. Next, we filter the redundant records and keep only the sequence line out of every four records. At this point, we have only the proper sequences from the input files. Then we generate K-mers and find the frequency of them. Finally, we apply the Top N design pattern in descending order.

First, the entire solution is presented as a set of 11 high-level steps (see Example 17-3), and then each step is implemented as a Java/Spark API.

Example 17-3. K-mer high-level solution in Spark

```
1 // Step 1: import required classes and interfaces
2 public class Kmer {
3     static JavaSparkContext createJavaSparkContext() throws Exception {...}
4
5     public static void main(String[] args) throws Exception {
6         // Step 2: handle input parameters
7         // Step 3: create a Spark context object (ctx)
8         // Step 4: broadcast K and N as global shared objects,
9         // which can be accessed from all cluster nodes
10        // Step 5: read FASTQ file from HDFS and create the first RDD
11        // Step 6: filter redundant records
12        // Step 7: generate K-mers
13        // Step 8: combine/reduce frequent K-mers
14        // Step 9: create a local top N for all partitions
15        // Step 10: collect local top Ns from all partitions
16        // and find final top N from all partitions
17        // Step 11: emit final top N, descending
18
19        // done
20        ctx.close()
21        System.exit(0);
```

```
22   }
23 }
```

Step 1: Import required classes and interfaces

The first step, shown in Example 17-4, imports all required Java classes and interfaces.

Example 17-4. Step 1: import required classes and interfaces

```
 1 // Step 1: import required classes and interfaces
 2 import java.util.Map;
 3 import java.util.SortedMap;
 4 import java.util.TreeMap;
 5 import java.util.List;
 6 import java.util.ArrayList;
 7 import java.util.Iterator;
 8 import java.util.Collections;
 9 import scala.Tuple2;
10 import scala.Tuple3;
11 import org.apache.spark.SparkConf;
12 import org.apache.spark.api.java.JavaRDD;
13 import org.apache.spark.api.java.JavaPairRDD;
14 import org.apache.spark.api.java.JavaSparkContext;
15 import org.apache.spark.api.java.function.PairFlatMapFunction;
16 import org.apache.spark.api.java.function.FlatMapFunction;
17 import org.apache.spark.api.java.function.Function;
18 import org.apache.spark.api.java.function.Function2;
19 import org.apache.spark.broadcast.Broadcast;
```

createJavaSparkContext() method

To create RDDs, you need an instance of `JavaSparkContext`, which is a factory class for creating `JavaRDD` and `JavaPairRDD` objects (see Example 17-5).

Example 17-5. createJavaSparkContext() method

```
1    static JavaSparkContext createJavaSparkContext() throws Exception {
2        JavaSparkContext ctx = new JavaSparkContext();
3        return ctx;
4    }
```

Step 2: Handle input parameters

This step, shown in Example 17-6, reads three required inputs from the command line: the FASTQ file, K (the size of the K-mer), and N (for the top *N*).

Example 17-6. Step 2: handle input parameters

```
1    // Step 2: handle input parameters
2    if (args.length < 3) {
3       System.err.println("Usage: Kmer <fastq-file> <K> <N>");
4       System.exit(1);
5    }
6    final String fastqFileName = args[0];      // FASTQ file as input
7    final  int K = Integer.parseInt(args[1]); // to find K-mers
8    final  int N = Integer.parseInt(args[2]); // to find top N
```

Step 3: Create a Spark context Object

We use `Kmer.createJavaSparkContext()` to create a `JavaSparkContext` object in this step (Example 17-7).

Example 17-7. Step 3: create a Spark context object

```
1    // Step 3: create a Spark context object
2    JavaSparkContext ctx = createJavaSparkContext();
```

Step 4: Broadcast global shared objects

In the Spark framework, to use shared objects in all cluster nodes we can broadcast them and read them from the `map()` and `reduce()` functions. To make an object sharable, we use the following API:

```
T t = <an-instance-of-T>;
Broadcast<T> broadcastT = ctx.broadcast(t);
```

To access the broadcasted (shared) object from any cluster node, we use the following API:

```
T t = broadcastT.value();
```

Since K (K-mer size) and N (for top N) are required from all cluster nodes, we broadcast these two values as shown in Example 17-8.

Example 17-8. Step 4: broadcast K and N as global shared objects

```
1    // Step 4: broadcast K and N as global shared objects,
2    // which can be accessed from all cluster nodes
3    final Broadcast<Integer> broadcastK = ctx.broadcast(K);
4    final Broadcast<Integer> broadcastN = ctx.broadcast(N);
```

Step 5: Read the FASTQ file from HDFS and create the first RDD

This step, shown in Example 17-9, reads the FASTQ file and creates a Jav aRDD<String> object, where each record of the FASTQ file is represented as a String object.

Example 17-9. Step 5: read FASTQ file from HDFS and create the first RDD

```
1    // Step 5: read FASTQ file from HDFS and create the first RDD
2    JavaRDD<String> records = ctx.textFile(fastqFileName, 1);
3    records.saveAsTextFile("/kmers/output/1");
```

Here is the output of this step:

```
# hadoop fs -cat /kmers/output/1/part*
@EAS54_6_R1_2_1_413_324
CCCTTCTTGTCCCCAGCGTTTCTCC
+
;;3;;;;;;;;;;;;7;;;;;;;;88
@EAS54_6_R1_2_1_540_792
TTGGCAGGCCAAGGCCGATGGATCA
+
;;;;;;;;;;;7;;;;;-;;;3;83
@EAS54_6_R1_2_1_443_348
GTTGCTTCTGGCGTGGGTGGGGGGG
+EAS54_6_R1_2_1_443_348
;;;;;;;;;;;9;7;;.7;393333
@EAS54_6_R1_2_1_413_324
CCCCCCTTGTCTTCAGCCCTTCTCC
+
;;3;;;;;;;;;;;;7;;;;;;;;88
@EAS54_6_R1_2_1_540_792
TTTTCAGGCCAAGGCCGATGGATCA
+
;;;;;;;;;;;7;;;;;-;;;3;83
@EAS54_6_R1_2_1_443_348
GTTGTTTCTGGCGTGGGTGGGGGGG
+EAS54_6_R1_2_1_443_348
;;;;;;;;;;;9;7;;.7;393333
@EAS54_6_R1_2_1_443_348
GTTGTTTCTGGCGTGGGTGGCCCCC
+EAS54_6_R1_2_1_443_348
;;;;;;;;;;;9;7;;.7;393333
```

Step 6: Filter redundant records

This step, shown in Example 17-10, uses a very powerful Spark API, JavaRDD.fil
ter(), to filter out the redundant records before applying the map() function. In a
FASTQ file, we just keep the records that represent DNA sequences.

Example 17-10. Step 6: filter redundant records

```
1    // Step 6: filter redundant records
2    // JavaRDD<T> filter(Function<T,Boolean> f)
3    // Return a new RDD containing only the elements that satisfy a predicate.
4    JavaRDD<String> filteredRDD = records.filter(new Function<String,Boolean>() {
5      public Boolean call(String record) {
```

```
6          String firstChar = record.substring(0,1);
7          if ( firstChar.equals("@") ||
8               firstChar.equals("+") ||
9               firstChar.equals(";") ||
10              firstChar.equals("!") ||
11              firstChar.equals("~") ) {
12            return false; // do not return these records
13          }
14          else {
15            return true;
16          }
17        }
18      });
19      filteredRDD.saveAsTextFile("/kmers/output/1.5");
```

Here is the output of this step:

```
# hadoop fs -cat /kmers/output/1.5/part*
CCCTTCTTGTCCCCAGCGTTTCTCC
TTGGCAGGCCAAGGCCGATGGATCA
GTTGCTTCTGGCGTGGGTGGGGGGG
CCCCCCTTGTCTTCAGCCCTTCTCC
TTTTCAGGCCAAGGCCGATGGATCA
GTTGTTTCTGGCGTGGGTGGGGGGG
GTTGTTTCTGGCGTGGGTGGCCCCC
```

Step 7: Generate K-mers

This step, shown in Example 17-11, implements the mapper for K-mers by using the
JavaRDD.flatMapToPair() function. The mapper accepts a sequence and K (the size
of K-mers) and then generates all (kmer, 1) pairs.

Example 17-11. Step 7: generate K-mers

```
1     // Step 7: generate K-mers
2     // PairFlatMapFunction<T, K, V>
3     // T => Iterable<Tuple2<K, V>>
4     JavaPairRDD<String,Integer> kmers =
5       filteredRDD.flatMapToPair(new PairFlatMapFunction<
6       String,        // T
7       String,        // K
8       Integer        // V
9     >() {
10      public Iterable<Tuple2<String,Integer>> call(String sequence) {
11        int K = broadcastK.value();
12        List<Tuple2<String,Integer>> list =
13          new ArrayList<Tuple2<String,Integer>>();
14        for (int i=0; i < sequence.length()-K+1 ; i++) {
15          String kmer = sequence.substring(i, K+i);
16          list.add(new Tuple2<String,Integer>(kmer, 1));
17        }
```

```
18          return list;
19       }
20    });
21    kmers.saveAsTextFile("/kmers/output/2");
```

Here is the partial output of this step:

```
# hadoop fs -cat /kmers/output/2/part*
(CCC,1)
(CCT,1)
(CTT,1)
...
(GGC,1)
(GCC,1)
(CCC,1)
(CCC,1)
(CCC,1)
```

Step 8: Combine/reduce frequent K-mers

As shown in Example 17-12, this step implements the reducer for K-mers by using the `JavaPairRDD.reduceByKey()` function. The reducer accepts a key (as K-mers) and values (frequencies of K-mers) and then generates a final count of K-mers.

Example 17-12. Step 8: combine/reduce frequent K-mers

```
1    // Step 8: combine/reduce frequent K-mers
2    JavaPairRDD<String, Integer> kmersGrouped =
3       kmers.reduceByKey(new Function2<Integer, Integer, Integer>() {
4       public Integer call(Integer i1, Integer i2) {
5          return i1 + i2;
6       }
7    });
8    kmersGrouped.saveAsTextFile("/kmers/output/3");
```

Here is the output of this step:

```
# hadoop fs -cat /kmers/output/3/part*
(CTC,2)
(AGC,2)
(CAA,2)
(TGC,1)
(GGC,9)
(GCC,6)
(GCT,1)
(CCT,3)
(TTT,5)
(TGG,12)
(TCC,3)
(CGA,2)
(CCC,11)
(AGG,4)
```

```
(GGT,3)
(GCA,1)
(CTG,3)
(TGT,4)
(TCA,4)
(GTG,6)
(CTT,6)
(TTC,8)
(CGT,4)
(GGG,13)
(CAG,4)
(GAT,4)
(TTG,6)
(CCA,3)
(AAG,2)
(TCT,7)
(GTT,6)
(GTC,2)
(GCG,4)
(ATG,2)
(CCG,2)
(GGA,2)
(ATC,2)
```

Step 9: Create a local top N for each partition

This step, shown in Example 17-13, partitions all (kmer, frequency) pairs into
many partitions and then finds a top *N* for every partition. For every partition, we
just keep the top *N* (frequency, kmer) pairs as a SortedMap, where TreeMap implements the SortedMap interface. Finding the local top *N* for each partition is handled
by the JavaPairRDD.mapPartitions() method.

Example 17-13. Step 9: create a local top N for all partitions

```
1     // Step 9: create a local top N for all partitions
2     // Now we have: (K=kmer,V=frequency).
3     // Next step is to find the top N K-mers
4     JavaRDD<SortedMap<Integer, String>> partitions = kmersGrouped.mapPartitions(
5       new FlatMapFunction<Iterator<Tuple2<String,Integer>>,
6                           SortedMap<Integer, String>
7                           >() {
8     @Override
9     public Iterable<SortedMap<Integer, String>>
10        call(Iterator<Tuple2<String,Integer>> iter) {
11        int N = broadcastN.value();
12        SortedMap<Integer, String> topN = new TreeMap<Integer, String>();
13        while (iter.hasNext()) {
14            Tuple2<String,Integer> tuple = iter.next();
15            String kmer = tuple._1;
16            int frequency = tuple._2;
17            topN.put(frequency, kmer);
```

```
18          // keep only top N
19          if (topN.size() > N) {
20              topN.remove(topN.firstKey());
21          }
22      }
23      System.out.println("topN="+topN);
24      return Collections.singletonList(topN);
25      }
26  });
```

Step 10: Find the final top N

This step, shown in Example 17-14, aggregates all top *N*s generated from all partitions and creates the final top *N* for all partitions. For this step, we need the value of *N*, which we read from a broadcasted variable (broadcastN).

Example 17-14. Step 10: find final top N

```
1   // Step 10: collect local top Ns from all partitions
2   // and find final top N from all partitions
3   SortedMap<Integer, String> finaltopN = new TreeMap<Integer, String>();
4   List<SortedMap<Integer, String>> alltopN = partitions.collect();
5   for (SortedMap<Integer, String> localtopN : alltopN) {
6       // frequency = tuple._1
7       // kmer = tuple._2
8       for (Map.Entry<Integer, String> entry : localtopN.entrySet()) {
9           finaltopN.put(entry.getKey(), entry.getValue());
10          // keep only top N
11          if (finaltopN.size() > N) {
12              finaltopN.remove(finaltopN.firstKey());
13          }
14      }
15  }
```

Step 11: Emit final top N

This step, shown in Example 17-15, emits the final top *N* for all K-mers.

Example 17-15. Step 11: emit final top N

```
1   // Step 11: emit final top N, descending
2   System.out.println("=== top " + N + " ===");
3   List<Integer> frequencies = new ArrayList<Integer>(finaltopN.keySet());
4   for(int i = frequencies.size()-1; i>=0; i--) {
5       System.out.println(frequencies.get(i) + "\t" +
6                       finaltopN.get(frequencies.get(i)));
7   }
```

Combining steps 9 and 10 into a single function

Steps 9 and 10 can be combined into a single Spark function, `JavaPairRDD.top()`. The `top()` function is defined as follows:

```
import java.util.List;
import java.util.Comparator;
...
List<T> top(int N, Comparator<T> comp)
// Returns the top N elements from this RDD as
// defined by the specified Comparator[T].
// Parameters:
//    N - the number of top elements to return
//    comp - the comparator that defines the order
```

The second parameter (`Comparator<T>`) of `top()` defines how the RDD elements will be sorted (you may sort elements in ascending or descending order). Next, we define a `Comparator`. The input RDD is `kmersGrouped`, which is a `JavaPairRDD<String,Integer>`; therefore, our comparator has to sort elements based on the frequencies (as `Integer`s) of K-mers (as `String`s):

Example 17-16 shows how to sort tuples in descending order.

Example 17-16. Descending comparator: TupleComparatorDescending

```
 1 static class TupleComparatorDescending
 2    implements Comparator<Tuple2<String, Integer>>, Serializable {
 3    final static TupleComparatorDescending INSTANCE =
 4       new TupleComparatorDescending();
 5    public int compare(Tuple2<String, Integer> t1,
 6                       Tuple2<String, Integer> t2) {
 7       // sorts RDD elements descending (use for top N)
 8       return -t1._2.compareTo(t2._2);
 9    }
10 }
```

And Example 17-17 shows how to sort tuples in ascending order.

Example 17-17. Ascending comparator: TupleComparatorAscending

```
 1 static class TupleComparatorAscending
 2    implements Comparator<Tuple2<String, Integer>>, Serializable {
 3    final static TupleComparatorAscending INSTANCE =
 4       new TupleComparatorAscending();
 5    public int compare(Tuple2<String, Integer> t1,
 6                       Tuple2<String, Integer> t2) {
 7       // sorts RDD elements ascending (use for bottom N)
 8       return -t1._2.compareTo(t2._2);
 9    }
10 }
```

Now, we are ready to apply the top() function (note that your comparator has to implement the Serializable interface since sorting algorithms are used in a distributed environment):

```
// to find top 10
List<Tuple2<String, Integer>> finalTop10 =
    kmersGrouped.top(10, TupleComparatorDescending.INSTANCE);

// to find bottom 10
List<Tuple2<String, Integer>> finalBottom10 =
    kmersGrouped.top(10, TupleComparatorAscending.INSTANCE);
```

Sample Run

YARN script for Spark

The script shown here runs our Spark program in the YARN environment:

```
 1 $ cat run_kmer.sh
 2 #!/bin/bash
 3 export JAVA_HOME=/usr/java/jdk7
 4 export SPARK_HOME=/usr/local/spark-1.1.0
 5 export HADOOP_HOME=/usr/local/hadoop-2.5.0
 6 export HADOOP_CONF_DIR=$HADOOP_HOME/etc/hadoop
 7 export YARN_CONF_DIR=$HADOOP_HOME/etc/hadoop
 8 export BOOK_HOME=/mp/data-algorithms-book
 9 export APP_JAR=$BOOK_HOME/dist/data_algorithms_book.jar
10 export SPARK_JAR=$BOOK_HOME/lib/spark-assembly-1.1.0-hadoop2.5.0.jar
11 #
12 export INPUT=/data/sample.fastq
13 export K=3
14 export N=5
15 prog=org.dataalgorithms.chap17.spark.Kmer
16 $SPARK_HOME/bin/spark-submit --class $prog \
17     --master yarn-cluster \
18     --num-executors 12 \
19     --driver-memory 3g \
20     --executor-memory 7g \
21     --executor-cores 12 \
22     $APP_JAR $INPUT $K $N
```

HDFS input

Next, we examine the input data in HDFS:

```
# hadoop fs -cat /data/sample.fastq
@EAS54_6_R1_2_1_413_324
CCCTTCTTGTCCCCAGCGTTTCTCC
+
;;3;;;;;;;;;;;;7;;;;;;;88
@EAS54_6_R1_2_1_540_792
TTGGCAGGCCAAGGCCGATGGATCA
```

```
+
;;;;;;;;;;;;7;;;;;-;;;3;83
@EAS54_6_R1_2_1_443_348
GTTGCTTCTGGCGTGGGTGGGGGGG
+EAS54_6_R1_2_1_443_348
;;;;;;;;;;;;9;7;;.7;393333
@EAS54_6_R1_2_1_413_324
CCCCCCTTGTCTTCAGCCCTTCTCC
+
;;3;;;;;;;;;;;;7;;;;;;;88
@EAS54_6_R1_2_1_540_792
TTTTCAGGCCAAGGCCGATGGATCA
+
;;;;;;;;;;;;7;;;;;-;;;3;83
@EAS54_6_R1_2_1_443_348
GTTGTTTCTGGCGTGGGTGGGGGGG
+EAS54_6_R1_2_1_443_348
;;;;;;;;;;;;9;7;;.7;393333
@EAS54_6_R1_2_1_443_348
GTTGTTTCTGGCGTGGGTGGCCCCC
+EAS54_6_R1_2_1_443_348
;;;;;;;;;;;;9;7;;.7;393333
```

Output for final top N

The final top 5 list (in descending order) is presented here:

```
=== top 5 ===
13   GGG
12   TGG
11   CCC
9    GGC
8    TTC
```

This chapter presented MapReduce/Hadoop and Spark solutions for counting K-mers for a given set of DNA sequences. We were able to apply the Top N design pattern from Chapter 3 to find the top K-mers. The next chapter introduces a very important concept in genomics: DNA sequencing, which finds *single nucleotide polymorphisms* (SNPs) for a given large set of DNA sequences.

## CHAPTER 18

DNA Sequencing

Today, genome sequencing machines (such as Illumina's HiSeq 4000) are able to generate thousands of gigabases of DNA and RNA sequencing data in a few hours for less than US$1,000 (a few years ago, the price was over US$100,000, and sequencing the first human genome cost about US$3 billion). Success in biology and the life sciences depends on our ability to properly analyze the big data sets that are generated by these technologies, which in turn requires us to adopt advances in informatics. Map-Reduce/Hadoop and Spark enable us to compute and analyze thousands of gigabytes/petabytes of data in hours (rather than days or weeks). For example, Spark was recently used to sort 100 TB of data using 206 machines in 23 minutes.[1]

In simple terms, DNA sequencing is the sequencing of whole genomes (such as human genomes). According to *http://dnasequencing.com*: "if finding DNA was the discovery of the exact substance holding our genetic makeup information, DNA sequencing is the discovery of the process that will allow us to *read* that information." The main function of DNA sequencing is to find the precise order of nucleotides within a DNA molecule. Also, DNA sequencing is used to determine the order of the four bases—adenine (A), guanine (G), cytosine (C), and thymine (T)—in a strand of DNA.

What are some of the challenges of DNA sequencing? There are many, but here are some of the most important ones:

- There are several sequencing technologies to generate FASTQ files, and the lengths of DNA sequences are different for each sequencing technology.

---

[1] *http://bit.ly/spark_2014_gray_sort*

- The input data (FASTQ data) size is *big* (a single DNA sequence sample can be up to 900 GB).

- With a single powerful server, it takes too long (up to 80 hours) to process one DNA sequence and extract variants such as single nucleotide polymorphisms (SNPs).

- There are many algorithms and steps involved in DNA sequencing, so selecting the proper combinations of open source tools is a serious challenge. For example, there are quite a few mapping/alignment algorithms and parameters.

- Scalability—that is, optimizing the number of mappers and reducers—is difficult to achieve.

A high-level DNA sequencing workflow is presented in Figure 18-1. Our focus in this chapter will be implementing DNA sequencing as a set of MapReduce programs that will accept a DNA data set as a FASTQ file and finally generate a VCF (variant call format) file, which has variants for a given DNA data set.

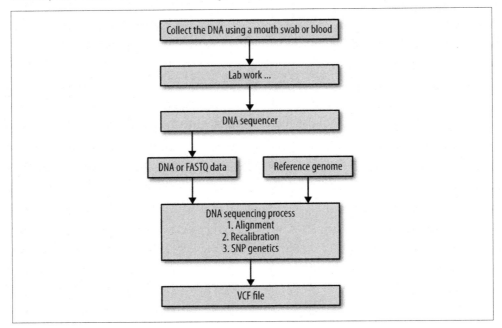

Figure 18-1. High-level view of DNA sequencing

One of the major goals of DNA sequencing is to find variants, since most of our DNA is identical; only a very small percent differs from person to person. One important example is the identification of single nucleotide polymorphisms (SNPs). The identification and extraction of SNPs from raw genetic sequences involves many algorithms and the application of a diverse set of tools.

The DNA sequencing pipeline is illustrated in Figure 18-2 and includes the following key steps:

1. Input data validation: performing quality control on input data such as FASTQ files

2. Alignment: mapping short reads to the reference genome

3. Recalibration: visualizing and post-processing the alignment, including base quality recalibration

4. Variant detection: executing the SNP calling procedure along with filtering SNP candidates

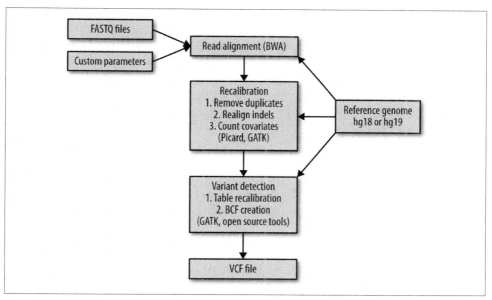

Figure 18-2. DNA sequencing pipeline

There is plenty of data (*http://www.1000genomes.org/data*) to analyze and apply DNA sequencing to, and there are lots of open source algorithms for completing the previous four steps. Note that your choice of these open source tools will significantly affect your final results, so it's important that you understand them well.

Input Data for DNA Sequencing

The most common format for DNA sequencing data is FASTQ, a text-based format for storing both a biological sequence and its quality scores. For a given FASTQ file, every four lines represent a single DNA sequence.

The general syntax of a FASTQ file is as follows:

```
<fastq>:= <block>+
<block>:=@<seqname>\n<seq>\n[<seqname>]\n<qual>\n
<seqname>:= [A-Za-z0-9_.:-]+
<seq>:= [A-Za-z\n\.~]+
<qual>:= [!-~\n]+
```

And here is an example:

```
@NCYC361-11a03.q1k bases 1 to 1576
GCGTGCCCGAAAAAATGCTTTTGGAGCCGCGCGTGAAAT...
+NCYC361-11a03.q1k bases 1 to 1576
!)))))****(((***%%((((*(((+,**(((+**+,-...
```

FASTQ data can be paired or nonpaired. If it is paired, then our input for the DNA sequencing will be a pair of files: *left_file.fastq* and *right_file.fastq*. If it is nonpaired, there will be a single file: *file.fastq*.

Now that you have an idea of what the input data looks like, let's take a closer look at the first few steps of our DNA sequencing pipeline. Then we'll see how MapReduce can help us solve the DNA sequencing problem.

Input Data Validation

The first step in the DNA sequencing pipeline is validating the format of FASTQ files. With validation, you want to verify the quality of the input files. Input data validation tools enable you to do some quality control checks on raw sequence data (for example, in the FASTQ file format) coming from high-throughput sequencing pipelines.

There are lots of open source tools for input data validation. For example, for FASTQ validation you have these options:

- FastQValidator (*http://bit.ly/fastqvalidator*)
- FastQC (*http://bit.ly/FastQC*)

The input data validation step is very simple and straightforward, so we will not cover it here. Our focus will be on mapping/alignment, recalibration, and variant detection algorithms using MapReduce.

DNA Sequence Alignment

Sequence alignment is the comparison of two or more DNA or protein sequences. The main purpose of sequence alignment is to highlight similarity between the sequences.

For global sequence alignment, consider the following example with two input sequences over the same alphabet:

- Sequence 1: GCGCATGGATTGAGCGA
- Sequence 2: TGCGCCATTGATGACCA

Our output is a possible alignment of the two sequences:

- **-GCGC-AT**G**GATTGA**G**CGA**
- **TGCGCCAT**T**GAT-GA**C**C-A**

We can observe three elements in the possible alignment output:

- Perfect matches (in **bold**)
- Mismatches (underlined)
- Insertions and deletions (called *indels*, presented without formatting)

For the alignment phase, we will use MapReduce/Hadoop along with the following open source tools:

- Burrows-Wheeler Aligner (BWA), an efficient program that aligns relatively short nucleotide sequences against a long reference sequence such as the human genome (see *http://bio-bwa.sourceforge.net/*)
- Sequence Alignment/Map (SAM) tools, which provide various utilities for manipulating alignments in the SAM format, including sorting, merging, indexing, and generating alignments in a per-position format (see *http://samtools.sourceforge.net/*)

We will be working with files in the BAM format, which is the binary format of a SAM file.

MapReduce Algorithms for DNA Sequencing

Typical DNA sequencing for a single data sample (about 400–900 GB in the FASTQ file format) might take 70+ hours for a very powerful single server. The goal of the MapReduce algorithm is to find the answer in a few hours and make the solution scalable.

Since most open source tools (such as BWA, SAMtools, and GATK (*https://www.broadinstitute.org/gatk/*)) for alignment, recalibration, and variant detection have Linux command-line interfaces, at each MapReduce phase our `map()` and `reduce()` functions will call Linux shell scripts and provide the proper parameters. To execute these shell scripts, we will use the FreeMarker templating language (*http://freemarker.org/*), which will merge Java objects and data structures with a template to create a proper shell script (see Figure 18-3). To distinguish one DNA sequence from another, for each analysis we will assign and utilize a unique GUID called the "analysis ID" (this helps us to keep our input and output directories organized).

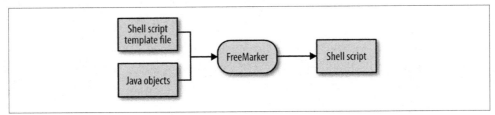

Figure 18-3. FreeMarker template engine

The MapReduce solution is presented in three steps, which are illustrated in Figures 18-4 and 18-5. These correspond to steps 2–4 in the DNA sequencing pipeline described at the beginning of this chapter.

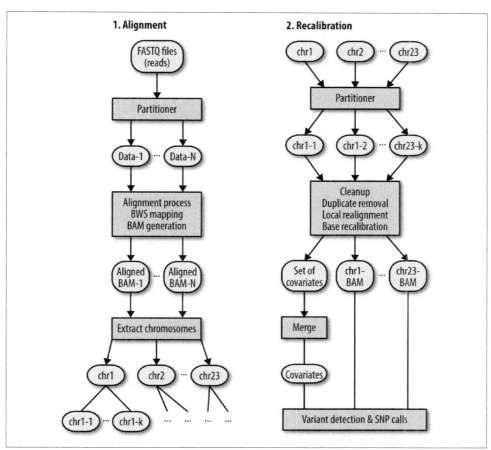

Figure 18-4. MapReduce solution (steps 1 and 2)

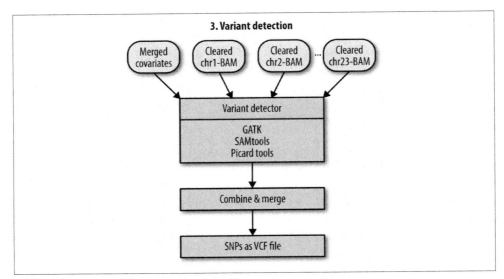

Figure 18-5. MapReduce solution (step 3)

The DNA sequencing data flow for our three-step MapReduce solution is presented in Figure 18-6. It shows how data is partitioned and merged during each stage.

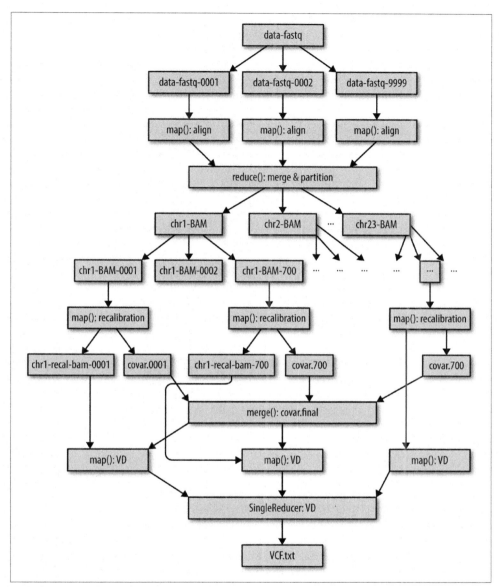

Figure 18-6. DNA sequencing data flow

Step 1: Alignment

A high-level workflow for the alignment phase is depicted in Figure 18-7.

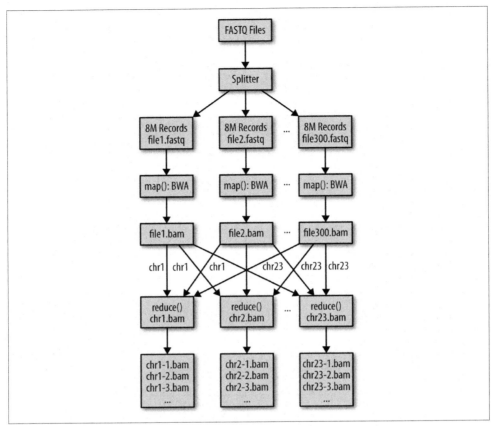

Figure 18-7. DNA sequencing alignment workflow

Before the alignment step starts, we partition our DNA sequence FASTQ file(s) into sets of 8 million lines (or 2 million sequences; remember, in FASTQ format, each group of four lines represents a single DNA sequence). As mentioned previously, if FASTQ data is paired, our input is a pair of files: *left_file.fastq* and *right_file.fastq*. If it is nonpaired, our input will be a single file: *file.fastq*. For paired data, we will partition as follows (for paired data, an alignment map() function will process *left_file.fastq.NNNN* and *right_file.fastq.NNNN* together):

```
left_file.fastq.0000 right_file.fastq.0000
left_file.fastq.0001 right_file.fastq.0001
left_file.fastq.0002 right_file.fastq.0002
...                  ...
```

For nonpaired data, we will partition as follows (for nonpaired data, an alignment map() function will process *file.fastq.NNNN*):

```
file.fastq.0000
file.fastq.0001
file.fastq.0002
...
```

Each partition (also known as a chunk) will be consumed by a `map()` function. Note that the partition size used here (8 million lines, equal to 2 million sequences) is just for illustration purposes; the size you use for your partitions should be determined by the size of your Hadoop cluster. That is, if you have a cluster of 50 nodes and each node can handle 4 mappers, then you should split your FASTQ file into 200 partitions. For example, if your total input size is about 400 GB, then you should partition your input into 2 GB chunks (this way, you will maximize the usage of all your mappers). The `map()` function will read the input file (one single chunk) and will generate an aligned file in BAM format. Here, the `map()` function uses BWA to perform the alignment process. Once the alignment is done, then it will extract all chromosomes (1, 2, ..., 22, 23[2]) and save them in the MapReduce filesystem (HDFS, for Hadoop). For example, if we have 800 partitions, we will have generated 800 files per chromosome (23 * 800 = 18,400 files). There will be only 23 reducers (one per chromosome). The reducer will concatenate (merge and sort) all chromosomes for a specific chromosome ID. All chromosomes 1 will be concatenated into a single file called *chr1.bam*, all chromosomes 2 will be concatenated into a single file called *chr2.bam*, and so on. Then each reducer will partition the merged BAM file into small files that will be used as input to the recalibration phase.

Mapper for the alignment phase

For the alignment mapper shown in Example 18-1, our solution will accept files in the FASTQ format as input and will generate partitioned chromosomes (chr1, chr2, ..., chr22, chr23).

Example 18-1. Alignment phase: map() function

```
1 /**
2  * @param key is a key generated by MapReduce framework
3  * @param value is a partitioned FASTQ file (may be 8M lines = 2M sequences)
4  */
5 map(key, value) {
6    // note: chr23 = concat(chrX, chrY, chrM)
7    alignedBAMFile = alignByBWA(value);
8    (chr1File, chr2File, ..., ch23File) = partitionByChromosome(alignedFile);
9    for (i=1, i < 24; i++) {
10       emit(chr<i>, chr<i>File);
```

---

2 There is no chromosome 23, but we concatenate chromosomes X, Y, and M and call the result chromosome 23.

```
11    }
12 }
```

The `alignByBWA()` function accepts a partitioned FASTQ file, performs the alignment, and finally partitions the aligned file by chromosome. All of these actions are done by a shell script template. Portions of this template are listed in Example 18-2.

Example 18-2. Alignment phase: nonpaired input

```
 1 #!/bin/bash
 2 ...
 3 export BWA=<bwa-install-dir>/bwa
 4 export SAMTOOLS=<samtools-install-dir>/samtools
 5 export BCFTOOLS=<bcftools-install-dir>/bcftools
 6 export VCFUTILS=<bcftools-install-dir>/vcfutils.pl
 7 export HADOOP_HOME=<hadoop-install-dir>
 8 export HADOOP_CONF_DIR=<hadoop-install-dir>/conf
 9 ...
10 # data directories
11 export TMP_HOME=<root-tmp-dir>/tmp
12 export BWA_INDEXES=<root-index-dir>/ref/bwa
13 ...
14 # define ref. genome
15 export REF=<root-reference-dir>/hg19.fasta
16
17 ### step 1: alignment
18 # the KEY uniquely identifies the input file
19 KEY={key}
20 # input_file
21 export INPUT_FILE=${input_file}
22 export ANALYSIS_ID=${analysis_id}
23 NUM_THREAD=3
24 cd $TMP_HOME
25 $BWA aln -t $NUM_THREAD $REF $INPUT_FILE > out.sai
26 $BWA samse -r $REF out.sai $INPUT_FILE | $SAMTOOLS view -Su -F 4 - | \
27     $SAMTOOLS sort - aln.flt
28
29 # start indexing aln.flt.bam file
30 $SAMTOOLS index aln.flt.bam
31
32 # partition aligned data
33 for i in {1..22}
34 do
35     CHR=chr$i
36     $SAMTOOLS view -b -o $CHR.bam aln.flt.bam $CHR
37     output_file=/genome/dnaseq/output/$ANALYSIS_ID/$CHR/$KEY.$CHR.bam
38     $HADOOP_HOME/bin/hadoop fs -put $CHR.bam $output_file
39 done
40
41 # do the same thing for X, Y and M chromosomes
42 $SAMTOOLS view -b -o chr23.bam aln.flt.bam chrX chrY chrM
```

```
43 output_file=/genome/dnaseq/output/$ANALYSIS_ID/chr23/$KEY.chr23.bam
44 $HADOOP_HOME/bin/hadoop fs -put chr23.bam $output_file
45
46 exit 0
```

The provided shell script handles nonpaired data only. If the input files are paired, then the preceding lines 25–27 are replaced by the code in Example 18-3.

Example 18-3. Alignment phase: paired input

```
25 $BWA aln -t $NUM_THREAD $REF $INPUT_FILE_1 > out1.sai
26 $BWA aln -t $NUM_THREAD $REF $INPUT_FILE_2 > out2.sai
27 $BWA sampe -r $INFO_RG $REF out1.sai out2.sai $INPUT_FILE_1 $INPUT_FILE_2 | \
28       $SAMTOOLS view -Su -F 4 - | $SAMTOOLS sort - aln.flt
```

Reducer for the alignment phase

For the alignment phase, there will be exactly 23 reducers (one reducer per chromosome). The reducer key will be a composite key of <chrID><;><analysisID>, where the chromosome ID is labeled {01, 02, 03, ..., 23}. Note the chromosome ID of 23 includes chrM, chrX, and chrY. Each reducer will merge all aligned *.bam* files into a single merged *chr<i>.bam* file:

```
chr<i>.bam = merge the following files:
            chr<i>.bam.0000
            chr<i>.bam.0001
            ...
            chr<i>.bam.0437
            ...
```

After merging all the files into a single *chr<i>.bam* file, we partition *chr<i>.bam* into many small *.bam* files to be fed to the recalibration mapper of step 2. The partitioned files will be:

```
chr<i>.bam.j (j = 1, 2, 3, ..., 100+)
```

The reduce() function for the alignment phase is presented in Example 18-4.

Example 18-4. Alignment phase: reduce() function

```
1 /**
2  * @param key is a <chrID><;><analysis_id>
3  *    where chrID is in (1, 2, 3, ..., 23)
4  * @param value is ignored (not used)
5  */
6 reduce(key, value) {
7    DNASeq.mergeAllChromosomesAndPartition(key);
8 }
```

The bulk of the work lies with the DNASeq.mergeAllChromosomesAndPartition() method, which merges all aligned *.bam* files for a specific chromosome (see Example 18-5). As mentioned previously, the final merged file is then partitioned for further processing by the recalibration phase (step 2).

Example 18-5. mergeAllChromosomesAndPartition() method

```
1 /**
2 * reducerKey=<chrID>;<analysis_id>
3 *    where chrID=1, 2, ..., 22, 23 (23 includes chrM, chrX, chrY)
4 */
5 public static void mergeAllChromosomesAndPartition(String reducerKey)
6    throws Exception {
7    // split the line: each line has two fields (fields are separated by ";")
8    String[] tokens = reducerKey.split(";");
9    String chrID = tokens[0];
10   String analysisID = tokens[1];
11   Map<String, String> templateMap = new HashMap<String, String>();
12   templateMap.put("chr_id", chrID);
13   templateMap.put("analysis_id", analysisID);
14   mergeAllChromosomesBamFiles(templateMap);
15   partitionSingleChromosomeBam(templateMap);
16 }
```

As you can see from the mergeAllChromosomesAndPartition() method, both of the helper methods, mergeAllChromosomesBamFiles() and partitionSingleChromosomeBam(), use the FreeMarker template engine to pass the required Java objects and then execute shell scripts on behalf of the reducers. The definition of the mergeAllChromosomesBamFiles() method is given in Example 18-6.

Example 18-6. mergeAllChromosomesBamFiles() method

```
1 /**
2 * This method will merge the following files and create a single chr<i>.bam file
3 * where i is in {1, 2, ..., 23}:
4 *
5 *    HDFS: /.../chr<i>/chr<i>.bam.0000
6 *    HDFS: /.../chr<i>/chr<i>.bam.0001
7 *    ...
8 *    HDFS: /.../chr<i>/chr<i>.bam.0437
9 *
10 * Then merge all these (.0000, .0001, ..., .0437) files and save the result in
11 * /data/tmp/<analysis_id>/chr<i>/chr<i>.bam
12 *
13 * Once chr<i>.bam is created, then we partition it into small .bam files,
14 * which will be fed to RecalibrationDriver (step 2 of DNA sequencing)
15 *
16 */
17 public static void mergeAllChromosomesBamFiles(Map<String, String> templateMap)
```

```
18     throws Exception {
19     TemplateEngine.initTemplatEngine();
20     String templateFileName = <freemarker-template-file-as-a-bash-script>;
21     // create the actual script from a template file
22     String chrID = templateMap.get("chr_id");
23     String analysisID = templateMap.get("analysis_id");
24     String scriptFileName = createScriptFileName(chrID, analysisID);
25     String logFileName = createLogFileName(chrID, analysisID);
26     File scriptFile = TemplateEngine.createDynamicContentAsFile(templateFileName,
27                                                      templateMap,
28                                                      scriptFileName);
29     if (scriptFile != null) {
30         ShellScriptUtil.callProcess(scriptFileName, logFileName);
31     }
32 }
```

The `TemplateEngine.createDynamicContentAsFile()` method does the magic: it takes two inputs (`templateFileName` and `templateMap`) and produces a `scriptFile Name`. Basically, all parameters are passed to `templateFileName` and then a new shell script is generated as a `scriptFileName`, which is then executed on a reducer's behalf. There are two important classes, `ShellScriptUtil` and `TemplateEngine`, that merit some discussion. The `ShellScriptUtil.callProcess()` method accepts a shell script file (first parameter), which it executes. It then writes all logs from the script execution to a logfile (second parameter). Logging is asynchronous, meaning that as you execute the script, the logfile immediately becomes available.

The `TemplateEngine` class is defined in Example 18-7. It just implements the basic notion of a templating engine: it accepts a template (as a text file with key holders) and key-value pairs as a Java map and then creates a brand new file in which all keys in the template are replaced by values.

Example 18-7. TemplateEngine class

```
1 import java.io.File;
2 import java.io.Writer;
3 import java.io.FileWriter;
4 import java.util.Map;
5 import java.util.concurrent.atomic.AtomicBoolean;
6 import freemarker.template.Template;
7 import freemarker.template.Configuration;
8 import freemarker.template.DefaultObjectWrapper;
9
10 /**
11  * This class uses FreeMarker (http://freemarker.sourceforge.net/).
12  * FreeMarker is a template engine, a generic tool to generate text
13  * output (anything from shell scripts to autogenerated source code)
14  * based on templates. It's a Java package, a class library for Java
15  * programmers. It's not an application for end users in itself, but
16  * something that programmers can embed into their products.
```

```
17   *
18   * @author Mahmoud Parsian
19   *
20   */
21  public class TemplateEngine {
22
23      // you usually do it only once in the whole application life cycle
24      private static Configuration TEMPLATE_CONFIGURATION = null;
25      private static AtomicBoolean initialized = new AtomicBoolean(false);
26
27      // the following template directories will be loaded from configuration file
28      private static String TEMPLATE_DIRECTORY = "/home/dnaseq/template";
29
30      public static void init() throws Exception {
31          if (initialized.get()) {
32          // it is already initialized and returning...
33           return;
34          }
35          initConfiguration();
36          initialized.compareAndSet(false, true);
37      }
38
39      static {
40          if (!initialized.get()) {
41              try {
42                  init();
43              }
44              catch(Exception e) {
45                  theLogger.error("TemplateEngine init failed at initialization.", e);
46              }
47          }
48      }
49
50      // this suppports a single template directory
51      private static void initConfiguration() throws Exception {
52          TEMPLATE_CONFIGURATION = new Configuration();
53          TEMPLATE_CONFIGURATION.setDirectoryForTemplateLoading(
54             new File(TEMPLATE_DIRECTORY));
55          TEMPLATE_CONFIGURATION.setObjectWrapper(new DefaultObjectWrapper());
56          TEMPLATE_CONFIGURATION.setWhitespaceStripping(true);
57          // if the following is set, then undefined keys will be set to ""
58          TEMPLATE_CONFIGURATION.setClassicCompatible(true);
59      }
60
61      public static File createDynamicContentAsFile(...){...}
```

The most important method of the TemplateEngine class, createDynamicContentAs
File(), is defined in Example 18-8. This method accepts a template file that has key
holders and a set of key-value pairs and then generates a new file by substituting the
given keys in the key holders.

Example 18-8. TemplateEngine.createDynamicContentAsFile() method

```
1    /**
2     * @param templateFile is a template filename such as script.sh.template
3     * @param keyValuePairs is a set of (K,V) pairs
4     * @param outputFileName is a generated filename from templateFile
5     */
6    public static File createDynamicContentAsFile(String templateFile,
7                                                  Map<String,String> keyValuePairs,
8                                                  String outputFileName)
9       throws Exception {
10      if ((templateFile == null) || (templateFile.length() == 0)) {
11         return null;
12      }
13
14      Writer writer = null;
15      try {
16         // create a template: example "cb_stage1.sh.template2"
17         Template template = TEMPLATE_CONFIGURATION.getTemplate(templateFile);
18         // merge data model with template
19         File outputFile = new File(outputFileName);
20         writer = new BufferedWriter(new FileWriter(outputFile));
21         template.process(keyValuePairs, writer);
22         writer.flush();
23         return outputFile;
24      }
25      finally {
26         if (writer != null) {
27            writer.close();
28         }
29      }
30   }
31 }
```

Step 2: Recalibration

Recalibration is the second phase of our MapReduce DNA sequencing pipeline. In the recalibration step, each map() function will work on a specific aligned chromosome. The mapper will perform duplicate marking, local realignment, and recalibration. The goal of map() is to create a local recalibration table filled with *covariates*. These local covariates will be merged by the single reducer to create the final single global file (recalibration table) that will be used by the map() function of the third and final step of DNA sequencing, variant detection.

The recalibration MapReduce algorithm (data flow) is presented in Figure 18-8.

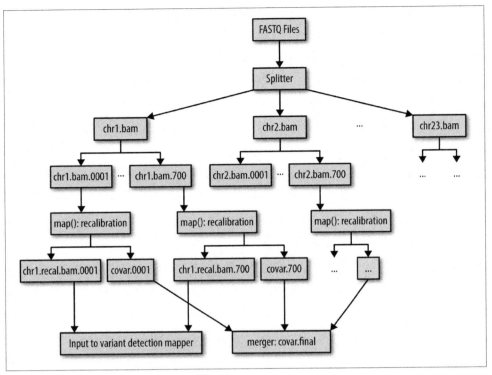

Figure 18-8. DNA sequencing: recalibration

Following the alignment phase, we create special metadata to be used by the recalibration mappers. This metadata has the following format:

```
<counter><;><partitioned-bam-file><;><ref_genome><;><analysis_id>
```

where:

- `<counter>` is an autogenerated sequence of numbers 0000, 0001, 0002, ...
- `<partitioned-bam-file>` is a chunk of partitioned aligned file.
- `<ref_genome>` refers to hg18 or hg19.
- `<analysis_id>` is a GUID for DNA sequencing (to distinguish one analysis from another).

Here is some sample input:

```
0001;chr07.bam.0001;hg19;208
0002;chr07.bam.0002;hg19;208
0003;chr07.bam.0003;hg19;208
...
```

The recalibration mapper is presented in Example 18-9.

Example 18-9. Recalibration phase: map() function

```
1  // key is MR generated, ignored here
2  // value is: <counter><;><partitioned-bam-file><;><ref_genome><;><analysis_id>
3  map(key, value) {
4      // actual file location will be:
5      //   /data/dnaseq/align/ANALYSIS_ID/merged.bam.<KEY>
6      Map<String, String> tokens =
7          DNASeq.tokenizeRecalibrationMapperInput(value);
8      String reducerKey = tokens.get("analysis_id");
9      DNASeq.recalibrationMapper(tokens);
10     emit(reducerKey, value);
11 }
12
13 public static void recalibrationMapper(Map<String, String> templateMap)
14     throws Exception {
15     TemplateEngine.init();
16     // create the actual script from a template file
17     String key = templateMap.get("key");
18     String analysisID = templateMap.get("analysis_id");
19     String scriptFileName = createScriptFileName("recalibration_mapper",
20                                                  key,
21                                                  analysisID);
22     String logFileName = createLogFileName("recalibration_mapper",
23                                            key,
24                                            analysisID);
25     File scriptFile = TemplateEngine.createDynamicContentAsFile(
26         "recalibration_mapper.template",
27         templateMap,
28         scriptFileName);
29     if (scriptFile != null) {
30         ShellScriptUtil.callProcess(scriptFileName, logFileName);
31     }
32 }
```

There will be only *one* reducer for each <analysis_id> (see Example 18-10).

Example 18-10. Recalibration phase: reduce() function

```
1 // key: analysisID
2 // values: ignored
3 reduce(key, Iterable<Object> values) {
4     DNASeq.recalibrationReducer(key);
5     emit(key, key);
6 }
```

The recalibrationReducer() method is defined in Example 18-11.

Example 18-11. recalibrationReducer() method

```
 1 public static void recalibrationReducer(String analysisID)
 2     throws Exception {
 3     TemplateEngine.init();
 4     String[] tokens = valueAsString.split(";");
 5     Map<String, String> templateMap = new HashMap<String, String>();
 6     templateMap.put("key", "-"); // key is undefined
 7     templateMap.put("analysis_id", key);
 8     // create the actual script from a template file
 9     String scriptFileName = createScriptFileName("recalibration_reducer",
10                                                  analysisID);
11     String logFileName = createLogFileName("recalibration_reducer",
12                                            analysisID);
13     File scriptFile = TemplateEngine.createDynamicContentAsFile(
14         "recalibration_reducer.template",
15         templateMap,
16         scriptFileName);
17     if (scriptFile != null) {
18         ShellScriptUtil.callProcess(scriptFileName, logFileName);
19     }
20 }
```

The recalibration mapper template is defined in Example 18-12.

Example 18-12. Recalibration mapper template

```
 1 #!/bin/bash
 2
 3 ###
 4 ### Recalibration mapper template
 5 ###
 6 ### call snp (get variants) up to calculation of ...recal.table.csv
 7 ### once recal.table.csv is created, it will be saved in HDFS
 8 ### input file: aligned bam file (partitioned from a chr<i>.bam)
 9 ...
10 ##
11 ## input file: aligned bam file (partitioned from a chr<i>.bam)
12 ## copy HDFS_BAM_FILE to LOCAL_BAM_FILE
13 HDFS_BAM_FILE=${hdfs_bam_file}
14 BAM_FILE='basename $HDFS_BAM_FILE';
15 $HADOOP_HOME/bin/hadoop fs -copyToLocal $HDFS_BAM_FILE.
16 ...
17 #
18 # put 4.recal.table.csv into GLOBAL/SHARED directory
19 #
20 export SHARED_RECAL_DIR=/dnaseq/recal/${analysis_id}
21 ...
22 ## marking duplicates
23 java        -Xmx4g\
24             -Djava.io.tmpdir=$JAVA_IO_TMPDIR \
25             -jar $PICARD_JAR/MarkDuplicates.jar \
```

```
26          I=$BAM_FILE \
27          O=2.mark.out.bam \
28          M=2.mark.out.metrics \
29          AS=true
30
31 ## local realignment
32 samtools index 2.mark.out.bam
33 java        -Xmx4g \
34          -Djava.io.tmpdir=$JAVA_IO_TMPDIR \
35          -jar $GATK_JAR/GenomeAnalysisTK.jar \
36          -T IndelRealigner \
37          -I 2.mark.out.bam \
38          -o 3.realigned.out.bam \
39          -R $REF \
40          -targetIntervals $DBSNP/dbsnp_indel.intervals \
41          -known $DBSNP/dbsnp_indel.vcf \
42          --consensusDeterminationModel KNOWNS_ONLY \
43          -LOD 0.4
44 ## base quality recalibration
45 java        -Xmx4g \
46          -Djava.io.tmpdir=$JAVA_IO_TMPDIR \
47          -jar $GATK_JAR/GenomeAnalysisTK.jar \
48          -T CountCovariates \
49          -I 3.realigned.out.bam \
50          -recalFile 4.recal.table.csv \
51          -R $REF \
52          -knownSites $DBSNP/dbsnp.vcf \
53          -cov QualityScoreCovariate \
54          -cov ReadGroupCovariate \
55          -cov PositionCovariate \
56          -cov DinucCovariate
57 # copy result to shared directory
58 cp -f 4.recal.table.csv $SHARED_RECAL_DIR/$KEY.4.recal.table.csv
59
60 ##
61 ## we also need to save 3.realigned.out.bam (which will be
62 ## needed in variant_detection_mapper.sh.template)
63 ##
64 cp -f 3.realigned.out.bam $SHARED_RECAL_DIR/$BAM_FILE.3.realigned.out.bam
65 ###
66 ### so we will have:
67 ###      $SHARED_RECAL_DIR/$KEY.4.recal.table.csv          for KEY=1, 2, 3, ....
68 ###      $SHARED_RECAL_DIR/$BAM_FILE.3.realigned.out.bam for KEY=1, 2, 3, ....
69 ###      (will be input to variant_detection_mapper.sh.template)
70 ###
```

The recalibration reducer template is defined in Example 18-13.

Example 18-13. Recalibration reducer template

```
 1 #!/bin/bash
 2 ###
 3 ### Merge all -.4.recal.table.csv files (generated by individual .bam files)
 4 ### into a single recal.table.merged.final.txt file.
 5 ###
 6 ### Once recal.table.merged.final.txt is created, it will be saved in
 7 ### /dnaseq/recal/${analysis_id}/ and will be fed into VariantDetectionMapper.
 8 ###
 9 ...
10 #
11 # All -.4.recal.table.csv files are in $SHARED_RECAL_DIR directory
12 #
13 export SHARED_RECAL_DIR=/dnaseq/recal/$ANALYSIS_ID/
14 recal_files='find $SHARED_RECAL_DIR -name '*.4.recal.table.csv' | sort'
15 num_of_recal_files='find $SHARED_RECAL_DIR -name '*.4.recal.table.csv' | wc -1'
16 ...
17 ### NOTE: all calculations will take place at $SHARED_RECAL_DIR
18 # prepare java input files
19 java_input_files=""
20 for file in $recal_files
21 do
22        echo "preparing java input file=$file"
23        java_input_files="$file $java_input_files"
24 done
25 ...
26 cd $SHARED_RECAL_DIR
27 current_dir='pwd'
28 export MERGE_COVARIATES=JavaMergeCovariates
29 $JAVA_HOME/bin/java -Xms4g -Xmx12g $MERGE_COVARIATES \
30  -i "$java_input_files" -o recal.txt.unsorted
31 #
32 # sort the file accordingly
33 #
34 /bin/sort -t, -k 2,2n -k3,3n -k4,4 recal.txt.unsorted > recal.txt.sorted
35 #
36 # The recal.txt.sorted file will be used by the Variant Detection Mapper.
```

Step 3: Variant Detection

Variant detection (also known as SNP calling) is the final phase of DNA sequencing. The goal of this step is to generate variants in *VCF* (*variant call format*; developed by the 1000 Genomes Project (*http://www.1000genomes.org/*)). The map() function will use the BAM file generated by the map() function of the recalibration step, and the final single "recalibration table" file. The map() function will use open source tools (such as GATK (*https://www.broadinstitute.org/gatk/*) and SAMtools) to generate partial variants (which are raw BCF—binary call format—files). The reducer will concatenate (sort and merge) the raw BCF files to generate a single VCF file. Once the VCF file is created, it can be used by many analytical algorithms, such as allelic frequency (covered in Chapter 21), family analysis, and the Cochran-Armitage trend test.

Variant detection is the process of finding bases in the NGS (next-generation sequencing) data that differ from the reference genome, such as hg18 or hg19; these refer to the version of the human genome assembly and determine the version of the corresponding reference annotations (for details, see *http://bit.ly/ build_36_1_genome*).

Mapper for the variant detection phase

The mapper accepts a chunked "realigned *.bam*" file and performs the following transformations on it:

- Base quality recalibration
- Variant calling and filtering

The bulk of the work is done by the DNASeq.theVariantDetectionMapper() method, which accepts the required parameters and creates a proper shell script from a given template. Finally, it executes the shell script. The mapper for the variant detection phase is provided in Example 18-14.

Example 18-14. Variant detection phase: map() function

```
1 // key: ignored, not used
2 // value: <counter><;><3.realigned.out.bam.<key>><;><ref_genome><;><analysis_id>
3 // index  <   0   > <        1            > <   2   > <   3   >
4 // value example-1:     0001;/<dir>/realigned.out.bam.0001;hg19;208
5 // value example-2:     0007;/<dir>/realigned.out.bam.0007;hg19;208
6 // NOTE: THERE WILL BE ONE SINGLE REDUCER for variant detection:
7 // the key for output of reducer will be <analysis_id>
8 map(key, value) {
9    Map<String, String> tokens = DNASeq.tokenizeTheVariantDetectionMapper(value);
10   String reducerKey = tokens.get("analysis_id");
11   DNASeq.theVariantDetectionMapper(tokens);
12   emit(reducerKey, reducerKey);
13 }
```

The theVariantDetectionMapper() method, shown in Example 18-15, accepts as a parameter the analysis_id (which uniquely identifies all file directories for a specific DNA sequencing run).

Example 18-15. theVariantDetectionMapper() method

```
1 public static void theVariantDetectionMapper(Map<String, String> templateMap)
2    throws Exception {
3    TemplateEngine.init();
```

```
4    // create the actual script from a template file
5    String scriptFileName = "/dnaseq/variant_detection_mapper_" +
6       templateMap.get("analysis_id") + "_" + templateMap.get("key") +".sh";
7    String logFileName =    "/dnaseq/variant_detection_mapper_" +
8       templateMap.get("analysis_id") + "_" + templateMap.get("key") +".log";
9    File scriptFile = TemplateEngine.createDynamicContentAsFile(
10      "variant_detection_mapper.template",
11      templateMap,
12      scriptFileName);
13   if (scriptFile != null) {
14      ShellScriptUtil.callProcess(scriptFileName, logFileName);
15   }
16 }
```

Portions of the *variant_detection_mapper.template* are provided in Example 18-16.

Example 18-16. Variant detection mapper template

```
1 #!/bin/bash
2 ...
3
4 # 1. perform base quality recalibration:
5 # GATK required that the BAM file extension has to be .bam
6 samtools index $REALIGNED_OUT_BAM_FILE
7 #
8 java -Xmx4g \
9     -Djava.io.tmpdir=$JAVA_IO_TMPDIR \
10    -jar $GATK_JAR/GenomeAnalysisTK.jar \
11    -T TableRecalibration \
12    -I $REALIGNED_OUT_BAM_FILE \
13    -o 4.recal.out.bam \
14    -R $REF \
15    -recalFile $SHARED_RECAL_DIR/recal.table.merged.final.txt
16 ...
17 # 2. variant calling and filtering
18 samtools mpileup -Duf $REF -q 1 4.recal.out.bam | bcftools view -bvg ] - > \
19 $REALIGNED_OUT_BAM_FILE.raw.bcf
```

Reducer for the variant detection phase

As noted previously, there will be *only one reducer* for all mappers (see
Example 18-17). This is because we will be merging values to create a single output: a
VCF file. Accordingly, the reducer does only one thing: creates a VCF file (see
Example 18-18).

Example 18-17. Variant detection phase: reducer() function

```
1 // key: <analysis_id>, which identifies all data uniquely
2 // values: ignored
3 reduce(key, values) {
```

```
4      DNASeq.theVariantDetectionReducer(key);
5      emit(key, key);
6 }
```

Example 18-18. theVariantDetectionReducer() method

```
1 public static void theVariantDetectionReducer(String analysisID)
2    throws Exception {
3      TemplateEngine.init();
4      Map<String, String> templateMap = new HashMap<String, String>();
5      templateMap.put("key", "-");
6      templateMap.put("analysis_id", analysisID);
7      // create the actual script from a template file
8      String scriptFileName = "/dnaseq/variant_detection_reducer_" +
9                       templateMap.get("analysis_id") +".sh";
10     String logFileName = "/dnaseq/variant_detection_reducer_" +
11                      templateMap.get("analysis_id") +".log";
12     File scriptFile = TemplateEngine.createDynamicContentAsFile(
13         "variant_detection_reducer.template",
14         templateMap,
15         scriptFileName);
16     if (scriptFile != null) {
17        ShellScriptUtil.callProcess(scriptFileName, logFileName);
18     }
19 }
```

Portions of the *variant_detection_reducer.template* are provided in Example 18-19.

Example 18-19. Variant detection reducer template

```
1 #!/bin/bash
2 ...
3 # call snp (get variants)
4 # concatenate all $KEY.raw.bcf files
5 #
6 FINAL_BCF_FILE=$FINAL_DIR/all.raw.bcf
7 VCF_FILE=$FINAL_DIR/var.flt.vcf
8 ...
9 ##
10 ## Concatenate BCF files. The input files are required to be
11 ## sorted and have identical samples appearing in the same order.
12 ##
13 ALL_BCF_FILES='find $RECAL_DIR/ -name '*.raw.bcf' | sort'
14 $BCFTOOLS cat $ALL_BCF_FILES > $FINAL_BCF_FILE
15 #
16 # begin bcftools & create final VCF file
17 $BCFTOOLS view $FINAL_BCF_FILE | $VCFUTILS varFilter > $VCF_FILE
```

This chapter presented a MapReduce solution for DNA sequencing, a very important task in the genome analysis ecosystem. Typically, DNA sequencing can be done by a powerful computer in 70 hours, but this time can be decreased to minutes by a MapReduce solution on a cluster of 100 nodes. The next chapter presents a scalable solution for Cox regression (or so-called survival analysis).

## CHAPTER 19

Cox Regression

In medical statistics, survival analysis describes the effect on survival times of a continuous variable (such as gene expression). Cox proportional hazards regression is a very important and popular regression algorithm used in survival analysis; its simplicity and lack of assumptions about survival distribution provide the relative risk for a unit change in the variable. For example, a unit change in the expression of a specific gene gives a twofold increase in relative risk. A simple example of Cox regression is: do men and women have different risks of developing brain cancer based on their consumption of alcoholic beverages? By constructing a Cox regression model with alcohol usage (ounces consumed per day) and gender entered as covariates, you can test hypotheses regarding the effects of gender and alcohol on time to onset for brain cancer.

A Cox regression model is a statistical technique used to explore the relationship between the survival of a patient and several explanatory variables such as `time` and `censor`. The Cox regression model was developed by statistics professor Sir David Cox. One important characteristic of Cox regression is that it estimates *relative* rather than *absolute* risk, and it does not assume any knowledge of absolute risk. By definition, Cox regression that implements the proportional hazards model is designed for the analysis of the time until an event occurs or the time between events. Cox regression uses one or more predictor variables, called *covariates*, to predict a status or event variable. In the example of survival analysis, time is the covariate and death is the event (i.e., we are analyzing the time from the diagnosis of illness until the event of death).

Cox regression is used extensively in the clinical and medical fields. Here are some example applications:

- Survival analysis using continuous variables such as gene expression or white blood count ([29])
- Combining gene signatures to improve prediction of breast cancer survival ([36])

For further details on Cox regression, see David Garson's book[9] and *http://bit.ly/cox_regression*.

The R programming language's (*http://www.r-project.org/*) implementation of Cox regression is an industry-standard reliable implementation (based on the coxph() function), and we will use it in our MapReduce solution. Unfortunately, there is no good implementation of Cox regression in Java.

This chapter will provide a two-phase MapReduce solution to Cox regression:

- Phase 1: prepare the proper input for Cox regression. Here, we aggregate, group, and generate data to prepare for calling R's coxph() function.
- Phase 2: use the output of phase 1 and apply R's coxph() function. Finally, analyze the generated results.

The Cox Model in a Nutshell

Cox regression is a relatively complex time-based statistical function. Its main purpose is to build a predictive model for time-to-event data. In a nutshell, the Cox regression model produces a survival function that predicts the probability that the event of interest has occurred at a given time t for given values of the predictor variables (for example, in lung cancer analysis, predictor variables might be the number of cigarettes smoked by people of different genders). The Cox regression is estimated from observed subjects and events during some time period.

The Cox proportional hazards model can be expressed as follows:

$$h_i(t) = h_0(t) \exp(\beta_1 x_{i1} + \beta_2 x_{i2} + ... + \beta_n x_{in})$$

where:

- $(x_{i1}, x_{i2}, ..., x_{in})$ are the predictor variables and are time-independent.
- $(\beta_1, \beta_2, ..., \beta_n)$ is a vector of regression parameters and is estimated by Cox regression.
- $h_0(t)$ is the baseline hazard, which is an unspecified function, making it a semi-parametric model—that is, it depends on time but not on the covariates.
- $\exp(\beta X)$ depends on the covariates but not on time.

The hazard ratio for two observations is independent of time t, which defines the proportional hazards property as:

$$\frac{h_i(t)}{h_j(t)} = \frac{h_0(t)e^{\theta_i}}{h_0(t)e^{\theta_j}} = \frac{e^{\theta_i}}{e^{\theta_j}}$$

We can divide both sides of the equation by $h_0(t)$. Then taking logarithms, we obtain:

$$ln\left(\frac{h_i(t)}{h_0(t)}\right) = \left(\beta_1 x_{i1} + \beta_2 x_{i2} + \ldots + \beta_n x_{in}\right)$$

We call $\frac{h_i(t)}{h_0(t)}$ the hazard ratio.

Cox Regression Basic Terminology

To use Cox regression in the context of survival analysis, we need to understand several key definitions. We borrow these definitions from Michael Walker (*http://bit.ly/ surv_analysis*):

Event
This is an application-dependent concept. Examples are death, disease recurrence, or recovery.

Time
This parameter plays an especially important role in the Cox regression definition. Events are time-based—for example, the time from the beginning of an observation period (e.g., surgery) to an event, the end of the study, or loss of contact or withdrawal from the study.

Censoring/censored observation
When test subjects do not have an event during the observation time, they are described as *censored*, meaning we cannot observe what has happened to them subsequently. A censored subject may or may not have an event after the observation time ends.

Survivor function, S(t)
This is the probability that a subject survives longer than time t.

Cox Regression Using R

The R programming language provides an implementation of the Cox regression model through coxph {survival}. The coxph() function fits a Cox proportional hazards regression model.[1]

R's Surv() function creates a survival object, which is used as a response variable. It accepts two parameters: Surv(time, censor), where:

- time is a vector of event times.

- censor is a vector of indicator values (denoting whether the event was observed or censored).

The following example shows some sample values for time and censor:

```
> time=c(5.880903491,11.07186858,10.97330596,1.347022587,8.246406571,
         6.209445585,1.80698152,6.899383984,1.281314168,5.650924025,
         10.25051335,2.036960986,6.800821355,6.932238193,6.800821355,
         2.595482546,8.344969199,5.848049281,4.238193019,5.815195072,
         6.340862423,2.529774127,2.628336756,0.689938398,1.347022587,
         2.694045175,6.078028747,1.21560575,8.410677618,8.509240246)
> censor=c(1,1,0,1,1,1,1,0,1,1,0,1,0,1,1,1,0,0,1,1,1,1,1,1,0,1,1,0,0)
```

We use the coxph() function as follows:

```
> library(survival) # load the package
> coxph(Surv(time, censor) ~ logRatio)
Call:
coxph(formula = Surv(time, censor) ~ logRatio)

            coef exp(coef)  se(coef)     z    p
logRatio -0.0247     0.976    0.0798 -0.31 0.76

Likelihood ratio test=0.1  on 1 df, p=0.758   n= 30, number of events= 21
```

Expression Data

The data for a specific gene (i.e., the changes in expression value) is expressed as a foldchange. Fold change (*http://en.wikipedia.org/wiki/Fold_change*) is a measure describing how much a quantity changes going from an initial to a final value:

```
> foldchange=c(20.3,-15.5,-8.04,4.85,5.5,2.16,1.94,-2.13,-52.5,-1.07,
               6.23,7.19,4.97,-39.8,-2.11,3.19,-1.24,1.24,2.73,-44.4,
               -35,-58.5,-1.79,1.74,-2.15,3.22,-1.7,-3.07,2.57,-1.41)
> convert=function(x){return(log2(max(x, -1/x)))}
```

---

[1] Time-dependent variables, time-dependent strata, multiple events per subject, and other extensions are incorporated using the counting process formulation of Andersen and Gill. (Source: *http://bit.ly/coxph*.)

```
> logRatio = sapply(foldchange, convert)

> logRatio
 [1]  4.3434078 -3.9541963 -3.0071955  2.2779847  2.4594316  1.1110313
 [7]  0.9560567 -1.0908534 -5.7142455 -0.0976108  2.6392322  2.8459918
[13]  2.3132459 -5.3146965 -1.0772430  1.6735564 -0.3103401  0.3103401
[19]  1.4489010 -5.4724878 -5.1292830 -5.8703647 -0.8399596  0.7990873
[25] -1.1043367  1.6870607 -0.7655347 -1.6182387  1.3617684 -0.4956952
```

From the coxph() function, we are interested in only two values:

- coef = -0.0247

- pValue = 0.758

Cox Regression Application

Now let's consider a sample application of Cox regression. Say we have a set of patients. Each patient has a set of biosets, and each bioset has a set of genes (for example, genes in the RNA gene expression data type) and their associated gene values (the fold change). Biosets are individually analyzed data signatures. They encompass data in the form of experimental sample comparisons (for transcriptomic, epigenetic, and copy-number variation data), as well as genotype signatures (for GWAS—genome-wide association study—and mutational data). A bioset is more commonly known as a *gene signature* (*http://bit.ly/gene_sig*).

There can be as many as 60,000 genes per bioset. This number differs depending on the type of bioset; for example, methylation biosets can have up to 20,000 genes, and gene expression biosets can have up to 50,000 genes. The problem can be stated as such: given a set of biosets, time, and censor, find the coef (coefficient) and pValue (probability value) for all genes contained in all biosets. If we are doing the Cox regression for a set of 100,000 samples, then we may have to analyze 100,000 × 60,000 = 6 billion data records. This problem is a good candidate for MapReduce.

Cox Regression POJO Solution

To help you better understand Cox regression, I'll now present a non-MapReduce solution. For each bioset data type (gene expression, copy-number variation, methylation) there is a fixed number of genes, identified by geneIdList. The objective of our algorithm is to create input like:

```
geneID_1 bioset1_value11 bioset2_value12, ..., biosetN_value1N
geneID_2 bioset1_value21 bioset2_value22, ..., biosetN_value2N
...
geneID_M bioset1_valueM1 bioset2_valueM2, ..., biosetN_valueMN
```

and then to pass this input to R's coxph() function. For example, for the copy-number variation (cnv) type, we can express our algorithm as shown in Example 19-1.

Example 19-1. Cox regression algorithm without MapReduce

```
 1 input: double[] time;
 2 input: int[] censor;
 3 input: List<Long> biosetIDs;
 4 input: List<Long> cnvGeneIdList; // prebuilt (key, value) database
 5 output: List<Tuple3<String, Double, Double>>
 6 //    as List<Tuple3<geneID, coef, p-value>>
 7 //
 8 // iterate through all genes
 9 for (geneID : cnvGeneIdList) {
10     // there is a key-value store per geneID
11     // where key is the biosetID and value is the gene value
12     mapDB = getMapDB(geneID);
13     int index = 0;
14     double[] geneValues = new double[time.length];
15     for (biosetID : biosetIDs) {
16         double geneValue = mapDB.get(biosetID);
17         geneValues[index++] = geneValue;
18     }
19
20     // call R's Cox regression as coxph() function
21     double[] result = coxph(time, censor, geneValues);
22     double coef = result[0];
23     double pValue = result[1];
24     emit(geneID, (coef, pValue));
25 }
```

For example, if we have 5,000 biosets, then we want to calculate coxph() for all genes (up to 40,000) contained in these biosets. This will require 40,000 coxph() calls, and each call will have three arrays of time[5,000], censor[5,000], and fold change[5,000] (where foldchange refers to gene values).

Running this algorithm will generate the following output:

```
geneID_1 coef_1 pValue_1
geneID_2 coef_2 pValue_2
...
geneID_M coef_M pValue_M
```

As you know, this solution does not use MapReduce. To make this happen, we create a persistent (key, value) store for each gene: the database name is the geneID, the key is the `biosetID`, and the `value` is the value associated with `geneID`. For our persistent store, we use MapDB.[2]

This is an efficient solution when the number of biosets is in the hundreds. When the number of biosets is in the thousands, the MapReduce/Hadoop solution will scale much better than the non-MapReduce solution.

Input for MapReduce

Typically, a patient has a set of biosets, and each bioset can be a different type (such as copy-number variation, methylation, or gene expression). Again, each bioset has thousands of records, and each record contains a `geneID`, reference (`{r1, r2, r3, r4}`) and a value associated with that `geneID`. A bioset is identified by a `biosetID`. For example, `biosetID 8800` has the following data:

```
$ head 8800.csv
13972,r1;2.45
4082,r1;1.8
40583,r1;1.8
16422,r1;1.8
21602,r1;1.8
45735,r1;1.8
43936,r1;1.8
26446,r1;1.8
16030,r1;-3
828,r1;0
```

where each row/record represents the `geneID`, and reference type, and associated value (e.g., for the first row, `13972` is the `geneID`, `r1` is a normal reference, and `2.45` is an associated fold change value). Given that the order of values per `geneID` is very important in Cox regression, we will generate another set of data from our existing key-value store that includes the `biosetID` as well. Here is our desired input for the `biosetID` of `8800` to be used in our MapReduce/Hadoop implementation:

```
$ head 8800_for_cox.csv
13972,r1;8800,2.45
4082,r1;8800,1.8
40583,r1;8800,1.8
16422,r1;8800,1.8
21602,r1;8800,1.8
45735,r1;8800,1.8
```

---

2 MapDB (*https://github.com/jankotek/MapDB*) provides concurrent `TreeMap` and `HashMap` functionality backed by disk storage or off-heap memory. It is a fast, scalable, and easy-to-use embedded Java database engine. It is tiny (a 160 KB JAR file), but it's packed with features such as transactions, space-efficient serialization, an instance cache, and transparent compression/encryption. It also has outstanding performance, rivaled only by native embedded database engines. MapDB is developed by Jan Kotek (*https://github.com/jankotek/*).

```
43936,r1;8800,1.8
26446,r1;8800,1.8
16030,r1;8800,-3
828,r1;8800,0
```

Input Format

Each bioset record will have the following format:

```
<geneID><,><referenceID><;><biosetID><,><geneValue>
```

where `referenceID` is one of `r1` = normal, `r2` = disease, `r3` = paired, or `r4` = unknown.

Note that we use two different delimiters (`;` and `,`) in our data, which will help us when tokenizing data in MapReduce's `map()` and `reduce()` functions.

Cox Regression Using MapReduce

As outlined previously in the chapter, we implement Cox regression in a two-phase MapReduce algorithm. Here's a reminder, along with a description of the roles of the mapper and reducer in each phase:

- Phase 1: generate data to prepare for calling the `coxph()` function.
  - `map()`: Group data by `<geneID><,><referenceID>` (the key).
  - `reduce()`: For each reducer, generate `<geneID><,><referenceID>` followed by all gene values in proper order of biosets (the order has to be preserved, or else the `coxph()` call will be meaningless).
- Phase 2: call `coxph()` and analyze the generated results.
  - `map()`: Call `coxph()` for the data generated by the `reduce()` function in phase 1.
  - `reduce()`: None.

Cox Regression Phase 1: map()

The `map()` function for phase 1, shown in Example 19-2, is an identity mapper. It accepts key-value pairs and emits the same key-value pairs.

Example 19-2. Cox regression algorithm phase 1: map() function

```
1 /**
2  * Each input record represents a key-value pair
3  * where the input record has the following format:
4  *     <geneID><,><referenceID><;><biosetID><,><geneValue>
```

```
 5  =* The mapper emits (K,V) pairs as:
 6  *      K: <geneID><,><referenceID>
 7  *      V: <biosetID><,><geneValue>
 8  */
 9 map(key, value) {
10     String[] tokens = StringUtil.split(value, ";");
11     String reducerKey = tokens[0];    // <geneID><,><referenceID>
12     String reducerValue = tokens[1];  // <biosetID><,><geneValue>
13     emit(reducerKey, reducerValue);
14 }
```

Cox Regression Phase 1: reduce()

Each reducer accepts a (`key`, `values`) pair, where key is a pair of (`geneID`, `referen ceID`) and `values` is a list of pairs of (`biosetID`, `geneValue`). As shown in Example 19-3, the reducer orders `geneValues` according to the order of biosets received at the `setup()` of the reducer class. For example, if `values` = {(B1, G1), (B3, G3), (B4, G4), (B2, G2)} and biosets are received as (B1, B2, B3, B4), then the reducer will generate the sorted gene values as (G1, G2, G3, G4).

Example 19-3. Cox regression algorithm phase 1: reduce()

```
 1 /**
 2  * @param key key is the <geneID><referenceID>
 3  * @param values is a list of {<biosetID><,><geneValue>}
 4  * NOTE: biosetIDs (List<Long>) will be passed from MapReduce driver and will
 5  * be saved at the reducer's setup() function (done once before reduce() starts)
 6  */
 7 reduce(key, values) {
 8     String[] doubleValues = new String[biosets.size()];
 9     int numberOfValues = 0;
10     for (pair : values) {
11         String[] tokens = StringUtils.split(pair, ",");
12         String biosetID = tokens[0];
13         String geneValue = tokens[1];
14
15         int index = biosets.indexOf(biosetID);
16         if (index == -1) {
17             // biosetID not found
18             return;
19         }
20
21         // biosetID found at location "index"
22         doublevalues[index] = geneValue;
23         numberOfValues++;
24     }
25
26     // values are candidates for Cox regression analysis
27     if (numberOfValues != biosets.size()) {
28         // there are not enough gene values for these biosets,
```

```
29          // cannot perform Cox regression
30          return;
31      }
32
33      // numberOfValues == biosets.size()
34      StringBuilder builder = new StringBuilder();
35      builder.append(key.toString());
36      builder.append(",");
37      for (int i=0; i < doublevalues.length; i++) {
38          builder.append(doublevalues[i]);
39          // check to see if we need to add comma
40          if (i < (doublevalues.length -1)) {
41              builder.append(",");
42          }
43      }
44
45      // prepare reducer for output
46      String reducerValue = builder.toString();
47      // reducerValue = <geneID><,><referenceID>, value1, value2, ..., valueN
48      context.write(null, reducerValue);
49 }
```

Cox Regression Phase 2: map()

The mapper in this phase accepts an HDFS input file and then executes coxph() with
this input. Output is then transferred to HDFS for final analysis. For this mapper, we
need a setup() function, which will be executed once. (See Examples 19-4 and 19-5
for setup() and map(), respectively.)

Example 19-4. Cox regression algorithm phase 2: setup()

```
1 /**
2  * map(key) = LongWritable (generated by Hadoop, ignored here)
3  * map(value) = Text (name of an HDFS file: /biomarker/output/rnae/0/part-r-00000)
4  *              which will be used as an input to Cox regression analysis
5  *
6  * reduce(key)   = none
7  * reduce(value) = none
8  */
9 public class CoxRegressionMapperPhase2
10     extends Mapper<LongWritable, Text, LongWritable, Text> {
11
12     private Configuration conf = null;
13     private FileSystem fs = null;
14     private String timeAsCommaSeparatedString = null;
15     private String censorAsCommaSeparatedString = null;
16     private String hadoopOutputPathAsString = null;
17
18     ...
19
```

```
20    // will be run only once
21    public void setup(Context context)
22       throws IOException, InterruptedException {
23       this.conf = context.getConfiguration();
24       this.fs = FileSystem.get(conf);
25       hadoopOutputPathAsString = conf.get("hadoopOutputPathAsString");
26       timeAsCommaSeparatedString = conf.get("time");
27       censorAsCommaSeparatedString = conf.get("censor");
28
29       //
30       // make sure /hadoop/home/cox_regression.r.template file does exist
31       // in local Unix filesystem; if it does not exist then copy it from
32       // hdfs:/biomarker/template/cox_regression.r.template
33       //
34       if (IOUtil.fileExists(
35          CoxRegressionUsingR.COX_REGRESSION_TEMPLATE_FILE_FULL_NAME)) {
36          THE_LOGGER.info("template file does exist: "+
37          CoxRegressionUsingR.COX_REGRESSION_TEMPLATE_FILE_FULL_NAME);
38       }
39       else {
40          // copy it from HDFS
41          copyHDFSFileToLocal(
41                CoxRegressionUsingR.COX_REGRESSION_TEMPLATE_FILE_HDFS_PATH,
42                   CoxRegressionUsingR.COX_REGRESSION_TEMPLATE_FILE_FULL_NAME);
43       }
44    }
45
46    // map() defined next
```

Example 19-5. Cox regression algorithm phase 2: map()

```
 1 /**
 2  * @param key is the key generated by the MapReduce framework (not used here)
 3  * @param value is name of HDFS input file generated by reduce() of phase 1
 4  * (for example: HDFS file like </biomarker/output/rnae/0><,><part-r-00019>)
 5  * NOTE: the following variables:
 6  *         timeAsCommaSeparatedString,
 7  *         censorAsCommaSeparatedString, and
 8  *         hadoopOutputPathAsString
 9  * are initialized in reducer's setup() function (done once).
10  */
11 map(key, value) {
12    String coxRegressionInputFileName = "/tmp/" + HadoopUtil.getRandomUUID();
13    // coxRegressionInputFileName = /tmp/a99817a0-c149-4cb2-a771-dbc7da86b56a
14    String coxRegressionOutputFileName = coxRegressionInputFileName + ".out.txt";
15    File coxRegressionInputFile = new File(coxRegressionInputFileName);
16
17    Path hdfsPartFile = new Path(valueAsString);
18    FileUtil.copy(fs,                        // FileSystem
19                  hdfsPartFile,              // src file
20                  coxRegressionInputFile,    // destination
21                  false,                     // boolean deleteSource
```

```
22              conf);
23
24    int coxCallStatus = -1; // failure
25    // perform Cox regression
26    coxCallStatus = CoxRegressionUsingR.callCoxRegression(
27         coxRegressionInputFileName,
28         coxRegressionOutputFileName,
29         timeAsCommaSeparatedString,
30         censorAsCommaSeparatedString);
31
32    if (coxCallStatus == 0) {
33        // it is success! then copy coxRegressionOutputFileName
34        // to HDFS (to hadoopOutputPathAsString)
35        File coxRegressionOutputFile = new File(coxRegressionOutputFileName);
36        if (coxRegressionOutputFile.exists()) {
37            FileUtil.copy(coxRegressionOutputFile, fs,
38                    new Path(hadoopOutputPathAsString), false, conf);
39        }
40    }
41
42    // send it to reducer (indication, we are done for logging purposes)
43    context.write(key, value);
44 }
```

Sample Output Generated by Phase 1 reduce() Function

Here are the sample output files generated by the reduce() function of phase 1:

```
$ hadoop fs -ls /biomarker/output/rnae/0/part*
Found 30 items
-rw-r--r--   3 ...   1047918 ... /biomarker/output/rnae/0/part-r-00000
-rw-r--r--   3 ...   1053398 ... /biomarker/output/rnae/0/part-r-00001
...
-rw-r--r--   3 ...   1030567 ... /biomarker/output/rnae/0/part-r-00026
-rw-r--r--   3 ...   1028483 ... /biomarker/output/rnae/0/part-r-00027
```

If our test example has 5,000 biosets, then we get:

```
$ hadoop fs -cat /biomarker/output/rnae/0/part-r-00005 | head
100174,r1,1.8619553641448698,1.8925853151926535, ..., <5000th-value>
100181,r1,0.40490312214513074,2.67581593117227, ..., <5000th-value>
100191,r2,-13.287712379549449,13.28771237954945, ..., <5000th-value>
100237,r1,0.8147554828098739,-0.3391373849195852, ..., <5000th-value>
100314,r1,2.103665482765696,2.254594043033141, ..., <5000th-value>
100478,r2,0.0,0.0, ..., <5000th-value>
100482,r1,1.5464623581670915,-2.5864044748950628, ..., <5000th-value>
100545,r1,-2.454965473634712,0.41359408240917517, ..., <5000th-value>
100555,r2,-13.287712379549449,-0.15055967657538144, ..., <5000th-value>
```

Sample Output Generated by the Phase 2 map() Function

In the following sample output, the first column is `<geneID><,><referenceID>`, the second column is `coef`, and the last column is `pValue`:

```
94893,r2   -0.04106195   0.7144141
94963,r2    0.2514287    0.02973554
95037,r1   -0.1822651    0.326605
95047,r2   -0.02349459   0.8174117
95338,r1    0.06733862   0.4429394
95425,r2   -0.1370884    0.3265356
95719,r2   -0.02158204   0.9071648
95891,r1    0.1033474    0.6061742
```

Cox Regression Script for MapReduce

The `CoxRegressionUsingR` class contains the core functionality for Cox regression. This class creates an `Rscript` from a template file. An instance of an `Rscript` is given in Example 19-6.

Example 19-6. Cox regression algorithm by Rscript

```
 1 #!/usr/local/bin/Rscript
 2
 3 input_file = "/tmp/f11d10f4-e0a6-4796-9a1c-34c6914be1e7"
 4 cat("input_file=", input_file, "\n")
 5 output_file = "/tmp/f11d10f4-e0a6-4796-9a1c-34c6914be1e7.out.txt"
 6 cat("output_file=", output_file, "\n")
 7
 8 library("survival")
 9
10 # a function for conversion
11 convert=function(x){return(log2(max(x, -1/x)))}
12
13 # a function to perform Cox regression
14 cox_regression <- function(line){
15     #cat(line, "\n")
16     # each line has this format:
17     # <geneID><;><V1,V2,...,Vn><;><T1,T2,...,Tn><;><C1,C2,...,Cn>
18     items = unlist(strsplit(line, ";"))
19     #
20     geneID = items[[1]]
21     #
22     value = as.double(unlist(strsplit(items[[2]], ",")))
23     #
24     time = as.double(unlist(strsplit(items[[3]], ",")))
25     #
26     censor = as.double(unlist(strsplit(items[[4]], ",")))
27     #
28     coxphoutput = coxph(Surv(time,censor) ~ value)
29     pValue = summary(coxphoutput)$waldtest[3]
```

```
30       cat(geneID, coxphoutput$coef, pValue, "\n", file=output_file, append=TRUE)
31 }
32
33 # driver section of Rscript
34 conn <- file(input_file, open="r")
35 while(length(line <- readLines(conn, 1)) > 0) {
36    try.output <- try( cox_regression(line) )
37 }
38 close.connection(conn)
```

Here's a breakdown of this code:

Lines 14–31

Here we define our custom function, cox_regression(), which calls R's coxph()
function. Line 18 tokenizes the input record. Finally, coxph() produces coef and
pValue.

Line 30

This line appends geneID, coef, and pValue to the output file.

Lines 34–38

This is the driver for the Rscript. It opens the file, reads line-by-line, and applies
the cox_regression() function. Finally, it closes the input file to release the
resources.

Here is the sample output:

```
$ head -4 /tmp/f11d10f4-e0a6-4796-9a1c-34c6914be1e7.out.txt
100007,r1,0.1038095,0.3594686
10017,r2,0.00613293,0.892313
100205,r1,-0.01681699,0.6164844
101583,r1,0.03383865,0.4736812
```

This chapter presented a distributed scalable Cox regression algorithm using MapRe-
duce/Hadoop. Cox regression is a very important technique in survival analysis for
clinical applications. The next chapter implements a MapReduce solution for the
Cochran-Armitage trend test, which is used for analysis of VCF (variant call format)
files.

## CHAPTER 20

Cochran-Armitage Test for Trend

The Cochran-Armitage test for trend (CATT) is used in analyzing germline (*https://en.wikipedia.org/wiki/Germline*) data. For example, variants in a VCF (variant call format) file generated by DNA sequencing can be labeled as germline data. The CATT is a statistical method of directing chi-squared tests toward narrow alternatives. If R is a set of response variables and E is a set of experimental variables, then the CATT is sensitive to the linearity between $R(s)$ and $E(s)$ and detects trends. The CATT can be expressed another way: if B is a binary outcome of some events {PASSED, FAILED} and C is a set of ordered categories $\{C_1, ..., C_n\}$, then the CATT can be used as a linear trend in proportions on B across levels of C. To apply the CATT, we build a contingency table: two rows with outcome values {PASSED, FAILED} and n columns as $\{C_1, ..., C_n\}$. The contingency table for the CATT is explained in the next sections.

According to Wikipedia (*http://bit.ly/cochran-armitage*):

> The Cochran-Armitage test for trend, named for William Cochran and Peter Armitage, is used in categorical data analysis when the aim is to assess for the presence of an association between a variable with two categories and a variable with k categories. It modifies the Pearson chi-squared test to incorporate a suspected ordering in the effects of the k categories of the second variable. For example, doses of a treatment can be ordered as "low," "medium," and "high," and we may suspect that the treatment benefit cannot become smaller as the dose increases. The trend test is often used as a genotype-based test for case-control genetic association studies.

And according to Stefan Wellek and Andreas Ziegler (*http://bit.ly/wellek_ziegler*)[30]:

> The Cochran-Armitage trend test based on the linear regression model has become a standard procedure for association testing in case-control studies.

Cochran-Armitage Algorithm

The CATT is applied when the data takes the form of a $2 \times k$ contingency table. The number of rows (2) indicates the outcome of an experiment, and the number of columns indicates a variable number (k) of experiments. For example, if $k = 3$, then the contingency table will be as shown in Table 20-1.

Table 20-1. 2 × 3 contingency table

Group	B = 1	B = 2	B = 3
A = 1	N_{11}	N_{12}	N_{13}
A = 2	N_{21}	N_{22}	N_{23}

This contingency table can be completed with the marginal totals of the two variables, as shown in Table 20-2.

Table 20-2. 2 × 3 contingency table with marginal totals

Group	B = 1	B = 2	B = 3	Sum
A = 1	N_{11}	N_{12}	N_{13}	R_1
A = 2	N_{21}	N_{22}	N_{23}	R_2
Sum	C_1	C_2	C_3	N

Where:

- $R_1 = N_{11} + N_{12} + N_{13}$
- $R_2 = N_{21} + N_{22} + N_{23}$
- $C_1 = N_{11} + N_{21}$
- $C_2 = N_{12} + N_{22}$
- $C_3 = N_{13} + N_{23}$
- $N = R_1 + R_2 = C_1 + C_2 + C_3 = N_{11} + N_{12} + N_{13} + N_{21} + N_{22} + N_{23}$

The trend test statistic is:

$$T \equiv \sum_{i=1}^{k} w_i \left(N_{1i} R_2 - N_{2i} R_1 \right)$$

where w_i is weight. In using CATT for alleles of germline data, we can apply three different tests based on the value of the weight:

- weight = {0, 1, 2}: for additive
- weight = {1, 1, 0}: for dominant
- weight = {0, 1, 1}: for recessive

The hypothesis of no association (known as the *null hypothesis*) can be expressed as:

$$\Pr(A = 1|B = 1) = \ldots = \Pr(A = 1|B = k)$$

Assuming that the null hypothesis holds, then using iterated expectation we can write:

$$E(T) = E(E(T|R_1, R_2)) = E(0) = 0$$

Given two discrete random variables X and Y, we can define the conditional expectation as:

$$E[X|Y = y] = \sum_x x \cdot P(X = x|Y = y)$$

Now, using all these definitions and formulas, we are ready to write our Cochran-Armitage algorithm in Java (Example 20-1). One major goal of the CATT is to compute the p-value (a probability value between 0.00 and 1.00). Using the algorithm defined in Wikipedia (*http://bit.ly/cochran-armitage*), we implement the CATT as a POJO class, CochranArmitage. This Java class will be used in our MapReduce solution.

Example 20-1. Cochran-Armitage algorithm

```
1 import java.io.BufferedReader;
2 import java.io.BufferedWriter;
3 import java.io.FileReader;
4 import java.io.FileWriter;
5 import java.io.IOException;
6
7 import org.apache.log4j.Logger;
8 import org.apache.commons.math3.distribution.NormalDistribution;
9
10 /**
11  * Class that calculates the Cochran-Armitage test for trend
12  * on a 2x3 contingency table.  Used to estimate association
13  * in additive genetic models of genotype data.
14  */
15 public class CochranArmitage {
16
```

```
17    private static final Logger THE_LOGGER =
18        Logger.getLogger(CochranArmitage.class);
19
20    // use weights corresponding to additive/codominant model
21    private static final int[] WEIGHTS = { 0, 1, 2 };
22
23    // dimensions of passed contingency table - must be 2 rows x 3 columns
24    private static final int NUMBER_OF_ROWS = 2;
25    private static final int NUMBER_OF_COLUMNS = 3;
26
27    // variables to hold variance, raw statistic, standardized statistic,
28    // and p-value
29    private double stat = 0.0;
30    private double standardStatistics = 0.0;
31    private double variance = 0.0;
32    private double pValue = -1.0; // range is 0.0 to 1.0 (-1.0 means undefined)
33
34    // NormalDistribution class from Apache used to calculate p-values
35    private static NormalDistribution normDist = new NormalDistribution();
36
37    /**
38     * Get the variance
39     */
40    public double getVariance() {
41        return variance;
42    }
43
44    /**
45     * Get the Stat
46     */
47    public double getStat() {
48        return stat;
49    }
50
51    /**
52     * Get the StandardStatistics
53     */
54    public double getStandardStatistics() {
55        return standardStatistics;
56    }
57
58    /**
59     * Get the p-value
60     */
61    public double getpValue() {
62        return pValue;
63    }
64
65    /**
66     * Computes the Cochran-Armitage test for trend for the passed
67     * 2 row by 3 column contingency table
68     * @param countTable = 2x3 contingency table.
```

```
69        * @return the p-value of the Cochran-Armitage statistic of the passed table
70        */
71       public double callCochranArmitageTest(int[][] countTable) {
72           // defined in Example 20-2
73       }
74
75
76       /**
77        * @param args input/output files for testing/debugging
78        * args[0] as input file
79        * args[1] as output file
80        */
81       public static void main(String[] args) throws IOException {
82           // defined in Example 20-3
83       }
84
85 }
```

The callCochranArmitageTest() method, defined in Example 20-2, is the core of the Cochran-Armitage algorithm.

Example 20-2. Cochran-Armitage algorithm: callCochranArmitageTest()

```
 1 /**
 2  * Computes the Cochran-Armitage test for trend for the passed
 3  * 2 row by 3 column contingency table
 4  * @param countTable = 2x3 contingency table.
 5  * @return the p-value of the Cochran-Armitage statistic of the passed table
 6  */
 7 public double callCochranArmitageTest(int[][] countTable) {
 8
 9    if (countTable == null) {
10       throw new IllegalArgumentException(
11          "contingency table cannot be null/empty.");
12    }
13
14    if ( (countTable.length != NUMBER_OF_ROWS) ||
15         (countTable[0].length != NUMBER_OF_COLUMNS) ) {
16       throw new IllegalArgumentException(
17          "contingency table must be 2 rows by 3 columns");
18    }
19
20    int totalSum=0;
21    int[] rowSum = new int[NUMBER_OF_ROWS];
22    int[] colSum = new int[NUMBER_OF_COLUMNS];
23
24    // calculate marginal and overall sums for the contingency table
25    for (int i=0; i<NUMBER_OF_ROWS; i++) {
26       for (int j=0; j<NUMBER_OF_COLUMNS; j++) {
27          rowSum[i] += countTable[i][j];
28          colSum[j] += countTable[i][j];
```

```
29          totalSum += countTable[i][j];
30       }
31    }
32
33    // calculate the test statistic and variance based on the formulae at
34    // http://en.wikipedia.org/wiki/Cochran-Armitage_test_for_trend
35    stat = 0.0;
36    variance = 0.0;
37    for (int j=0; j<NUMBER_OF_COLUMNS; j++) {
38       stat += WEIGHTS[j] * (countTable[0][j]*rowSum[1] -
39                    countTable[1][j]*rowSum[0]);
40       variance += WEIGHTS[j]*WEIGHTS[j]*colSum[j]*(totalSum-colSum[j]);
41
42       if (j!=NUMBER_OF_COLUMNS-1) {
43          for (int k=j+1;k<NUMBER_OF_COLUMNS;k++) {
44             variance -= 2*WEIGHTS[j]*WEIGHTS[k]*colSum[j]*colSum[k];
45          }
46       }
47    }
48    variance *= rowSum[0]*rowSum[1]/totalSum;
49
50    // standardized statistic is stat divided by SD
51    standardStatistics = stat/Math.sqrt(variance);
52
53    // use Apache Commons normal distribution to calculate two-tailed p-value
54    pValue = 2*normDist.cumulativeProbability(-Math.abs(standardStatistics));
55
56    // return the p-value
57    return pValue;
58 }
```

The program shown in Example 20-3 tests the Cochran-Armitage algorithm.

Example 20-3. Cochran-Armitage algorithm: main()

```
1 /**
2  * @param args input/output files for testing/debugging
3  * args[0] as input file
4  * args[1] as output file
5  */
6 public static void main(String[] args) throws IOException {
7    if (args.length != 2) {
8       THE_LOGGER.info("usage: java CochranArmitage " +
9             "<input-filename> <output-filename>");
10      throw new IOException("must provide input and output files for testing.");
11   }
12
13   long startTime = System.currentTimeMillis();
14   String inputFileName = args[0];
15   String outputFileName = args[1];
16   BufferedWriter outfile = new BufferedWriter(new FileWriter(outputFileName));
17   outfile.write("score\tp-value\n");
```

```
18    BufferedReader infile = new BufferedReader(new FileReader(inputFileName));
19
20    int[][] countTable = new int[2][3];
21    String line = null;
22    while (( line = infile.readLine()) != null) {
23        String[] tokens = line.split("\t");
24        int index=0;
25
26        // populate 2x3 contingency table
27        for(int i=0; i<2; i++) {
28            for(int j=0; j<3; j++) {
29                countTable[i][j] = Integer.parseInt(tokens[index++]);
30            }
31        }
32
33        CochranArmitage catest = new CochranArmitage();
34        double pValue = catest.callCochranArmitageTest(countTable);
35        outfile.write(String.format("%f\t%f\n",
36          catest.getStandardStatistics(), pValue));
37    }
38
39    long elapsedTime = System.currentTimeMillis() - startTime;
40    THE_LOGGER.info("run time (in milliseconds): " + elapsedTime);
41
42    infile.close();
43    outfile.close();
44 }
```

The following is a sample run of the Cochran-Armitage algorithm. First, we compile the algorithm and define the input:

```
$ javac CochranArmitage.java
$ cat test3.txt
1386   1565   401   1342   1579   434
2716    672    13   2689    695     9
2062   1144   151   2021   1184   173
```

Then we run the algorithm:

```
$java CochranArmitage test3.txt test3.txt.out
[main] [INFO ] [CochranArmitage] - run time (in milliseconds): 9
```

The expected output looks like this:

```
$ cat test3.txt.out
score       p-value
-1.414843   0.157114
-0.488857   0.624943
-1.555344   0.119864
```

Application of Cochran-Armitage

In genome analysis, the CATT is applied for statistical tests for differences in *genotype frequency*, in which each individual should be coded as {0, 1, 2} based on the number of the particular variant allele in that individual. These counts can be used to assemble a contingency table consisting of two rows and three columns (each row representing a specific group and each column representing the outcome of an experiment such as an allele count) that can be analyzed by standard statistical methods. The CATT is used to approximate an additive genetic model.

The real example in genomic analysis can be stated as follows: let Group A denote a set of biosets (generated from VCF files) for a set of patients, and let Group B denote another set of biosets (also generated from VCF files) for another set of patients. The goal is to apply the CATT to a set of alleles found at a specific chromosome[1] with a given start position and stop position (for details on chromosomes, visit the National Institute of Health website (*http://bit.ly/chromosome_nih*)). This data can be truly huge. Each bioset generated from a (human sample) VCF file may have over 4,000,000 chromosomes. If Group A has 3,000 samples and Group B has 5,000 samples, then to compare genotype frequency we have to analyze 32 billion records (obviously, this is a big data problem!):

Group A records = 3,000 × 4,000,000 = 12,000,000,000
Group B records = 5,000 × 4,000,000 = 20,000,000,000
Total records = 12,000,000,000 + 20,000,000,000 = 32,000,000,000

To use the CATT for genotype frequency we form a 2 × 3 contingency table for each allele found at the common key of a specific chromosome (identified by its start position and end position). See Table 20-3.

Table 20-3. Contingency table for each allele

Group	Count of 0	Count of 1	Count of 2
Group A	N_{11}	N_{12}	N_{13}
Group B	N_{21}	N_{22}	N_{23}

I will demonstrate building a 2 × 3 contingency table for each allele through the following example. Let Group A be a set of six biosets identified by $\{B_1, B_2, B_3, B_4, B_5, B_6\}$ (see Table 20-4) and let Group B be a set of five biosets identified by $\{B_7, B_8, B_9, B_{10}, B_{11}\}$ (see Table 20-5). Note that this data is for a very specific chromosome at a defined start and stop position.

---

1 Humans normally have 46 chromosomes in each cell, divided into 23 pairs. Two copies of chromosome 1, one copy inherited from each parent, form one of the pairs. (Source: *http://ghr.nlm.nih.gov/chromosome/1.*)

Table 20-4. Group A biosets

Bioset ID	Allele1	Allele2
B_1	A	C
B_2	A	A
B_3	A	C
B_4	G	G
B_5	A	A
B_6	AC	T

Table 20-5. Group B biosets

Bioset ID	Allele1	Allele2
B_7	A	A
B_8	C	C
B_9	A	C
B_{10}	A	A
B_{11}	A	A

Before generating/building contingency tables, we need to build some data structures, as outlined in Table 20-6.

Table 20-6. Genotype frequency

Bioset ID	Group	A count	C count	G count	T count	AC count
B_1	Group A	1	1	0	0	0
B_2	Group A	2	0	0	0	0
B_3	Group A	1	1	0	0	0
B_4	Group A	0	0	2	0	0
B_5	Group A	2	0	0	0	0
B_6	Group A	0	0	0	1	1
B_7	Group B	2	0	0	0	0
B_8	Group B	0	2	0	0	0
B_9	Group B	1	1	0	0	0
B_{10}	Group B	2	0	0	0	0
B_{11}	Group B	2	0	0	0	0

Now, we can generate a contingency table for each allele (A, C, G, T, and AC; see Tables 20-7 through 20-11), after which we may apply the CATT algorithm. In our MapReduce algorithm, each reducer for (Key_2, $Value_2$) will generate a set of contingency tables (where Key_2 is a composite key of chromosomeID:start:stop).

Table 20-7. Contingency table for allele A

Group	Count of 0	Count of 1	Count of 2
Group A	2	2	2
Group B	1	1	3

Table 20-8. Contingency table for allele C

Group	Count of 0	Count of 1	Count of 2
Group A	4	2	0
Group B	3	1	1

Table 20-9. Contingency table for allele G

Group	Count of 0	Count of 1	Count of 2
Group A	5	0	1
Group B	5	0	0

Table 20-10. Contingency table for allele T

Group	Count of 0	Count of 1	Count of 2
Group A	5	1	0
Group B	5	0	0

Table 20-11. Contingency table for allele AC

Group	Count of 0	Count of 1	Count of 2
Group A	5	1	0
Group B	5	0	0

MapReduce Solution

This section will present a MapReduce algorithm for the CATT that can be implemented by Hadoop and Spark. Our implementation is based on MapReduce/Hadoop.

Input

Since the same bioset can be selected for both groups of biosets (A and B), we will generate two types of data (the only difference will be the GROUP-NAME; for Group A,

GROUP-NAME will be a and for Group B, GROUP-NAME will be b, which will enable us to distinguish one group from the other).

Each bioset record will have the following format:

```
<chromosome-ID>
<:>
<chromosome-start-position>
<:>
<chromosome-stop-position>
<;>
<GROUP-NAME>
<:>
<allele1>
<:>
<allele2>
<:>
<reference>
<:>
<snp-id>
<:>
<mutation-class-ID>
<:>
<gene-id>
<:>
<bioset_Id>
```

For example, if we select six biosets for Group A, then we will have:

```
7:10005296:10005296;a:A:C:A:snpid:mc:geneid:1000
7:10005296:10005296;a:A:A:A:snpid:mc:geneid:2000
7:10005296:10005296;a:A:C:C:snpid:mc:geneid:3000
7:10005296:10005296;a:G:G:G:snpid:mc:geneid:4000
7:10005296:10005296;a:A:A:A:snpid:mc:geneid:5000
7:10005296:10005296;a:AC:T:A:snpid:mc:geneid:6000
```

And if we select five biosets for Group B, then we will have:

```
7:10005296:10005296;b:A:A:A:snpid:mc:geneid:7000
7:10005296:10005296;b:C:C:C:snpid:mc:geneid:7100
7:10005296:10005296;b:A:C:C:snpid:mc:geneid:7200
7:10005296:10005296;b:A:A:A:snpid:mc:geneid:7300
7:10005296:10005296;b:A:A:A:snpid:mc:geneid:7400
```

Expected Output

Each result record (the p-value generated by the Cochran-Armitage test) will have the following format:

```
<pValue>
<:>
<chromosome-ID>
<:>
```

```
<chromosome-start-position>
<:>
<chromosome-stop-position>
<:>
<gene-id>
<:>
<mutation-class-ID>
<:>
<reference>
<:>
<alternate-allele>
<:>
<N11>
<:>
<N12>
<:>
<N13>
<:>
<N21>
<:>
<N22>
<:>
<N23>
<:>
<snp-id>
```

Mapper

The mapper (see Example 20-4) will generate a key-value pair for each record, where the key will be:

```
<chromosome-ID><:><chromosome-start-position><:><chromosome-stop-position>
```

and the value will be the remaining attributes:

```
<GROUP-NAME>
<:>
<allele1>
<:>
<allele2>
<:>
<reference>
<:>
<snp-id>
<:>
<mutation-class-ID>
<:>
<gene-id>
<:>
<bioset_Id>
```

Example 20-4. Cochran-Armitage: map() function

```
 1 /**
 2  * @param key is the key generated by Hadoop, ignored here
 3  * @param value has the following format:
 4  *   <chr-ID><:><start><:><stop><;><GROUP><|><allele1><|><allele2><|>
 5  *     <ref><|><snp-id><|><mutation-class><|><gene-id>|<bioset_Id>
 6  *   where GROUP can be in {"a" , "b"}
 7  *
 8  * reducerKey = Text:  <chr-ID><:><start><:><stop>
 9  * reducerValue = Text: <GROUP><|><allele1><|><allele2><|><ref><|>
10  *                      <snp-id><|><mutation-class><|><gene-id>|<bioset_Id>
11  */
12 map(Object key, Text value) {
13     String[] tokens = StringUtils.split(line, ";");
14     if (tokens.length == 2) {
15         String reducerKey = tokens[0];
16         String reducerValue = tokens[1];
17         emit(reducerKey, reducerValue);
18     }
19 }
```

Reducer

The main task for the CATT is done by reducers. Each reducer's key will be the key generated by the mappers. The value of each reducer will be a list of values generated by the mappers. Therefore, a reducer that has a key of 7:10005296:10005296 will have the following values:

```
a:A:C:A:snpid:mc:geneid:1000
a:A:A:A:snpid:mc:geneid:2000
a:A:C:C:snpid:mc:geneid:3000
a:G:G:G:snpid:mc:geneid:4000
a:A:A:A:snpid:mc:geneid:5000
a:AC:T:A:snpid:mc:geneid:6000
b:A:A:A:snpid:mc:geneid:7000
b:C:C:C:snpid:mc:geneid:7100
b:A:C:C:snpid:mc:geneid:7200
b:A:A:A:snpid:mc:geneid:7300
b:A:A:A:snpid:mc:geneid:7400
```

To implement reduce() (see Example 20-5), we need three data structures:

```
// all alleles in Group A and Group B
Map<String, String[]> allAlleles = new HashMap<String, String[]>();

// all alleles in Group A
List<String[]> groupA = new ArrayList<String[]>();

// all alleles in Group B
List<String[]> groupB = new ArrayList<String[]>();
```

After these three data structures are populated, we will generate contingency tables and then apply the Cochran-Armitage trend test.

Example 20-5. Cochran-Armitage: reduce() function

```
1  /**
2   * @param key is the key: Text: <chr-ID><:><start><:><stop>
3   * @param values is a list of {value}, where each value has the following format:
4   *    <GROUP><:><allele1><:><allele2><:><ref><:><snp-id><:>
5   *       <mutation-class><:><gene-id>:<bioset_Id>
6   *     where GROUP can be in {"a" , "b"}
7   *
8   * outputKey = null
9   * outputValue = built by buildOutputValue() method
10  */
11  reduce(Text key, Iterable<Text> values) {
12      //  tokens[index]              0           1           2           3           4
13      //  reduce(value) = Text: <GROUP><:><allele1><:><allele2><:><ref><:><snp-id><:>
14      //  tokens[index]              5                   6           7
15      //  reduce(value) = Text: <mutation-class><:><gene-id>:<bioset_Id>
16
17      Map<String, String[]> allAlleles = new HashMap<String, String[]>();
18      List<String[]> groupA = new ArrayList<String[]>();
19      List<String[]> groupB = new ArrayList<String[]>();
20
21      for (Text valueAsText : values) {
22          String value = valueAsText.toString();
23          String[] tokens = StringUtils.split(value, "|");
24          if (tokens.length != 8) {
25              continue;
26          }
27
28          String group = tokens[0];
29          String allele1 = tokens[1];
30          String allele2 = tokens[2];
31          if (!allAlleles.containsKey(allele1)) {
32              allAlleles.put(allele1, tokens);
33          }
34          if (!allAlleles.containsKey(allele2)) {
35              allAlleles.put(allele2, tokens);
36          }
37
38          if (group.equals("a")) {
39              // it is either group "a"
40              groupA.add(tokens);
41          }
42          else {
43              // or group "b"
44              groupB.add(tokens);
45          }
46      } // end for-loop
```

```
47
48    if ( (groupA.isEmpty()) & (groupB.isEmpty()) ) {
49      return;
50    }
51
52    // iterate through allAlleles and do analysis
53    int[][] contingencyTable = new int[2][3]; // create a contingency table
54    for (Map.Entry<String, String[]> entry : allAlleles.entrySet()) {
55      String allele = entry.getKey();        // key
56      String[] tokens = entry.getValue();    // value
57
58      // -------------------------------------------------
59      // create the following table:
60      //
61      //           0    1    2    <-- counts
62      //         ------------------
63      // groupA   n10  n11  n12    (index 0 is groupA)
64      // groupB   n20  n21  n22    (index 1 is groupB)
65      //
66      //   Then pass this array of 2x3 to CochranArmitage Test
67      // -------------------------------------------------
68
69      clearContingencyTable(contingencyTable);
70      fillContingencyTable(groupA, groupB, contingencyTable);
71      double pValue = CochranArmitage.callTrendTest(contingencyTable);
72      String outputValue = buildOutputValue(pValue, key, allele, tokens,
73                                      contingencyTable);
74      // prepare reducer for output
75      emit(null, outputValue);
76    }
77 }
```

Example 20-6 defines the helper functions for the Cochran-Armitage trend test.

Example 20-6. Cochran-Armitage: helper functions

```
1 private static void clearContingencyTable(int[][] contingencyTable) {
2    for (int i=0; i < 2; i++) {
3      for (int j=0; j < 3; j++) {
4        contingencyTable[i][j] = 0;
5      }
6    }
7 }
8
9 private static void fillContingencyTable(List<String[]> groupA,
10                                         List<String[]> groupB,
11                                         int[][] contingencyTable) {
12    for (String[] tokensA: groupA) {
13      int count = countAlleles(tokensA, allele);
14      // here count = 0, 1, or 2
15      contingencyTable[0][count]++; // (index 0 is groupA)
16    }
```

```
17
18       for (String[] tokensB: groupB) {
19           int count = countAlleles(tokensB, allele);
20           // here count = 0, 1, or 2
21           contingencyTable[1][count]++; // (index 1 is groupB)
22       }
23 }
24
25 private static int countAlleles(String[] tokens, String allele) {
26       int count = 0;
27       if (allele.equals(tokens[1])) {
28           count++;
29       }
30       if (allele.equals(tokens[2])) {
31           count++;
32       }
33       // here count = 0, 1, or 2
34       return count;
35 }
```

The buildOutputValue() method, defined in Example 20-7, builds the final output to be emitted by reducers.

Example 20-7. Cochran-Armitage: buildOutputValue() function

```
 1 String buildOutputValue(pValue, key, allele, tokens, contingencyTable) {
 2     // tokens:              <GROUP></><allele1></><allele2></><ref></><snp-id></>
 3     // tokens[index]          0        1          2           3         4
 4     // tokens:              <mutation-class><|><gene-id>|<bioset_Id>
 5     // tokens[index]          5              6         7
 6     StringBuilder outputValue    = new StringBuilder();
 7     outputValue.append(pValue);                        // p-value
 8     outputValue.append(":");
 9     outputValue.append(key.toString()); // reduce(key)=<chr-ID><:><start><:><stop>
10     outputValue.append(":");
11     outputValue.append(tokens[6]);                     // <gene-id>
12     outputValue.append(":");
13     outputValue.append(tokens[5]);                     // <mutation-class>
14     outputValue.append(":");
15     outputValue.append(tokens[3]);                     // <ref>
16     outputValue.append(":");
17     outputValue.append(allele);                        // alternate allele
18     outputValue.append(":");
19     outputValue.append(contingencyTable[0][0]);   // n10 (group A, count 0)
20     outputValue.append(":");
21     outputValue.append(contingencyTable[0][1]);   // n11 (group A, count 1)
22     outputValue.append(":");
23     outputValue.append(contingencyTable[0][2]);   // n12 (group A, count 2)
24     outputValue.append(":");
25     outputValue.append(contingencyTable[1][0]);   // n20 (group B, count 0)
26     outputValue.append(":");
```

```
27    outputValue.append(contingencyTable[1][1]);    // n21 (group B, count 1)
28    outputValue.append(":");
29    outputValue.append(contingencyTable[1][2]);    // n22 (group B, count 2)
30    outputValue.append(":");
31    outputValue.append(tokens[4]);                 // snp-id
32    return outputValue.toString();
33 }
```

MapReduce/Hadoop Implementation Classes

The Hadoop implementation for the CATT is comprised of the classes shown in Table 20-12.

Table 20-12. Hadoop implementation classes

Class name	Class description
CochranArmitage	Cochran-Armitage trend test algorithm
CochranArmitageAnalyzer	Reads and analyzes result generated by MapReduce program
CochranArmitageClient	Simple class to submit MapReduce jobs
CochranArmitageDriver	Actual driver to submit MapReduce jobs
CochranArmitageItem	Output record is mapped into this bean class
CochranArmitageItemFactory	Factory class to generate CochranArmitageItem object
CochranArmitageItemImpl	Implementation of CochranArmitageItem
CochranArmitageMapper	Defines Hadoop map() for Cochran-Armitage trend test algorithm
CochranArmitageReducer	Defines Hadoop reduce() for Cochran-Armitage trend test algorithm
PaginatedObject	How to paginate result for frontend
ResultObject	Result object for Cochran-Armitage trend test algorithm

Sample Run

The following subsections outline the input, sample run log, and generated output for our sample run of the MapReduce/Hadoop implementation of the Cochran-Armitage trend test.

Input

```
$ cat run_CochranArmitage.sh
#!/bin/bash
client=CochranArmitageClient
java $client interactive 0out groupA_0.txt groupB_0.txt

$ cat groupA_0.txt
0

$ cat groupB_0.txt
0
```

```
$ hadoop fs -cat /germline/groupA/0/*
7:100:200;a|A|C|Ref|snpid|mc|geneid|1000
7:100:200;a|A|A|Ref|snpid|mc|geneid|2000
7:100:200;a|A|C|Ref|snpid|mc|geneid|3000
7:100:200;a|G|G|Ref|snpid|mc|geneid|4000
7:100:200;a|A|A|Ref|snpid|mc|geneid|5000
7:100:200;a|AC|T|Ref|snpid|mc|geneid|6000

$ hadoop fs -cat /germline/groupB/0/*
7:100:200;b|A|A|Ref|snpid|mc|geneid|7000
7:100:200;b|C|C|Ref|snpid|mc|geneid|7100
7:100:200;b|A|C|Ref|snpid|mc|geneid|7200
7:100:200;b|A|A|Ref|snpid|mc|geneid|7300
7:100:200;b|A|A|Ref|snpid|mc|geneid|7400
```

Log of sample run

The log output of a sample run is shown here, formatted and edited to fit the page:

```
$ ./run_CochranArmitage.sh
16:34:40 [main] [INFO ] [CATT] - executionType: interactive
16:34:40 [main] [INFO ] [CATT] - requestID: 0out
16:34:40 [main] [INFO ] [CATT] - biosetIDsFilenameGroupA: groupA_0.txt
16:34:40 [main] [INFO ] [CATT] - biosetIDsFilenameGroupB: groupB_0.txt
...
16:34:42 [main] [INFO ] [...JobClient] - map 0% reduce 0%
...
16:35:13 [main] [INFO ] [...JobClient] - map 100% reduce 100%
16:35:18 [main] [INFO ] [CATT] - run(): Job Finished in 37.782 seconds
16:35:18 [main] [INFO ] [CATT - run(): jobid=job_201307110717_0285
16:35:18 [main] [INFO ] [CATT] - submitJob(): runStatus=0
```

Generated output

```
$ hadoop fs -cat /biomarker/output/germline/0out/part*
0.2635524772829726:7:100:200:geneid:mc:Ref:AC:5:1:0:5:0:0:snpid
0.2635524772829726:7:100:200:geneid:mc:Ref:T:5:1:0:5:0:0:snpid
0.2635524772829726:7:100:200:geneid:mc:Ref:G:5:0:1:5:0:0:snpid
0.3545394797735012:7:100:200:geneid:mc:Ref:A:2:2:2:1:1:3:snpid
0.43276758066778453:7:100:200:geneid:mc:Ref:C:4:2:0:3:1:1:snpid
```

This chapter implemented the Cochran-Armitage trend test for inputs of germline data (expressed as VCF files) using MapReduce/Hadoop. The next chapter implements a scalable solution for allelic frequency analysis, which also uses germline data as input.

## CHAPTER 21

Allelic Frequency

Allelic frequency analysis is a technique used to find the frequency of alleles for genomic (*http://bit.ly/genomic_data*) data (especially for the germline (*http://bit.ly/germline_cells*) data type). An allelic frequency (*http://bit.ly/allele_freq*) is defined as "the percentage of a population of a species that carries a particular allele on a given chromosome locus." In this chapter, we'll develop a MapReduce solution to aggregate all genomic data for each desired key (composed of [chromosome, start-position, stop-position]), then apply Fisher's Exact Test (*http://bit.ly/fishers_exact_test*), a statistical test to determine if there are nonrandom associations between two groups of variables (these two groups of variables can be patient biosets, which will be discussed shortly). We will then analyze and plot the output of the MapReduce program. The input for allelic frequency calculation comes from VCF files generated by DNA sequencing pipelines. Typically each VCF record includes chromosome, start-position, stop-position, genome-reference, and two alleles (labeled allele1 and allele2—one from the mother and one from the father). This information will be sufficient for us to perform an allelic frequency analysis for two sets of data.

The main goal of this chapter is to present a MapReduce solution to allelic frequency calculation using Fisher's Exact Test, comprising three MapReduce jobs.

To comprehend the importance and the impact of allelic frequency, you must first understand the meaning of *mutations*, *migrations*, and *selections*. For details on these concepts, see the DNA and Mutations article (*http://bit.ly/dna_and_mutations*) from the Understanding Evolution project. Calculating an allelic frequency is very important for biology scientists: if there are changes over time in allelic frequencies, this can imply that genetic drift is occurring or that new mutations have been introduced into the population.

An example of a mutation is illustrated in Figure 21-1. The image shows how populations change genetically away from the Hardy-Weinberg equilibrium (*http://bit.ly/hardy-weinberg_equil*).

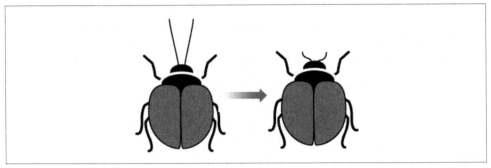

Figure 21-1. Mutation example

In this chapter we will:

1. Find the p-value (probability value in the range of 0.00 to 1.00) for every triad of (chromosome, start-position, stop-position) between two given groups (A and B) of biosets (defined shortly). This will be accomplished by MapReduce phase 1. For efficient runtime processing, for a given bioset we will create two identical copies of the original data and differentiate them by adding a groupID of a or b.

2. Find the 100 smallest p-values *among all chromosomes*—that is, those that are closest to 0.00 (as p-values get closer to 0.00, they become more interesting). This means that if we sort all p-values in ascending order, then our desired solution will be the first 100 p-values. This is implemented by the MapReduce phase 2 program. The output of phase 1 will also be used as input to phase 2.

3. Find the 100 smallest p-values *per chromosome*—that is, those that are closest to 0.00. This is implemented by the MapReduce phase 3 program. The output of phase 1 will also be used as input to phase 3.

Basic Definitions

Before we go over our MapReduce solution, we need to define a few important terms.

Chromosome

A chromosome is an organized structure of DNA, protein, and RNA found in cells. Human cells have 23 pairs of chromosomes labeled {1, 2, ..., 22, X, Y}.

Bioset

Biosets are individually analyzed data signatures; they encompass data in the form of experimental sample comparisons (for transcriptomic, epigenetic, and copy-number variation data), as well as genotype signatures (for GWAS—genome-wide association study—and mutational data). Biosets are more commonly referred to as *gene signatures*. A sample record of a bioset will contain a chromosome, its start and stop positions, two alleles, and other related information. A bioset also has an associated data type, which can be gene expression, protein expression, methylation, copy-number variation, miRNA, or somatic mutation. Say we have a set of patients. Each patient has a set of biosets (which are created directly from VCF files—each record of the VCF file contains information about a position in the genome), and each bioset has a set of genes and their associated fold change values. The number of entries/records per bioset depends on its data type. For example, a germline bioset can have 4.3 million records, while a gene expression bioset can have up to 50,000 records.

Allele and Allelic Frequency

An allele (*http://bit.ly/allele_def*) is a viable DNA (deoxyribonucleic acid) coding that occupies a given locus (position) on a chromosome. There are two alleles per chromosome position: allele1 and allele2. As stated earlier, allelic frequency is a measure of "the percentage of a population of a species that carries a particular allele on a given chromosome locus." Alternatively, allelic frequency can be defined as the frequency of an allele relative to that of other alleles of the same gene in a population. Typically, Fisher's Exact Test is used to calculate the p-value (probability value) for allelic frequency. Fisher's Exact Test uses a 2×2 contingency table, which represents how different treatments have produced different outcomes. Furthermore, Fisher's Exact Test is based on a *null hypothesis*, which assumes that treatments do not affect outcomes (i.e., that the two are independent).

Source of Data for Allelic Frequency

Shotgun sequencing machines generate DNA sequence data, in FASTQ (*http://bit.ly/fastq_format*) and other well-known formats, from biological (including human) samples. Then this FASTQ data (the size of these samples can be up to 800 GB) is analyzed by DNA sequencing (*http://bit.ly/dna_sequencing*) software and workflows, which eventually generate VCF files (*http://bit.ly/vc_format*). The VCF files we will be working with are is the result of DNA sequencing on germline data. VCF is a text file format, and VCF files are partitioned into metadata (about what kind of data they represent, the quality of the data, etc.) and data. Once a VCF file is available, we can create biosets and biomarkers (which are used in further analysis of genomes contained in groups of biosets/biomarkers). One such analysis is allelic frequency, the focus of this chapter. A workflow diagram for allelic frequency is presented in Figure 21-2.

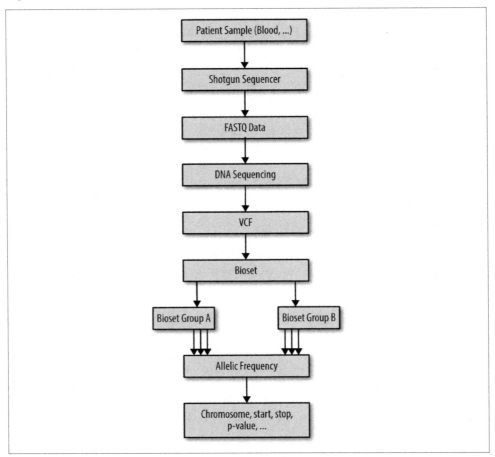

Figure 21-2. Allelic frequency workflow

Allelic frequency analysis for germline data is a big data problem: each germline bioset has about 4.3 million records containing genomic information such as chromosome ID, chromosome start position, chromosome end position, reference genome, allele1, and allele2. Imagine we have two groups of germline biosets: A and B. If Group A has 2,000 biosets and Group B has 4,000 biosets and we want to find an allelic frequency of the two groups' biosets, then we have to analyze:

$$4,300,000 \times (2,000 + 4,000) = 25,800,000,000 \text{ records}$$

To do an allelic frequency analysis (such as Fisher's Exact Test) on all alleles (`allele1`, `allele2`, etc.) in Groups A and B would take about 20 minutes for a 15-node Hadoop cluster; with 100 nodes it might take just under 4 minutes.

Allelic Frequency Analysis Using Fisher's Exact Test

Typically, after we find the allelic frequency for a given chromosome (identified by its chromosome ID, start position, and stop position), we apply Fisher's Exact Test to find the `pValue` (where $0.0 \leq pValue \leq 1.0$). As the `pValue` gets closer to 1.0, the association between rows (groups) and columns (outcomes) is considered not statistically significant; and as the `pValue` moves closer to 0.0, the association between rows (groups) and columns (outcomes) is considered statistically significant.

Fisher's Exact Test

Fisher's Exact Test (*http://bit.ly/fishers_exact_def*) is "a statistical test of independence much used in medical research. It tests the independence of rows and columns in a 2 × 2 contingency table (with 2 horizontal rows crossing 2 vertical columns creating 4 places for data) based on the exact sampling distribution of the observed frequencies. Hence it is an exact test." Fisher's Exact Test was devised by Sir Ronald Aylmer Fisher (*http://bit.ly/ronald_fisher*).

Typically, Fisher's Exact Test is conducted for two groups (Group 1 and Group 2) with two outcomes (Outcome 1 and Outcome 2), as shown in Table 21-1. Actual data values are shown in bold.

Table 21-1. Fisher's Exact Test

	Outcome 1	Outcome 2	Row totals
Group 1	*a*	*b*	$a + b$
Group 2	*c*	*d*	$c + d$
Column totals	$a + c$	$b + d$	$n = a+b+c+d$

The formula for Fisher's Exact Test is as follows:

$$p = \frac{\binom{a+b}{a}\binom{c+d}{c}}{\binom{n}{a+c}} = \frac{(a+b)!}{a!}\ \frac{(c+d)!}{b!}\ \frac{(a+c)!}{c!}\ \frac{(b+d)!}{d!\ n!}$$

where $\binom{n}{k}$ is a binomial coefficient and $n!$ is a factorial of n.

What do we determine with Fisher's Exact Test? The test allows us to statistically determine whether an association exists between two categorical variable with two levels each. It returns a p-value indicating the probability of observing data as extreme as or more extreme than the observed data, if the null hypothesis is true (i.e., if there is no difference between the two levels).

Let's look at two simple examples.

Table 21-2 shows a 2 × 2 contingency table.

Table 21-2. 2 × 2 contingency table (n = 34)

	Success	Failure	Row totals
Group 1	4	12	16
Group 2	8	10	18
Column totals	12	22	$n = 34$

According to Fisher's Exact Test, the two-tailed p-value equals 0.2966. The association between rows (groups) and columns (outcomes) is considered to be not statistically significant. A p-value can be calculated with either one or two tails. It is recommended that you use two-tailed (also called two-sided) p-values. (For details on one-tailed versus two-tailed p-values, see [2].)

For example, in the R programming language, we can perform Fisher's Exact Test as follows:

```
# R
R version 2.15.1 (2012-06-22)
> mytable = rbind ( c(4, 12), c(8, 10) );
> mytable
     [,1] [,2]
[1,]   4   12
[2,]   8   10
> fisher.test(mytable)
  Fisher's Exact Test for Count Data
  data:   mytable
  p-value = 0.2966
```

Let's look at another example, in Table 21-3.

Table 21-3. 2 × 2 contingency table (n = 26)

	Success	Failure	Row totals
Group 1	12	2	14
Group 2	2	10	12
Column totals	14	12	$n = 26$

According to Fisher's Exact Test, the two-tailed p-value here equals 0.0011. The association between rows (groups) and columns (outcomes) is considered to be very statistically significant.

Formal Problem Statement

Let A (denoted by a `groupID` of `a`) and B (denoted by a `groupID` of `b`) be sets of biosets for germline data (as you've learned, these biosets are created from VCF files generated by DNA sequencing). The size of set A is m and the size of set B is n. Note that m and n can be the same or different sizes. Given A and B, we want to find the allelic frequency for these two groups using Fisher's Exact Test. Each bioset record represents a variant and will be identified by the following attributes. Note that a bioset record may have over 50 attributes, but for allelic frequency the following attributes will be sufficient:

- Bioset's key attributes:
  — Chromosome ID: 1, 2, 3, etc.
  — Chromosome start position
  — Chromosome stop position
- Bioset's value attributes:
  — Group ID: a, b
  — `allele1`
  — `allele2`
  — Reference
  — SNP ID
  — Mutation class ID
  — Gene ID
  — Bioset ID

MapReduce Solution for Allelic Frequency

We implement allelic frequency analysis through a three-phase MapReduce algorithm:

- Phase 1: aggregate, group, and generate p-values by calling Fisher's Exact Test.
- Phase 2: use the output of phase 1 and find the bottom 100 (smallest) p-values among *all chromosomes*. We have designed this algorithm in such a way that we

will be able to find the bottom N for any N—for example, the bottom 50 or bottom 500).

- Phase 3: find the smallest 100 p-values *per chromosome*—that is, those that are closest to 0.00. For example, what are the smallest 100 p-values for chromosome 5?

MapReduce Solution, Phase 1

This phase finds the p-value for every triad of (chromosome, start-position, stop-position) between two given groups (A and B) of biosets. The map() function will group input records by a key of (chromosome, start-position, stop-position). The reduce() function will construct a 2 × 2 contingency table and finally call Fisher's Exact Test. It is not possible to provide a combine() function, since we need all alleles for each reducer.

Input

Since the same bioset can be selected for both sets (A and B), we will generate two types of data (the only difference will be the group-name: for Group A, GROUP-NAME will be a, and for Group B, GROUP-NAME will be b, which will enable us to distinguish one group from the other).

Each bioset record will have the following format:

```
<chromosome-ID>
<:>
<chromosome-start-position>
<:>
<chromosome-stop-position>
<;>
<GROUP-NAME>
<:>
<allele1>
<:>
<allele2>
<:>
<reference>
<:>
<snpID>
<:>
<mutationClassID>
<:>
<geneID>
<:>
<biosetID>
```

For example, if we select six biosets for Group A, then for chromosome 7 we might have the following data:

```
7:10005296:10005296;a:A:C:A:snpid:mc:geneid:1000
7:10005296:10005296;a:A:A:A:snpid:mc:geneid:2000
7:10005296:10005296;a:A:C:C:snpid:mc:geneid:3000
7:10005296:10005296;a:G:G:G:snpid:mc:geneid:4000
7:10005296:10005296;a:A:A:A:snpid:mc:geneid:5000
7:10005296:10005296;a:AC:T:A:snpid:mc:geneid:6000
```

And if we select five biosets for Group B, then for chromosome 7 we might have the following data:

```
7:10005296:10005296;b:A:A:A:snpid:mc:geneid:7000
7:10005296:10005296;b:C:C:C:snpid:mc:geneid:7100
7:10005296:10005296;b:A:C:C:snpid:mc:geneid:7200
7:10005296:10005296;b:A:A:A:snpid:mc:geneid:7300
7:10005296:10005296;b:A:A:A:snpid:mc:geneid:7400
```

Output/Result

Each output/result record (the p-value is generated by Fisher's Exact Test per chromosome-ID, chromosome-start-position, and chromosome-stop-position) will have the following format:

```
<pValue>
<:>
<chromosome-ID>
<:>
<chromosome-start-position>
<:>
<chromosome-stop-position>
<:>
<geneID>
<:>
<mutationClassID>
<:>
<reference>
<:>
<alternate-allele>
<:>
<N11>
<:>
<N12>
<:>
<N21>
<:>
<N22>
<:>
<snpID>
```

Note that N_{11}, N_{12}, N_{21}, and N_{22} refer to the values that we generate as a 2 × 2 contingency table, shown in Table 21-4.

Table 21-4. 2 x 2 contingency table for N_{11}, N_{12}, N_{21}, N_{22} values

	Known	Others	Row totals
Group A	N_{11}	N_{12}	$N_{11} + N_{12}$
Group B	N_{21}	N_{22}	$N_{21} + N_{22}$
Column totals	$N_{11} + N_{21}$	$N_{12} + N_{22}$	$n = N_{11} + N_{12} + N_{21} + N_{22}$

An allelic frequency analysis using Fisher's Exact Test will generate the following output:

```
1.0:7:10005296:10005296:geneid:mc:A:AC:1:11:0:10:snpid
1.0:7:10005296:10005296:geneid:mc:A:T:1:11:0:10:snpid
0.480519480519484:7:10005296:10005296:geneid:mc:G:G:2:10:0:10:snpid
0.4148606811145488:7:10005296:10005296:geneid:mc:A:A:6:6:7:3:snpid
0.6240601503759411:7:10005296:10005296:geneid:mc:C:C:2:10:3:7:snpid
```

Phase 1 Mapper

The mapper, shown in Example 21-1, will generate a key-value pair for each record, where the key will be:

```
<chromosome-ID><:><chromosome-start-position><:><chromosome-stop-position>
```

and the value will be the remaining attributes:

```
<GROUP-NAME>
<:>
<allele1>
<:>
<allele2>
<:>
<reference>
<:>
<snpID>
<:>
<mutationClassID>
<:>
<geneID>
<:>
<biosetID>
```

Example 21-1. Allelic frequency: map() function

```
1  /**
2   * @param key is the key generated by Hadoop, ignored here
3   * @param value has the following format:
4   *   <chrID><:><start><:><stop><;><GROUP><|><allele1><|><allele2><|><ref><|>
```

```
 5  *       <snpID><|><mutationClassID><|><geneID>|<biosetID>
 6  * where GROUP can be in {"a" , "b"}
 7  *
 8  * reducerKey = Text: <chrID><:><start><:><stop>
 9  * reducerValue = Text: <GROUP><|><allele1><|><allele2><|><ref><|>
10  *       <snpID><|><mutationClassID><|><geneID>|<biosetID>
11  */
12 map(Text key, Text value) {
13     String[] tokens = StringUtils.split(line, ";");
14     if (tokens.length == 2) {
15         String reducerKey = tokens[0];
16         String reducerValue = tokens[1];
17         emit(reducerKey, reducerValue);
18     }
19 }
```

The mapper function generates key-value pairs, where the key is composed of {chrID, start, stop}, and the value is composed of {GROUP, allele1, allele2, ref, snpID, mutationClassID, geneID, biosetID}. Therefore, each reducer will receive a key as <chrID><:><start><:><stop> and values as a list of the mappers' emitted values.

Phase 1 Reducer

The main task is done by the reducers. Each reducer's key will be the key generated by the mappers. The value of each reducer will be a list of values generated by the mappers. Therefore, a reducer that has a key of 7:10005296:10005296 will have the following values:

```
a:A:C:A:snpid:mc:geneid:1000
a:A:A:A:snpid:mc:geneid:2000
a:A:C:C:snpid:mc:geneid:3000
a:G:G:G:snpid:mc:geneid:4000
a:A:A:A:snpid:mc:geneid:5000
a:AC:T:A:snpid:mc:geneid:6000
b:A:A:A:snpid:mc:geneid:7000
b:C:C:C:snpid:mc:geneid:7100
b:A:C:C:snpid:mc:geneid:7200
b:A:A:A:snpid:mc:geneid:7300
b:A:A:A:snpid:mc:geneid:7400
```

To implement the reducer (see Example 21-2), we need three basic hash tables:

groupA

    Alleles that are only in Group A

```
    Map<String, Integer> groupA = new HashMap<String, Integer>();
```

groupB

    Alleles that are only in Group B

```
Map<String, Integer> groupB = new HashMap<String, Integer>();
```

globalMap

Alleles that are in Group A or Group B

```
Map<String, String[]> globalMap = new HashMap<String, String[]>();
```

After these three tables are populated for each key (as `<chrID><:><start><:><stop>`), we will iterate over `globalMap` to find all allelic frequencies. (See Examples 21-3 through 21-5.)

Example 21-2. Allelic frequency: reduce() function

```
 1 /**
 2  * @param key is the key: Text: <chrID><:><start><:><stop>
 3  * @param values is a list of {value}, where each value has the following format:
 4  *    <GROUP><:><allele1><:><allele2><:><ref><:><snpID><:>
 5  *       <mutationClassID><:><geneID>:<biosetID>
 6  * where GROUP can be in {"a" , "b"}
 7  *
 8  * outputKey = null (no key is required)
 9  * outputValue = built by buildOutputValue() method
10  */
11 reduce(Text key, Iterable<Text> values) {
12
13     int totalNumOfBiosetsInGroupA = 0;
14     int totalNumOfBiosetsInGroupB = 0;
15
16     Map<String, String[]> globalMap = new HashMap<String, String[]>();
17     Map<String, Integer> groupA = new HashMap<String, Integer>();
18     Map<String, Integer> groupB = new HashMap<String, Integer>();
19
20     // Step 1: populate tables by iterating over values (see Example 21-3)
21
22     // Step 2: create an instance of Fisher's Exact Test
23     FisherExactTest theFisherExactTest = new FisherExactTest();
24
25     // Step 3: find allelic frequencies by iterating
26     // over tables built (see Example 21-4)
27 }
```

Example 21-3. Step 1: populate tables by iterating over values

```
1    for (Text valueAsText: values) {
2        String value = valueAsText.toString();
3        String[] tokens = StringUtils.split(value, ":");
4        if (tokens.length != 8) {
5            continue;
6        }
7
```

```
 8      // reduce(value) = <GROUP><:><allele1><:><allele2><:><ref><:><snpID><:>
 9      // tokens[index]        0           1           2          3       4
10      // reduce(value) = <mutationClassID><:><geneID>:<biosetID>
11      // tokens[index]            5               6        7
12      String group = tokens[0];
13      String allele1 = tokens[1];
14      String allele2 = tokens[2];
15       if (group.equals("a")) {
16          // it is group "a"
17          totalNumOfBiosetsInGroupA++;
18          // handle allele1
19          Integer count = groupA.get(allele1);
20          if (count == null) {
21              groupA.put(allele1, 1);
22              globalMap.put(allele1, tokens);
23          }
24          else {
25              groupA.put(allele1, Integer.valueOf(count.intValue() + 1));
26          }
27          // handle allele2
28          Integer count2 = groupA.get(allele2);
29          if (count2 == null) {
30              groupA.put(allele2, 1);
31              globalMap.put(allele2, tokens);
32          }
33          else {
34              groupA.put(allele2, Integer.valueOf(count2.intValue() + 1));
35          }
36       }
37      else {
38          // handle allele1 for group "b"
39          totalNumOfBiosetsInGroupB++;
40          Integer count = groupB.get(allele1);
41          if (count == null) {
42             groupB.put(allele1, 1);
43             // check to see if we want to add this allele or not
44             if (!globalMap.containsKey(allele1)) {
45                 globalMap.put(allele1, tokens);
46             }
47          }
48          else {
49              groupB.put(allele1, Integer.valueOf(count.intValue() + 1));
50          }
51          // handle allele2
52          Integer count2 = groupB.get(allele2);
53          if (count2 == null) {
54             groupB.put(allele2, 1);
55             // check to see if we want to add this allele or not
56             if (!globalMap.containsKey(allele2)) {
57                 globalMap.put(allele2, tokens);
58             }
59          }
```

```
60          else {
61              groupB.put(allele2, Integer.valueOf(count2.intValue() + 1));
62          }
63      }
64
65  } // end while-loop
66
67  if ( (groupA.size() == 0) || (groupB.size() == 0) ) {
68      return;
69  }
```

Example 21-4. Step 3: find allelic frequencies by iterating over tables built

```
1   // now all of our three required hash tables are created:
2   //      groupA<String, Integer>
3   //      groupB<String, Integer>
4   //      globalMap<allele, tokens[]>
5   //
6   // next, iterate through globalMap<allele, tokens[]) and do analysis;
7   // note that globalMap<allele, tokens[]) has all alleles
8   for (Map.Entry<String, String[]> entry : globalMap.entrySet()) {
9       String allele = entry.getKey(); // key
10      String[] tokens = entry.getValue();
11
12      int n11 = 0;
13      int n12 = 0;
14      int n21 = 0;
15      int n22 = 0;
16
17      // check to see if groupA has this allele:
18      Integer countOfAllelesInGroupA = groupA.get(allele);
19      Integer countOfAllelesInGroupB = groupB.get(allele);
20      if (countOfAllelesInGroupA == null) {
21          // then this allele must be only in groupB
22          n11 = 0;
23          n12 = (2 * totalNumOfBiosetsInGroupA);
24          n21 = countOfAllelesInGroupB;
25          n22 = (2 * totalNumOfBiosetsInGroupB) - n21;
26      }
27      else if (countOfAllelesInGroupB == null) {
28          // then this allele must be only in groupA
29          n11 = countOfAllelesInGroupA;
30          n12 = (2 * totalNumOfBiosetsInGroupA) - n11;
31          n21 = 0;
32          n22 = (2 * totalNumOfBiosetsInGroupB);
33      }
34      else {
35          // then this allele must be in both (groupA and groupB)
36          n11 = countOfAllelesInGroupA;
37          n12 = (2 * totalNumOfBiosetsInGroupA) - n11;
38          n21 = countOfAllelesInGroupB;
39          n22 = (2 * totalNumOfBiosetsInGroupB) - n21;
```

```
40            }
41
42            theFisherExactTest.init(n11, n12, n21, n22);
43            double pValue = theFisherExactTest.get2Tail();
44            String outputValue = buildOutputValue(pValue, key, allele,
45                                            tokens, n11, n12, n21, n22);
46            // prepare reducer for output
47            emit(null, outputValue);
48        } // end for-loop
49 }
```

Example 21-5. Allelic frequency: buildOutputValue() function

```
 1 String buildOutputValue(pValue, key, allele, tokens, n11, n12, n21, n22) {
 2     StringBuilder outputValue = new StringBuilder();
 3     outputValue.append(pValue);           // p-value
 4     outputValue.append(":");
 5     outputValue.append(key.toString()); // key = <chrID><:><start><:><stop>
 6     outputValue.append(":");
 7     outputValue.append(tokens[6]);        // <geneID>
 8     outputValue.append(":");
 9     outputValue.append(tokens[5]);        // <mutationClassID>
10     outputValue.append(":");
11     outputValue.append(tokens[3]);        // <ref>
12     outputValue.append(":");
13     outputValue.append(allele);           // alternate allele
14     outputValue.append(":");
15     outputValue.append(n11);              // n11
16     outputValue.append(":");
17     outputValue.append(n12);              // n12
18     outputValue.append(":");
19     outputValue.append(n21);              // n21
20     outputValue.append(":");
21     outputValue.append(n22);              // n22
22     outputValue.append(":");
23     outputValue.append(tokens[4]);        // snpID
24     return outputValue.toString();
25 }
```

Sample Run of Phase 1 MapReduce/Hadoop Implementation

The following subsections provide the script, input, run log, and generated output for
our phase 1 MapReduce/Hadoop implementation of allelic frequency calculation.

The script

```
# cat run_test.sh
#!/bin/bash
groupA=/bioset/input/groupA/groupA.txt
groupB=/bioset/input/groupB/groupB.txt
```

```
output=/bioset/output
java AllelicFrequencyClient interactive  $groupA $groupB $output
```

Input

```
# hadoop fs -cat /bioset/input/groupA/groupA.txt
7:100:200;a|A|C|Ref|snpid|mc|geneid|1000
7:100:200;a|A|A|Ref|snpid|mc|geneid|2000
7:100:200;a|A|C|Ref|snpid|mc|geneid|3000
7:100:200;a|G|G|Ref|snpid|mc|geneid|4000
7:100:200;a|A|A|Ref|snpid|mc|geneid|5000
7:100:200;a|AC|T|Ref|snpid|mc|geneid|6000

# hadoop fs -cat /bioset/input/groupB/groupB.txt
7:100:200;b|A|A|Ref|snpid|mc|geneid|7000
7:100:200;b|C|C|Ref|snpid|mc|geneid|7100
7:100:200;b|A|C|Ref|snpid|mc|geneid|7200
7:100:200;b|A|A|Ref|snpid|mc|geneid|7300
7:100:200;b|A|A|Ref|snpid|mc|geneid|7400
```

Running the script

Log output from a sample run is shown here; it has been edited and formatted to fit
the page:

```
# ./run_test.sh
...
16:01:50  [AllelicFrequencyClient] - biosetIDsFilenameGroupA: groupA.txt
16:01:50  [AllelicFrequencyClient] - biosetIDsFilenameGroupB: groupB.txt
...
16:01:51  [AllelicFrequencyDriver] - GroupA biosetPath::/bioset/input/groupA::
16:01:51  [AllelicFrequencyDriver] - GroupB biosetPath::/bioset/input/groupB::
...
16:01:51  [org.apache.hadoop.mapred.JobClient] - Running job: job_201307110717
16:01:52  [org.apache.hadoop.mapred.JobClient] - map 0% reduce 0%
...
16:03:07  [org.apache.hadoop.mapred.JobClient] - map 100% reduce 100%
16:03:12  [AllelicFrequencyDriver] - run(): Job Finished in 80.862 seconds
16:03:12  [AllelicFrequencyDriver] - submitJob(): runStatus=0
```

Generated output

```
# hadoop fs -cat /bioset/output/part*
1.0:7:100:200:geneid:mc:Ref:AC:1:11:0:10:snpid
1.0:7:100:200:geneid:mc:Ref:T:1:11:0:10:snpid
0.480519480519484:7:100:200:geneid:mc:Ref:G:2:10:0:10:snpid
0.4148606811145488:7:100:200:geneid:mc:Ref:A:6:6:7:3:snpid
0.6240601503759411:7:100:200:geneid:mc:Ref:C:2:10:3:7:snpid
```

Sample Plot of P-Values

Let's say we have extracted p-values from the allelic frequency output into a file called *pvalue.txt*, and we want to plot these values (I have just extracted about 40 p-values here, out of 4.3 million). Using the R programming language, this is straightforward:

```
# R
R version 2.15.1 (2012-06-22) -- "Roasted Marshmallows"
> p = read.table('pvalue.txt');
> p
     V1
1  0.00
2  0.05
...
36 0.90
37 1.00
38 1.00
> plot(table(p));
> title(main="Allelic Frequency");
> q();
```

The output will be a PDF file, as illustrated in Figure 21-3.

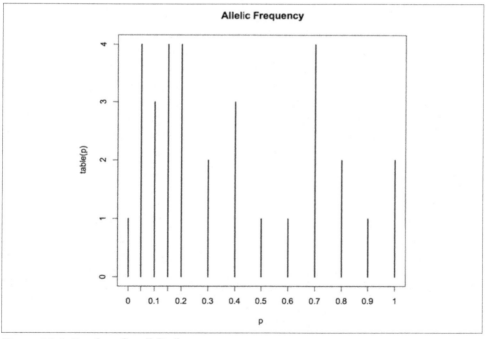

Figure 21-3. P-values for allelic frequency

MapReduce Solution, Phase 2

The goal of this phase is to find the first smallest 100 p-values among all chromosomes—that is, those that are closest to 0.00. The output of phase 1 will be used as input to phase 2. The easiest solution is to sort (in ascending order) the output of phase 1 by p-value and then output the first 100 records (which will be the desired output). Since the output of phase 1 may be big, however, sorting is not a good option, so instead we'll solve this using another MapReduce job. Were we using a relational database such as Oracle or MySQL, we could answer this question with a SQL query (assuming that `allele_frequency_table` is a table that contains `pValue` and `<other>` columns and that data is loaded to this table from the output of phase 1):

```
SELECT *
  FROM allele_frequency_table
    ORDER BY pValue LIMIT 100;
```

However, as explained earlier in this book, because of the high volumes of data we are dealing with this task is much better suited to a MapReduce solution.

Using the allelic frequency algorithm (from phase 1), we were able to generate (`pValue, chromosomeID, start, stop, ...`) for all chromosomes for all given biosets in both groups. Now we need to do the sorting (in ascending order) to find the smallest 100 p-values among the generated records. Sorting all the output generated by our allelic frequency algorithm is not a good solution at all, however, as previously noted. If the output of phase 1 is huge, we might run out of memory. So, we choose the other option: using another MapReduce program that reads the output of the allelic frequency algorithm and then generates the smallest 100 p-values among all chromosomes. Our new MapReduce algorithm is pretty simple:

- Mapper:
  — Each mapper finds its local bottom 100 p-values and sends that bottom 100 list to the reducer.
  — We will use many mappers.
- Reducer
  — The reducer finds the final bottom 100 p-values from the bottom 100 lists sent from the mappers.
  — We will use a single reducer for the final bottom 100.

Phase 2 Mapper for Bottom 100 P-Values

The mappers will consume the outputs generated by our allelic frequency algorithm in phase 1. Each mapper will read (`pValue, chromosomeID, start, stop, ...`) and then emit its bottom 100 p-values, using a list data structure. We will use Java's

TreeMap[1] data structure to keep track of the bottom 100 list. The sort order of the list will be preserved by the p-value, as a Double key ($0 \leq pValue \leq 1$):

```
import java.util.TreeMap;
import java.util.SortedMap;
SortedMap<Double, String> bottom100 = new TreeMap<Double, String>();
```

We have to make sure that our bottom100 data structure just holds the bottom 100 p-values. Example 21-6 defines the map() function inside the Bottom100Mapper class: the map() function itself will not emit any key-value pairs, but it will maintain and update the bottom100 data structure. When map() has completed its function, the cleanup() function will emit the bottom 100 list.

Example 21-6. Bottom100Mapper class

```
 1 public class Bottom100Mapper ... {
 2
 3     private SortedMap<Double, String> bottom100 =
 4         new TreeMap<Double, String>();
 5
 6     // key is the p-value of Double type and range is 0.00 to 1.00
 7     // value is the entire record of allelic frequency output (includes p-value)
 8     map(Double key, String entireRecord) {
 9         bottom100.put(key, value); // sort by p-value
10         if (bottom100.size() > 100) {
11             // remove the greatest p-value
12             bottom100.remove(bottom100.lastKey());
13         }
14     }
15
16     // called once at the end of the mapper task
17     cleanup() {
18         for (Map.Entry<Double, String> entry : bottom100.entrySet() {
19             Double pValue = entry.getKey();
20             String entireRecord = entry.getValue();
21             String outputValue = pair(pValue, entireRecord);
22             // NULL key will send all key-value
23             // pairs to a single reducer only
24             emit(NULL, outputValue);
25         }
26     }
27 }
```

---

1 The java.util.TreeMap is a red-black tree-based NavigableMap implementation. The map is sorted according to the natural ordering of its keys, or by a Comparator provided at the time of the map's creation, depending on which constructor is used. This implementation provides guaranteed log(n) time cost for the containsKey, get, put, and remove operations.

Phase 2 Reducer for Bottom 100 P-Values

The bottom 100 algorithm is designed such that only one reducer will aggregate all the bottom 100 lists generated by all the mappers. The key for our single reducer is NULL (in Hadoop this will be an instance of NullWritable). To guarantee that we will have only one reducer, we will also set the number of reduce tasks (setNumOfReduce Tasks()) to 1 in our job driver class, as shown in Example 21-7.

Example 21-7. Bottom100Driver

```
 1 public class Bottom100Driver {
 2    ...
 3    void run(String[] args) {
 4        ...
 5        Job job = new Job(...);
 6        ...
 7        job.setNumReduceTasks(1);
 8        ...
 9    }
10    ...
11 }
```

The job of the single reducer is to generate the final bottom 100 list from all bottom 100 lists generated by all mappers. So, the reducer's functionality (defined in Example 21-8) is very similar to that of the mappers.

Example 21-8. Bottom100Reducer

```
 1 public class Bottom100Reducer ... {
 2
 3    reduce(NullWritable key, Iterable<pair<Double, String>> values) {
 4        SortedMap<Double, String> finalBottom100 =
 5            new TreeMap<Double, String>();
 6
 7        for (pair(Double, String) value : values) {
 8            Double pValue = value.pValue;
 9            String entireRecord = value.entireRecord;
10            finalBottom100.put(pValue, entireRecord);
11
12            if (finalBottom100.size() > 100) {
13                // remove the greatest p-value
14                finalBottom100.remove(finalBottom100.lastKey());
15            }
16        }
17
18        // now, we have the final bottom 100 list
19        for (Map.Entry<Double, String> entry : finalBottom100.entrySet() {
20            Double pValue = entry.getKey();
21            String entireRecord = entry.getValue();
```

```
22              emit(pValue, entireRecord);
23          }
24      }
25 }
```

Is Our Bottom 100 List a Monoid?

Next we will determine whether our bottom 100 list is a monoid.[2] If it is, then we can provide a combiner for our bottom 100 list. As you will see, bottom100 is a commutative monoid.

bottom100 is defined as follows:

```
bottom100 = MONOID(S, e, f),
```

where:

S

$\{(p, w), 0 \le p \le 1, w \text{ is a unique chromosome record}\}$

e

$\{\}$ is an empty set

f

Is the bottom100 function

The bottom100 commutative property is defined as follows:

```
bottom100(a) = {(p1, w1), ..., (p100, w100)
where 0 ≤ p1 ≤ ... ≤ p100 ≤ 1}
bottom100(a, b) = bottom100(a ∪ b) =
bottom100(b ∪ a) = bottom100(b, a)
bottom100(a, b) = c ∈ S
```

And, finally, the bottom100 identity element property can be stated as: let a, b ∈ S. Then:

```
bottom100(a, e) = a
bottom100(e, a) = a
```

In mathematical notation, we can write these as follows:

---

2 Monoids in the context of MapReduce are explained in Chapter 28.

Closure

$$\forall a, b \in S : \text{bottom100}(a, b) \in S$$

Associativity

$$\forall a, b, c \in S : \text{bottom100}(a, \text{bottom100}(b, c)) = \text{bottom100}(\text{bottom100}(a, b), c))$$

Identity element

$$\exists e \in S : \forall a \in S : \text{bottom100}(a, e) = a = \text{bottom100}(e, a)$$

Commutative

$$\forall a, b \in S : \text{bottom100}(a, b) = \text{bottom100}(b, a)$$

Hadoop Implementation Classes for Bottom 100 List

The Java classes used in the bottom 100 list MapReduce solution are listed in Table 21-5. In our solution, we utilized the `PairOfDoubleString`[3] class as a Hadoop `WritableComparable` representing a pair consisting of a `Double` and a `String`.

Table 21-5. Java classes used in Hadoop solution for bottom 100 list

Class name	Description
`Bottom100Driver`	A driver program to submit Hadoop jobs
`Bottom100Mapper`	Defines `map()`
`Bottom100Combiner`	Defines `combine()`
`Bottom100Reducer`	Defines `reduce()`
`HadoopUtil`	Defines some utility functions
`PairOfDoubleString`	`WritableComparable` representing a pair consisting of a `Double` and a `String`

MapReduce Solution, Phase 3

In phase 2 we found the 100 smallest p-values *among all chromosomes* (i.e., those closest to 0.00). In phase 3, we will find the 100 smallest p-values *per chromosome* (again, those closest to 0.00). That is, we want to find the smallest 100 p-values for:

- Chromosome 1
- Chromosome 2
- ...
- Chromosome 22

---

3 This is part of the Cloud9 toolkit developed by Jimmy Lin, a collection of Hadoop tools that tries to make working with big data a bit easier.

- Chromosome X
- Chromosome Y

Therefore, we want to generate 24 outputs. The output of phase 1 will be used as input to phase 3. The easiest solution is to sort (in ascending order) the output of phase 1 by p-value and then group by chromosome, and finally output the first 100 records for each chromosome. Given that the output of phase 1 may be big, though, sorting is not a good option. Instead, we will solve this using another MapReduce job. Were we using a relational database (such as Oracle or MySQL), we could answer this question with a SQL query (assuming that `allele_frequency_table` is a table that contains `pValue` and `<other>` columns and that data is loaded to this table from the output of phase 1). We could run the following SQL query for each chromosome:

```
for (id in (1, 2, 3, ..., 21, 22, X, Y)) {
    SELECT *
        FROM allele_frequency_table
            WHERE chromosome_id = id
            ORDER BY pValue LIMIT 100;

}
```

The MapReduce phase 3 algorithm is pretty simple:

- Mapper:
  - Each mapper finds its local bottom 100 p-values for each chromosome and sends that bottom 100 list to the reducer (one reducer per chromosome, for a total of 24 reducers).
  - We will use many mappers.
- Reducer
  - Each reducer finds the final bottom 100 p-values from the bottom 100 lists sent from the mappers.
  - We will use a single reducer for each chromosome for the final bottom 100.

Phase 3 Mapper for Bottom 100 P-Values

The mappers will consume the outputs generated by our allelic frequency algorithm from phase 1. Each mapper will read (`pValue`, `chromosomeID`, `start`, `stop`, ...) and then emit its bottom 100 p-values for each chromosome, using a list data structure. As shown in Example 21-9, we will use Java's `TreeMap` data structure to keep track of the bottom 100 lists: the sort order will be preserved by the p-value as a `Dou ble` key ($0 \leq pValue \leq 1$).

Example 21-9. Required data structures

```
1 import java.util.Map;
2 import java.util.HashMap;
3 import java.util.SortedMap;
4 import java.util.TreeMap;
5 ...
6 // map<chromosomeID, SortedMap<p-value, record>>
7 private Map<String, SortedMap<Double, String>> chromosomes =
8     new HashMap<String, TreeMap<Double, String>>();
```

We have to make sure that our bottom100 data structure just holds the bottom 100 p-values. Example 21-10 defines the map() function inside the Bottom100MapperPhase3 class: the map() function itself will not emit any key-value pairs, but it will maintain and update the bottom100 data structure. When map() has completed its function, then the cleanup() function will emit the bottom 100 list for each chromosome.

Example 21-10. Bottom100MapperPhase3

```
1 public class Bottom100MapperPhase3 ... {
2     // map<chromosomeID, treemap<p-value, record>>
3     private Map<String, SortedMap<Double, String>> chromosomes =
4         new HashMap<String, TreeMap<Double, String>>();
5
6     // key is the p-value of Double type and range is 0.00 to 1.00
7     // value is the entire record of allelic frequency output (includes p-value)
8     map(Double key, String entireRecord) {
9         String chromosomeID = extract(entireRecord);
10        SortedMap<Double, String> bottom100 = chromosomes.get(chromosomeID);
11        if (bottom100 == null) {
12            bottom100 = new TreeMap<Double, String>();
13        }
14        bottom100.put(key, value); // sort by p-value
15        if (bottom100.size() > 100) {
16            // remove the greatest p-value
17            bottom100.remove(bottom100.lastKey());
18        }
19    }
20
21    // called once at the end of the mapper task
22    cleanup() {
23        for (Map.Entry<String, SortedMap<Double, String>>> entry :
24        chromosomes.entrySet() {
25            String chromosomeID = entry.getKey();
26            SortedMap<Double, String> bottom100 = = entry.getValue();
27            for (Map.Entry<Double, String> row : bottom100.entrySet() {
28                Double pValue = row.getKey();
29                String entireRecord = row.getValue();
30                String outputValue = pair(pValue, entireRecord);
31                // pairs to a specific chromosome
```

```
32              emit(chromosomeID, outputValue);
33          }
34      }
35  }
36 }
```

Phase 3 Reducer for Bottom 100 P-Values

The bottom 100 algorithm is designed such that only one reducer per chromosome will aggregate all the bottom 100 lists generated by all the mappers (note that each reducer will work on the bottom 100 for a single chromosome, as opposed to all chromosomes as in phase 2). The key for our single reducer is chromosomeID.

The job of each reducer is to generate the final bottom 100 list from all bottom 100 lists generated by all mappers (for a particular chromosome). So, the reducer's functionality (defined in Example 21-11) is very similar to that of the mappers.

Example 21-11. Bottom100ReducerPhase3

```
1 public class Bottom100ReducerPhase3 ... {
2
3      // key is a chromosomeID in {1, 2, ..., 22, X, Y}
4      reduce(String key, Iterable<pair<Double, String>> values) {
5          SortedMap<Double, String> finalBottom100 =
6              new TreeMap<Double, String>();
7
8          for (pair(Double, String) value : values) {
9              Double pValue = value.pValue;
10             String entireRecord = value.entireRecord;
11             finalBottom100.put(pValue, entireRecord);
12
13             if (finalBottom100.size() > 100) {
14                 // remove the greatest p-value
15                 finalBottom100.remove(finalBottom100.lastKey());
16             }
17         }
18
19         // now, we have the final bottom 100 list
20         for (Map.Entry<Double, String> entry : finalBottom100.entrySet() {
21             Double pValue = entry.getKey();
22             String entireRecord = entry.getValue();
23             emit(key, (pValue + entireRecord));
24         }
25     }
26 }
```

Hadoop Implementation Classes for Bottom 100 List for Each Chromosome

The Java classes used in our MapReduce solution for the bottom 100 list per chromosome are listed in Table 21-6. In our solution, we utilized the `PairOfDoubleString` class as a Hadoop `WritableComparable` representing a pair consisting of a `Double` and a `String`.

Table 21-6. Java classes used in Hadoop solution for bottom 100 list per chromosome

Class name	Description
`Bottom100DriverPhase3`	A driver program to submit Hadoop jobs
`Bottom100MapperPhase3`	Defines `map()`
`Bottom100CombinerPhase3`	Defines `combine()`
`Bottom100ReducerPhase3`	Defines `reduce()`
`HadoopUtil`	Defines some utility functions
`PairOfDoubleString`	`WritableComparable` representing a pair consisting of a `Double` and a `String`

Special Handling of Chromosomes X and Y

To properly calculate allelic frequencies for a given set of biomarkers/biosets, we need to treat gender chromosomes (chromosomes X and Y) differently than all other chromosomes. This means we need to modify the algorithm for handling chromosomes X and Y for a given germline dataset. Specifically, alleles in non-pseudoautosomal regions (non-PARs) of chromosomes X and Y for male samples should be counted once instead of twice. There are two PARs on chromosomes X and Y:

- PAR1:
  — Chromosome X: 60,001–2,699,520
  — Chromosome Y: 10,001–2,649,520
- PAR2:
  — Chromosome X: 154,931,044–155,260,560
  — Chromosome Y: 59,034,050–59,373,566

Implementation of this algorithm (with proper handling of chromosomes X and Y) is left as an exercise to the interested reader.

This chapter presented a scalable MapReduce solution for finding allelic frequencies for a large set of germline data (represented as VCF files). The next chapter presents MapReduce and Spark solutions for the t-test.

## CHAPTER 22

The T-Test

The t-test (also known as the two-sample t-test) is used in clinical applications and genome analysis to test statistical hypotheses. The t-test for independent samples compares the means (μ, also known as the average) of two samples. In statistics, to compare two data sets, we convert the data to a simpler form, such as the means of the data, and then compute and compare the means. Since we are comparing random samples, there is room for random errors (usually denoted by the sample's standard deviation, σ). The standard deviation equation for a population of N samples is defined as:

$$\sigma = \sqrt{\frac{\sum\limits_{i=1}^{N}(X_i - \mu)^2}{N}}$$

where:

σ = the standard deviation
X_i = i^{th} value in the population
μ = the mean of the values in the population

In factoring a random error, therefore, we might be comparing $\mu \pm \sigma$. According to Sarah Boslaugh's book *Statistics in a Nutshell* (O'Reilly), "The purpose of [the t-test] is to determine whether the means of the populations from which the samples were drawn are the same. The subjects in the two samples are assumed to be unrelated and to have been independently selected from their populations."

This chapter will provide MapReduce/Hadoop and Spark solutions for the t-test. The MapReduce algorithm presented here is generic and can be used for any high volume of data.

Performing the T-Test on Biosets

In genome analysis and especially in somatic mutations, the t-test is used for a pair of samples drawn for the same gene (identified as a `geneID`). Given a set of biosets/biomarkers identified by $B = \{B_1, B_2, ..., B_n\}$ (where each bioset contains "pairs of `geneID` and `geneValue`"[1]) and given a survival time identified by $\{S_1, S_2, ..., S_n\}$ (note that S_i corresponds to B_i), our goal is to create two sample sets: `Exist-Set` and `Non-Exist-Set`. Given this input, we create $\{G_1, G_2, ..., G_m\}$, where B_i represents a set of biosets and G_i is a `geneID` in one of those biosets (G_i acts as a reverse index to biosets). So, we have:

- `Exist-Set` sample: $\{S_i | B_i \in G_k\}$
- `Non-Exist-Set` sample: $\{S_i | B_i \notin G_k\}$

Then we apply the `ttest()` function to `Exist-Set` and `Non-Exist-Set`. Table 22-1 is a concrete example with four biosets (B_i is a GUID and T_i is a primitive double data type).

Table 22-1. Sample data

biosetID	Survival time
B_1	T_1
B_2	T_2
B_3	T_3
B_4	T_4

Further, assume that the biosets have the `geneID` and `geneValue` pairs shown in Table 22-2.

Table 22-2. Bioset data

Bioset	geneID	geneValue
B_1	G1	V11
	G2	V12
	G3	V13
B_2	G1	V21
	G2	V22
	G4	V24

---

1 Note that the number of pairs depends on the bioset type. For example, for the RNA gene expression data type we might have 40,000+ pairs, and for the methylation data type we might have 20,000+ pairs.

Bioset	geneID	geneValue
B_3	G1	V31
	G3	V32
	G4	V33
	G5	V34
	G6	V35
B_4	G2	V41
	G5	V42
	G6	V43

Then we will have the containment table shown in Table 22-3.

Table 22-3. Containment table

geneID	Time T_1	T_2	T_3	T_4
G1	B_1	B_2	B_3	–
G2	B_1	B_2	–	B_4
G3	B_1	–	B_3	–
G4	–	B_2	B_3	–
G5	–	–	B_3	B_4
G6	–	–	B_3	B_4

For example, the first row in Table 22-2 indicates that G1 is contained in biosets $\{B_1, B_2, B_3\}$, but not contained in $\{B_4\}$. The information in this table leads us to call up the following functions:

```
G1: ttest({T1, T2, T3}, {T4})
G2: ttest({T1, T2, T4}, {T3})
G3: ttest({T1, T3}, {T2, T4})
G4: ttest({T2, T3}, {T1, T4})
G5: ttest({T3, T4}, {T1, T2})
G6: ttest({T3, T4}, {T1, T2})
```

For a single `ttest()` implementation, we will use the following objects from the Apache Commons Math project:

- Interface: `org.apache.commons.math.stat.inference.TTest`
- Implementation class: `org.apache.commons.math.stat.inference.TTestImpl`

The implementation of `ttest()` (used in the `TTestImpl` class) can be described as follows. This statistic can be used to perform a two-sample (*sample1* and *sample2*) t-test to compare sample means. The returned t-statistic is as follows:

$$t = \frac{(m_1 - m_2)}{\sqrt{\dfrac{v_1}{n_1} + \dfrac{v_2}{n_2}}}$$

where:

- n_1 is the size of the first sample (*sample1*).
- n_2 is the size of the second sample (*sample2*).
- m_1 is the mean of the first sample.
- m_2 is the mean of the second sample.
- v_1 is the variance of the first sample.
- v_2 is the variance of the second sample.

How do we use these objects to implement `ttest()`? Example 22-1 shows a simple implementation.

Example 22-1. ttest() implementation

```
1 import org.apache.commons.math.stat.inference.TTest;
2 import org.apache.commons.math.stat.inference.TTestImpl;
3 import org.apache.commons.math.MathException;
4
5 public class MathUtil {
6    /**
7     * @param sample1 = array of sample data values
8     * @param sample2 = array of sample data values
9     * @return the observed significance level, or
10    * p-value, associated with a two-sample, two-tailed
11    * t-test comparing the means of the input arrays
12    */
13   public static double ttest(double[] sample1, double[] sample2) {
14       if ( (sample1 == null) ||
15            (sample2 == null) ||
16            (sample1.length == 0) ||
17            (sample2.length == 0) ) {
18           // return a nonexistent value
19           return Double.MAX_VALUE;
20       }
21
22       if ((sample1.length == 1) && (sample2.length == 1)) {
23           // return a nonexistent value
24           return Double.MAX_VALUE;
25       }
26       return calculateTtest(sample1, sample2);
27   }
28
```

```
29        private static double calculateTtest(double[] sample1, double[] sample2) {
30        ...
31        }
32 }
```

The `calculateTtest()` method is implemented in Example 22-2.

Example 22-2. The calculateTtest() method

```
 1 /**
 2  * @param sample1 = array of sample data values
 3  * @param sample2 = array of sample data values
 4  * @return p-value, associated with sample1 and sample2
 5  */
 6 private static double calculateTtest(double[] sample1, double[] sample2) {
 7     double pValue = 0.0d;
 8     TTest ttest = new TTestImpl();
 9     try {
10         if (sample1.length == 1) {
11             pValue = ttest.tTest(sample1[0], sample2);
12         }
13         else if (sample2.length == 1) {
14             pValue = ttest.tTest(sample2[0], sample1);
15         }
16         else {
17             pValue = ttest.tTest(sample1, sample2);
18         }
19     }
20     catch(MathException me) {
21         System.out.println("ttest() failed. +", me.getMessage());
22         pValue = 0.0d;
23     }
24
25     return pValue;
26 }
```

MapReduce Problem Statement

Given a set of biosets,[2] where a bioset may have up to 100,000 genes, we want to apply the `ttest()`) function to each gene for all biosets. Typically, in genome analysis, the t-test is applied to the gene expression, methylation, somatic mutation, and copy-number variation bioset data types. This kind of analysis involves reading and processing hundreds of millions of records. For example, to process 200,000 biosets (the normal number of biosets in patient-centric applications) with each having 50,000 unique `geneID`s, the MapReduce solution has to handle 10 billion

---

2 For details on biosets, please refer to Appendix A.

(10,000,000,000) records. This volume of data and `ttest()` processing cannot be handled by a single server.

Input

Our input for the t-test has two parts (B_i corresponds to S_i):

- List of biosets (B_1, B_2, ..., B_n)
- Survival times for these biosets (S_1, S_2, ..., S_n)

Each record of a bioset will have the following format:

```
<geneID><,><biosetID><,><geneValue>
```

For example:

```
7562135,778800,1.04
```

or:

```
7570769,778800,-1.09
```

The bioset files persist in HDFS and will be read by the MapReduce framework (during the `map()` execution). How will we pass these two additional dynamic parameters (the list of bioset IDs, and the survival times for biosets) from the MapReduce driver to the `map()` and `reduce()` functions? Using the MapReduce/Hadoop `Configuration` object, we can set these values through `Configuration.set()` and retrieve them through `Configuration.get()` in the `setup()` function of `map()` or `reduce()`. An alternative method is to use Hadoop's `DistributedCache`[3] class, which can distribute large, application-specific, read-only files efficiently.

Expected Output

For each `geneID` (contained in all of the biosets), we need to generate:

```
<geneID><,><RESULT-of-TTEST-FUNCTION>
```

where `<RESULT-of-TTEST-FUNCTION>` is a p-value.

MapReduce Solution

The goal of our MapReduce solution is to apply the t-test algorithm to all genes contained in these biosets. The mapper gets `<geneID><,><biosetID><,><geneValue>`

---

3 The full name is `org.apache.hadoop.filecache.DistributedCache`. `DistributedCache` is a class provided by Hadoop's MapReduce framework to cache files needed by applications.

and emits a key-value pair, where the key is the geneID and the value is the biosetID. The reducer function's job is to create two lists (Exist-Set and Non-Exist-Set) and then apply the t-test to them.

As shown in Example 22-3, map() is a simple function that emits pairs of (geneID, biosetID).

Example 22-3. T-test: map() function

```
 1 /**
 2  * @param key is generated by MapReduce framework, ignored here
 3  * @param value is a String with the following format:
 4  *      <geneID><,><biosetID><,><geneValue>
 5  * Note that <geneValue> is not used in the t-test.
 6  */
 7 map(key, value) {
 8     String[] tokens = value.split(",");
 9     String geneID = tokens[0];
10     String biosetID = tokens[1];
11     emit(geneID, biosetID);
12 }
```

The main function of the reducer (defined in Example 22-4) is to create a reverse index of genes based on biosetIDs and finally apply the t-test algorithm to two sets: Exist-Set and Non-Exist-Set. The reduce() function implements the t-test and preserves the order of biosetIDs and survival times.

Example 22-4. Reducer for t-test

```
 1 public class TtestReducer {
 2
 3     // instance variables
 4     private Configuration conf = null;
 5     // biosetIDs as Strings : NOTE order of biosets is VERY IMPORTANT
 6     public List<String> biosets = null;
 7     // survival time : NOTE order of time items is VERY IMPORTANT
 8     public List<Double> time = null;
 9
10     // will be run only once
11     public void setup(Context context) {
12         this.conf = context.getConfiguration();
13
14         // get parameters from Hadoop's configuration
15         String biosetsAsString = conf.get("biosets");
16         this.biosets = DataStructuresUtil.splitOnToListOfString(biosetsAsString,
17                                                         ",");
18
19         String timeAsCommaSeparatedString = conf.get("time");
20         this.time = DataStructuresUtil.toListOfDouble(timeAsCommaSeparatedString);
```

```
21    }
22
23    // key = geneID
24    // values = list of { biosetID }
25    public void reduce(Text key, Iterable<Text> values) {
26        // solution is given next
27      }
28 }
```

The `reduce()` function for our t-test implementation is presented in Example 22-5.

Example 22-5. T-test: reduce() function

```
 1 // key = geneID
 2 // values = list of { biosetID }
 3 public void reduce(Text key, Iterable<Text> values) {
 4    Iterator<Text> iter = values.iterator();
 5    List<Double> exist = new ArrayList<Double>();
 6    List<Double> notexist = new ArrayList<Double>();
 7    List<String> genebiosets = new ArrayList<String>();
 8    while (iter.hasNext()) {
 9       String biosetID = iter.next();
10       genebiosets.add(biosetID);
11    }
12
13    for (int i=0; i < biosets.size(); i++) {
14       // check to see if this biosetID does exist in genes
15       int index = genebiosets.indexOf(biosets.get(i));
16       if (index == -1) {
17          // biosetID not found
18          notexist.add(time.get(i));
19       }
20       else {
21          // biosetID found
22          exist.add(time.get(i));
23       }
24    }
25
26    if (exist.isEmpty()) {
27       // no need to include it
28       return;
29    }
30
31    if (notexist.isEmpty()) {
32       // no need to include it
33       return;
34    }
35
36    //
37    // here we have:
38    //     (exist.size() > 0) && (notexist.size() > 0)
39    //
```

```
40   // prepare final value(s) for reducer
41   //
42   double pValue = MathUtil.ttest(exist, notexist); // calls ttest()
43   emit(key, pValue);
44 }
```

Hadoop Implementation Classes

This section implemented a MapReduce t-test solution using Hadoop. Our Hadoop solution is composed of the Java classes shown in Table 22-4.

Table 22-4. T-test implementation classes using MapReduce/Hadoop

Class name	Description
TtestDriver	The driver class for submitting MapReduce jobs
TtestMapper	Defines the map() function
TtestReducer	Defines the reduce() function
TtestAnalyzer	Reads output data generated by reducers

Spark Implementation

This section implements a MapReduce t-test solution using Spark. The Spark solution is a single driver Java class using RDDs. Three types of input are involved for the t-test:

- List of biosetIDs $\{B_1, B_2, ..., B_n\}$, where $n > 0$ and each B_i is a bioset ID.
- List of survival times $\{T_1, T_2, ..., T_n\}$, where each T_i is a Double data type. Each B_i corresponds to T_i.
- List of n files (one file per bioset): {B1.txt, B2.txt, ..., Bn.txt}. Each record in the bioset files has the following format (note that for ttest, geneValue will not be used):

  `<geneID><,><biosetID><,><geneValue>`

Since each B_i corresponds to T_i, we will combine these two data points into a single file, called *timetable.txt*, where each record will have two columns: <bioset_id> and <survival_time>. Therefore, we assume the following input files:

```
/<hdfs-directory>/timetable/timetable.txt
/<hdfs-directory>/biosets/bioset_1.txt
/<hdfs-directory>/biosets/bioset_2.txt
/<hdfs-directory>/biosets/bioset_3.txt
...
/<hdfs-directory>/biosets/bioset_n.txt
```

High-Level Steps

Using these input files, the Spark t-test workflow is presented in Figure 22-1.

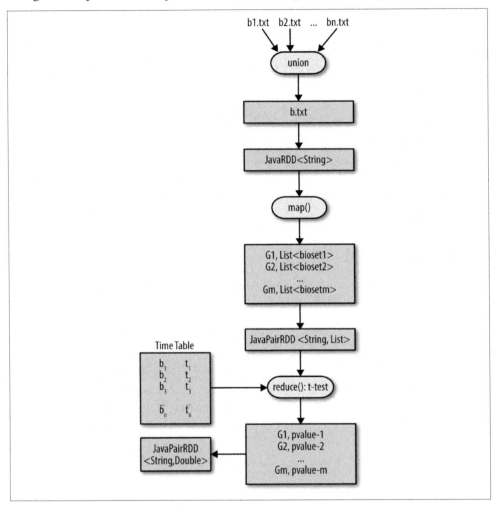

Figure 22-1. Spark t-test workflow

The high-level implementation of the Spark workflow is as follows (see Example 22-6):

1. Concatenate all bioset files (*B1.txt*, *B2.txt*, ..., *Bn.txt*) and create a `JavaRDD<String>`, where each item (as a `String` object) of this RDD has the format:

   ```
   <geneID><,><biosetID><,><geneValue>
   ```

2. Map the `JavaRDD<String>` into a `JavaRDD<String, Iterable<String>>`, where the key (as a `String`) is a `geneID` and the value is a list of biosets.

3. Read time table data as pairs of (`biosetID, survival-time`) and reduce the `JavaRDD<String, Iterable<String>>` using the t-test algorithm into a final `JavaRDD<String, Double>` where the key (as a `String`) is a `geneID` and the value is a p-value (output of the t-test algorithm).

4. Save the final `JavaPairRDD` in HDFS.

Example 22-6. Spark solution: high-level steps

```
1 // Step 1: import required classes and interfaces
2 public class SparkTtest {
3     static JavaSparkContext createJavaSparkContext() {...}
4     static Map<String, Double> createTimeTable(String filename) {...}
5     static JavaRDD<String> readBiosetFiles(JavaSparkContext ctx,
6                                            String biosetFiles) {...}
7
8     public static void main(String[] args) throws Exception {
9         // Step 2: handle input parameters
10         // Step 3: create time table data structure
11         // Step 4: create a Spark context object (ctx)
12         // Step 5: broadcast shared variables used by all cluster nodes
13         // Step 6: create RDD for all biosets, where
14         // each RDD element has: <geneID><,><biosetID><,><geneValue>
15         // Step 7: map bioset records into JavaPairRDD<K,V> pairs
16         // where K = <geneID>, V = <biosetID>
17         // Step 8: group biosets by geneID;
18         // now, for each geneID we have a List<biosetID>
19         // Step 9: perform t-test for every geneID
20
21         // done
22         ctx.close();
23         System.exit(0);
24     }
25 }
```

Create JavaSparkContext

The `createJavaSparkContext()` method (illustrated in Example 22-7) is used to create a `JavaSparkContext` object, a factory for creating new RDDs.

Example 22-7. createJavaSpark() method

```
1 static JavaSparkContext createJavaSparkContext() throws Exception {
2     return new JavaSparkContext();
3 }
```

createTimeTable() method

The createTimeTable() method, shown in Example 22-8, creates our TimeTable data structure, which is a hash table of (K,V) pairs where K is a biosetID and V is a time associated with K.

Example 22-8. Create TimeTable data structure

```
1   static Map<String, Double> createTimeTable(String filename) throws Exception {
2       Map<String, Double> map = new HashMap<String, Double>();
3       BufferedReader in = null;
4       try {
5           in = new BufferedReader(new FileReader(filename));
6           String line = null;
7           while ((line = in.readLine()) != null) {
8               String value = line.trim();
9               String[] tokens = value.split("\t");
10              String biosetID = tokens[0];
11              Double time = new Double(tokens[1]);
12              map.put(biosetID, time);
13          }
14          System.out.println("createTimeTable() map="+map);
15      }
16      finally {
17          if (in != null) {
18              in.close();
19          }
20      }
21      return map;
22  }
```

readBiosetFiles() method

We will use the JavaSparkContext to create an RDD for all given biosets, which we populate by reading in the bioset files with the readBiosetFiles() method. This method then partitions the RDD into 14 partitions (an arbitrary number is used here for illustration purposes; the number of partitions you need will depend on the size of your data and cluster) for further distributed and parallel processing (see Example 22-9). Determining the right number of partitions is very important to the performance of your program.

Example 22-9. Create RDD for all biosets, and partition it

```
1 static JavaRDD<String> readBiosetFiles(JavaSparkContext ctx,
2                                        String biosetFiles)
3       throws Exception {
4       StringBuilder unionPath = new StringBuilder();
5       BufferedReader in = null;
6       try {
```

```
7        in = new BufferedReader(new FileReader(biosetFiles));
8        String singleBiosetFile = null;
9        while ((singleBiosetFile = in.readLine()) != null) {
10           singleBiosetFile = singleBiosetFile.trim();
11           unionPath.append(singleBiosetFile);
12           unionPath.append(",");
13        }
14        //System.out.println("readBiosetFiles() unionPath="+unionPath);
15     }
16     finally {
17        if (in != null) {
18           in.close();
19        }
20     }
21     // remove the last comma ","
22     String unionPathAsString = unionPath.toString();
23     unionPathAsString = unionPathAsString.substring(0,
24                    unionPathAsString.length()-1);
25     // create RDD
26     JavaRDD<String> allBiosets = ctx.textFile(unionPathAsString);
27     JavaRDD<String> partitioned = allBiosets.coalesce(14);
28     return partitioned;
29 }
```

Step 1: Import required classes and interfaces

Example 22-10 imports the required classes and interfaces for our Spark implementation.

Example 22-10. Step 1: import required classes and interfaces

```
1    // Step 1: import required classes and interfaces
2    import scala.Tuple2;
3    import org.apache.spark.api.java.JavaRDD;
4    import org.apache.spark.api.java.JavaPairRDD;
5    import org.apache.spark.api.java.JavaSparkContext;
6    import org.apache.spark.api.java.function.Function;
7    import org.apache.spark.api.java.function.PairFunction;
8    import org.apache.commons.lang.StringUtils;
9    import org.apache.spark.broadcast.Broadcast;
10   import org.apache.spark.SparkConf;
11
12   import java.util.Map;
13   import java.util.HashMap;
14   import java.util.Set;
15   import java.util.HashSet;
16   import java.util.List;
17   import java.util.ArrayList;
18   import java.io.FileReader;
19   import java.io.BufferedReader;
```

Step 2: Handle input parameters

This step, shown in Example 22-11, reads two input parameters: the time table file and the bioset file.

Example 22-11. Step 2: handle input parameters

```
1 // Step 2: handle input parameters
2 if (args.length != 2) {
3    System.err.println("Usage: SparkTtest <timetable-file> <bioset-file>");
4    System.exit(1);
5 }
6 String timeTableFileName = args[0];
7 System.out.println("<timetable-file>="+timeTableFileName);
8 String biosetFileNames = args[1];
9 System.out.println("<bioset-file>="+biosetFileNames);
```

Step 3: Create TimeTable data structure

This step, shown in Example 22-12, creates a `TimeTable` data structure as a hash table of `Map<biosetID, time>`.

Example 22-12. Step 3: create time table data structure

```
1       // Step 3: create time table data structure
2       Map<String, Double> timetable = createTimeTable(timeTableFileName);
```

Step 4: Create a Spark context object

This step, shown in Example 22-13, creates an instance of `JavaSparkContext`, a factory class used to create new RDDs.

Example 22-13. Step 4: create a Spark context object

```
1       // Step 4: create a Spark context object
2       JavaSparkContext ctx = createJavaSparkContext();
```

Step 5: Broadcast shared data structures

Spark's `Broadcast` class is used to broadcast and share global data structures among all cluster nodes. Once a data structure is broadcasted, you may read/retrieve it from any cluster node (by using Spark's transformations) using the `Broadcast.value()` method. See Example 22-14.

Example 22-14. Step 5: broadcast shared data structures

```
1       // Step 5: broadcast shared data structures and variables
2       // used by all cluster nodes; we need this shared data structure
```

```
3        // when we want to find Exist-Set and Not-Exist-Set sets after
4        // grouping data by geneID.
5        final Broadcast<Map<String, Double>> broadcastTimeTable =
6            ctx.broadcast(timetable);
```

Step 6: Create RDD for all biosets

This step, shown in Example 22-15, reads all input data and creates an RDD for all input biosets.

Example 22-15. Step 6: create RDD for all biosets

```
1        // Step 6: create RDD for all biosets;
2        // each RDD element has: <geneID><,><biosetID><,><geneValue>
3        JavaRDD<String> biosets = readBiosetFiles(ctx, biosetFileNames);
4        biosets.saveAsTextFile("/ttest/output/1");
```

Step 7: Map bioset records into JavaPairRDD<K,V> pairs

This step, shown in Example 22-16, converts JavaRDD<String> biosets into Java PairRDD<geneID, biosetID> pairs.

Example 22-16. Step 7: map bioset records into JavaPairRDD<K,V> pairs

```
1        // Step 7: map bioset records into JavaPairRDD<K,V> pairs
2        // where K = <geneID>
3        //       V = <biosetID>
4        // Note that for ttest, <geneValue> is not used (ignored here).
5        JavaPairRDD<String, String> pairs = biosets.mapToPair(
6            new PairFunction<
7                            String, // T
8                            String, // K
9                            String  // V
10                           >() {
11           public Tuple2<String, String> call(String biosetRecord) {
12               String[] tokens = StringUtils.split(biosetRecord, ",");
13               String geneID = tokens[0];   // K
14               String biosetID = tokens[1]; // V
15               return new Tuple2<String,String>(geneID, biosetID);
16           }
17        });
18        pairs.saveAsTextFile("/ttest/output/2");
```

Step 8: Group biosets by geneID

As shown in Example 22-17, this step uses JavaPairRDD.groupByKey() to group all gene values for a single geneID.

Example 22-17. Step 8: group biosets by geneID

```
1    // Step 8: group biosets by geneID
2    JavaPairRDD<String, Iterable<String>> grouped = pairs.groupByKey();
3    // now, for each geneID we have a List<biosetID>
4    grouped.saveAsTextFile("/ttest/output/3");
```

Step 9: Perform T-Test for Every geneID

In this step, shown in Example 22-18, the actual t-test algorithm is applied to gene values.

Example 22-18. Step 9: perform t-test for every geneID

```
1    // Step 9: perform t-test for every geneID
2    // mapValues[U](f: (V) => U): JavaPairRDD[K, U]
3    // Pass each value in the key-value pair RDD through a map function without
4    // changing the keys; this also retains the original RDD's partitioning.
5    JavaPairRDD<String, Double> ttest = grouped.mapValues(
6        new Function<
7                    Iterable<String>, // input
8                    Double          // output (result of ttest)
9                    >() {
10       public Double call(Iterable<String> biosets) {
11           Set<String> geneBiosets = new HashSet<String>();
12           for (String biosetID : biosets) {
13               geneBiosets.add(biosetID);
14           }
15
16           // now we need a shared Map data structure to iterate over its items
17           Map<String, Double> timetable = broadcastTimeTable.value();
18           // the following two lists are needed for ttest(exist, notexist)
19           List<Double> exist = new ArrayList<Double>();
20           List<Double> notexist = new ArrayList<Double>();
21           for (Map.Entry<String, Double> entry : timetable.entrySet()) {
22               String biosetID = entry.getKey();
23               Double time = entry.getValue();
24               if (geneBiosets.contains(biosetID)) {
25                   exist.add(time);
26               }
27               else {
28                   notexist.add(time);
29               }
30           }
31
32           // perform the ttest(exist, notexist)
33           double ttest = MathUtil.ttest(exist, notexist);
34           return ttest;
35       }
36   });
37   ttest.saveAsTextFile("/ttest/output/4");
```

T-Test Algorithm

For the t-test algorithm (Example 22-19) we use the solution from Apache Commons
Math (*http://bit.ly/commons_math*), where:

TTest
>   Is an interface that specifies several t-test algorithms

TTestImpl
>   Is the class that implements the TTest interface

Example 22-19. T-test algorithm solution from Apache Commons Math

```
 1 import java.util.List;
 2 import java.util.ArrayList;
 3 import org.apache.commons.math.stat.inference.TTest;
 4 import org.apache.commons.math.stat.inference.TTestImpl;
 5
 6 public class MathUtil {
 7
 8     private static final TTest ttest = new TTestImpl();
 9
10     public static double ttest(double[] arrA, double[] arrB) {
11         if ((arrA.length == 1) && (arrB.length == 1)) {
12             // return a NULL value for score (does not make sense)
13             return Double.NaN;
14         }
15
16         double score = Double.NaN;
17         try {
18             if (arrA.length == 1) {
19                 score = ttest.tTest(arrA[0], arrB);
20             }
21             else if (arrB.length == 1) {
22                 score = ttest.tTest(arrB[0], arrA);
23             }
24             else {
25                 score = ttest.tTest(arrA, arrB);
26             }
27         }
28         catch(Exception e) {
29             e.printStackTrace();
30             score = Double.NaN;
31         }
32         return score;
33     }
34
35     public static double ttest(List<Double> groupA, List<Double> groupB) {
36         if ((groupA.size() == 1) && (groupB.size() == 1)) {
37             return Double.NaN;
38         }
```

```java
39
40          double score;
41          if (groupA.size() == 1) {
42              score = tTest(groupA.get(0), groupB);
43          }
44          else if (groupB.size() == 1) {
45              score = tTest(groupB.get(0), groupA);
46          }
47          else {
48              score = tTest(groupA, groupB);
49          }
50          return score;
51      }
52
53      private static double tTest(double d, List<Double> group) {
54          try {
55              double[] arr = listToArray(group);
56              return ttest.tTest(d, arr);
57          }
58          catch(Exception e) {
59              e.printStackTrace();
60              return Double.NaN;
61          }
62      }
63
64      private static double tTest(List<Double> groupA, List<Double> groupB) {
65          try {
66              double[] arrA = listToArray(groupA);
67              double[] arrB = listToArray(groupB);
68              return ttest.tTest(arrA, arrB);
69          }
70          catch(Exception e) {
71              e.printStackTrace();
72              return 0.0d;
73          }
74      }
75
76      static double[] listToArray(List<Double> list) {
77          if ( (list == null) || (list.isEmpty()) ) {
78              return null;
79          }
80
81          double[] arr = new double[list.size()];
82          for (int i=0; i < arr.length; i++) {
83              arr[i] = list.get(i);
84          }
85          return arr;
86      }
87 }
```

Sample Run

Input

We have two inputs for the Spark t-test program, the time table and biosets, which are described as follows:

```
# cat ttestinput/timetable.txt
b1      0.9
b2      0.75
b3      0.5
b4      1.1

# cat ttestinput/biosets.txt
/ttest/input/b1.txt
/ttest/input/b2.txt
/ttest/input/b3.txt
/ttest/input/b4.txt

# hadoop fs -ls /ttest/input/
Found 4 items
-rw-r--r--   3 hadoop root,hadoop   52 2014-07-06 22:10 /ttest/input/b1.txt
-rw-r--r--   3 hadoop root,hadoop   33 2014-07-06 22:10 /ttest/input/b2.txt
-rw-r--r--   3 hadoop root,hadoop   31 2014-07-06 22:10 /ttest/input/b3.txt
-rw-r--r--   3 hadoop root,hadoop   31 2014-07-06 22:10 /ttest/input/b4.txt

# hadoop fs -cat /ttest/input/b1.txt
G1,b1,1.0
G2,b1,0.6
G3,b1,0.09
G4,b1,2.2
G5,b1,1.03

# hadoop fs -cat /ttest/input/b2.txt
G1,b2,2.09
G2,b2,1.07
G3,b2,1.00

# hadoop fs -cat /ttest/input/b3.txt
G2,b3,2.9
G3,b3,1.03
G5,b3,2.9

# hadoop fs -cat /ttest/input/b4.txt
G1,b4,2.9
G2,b4,1.8
G4,b4,1.05
```

YARN shell script

The following shell script runs our Spark program in a YARN environment:

```
# cat ./run_ttest.sh
#!/bin/bash
export JAVA_HOME=/usr/java/jdk7
export BOOK_HOME=/mp/data-algorithms-book
export SPARK_HOME=/usr/local/spark-1.0.0
export HADOOP_HOME=/usr/local/hadoop-2.5.0
export HADOOP_CONF_DIR=$HADOOP_HOME/etc/hadoop
export YARN_CONF_DIR=$HADOOP_HOME/etc/hadoop
APP_JAR=$BOOK_HOME/dist/data_algorithms_book.jar
LIB=$BOOK_HOME/lib
EXTRA_JARS=$LIB/commons-math-2.2.jar,$LIB/commons-math3-3.0.jar
TIMETABLE=$BOOK_HOME/data/timetable.txt
BIOSETS=$DAB_HOME/data/biosets.txt
$SPARK_HOME/bin/spark-submit
    --class org.dataalgorithms.chap22.spark.SparkTtest \
    --master yarn-cluster \
    --num-executors 12 \
    --driver-memory 3g \
    --executor-memory 7g \
    --executor-cores 12 \
    --jars $EXTRA_JARS \
    $APP_JAR $TIMETABLE $BIOSETS
```

Log of sample run

The following is the log output from a sample run of our script:

```
# ./run_ttest.sh
<timetable-file>=/home/mp/data-algorithms-book/ttestinput/timetable.txt
<bioset-file>=/home/mp/data-algorithms-book/ttestinput/biosets.txt
createTimeTable() map={b1=0.9, b3=0.5, b2=0.75, b4=1.1}
...
```

Generated debugging output

Here is the debugging output for our script:

```
# hadoop fs -cat /ttest/output/1/part*
G1,b1,1.0
G2,b1,0.6
G3,b1,0.09
G4,b1,2.2
G5,b1,1.03
G1,b4,2.9
G2,b4,1.8
G4,b4,1.05
G1,b2,2.09
G2,b2,1.07
```

```
G3,b2,1.00
G2,b3,2.9
G3,b3,1.03
G5,b3,2.9

# hadoop fs -cat /ttest/output/2/part*
(G1,b1)
(G2,b1)
(G3,b1)
(G4,b1)
(G5,b1)
(G1,b4)
(G2,b4)
(G4,b4)
(G1,b2)
(G2,b2)
(G3,b2)
(G2,b3)
(G3,b3)
(G5,b3)

# hadoop fs -cat /ttest/output/3/part*
(G3,[b3, b1, b2])
(G4,[b1, b4])
(G5,[b1, b3])
(G1,[b1, b4, b2])
(G2,[b1, b4, b2, b3])
```

Generated final output

And here is the final output of our program:

```
# hadoop fs -cat /ttest/output/4/part*
(G3,0.08146847659449757)
(G4,0.14994028688738084)
(G5,0.48769401782708255)
(G1,0.05441315690970782)
(G2,0.0)
```

This chapter presented scalable MapReduce/Hadoop and Spark solutions for t-tests using biosets (if you prefer, you may utilize a different type of data, but the t-test is usually performed in the clinical laboratory using biosets). As you've learned here, the t-test examines whether the means of two groups are statistically different from each other.

## CHAPTER 23

Pearson Correlation

Introduction

The Pearson[1] correlation measures how well two sets of data are related (linear relationship). It is the most common measure of correlation in mathematics and statistics. In a nutshell, the Pearson correlation answers this question: is it possible to draw a line graph to represent the data? According to *onlinestatbook*:

> The Pearson product-moment correlation coefficient is a measure of the strength of the linear relationship between two variables. It is referred to as *Pearson's correlation* or simply as the *correlation coefficient*. If the relationship between the variables is not linear, then the correlation coefficient does not adequately represent the strength of the relationship between the variables.

This chapter will provide two MapReduce solutions for the Pearson correlation:

- A simple solution using classical MapReduce/Hadoop
- A Spark implementation that will correlate all vs. all (defined shortly)

The algorithms presented for Pearson correlations can be easily adapted to Spearman ranked correlations (*http://bit.ly/spearman_coeff*). To perform a Spearman ranked correlation, I have provided a Java wrapper class called `Spearman.java`. By the end of this chapter, you will be able to replace a Pearson correlation with Spearman's ranked correlation algorithm.

---

[1] Karl Pearson (1857–1936) was an English mathematician who has been credited with establishing the discipline of mathematical statistics.

Pearson Correlation Formula

The formula for the Pearson correlation can be written in many different equivalent forms. Let $x = (x_1, x_2, ..., x_n)$ and $y = (y_1, y_2, ..., y_n)$. Then the Pearson correlation for x and y can be expressed as:

$$r = \frac{\Sigma(x_i - \bar{x})(y_i - \bar{y})}{\sqrt{\Sigma(x_i - \bar{x})^2 \Sigma(y_i - \bar{y})^2}}$$

$$r = \frac{\Sigma xy - \frac{\Sigma x \Sigma y}{n}}{\sqrt{\left(\Sigma x^2 - \frac{(\Sigma x)^2}{n}\right)\left(\Sigma y^2 - \frac{(\Sigma y)^2}{n}\right)}}$$

where:

$$\bar{x} = \frac{\Sigma x}{n}$$

$$\bar{y} = \frac{\Sigma y}{n}$$

The Pearson correlation has the following properties:

- It has a range of $-1.00 \le r \le 1.00$.
- The correlation coefficient is a unitless index of the strength of the association between two variables:
  - $r > 0$ means a positive association.
  - $r < 0$ means a negative association.
  - $r = 0$ means no association.
- It measures the linear relationship between x and y.

Given two sets of data, what are the possible values for the Pearson correlation? The results will be between -1.00 and 1.00. The values can be classified as follows:

- High/positive correlation: 0.6 to 1.0 or -0.6 to -1.0 (see Figure 23-1).
- Medium correlation: 0.3 to 0.6 or -0.3 to -0.6.
- Low/negative correlation: 0.1 to 0.3 or -0.1 to -0.3 (see Figure 23-2).
- No correlation: close to 0.00 (see Figure 23-3).

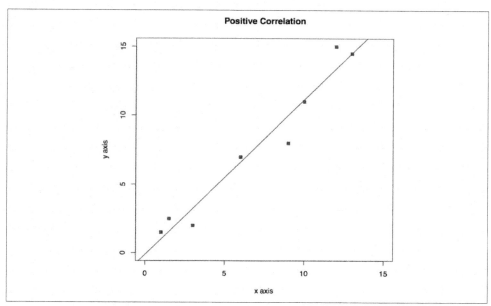

Figure 23-1. Positive correlation

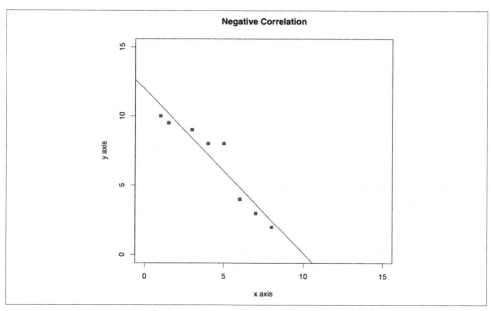

Figure 23-2. Negative correlation

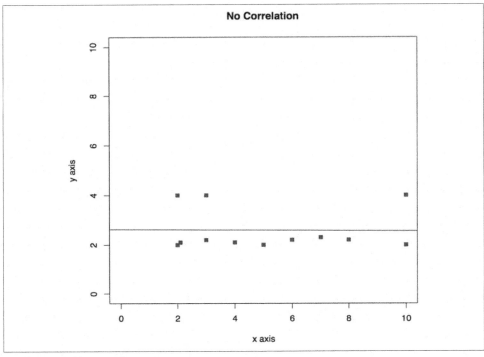

Figure 23-3. No correlation

Pearson Correlation Example

Table 23-1 shows the number of years in college (x) and subsequent yearly income for seven participants (y). Income here is in thousands of dollars, but this fact does not require any changes in our computations.

Table 23-1. Participants' years of college and annual income

Participant	x	y	x^2	y^2	xy
Alex	0	15	0	225	0
Mary	1	18	0	225	15
Jane	3	20	9	400	60
John	4	25	16	625	100
Rafa	4	30	16	900	120
Roger	6	35	36	1225	210
Ken	7	40	36	1225	210
	$\Sigma x = 18$	$\Sigma y = 140$	$\Sigma x^2 = 78$	$\Sigma y^2 = 3600$	$\Sigma xy = 505$

Plugging the values into the formula for the Pearson correlation results in $r = 0.95$, a high correlation.

Data Set for Pearson Correlation

We want to process a generalized data set as a matrix (in CSV format), where the columns correspond to variables (such as x, y, z) and rows correspond to instances. The sample data might look like the following:

```
ROW-1: 1, 1, 3, -1
ROW-2: 2, 2, 1, -2
ROW-3: 3, 3, 8, -3
...
```

POJO Solution for Pearson Correlation

Let data be a two-dimensional array of doubles; then we can compute the pairwise correlation as shown in Example 23-1.

Example 23-1. Computing pairwise correlations

```
1 public void computeAllPairwiseCorrelations(double[][] data) {
2    int numColumns = data[0].length;
3    for(int i=0; i < numColumns; i++) {
4        for(int j=i+1; j < numColumns; j++) {
5            // compute the correlation between the i-th and j-th columns/variables
6            double correlation = computeCorrelation(i, j, data);
7            System.out.println("i="+i+" j="+j+" correlation="+correlation);
8        }
9    }
10 }
```

The Java method to compute the pairwise Pearson correlation might look like Example 23-2.

Example 23-2. Computing Pearson correlation

```
1 public double computePearsonCorrelation(int i, int j, double[][] data) {
2    double x = 0;
3    double y = 0;
4    double xx = 0;
5    double yy = 0;
6    double xy = 0;
7    double n = data.length;
8    for(int row=0; row < data.length; row++) {
9        x += data[row][i];
10       y += data[row][j];
11       xx += Math.pow(data[row][i], 2.0d);
```

```
12          yy += Math.pow(data[row][j], 2.0d);
13          xy += data[row][i] * data[row][j];
14      }
15      double numerator = xy - ((x * y) / n);
16      double denominator1 = xx - (Math.pow(x, 2.0d) / n);
17      double denominator2 = yy - (Math.pow(y, 2.0d) / n);
18      double denominator = Math.sqrt(xx * yy);
19      double correlation = numerator / denominator;
20      return correlation;
21 }
```

POJO Solution Test Drive

To test-drive the Pearson correlation, we use a small sample, as shown in Example 23-3.

Example 23-3. Test-drive of Pearson correlation

```
1 public class PearsonCorrelation {
2      public void computeAllPairwiseCorrelations(double[][] data) {...}
3      public double computeCorrelation(int i, int j, double[][] data) {...}
4
5      public static void main(String[] args) throws Exception {
6          double[][] matrix = new double[][] {
7              {1, 1, 3, -1},
8              {2, 2, 1, -2},
9              {3, 3, 8, -3}
10         };
11         PearsonCorrelation pc = new PearsonCorrelation();
12         pc.computeAllPairwiseCorrelations(matrix);
13         System.exit(0);
14     }
15 }
```

Here is the output of a sample run:

```
$ javac PearsonCorrelation.java
$ java PearsonCorrelation
i=0 j=1 correlation=0.14285714285714285
i=0 j=2 correlation=0.15534244150030002
i=0 j=3 correlation=-0.14285714285714285
i=1 j=2 correlation=0.15534244150030002
i=1 j=3 correlation=-0.14285714285714285
i=2 j=3 correlation=-0.15534244150030002
```

From this output we can conclude that our MapReduce solution has to generate six unique reducer keys.

MapReduce Solution for Pearson Correlation

For our MapReduce solution, we will focus on the map() and reduce() functions.

map() Function for Pearson Correlation

Example 23-4 defines the mapper for the Pearson correlation.

Example 23-4. Pearson correlation: map() function

```
 1 /**
 2  * key is MapReduce generated, ignored here
 3  * value is one row of the matrix
 4  */
 5 map(key, value) {
 6   double[] arr = line.split(",");
 7   int size = arr.length;
 8   for(int i=0; i < size -1; i++) {
 9     for(int j=i+1; j < size; j++) {
10       reducerKey = PairOfLongs(i, j);
11       reducerValue = PairOfDoubles(arr[i], arr[j]);
12       emit(reducerKey, reducerValue);
13     }
14   }
15 }
```

Now let's see what each map() function will generate. map(ROW-1) will generate:

- K2=(0,1) and V2=(1,1)
- K2=(0,2) and V2=(1,3)
- K2=(0,3) and V2=(1,-1)
- K2=(1,2) and V2=(1,3)
- K2=(1,3) and V2=(1,-1)
- K2=(2,3) and V2=(3,-1)

map(ROW-2) generates:

- K2=(0,1) and V2=(2,2)
- K2=(0,2) and V2=(2,1)
- K2=(0,3) and V2=(2,-2)
- K2=(1,2) and V2=(2,1)
- K2=(1,3) and V2=(1,-2)
- K2=(2,3) and V2=(1,-2)

map(ROW-3) generates:

- K2=(0,1) and V2=(3,3)
- K2=(0,2) and V2=(3,8)
- K2=(0,3) and V2=(3,-3)
- K2=(1,2) and V2=(3,8)
- K2=(1,3) and V2=(3,-3)
- K2=(2,3) and V2=(8,-3)

reduce() Function for Pearson Correlation

As mentioned earlier, six unique keys are generated for reducers:

- K2=(0,1) and List_of_V2=[(1,1), (2,2), (3,3)]
- K2=(0,2) and List_of_V2=[(1,3), (2,1), (3,8)]
- K2=(0,3) and List_of_V2=[(1,-1), (2,-2), (3,-3)]
- K2=(1,2) and List_of_V2=[(1,3), (2,1), (3,8)]
- K2=(1,3) and List_of_V2=[(1,-1), (1,-2), (3,-3)]
- K2=(2,3) and List_of_V2=[(3,-1), (1,-2), (8,-3)]

Example 23-5 defines the reducer for the Pearson correlation.

Example 23-5. Pearson correlation: reduce() function

```
1 reduce(PairOfLongs key, Iterable<PairOfDoubles> values) {
2     double x = 0.0d;
3     double y = 0.0d;
4     double xx = 0.0d;
5     double yy = 0.0d;
6     double xy = 0.0d;
7     double n = 0.0d;
8
9     for(PairOfDoubles pair : values) {
10        x += pair.getLeftElement();
11        y += pair.getRightElement();
12        xx += Math.pow(pair.getLeftElement(), 2.0d);
13        yy += Math.pow(pair.getRightElement(), 2.0d);
14        xy += (pair.getLeftElement() * pair.getRightElement());
15        n += 1.0d;
16    }
17
18    PearsonComputation pearson = new PearsonComputation(x, y, xx, yy, xy, n);
19    emit(key, pearson);
20 }
```

Hadoop Implementation Classes

For our Hadoop implementation, we provide a driver, classes that define the `map()` and `reduce()` functions, and some custom data structures and classes (all shown in Table 23-2) to hold intermediate values for the Pearson correlation.

Table 23-2. Classes and data structures for Hadoop implementation of the Pearson correlation

Class name	Description
PearsonCorrelationDriver	A driver program to submit Hadoop jobs
PearsonCorrelationMapper	Defines map()
PearsonCorrelationReducer	Defines reduce()
PearsonCorrelation	Implements Pearson correlation algorithm
HadoopUtil	Defines some utility functions
TestDataGeneration	Generates test data for Pearson correlation
PairOfWritables<L,R>	edu.umd.cloud9.io.pair.PairOfWritables<L,R>

In our Hadoop implementation, we use a `PairOfWritables<L,R>` class, which can be instantiated to generate `PairOfWritables<Long,Long>` and `PairOfWritables<Double,Double>`. `PairOfWritables` (a class representing a pair of `Writables`) is defined in Example 23-6.

Example 23-6. PairOfWritables class

```
1 package edu.umd.cloud9.io.pair;
2
3 import java.io.DataInput;
4 import java.io.DataOutput;
5 import java.io.IOException;
6 import org.apache.hadoop.io.Writable;
7
8 public class PairOfWritables<L extends Writable, R extends Writable>
9     implements Writable {
10
11     private L leftElement;
12     private R rightElement;
13     ...
14 }
```

We use `PairOfWritables.getLeftElement()` and `PairOfWritables.getRightElement()` to retrieve `leftElement` and `rightElement`, respectively.

Spark Solution for Pearson Correlation

In this section we will correlate all vs. all. What does this mean? Let's define a specific problem case first, and then I'll explain all vs. all correlation. Note that you may easily adapt the algorithm presented here to your specific input data (input data formats will certainly differ for different application domains). Let $P = \{P_1, P_2, ..., P_n\}$ be a set of patients (where each patient is identified by a `Patient-ID`). Let each patient have a finite set of biomarker data in the following format:

```
<Gene-ID><,><Reference><,><Patient-ID><,><Gene-Value-As-Double-Data-Type>
```

where:

```
Reference = {
                    r1, // normal
                    r2, // disease
                    r3, // paired
                    r4 // unknown
            }
```

To achieve the correct correlation results, we use only one type of "reference" (which will be used as a filter). For example, two sample biomarker rows might look like:

```
G1234,r3,P100,0.04
G1345,r1,P200,0.90
G2155,r2,P200,0.86
```

Let $G = \{G_1, G_2, ..., G_m\}$ be a set of genes (expressed as `Gene-IDs`). For example, for the RNA gene expression data type the number of unique genes might be about 40,000. Thus, the correlation of all vs. all will generate:

$$40,000 \times 40,000 = 1,600,000,000$$

Pearson correlation data points. But since the correlation of (G_i, G_j) is the same as that of (G_j, G_i), this calculation can be reduced to the following (where $N = 40,000$):

$$\frac{N \times (N-1)}{2}$$

Therefore, for example, if $G = \{G_1, G_2, G_3, G_4, G_5\}$, we will generate the Pearson correlation for the following pairs:

(G_1, G_2)

(G_1, G_3)

(G_1, G_4)

(G_1, G_5)

(G_2, G_3)

(G_2, G_4)

(G_2, G_5)

(G_3, G_4)

(G_3, G_5)

(G_4, G_5)

To generate the correct pair of genes for correlation, we will make sure that:

$$G_i < G_j$$

This will guarantee that we do not generate both (G_i, G_j) and (G_j, G_i).

Input

We will read biomarker data from HDFS. We will assume that the following data exists in HDFS (biomarker data is in text format and identified by text files {b1, b2, b3, ...}:

```
/biomarker/input/b1
/biomarker/input/b2
/biomarker/input/b3
...
```

where each record in these biomarker files has the following format:

```
<Gene-ID><,><Reference><,><Patient-ID><,><Gene-Value-As-Double-Data-Type>
```

Output

Let $G = \{G_1, G_2, ..., G_m\}$ be a set of gene IDs. The goal is to generate the following set of output records for every pair of genes (G_i, G_j):

$(G_i, G_j),$ (pearson-correlation, pValue)

where:

- $G_i < G_j$
- $G_i \in \{G_1, G_2, ..., G_m\}$
- $G_j \in \{G_1, G_2, ..., G_m\}$

- $0.00 \leq$ pValue ≤ 1.00
- $-1.00 \leq$ pearson-correlation $\leq +1.00$

Spark Solution

Our Spark solution is presented as a single Java driver class that uses the rich Spark API (which includes functions such as `filter()` and `cartesian()`) to find the correlation of all vs. all genes. Note that here we present a Spark solution for all genes vs. all genes, but you may apply this technique to any kind of data. The input to our Spark program will be a set of biomarker files and a `reference` (where the value will be in {`r1`, `r2`, `r3`, `r4`}). All biomarker inputs are read from HDFS into a single `JavaRDD` and then partitioned by the following Spark method:

```
public JavaRDD<T> coalesce(int numberOfPartitions)
// Description: return a new RDD that is
// reduced into numberOfPartitions partitions.
```

After the `JavaRDD` is created and partitioned, we filter all biomarkers by `reference` value. For example, if `reference = r2`, then all records that do not have a `reference` value of `r2` are tossed out. We accomplish this using the `JavaRDD.filter()` function. Next we map all filtered records by using the `JavaRDD.mapToPair()` function, which generates the following `JavaPairRDD<K,V>`:

- K = Gene-ID (as a `String`)
- V = `Tuple2<String, Double>(patientID, geneValue)`

The next step is to group all biomarker data by `Gene-ID`, which generates the following `JavaPairRDD` (which we'll call `grouped`):

```
JavaPairRDD<String, Iterable<Tuple2<String,Double>>>
```

where:

- K = `Gene-ID`
- V = `Iterable<Tuple2(patientID, geneValue)>`

To correlate all vs. all genes, we have to create the Cartesian product of grouped by grouped: this will generate all possible combinations of (G_i, G_j). Let's call the result of the Cartesian product `cart`. Before doing any correlation, we will filter the Cartesian product result (`cart`) and keep only pairs where $G_i < G_j$. Filtering is accomplished by:

```
cart.filter(...);
```

After filtering the Cartesian product, we are ready to calculate the Pearson correlation and its associated p-value for all possible combinations of (G_i, G_j). To compute the Pearson correlation for (G_i, G_j), we will make the matrix shown in Table 23-3.

Table 23-3. Matrix to calculate Pearson correlation for G_1 and G_j

	Patient-ID$_1$	Patient-ID$_2$	Patient-ID$_3$	...
G_i	avg(values)	avg(values)	avg(values)	...
G_j	avg(values)	avg(values)	avg(values)	...

Now we are ready to present a complete solution using the Spark API. First, I present the entire structure of the Spark program as a set of high-level steps and then we'll discuss each step in detail.

High-Level Steps

A workflow for the Spark solution is presented in Example 23-7 (see also Figure 23-4).

Example 23-7. Spark solution: high-level steps

```
 1 // Step 1: import required classes and interfaces
 2 /**
 3  * What does all vs. all correlation mean?
 4  *
 5  * Let selected genes be: G = (g1, g2, g3, g4).
 6  * Then all vs. all will correlate between the following pairs of genes:
 7  *
 8  *   (g1, g2)
 9  *   (g1, g3)
10  *   (g1, g4)
11  *   (g2, g3)
12  *   (g2, g4)
13  *   (g3, g4)
14  *
15  * Note that pairs (Ga, Gb) are generated if and only if (Ga < Gb).
16  * Correlation of (Ga, Gb) and (Gb, Ga) is the same, so there is no
17  * need to calculate correlations for duplicate genes.
18  *
19  *   Biomarker record example:
20  *      format:   <geneID><,><r{1,2,3,4}><,><patientID><,><geneValue>
```

```
21  *      example:  37761,r2,p10001,1.287
22  *
23  * @author Mahmoud Parsian
24  *
25  */
26 public class AllVersusAllCorrelation implements java.io.Serializable {
27
28    static boolean smaller(String g1, String g2) {...}
29    static class MutableDouble implements java.io.Serializable {...}
30    static Map<String, MutableDouble> toMap(List<Tuple2<String,Double>> list)
31       {...}
32    static List<String> toListOfString(Path hdfsFile) throws Exception {...}
33    static JavaRDD<String> readBiosets(JavaSparkContext ctx, List<String>
34                                       biosets) {...}
35
36    public static void main(String[] args) throws Exception {
37      // Step 2: handle input parameters
38      // Step 3: create Spark context object (ctx)
39      // Step 4: create list of input files/biomarkers
40      // Step 5: broadcast reference as global shared object,
41      //         which can be accessed from all cluster nodes
42      // Step 6: read all biomarkers from HDFS and create the first RDD
43      // Step 7: filter biomarkers by reference
44      // Step 8: create (Gene-ID, (Patient-ID, Gene-Value)) pairs
45      // Step 9: group biomarkers by Gene-ID
46      // Step 10: create Cartesian product of all genes
47      // Step 11: filter redundant pairs of genes
48      // Step 12: calculate Pearson correlation and p-value
49
50      // done
51      ctx.close();
52      System.exit(0);
53    }
54 }
```

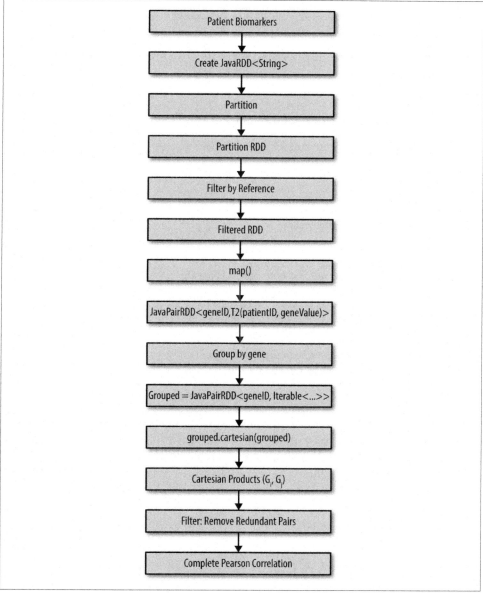

Figure 23-4. Pearson correlation of all vs. all

Step 1: Import required classes and interfaces

This step, shown in Example 23-8, imports the classes and interfaces we need for our solution, which are contained in the following Spark packages:

- `org.apache.spark.api.java` (contains the `JavaPairRDD`, `JavaRDD`, and `JavaS parkContext` classes).

- `org.apache.spark.api.java.function` (contains the `Function` and `PairFunc tion` interfaces).

Example 23-8. Step 1: import required classes and interfaces

```
1 // Step 1: import required classes and interfaces
2 import java.util.Map;
3 import java.util.HashMap;
4 import java.util.List;
5 import java.util.ArrayList;
6 import java.io.BufferedReader;
7 import java.io.InputStreamReader;
8 import scala.Tuple2;
9 import org.apache.spark.api.java.JavaRDD;
10 import org.apache.spark.api.java.JavaPairRDD;
11 import org.apache.spark.api.java.JavaSparkContext;
12 import org.apache.spark.api.java.function.PairFunction;
13 import org.apache.spark.api.java.function.Function;
14 import org.apache.spark.broadcast.Broadcast;
15 import org.apache.hadoop.fs.Path;
16 import org.apache.hadoop.fs.FileSystem;
17 import org.apache.hadoop.fs.FSDataInputStream;
18 import org.apache.hadoop.conf.Configuration;
```

smaller() method

The `smaller()` method, defined in Example 23-9, enables us to avoid generating duplicate pairs of genes. The pairs (g_1, g_2) and (g_2, g_1) will generate the same correlation, so we will generate only a single pair, (g_1, g_2), where g_1 is smaller than g_2. After the Cartesian product of genes is generated (via the `cartesian()` function), we will use the `smaller()` method to filter out the unnecessary pairs of genes.

Example 23-9. smaller() method

```
1 static boolean smaller(String g1, String g2) {
2     if (g1.compareTo(g2) < 0) {
3         return true;
4     }
5     else {
6         return false;
7     }
8 }
```

MutableDouble class

The MutableDouble class, defined in Example 23-10, is used to store all biomarker values for a single patient. This class sums up the double values, keeps the count, and provides a convenient avg() method. This class will hold all values for a single gene and a single patient.

Example 23-10. MutableDouble class

```
 1 static class MutableDouble implements java.io.Serializable {
 2     private double value = 0.0;
 3     private double count = 0.0;
 4
 5     public MutableDouble(double d) {
 6         value = d;
 7         count = 1.0;
 8     }
 9     public MutableDouble(Double d) {
10         if (d == null) {
11             value = 0.0;
12         }
13         else {
14             value = d;
15         }
16         count = 1.0;
17     }
18
19     public void increment(Double d) {
20         if (d == null) {
21             // value does not change
22         }
23         else {
24             value += d;
25         }
26         count++;
27     }
28
29     public void increment(double d) {
30         count++;
31         value += d;
32     }
33
34     public double avg() {
35         return value/count;
36     }
37 }
```

toMap() method

The toMap() method, defined in Example 23-11, converts a list of Tuple2<PatientID, GeneValue> items into a Map<PatientID, MutableDouble> (i.e., it basically aggregates values for all patients for a single gene).

Example 23-11. toMap() method

```
1 static Map<String, MutableDouble> toMap(Iterable<Tuple2<String,Double>> list) {
2    Map<String, MutableDouble> map = new HashMap<String, MutableDouble>();
3    for (Tuple2<String,Double> entry : list) {
4        MutableDouble md = map.get(entry._1);
5        if (md == null) {
6            map.put(entry._1, new MutableDouble(entry._2));
7        }
8        else {
9            md.increment(entry._2);
10       }
11   }
12   return map;
13 }
```

toListOfString() method

The toListOfString() method creates a List<String>, where each element is an HDFS file representing a biomarker file for a patient (each patient may have any number of biomarker files). The input to this method is an HDFS file, which contains all biomarker files involved for the Pearson correlation. To help you understand this method, I provide the following demo:

```
# hadoop fs -cat /biomarkers/biomarkers.txt
/biomarker/input/b1
/biomarker/input/b2
/biomarker/input/b3
/biomarker/input/b4
/biomarker/input/b5
/biomarker/input/b6
/biomarker/input/b7
/biomarker/input/b8
/biomarker/input/b9
/biomarker/input/b10
/biomarker/input/b11
/biomarker/input/b12
/biomarker/input/b13
/biomarker/input/b14
/biomarker/input/b15

# hadoop fs -cat /biomarker/input/b1
g1,r2,p1,1.86
g2,r2,p1,0.74
```

```
g3,r2,p1,1.24
...

# hadoop fs -cat /biomarker/input/b2
g1,r2,p2,2.46
g2,r2,p2,3.24
g3,r1,p2,1.44
...
```

For this example, the result is a List<String>, which contains the following Strings:

```
/biomarker/input/b1
/biomarker/input/b2
...
/biomarker/input/b14
/biomarker/input/b15
```

The method is defined in Example 23-12

Example 23-12. toListOfString() method

```
 1 static List<String> toListOfString(Path hdfsFile) throws Exception {
 2      FSDataInputStream fis = null;
 3      BufferedReader br = null;
 4      FileSystem fs = FileSystem.get(new Configuration());
 5      List<String> list = new ArrayList<String>();
 6      try {
 7          fis = fs.open(hdfsFile);
 8          br = new BufferedReader(new InputStreamReader(fis));
 9          String line = null;
10          while ((line = br.readLine()) != null) {
11              String value = line.trim();
12              list.add(value);
13          }
14      }
15      finally {
16          if (br != null) {
17              br.close();
18          }
19      }
20      return list;
21 }
```

readBiosets() method

The readBiosets() method, defined in Example 23-13, reads all biomarkers (files in HDFS) and generates the first RDD for further processing. Each RDD element is a record of the biomarker file.

Example 23-13. readBiosets() method

```
1 static JavaRDD<String> readBiosets(JavaSparkContext ctx,
2                                     List<String> biosets) {
3     int size = biosets.size();
4     int counter = 0;
5     StringBuilder paths = new StringBuilder();
6     for (String biosetFile : biosets) {
7         counter++;
8         paths.append(biosetFile);
9         if (counter < size) {
10            paths.append(",");
11        }
12    }
13    JavaRDD<String> rdd = ctx.textFile(paths.toString());
14    return rdd;
15 }
```

You may further partition this RDD by using the following `coalesce()` method of the Spark API:

```
public JavaRDD<T> coalesce(int numPartitions)
// Description: return a new RDD that is reduced
// into numPartitions partitions.
```

The question is how to select the right number of partitions for an RDD. The answer depends on the number of cluster nodes, number of cores per server, and amount of RAM. There is no silver-bullet formula for finding the right number of partitions for an RDD (that is, you will need to find and set this for your environment through some trial and error).

Now, with the method definitions out of the way, we can get back to fleshing out the individual steps of the high-level solution presented in Example 23-7.

Step 2: Handle input parameters

This step, shown in Example 23-14, reads two parameters:

- A reference value, which can be any of {r1, r2, r3, r4}
- An HDFS file, which contains the list of all biomarker files (persisted as HDFS files) required for the Pearson correlation

Example 23-14. Step 2: handle input parameters

```
1 // Step 2: handle input parameters
2 if (args.length < 2) {
3     System.err.println(
4         "Usage: AllVersusAllCorrelation <reference> <all-bioset-ids-as-filename>");
5     System.err.println(
```

```
6              "Usage: OneVersusAllCorrelation r2 <all-bioset-ids-as-filename>");
7       System.exit(1);
8 }
9 final String reference = args[1]; // {"r1", "r2", "r3", "r4"}
10 final String biomarkersFileName = args[2];
```

Step 3: Create a Spark context object

This step creates a JavaSparkContext object. An instance of JavaSparkContext can be created in many different ways; for example, the SparkUtil class provides a few convenient methods to do so. SparkUtil's methods are shown in Example 23-15, and the Spark context object is created in Example 23-16.

Example 23-15. SparkUtil methods for creating JavaSparkContext

```
1 public class SparkUtil {
2    /**
3     * Create a JavaSparkContext object
4     *
5     * @param appName is an application name
6     * @return a JavaSparkContext
7     *
8     */
9    public static JavaSparkContext createJavaSparkContext(String appName)
10        throws Exception {...}
11
12    /**
13     * Create a JavaSparkContext object from a given Spark master URL
14     *
15     * @param sparkMasterURL Spark master URL as
16     *     "spark://<spark-master-host-name>:7077"
17     * @param description program description
18     * @return a JavaSparkContext
19     *
20     */
21    public static JavaSparkContext
22        createJavaSparkContext(String sparkMasterURL, String description)
23        throws Exception {...}
24 }
```

Example 23-16. Step 3: create a Spark context object

```
1    // Step 3: create Spark context object
2    JavaSparkContext ctx = SparkUtil.createJavaSparkContext("pearson-correlation");
```

Step 4: Create list of input files/biomarkers

This step, shown in Example 23-17, reads the file identified by `biomarkersFileName`, a text HDFS file that contains all input biomarker files (one biomarker file per line) for our Pearson correlation.

Example 23-17. Step 4: create list of input files/biomarkers

```
1    Step 4: create list of input files/biomarkers
2    List<String> list = toListOfString(new Path(biomarkersFileName));
```

Step 5: Broadcast reference as global shared object

Since the `reference` value (`{r1, r2, r3, r4}`) is used for filtering RDD elements, it should be broadcasted to all cluster nodes. In Spark, to broadcast (as a read-only shared object) a data structure, we use the `Broadcast` class as follows.

- To broadcast a shared data structure of type `T`:
  ```
  T t = <create-object-of-type-T>;
  final Broadcast<T> broadcastT = ctx.broadcast(t);
  ```
- To read/access a broadcasted shared data structure of type `T`:
  ```
  T t = broadcastT.value();
  ```

In MapReduce/Hadoop, you can broadcast a shared data structure to the `map()` or `reduce()` functions by using Hadoop's `Configuration` object. You use `Configuration.set(...)` to broadcast, and `Configuration.get(...)` to read/access broadcasted objects. Spark's API is much richer than Hadoop's API, as it allows you to broadcast any type of data structure. The implementation of this step is shown in Example 23-18.

Example 23-18. Step 5: broadcast reference as global shared object

```
1    // Step 5: broadcast reference as global shared object
2    //         that can be accessed from all cluster nodes
3    final Broadcast<String> REF = ctx.broadcast(reference); // "r2"
```

Step 6: Read all biomarkers from HDFS and create the first RDD

This step, shown in Example 23-19, reads all biomarker files and creates a single `JavaRDD<String>`, which can be partitioned further through the following method:

```
JavaRDD<T> coalesce(int numPartitions)
```

Example 23-19. Step 6: read all biomarkers from HDFS and create the first RDD

```
1 // Step 6: read all biomarkers from HDFS and create the first RDD
2 JavaRDD<String> biosets = readBiosets(ctx, list);
3 biosets.saveAsTextFile("/output/1");
```

Sample output of this step is provided here for debugging purposes:

```
# hadoop fs -cat /output/1/*
g1,r2,p1,1.86
g2,r2,p1,0.74
g3,r2,p1,1.24
g4,r1,p1,2.44
g5,r2,p1,1.69
g6,r2,p1,0.93
g7,r2,p1,1.44
g8,r2,p1,2.11
g1,r2,p2,2.46
g2,r2,p2,3.24
...
```

Note that the methods `JavaRDD.saveAsTextFile()` and `JavaPairRDD.saveAsText File()` are not required for our Spark solution (they save the RDDs in HDFS). These methods are provided for debugging and to enhance your understanding of the process.

Step 7: Filter biomarkers by reference

Spark provides a very simple and powerful API for filtering RDDs. To filter elements, we just need to implement a `filter()` function: it returns `true` for the records you want to keep, and `false` for the records you want to toss out. See Example 23-20.

Example 23-20. Step 7: filter biomarkers by reference

```
1  // JavaRDD<T> filter(Function<T,Boolean> f)
2  // Return a new RDD containing only the elements that satisfy a predicate.
3  JavaRDD<String> filtered = biosets.filter(new Function<String,Boolean>() {
4      public Boolean call(String record) {
5          String ref = REF.value();
6          String[] tokens = record.split(",");
7          if (ref.equals(tokens[1])) {
8              return true; // do return these records
9          }
10         else {
11             return false; // do not return these records
12         }
13     }
14 });
15 filtered.saveAsTextFile("/output/2");
```

Sample output of this step is provided for debugging purposes; note that only r2 references appear in the output (all other references {r1, r3, r4} are dropped from the resulting RDD):

```
# hadoop fs -cat /output/2/*
g1,r2,p1,1.86
g2,r2,p1,0.74
g3,r2,p1,1.24
g5,r2,p1,1.69
g6,r2,p1,0.93
g7,r2,p1,1.44
g8,r2,p1,2.11
g1,r2,p2,2.46
g2,r2,p2,3.24
g4,r2,p2,2.11
g5,r2,p2,1.69
g6,r2,p2,1.25
...
```

Step 8: Create (Gene-ID, (Patient-ID, Gene-Value)) pairs

This step, shown in Example 23-21, implements a map() function that transforms:

```
<Gene-ID><,><reference><,><Patient-ID><,><Gene-Value>
```

into a (K, V) pair, where:

```
K = Gene-ID
V = Tuple2<Patient-ID, Gene-Value>
```

Note that from this step onward, reference is not needed.

Example 23-21. Step 8: create (Gene-ID, (Patient-ID, Gene-Value)) pairs

```
1    // Step 8: create (Gene-ID, (Patient-ID, Gene-Value)) pairs
2    // PairMapFunction<T, K, V>
3    // T => Tuple2<K, V> = Tuple2<geneID, Tuple2<patientID, geneValue>>
4    //
5    JavaPairRDD<String,Tuple2<String,Double>> pairs =
         filtered.mapToPair(new PairFunction<
6       String,                     // T
7       String,                     // K = g1234 (a Gene-ID)
8       Tuple2<String,Double>       // V = <Patient-ID, Gene-Value>
9       >() {
10      public Tuple2<String,Tuple2<String,Double>> call(String rec) {
11          String[] tokens = rec.split(",");
12          // tokens[0] = 1234
13          // tokens[1] = 2 (this is a ref in {"1", "2", "3", "4"}
14          // tokens[2] = patientID
15          // tokens[3] = value
16          Tuple2<String,Double> V =
17              new Tuple2<String,Double>(tokens[2], Double.valueOf(tokens[3]));
```

```
18              return new Tuple2<String,Tuple2<String,Double>>(tokens[0], V);
19          }
20      });
21      pairs.saveAsTextFile("/output/3");
```

Sample output of this step is provided for debugging purposes:

```
# hadoop fs -cat /output/3/*
(g1,(p1,1.86))
(g2,(p1,0.74))
(g3,(p1,1.24))
(g5,(p1,1.69))
(g6,(p1,0.93))
(g7,(p1,1.44))
(g8,(p1,2.11))
(g1,(p2,2.46))
(g2,(p2,3.24))
...
```

Step 9: Group by gene

This step, shown in Example 23-22, groups data by Gene-ID. The result of this grouping is a new RDD in the format:

```
JavaPairRDD<String, Iterable<Tuple2<String,Double>>>
```

where:

```
K = Gene-ID
V = Iterable<Tuple2<Patient-ID, Gene-Value>>
```

Example 23-22. Step 9: group by gene

```
1   // Step 9: group biomarkers by Gene-ID
2   JavaPairRDD<String, Iterable<Tuple2<String,Double>>>  grouped =
3       pairs.groupByKey();
4   grouped.saveAsTextFile("/output/4");
5   // grouped = (K, V)
6   //     where
7   //          K = Gene-ID
8   //          V = Iterable<Tuple2<Patient-ID,Gene-Value>>
9   grouped.saveAsTextFile("/output/5");
```

Partial sample output of this step is provided for debugging purposes; the output is formatted to fit the page:

```
# hadoop fs -cat /output/5/*
(g1,[(p1,1.86), (p1,1.76), (p1,1.16), (p3,1.06),
     (p1,1.86), (p2,1.46), (p2,1.33), (p2,2.46),
     (p2,2.46), (p2,1.33), (p3,2.61), (p1,2.86),
     (p2,2.06), (p2,1.43)])
(g2,[(p2,3.24), (p2,1.24), (p2,2.0), (p3,1.55),
```

```
            (p1,1.74), (p2,3.2), (p2,2.5), (p1,0.74),
            (p1,2.84), (p1,1.33), (p3,1.24), (p3,2.1),
            (p1,2.74), (p2,2.24), (p2,2.0)])
      ...
```

Step 10: Create Cartesian product of all genes

To perform an all genes vs. all genes correlation, we have to create a Cartesian product of all genes. We accomplish this through the `JavaPairRDD.cartesian()` function, as shown in Example 23-23.

Example 23-23. Step 10: Create Cartesian product of all genes

```
1    // Step 10: create Cartesian product of all genes
2    // <U> JavaPairRDD<T,U> cartesian(JavaRDDLike<U,?> other)
3    // Return the Cartesian product of this RDD and another one;
4    // that is, the RDD of all pairs of elements (a, b)
5    // where a is in this and b is in other.
6    JavaPairRDD< Tuple2<String, Iterable<Tuple2<String,Double>>>,
7                 Tuple2<String, Iterable<Tuple2<String,Double>>>
8           > cart = grouped.cartesian(grouped);
9    cart.saveAsTextFile("/output/6");
10   // cart =
11   //      (g1, g1), (g1, g2), (g1, g3), (g1, g4)
12   //      (g2, g1), (g2, g2), (g2, g3), (g2, g4)
13   //      (g3, g1), (g3, g2), (g3, g3), (g3, g4)
14   //      (g4, g1), (g4, g2), (g4, g3), (g4, g4)
```

Step 11: Filter redundant pairs of genes

Let g1 and g2 be two genes; since the Pearson correlation for (g1, g2) is the same as for (g2, g1), to reduce computation time we will filter duplicate pairs (see Example 23-24). We keep the gene pairs of (g1, g2) if and only if g1 < g2.

Example 23-24. Step 11: filter redundant pairs of genes

```
1    // Step 11: filter redundant pairs of genes
2    // Keep pairs (g1, g2) if and only if (g1 < g2).
3    // After filtering, we will have:
4    // filtered2 =
5    //      (g1, g2), (g1, g3), (g1, g4)
6    //      (g2, g3), (g2, g4)
7    //      (g3, g4)
8    //
9    // JavaRDD<T> filter(Function<T,Boolean> f)
10   // Return a new RDD containing only the elements that satisfy a predicate.
11   JavaPairRDD<Tuple2<String, Iterable<Tuple2<String,Double>>>,
12        Tuple2<String, Iterable<Tuple2<String,Double>>>> filtered2 =
13        cart.filter(new Function<
14        Tuple2<Tuple2<String, Iterable<Tuple2<String,Double>>>,
```

```
15                Tuple2<String, Iterable<Tuple2<String,Double>>>
16            >,
17          Boolean>() {
18       public Boolean call(Tuple2<
19          Tuple2<String, Iterable<Tuple2<String,Double>>>,
20          Tuple2<String, Iterable<Tuple2<String,Double>>>> pair) {
21          // pair._1 = Tuple2<String, Iterable<Tuple2<String,Double>>>
22          // pair._2 = Tuple2<String, Iterable<Tuple2<String,Double>>>
23          if (smaller(pair._1._1, pair._2._1)) {
24             return true; // do return these records
25          }
26          else {
27             return false; // do not return these records
28          }
29       }
30    });
31    filtered2.saveAsTextFile("/output/7");
```

Partial output of this step is displayed here for debugging purposes. The output is formatted to fit the page:

```
# hadoop fs -cat /output/7/*

...
((g1,[(p2,2.46), (p2,2.46), (p2,1.33), (p3,2.61), (p1,2.86),
     (p2,2.06), (p2,1.43), (p1,1.86), (p1,1.76), (p1,1.16),
     (p3,1.06), (p1,1.86), (p2,1.46), (p2,1.33)]),
 (g2,[(p2,3.24), (p2,1.24), (p2,2.0), (p3,1.55), (p1,1.74),
     (p2,3.2), (p1,0.74), (p1,2.84), (p1,1.33), (p3,1.24),
     (p3,2.1), (p1,2.74), (p2,2.24), (p2,2.0), (p2,2.5)])
)
...
((g3,[(p1,1.24), (p1,1.24), (p1,1.64), (p1,2.66),
     (p3,2.22), (p1,1.24)]),
 (g4,[(p2,2.11), (p2,2.11), (p2,1.77), (p2,2.01),
     (p3,2.87), (p2,1.11), (p2,1.77), (p2,1.78)])
)
...
```

Step 12: Calculate Pearson correlation and p-value

Now our generated pairs are aggregated with proper data, and it is time to perform the Pearson correlation and find its associated p-value (see Example 23-25). If there is not sufficient data for correlation, then we return Double.NaN for the correlation and p-value. We implement the Pearson correlation using the Apache Commons Math3 package (provided in the following sections).

Example 23-25. Step 12: calculate Pearson correlation and p-value

```
1    // Step 12: calculate Pearson correlation and p-value
2    // Next, iterate through all mapped values
3    // JavaPairRDD<String, List<Tuple2<String,Double>>> mappedvalues
4    // Create (K,V), where
5    //      K = Tuple2<String,String>(g1, g2)
6    //      V = Tuple2<Double,Double>(corr, pValue)
7    //
8    JavaPairRDD<Tuple2<String,String>,Tuple2<Double,Double>> finalresult =
9            filtered2.mapToPair(new PairFunction<
10              Tuple2<Tuple2<String,Iterable<Tuple2<String,Double>>>,
11                    Tuple2<String,Iterable<Tuple2<String,Double>>>>, // input
12              Tuple2<String,String>,                                 // K
13              Tuple2<Double,Double>                                  // V
14          >() {
15        public Tuple2<Tuple2<String,String>,Tuple2<Double,Double>>
16          call(Tuple2<Tuple2<String,Iterable<Tuple2<String,Double>>>,
17                 Tuple2<String,Iterable<Tuple2<String,Double>>>> t) {
18        Tuple2<String,Iterable<Tuple2<String,Double>>> g1 = t._1;
19        Tuple2<String,Iterable<Tuple2<String,Double>>> g2 = t._2;
20
21        Map<String, MutableDouble> g1map = toMap(g1._2);
22        Map<String, MutableDouble> g2map = toMap(g2._2);
23        // now perform a correlation(one, other)
24        // make sure we order the values accordingly by Patient-ID
25        // each Patient-ID may have one or more values
26        List<Double> x = new ArrayList<Double>();
27        List<Double> y = new ArrayList<Double>();
28        for (Map.Entry<String, MutableDouble> g1Entry : g1map.entrySet()) {
29            String g1PatientID = g1Entry.getKey();
30            MutableDouble g2MD = g2map.get(g1PatientID);
31            if (g2MD != null) {
32                // both one and other for Patient-ID have values
33                x.add(g1Entry.getValue().avg());
34                y.add(g2MD.avg());
35            }
36        }
37
38        System.out.println("x="+x);
39        System.out.println("y="+y);
40        // K = pair of genes
41        Tuple2<String,String> K = new Tuple2<String,String>(g1._1,g2._1);
42        if (x.size() < 3) {
43            // not enough data to perform correlation
44            return new Tuple2<Tuple2<String,String>,Tuple2<Double,Double>>
45                (K, new Tuple2<Double,Double>(Double.NaN, Double.NaN));
46
47        }
48        else {
49            // Pearson
```

```
50              double correlation = Pearson.getCorrelation(x, y);
51              double pValue = Pearson.getpValue(correlation, (double) x.size() );
52              return new Tuple2<Tuple2<String,String>,Tuple2<Double,Double>>
53                (K, new Tuple2<Double,Double>(correlation, pValue));
54          }
55      }
56    });
57    finalresult.saveAsTextFile("/output/corr");
```

The complete output of the final step is provided here for debugging purposes. Note that if two genes do have not enough data to correlate, then for lack of a proper value we emit Double.NaN:

```
# hadoop fs -cat /output/corr/part*
((g1,g2),(-0.5600331663273436,0.6215767617117369))
((g1,g3),(NaN,NaN))
((g1,g4),(NaN,NaN))
((g1,g5),(-0.02711004213333685,0.9827390963782845))
((g1,g6),(0.19358340989347553,0.8759779754044315))
((g1,g7),(-0.8164277145788058,0.3919024816433061))
((g1,g8),(0.1671231007563918,0.8931045335800389))
((g1,g9),(0.6066217061857698,0.5850485651167254))
((g2,g3),(NaN,NaN))
((g2,g4),(NaN,NaN))
((g2,g5),(-0.8129831655334596,0.3956841419099777))
((g2,g6),(-0.9212118275674606,0.25440121369269475))
((g2,g7),(0.9356247601371344,0.22967428006843038))
((g2,g8),(-0.9104130933946509,0.271527771868302))
((g2,g9),(-0.9983543136507176,0.036528196595012385))
((g3,g4),(NaN,NaN))
((g3,g5),(NaN,NaN))
((g3,g6),(NaN,NaN))
((g3,g7),(NaN,NaN))
((g3,g8),(NaN,NaN))
((g3,g9),(NaN,NaN))
((g4,g5),(NaN,NaN))
((g4,g6),(NaN,NaN))
((g4,g7),(NaN,NaN))
((g4,g8),(NaN,NaN))
((g4,g9),(NaN,NaN))
((g5,g6),(0.9754751741958164,0.1412829282172836))
((g5,g7),(-0.5551020210096935,0.625358421978409))
((g5,g8),(0.9810429471659294,0.12415637004167612))
((g5,g9),(0.7782528977513095,0.4322123385049901))
((g6,g7),(-0.7245714063087034,0.4840754937611247))
((g6,g8),(0.9996381540187659,0.017126558175602602))
((g6,g9),(0.8973843455132996,0.2909294102877069))
((g7,g8),(-0.7057703774748613,0.5012020519367326))
((g7,g9),(-0.9543282445223156,0.19314608347341866))
((g8,g9),(0.885190414128154,0.30805596846331396))
```

Pearson Correlation Wrapper Class

Pearson is a wrapper class, defined in Example 23-26, that provides two methods: getCorrelation() and getpValue(). The underlying implementation uses the Apache Commons Math3 package (*http://bit.ly/ap-com-math*).

Example 23-26. Pearson wrapper class

```
 1 import java.util.List;
 2 import java.util.Arrays;
 3 import org.apache.commons.math3.distribution.TDistribution;
 4 import org.apache.commons.math3.stat.correlation.PearsonsCorrelation;
 5 /**
 6  * Class for calculating the Pearson correlation coefficient and p-value
 7  *
 8  */
 9 public class Pearson {
10
11     final static PearsonsCorrelation PC = new PearsonsCorrelation();
12
13     public static double getCorrelation(List<Double> X, List<Double> Y) {
14         double[] xArray = toDoubleArray(X);
15         double[] yArray = toDoubleArray(Y);
16         double corr = PC.correlation(xArray, yArray);
17         return corr;
18     }
19
20     private static double[] toDoubleArray(List<Double> list) {
21         if (list == null) {
22             return null;
23         }
24         double[] arr = new double[list.size()];
25         for (int i=0; i < list.size(); i++) {
26             arr[i] = list.get(i);
27         }
28         return arr;
29     }
30
31     public static double getpValue(final double corr, final int n) {
32         return getpValue(corr, (double) n);
33     }
34
35     public static double getpValue(final double corr, final double n) {
36         double t = Math.abs(corr * Math.sqrt( (n-2.0) / (1.0 - (corr * corr)) ));
37         System.out.println(" t =" + t);
38         TDistribution tdist = new TDistribution(n-2);
39         double pValue = 2* (1.0 - tdist.cumulativeProbability(t));
40         return pValue;
41     }
42 }
```

Testing the Pearson Class

In Example 23-27, we test our wrapper class.

Example 23-27. Testing the Pearson wrapper class

```
 1 import java.util.List;
 2 import java.util.Arrays;
 3 public class TestPearson {
 4
 5    public static void main(String[] args) {
 6        test(args);
 7    }
 8
 9    /**
10     * test/debug
11     */
12    public static void test(String[] args) {
13          // index                  0   1   2   3   4
14       List<Double> X = Arrays.asList(2.0, 4.0, 45.0, 6.0, 7.0);
15       List<Double> Y = Arrays.asList(23.0, 5.0, 54.0, 6.0, 7.0);
16       double n = X.size(); // 5.0;
17       double corr = Pearson.getCorrelation(X, Y);
18       double pValue = Pearson.getpValue(corr, n);
19       System.out.println("corr =" + corr);
20       System.out.println("pValue =" + pValue);
21    }
22 }
```

Pearson Correlation Using R

Example 23-28 shows how to use the R language for Pearson correlation. You may use this example to compare our Java implementation with R.

Example 23-28. Pearson correlation using R

```
 1 > x=c(2,4,45,6,7)
 2 > y=c(23,5,54,6,7)
 3 > cor.test(x,y)
 4
 5 Pearson's product-moment correlation
 6
 7 data:  x and y
 8 t = 3.6026, df = 3, p-value = 0.03669
 9 alternative hypothesis: true correlation is not equal to 0
10 95 percent confidence interval:
11  0.09266873 0.99352355
12 sample estimates:
13       cor
14 0.9012503
```

YARN Script to Run Spark Program

To run our Spark program, *AllVersusAllCorrelation*, in YARN, we use the shell script shown:

```
# cat run_all_vs_all.sh
#!/bin/bash
SPARK_HOME=/usr/local/spark-1.0.0
# app jar:
BOOK_HOME=/mp/data-algorithms-book
APP_JAR=$BOOK_HOME/dist/data_algorithms_book.jar
prog=org.dataalgorithms.chap23.spark.AllVersusAllCorrelation
reference=r2
biomarkers=/mp/biomarkers.txt
$SPARK_HOME/bin/spark-submit --class $prog \
    --master yarn-cluster \
    --num-executors 12 \
    --driver-memory 3g \
    --executor-memory 7g \
    --executor-cores 12 \
    $APP_JAR  $reference  $biomarkers
```

Spearman Correlation Using Spark

To calculate the Spearman correlation instead of Pearson, you just need to replace the following two lines in step 12 ("Step 12: Calculate Pearson correlation and p-value" on page 539):

```
// Pearson
double correlation = Pearson.getCorrelation(x, y);
double pValue = Pearson.getpValue(correlation, (double) x.size() );
```

with:

```
// Spearman
double correlation = Spearman.getCorrelation(x, y);
double pValue = Spearman.getpValue(correlation, (double) x.size() );
```

and then use the Spearman wrapper class provided in the next section.

Spearman Correlation Wrapper Class

The Spearman wrapper class, defined in Example 23-29, provides two methods: get Correlation() and getpValue(). The underlying implementation uses the Apache Commons Math3 package.

Example 23-29. Spearman wrapper class

```
1 import java.util.Arrays;
2 import java.util.List;
```

```
 3 import java.util.ArrayList;
 4 import org.apache.commons.math3.distribution.TDistribution;
 5 import org.apache.commons.math3.stat.correlation.SpearmansCorrelation;
 6
 7 /**
 8  * Class for calculating Spearman's rank correlation between two vectors.
 9  *
10  * @author Mahmoud Parsian
11  *
12  */
13 public class Spearman {
14
15     final static SpearmansCorrelation SC = new SpearmansCorrelation();
16
17     public static double getCorrelation(List<Double> X, List<Double> Y) {
18         double[] xArray = toDoubleArray(X);
19         double[] yArray = toDoubleArray(Y);
20         double corr = SC.correlation(xArray, yArray);
21         return corr;
22     }
23
24     public static double getpValue(double corr, double n) {
25         double t = Math.abs(corr * Math.sqrt( (n-2.0) / (1.0 - (corr * corr)) ));
26         System.out.println("    t =" + t);
27         TDistribution tdist = new TDistribution(n-2);
28         double pValue = 2.0 * (1.0 - tdist.cumulativeProbability(t));
29         return pValue;
30     }
31
32     static double[] toDoubleArray(List<Double> list) {
33         double[] arr = new double[list.size()];
34         for (int i=0; i < list.size(); i++) {
35             arr[i] = list.get(i);
36         }
37         return arr;
38     }
39 }
```

Testing the Spearman Correlation Wrapper Class

Example 23-30 tests Spearman's wrapper class.

Example 23-30. Testing the Spearman wrapper class

```
1 import java.util.Arrays;
2 import java.util.List;
3 public class TestSpearman {
4
5     public static void main(String[] args) {
6         test(args);
7     }
```

```
 8
 9     public static void test(String[] args) {
10         //                            1    2    3    4    5
11         List<Double> X = Arrays.asList(2.0, 4.0, 45.0, 6.0, 7.0);
12         List<Double> Y = Arrays.asList(23.0, 5.0, 54.0, 6.0, 7.0);
13         double n = X.size(); // 5.0;
14         double corr = getCorrelation(X, Y);
15         double pValue = getpValue(corr, n);
16         System.out.println("corr   =" + corr);
17         System.out.println("pValue =" + pValue);
18         //                             1     2     3     4     5
19         List<Double> X2 = Arrays.asList(12.0, 14.0, 45.0, 6.0, 17.0);
20         List<Double> Y2 = Arrays.asList(3.0, 5.0, 15.0, 16.0, 17.0);
21         double n2 = X2.size(); // 5.0;
22         double corr2 = getCorrelation(X2, Y2);
23         double pValue2 = getpValue(corr2, n2);
24         System.out.println("corr2   =" + corr2);
25         System.out.println("pValue2 =" + pValue2);
26     }
27 }
```

This chapter provided two scalable distributed solutions (MapReduce/Hadoop and Spark) for performing Pearson correlations, which are very important in clinical applications. We also saw how to calculate the Spearman correlation using our Spark solution. The next chapter provides distributed algorithms for DNA base counting, which is used in genome algorithms and applications.

## CHAPTER 24

DNA Base Count

This chapter provides four solutions for DNA base counting:

- A MapReduce/Hadoop solution using FASTA format
- A MapReduce/Hadoop solution using FASTQ format
- A Spark solution using FASTA format
- A Spark solution using FASTQ format

The purpose of this chapter is to count DNA[1] bases. Human DNA's code is written using only four letters—A, C, T, and G—and when we cannot recognize the code, we label it as N. The meaning of this DNA code lies in the sequence of the letters A, T, C, and G in the same way that the meaning of a word in the English language lies in the sequence of alphabet letters (A–Z).

In this chapter we'll find the frequencies (or percentages) of A, T, C, G, and N in a given set of DNA sequences. We'll also provide custom record readers for Hadoop's input files.

So what do the letters *ATCG* stand for in the context of DNA? They refer to four of the nitrogenous bases associated with DNA:

---

1 Deoxyribonucleic acid (DNA) is a molecule that encodes the genetic instructions used in the development and functioning of all known living organisms and many viruses. DNA is a nucleic acid; alongside proteins and carbohydrates, nucleic acids compose the three major macromolecules essential for all known forms of life. Most DNA molecules consist of two biopolymer strands coiled around each other to form a double helix. The two DNA strands are known as polynucleotides since they are composed of simpler units called nucleotides. Each nucleotide is composed of a nitrogen-containing nucleobase—either guanine (G), adenine (A), thymine (T), or cytosine (C)—as well as a monosaccharide sugar called deoxyribose and a phosphate group. (Source: Wikipedia (*http://en.wikipedia.org/wiki/DNA*).)

- A = Adenine
- T = Thymine
- C = Cytosine
- G = Guanine

For example, ACGGGTACGAAT is a very small DNA sequence. DNA sequences can be huge.[2] DNA base counting for our example will generate the results shown in Table 24-1.

Table 24-1. DNA base count example

Base	Count
a	4
t	2
c	2
g	4
n	0

DNA sequences can be represented in many different formats, including the popular FASTA and FASTQ text-based formats, which are what we'll use in our solutions. Note that Hadoop's default record reader reads records line by line, and therefore we cannot use Hadoop's default record reader for reading files in FASTQ format, where a record is made up of a sequence of four lines. We need to plug in (inject custom record readers) `FastaInputFormat` and `FastqInputFormat` to read FASTA and FASTQ file formats, respectively. If we do not use custom record readers, we have to toss out the unneeded records (lines) in our DNA base counting, which is easy to do for the FASTA format, but not for FASTQ.

FASTA Format

A sequence file in FASTA format can contain several sequences. Each sequence in FASTA format begins with a single-line description, followed by one or many lines of sequence data. The description line must begin with a greater-than (>) symbol in the first column.

---

2 Haploid human genomes (contained in egg and sperm cells) consists of three billion DNA base pairs, while diploid genomes (found in somatic cells) have twice the DNA content." (Source: Wikipedia (*http://bit.ly/h_sapiens_genome*).)

FASTA Format Example

The following is an example sequence in FASTA format (this file has four sequences and is not case-sensitive:

```
# cat test_fasta.fasta
>seq1
cGTAaccaataaaaaaacaagcttaacctaattc
>seq2
agcttagTTTGGatctggccggg
>seq3
gcggatttactcCCCCCAAAAANNagggagagcccagataaatggagtctgtgcgtccaca
gaattcgcacca
AATAAAACCTCACCCAT
agagcccagaatttactcCCC
>seq4
gcggatttactcaggggagagcccagGGataaatggagtctgtgcgtccaca
gaattcgcacca
```

FASTQ Format

FASTQ is a text-based format for storing both a biological sequence (usually a nucleotide sequence) and its corresponding quality scores. Both the sequence letter and quality score are encoded with a single ASCII character for brevity. A FASTQ file normally uses four lines per sequence, as follows:

- Line 1 begins with an @ character and is followed by a sequence identifier and an optional description.

- Line 2 is the raw sequence letters (e.g., A, T, C, G).

- Line 3 begins with a + character and is optionally followed by the same sequence identifier (and any description) again.

- Line 4 encodes the quality values for the sequence in line 2, and must contain the same number of symbols as there are letters in the sequence.

FASTQ Format Example

A FASTQ file containing a single DNA sequence might look like this:

```
@SEQ_ID
GATTTGGGGTTCAAAGCAGTATCGATCAAATAGTAAATCCATTTGTTCAACTCACAGTTT
+
!''*((((***+))%%%++)(%%%%).1***-+*''))**55CCF>>>>>>CCCCCCC65
```

MapReduce Solution: FASTA Format

For DNA base counting, we use a mapper, a reducer, and a custom FASTA format reader (we implement the FASTA reader by injecting the `FastaInputFormat` class in to the `Job.setInputFormatClass()` method).

Reading FASTA Files

How do we instruct the MapReduce/Hadoop framework to read FASTA data? The default reader in Hadoop reads input records line by line, but a FASTA record may span many lines. Hadoop provides a plug-in framework for "input format" and "record reader." We develop two custom plug-in classes, `FastaInputFormat` and `Fas taRecordReader`, to enable us to read the FASTA format. In Hadoop, the default input format is provided by the `TextInputFormat` class. Our custom class `FastaInput Format` extends this class and overrides two methods: `createRecordReader()` and `isSplitable()`. The overridden `createRecordReader()` method returns a new custom record reader called `FastaRecordReader`.

MapReduce FASTA Solution: map()

To find the count of DNA bases, the `map()` function will get a FASTA record, which can be one or more lines of DNA sequences. The `map()` function will then tokenize each line and count the bases. To make our mapper more efficient, we will not `emit(letter, 1)` for each letter, but rather we will emit a total for each base by using a hash table (`Map<Character, Long>`). Finally, by using Hadoop's `cleanup()` method, we will iterate the hash table and `emit(letter, countOfLetter)`. The hash table is a very efficient solution, since the number of keys is limited to the very small number of DNA letters. Furthermore, this smart `map()` algorithm reduces the network traffic by emitting only the minimum number of (`letter, countOfLetter`) pairs to the MapReduce framework. The mapper class, `FastaCountBaseMapper`, will have the structure shown in Example 24-1.

Example 24-1. FastaCountBaseMapper class

```
 1 public class FastaCountBaseMapper ... {
 2
 3    Map<Character, Long> dnaBasesCounter = null;
 4
 5    // this function is called once at the beginning of the map task
 6    setup() {
 7        dnaBasesCounter = new HashMap<Character, Long>();
 8    }
 9
10    map(Object key, String value) {
11        ...
```

```
12    }
13
14    // called once at the end of the map task
15    cleanup() {
16        // now iterate the baseCounter and emit <key, value>
17        for (Map.Entry<Character, Long> entry : dnaBaseCounter.entrySet()) {
18            emit(entry.getKey(), entry.getValue());
19        }
20    }
21 }
```

The map() function is listed in Example 24-2.

Example 24-2. DNA base count: map() function

```
1 /**
2 * @param key is the key generated by Hadoop (ignored here)
3 * @param value is one line of input for a given document
4 */
5 map(Object key, String value) {
6    // fasta is a string composed of many DNA-seq lines
7    String fasta = value.trim().toLowerCase();
8    String[] lines = fasta.split("[\\r\\n]+");
9    for (int i=1; i < lines.length; i++) {
10       char[] array = lines[i].toCharArray();
11       for(char c : array) {
12          Long v = dnaBaseCounter.get(c);
13          if (v == null) {
14             dnaBaseCounter.put(c, 1);
15          }
16          else {
17             dnaBaseCounter.put(c, v+1);
18          }
19       }
20    }
21 }
```

MapReduce FASTA Solution: reduce()

Since the number of letters in the DNA alphabet is very limited, we might just set the number of reducers to 5 (one for every DNA letter). The reducer is almost identical to the classic word count reducer; it just sums up the counters for each DNA letter (see Example 24-3).

Example 24-3. DNA base count: reduce() function

```
1 /**
2 * @param key is the unique DNA letter generated by the mapper
3 * @param value is a list of integers (partial count of a unique word)
4 */
```

```
 5 reduce(String key, List<long> value) {
 6    long sum = 0;
 7    for (int count : value) {
 8        sum += count;
 9    }
10    emit(key, sum);
11 }
```

Sample Run

This section includes a sample run and the generated output of our Hadoop FASTA format solution.

Log of sample run

Here is the log output from a sample run of our Hadoop solution (edited and formatted to fit the page):

```
# ./run.sh
...
Deleted hdfs://localhost:9000/dna-base-count/output
13/03/15 09:16:22 INFO CountBaseDriver: inputDir=/dna-base-count/input
13/03/15 09:16:22 INFO CountBaseDriver: outputDir=/dna-base-count/output
...
13/03/15 09:16:24 INFO mapred.JobClient: map 0% reduce 0%
...
13/03/15 09:17:53 INFO mapred.JobClient: map 100% reduce 100%
...
13/03/15 09:17:58 INFO mapred.JobClient: Map-Reduce Framework
13/03/15 09:17:58 INFO mapred.JobClient: Map input records=7
13/03/15 09:17:58 INFO mapred.JobClient: Reduce input records=44
13/03/15 09:17:58 INFO mapred.JobClient: Reduce input groups=9
13/03/15 09:17:58 INFO mapred.JobClient: Reduce output records=9
13/03/15 09:17:58 INFO mapred.JobClient: Map output records=44
13/03/15 09:17:58 INFO CountBaseDriver: run(): status=true
13/03/15 09:17:58 INFO CountBaseDriver: returnStatus=0
```

Generated output

The following is the generated output for our Hadoop FASTA solution:

```
$ hadoop fs -cat /dna-base-count/output/p*
c    82
G    10
g    80
T     5
A     7
t    82
C     7
a    110
N     5
```

Custom Sorting

What if you wanted to send a and A to the same reducer and wanted to sum up a's with A's (since they are the same DNA letter)? There are at least two ways to accomplish this:

Option 1:

> Convert all input for map() to lowercase letters. We can do this very easily in the mapper code (map() function) by replacing the following line:

```
String fasta = value.toString();
```

> with this one:

```
String fasta = value.toString().toLowerCase();
```

Option 2

> Provide an outcome sorter that will be injected into the MapReduce framework. We can define the comparator that controls how the keys are sorted before they are passed to the reducer as follows:

```
job.setSortComparatorClass(BaseComparator.class);
```

Example 24-4 shows how we implement our comparator for option #2.

Example 24-4. Custom comparator: BaseComparator

```
 1 import org.apache.hadoop.io.Text;
 2 import org.apache.hadoop.io.WritableComparator;
 3 import org.apache.hadoop.io.WritableComparable;
 4
 5 public class BaseComparator extends WritableComparator {
 6     protected BaseComparator() {
 7         super(Text.class, true);
 8     }
 9
10     @Override
11     public int compare(WritableComparable w1, WritableComparable w2) {
12         Text t1 = (Text) w1;
13         Text t2 = (Text) w2;
14         String s1 = t1.toString().toUpperCase();
15         String s2 = t2.toString().toUpperCase();
16         int cmp = s1.compareTo(s2);
17         return cmp;
18     }
19 }
```

In Hadoop, to write a custom comparator, you just need to extend the org.apache.hadoop.io.WritableComparator class and implement the compare()

method. Here, the custom comparator (BaseComparator class) sorts the keys (a, A, t, T, c, C, g, G, n, N), ignoring case so that the uppercase and lowercase versions of a DNA base will be next to each other. By default, classes injected into the methods setSortComparatorClass() and setGroupingComparatorClass() use the same comparator. For example, if we set setSortComparatorClass() and leave setGroupingComparatorClass() unset, setGroupingComparatorClass() will use the same comparator that we set for setSortComparatorClass() (although the opposite case is not true). You can use this example to test and verify it.

Custom Partitioning

What if we wanted to send all of our keys to only five reducers (one reducer per DNA letter)? The answer is to provide a custom partitioner. The default partitioner in Hadoop is the HashPartitioner, which hashes a mapper-generated key to determine which partition (which reducer) the (key, value) belongs in. The number of partitions is then equal to the number of reduce tasks for the job. So the main question is, when a map() generates a (key, value), does it have to be sent to a reducer? If so, which one? We can use the Job.setPartitionerClass() method to enable our custom partitioner by sending all keys with letter a/A to reducer 1, b/B to reducer 2, and so on (see Example 24-5).

What if we wanted to send all of our keys to only five reducers (one reducer per DNA letter)? The answer is to provide a custom partitioner. The default partitioner in Hadoop is the HashPartitioner, which hashes a mapper-generated key to determine which partition (which reducer) the (key, value) belongs in. The number of partitions is then equal to the number of reduce tasks for the job. So the main question is when a map() generates a (key, value), does it have to be sent to a reducer? If so, which one? We can use the Job.setPartitionerClass() method to enable our custom partitioner by sending all keys with letter a/A to reducer 1, b/B to reducer 2, and so on (see Example 24-5).

Example 24-5. Custom partitioner

```
1 import org.apache.hadoop.mapreduce.Partitioner;
2
3 /** Partition keys by bases{A,T,G,C,a,t,g,c}. */
4 public class BasePartitioner<K, V> extends Partitioner<K, V> {
5    public int getPartition(K key, V value, int numReduceTasks) {
6        String base = key.toString();
7        if (base.compareToIgnoreCase("A") == 0) {
8            return 0;
9        }
10       else if (base.compareToIgnoreCase("C") == 0) {
11           return 1;
12       }
```

```
13          else if (base.compareToIgnoreCase("G") == 0) {
14              return 2;
15          }
16          else if(base.compareToIgnoreCase("T") == 0) {
17              return 3;
18          }
19          else {
20              return 4;
21          }
22      }
23 }
```

Then in our driver class, we inject our custom classes as shown in Example 24-6.

Example 24-6. DNA base count driver

```
 1 public class CountBaseDriver extends Configured implements Tool {
 2
 3      public int run(String[] args) throws Exception {
 4          Job job = new Job(getConf(), "count-dns-bases");
 5          job.setJarByClass(CountBaseMapper.class);
 6          job.setMapperClass(CountBaseMapper.class);
 7          job.setReducerClass(CountBaseReducer.class);
 8          job.setNumReduceTasks(5);
 9          //job.setCombinerClass(CountBaseCombiner.class);
10          job.setInputFormatClass(FastaInputFormat.class);
11          job.setPartitionerClass(BasePartitioner.class);
12          job.setSortComparatorClass(BaseComparator.class);
13          job.setGroupingComparatorClass(BaseComparator.class);
14          job.setOutputKeyClass(Text.class);
15          job.setOutputValueClass(LongWritable.class);
16          FileInputFormat.addInputPath(job, new Path(args[0]));
17          FileOutputFormat.setOutputPath(job, new Path(args[1]));
18
19          boolean status = job.waitForCompletion(true);
20          theLogger.info("run(): status="+status);
21          return status ? 0 : 1;
22      }
23      ...
24 }
```

Now, when we run our job, we will have the following (output is edited and formatted to fit the page):

```
$ ./run.sh
...
Deleted hdfs://localhost:9000/dna-base-count/output
13/03/15 09:44:26 INFO CountBaseDriver: inputDir=/dna-base-count/input
13/03/15 09:44:26 INFO CountBaseDriver: outputDir=/dna-base-count/output
13/03/15 09:44:27 INFO input.FileInputFormat: Total input paths to process : 1
13/03/15 09:44:27 INFO mapred.JobClient: Running job: job_201303150852_0004
13/03/15 09:44:28 INFO mapred.JobClient: map 0% reduce 0%
```

```
...
13/03/15 09:45:58 INFO mapred.JobClient: map 100% reduce 100%
13/03/15 09:46:03 INFO mapred.JobClient: Job complete: job_201303150852_0004
...
13/03/15 09:46:03 INFO mapred.JobClient: Map-Reduce Framework
13/03/15 09:46:03 INFO mapred.JobClient: Map input records=7
13/03/15 09:46:03 INFO mapred.JobClient: Reduce input records=44
13/03/15 09:46:03 INFO mapred.JobClient: Reduce input groups=5
13/03/15 09:46:03 INFO mapred.JobClient: Reduce output records=5
13/03/15 09:46:03 INFO mapred.JobClient: Map output records=44
13/03/15 09:46:03 INFO CountBaseDriver: run(): status=true
13/03/15 09:46:03 INFO CountBaseDriver: returnStatus=0
```

Now we have only five reducers:

```
$ hadoop fs -ls /dna-base-count/output/p*
-rw-r--r-- ... 6 2013-03-15 10:06 /dna-base-count/output/part-r-00000
-rw-r--r-- ... 5 2013-03-15 10:06 /dna-base-count/output/part-r-00001
-rw-r--r-- ... 5 2013-03-15 10:06 /dna-base-count/output/part-r-00002
-rw-r--r-- ... 5 2013-03-15 10:06 /dna-base-count/output/part-r-00003
-rw-r--r-- ... 4 2013-03-15 10:06 /dna-base-count/output/part-r-00004

$ hadoop fs -cat /dna-base-count/output/p*

a    117
c     89
g     90
t     87
n      5
```

MapReduce Solution: FASTQ Format

For DNA base counting, we use a mapper and a reducer. This solution for FASTQ is very similar to the FASTA solution, except we'll be injecting a different class for handling the input format. For the FASTQ format, we will inject the FastqInputFormat class:

```
job.setInputFormatClass(FastqInputFormat.class);
```

Using FastqInputFormat, the mapper will get a key-value pair, where the key is a LongWritable and the value is a Text object in the following format (the line delimiter is ,;,):

```
<line-1><,;,><line-2><,;,><line-3><,;,><line-4>
```

We have four lines for each mapper value, since each FASTQ record corresponds to four lines of data. The mapper class for the FASTQ format will be different from the FASTA classes because the input formats are different, but the reducer class will not change.

Reading FASTQ Files

How do we instruct the MapReduce/Hadoop framework to read FASTQ data? The default reader in Hadoop reads input records line by line, but for the FASTQ format we need to read four lines by four lines, as each set of four lines is a FASTQ record. It is not possible to determine reliably if a line is a sequence name, a sequence itself, or a quality line by just looking at the letters it contains, so we need all four lines. The second line of each set contains the sequence, so we need to use the line numbers of a FASTQ file. Hadoop provides a plug-in framework for "input format" and "record reader." We develop two custom plug-in classes, FastqInputFormat and FastqRecordReader, to enable us to read the FASTQ format. In Hadoop, the default input format is provided by the TextInputFormat class. Our custom class, FastqInputFormat, extends this class and overrides two methods: createRecordReader() and isSplitable(). The overridden createRecordReader() method returns a new custom record reader called FastqRecordReader. Example 24-7 shows how the FastqInputFormat class is implemented.

Example 24-7. FastqInputFormat: custom InputFormat class

```
 1 import org.apache.hadoop.fs.Path;
 2 import org.apache.hadoop.io.LongWritable;
 3 import org.apache.hadoop.io.Text;
 4 import org.apache.hadoop.mapreduce.InputSplit;
 5 import org.apache.hadoop.mapreduce.RecordReader;
 6 import org.apache.hadoop.mapreduce.TaskAttemptContext;
 7 import org.apache.hadoop.mapreduce.lib.input.TextInputFormat;
 8 import org.apache.hadoop.mapreduce.JobContext;
 9 /**
10  * This class defines an InputFormat for FASTQ
11  * files for the Hadoop MapReduce framework.
12  */
13 public class FastqInputFormat extends TextInputFormat {
14    @Override
15    public RecordReader<LongWritable, Text> createRecordReader(
16            InputSplit inputSplit,
17            TaskAttemptContext taskAttemptContext) {
18      return new FastqRecordReader();
19    }
20
21    @Override
22    public boolean isSplitable(JobContext context, Path file) {
23        return false;
24    }
25 }
```

The other custom class is FastqRecordReader, which extends the Record Reader<LongWritable, Text> class (see). The FastqRecordReader class breaks the input data into key-value pairs for input to the mapper. In this case, `FastqRecor dReader` creates values (as `String` objects) that can hold the four lines of a FASTQ record.

Example 24-8. FastqRecordReader: custom RecordReader class

```
1 import ...
2 import org.apache.hadoop.mapreduce.RecordReader;
3
4 /**
5  * This class define a RecordReader for FASTQ files
6  * for the Hadoop MapReduce framework.
7  */
8 public class FastqRecordReader extends RecordReader<LongWritable, Text> {
9     ...
10 }
```

MapReduce FASTQ Solution: map()

To find the count of DNA bases, the `map()` function will get a FASTQ record, which is exactly four lines of text wherein only the second line contains a DNA sequence. The `map()` function will then tokenize the second line (containing the DNA sequence) and count the bases. To make our mapper more efficient, we will not `emit(letter, 1)` for each letter, but rather we will emit the total of each base by using a hash table (`Map<Character, Long>`). Finally, by using Hadoop's `cleanup()` method, we will iterate through the hash table and `emit(letter, countOfLetter)`. The hash table is a very efficient solution, since the number of keys is limited to the very small number of DNA letters. Furthermore, this smart `map()` algorithm reduces the network traffic by emitting only the minimum number of (`letter, countOfLetter`) pairs to the MapReduce framework. See Example 24-9.

Example 24-9. DNA base count: map() function using FASTQ format

```
1 Map<Character, Long> dnaBasesCounter = null;
2 /**
3  * This function is called once at the beginning of the map task.
4  */
5 setup() {
6     dnaBasesCounter = new HashMap<Character, Long>();
7 }
8
9 /**
10  * @param key is the key generated by Hadoop (ignored here)
11  * @param value is one line of input for a given document
12  */
13 map(Object key, String value) {
14     String fastq = value.toString();
```

```
15    // 4 lines are separated by a special delimiter: ",;,"
16    String[] lines = fastq.split(",;,");
17    // 2nd line = lines[1] = the DNA sequence
18    char[] array = lines[1].toCharArray();
19    for(char c : array) {
20        Long v = dnaBaseCounter.get(c);
21        if (v == null) {
22            dnaBaseCounter.put(c, 1);
23        }
24        else {
25            dnaBaseCounter.put(c, v+1);
26        }
27    }
28 }
29
30 /**
31  * Called once at the end of the map task.
32  */
33 cleanup() {
34    // now iterate the baseCounter and emit <key, value>
35    for (Map.Entry<Character, Long> entry : dnaBaseCounter.entrySet()) {
36        emit(entry.getKey(), entry.getValue());
37    }
38 }
```

MapReduce FASTQ Solution: reduce()

Since the number of letters in the DNA alphabet is very limited, we might just set the
number of reducers to 5 (one for every DNA letter). The reducer is again almost
identical to our word count reducer; it just sums up the counters for each DNA letter.
See Example 24-10.

Example 24-10. DNA base count: reduce() function using FASTQ format

```
1 /**
2  * @param key is the unique DNA letter generated by the mapper
3  * @param value is a list of integers (partial count of a unique word)
4  */
5 reduce(String key, List<long> value) {
6    long sum = 0;
7    for (int count : value) {
8        sum += count;
9    }
10    emit(key, sum);
11 }
```

Hadoop Implementation Classes: FASTQ Format

The Hadoop implementation consists of the classes shown in Table 24-2.

Table 24-2. Hadoop implementation classes

Class name	Description
BaseComparator	Comparator class for DNA bases
BasePartitioner	Custom partitioner class
FastqCountBaseDriver	Class that submits Hadoop jobs
FastqCountBaseMapper	Mapper class
FastqCountBaseReducer	Reducer class
FastqInputFormat	Custom InputFormat class
FastqRecordReader	Custom RecordReader class

Sample Run

This section includes a sample run and the generated output of our Hadoop FASTQ format solution.

Log of sample run

The following shows the log of a sample run (edited and formatted to fit the page) of our Hadoop implementation for the FASTQ format:

```
$ ./run_fastq.sh
...
Deleted hdfs://localhost:9000/fastq/output
...
13/03/19 09:24:45 INFO FastqCountBaseDriver: run(): input args[0]=/fastq/input
13/03/19 09:24:45 INFO FastqCountBaseDriver: run(): output args[1]=/fastq/output
13/03/19 09:24:47 INFO mapred.JobClient: map 0% reduce 0%
...
13/03/19 09:26:03 INFO mapred.JobClient: map 100% reduce 100%
...
13/03/19 09:26:08 INFO mapred.JobClient: Map input records=5
...
13/03/19 09:26:08 INFO mapred.JobClient: Reduce output records=4
13/03/19 09:26:08 INFO mapred.JobClient: Map output records=4
13/03/19 09:26:08 INFO FastqCountBaseDriver: run(): status=true
```

Generated output

The generated output for our Hadoop FASTQ solution is as follows:

```
$ hadoop fs -ls /fastq/output/
-rw-r--r--   1 ...   5 2013-03-19 09:25 /fastq/output/part-r-00000
...
-rw-r--r--   1 ...   5 2013-03-19 09:25 /fastq/output/part-r-00008
-rw-r--r--   1 ...   0 2013-03-19 09:25 /fastq/output/part-r-00009

$ hadoop fs -cat /fastq/output/p*
c  36
g  22
t  67
a  55
```

Spark Solution: FASTA Format

This section solves the DNA base count problem for the FASTA format using Spark. Identifying DNA sequences in FASTA format is much easier than in FASTQ: if a line starts with > it is a comment line (i.e., it's not part of a DNA sequence and will be ignored); otherwise, it is a valid DNA sequence. This is our algorithm: read input in FASTA format, partition the input, create a hash table for each partition (the keys for the hash table will be DNA codes {A, T, C, G} and the values will be the frequencies of these DNA codes), and finally combine/merge all hash tables from all partitions into a final single hash table. The entire solution is presented in a single Java class using the Spark API. First, I will present the high-level steps, and then I'll present each step as a Spark transformation or action.

High-Level Steps

shows the high-level steps of our Spark solution to finding the DNA base count for the FASTA format.

Example 24-11. High-level steps

```
1 package org.dataalgorithms.spark.chap24;
2 // Step 1: import required classes and interfaces
3 public class SparkDNABaseCountFASTA {
4    public static void main(String[] args) throws Exception {
5        // Step 2: handle input parameters
6        // Step 3: create an RDD from FASTA input
7        // Step 4: map partitions
8        // Step 5: collect all DNA base counts
9        // Step 6: emit final counts
10
11       // done
```

```
12    ctx.close(); // close JavaSparkContext object
13    System.exit(0);
14  }
15 }
```

Step 1: Import required classes and interfaces

In this step, shown in Example 24-12, we import the required classes and interfaces for our solution.

Example 24-12. Step 1: import required classes and interfaces

```
1 // Step 1: import required classes and interfaces
2 import java.util.Map;
3 import java.util.List;
4 import java.util.HashMap;
5 import java.util.Iterator;
6 import java.util.Collections;
7 import org.apache.spark.api.java.JavaRDD;
8 import org.apache.spark.api.java.JavaSparkContext;
9 import org.apache.spark.api.java.function.FlatMapFunction;
```

Step 2: Handle input parameters

shows how we handle the input parameters.

Example 24-13. Step 2: handle input parameters

```
1    // Step 2: handle input parameters
2    if (args.length != 1) {
3        System.err.println("Usage: SparkDNABaseCountFASTA <input-path>");
4        System.exit(1);
5    }
6    final String inputPath = args[0];
```

Step 3: Create an RDD from FASTA input

In this step, shown in Example 24-14, we create an RDD from the FASTA input.

Example 24-14. Step 3: create an RDD from FASTA input

```
1    // Step 3: create an RDD from FASTA input
2    JavaSparkContext ctx = new JavaSparkContext();
3    JavaRDD<String> fastaRDD = ctx.textFile(inputPath, 1);
```

Step 4: Map partitions

In Example 24-15, each partition creates a hash table of (K,V), where K is a DNA code and V is the associated frequency of the DNA code.

Example 24-15. Step 4: map partitions

```
1    // Step 4: map partitions
2    // <U> JavaRDD<U> mapPartitions(FlatMapFunction<Iterator<T>,U> f)
3    // Return a new RDD by applying a function to each partition of this RDD.
4    JavaRDD<Map<Character, Long>> partitions = fastaRDD.mapPartitions(
5        new FlatMapFunction<Iterator<String>, Map<Character,Long>>() {
6        @Override
7        public Iterable<Map<Character,Long>> call(Iterator<String> iter) {
8            Map<Character,Long> baseCounts = new HashMap<Character,Long>();
9            while (iter.hasNext()) {
10               String record = iter.next();
11               if (record.startsWith(">")) {
12                   // it is a FASTA comment record, ignore it
13               }
14               else {
15                   String str = record.toUpperCase();
16                   for (int i = 0; i < str.length(); i++) {
17                       char c = str.charAt(i);
18                       Long count = baseCounts.get(c);
19                       if (count == null) {
20                           baseCounts.put(c, 1l);
21                       }
22                       else {
23                           baseCounts.put(c, count+1l);
24                       }
25                   }
26               }
27           }
28           return Collections.singletonList(baseCounts);
29        }
30    });
```

Step 5: Collect all DNA base counts

In Example 24-16, we collect all the DNA base counts.

Example 24-16. Step 5: collect all DNA base counts

```
1    // Step 5: collect all DNA base counts
2    List<Map<Character, Long>> list = partitions.collect();
3    System.out.println("list="+list);
4    Map<Character, Long> allBaseCounts = list.get(0);
5    for (int i=1; i < list.size(); i++) {
6        Map<Character, Long> aBaseCount = list.get(i);
```

```
7            for (Map.Entry<Character, Long> entry : aBaseCount.entrySet()) {
8                char base = entry.getKey();
9                Long count = allBaseCounts.get(base);
10               if (count == null) {
11                   allBaseCounts.put(base, entry.getValue());
12               }
13               else {
14                   allBaseCounts.put(base, (count + entry.getValue()));
15               }
16           }
17       }
```

Step 6: Emit final counts

In this step, shown in Example 24-17, we emit the final DNA base counts.

Example 24-17. Step 6: emit final counts

```
1        // Step 6: emit final counts
2        for (Map.Entry<Character, Long> entry : allBaseCounts.entrySet()) {
3            System.out.println(entry.getKey() + "\t" + entry.getValue());
4        }
```

Sample Run

The following subsections provide the input, script, and generated output for a sample run of our Spark FASTA solution.

Input

```
$ hadoop fs -cat /home/hadoop/testspark/fasta.txt
>seq1
cGTAaccaataaaaaaacaagcttaacctaattc
>seq2
agcttagTTTGGatctggccgggg
>seq3
gcggatttactcCCCCCAAAAANNaggggagagcccagataaatggagtctgtgcgtccaca
gaattcgcacca
AATAAAACCTCACCCAT
agagcccagaatttactcCCC
>seq4
gcggatttactcaggggagagcccagGGataaatggagtctgtgcgtccaca
gaattcgcacca
```

Script

The following is the script to run our Spark DNA base count solution for FASTA:

```
$ cat run_spark_dna_base_count_fasta.sh
#!/bin/bash
export JAVA_HOME=/usr/java/jdk7
```

```
export SPARK_HOME=/usr/local/spark-1.1.0
export SPARK_MASTER=spark://myserver100:7077
export BOOK_HOME=/mp/data-algorithms-book
export APP_JAR=$BOOK_HOME/dist/data_algorithms_book.jar
INPUT=/home/hadoop/testspark/fasta.txt
# Run on a Spark standalone cluster
$SPARK_HOME/bin/spark-submit \
  --class org.dataalgorithms.chap24.spark.SparkDNABaseCountFASTA \
  --master $SPARK_MASTER \
  --executor-memory 2G \
  --total-executor-cores 20 \
  $APP_JAR \
  $INPUT
```

Log of sample run

Our script was run in a three-node ({myserver100, myserver200, myserver300})
Spark cluster environment. The output has been edited to fit the page:

```
# ./run_spark_dna_base_count_fasta.sh
...
INFO : Remoting started; listening on addresses :
  [akka.tcp://sparkDriver@myserver100:59451]
INFO : Remoting now listens on addresses:
  [akka.tcp://sparkDriver@myserver100:59451]
INFO : Successfully started service 'sparkDriver' on port 59451.
...
INFO : Executor added: app-20141114113127-0023/0 on worker-20141016164917-
  myserver200-34042 (myserver200:34042) with 2 cores
INFO : Granted executor ID app-20141114113127-0023/0 on hostPort
  myserver200:34042 with 2 cores, 2.0 GB RAM
INFO : Executor added: app-20141114113127-0023/1 on
  worker-20141016164917-myserver300-52001 (myserver300:52001) with 2 cores
INFO : Granted executor ID app-20141114113127-0023/1 on hostPort
  myserver300:52001 with 2 cores, 2.0 GB RAM
INFO : Executor added: app-20141114113127-0023/2 on
  worker-20141016164917-myserver100-58455 (myserver100:58455) with 2 cores
INFO : Granted executor ID app-20141114113127-0023/2 on hostPort
  myserver100:58455 with 2 cores, 2.0 GB RAM
INFO : Executor updated: app-20141114113127-0023/0 is now RUNNING
INFO : Executor updated: app-20141114113127-0023/1 is now RUNNING
INFO : Executor updated: app-20141114113127-0023/2 is now RUNNING
...
INFO : Job finished: collect at SparkDNABaseCountFASTA.java:67,
  took 0.069880929 s
INFO : Removed TaskSet 2.0, whose tasks have all completed, from pool
list=[{T=45, N=2, G=53, A=73, C=61}]
T     45
N     2
G     53
A     73
```

Spark Solution: FASTQ Format

This section solves the DNA base count problem for the FASTQ format using Spark. In FASTQ format, each DNA sequence is presented as a list of four continuous lines/records. For DNA base counting, we are interested only in the second line, which is the actual DNA sequence (the other three records will be ignored). In Spark, the default record reader reads files line by line. For FASTQ, we cannot use the default record reader because identifying the actual DNA sequence from a given line/record is not deterministic. If it were, we could read line by line and process only the actual DNA sequences. Since identifying the DNA sequence from a given line of a FASTQ file is not possible, we will read the FASTQ files four lines at a time (again, each set of four lines represents a single record of a FASTQ file).

But how do we read a FASTQ file record by record (i.e., in sets of four lines)? The answer is to write a custom `InputFormat` (as a plug-in class) that will return four lines of input instead of one line of input. We accomplish this with `FastqInputFormat`, which extends `TextInputFormat` (note that FASTQ files are regular text files). This is our algorithm: read input in FASTQ format with a custom `FastqInputFormat` (this will return four lines, but only the line representing the DNA sequence will be processed), partition the input, create a hash table for each partition (the keys for the hash table will be DNA codes {A, T, C, G} and the values will be the frequencies of these DNA codes), and finally combine/merge all hash tables from all partitions into a final single hash table. The entire solution is presented in a single Java class using the Spark API. First, I'll show the high-level steps, and then I'll present each step as a Spark transformation or action.

High-Level Steps

Example 24-18 shows the high-level steps of our Spark solution to finding the DNA base count for the FASTQ format.

Example 24-18. High-level steps

```
1 package org.dataalgorithms.spark.chap24;
2 // Step 1: import required classes and interfaces
3 public class SparkDNABaseCountFASTQ {
4    public static void main(String[] args) throws Exception {
5       // Step 2: handle input parameters
6       // Step 3: create a JavaPairRDD from FASTQ input format
7       // Step 4: map partitions
8       // Step 5: collect all DNA base counts
9       // Step 6: emit final counts
```

```
10
11          // done
12          ctx.close(); // close JavaSparkContext object
13          System.exit(0);
14      }
15 }
```

Step 1: Import required classes and interfaces

In this step, shown in Example 24-19, we import the required classes and interfaces
for our solution.

Example 24-19. Step 1: import required classes and interfaces

```
1 // Step 1: import required classes and interfaces
2 import scala.Tuple2;
3
4 import java.util.Map;
5 import java.util.List;
6 import java.util.HashMap;
7 import java.util.Iterator;
8 import java.util.Collections;
9
10 import org.apache.spark.api.java.JavaRDD;
11 import org.apache.spark.api.java.JavaPairRDD;
12 import org.apache.spark.api.java.JavaSparkContext;
13 import org.apache.spark.api.java.function.FlatMapFunction;
14
15 import org.apache.hadoop.io.Text;
16 import org.apache.hadoop.io.LongWritable;
17 import org.apache.hadoop.conf.Configuration;
```

Step 2: Handle input parameters

Example 24-20 shows how we handle the input parameters.

Example 24-20. Step 2: handle input parameters

```
1 // Step 2: handle input parameters
2 if (args.length != 1) {
3    System.err.println("Usage: SparkDNABaseCountFASTQ <input-path>");
4    System.exit(1);
5 }
6 final String inputPath = args[0];
```

Step 3: Create a JavaPairRDD from FASTQ input

In this step, shown in Example 24-21, we create an RDD from the FASTQ input.

Example 24-21. Step 3: create a JavaPairRDD from FASTQ input

```
1 // Step 3: create an JavaPairRDD from FASTQ input
2 JavaSparkContext ctx = new JavaSparkContext();
3
4 // import org.apache.hadoop.mapreduce.InputFormat;
5 // public <K,V,F extends InputFormat<K,V>> JavaPairRDD<K,V> newAPIHadoopFile(
6 //            String path,
7 //            Class<F> fClass,
8 //            Class<K> kClass,
9 //            Class<V> vClass,
10 //            org.apache.hadoop.conf.Configuration conf)
11 // Get an RDD for a given Hadoop file with an arbitrary new API InputFormat
12 // and extra configuration options to pass to the input format.
13 // Note: Because Hadoop's RecordReader class reuses the same Writable
14 // object for each record, directly caching the returned RDD will create
15 // many references to the same object. If you plan to directly cache Hadoop
16 // Writable objects, you should first copy them using a map function.
17
18 //// you may partition your data by coalesce()
19 ////    public JavaPairRDD<T> coalesce(int N)
20 ////    Return a new RDD that is reduced into N partitions.
21 JavaPairRDD<LongWritable ,Text> fastqRDD = ctx.newAPIHadoopFile(
22             inputPath,              // input path
23             FastqInputFormat.class, // custom InputFormat
24             LongWritable.class,     // Key returned by custom InputFormat
25             Text.class,             // Value returned by custom InputFormat
26             new Configuration()     // Hadoop configuration object
27 );
```

Step 4: Map partitions

Step 4, shown in Example 24-22, shows how to map partitions and create local `Map<Character, Long>` objects.

Example 24-22. Step 4: map partitions

```
1 // Step 4: map partitions
2 // <U> JavaRDD<U> mapPartitions(FlatMapFunction<Iterator<T>,U> f)
3 // Return a new RDD by applying a function to each partition of this RDD.
4 JavaRDD<Map<Character, Long>> partitions = fastqRDD.mapPartitions(
5    new FlatMapFunction<Iterator<Tuple2<LongWritable ,Text>>,
6                        Map<Character,Long>
7                        >() {
8    @Override
```

```
 9      public Iterable<Map<Character,Long>> call(
10        Iterator<Tuple2<LongWritable ,Text>> iter) {
11        Map<Character,Long> baseCounts = new HashMap<Character,Long>();
12        while (iter.hasNext()) {
13          Tuple2<LongWritable ,Text> kv = iter.next();
14          String fastqRecord = kv._2.toString(); // get a FASTQ record
15          String[] lines = fastqRecord.split(",;,");
16          // 2nd line (i.e., lines[1]) is the DNA sequence
17          String sequence = lines[1].toUpperCase();
18          for (int i = 0; i < sequence.length(); i++) {
19            char c = sequence.charAt(i);
20            Long count = baseCounts.get(c);
21            if (count == null) {
22              baseCounts.put(c, 1l);
23            }
24            else {
25              baseCounts.put(c, count+1l);
26            }
27          }
28        }
29        return Collections.singletonList(baseCounts);
30     }
31 });
```

Step 5: Collect all DNA base counts

In Example 24-23, we collect all the DNA base counts.

Example 24-23. Step 5: collect all DNA base counts

```
 1 // Step 5: collect all DNA base counts
 2 List<Map<Character, Long>> list = partitions.collect();
 3 System.out.println("list="+list);
 4 Map<Character, Long> allBaseCounts = list.get(0);
 5 for (int i=1; i < list.size(); i++) {
 6     Map<Character, Long> aBaseCount = list.get(i);
 7     for (Map.Entry<Character, Long> entry : aBaseCount.entrySet()) {
 8         char base = entry.getKey();
 9         Long count = allBaseCounts.get(base);
10         if (count == null) {
11             allBaseCounts.put(base, entry.getValue());
12         }
13         else {
14             allBaseCounts.put(base, (count + entry.getValue()));
15         }
16     }
17 }
```

Step 6: Emit Final Counts

In this step, shown in Example 24-24, we emit the final DNA base counts.

Example 24-24. Step 6: emit final counts

```
1 // Step 6: emit final counts
2 for (Map.Entry<Character, Long> entry : allBaseCounts.entrySet()) {
3     System.out.println(entry.getKey() + "\t" + entry.getValue());
4 }
```

Sample Run

The following subsections provide the input, script, and generated output for a sample run of our Spark FASTQ solution.

Input

```
$ hadoop fs -cat /home/hadoop/testspark/sample.fastq
@EAS54_6_R1_2_1_413_324
CCCTTCTTGTCTTCAGCGTTTCTCC
+
;;3;;;;;;;;;;;7;;;;;;;88
@EAS54_6_R1_2_1_540_792
TTGGCAGGCCAAGGCCGATGGATCA
+
;;;;;;;;;;;7;;;;;-;;;3;83
@EAS54_6_R1_2_1_443_348
GTTGCTTCTGGCGTGGGTGGGGGGG
+EAS54_6_R1_2_1_443_348
;;;;;;;;;;;9;7;;.7;393333
```

Script

The following is the script to run our Spark DNA base count solution for FASTQ:

```
$ cat ./run_spark_dna_base_count_fastq.sh
#!/bin/bash
export JAVA_HOME=/usr/java/jdk7
export BOOK_HOME=/mp/data-algorithms-book
export SPARK_HOME=/usr/local/spark-1.1.0
export SPARK_MASTER=spark://myserver100:7077
export SPARK_JAR=$BOOK_HOME/lib/spark-assembly-1.1.0-hadoop2.5.0.jar
export APP_JAR=$BOOK_HOME/dist/data_algorithms_book.jar
#
# build all other dependent jars in OTHER_JARS
JARS='find $BOOK_HOME/lib -name '*.jar''
OTHER_JARS=""
for J in $JARS ; do
    OTHER_JARS=$J,$OTHER_JARS
```

```
done
#
INPUT=/home/hadoop/testspark/sample.fastq
DRIVER=org.dataalgorithms.chap24.spark.SparkDNABaseCountFASTQ
  --class $DRIVER \
  --master $SPARK_MASTER \
  --jars $OTHER_JARS \
  $APP_JAR $INPUT
```

Log of sample run

Our script was run in a three-node (myserver100, myserver200, myserver300) Spark cluster environment. The output page has been edited to fit the page:

```
$ ./run_spark_dna_base_count_fastq.sh
...
INFO : Remoting started; listening on addresses :
  [akka.tcp://sparkDriver@myserver100:52511]
INFO : Remoting now listens on addresses:
  [akka.tcp://sparkDriver@myserver100:52511]
INFO : Successfully started service 'sparkDriver' on port 52511.
...
INFO : Stage 0 (collect at SparkDNABaseCountFASTQ.java:102)
  finished in 7.367 s
INFO : Job finished: collect at SparkDNABaseCountFASTQ.java:102,
  took 7.446341308 s
T 22
G 27
A 7
C 19
```

This chapter presented multiple MapReduce and Spark solutions for DNA base counting, which is used in genome-based applications. The next chapter presents a MapReduce/Hadoop solution to RNA sequencing, which is used for genome and clinical applications.

## CHAPTER 25

RNA Sequencing

In recent years, RNA (ribonucleic acid) sequencing has revolutionized the exploration of gene expression. Improvements in RNA sequencing methods have enabled researchers to rapidly profile and investigate the transcriptome. Dr. Ananya Mandel (*http://bit.ly/what_is_rna*) defines RNA as "an important molecule with long chains of nucleotides. A nucleotide contains a nitrogenous base, a ribose sugar, and a phosphate. Just like DNA, RNA is vital for living beings." RNA's main function is to transfer the genetic code needed for the creation of proteins from the nucleus to the ribosome. According to Dr. Mandel: "This process prevents the DNA from having to leave the nucleus. This keeps the DNA and genetic code protected from damage. Without RNA, proteins could never be made."

This chapter will provide a complete MapReduce solution for a computational pipeline for analyzing RNA sequencing (RNA-Seq) data for differential gene expression. In our implementation, we will utilize two open source packages:

TopHat (http://bit.ly/TopHat-tool)
> A fast splice junction mapper for RNA-Seq reads. It aligns RNA-Seq reads to mammalian-sized genomes using the ultra-high-throughput short read aligner Bowtie, and then analyzes the mapping results to identify splice junctions between exons.

Cufflinks (http://bit.ly/cufflinks_tool)
> Assembles transcripts, estimates their abundances, and tests for differential expression and regulation in RNA-Seq samples. It accepts aligned RNA-Seq reads and assembles the alignments into a parsimonious set of transcripts. Cufflinks then estimates the relative abundances of these transcripts based on how many reads support each one, taking into account biases in library preparation protocols.

Data Size and Format

RNA-Seq data can be presented in FASTA, FASTQ, BAM, and many other formats. The TopHat package handles the FASTA and FASTQ data formats. Each sample of RNA-Seq data can be from 30 GB to 300 GB in size (a single RNA-Seq analysis can constitute up to 1 TB of data or more).

MapReduce Workflow

The RNA sequencing pipeline includes the following main steps:

1. Input data validation (quality control of input data such as FASTQ files)
2. Alignment (mapping of short reads to the reference genome)
3. Transcript assembly (using the Cufflinks and Cuffdiff tools)

The RNA-Seq workflow is presented in Figure 25-1.

Input Data Validation

This step validates the format of FASTQ files. With validation, you want to guarantee the quality of the input files. Input data validation tools enable you to do some quality control checks on raw sequence data (for example, in the FASTQ file format) coming from high-throughput sequencing pipelines.

There are lots of open source tools for input data validation. For example, for FASTQ validation you have these options:

- FastQValidator (*http://bit.ly/fastqvalidator*)
- FastQC (*http://bit.ly/FastQC*)

The input data validation step is very simple and straightforward, so we will not cover it here. Our focus will be on the core of RNA sequencing: mapping/alignment and testing for differential expression and regulation in RNA-Seq samples.

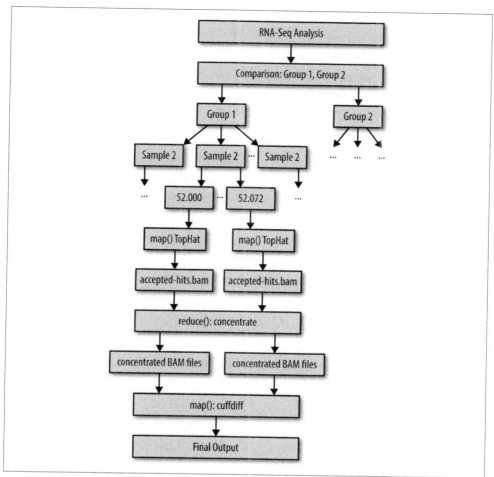

Figure 25-1. RNA-Seq workflow

RNA Sequencing Analysis Overview

Before we delve into MapReduce algorithms for RNA sequencing, you need to understand how data/samples are used in RNA-Seq analysis. To perform an RNA-Seq analysis, we need to compare two groups of RNA-Seq data samples (this is a single
comparison; an RNA-Seq analysis may have one or more comparisons):

Group 1

A set of samples where each sample may have one or more FASTQ files. For
example, this group might be a set of "normal" samples.

Group 2

A set of samples where each sample may have one or more FASTQ files. For example, this group might be set of "cancer" (disease) samples.

The goal is to find significant changes in transcript expression, splicing, and promoter use between samples of Group 1 and Group 2 (typically, we will use Cufflinks's Cuffdiff program to perform the RNA-Seq analysis between two groups). Typically, an input to an RNA-Seq analysis has one or more comparisons. Each comparison has exactly two groups (Group 1 and Group 2, as just discussed).

For example, the following is a sample input for RNA-Seq analysis. This analysis has three comparisons (Comparison 1, Comparison 2, and Comparison 3). Each comparison has exactly two groups: Group 1 and Group 2. Comparison 1's Group 1 has four samples and Group 2 has three samples (the sample data for Comparison 2 and Comparison 3 is not shown here):

- Comparison 1

    Group 1: {Sample 1, Sample 2, Sample 3, Sample 4}
    Group 2: {Sample 7, Sample 8, Sample 9}
    where

        Sample 1 = {file11.fastq, file12.fastq, file13.fastq}
        Sample 2 = {file21.fastq, file22.fastq}
        Sample 3 = {file31.fastq, file32.fastq, file33.fastq, file34.fastq}
        Sample 4 = {file41.fastq}
        ...
        Sample 7 = {file71.fastq, file72.fastq}
        Sample 8 = {file81.fastq, file82.fastq, file83.fastq}
        Sample 9 = {file91.fastq, file92.fastq, file93.fastq}

- Comparison 2

    Group 1: {...}
    Group 2: {...}

- Comparison 3

    Group 1: {...}
    Group 2: {...}

The RNA-Seq data structures are presented in Figure 25-2.

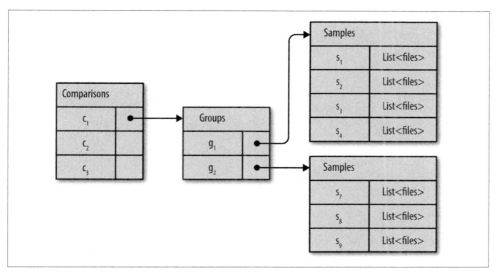

Figure 25-2. RNA-Seq data structures

The input data for RNA-Seq can easily be represented by the Java class and data structures shown in Example 25-1.

Example 25-1. RNA-Seq data structures

```
1 import java.util.Arrays;
2 import java.util.Map;
3 import java.util.HashMap;
4 import java.util.List;
5 import java.util.ArrayList;
6
7 public class Comparison {
8     private Map<String, List<String>> group1 = null;
9     private Map<String, List<String>> group2 = null;
10    public void setGroup1(Map<String, List<String>> group1) {
11        this.group1 = group1;
12    }
13    public void setGroup2(Map<String, List<String>> group2) {
14        this.group2 = group2;
15    }
16    public Map<String, List<String>> getGroup1() {
17        return this.group1;
18    }
19    public Map<String, List<String>> getGroup2() {
20        return this.group2;
21    }
22 }
```

Now we may use the `Comparison` class to create the proper RNA-Seq data structures, as shown in Example 25-2.

Example 25-2. RNA-Seq data structures usage

```
1 // create all three comparisons:
2 List<Comparison> comparisons = new ArrayList<Comparison>();
3 Comparison comparison_1 = new Comparison();
4 Comparison comparison_2 = new Comparison();
5 Comparison comparison_3 = new Comparison();
6 comparisons.add(comparison_1);
7 comparisons.add(comparison_2);
8 comparisons.add(comparison_3);
9
10 // prepare Group 1 for comparison_1
11 Map<String, List<String>> group1 = new HashMap<String, List<String>>()
12 group1.put("Sample-1w"1, new ArrayList<String>(
13   Arrays.asList("file11.fastq", "file12.fastq", "file13.fastq")));
14 group1.put("Sample-2", new ArrayList<String>(
15   Arrays.asList("file21.fastq", "file22.fastq")));
16 group1.put("Sample-3", new ArrayList<String>(
17   Arrays.asList("file31.fastq", "file32.fastq", "file33.fastq", "file34.fastq")));
18 group1.put("Sample-4", new ArrayList<String>(Arrays.asList("file41.fastq")));
19
20 // prepare Group 2 for comparison_1
21 Map<String, List<String>> group2 = new HashMap<String, List<String>>()
22 group2.put("Sample-7", new ArrayList<String>(
23   Arrays.asList("file71.fastq", "file72.fastq")));
24 group2.put("Sample-8", new ArrayList<String>(
25   Arrays.asList("file81.fastq", "file82.fastq", "file83.fastq")));
26 group2.put("Sample-9", new ArrayList<String>(
27   Arrays.asList("file91.fastq", "file92.fastq", "file93.fastq")));
28 comparison_1.setGroup1(group1);
29 comparison_1.setGroup2(group2);
30 ...
```

We further split the *<filename>.fastq* files (using Linux's `split()` function) into 8 million records (exactly 2 million FASTQ records, since each four lines is one FASTQ record). The reason for this split is to make sure that every mapper will get its fair share of input records.

MapReduce Algorithms for RNA Sequencing

Our solution for RNA-Seq analysis has two MapReduce algorithm steps:

1. MapReduce TopHat mapping
2. MapReduce Cuffdiff calling

Step 1: MapReduce TopHat Mapping

This step comprises the `map()` and `reduce()` functions: the mappers use TopHat to align the input data, and then the reducers concatenate the mappers' output. The driver program for step 1 partitions data into small chunks and passes each input file to a mapper. For example, an input for an RNA-Seq analysis might be the HDFS directory */rnaseq/input/2397/* (where *2397* is an `analysisID` that uniquely identifies the RNA-Seq analysis):

```
# hadoop fs -ls /rnaseq/input/2397/
0000.txt
0001.txt
0002.txt
..
0090.txt
0091.txt
```

Each input file has one single record composed of many tokens (note that since each record is too long, it is formatted for print; each line here contains one token with a delimiter of ;):

```
# hadoop fs -cat /rnaseq/input/2397/0090.txt
0090;                            # counter
g1_vs_g2;                        # comparison ID
10332;                           # group ID
62586;                           # sample ID
annotation;                      # RNA-Seq input type
2397;                            # GUID as analysis ID
2;                               # segment mismatches
fr-unstranded;                   # library type
55;                              # segment length
Refseq;                          # gene model
hg18;                            # reference genome
/data/GSE29006/SRR192334_1_0026, # paired left file
/data/GSE29006/SRR192334_2_0026  # paired right file
```

The map() function

The `map()` function calls a bash shell script[1] that applies TopHat and generates intermediate BAM files (see Example 25-3). The output of each TopHat mapper will be an *accepted_hits.bam* file, which is a list of read alignments in SAM format. SAM is a compact short read alignment format that has been increasingly adopted.

---

[1] I used FreeMarker (*http://freemarker.sourceforge.net/*), a generic tool for generating text output based on templates, to generate the shell scripts.

Example 25-3. Step 1: map() function

```
1  // key is MR generated, ignored here
2  // value represents one record of input
3  map(key, value) {
4     Map<String, String> tokens = tokenizeMapperRecord(value);
5     // The reducer key will be:
6     // "<analysis_id><;><comparison_id><;><group_id><;><sample_id>"
7     String reducerKey = getReducerKey(tokens);
8     RNASeq.tophat(tokens);
9     emit(reducerKey, value);
10 }
11
12 public static void tophat(Map<String, String> tokens)
13    throws Exception {
14    TemplateEngine.init();
15    Map<String, String> templateMap = new HashMap<String, String>();
16    templateMap.put("key", tokens.get("counter"));
17    templateMap.put("counter", tokens.get("counter"));
18    templateMap.put("comparison_id", tokens.get("comparison_id"));
19    templateMap.put("group_id", tokens.get("group_id"));
20    templateMap.put("sample_id", tokens.get("sample_id"));
21    templateMap.put("rna_seq_input_type", tokens.get("rna_seq_input_type"));
22    templateMap.put("analysis_id", tokens.get("analysis_id"));
23    templateMap.put("rna_seq_tophat_segment_mismatches",
24       tokens.get("rna_seq_tophat_segment_mismatches"));
25    templateMap.put("rna_seq_tophat_library_type",
26       tokens.get("rna_seq_tophat_library_type"));
27    templateMap.put("rna_seq_tophat_segment_length",
28       tokens.get("rna_seq_tophat_segment_length"));
29    templateMap.put("rna_seq_tophat_gene_model",
30       tokens.get("rna_seq_tophat_gene_model"));
31    templateMap.put("rna_seq_tophat_reference_genome",
32       tokens.get("rna_seq_tophat_reference_genome"));
33    // create the actual script from a template file
34    String scriptFileName = "/rnaseq/scripts/tophat." +
35       tokens.get("analysis_id") + "." + tokens.get("counter") + ".sh";
36    String logFileName = "/rnaseq/logs/tophat." +
37       tokens.get("analysis_id") + "." + tokens.get("counter") + ".log";
38    File scriptFile = TemplateEngine.createDynamicContentAsFile("tophat.template",
39       templateMap, scriptFileName);
40    if (scriptFile != null) {
41       ShellScriptUtil.callProcess(scriptFileName, logFileName);
42    }
43 }
```

The reduce() function

The reduce() function calls a bash shell script that uses the SAMtools cat function to concatenate accepted hits BAM files (*accepted_hits.bam*). Then the script uses the

SAMtools `sort` function to generate the sorted BAM file. So, for our example, for Comparison 1 the reducers will generate the following sorted BAM files in HDFS:

```
/<hdfs-dir>/${analysis_id}/comparison_1/group_1/sample_1/reducer/sorted.bam
/<hdfs-dir>/${analysis_id}/comparison_1/group_1/sample_2/reducer/sorted.bam
/<hdfs-dir>/${analysis_id}/comparison_1/group_1/sample_3/reducer/sorted.bam
/<hdfs-dir>/${analysis_id}/comparison_1/group_1/sample_4/reducer/sorted.bam

/<hdfs-dir>/${analysis_id}/comparison_1/group_2/sample_7/reducer/sorted.bam
/<hdfs-dir>/${analysis_id}/comparison_1/group_2/sample_8/reducer/sorted.bam
/<hdfs-dir>/${analysis_id}/comparison_1/group_2/sample_9/reducer/sorted.bam
```

The reducer is defined in Example 25-4.

Example 25-4. Step 1: reduce() function

```
1 // key: "<analysis_id><;><comparison_id><;><group_id><;><sample_id>"
2 // values: not used
3 reduce(key, values) {
4     RNASeqTophat.catenatePartitionedBamFiles(key);
5     emit(key, key);
6 }
7
8 /**
9  * This method concatenates small/partitioned accepted_hits.bam files
10  * and creates a single sorted.bam file.
11  * @param key: "<analysis_id><;><comparison_id><;><group_id><;><sample_id>"
12  */
13 public static void catenatePartitionedBamFiles(String key) {
14     throws Exception {
15     TemplateEngine.init();
16     // split the key (fields are separated by ";")
17     String[] tokens = reducerKey.split(";");
18     String analysisID = tokens[0];
19     String comparisonID = tokens[1];
20     String groupID = tokens[2];
21     String sampleID = tokens[3];
22     // create a template map to be passed to FreeMarker template
23     Map<String, String> templateMap = new HashMap<String, String>();
24     templateMap.put("analysis_id", analysisID);
25     templateMap.put("comparison_id", comparisonID);
26     templateMap.put("group_id", groupID);
27     templateMap.put("sample_id", sampleID);
28
29     // create the actual script from a template file
30     String scriptFileName = "/rnaseq/scripts/catenate_partitioned_bam_files." +
31         analysisID + "." + comparisonID + "." + groupID + "." + sampleID + ".sh";
32     String logFileName = "/rnaseq/scripts/catenate_partitioned_bam_files." +
33         analysisID + "." + comparisonID + "." + groupID + "." + sampleID + ".log";
34     File scriptFile = TemplateEngine.createDynamicContentAsFile(
35         "cat_bam_files_partitioned.template.sh", templateMap, scriptFileName);
36     if (scriptFile != null) {
```

```
37        ShellScriptUtil.callProcess(scriptFileName, logFileName);
38    }
39 }
```

Step 2: MapReduce Calling Cuffdiff

This step also comprises `map()` and `reduce()` functions (the reducer is optional but may be used for further analysis). The mapper calls the `cuffdiff` function for two groups for any given comparison, and then the reducers generate the final desired output as biosets/biomarkers for further analysis.

The map() function

The mapper will call the `cuffdiff` function for every comparison (i.e., in our example, we have three comparisons, so `cuffdiff` will be called three times). For example, for Comparison 1, `cuffdiff` will be called as follows:

```
group_1= {
/<hdfs-dir>/${analysis_id}/comparison_1/group_1/sample_1/reducer/sorted.bam
/<hdfs-dir>/${analysis_id}/comparison_1/group_1/sample_2/reducer/sorted.bam
/<hdfs-dir>/${analysis_id}/comparison_1/group_1/sample_3/reducer/sorted.bam
/<hdfs-dir>/${analysis_id}/comparison_1/group_1/sample_4/reducer/sorted.bam
}

group_2= {
/<hdfs-dir>/${analysis_id}/comparison_1/group_2/sample_7/reducer/sorted.bam
/<hdfs-dir>/${analysis_id}/comparison_1/group_2/sample_8/reducer/sorted.bam
/<hdfs-dir>/${analysis_id}/comparison_1/group_2/sample_9/reducer/sorted.bam
}

cuffdiff $group_1 $group_2
```

`cuffdiff` generates the following output files, which will be saved in HDFS:

- *isoform_exp.diff*
- *isoforms.read_group_tracking*
- *read_groups.info*

The mapper for step 2 is presented in Example 25-5.

Example 25-5. Step 2: map() function

```
1 /**
2  * The mapper calls the cuffdiff function for two groups of data.
3  *
4  * @param key will be:
5  *   "<analysis_id><;><comparison_id><;><group_id><;><sample_id>"
6  * @param value is a String of 11 tokens:
7  * index content
```

```
 8  *  ---- ---------
 9  *   0    <counter-as-key>; (such as 0000, 0001, )
10  *   1    <comparison_id>;
11  *   2    <group1_id>;
12  *   3    <group2_id>;
13  *   4    constant "cuffdiff"; (ignored)
14  *   5    <analysis_id>;
15  *   6    <segment_mismatches>;
16  *   7    <library_type>;
17  *   8    <segment_length>;
18  *   9    <gene_model>;
19  *  10    <reference_genome>;
20  *
21  */
22  map(key, value) {
23      Map<String, String> tokens = tokenizeMapperRecord(value);
24      //  reducerKey =   <analysis_id><;><comparison_id>
25      String reducerKey = getReducerKey(tokens);
26      RNASeqCuffDiff.cuffdiff(tokens);
27      emit(reducerKey, value);
28  }
30
31  public static void cuffdiff(Map<String, String> tokens) throws Exception {
32      TemplateEngine.init();
33      String scriptFileName = "/rnaseq/scripts/run_cuffdiff." +
34          tokens.get("analysis_id") + "." + tokens.get("comparison_id") + ".sh";
35      String logFileName = "/rnaseq/logs/run_cuffdiff." +
36          tokens.get("analysis_id") + "." + tokens.get("comparison_id") + ".log";
37      File scriptFile = TemplateEngine.createDynamicContentAsFile(
38          "cuffdiff.sh.template", tokens, scriptFileName);
39      if (scriptFile != null) {
40          ShellScriptUtil.callProcess(scriptFileName, logFileName);
41      }
42  }
```

The reduce() function

There is no reducer for step 2, but you can use reducers to read the output of the cuffdiff function and generate biosets/biomarkers, so you might find them useful for further analysis and evaluation of RNA-Seq samples.

This chapter presented a generic high-level MapReduce solution for RNA sequencing. I presented a concrete MapReduce solution along with open source tools. The next chapter provides scalable distributed solutions for gene aggregation (also known as marker frequency in clinical applications).

## CHAPTER 26

Gene Aggregation

This chapter provides four distinct solutions to gene aggregation (also known as *marker frequency* in clinical applications), in MapReduce/Hadoop and Spark. The input data for gene aggregation is patients' biosets. As discussed in previous chapters, a *bioset*, also called a *gene signature*, encompasses data in the form of experimental sample comparisons (for transcriptomic, epigenetic, and copy-number variation data), as well as genotype signatures (for GWAS and mutational data). In simple terms, a bioset is a list of key-value pairs, where the key is a `geneID` and the value is a list of associated attributes. Gene aggregation is used in clinical applications to identify transcriptional signatures and patterns of gene expression data. Gene aggregation is also used to see how genes are grouped together and how this affects the overall analysis. Gene aggregation is an evolutionary method and depends on chromosomal folding and higher-order structures.

Gene aggregation is achieved through three metrics:

- *Reference type* refers to the type of patient data:
  - r1 = normal
  - r2 = disease
  - r3 = paired
  - r4 = unknown
- *Gene filter type* refers to the type of filter applied to the data. The filter type indicates how gene values will be grouped and analyzed. For example, if a filter type is up, then only gene values that are greater than a filter value threshold will be considered for further analysis. There are three gene filter types:

- — Absolute value (abs)
- — Greater than (up)
- — Less than (down)
- *Filter value threshold* is used by the gene filter type to exclude the genes that do not meet the threshold value.

Each bioset belongs to a patient identified by a `patientID`. Given a set of biosets (numbering in the thousands or tens of thousands), where each bioset may have up to 50,000 genes, we want to find the frequency of each gene that satisfies the aforementioned three metrics: reference type, gene filter type, and filter value threshold. The filter type indicates how the gene value should be compared to the filter value threshold (i.e., should we use absolute value, greater than, or less than?). The number of genes per bioset depends on the bioset data type: copy-number variation, gene expression, methylation, or somatic mutation. Before we delve into the MapReduce algorithm for gene aggregation, let's discuss the input/output data.

Input

Each bioset may have 20,000 to 50,000 records, and each record will have the following format (in the following examples, patients are identified by `p100` and `p200`):

```
<geneID><,><referenceType><;><patientID><,><geneValue>
```

For example:

```
7562135,r1;p100,1.04
```

Or:

```
7570769,r1;p200,-1.09
```

Output

The goal of gene aggregation is to find the frequency of each gene along with its reference type (`r1`, `r2`, `r3`, or `r4`). The MapReduce solution will generate the following output format in a distributed filesystem (for example, HDFS):

```
<geneID><,><referenceType><TAB><frequency-count>
```

For example:

```
7562135,r1    1205
```

Or:

```
7570769,r3    14067
```

Eventually, this output can be read into a Java object such as GeneAggregationFre
quencyCount, which will be discussed in the section "Analysis of Output" on page
597.

MapReduce Solutions (Filter by Individual and by Average)

The question in our gene aggregation algorithm is this: per patient, do we filter by
individual gene values (patientID is ignored) or by an *average of gene values*
(patientID is used)? For example, if we have 10 values for GENE-1 (using real data,
the number of values per geneID can be in the thousands; to help you understand the
algorithms, I use toy data here) for three patients (identified by p100, p200, p300)
with a reference type of r1, a gene filter type of up, and a filter value threshold of
1.04:

```
GENE-1,r1;p100,1.00
GENE-1,r1;p100,1.06
GENE-1,r1;p100,1.10
GENE-1,r1;p100,1.20

GENE-1,r1;p200,1.00
GENE-1,r1;p200,1.02
GENE-1,r1;p200,1.04

GENE-1,r1;p300,1.01
GENE-1,r1;p300,1.06
GENE-1,r1;p300,1.08
```

then we get the following different values (based on whether we filter by individual
gene values or by the average of gene values):

- If we filter by individual gene values we get the following output:

  ```
  GENE-1,r1    6
  ```

  since only six records' gene values are greater than or equal to 1.04, which passes
  the filter.

- If we filter by the average of gene values, we get the following output:

  ```
  GENE-1,r1    2
  ```

  since the average of values $\left(\frac{1.00 + 1.06 + 1.10 + 1.20}{4}\right)$ for patient p100 is 1.09, which
  is greater than 1.04 (passes the filter), the average of values $\left(\frac{1.00 + 1.02 + 1.04}{3}\right)$ for
  patient p200 is 1.02 (which does not pass the filter), and the average of values

$\left(\frac{1.01 + 1.06 + 1.08}{3}\right)$ for patient p300 is 1.05 (which passes the filter). Therefore, only two patients passed the test by average, so the frequency is 2.

We provide two distinct MapReduce solutions, which handle filtering by individual gene values as well as by the average of gene values.

How will we pass these three dynamic parameters (reference type, gene filter type, and filter value threshold) from the MapReduce driver to the map() and reduce() functions? Using the MapReduce/Hadoop Configuration object, we can set these values through Configuration.set() and retrieve them through Configuration.get() in the setup() function of map() or reduce().

The mapper gets one record of a bioset and tokenizes the input into a <geneID><,><referenceType> and geneValue. If the <geneID><,><referenceType> contains the desired reference type, then we check the geneValue to see if it meets the filter value threshold. If both conditions are satisfied, then we emit key-value pairs where the key is the <geneID><,><referenceType> and the value is the integer 1. The reducer sums up the frequencies for a specific <geneID><,><referenceType> and emits a key-value pair, where the key is the <geneID><,><referenceType> and the value is the final frequency count.

Mapper: Filter by Individual

For our filter by individual solution the mapper's setup() function, defined in Example 26-1, will retrieve the desired parameters (i.e., the metrics needed for gene aggregation) to be used in the map() function, defined in Example 26-2. The checkFilter() function is defined in Example 26-3.

Example 26-1. Gene aggregator: setup() function for filtering by individual

```
 1 public class GeneAggregatorMapperByIndividual ... {
 2
 3   private String referenceType = null;
 4   private String filterType = null;
 5   private double filterValueThreshold;
 6
 7   /**
 8    * will be run only once
 9    */
10   public void setup(Context context) {
11     Configuration conf = context.getConfiguration();
12     this.referenceType = conf.get("gene.reference.type");
13     this.filterType = conf.get("gene.filter.type");
14     this.filterValueThreshold =
15       Double.parseDouble(conf.get("gene.filter.value.threshold"));
16   }
```

Example 26-2. Gene aggregator: map() function for filtering by individual

```
 1 /**
 2  * @param key is the key generated by MapReduce partitioner (ignored here)
 3  * @param value is one record of a bioset as:
 4  *    <geneID><,><referenceType><;><patientID><,><geneValue>
 5  */
 6 map(Long key, String value) {
 7    String[] tokens = StringUtil.split(value, ";");
 8    String geneIDAndReferenceType = tokens[0];
 9    String patientIDAndGeneValue = tokens[1];
10    String[] val = StringUtil.split(patientIDAndGeneValue, ",");
11    // val[0] = patientID
12    // val[1] = geneValue
13    double geneValue = Double.parseDouble(val[1]);
14
15    String[] arr = StringUtil.split(geneIDAndReferenceType, ",");
16    // arr[0] = geneID
17    // arr[1] = referenceType
18    // check referenceType
19    if (arr[1].equals(this.referenceType)) {
20       if (checkFilter(geneValue)) {
21          // Then create a counter for the reducer;
22          // otherwise nothing will be written.
23          // Prepare key-value for reducer and send it to reducer.
24          emit(geneIDAndReferenceType, 1);
25       }
26    }
27 }
```

Example 26-3. Gene aggregator: checkFilter() function for filtering by individual

```
 1 public boolean checkFilter(double value) {
 2    if (filterType.equals("abs")) {
 3       if (Math.abs(value) >= this.filterValueThreshold) {
 4          return true;
 5       }
 6       else {
 7          return false;
 8       }
 9    }
10    if (filterType.equals("up")) {
11       if (value >= this.filterValueThreshold) {
12          return true;
13       }
14       else {
15          return false;
16       }
17    }
18    if (filterType.equals("down")) {
19       if (value <= this.filterValueThreshold) {
20          return true;
```

```
21      }
22      else {
23          return false;
24      }
25  }
26  return false;
27 }
```

Since the `filterType` is passed from the MapReduce driver to `map()`, we know the value of `filterType` before any `map()` starts. Therefore, in our MapReduce/Hadoop implementation, we will be able to use custom mappers to avoid the `if` statement so many times per `map()`. Note that in our MapReduce solution, for readability purposes I have avoided all exception checking and handling.

Reducer: Filter by Individual

The reducer will receive a (`key`, `List<Integer>`) pair, where `key` is the unique `geneAndReferenceType` and `List<Integer>` is a partial frequency of the unique `geneAndReferenceAsString`.

The reducer's job is to sum up the number of occurrences of unique `geneAndReferenceTypes`. Example 26-4 defines the `reduce()` function.

Example 26-4. Gene aggregator: reduce() function for filtering by individual

```
 1 /**
 2  * @param key is the unique geneAndReferenceAsString generated by the mapper
 3  * @param values is a list of integers
 4  *     (partial count of a unique geneIDAndReferenceType)
 5  */
 6 reduce(String key, List<Integer> values) {
 7     int sum = 0;
 8     for (int count : values) {
 9         sum += count;
10     }
11     emit(key, sum);
12 }
```

Mapper: Filter by Average

For our filter by average solution the mapper's `setup()` function, defined in Example 26-5, will retrieve the desired parameters (i.e., the metrics needed for gene aggregation) to be used in the `map()` function, defined in Example 26-6. Since we are filtering by the average of gene values per patient, we have to pass the `patientIDs` along with the gene values to the reducers.

Example 26-5. Gene aggregator: setup() function for filtering by average

```
1 public class GeneAggregatorMapperByIndividual ... {
2
3     private String referenceType = null;
4     private String filterType = null;
5     private double filterValueThreshold;
6
7     /**
8      * will be run only once
9      */
10    public void setup(Context context) {
11        Configuration conf = context.getConfiguration();
12        this.referenceType = conf.get("gene.reference.type");
13        this.filterType = conf.get("gene.filter.type");
14        this.filterValueThreshold =
15            Double.parseDouble(conf.get("gene.filter.value.threshold"));
16    }
```

Example 26-6. Gene aggregator: map() function for filtering by average

```
1 /**
2  * @param key is the key generated by MapReduce partitioner (ignored here)
3  * @param value is one record of a bioset as:
4  *    <geneID><,><referenceType><;><patientID><,><geneValue>
5  */
6 map(Long key, String value) {
7     String[] tokens = StringUtil.split(value, ";");
8     String geneIDAndReferenceType = tokens[0];
9     String patientIDAndGeneValue = tokens[1];
10
11    String[] arr = StringUtil.split(geneIDAndReferenceType, ",");
12    // arr[0] = geneID
13    // arr[1] = referenceType
14    // check referenceType
15    if (arr[1].equals(this.referenceType)) {
16        // prepare key-value for reducer and send it to reducer
17        emit(geneIDAndReferenceType, patientIDAndGeneValue);
18    }
19 }
```

Since the filterType is passed from the MapReduce driver to map(), we know the value of filterType before any map() starts. Therefore, in our MapReduce/Hadoop implementation, we will be able to use custom mappers to avoid the if statement so many times per map(). Note that in our MapReduce solution, for readability purposes I have avoided all exception checking and handling.

Reducer: Filter by Average

The reducer will receive a (K, List<V>) pair, where K is the unique geneIDAndRefer enceType and V is a patientIDAndGeneValue. The reducer's job is to sum up the number of occurrences of unique geneIDAndReferenceTypes by filtering the average of gene values.

Example 26-7 defines the reduce() function.

Example 26-7. Gene aggregator: reduce() function for filtering by average

```
 1 /**
 2  * @param key is the unique geneIDAndReferenceType generated by mappers
 3  * @param values is a List<V> and V is a patientIDAndGeneValue
 4  */
 5 reduce(String key, List<String> values) {
 6      Map<String, Tuple2<Double,Integer>> patients =
 7         GeneAggregatorUtil.buildPatientsMap(values);
 8      int passedTheTest = GeneAggregatorUtil.getNumberOfPatientsPassedTheTest(
 9         patients,
10         this.filterType,
11         this.filterValueThreshold
12      );
13
14      // emit the output of reducer
15      emit(key, passedTheTest);
16 }
```

Computing Gene Aggregation

Computing gene aggregation is handled by a utility class called GeneAggregatorUtil. This class has two static methods:

buildPatientsMap()
> This method, defined in Example 26-8, accepts a List<Tuple2<patientID, gene Value>> and builds a Map<patientID, sumOfGeneValues>.

getNumberOfPatientsPassedTheTest()
> This method, defined in Example 26-9, counts to see how many patients passed the test (i.e., satisfied the filter criteria). It achieves this by examining each entry of Map built by the buildPatientsMap() method.

Also, we use a simple class, PairOfDoubleInteger, to represent a Tuple2<Double, Integer> and enable us to update its values.

Example 26-8. GeneAggregatorUtil.buildPatientsMap()

```
 1 /**
 2  * @param values = List<Tuple2<patientID, geneValue>>
 3  *
 4  * THE RESULT Map:
 5  * make sure we do not count more than once for the same patient
 6  *     patients.key = patientID
 7  *     patients.value = Tuple2<D, I>
 8  *        where D = sum of values for the patientID
 9  *              I = number of values (counter)
10  */
11 public static Map<String, PairOfDoubleInteger> buildPatientsMap(
12    Iterable<Text> values) throws IOException, InterruptedException {
13    Map<String, PairOfDoubleInteger> patients =
14       new HashMap<String, PairOfDoubleInteger>();
15    for (Text patientIdAndGeneValue : values) {
16       String[] tokens =
17          StringUtils.split(patientIdAndGeneValue.toString(), ",");
18       String patientID = tokens[0];
19       //tokens[1] = geneValue
20       double geneValue = Double.parseDouble(tokens[1]);
21       PairOfDoubleInteger pair = patients.get(patientID);
22       if (pair == null) {
23          pair = new PairOfDoubleInteger(geneValue, 1);
24          patients.put(patientID, pair);
25       }
26       else {
27          pair.increment(geneValue);
28       }
29    }
30    return patients;
31 }
```

Example 26-9. GeneAggregatorUtil.getNumberOfPatientsPassedTheTest()

```
 1 public static int getNumberOfPatientsPassedTheTest(
 2       Map<String, PairOfDoubleInteger> patients,
 3       double filterValue,
 4       String filterType) {  // filterType = {"up", "down", "abs"}
 5    if (patients == null) {
 6       return 0;
 7    }
 8
 9    // now, we will average the values and see which
10    // patients pass the threshold
11    int passedTheTest = 0;
12    for (Map.Entry<String, PairOfDoubleInteger>
13          entry : patients.entrySet()) {
14       //String patientID = entry.getKey();
15       PairOfDoubleInteger pair = entry.getValue();
16       double avg = pair.avg();
```

```
17          if (filterType.equals("up")) {
18              if (avg >= filterValue) {
19                  passedTheTest++;
20              }
21          }
22          if (filterType.equals("down")) {
23              if (avg <= filterValue) {
24                  passedTheTest++;
25              }
26          }
27          else if (filterType.equals("abs")) {
28              if (Math.abs(avg) >= filterValue) {
29                  passedTheTest++;
30              }
31          }
32      }
33      return  passedTheTest;
34 }
```

Hadoop Implementation Classes

We have a simple MapReduce solution for gene aggregation. The following classes are used to implement the MapReduce solution in Hadoop.

GeneAggregationDriverByIndividual
   A driver for setting input/output and launching the job

GeneAggregationMapperByIndividual
   A mapper to filter by individual values

GeneAggregationReducerByIndividual
   A reducer to filter by individual values

GeneAggregationDriverByAverage
   A driver for setting input/output and launching the job

GeneAggregationMapperByAverage
   A mapper to filter by the average of values

GeneAggregationReducerByAverage
   A reducer to filter by the average of values

In order to achieve better performance, we'll use separate classes for handling each filter type (up, down, abs). Therefore, GeneAggregationMapperByIndividual can be replaced by these three plug-in classes:

GeneAggregationMapperByIndividualUP
   When filterType = up

GeneAggregationMapperByIndividualDOWN
    When `filterType = down`

GeneAggregationMapperByIndividualABS
    When `filterType = abs`

Note that for performance efficiency purposes, I provided three mappers (one for each gene filter type). This enables us to avoid gene filter type checking by an `if` statement. For example, if we are processing 20,000 biosets and each bioset has over 40,000 `geneID`s, then we have avoided executing 800 million unnecessary `if` statements.

Likewise, the `GeneAggregationReducerByAverage` reducer class can be optimized through these three plug-in classes:

GeneAggregationReducerByAverageUP
    When `filterType = up`

GeneAggregationReducerByAverageDOWN
    When `filterType = down`

GeneAggregationReducerByAverageABS
    When `filterType = abs`

Similar to the plug-in mapper classes, these custom plug-in reducers avoid unnecessary `if` statement checks.

We set the plug-in mapper classes in the driver class when we check gene values individually, as shown in Example 26-10.

Example 26-10. GeneAggregationDriverByIndividual class

```
1 public class GeneAggregationDriverByIndividual extends Configured
2     implements Tool {
3     String filterType = ...;
4
5     public int run(String[] args) throws Exception {
6         Job job = ...;
7         ...
8         // set the optimized mapper class
9         if (filterType.equals("up")) {
10            job.setMapper(GeneAggregationMapperByIndividualUP.class);
11        else if (filterType.equals("down")) {
12            job.setMapper(GeneAggregationMapperByIndividualDOWN.class);
13        }
14        else if (filterType.equals("abs")) {
15            job.setMapper(GeneAggregationMapperByIndividualABS.class);
16        }
17        else {
```

```
18          throw new Exception("filterType is undefined");
19      }
20
21      // set the reducer class
22      job.setReducer(GeneAggregationReducerByIndividualDOWN.class);
23      ...
24  }
25 }
```

We set the plug-in reducer classes in the driver class when we check gene values by average, as shown in Example 26-11.

Example 26-11. GeneAggregationDriverByAverage class

```
1 public class GeneAggregationDriverByAverage extends Configured implements Tool {
2      String filterType = ...;
3
4      public int run(String[] args) throws Exception {
5          Job job = ...;
6          ...
7          // set the mapper class
8          job.setMapper(GeneAggregationMapperByAverage.class);
9
10         // set the optimized reducer class
11         if (filterType.equals("up")) {
12             job.setReducer(GeneAggregationReducerByAverageUP.class);
13         else if (filterType.equals("down")) {
14             job.setReducer(GeneAggregationReducerByAverageDOWN.class);
15         }
16         else if (filterType.equals("abs")) {
17             job.setReducer(GeneAggregationReducerByAverageABS.class);
18         }
19         else {
20             throw new Exception("filterType is undefined");
21         }
22         ...
23     }
24 }
```

Next, the checkFilter() method is broken down into three segments (one segment per mapper class), as shown in Examples 26-12 through 26-14. Since we have a custom plug-in mapper class for each filterType, the if statement(s) are dropped. Now, each mapper class knows the exact filterType value.

Example 26-12. checkFilter() for GeneAggregationMapperByIndividualUP class

```
1 public boolean checkFilter(double value) {
2      //if (filterType.equals("up")) {
3          if (value >= this.filterValueThreshold) {
4              return true;
```

```
5      }
6      else {
7          return false;
8      }
9  //}
10 }
```

Example 26-13. checkFilter() for GeneAggregationMapperByIndividualDOWN class

```
1 public boolean checkFilter(double value) {
2     //if (filterType.equals("down")) {
3         if (value <= this.filterValueThreshold) {
4             return true;
5         }
6         else {
7             return false;
8         }
9     //}
10 }
```

Example 26-14. checkFilter() for GeneAggregationMapperByIndividualABS class

```
1 public boolean checkFilter(double value) {
2     //if (filterType.equals("abs")) {
3         if (Math.abs(value) >= this.filterValueThreshold) {
4             return true;
5         }
6         else {
7             return false;
8         }
9     //}
10 }
```

Analysis of Output

The output (saved in HDFS as a SequenceFile—that is, binary key-value pairs) of our MapReduce/Hadoop solution will have the following format:

    <geneID><,><referenceType><TAB><frequency-count>

For example:

    7562135,r1   1205

Or:

    7570769,r1   14067

We can easily read these output files and pass the values into Java objects.

The FrequencyItem interface, shown in Example 26-15, is used for returning the results of gene aggregation.

Example 26-15. FrequencyItem interface

```
1 public interface FrequencyItem {
2    public Integer getGeneId();
3    public void setGeneId(Integer id);
4
5    public Integer getFrequency();
6    public void setFrequency(Integer frequency);
7
8    public String getReferenceType();
9    public void setReferenceType(String referenceType);
10
11   public String toString();
12 }
```

Then we invoke the following, where dir is the Hadoop output path:

```
List<FrequencyItem> list = readDirectoryIntoFrequencyItem(dir);
```

The GeneAggregatorAnalyzerUsingFrequencyItem class is defined in Examples 26-16 through 26-20. This class reads the output directory of the HDFS and returns the result as a List<FrequencyItem> object.

Example 26-16. GeneAggregatorAnalyzerUsingFrequencyItem class

```
1 GeneAggregatorAnalyzerUsingFrequencyItem {
2
3    static List<FrequencyItem> readDirectoryIntoFrequencyItem(String pathAsString) {
4       return readDirectoryIntoFrequencyItem(new Path(pathAsString));
5    }
6
6    static List<FrequencyItem> readDirectoryIntoFrequencyItem(Path path) {
7       // definition is provided in Example 26-17
8    }
9
10   @SuppressWarnings("unchecked")
11   public static List<FrequencyItem> readFileIntoFrequencyItem(Path path,
12                                                   FileSystem fs) {
13      // definition is provided in Example 26-18
14   }
15
16   private static FrequencyItem createFrequencyItem(Text key,
17                                                   IntWritable frequency) {
18      // definition is provided in Example 26-19
19   }
20
21   static void closeAndIgnoreException(SequenceFile.Reader reader) {
22      // definition is provided in Example 26-20
23   }
24
25   public static void main(String[] args) throws Exception {
```

```
26        //test1(args);
27        Path path = new Path(args[0]);
28        List<FrequencyItem> list = readDirectoryIntoFrequencyItem(path);
29        THE_LOGGER.info("list="+list.toString());
30    }
31 }
```

Example 26-17. readDirectoryIntoFrequencyItem() method

```
1 static List<FrequencyItem> readDirectoryIntoFrequencyItem(Path path) {
2     FileSystem fs = null;
3     try {
4         fs = FileSystem.get(new Configuration());
5     }
6     catch (IOException e) {
7         THE_LOGGER.error("Unable to access the hadoop file system!", e);
8         throw new RuntimeException("Unable to access the hadoop file system!");
9     }
10
11    List<FrequencyItem> list = new ArrayList<FrequencyItem>();
12    try {
13        FileStatus[] status = fs.listStatus(path);
14        for (int i = 0; i < status.length; ++i) {
15            Path hdfsFile = status[i].getPath();
16            if (hdfsFile.getName().startsWith("part")) {
17                List<FrequencyItem> pairs = readFileIntoFrequencyItem(hdfsFile, fs);
18                list.addAll(pairs);
19            }
20        }
21    }
22    catch (IOException e) {
23        THE_LOGGER.error("Unable to access the hadoop file system!", e);
24        throw new RuntimeException("Error reading the hadoop file system!");
25    }
26    return list;
27 }
```

Example 26-18. readFileIntoFrequencyItem() method

```
1 @SuppressWarnings("unchecked")
2 public static List<FrequencyItem> readFileIntoFrequencyItem(Path path,
3                                                    FileSystem fs) {
4     List<FrequencyItem> list = new ArrayList<FrequencyItem>();
5     SequenceFile.Reader reader = null;
6     try {
7         reader = new SequenceFile.Reader(fs, path, fs.getConf());
8         Text key = (Text) reader.getKeyClass().newInstance();
9         IntWritable value = (IntWritable) reader.getValueClass().newInstance();
10        while (reader.next(key, value)) {
11            list.add(createFrequencyItem(key, value));
12            key = (Text) reader.getKeyClass().newInstance();
```

```
13              value = (IntWritable) reader.getValueClass().newInstance();
14      }
15  }
16  catch (Exception e) {
17      THE_LOGGER.error("Error reading SequenceFile " + path, e);
18      throw new RuntimeException("Error reading SequenceFile " + path);
19  }
20  finally {
21      closeAndIgnoreException(reader);
22  }
23  return list;
24 }
```

Example 26-19. createFrequencyItem() method

```
1 private static FrequencyItem createFrequencyItem(Text key,
2                                                   IntWritable frequency) {
3    // key = <geneID><,><referenceType> where referenceType in {r1, r2, r3, r4}
4    // value = integer
5    if (key == null) {
6       return null;
7    }
8    String geneIDAndReference = key.toString();
9    String[] tokens = StringUtils.split(geneIDAndReference, ",");
10    String geneID = tokens[0];
11    String referenceType =  tokens[0];
12    FrequencyItem item = FrequencyItemFactory.createFrequencyItem(
13        geneID, referenceType, frequency.get());
14    return item;
15 }
```

Example 26-20. closeAndIgnoreException() method

```
1 static void closeAndIgnoreException(SequenceFile.Reader reader) {
2    if (reader == null) {
3        return;
4    }
5
6    try {
7        reader.close();
8    }
9    catch(Exception ignore) {
10        THE_LOGGER.error("Error closing SequenceFile.Reader.", ignore);
11    }
12 }
```

Gene Aggregation in Spark

The following sections present two Spark solutions for gene aggregation. From HDFS input files, we will create RDDs and manipulate them in Spark. Spark's main data representation is an RDD that enables parallel operations (such as the map(), reduce(), and groupByKey() functions) on the data. Spark can read and save RDDs from many different sources (including HDFS and the Linux filesystem). Another way to create RDDs is from Java collection objects.

As with the Hadoop solution, we provide two distinct Spark solutions for gene aggregation (in each case, the entire Spark solution is presented in one Java driver class):

- Filtering by individual gene values is implemented by the SparkGeneAggregation ByIndividual class.

- Filtering by the average of gene values is implemented by the SparkGeneAggrega tionByAverage class.

Spark Solution: Filter by Individual

The first step to filtering by individual is to create a JavaRDD<String> for all input biosets, where each item of the RDD will be a record of a bioset. The second step is to filter out the values that do not meet the reference type and filter value threshold values. The third step will be to map the RDD items (generated by the second step) into JavaPairRDD<K,V> pairs, where K is a <geneID><,><referenceType> and V is an integer, 1 (similar to the classic word count example). The final step will be to group by K.

Sharing Data Between Cluster Nodes

The question now is how to pass the three metric values (referenceType, filter Type, and filterValueThreshold) to Spark's actions and transformations for manipulating RDDs. Spark provides the Broadcast<T>[1] class for sharing read-only variables among all cluster nodes. In MapReduce/Hadoop, sharing variables among mappers and reducers is accomplished through the Hadoop Configuration object. The driver class (which submits jobs to the MapReduce framework) sets/defines shared variables and the map() or reduce() function uses these shared variables. Sharing is achieved through the mapper's or reducer's setup() function, which is called once for each mapper or reducer. Also, in Hadoop, you may use DistributedCache.[2]

---

1 org.apache.spark.broadcast.Broadcast. Spark's Broadcast variables allow the programmer to keep a read-only variable cached on each cluster node rather than shipping a copy of it with MapReduce tasks. Broadcast variables provide every cluster node with a copy of an input data set in an efficient manner. Spark attempts to distribute Broadcast variables using efficient broadcast algorithms to reduce communication cost.

2 org.apache.hadoop.filecache.DistributedCache is a facility provided by the MapReduce framework to cache files (text, archives, JARs, etc.) needed by applications.

In Spark, for our three metric values, we define three `Broadcast` objects; and when we need them for manipulating RDDs (using the `map()` and `reduce()` functions), we read them. This is how we define the `Broadcast` objects:

```
JavaSparkContext ctx = new JavaSparkContext();
...
Broadcast<String> broadcastVarReferenceType =
    ctx.broadcast(referenceType);
Broadcast<String> broadcastVarFilterType =
    ctx.broadcast(filterType);
Broadcast<Double> broadcastVarFilterValueThreshold =
    ctx.broadcast(filterValueThreshold);
```

and this is how we use/read them when needed:

```
String referenceType = (String) broadcastVarReferenceType.value();
String filterType = (String) broadcastVarFilterType.value();
Double filterValueThreshold =
    (Double) broadcastVarFilterValueThreshold.value();
```

The general form of using `Broadcast<T>` is defined as follows:

```
DEFINITION:
    JavaSparkContext ctx = new JavaSparkContext();
    T t = <some-data-structure-of-type-T>;
    final Broadcast<T> broadcastVariable = ctx.broadcast(t);
USAGE:
    T t = (T) broadcastVariable.value();
```

The Spark API indicates that after the `Broadcast` variable is created, it should be used instead of the value `t` in any functions run on the cluster so that `t` is not shipped to the nodes more than once.

High-Level Steps

The Spark solution is a single Java driver class manipulating several RDDs. This section provides the main steps of the Java driver class (Example 26-21), and then I will provide details for each step.

Example 26-21. SparkGeneAggregationByIndividual class

```
 1 //Step 1: import required classes and interfaces
 2 public class SparkGeneAggregationByIndividual {
 3
 4    public static void main(String[] args) throws Exception {
 5        //Step 2: handle input parameters
 6        //Step 3: create a Spark context object (ctx)
 7        //Step 4: broadcast shared variables
 8        //Step 5: create a single JavaRDD from all bioset files
 9        //Step 6: map bioset records into JavaPairRDD<K,V> pairs
10        //         where K = "<geneID><,><referenceType>", V = 1
```

```
11        //Step 7: filter out the redundant RDD elements
12        //Step 8: reduce by key and sum up the frequency count
13        //Step 9: prepare the final output
14
15        // done
16        ctx.close();
17        System.exit(0);
18    }
19 }
```

Step 1: Import required classes and interfaces

To use RDDs, we need Spark's `org.apache.spark.api.java` package. The `org.apache.spark.api.java.function` package defines functions for actions and transformations. Also, we need the `org.apache.spark.broadcast.Broadcast` class to define/broadcast shared global data structures among all cluster nodes.

Example 26-22. Step 1: import required classes and interfaces

```
 1 //Step 1: import required classes and interfaces
 2 import scala.Tuple2;
 3 import org.apache.spark.api.java.JavaPairRDD;
 4 import org.apache.spark.api.java.JavaRDD;
 5 import org.apache.spark.api.java.JavaSparkContext;
 6 import org.apache.spark.api.java.function.Function;
 7 import org.apache.spark.api.java.function.Function2;
 8 import org.apache.spark.api.java.function.PairFunction;
 9 import org.apache.commons.lang.StringUtils;
10 import org.apache.spark.broadcast.Broadcast;
11
12 import java.util.Arrays;
13 import java.util.List;
14 import java.util.ArrayList;
15 import java.io.FileReader;
16 import java.io.BufferedReader;
```

Step 2: Handle input parameters

This step, shown in Example 26-23, reads the three parameters (`referenceType`, `fil terType`, `filterValueThreshold`) for gene aggregation and all biosets involved in the analysis. Each bioset is identified by an HDFS file.

Example 26-23. Step 2: handle input parameters

```
 1        //Step 2: handle input parameters
 2        if (args.length != 4) {
 3            System.err.println("Usage: SparkGeneAggregationByIndividual "
 4                            + "<referenceType><filterType> "
 5                            + "<filterValueThreshold> <biosets>");
 6            System.exit(1);
```

```
7        }
8
9        final String referenceType = args[0];    // {"r1", "r2", "r3", "r4"}
10       final String filterType = args[1];       // {"up", "down", "abs"}
11       final Double filterValueThreshold = new Double(args[2]);
12       final String biosets = args[3];
13
14       System.out.println("args[0]: <referenceType>="+referenceType);
15       System.out.println("args[1]: <filterType>="+filterType);
16       System.out.println("args[2]: <filterValueThreshold>="+filterValueThreshold);
17       System.out.println("args[3]: <biosets>="+biosets);
```

Step 3: Create a Spark context object

This step, shown in Example 26-24, creates the `JavaSparkContext` object, which we need for the creation of RDDs. The context object can be created in many different ways.

Example 26-24. Step 3: create a Spark context object

```
1        //Step 3: create a Spark context object
2        JavaSparkContext ctx = new JavaSparkContext();
```

Step 4: Broadcast shared variables

As described earlier, Spark enables sharing variables and data structures among cluster nodes through the `Broadcast<T>` class, where `T` is a type of shared data (see Example 26-25). Spark has an efficient mechanism for broadcasting shared variables and objects. Shared variables can be accessed in Spark's `map()` and `reduce()` functions.

Example 26-25. Step 4: broadcast shared variables

```
1    //Step 4: broadcast shared variables
2    final Broadcast<String> broadcastVarReferenceType = ctx.broadcast(referenceType);
3    final Broadcast<String> broadcastVarFilterType = ctx.broadcast(filterType);
4    final Broadcast<Double> broadcastVarFilterValueThreshold =
5        ctx.broadcast(filterValueThreshold);
```

Step 5: Create a JavaRDD for biosets

The main data for gene aggregation analysis comes from bioset files. This step, shown in Example 26-26, creates a single `JavaRDD<String>` for all records of biosets involved in the analysis. A debugging step has been included as well.

Example 26-26. Step 5: create a single JavaRDD from all bioset files

```
1      //Step 5: create a single JavaRDD from all bioset files
2      JavaRDD<String> records = readInputFiles(ctx, biosets);
```

The code to debug this setp follows:

```
1 // debug1
2 List<String> debug1 = records.collect();
3 for (String rec : debug1) {
4    System.out.println("debug1 => "+ rec);
5 }
```

Step 6: Map bioset records into JavaPairRDD<K,V> pairs

This step creates a JavaPairRDD<K,V> object from each bioset record, where K = "<geneID><,><referenceType>" and V = 1. This will enable us to count the frequency of genes for all patients represented by biosets. When a bioset record does not match our metric criteria, we create a dummy object, Tuple2("null", 0), which will be filtered out before the output is finalized. In Spark, mapToPair() is not allowed to return Java null objects, which is why we create replacement objects such as Tuple2Null instead.

Example 26-27. Step 6: map bioset records into JavaPairRDD<K,V> pairs

```
1      //Step 6: map bioset records into JavaPairRDD<K,V> pairs
2      // where K = "<geneID><,><referenceType>", V = 1
3      JavaPairRDD<String, Integer> genes =
4             records.mapToPair(new PairFunction<String, String, Integer>() {
5        public Tuple2<String, Integer> call(String record) {
6           String[] tokens = StringUtils.split(record, ";");
7           String geneIDAndReferenceType = tokens[0];
8           String patientIDAndGeneValue = tokens[1];
9           String[] val = StringUtils.split(patientIDAndGeneValue, ",");
10          // val[0] = patientID
11          // val[1] = geneValue
12          double geneValue = Double.parseDouble(val[1]);
13          String[] arr = StringUtils.split(geneIDAndReferenceType, ",");
14          // arr[0] = geneID
15          // arr[1] = referenceType
16          // check referenceType and geneValue
17          String referenceType = (String) broadcastVarReferenceType.value();
18          String filterType = (String) broadcastVarFilterType.value();
19          Double filterValueThreshold =
20              (Double) broadcastVarFilterValueThreshold.value();
21
22          if ( (arr[1].equals(referenceType)) &&
23              (checkFilter(geneValue, filterType, filterValueThreshold)) ) {
24              // prepare key-value for reducer and send it to reducer
25              return new Tuple2<String, Integer>(geneIDAndReferenceType, 1);
```

```
26                }
27            else {
28                // otherwise nothing will be counted
29                // later we will filter out these "null" keys
30                return Tuple2Null;
31            }
32        }
33    });
```

The following debugs Step 6:

```
// debug2
List<Tuple2<String, Integer>> debug2 = genes.collect();
for (Tuple2<String, Integer> pair : debug2) {
    System.out.println("debug2 => key="+ pair._1 + "\tvalue="+pair._2);

}
```

Step 7: Filter out the redundant RDD elements

Step 6 created redundant (K,V) = ("null", 0) pairs. This step, shown in Example 26-28, filters out unnecessary data and provides a clean Java PairRDD<String,Integer>. We accomplish this by implementing Spark's filter() function, which is defined as:

```
public JavaPairRDD<K,V> filter(Function<Tuple2<K,V>,Boolean> f)

Description: Return a new RDD containing only the
            elements that satisfy a predicate;
```

Example 26-28 shows the filter implementation.

Example 26-28. Step 7: filter out the redundant RDD elements

```
1       //Step 7: filter out the redundant RDD elements
2       // If a counter (i.e., V) is 0, then exclude them.
3       JavaPairRDD<String,Integer> filteredGenes =
4           genes.filter(new Function<Tuple2<String,Integer>,Boolean>() {
5         public Boolean call(Tuple2<String, Integer> s) {
6           int counter = s._2;
7           if (counter > 0) {
8               return true;
9           }
10          else {
11              return false;
12          }
13        }
14      });
```

Step 8: Reduce by key and sum up the frequency count

This step, shown in Example 26-29, implements the reduce() function. It basically groups the genes by geneID and sums up the frequency counts.

Example 26-29. Step 8: reduce by key and sum up the frequency count

```
1    //Step 8: reduce by key and sum up the frequency count
2    JavaPairRDD<String, Integer> counts =
3        filteredGenes.reduceByKey(new Function2<Integer, Integer, Integer>() {
4        public Integer call(Integer i1, Integer i2) {
5            return i1 + i2;
6        }
7    });
```

Step 9: Prepare the final output

This step (Example 26-30) emits the final desired output for our gene aggregation analysis.

Example 26-30. Step 9: prepare the final output

```
1    //Step 9: prepare the final output
2    List<Tuple2<String, Integer>> output = counts.collect();
3    for (Tuple2<String, Integer> tuple : output) {
4        System.out.println("final output => "+ tuple._1 + ": " + tuple._2);
5    }
```

Utility Functions

Example 26-31 through Example 26-33 present utility methods that are used in our Spark implementation. The toList() method accepts a file containing all biosets involved in the analysis phase (see Example 26-31). Each record of the input file is an HDFS file that represents a single bioset.

Example 26-31. toList() utility function

```
1    /**
2     * Convert all bioset files into a List<biosetFileName>
3     *
4     * @param biosets is a filename, which holds all bioset files as HDFS entries
5     * An example will be:
6     *      /biosets/1000.txt
7     *      /biosets/1001.txt
8     *      ...
9     *      /biosets/1408.txt
10    */
11   private static List<String> toList(String biosets) throws Exception {
12       List<String> biosetFiles = new ArrayList<String>();
```

```
13        BufferedReader in = new BufferedReader(new FileReader(biosets));
14        String line = null;
15        while ((line = in.readLine()) != null) {
16            String aBiosetFile = line.trim();
17            biosetFiles.add(aBiosetFile);
18        }
19        in.close();
20        return biosetFiles;
21    }
```

Example 26-32. readInputFiles() utility function

```
1    static JavaRDD<String> readInputFiles(JavaSparkContext ctx,
2                                          String filename)
3      throws Exception {
4      List<String> biosetFiles = toList(filename);
5      int counter = 0;
6      JavaRDD[] rdds = new JavaRDD[biosetFiles.size()];
7      for (String biosetFileName : biosetFiles) {
8          System.out.println("readInputFiles(): biosetFileName=" + biosetFileName);
9          JavaRDD<String> record = ctx.textFile(biosetFileName);
10         rdds[counter] = record;
11         counter++;
12     }
13     JavaRDD<String> allBiosets = ctx.union(rdds);
14     return allBiosets;
15   }
```

Example 26-33. checkFilter() utility function

```
1 static  boolean checkFilter(double value,
2                             String filterType,
3                             Double filterValueThreshold) {
4      if (filterType.equals("abs")) {
5          if (Math.abs(value) >= filterValueThreshold) {
6              return true;
7          }
8          else {
9              return false;
10         }
11     }
12     if (filterType.equals("up")) {
13         if (value >= filterValueThreshold) {
14             return true;
15         }
16         else {
17             return false;
18         }
19     }
20     if (filterType.equals("down")) {
21         if (value <= filterValueThreshold) {
```

```
22          return true;
23        }
24        else {
25            return false;
26        }
27    }
28    return false;
29 }
```

Sample Run

The following subsections provide the input, script, and log output for a sample run of our Spark solution in the YARN environment.

Input

Here is the input for SparkGeneAggregationByIndividual:

```
# cat biosets.txt
/biosets/b1.txt
/biosets/b2.txt
/biosets/b3.txt
# hadoop fs -cat /biosets/b1.txt
GENE-1,r1;p100,1.00
GENE-1,r1;p100,1.06
GENE-1,r1;p100,1.10
GENE-1,r1;p100,1.20
# hadoop fs -cat /biosets/b2.txt
GENE-1,r1;p200,1.00
GENE-1,r1;p200,1.02
GENE-1,r1;p200,1.04
# hadoop fs -cat /biosets/b3.txt
GENE-1,r1;p300,1.01
GENE-1,r1;p300,1.06
GENE-1,r1;p300,1.08
```

Script

The following is the script to run SparkGeneAggregationByIndividual:

```
$ cat run_gene_aggregation_by_individual_yarn.sh
#!/bin/bash
export JAVA_HOME=/usr/java/jdk7
export HADOOP_HOME=/usr/local/hadoop-2.5.0
export HADOOP_CONF_DIR=$HADOOP_HOME/etc/hadoop
export YARN_CONF_DIR=$HADOOP_CONF_DIR
export SPARK_HOME=/home/hadoop/spark-1.1.0
export BOOK_HOME=/home/data-algorithms-book
export APP_JAR=$BOOK_HOME/data_algorithms_book.jar
prog=org.dataalgorithms.chap26.spark.SparkGeneAggregationByIndividual
biosets=$BOOK_HOME/data/biosets.txt
referenceType=r1
```

```
#{"r1", "r2", "r3", "r4"}
filterType=up
# {"up", "down", "abs"}
filterValueThreshold=1.04
$SPARK_HOME/bin/spark-submit --class $prog \
    --master yarn-cluster \
    --num-executors 6 \
    --driver-memory 1g \
    --executor-memory 1g \
    --executor-cores 12 \
    $APP_JAR $referenceType $filterType $filterValueThreshold $biosets
```

Log of sample run

```
# ./run_gene_aggregation_by_individual_yarn.sh

args[0]: <referenceType>=r1
args[1]: <filterType>=up
args[2]: <filterValueThreshold>=1.04
args[3]: <biosets>=/home/data-algorithms-book/data/biosets.txt

readInputFiles(): biosetFileName=/biosets/b1.txt
readInputFiles(): biosetFileName=/biosets/b2.txt
readInputFiles(): biosetFileName=/biosets/b3.txt

debug2 => key=null    value=0
debug2 => key=GENE-1,r1    value=1
debug2 => key=GENE-1,r1    value=1
debug2 => key=GENE-1,r1    value=1
debug2 => key=null    value=0
debug2 => key=null    value=0
debug2 => key=GENE-1,r1    value=1
debug2 => key=null    value=0
debug2 => key=GENE-1,r1    value=1
debug2 => key=GENE-1,r1    value=1

final output => GENE-1,r1: 6
```

Spark Solution: Filter by Average

This section presents a Spark solution for gene aggregation using the *filter by average* method. The first step to filtering by average is to create a JavaRDD<String> for all input biosets, where each item of the RDD will be a record of a bioset. The second step is to create a JavaPairRDD<K,V> object for each item, where K is a <gen eID><,><referenceType> and V is a <patientID><,><geneValue>. The third step is to group by K. The final step is to find the frequencies of each geneID by the average values of the genes (for each patient), which satisfies all given metrics. This example illustrates the core of gene aggregation using the filter by average.

To find the average for each patient, using V, we build a hash table as follows:

```
Map(patientID, Tuple2(sum(geneValue), count))
```

Next, we find the average for each patient as Map(patientID, average), where aver
age = sum(geneValue)/count. If the average passes the filter value threshold, then
that will be counted as 1 (meaning it passed the test); otherwise, it will be counted as
0 (meaning it did not pass the test).

High-Level Steps

As usual, I will present the main steps for the Spark solution first (see
Example 26-34), and in the subsequent sections I'll present the details of each step.

Example 26-34. Gene aggregation by average: high-level steps

```
1 //Step 1: import required classes and interfaces
2
3 public class SparkGeneAggregationByAverage {
4
5     // used as a dummy object for filtering
6     static final Tuple2<String, String> Tuple2Null =
7        new Tuple2<String, String>("n", "n");
8
9     public static void main(String[] args) throws Exception {
10        //Step 2: handle input parameters
11        //Step 3: create a Java Spark context object (ctx)
12        //Step 4: share global variables in all cluster nodes
13        //Step 5: read all bioset records and create an RDD
14        //Step 6: map bioset records and create a JavaPairRDD<K, V> from each
15        //   where K = "<geneID><,><referenceType>",
16        //           V = "<patientID><,><geneValue>"
17        //Step 7: filter redundant records created by step 6
18        //Step 8: group biosets by "<geneID><,><referenceType>"
19        //      genesByID = JavaPairRDD<K, List<V>>
20        //           where K = "<geneID><,><referenceType>"
21        //               V = "<patientID><,><geneValue>"
22        //Step 9: prepare the final desired output
23        //Step 10: emit the final output
24
25        // done
26        ctx.close();
27        System.exit(0);
28    }
29 }
```

Step 1: Import required classes and interfaces

In this step, shown in Example 26-35, we import the classes and interfaces we need
for our Spark solution to filtering by average.

Example 26-35. Step 1: import required classes and interfaces

```
1 //Step 1: import required classes and interfaces
2 import scala.Tuple2;
3 import org.apache.spark.api.java.JavaRDD;
4 import org.apache.spark.api.java.JavaPairRDD;
5 import org.apache.spark.api.java.JavaSparkContext;
6 import org.apache.spark.api.java.function.Function;
7 import org.apache.spark.api.java.function.PairFunction;
8 import org.apache.commons.lang.StringUtils;
9 import org.apache.spark.broadcast.Broadcast;
10
11 import java.io.FileReader;
12 import java.io.BufferedReader;
13 import java.util.Map;
14 import java.util.HashMap;
15 import java.util.List;
16 import java.util.ArrayList;
```

Step 2: Handle input parameters

Example 26-36 shows how we handle the input parameters for our solution.

Example 26-36. Step 2: handle input parameters

```
1    //Step 2: handle input parameters
2    if (args.length != 4) {
3      System.err.println("Usage: SparkGeneAggregationByAverage"+
4        " <referenceType> <filterType> <filterValueThreshold> <biosets>");
5      System.exit(1);
6    }
7
8    final String referenceType = args[0];      // {"r1", "r2", "r3", "r4"}
9    final String filterType = args[1];         // {"up", "down", "abs"}
10   final Double filterValueThreshold = new Double(args[2]);
11   final String biosets = args[3];
12
13   System.out.println("args[0]: <referenceType>="+referenceType);
14   System.out.println("args[1]: <filterType>="+filterType);
15   System.out.println("args[2]: <filterValueThreshold>="+filterValueThreshold);
16   System.out.println("args[3]: <biosets>="+biosets);
```

Step 3: Create a Java Spark context object

You need to create a JavaSparkContext object (as shown in Example 26-37) in order to create and manipulate your RDDs. There are many ways to create this context object. For details, see the Spark API documentation.

Example 26-37. Step 3: create a Java Spark context object

```
1    //Step 3: create a Java Spark context object
2    JavaSparkContext ctx = new JavaSparkContext();
```

Step 4: Share global variables in all cluster nodes

In Spark, the `Broadcast<T>` class enables us to share data structures of type `T` among all cluster nodes. Basically, you can share/broadcast your data structures in your driver program (the class submitting the job to the Spark or YARN cluster), and then you may read them from any cluster node inside the `map()` and `reduceByKey()` functions. For our three global variables, we do this as shown in Example 26-38.

Example 26-38. Step 4: share global variables in all cluster nodes

```
1    //Step 4: share global variables in all cluster nodes
2    final Broadcast<String> broadcastVarReferenceType =
3        ctx.broadcast(referenceType);
4    final Broadcast<String> broadcastVarFilterType =
6        ctx.broadcast(filterType);
7    final Broadcast<Double> broadcastVarFilterValueThreshold =
8        ctx.broadcast(filterValueThreshold);
```

Step 5: Read all bioset records and create an RDD

This step, shown in Example 26-39, reads all bioset files from HDFS and creates a single RDD (`JavaRDD<String>`). This functionality is explained in detail when we discuss the `readInputFiles()` method.

Example 26-39. Step 5: read all bioset records and create an RDD

```
1    //Step 5: read all bioset records and create an RDD
2    JavaRDD<String> records = readInputFiles(ctx, biosets);
```

We debug this step using the `JavaRDD.collect()` method:

```
1 // debug1
2 List<String> debug1 = records.collect();
3 for (String rec : debug1) {
4   System.out.println("debug1 => "+ rec);
5 }
```

Step 6: Map bioset records into JavaPairRDD <K,V> pairs

This step, shown in Example 26-40, creates `JavaPairRDD<K,V>` objects from all bioset records, where K = `<geneID><,><referenceType>` and V = `<patientID><,><gene Value>`. This will enable us to count the frequency of genes by average for all patients represented by biosets. When a bioset record does not match our metric criteria, we create a dummy object (marked as a null object), Tuple2("n", "n"), which will be filtered out before the output is finalized. In Spark, RDD elements cannot be Java null objects, which is why we create replacement objects such as Tuple2Null instead. Note that Spark's approach for ignoring some RDD elements is different from that of MapReduce/Hadoop, which just ignores them without emitting any redundant key-value pairs. For example, in MapReduce/Hadoop, if your mapper/reducer input does not meet your desired criteria, then you may generate zero key-value pairs (i.e., no output at all). But in Spark, the mapToPair() method has to return a non-null key-value pair (which you may filter out using the filter() method).

Example 26-40. Step 6: map bioset records into JavaPairRDD <K, V> pairs

```
1    //Step 6: map bioset records into JavaPairRDD<K, V> pairs
2    //    where K = "<geneID><,><referenceType>",
3    //          V = "<patientID><,><geneValue>"
4    JavaPairRDD<String, String> genes =
5        records.mapToPair(new PairFunction<String, String, String>() {
6      public Tuple2<String, String> call(String record) {
7        String[] tokens = StringUtils.split(record, ";");
8        String geneIDAndReferenceType = tokens[0];
9        String patientIDAndGeneValue = tokens[1];
10       String[] arr = StringUtils.split(geneIDAndReferenceType, ",");
11       // arr[0] = geneID
12       // arr[1] = referenceType
13       // check referenceType and geneValue
14       String referenceType = (String) broadcastVarReferenceType.value();
15       if ( arr[1].equals(referenceType) ) {
16           // prepare key-value for reducer and send it to reducer
17           return new Tuple2<String, String>(geneIDAndReferenceType,
18                                             patientIDAndGeneValue);
19       }
20       else {
21           // otherwise nothing will be counted
22           // later we will filter out these "null" keys
23           return Tuple2Null;
24       }
25     }
26   });
```

Step 7: Filter redundant records created by step 6

Step 6 created redundant (K,V) = Tuple2("n", "n") pairs as a replacement for Java null values. This step filters out redundant data and provides a clean Java PairRDD<String,String>. We accomplish this by implementing Spark's filter() function, which is defined as:

```
public JavaPairRDD<K,V> filter(Function<Tuple2<K,V>,Boolean> f)
// DESCRIPTION: Return a new RDD containing only the elements
//              that satisfy a predicate defined by function f.
```

Example 26-41 shows the filter implementation.

Example 26-41. Step 7: Filter redundant records created by step 6

```
1    //Step 7: filter redundant records created by step 6
2    // public JavaPairRDD<K,V> filter(Function<Tuple2<K,V>,Boolean> f)
3    // Return a new RDD containing only the elements that satisfy a predicate;
4    // If K = "n", then exclude them
5    JavaPairRDD<String,String> filteredGenes =
6        genes.filter(new Function<Tuple2<String,String>,Boolean>() {
7      public Boolean call(Tuple2<String, String> s) {
8         String value = s._1;
9         if (value.equals("n")) {
10            // exclude null entries
11            return false;
12        }
13        else {
14            return true;
15        }
16    }
17  });
```

Step 8: Group biosets by geneID and referenceType

This step, shown in Example 26-42, groups all bioset records by <geneID><,><refer enceType>. The grouped values will be ready for the final reduction which we will calculate gene aggregation by average per patient.

Example 26-42. Step 8: group biosets by <geneID><,><referenceType>

```
1 // Step 8: group biosets by <geneID><,><referenceType>
2 // genesByID = JavaPairRDD<K, List<V>>
3 //    where K = <geneID><,><referenceType>
4 //          V = <patientID><,><geneValue>
5 JavaPairRDD<String, Iterable<String>> genesByID = filteredGenes.groupByKey();
```

Step 9: Prepare the final desired output

This step applies the core "gene aggregation by average" algorithm to all bioset records. Now we have a list of <patientID><,><geneValue> for each <gen eID><,><referenceType>. This step is implemented by the mapValues() method as follows:

```
mapValues[U](f: (V) => U): JavaPairRDD[K, U]

Description: Pass each value in the key-value
             pair RDD through a map function
             without changing the keys; this also
             retains the original RDD's partitioning.
```

This step, shown in Example 26-43, uses Spark's broadcasted global variables (i.e., shared variables). You can define shared data structures by creating `Broadcast<T>` (where T is your data structure). To use shared/broadcasted variables, you use the `Broadcast.value()` method (this is how we read shared variables in all cluster nodes: the `value()` method returns a data structure of type T).

Example 26-43. Step 9: prepare the final desired output

```
1 // Step 9: prepare the final desired output
2 JavaPairRDD<String, Integer> frequency =
3   genesByID.mapValues(new Function<Iterable<String>, // input
4                                    Integer          // output
5                                    >() {
6   public Integer call(Iterable<String> values) {
7       Map<String, PairOfDoubleInteger> patients = buildPatientsMap(values);
8       String filterType = (String) broadcastVarFilterType.value();
9       Double filterValueThreshold =
10          (Double) broadcastVarFilterValueThreshold.value();
11      int passedTheTest = getNumberOfPatientsPassedTheTest(
12          patients,
13          filterType,
14          filterValueThreshold);
15      return passedTheTest;
16   }
17 });
```

Step 10: Emit the final output

This step, shown in Example 26-44, prints the final desired output.

Example 26-44. Step 10: emit the final output

```
1 //Step 10: emit the final output
2 List<Tuple2<String, Integer>> finalOutput = frequency.collect();
3 for (Tuple2<String, Integer> tuple : finalOutput) {
4     System.out.println("final output => "+ tuple._1 + ": " + tuple._2);
5 }
```

The following sections provide an explanation of some of the important methods used in our filter by average gene aggregation solution.

Utility Functions

The `toList()` method, shown in Example 26-45, collects all HDFS bioset files and saves them as a `List<String>`, where each list element is an HDFS bioset file.

Example 26-45. toList() support method

```
1    /**
2     * Convert all bioset files into a List<biosetFileName>
3     *
4     * @param biosets is a filename, which holds all bioset files as
5     * HDFS entries; an example will be:
6     *        /biosets/1000.txt
7     *        /biosets/1001.txt
8     *        ...
9     *        /biosets/1408.txt
10   */
11   private static List<String> toList(String biosets) throws Exception {
12       List<String> biosetFiles = new ArrayList<String>();
13       BufferedReader in = new BufferedReader(new FileReader(biosets));
14       String line = null;
15       while ((line = in.readLine()) != null) {
16           String aBiosetFile = line.trim();
17           biosetFiles.add(aBiosetFile);
18       }
19       in.close();
20       return biosetFiles;
21   }
```

The `readInputFiles()` method, shown in Example 26-46, reads all HDFS bioset files
and creates a new RDD as a `JavaRDD<String>`, where each element is a bioset record.
All bioset records are merged through the `JavaSparkContext.union()` method. Then
we partition this RDD by applying the `JavaRDD.coalesce()` method for further parallel processing.

Example 26-46. readInputFiles() support method

```
1    private static JavaRDD<String> readInputFiles(JavaSparkContext ctx,
2                                                  String filename)
3        throws Exception {
4        List<String> biosetFiles = toList(filename);
5        int counter = 0;
6        JavaRDD[] rdds = new JavaRDD[biosetFiles.size()];
7        for (String biosetFileName : biosetFiles) {
8            System.out.println("debug1 biosetFileName=" + biosetFileName);
9            JavaRDD<String> record = ctx.textFile(biosetFileName);
10           rdds[counter] = record;
11           counter++;
12       }
13       JavaRDD<String> allBiosets = ctx.union(rdds);
14       return allBiosets.coalesce(9, false);
15   }
```

The buildPatientsMap() method, shown in Example 26-47, builds a Map<String, PairOfDoubleInteger>, where the key is a patientID and the value is a PairOfDou bleInteger object, which keeps track of the sum of gene values and its count.

Example 26-47. buildPatientsMap() support method

```
1 private static Map<String,PairOfDoubleInteger>
2   buildPatientsMap(Iterable<String> values) {
3   Map<String, PairOfDoubleInteger> patients =
4      new HashMap<String, PairOfDoubleInteger>();
5   for (String patientIdAndGeneValue : values) {
6      String[] tokens = StringUtils.split(patientIdAndGeneValue, ",");
7      String patientID = tokens[0];
8      // tokens[1] = geneValue
9      double geneValue = Double.parseDouble(tokens[1]);
10      PairOfDoubleInteger pair = patients.get(patientID);
11      if (pair == null) {
12         pair = new PairOfDoubleInteger(geneValue, 1);
13         patients.put(patientID, pair);
14      }
15      else {
16         pair.increment(geneValue);
17      }
18   }
19   return patients;
20 }
```

The getNumberOfPatientsPassedTheTest() method, shown in Example 26-48, iterates through the Map<String, PairOfDoubleInteger> built by the buildPatients Map() method. Each entry of this map denotes a single patient. If a patient passes the desired metrics (i.e., the average of the gene values passes the defined metrics, filter Type and filterValueThreshold), then the patient is counted as passing the test.

Example 26-48. getNumberOfPatientsPassedTheTest() support method

```
1 private static int getNumberOfPatientsPassedTheTest(
2          Map<String, PairOfDoubleInteger> patients,
3          String filterType,
4          Double filterValueThreshold) {
5   if (patients == null) {
6      return 0;
7   }
8
9   // now, we will average the values and see which
10   // patients pass the threshhold
11   int passedTheTest = 0;
12   for (Map.Entry<String, PairOfDoubleInteger> entry : patients.entrySet()) {
13      //String patientID = entry.getKey();
14      PairOfDoubleInteger pair = entry.getValue();
```

```
15        double avg = pair.avg();
16        if (filterType.equals("up")) {
17            if (avg >= filterValueThreshold) {
18                passedTheTest++;
19            }
20        }
21        if (filterType.equals("down")) {
22            if (avg <= filterValueThreshold) {
23                passedTheTest++;
24            }
25        }
26        else if (filterType.equals("abs")) {
27            if (Math.abs(avg) >= filterValueThreshold) {
28                passedTheTest++;
29            }
30        }
31     }
32     return passedTheTest;
33 }
```

Sample Run

The next subsections walk you through the input, script, and log output for a sample run of our Spark solution in the YARN environment.

Input

Here is the input to our Spark solution in YARN:

```
# cat biosets.txt
/biosets/b1.txt
/biosets/b2.txt
/biosets/b3.txt
# hadoop fs -cat /biosets/b1.txt
GENE-1,r1;p100,1.00
GENE-1,r1;p100,1.06
GENE-1,r1;p100,1.10
GENE-1,r1;p100,1.20
# hadoop fs -cat /biosets/b2.txt
GENE-1,r1;p200,1.00
GENE-1,r1;p200,1.02
GENE-1,r1;p200,1.04
# hadoop fs -cat /biosets/b3.txt
GENE-1,r1;p300,1.01
GENE-1,r1;p300,1.06
GENE-1,r1;p300,1.08
```

Script

The following is the script for running `SparkGeneAggregationByAverage` in YARN:

```
$ cat run_gene_aggregation_by_average_yarn.sh
#!/bin/bash
export JAVA_HOME=/usr/java/jdk7
export HADOOP_HOME=/usr/local/hadoop-2.5.0
export HADOOP_CONF_DIR=$HADOOP_HOME/etc/hadoop
export YARN_CONF_DIR=$HADOOP_CONF_DIR
export SPARK_HOME=/usr/local/spark-1.1.0
export BOOK_HOME=/home/data-algorithms-book
export APP_JAR=$BOOK_HOME/dist/data_algorithms_book.jar
prog=org.dataalgorithms.chap26.spark.SparkGeneAggregationByAverage
biosets=$BOOK_HOME/data/biosets.txt
referenceType=r1
#{"r1", "r2", "r3", "r4"}
filterType=up
# {"up", "down", "abs"}
filterValueThreshold=1.04
$SPARK_HOME/bin/spark-submit --class $prog \
    --master yarn-cluster \
    --num-executors 6 \
    --driver-memory 1g \
    --executor-memory 1g \
    --executor-cores 12 \
    $APP_JAR $referenceType $filterType $filterValueThreshold $biosets
```

Log of sample run

The log output from a sample run is as follows:

```
# ./run_gene_aggregation_by_average_yarn.sh

args[0]: <referenceType>=r1
args[1]: <filterType>=up
args[2]: <filterValueThreshold>=1.04
args[3]: <biosets>=/home/data-algorithms-book/data/biosets.txt

debug1 biosetFileName=/biosets/b1.txt
debug1 biosetFileName=/biosets/b2.txt
debug1 biosetFileName=/biosets/b3.txt

final output => GENE-1,r1: 2
```

This chapter provided multiple MapReduce and Spark solutions for gene aggregation (aka marker frequency), and presented Spark's superior API for filtering and broadcasting data structures to all cluster nodes. Chapter 27 discusses linear regression and provides scalable distributed solutions for it.

Linear Regression

This chapter presents a very important statistical concept, linear regression,[3] which has many uses, including clinical applications such as genome analysis using patient sample data. According to Wikipedia: "Linear regression (*http://bit.ly/linear_regres sion*) is widely used in biological, behavioral and social sciences to describe possible relationships between variables. It ranks as one of the most important tools used in these disciplines." Implementing linear regression for small data is very straightforward: we can use many existing Java classes, such as `SimpleRegression` from Apache Commons.[4] However, these classes and packages can not handle a huge amount of data due to the limited memory and CPU resources in a single server. Our primary goal in this chapter is to implement linear regression for huge data sets (such as genomic data represented by biosets for many patients' sample data).

This chapter provides two distinct MapReduce/Hadoop solutions for linear regression:

- The first solution utilizes Apache Commons's `SimpleRegression`.
- The second solution implements MapReduce by using R's linear model.

Spark provides the Machine Learning Library package, or MLlib (*http://bit.ly/ mllib_guide*), which includes linear methods (MLlib is under active development).

---

3 The linear regression model analyzes the relationship between the response or dependent variable and a set of independent or predictor variables. This relationship is expressed as an equation that predicts the response variable as a linear function of the parameters. These parameters are adjusted so that a measure of fit is optimized. Much of the effort in model fitting is focused on minimizing the size of the residual, as well as ensuring that it is randomly distributed with respect to the model predictions. (Source: *http://en.wikipedia.org/wiki/ Predictive_analytics.*)

4 `org.apache.commons.math3.stat.regression.SimpleRegression`

The most common form of linear regression is *least squares fitting* (*http://bit.ly/least_squares_fitting*). Before getting into the details of implementing linear regression, let's define what it is and what it tells us. In simple terms, we are trying to fit an equation to a real set of data (kind of like predicting the future by observing a real set of data).

Basic Definitions

Here are some facts about linear regression, some of which come from *http://bit.ly/linear_regression_intro*:

- Linear regression is modeled by the linear equation $y = ax + b$. In a nutshell, regression analysis is used to find equations that fit data, where data is represented by a set of (x, y).

- Linear regression uses the fact that there is a statistically significant correlation between two variables to allow you to make predictions about one variable based on your knowledge of the other.

- You should not do linear regression unless your correlation coefficient is statistically significant.

- For linear regression to work, there must be a linear relationship between the variables.

Next we need some definitions for regression and linear regression. A regression is a statistical analysis assessing the association between variables (such as x and y in the regression equation $y = ax + b$). In its simplest form, regression is used to find the relationship between two variables x and y, but you may use more than two variables. Therefore, linear regression defines/estimates the relationship between variables when the regression equation is linear; for example, $y = ax + b$, where a is the intercept point of the regression line and the y-axis and b is the slope of the regression line. So, the main goal of the linear regression is to find a (i.e., the intercept point— the value of y when $x = 0$) and b (the slope) for a given set of (x, y). Typically x is the explanatory variable and y is the dependent variable.

Simple Example

Here I present a simple example to demonstrate the basic concept of a linear regression. The goal of linear regression analysis is to find the linear equation(s) that fit the data. Once we have the linear equation ($y = ax + b$), we can use the linear regression model (expressed as a linear equation) to make predictions. Here, I show you how to use sample data to calculate linear regression and find the equation $y = ax + b$. Our two variables are age and glucose level, for a very small set of patients. First we make a chart of our data, as shown in Table 27-1.

Table 27-1. Data chart for patient age and glucose level

Subject	Age (x)	Glucose level (y)	xy	x^2	y^2
1	41	90	3,690	1,681	8,100
2	42	93	3,906	1,764	8,649
3	43	98	4,214	1,849	9,604
4	20	64	1,280	400	4,096
5	25	78	1,950	625	6,084
6	40	71	2,840	1,600	5,041
7	58	88	5,104	3,364	7,744
8	60	86	5,160	3,600	7,396
Sum	329	668	28,144	14,883	56,714

Next, we use the following formulas to calculate *a* and *b*:

$$a = \frac{(\Sigma y)\left(\Sigma x^2\right) - (\Sigma x)(\Sigma xy)}{n\left(\Sigma x^2\right) - (\Sigma x)^2}$$

$$b = \frac{n(\Sigma xy) - (\Sigma x)(\Sigma y)}{n\left(\Sigma x^2\right) - (\Sigma x)^2}$$

Note that *n* is the number of samples for regression (in our example, $n = 8$). Now, by plugging in the precalculated values, we get:

$a = 63.05$

$b = 0.497$

Next, we plot linear regression using the R programming language (see Figure 27-1):

```
# R
R version 2.15.1 (2012-06-22) -- "Roasted Marshmallows"
> x <- c(41, 42, 43, 20, 25, 40, 58, 60)
> y <- c(90, 93, 98, 64, 78, 71, 88, 86)
> mod1 <- lm(y ~ x)
> plot(x, y, xlim=c(min(x)-5, max(x)+5), ylim=c(min(y)-10, max(y)+10))
> abline(mod1, lwd=2)
```

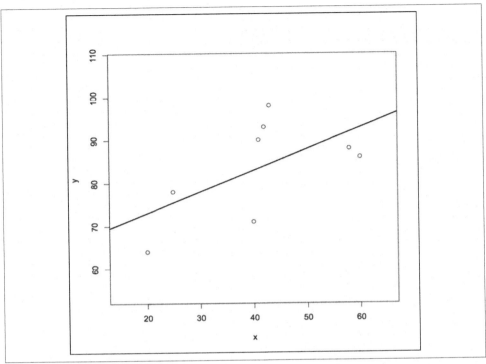

Figure 27-1. Linear regression in R

As you can observe from the plot, linear regression attempts to model the relationship between two variables (*x* and *y*) by fitting a linear equation to the observed data (the most common algorithm for fitting a regression line is the method of least squares).

Problem Statement

Assume we have a set of patient data for a clinical trial of some medication or treatment. We further assume that each patient may have a set of biosets/biomarkers, and each bioset/biomarker has a set of key-value pairs where the key is the Gene-ID and the value can represent segment value, copy change number, or some other related genomic data value (here the value represents variable *x*, and variable *y* is the survival time of that specific patient for this treatment). The number of key-value pairs for each biomarker depends on the type of bioset (the bioset data types are methylation, copy-number variation, gene expression, and somatic mutation). For example, for the gene expression type, each biomarker will have up to 50,000 key-value pairs. Imagine you want to do a linear regression for 40,000 biosets: this will yield 2 billion data points, which makes it impossible to do the linear regression computation on a single server. Here our interest is to do a linear regression for each Gene-ID. Explicitly, our objective is to find the following for each Gene-ID:

- Intercept (the intercept point of the estimated regression line)
- Slope (the slope of the estimated regression line)
- Significance (the p-value or significance level of the slope correlation)

Input Data

Our input data will be composed of a set of biosets/biomarkers, with each bioset identified by a unique bioset_id. Each bioset is composed of up to 60,000 records, and each record will be formatted as follows (here, we consider gene_value as variable x):

```
<gene_id><,><reference><;><bioset_id><,><gene_value>
```

where <gene_id> is a gene represented by an ID and <reference> will be one of the following:

- r1 = reference to normal patient
- r2 = reference to disease
- r3 = reference to paired
- r4 = none

For example:

```
1234,r2;3344550,0.43
```

Or:

```
122765,r1;3344550,1.78
```

Also, we will have another input vector (to represent variable y), such as survival time for patients (which is an array of the Double data type; each item corresponds to a bioset). For example, to analyze 5,000 biosets, we need to pass an array of survival times with a size of 5,000.

Expected Output

After our linear regression job is completed, our analysis will be in the following format (one record per Gene-ID):

```
<gene_id><,><reference><,><slope><,><intercept><,><pValue>
```

For example:

```
1234,r2,1.002,3.12007,0.000098
```

MapReduce Solution Using SimpleRegression

Our MapReduce solution for linear regression comprises a mapper and a reducer. The main task of the `map()` function is to identify variable *x* and pass it to a reducer. (Each reducer will receive and handle a key-value pair. The key will be the `gene_id` and `reference` and its associated value will be the `gene_value` (variable *x* in the linear regression). Variable *y* in our example is the survival time and is passed from the driver class to the MapReduce/Hadoop `Configuration` object. The `reduce()` function will get the *y* values from the `Configuration` object (in Hadoop this will be done by the `setup()` method). Once we have the *x* and *y* variables, we will use the `SimpleRegression`[3] class to perform our linear regression and then write the result (`slope`, `intercept`, and `pValue`) back to HDFS. Using the `SimpleRegression` class is very simple:

```
// y = intercept + slope * x
SimpleRegression sr = new SimpleRegression();
sr.addData(1d, 2d); // x = 1, y = 2
sr.addData(3d, 3d); // x = 3, y = 3
sr.addData(2d, 4d); // x = 2, y = 4
// we may add any number of sr.addData(x, y)
// now all statistics are defined.
double pValue = sr.getSignificance());
double intercept = sr.getIntercept());
double slope = sr.getSlope());
```

Note that the `gene_value` represents *x*s, and we will pass `bioset_ids` and survival times (representing *y*s). We need to pass the `bioset_ids` because `bioset_id[i]` corresponds with `survival_time[i]`, and we have to make sure that we are using the proper *x*s and *y*s for linear regression. The mapper is presented in Example 27-1.

Example 27-1. Linear regression: map() function

```
1 /**
2  * @param key is generated by Hadoop (ignored here)
3  * @param value's format: <gene_id><,><reference><;><bioset_id><,><gene_value>
4  */
5 map(key, value) {
6     String line = value.toString().trim();
7     if ((line == null) || (line.length() == 0)) {
8         return;
9     }
10
11    String[] tokens = StringUtils.split(line, ";");
12    // tokens[0] = <gene_id><,><reference>
```

---

3 `org.apache.commons.math3.stat.regression.SimpleRegression` (Apache Commons Math)

```
13      // tokens[1] = <bioset_id><,><gene_value>
14      if (tokens.length == 2) {
15          // prepare (key, value) for reducer
16          emit(tokens[0], tokens[1]);
17      }
18  }
```

The reducer class, LinearRegressionReducer, is presented in Example 27-2, and the reduce() function is defined in Example 27-3 .

Example 27-2. LinearRegressionReducer for linear regression

```
1 public class LinearRegressionReducer ... {
2      // instance variables
3      private Configuration conf = null;
4      private List<Double> time = null;
5      // biosetIDs as Strings : NOTE order of biosets is VERY IMPORTANT
6      private List<String> biosets = null;
7
8      // will be run only once
9 public void setup(Context context)
10      this.conf = context.getConfiguration();
11      // get parameters from Hadoop's configuration
12      String biosetsAsString = conf.get("biosets");
13      this.biosets =
14          DataStructuresUtil.splitOnToListOfString(biosetsAsString, ",");
15      String timeAsCommaSeparatedString = conf.get("time");
16      this.time = DataStructuresUtil.splitOnToListOfDouble(
17          timeAsCommaSeparatedString, ",");
18  }
19
20      // key = <gene_id><,><reference>
21      // values = { bioset_id,value }
22      // biosets are: B1, B2, B3, ..., Bn
23      // times are : T1, T2, T3, ..., Tn
24      public void reduce(Text key, Iterable<Text> values) {
25          // see Example 27-3 ...
26      }
27 }
```

Example 27-3. Linear regression: reduce() function

```
1 public class LinearRegressionReducer ... {
2      ...
3      // key = <gene_id><,><reference>
4      // values = { bioset_id,value }
5      // biosets are: B1, B2, B3, ..., Bn
6      // times are : T1, T2, T3, ..., Tn
7      public void reduce(Text key, Iterable<Text> values) {
8          int numberOfValues = 0;
```

```
9        SimpleRegression sr = new SimpleRegression();
10       Iterator<Text> iter = values.iterator();
11       while (iter.hasNext()) {
12           Text pairAsText = iter.next();
13           if (pairAsText == null) {
14               continue;
15           }
16           String pairAsString = pairAsText.toString();
17           String[] tokens = StringUtils.split(pairAsString, ",");
18           // biosetID = tokens[0]
19           // value    = tokens[1]
20           if (tokens.length != 2) {
21               // then ignore that (value, time) from regression
22               continue;
23           }
24
25           int index = biosets.indexOf(tokens[0]);
26           if (index == -1) {
27               // biosetID not found
28               continue;
29           }
30
31           // biosetID found at index
32           // sr.addData(xPos.get(i), yPos.get(i));
33           double dvalue = Double.parseDouble(tokens[1]);
34           sr.addData(dvalue, time.get(index));
35           numberOfValues++;
36       }
37
38       if (numberOfValues > 0) {
39           StringBuilder builder = new StringBuilder();
40           builder.append(key.toString()); // gene_id_and_reference: 1234,r2
41           builder.append(",");
42           builder.append(sr.getSignificance()); // p-value
43           builder.append(",");
44           builder.append(sr.getIntercept()); // intercept
45           builder.append(",");
46           builder.append(sr.getSlope()); // slope
47           // prepare reducer for output
48           // p-value,intercept,slope
49           Text reducerValue = new Text(builder.toString());
50           emit(null, reducerValue);
51       }
52   }
53 }
```

Hadoop Implementation Classes

Our MapReduce/Hadoop implementation is composed of the classes shown in Table 27-2.

Table 27-2. Required classes for our MapReduce/Hadoop implementation

Class name	Class description
LinearRegressionDriver	The driver class, which defines input/output and registers plug-in classes
LinearRegressionMapper	Defines the map() function
LinearRegressionReducer	Defines the reduce() function
LinearRegressionAnalyzer	Defines how output data will be read from HDFS
LinearRegressionClient	Client class to submit job

MapReduce Solution Using R's Linear Model

Our MapReduce solution for linear regression using R's linear model comprises two MapReduce jobs. The first job aggregates the required data and generates input files to be read/used in the second MapReduce job. The second MapReduce job reads that input and then applies R's linear model function, lm() (for details, see *http://bit.ly/ r_linear_models*). R's linear model is more accurate and comprehensive than Apache's SimpleRegression class. The reason for having a second MapReduce job is to avoid calling the lm() function for every single gene_id (note that calling R for every single gene_id does not scale well, but calling R for many other inputs does scale well). We basically collect as many IDs as possible in a text file and then call the lm() function.

Before I describe the two-phase MapReduce solution, I'll show you how R's lm() function can be used:

```
# R
R version 2.15.1 (2012-06-22) -- "Roasted Marshmallows"
> x <- c(-1.0, 1.1, 2.2, 3.3, 4.4, 5.5, -1.5)
> y <- c(-1.1, 1.88, 2.88, 3.44, 4.44, 5.99, -1.8)
> fit = lm(x ~ y)
> intercept = fit$coef[1]
> intercept
(Intercept)
-0.07142071
> slope = fit$coef[2]
> slope
        y
0.921802
> pValue = anova(fit)$'Pr(>F)'[1]
> pValue
[1] 1.279226e-05
> rsquare = summary(fit)$r.squared
> rsquare
[1] 0.9830423
> plot(x, y, xlim=c(min(x)-2, max(x)+2), ylim=c(min(y)-5, max(y)+5))
> abline(fit, lwd=1)
```

Plotting by R's `plot()` and `abline()` functions generates the linear model, which is illustrated in Figure 27-2.

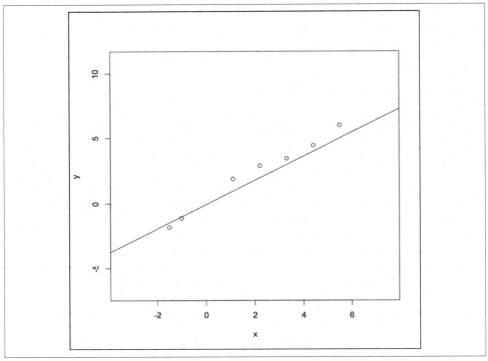

Figure 27-2. Linear regression model

Phase 1

The main task of the `map()` function for phase 1 is to identify variable x and pass it to a reducer—the reducer will receive as a key the `gene_id` and `reference`, and its associated value will be the `gene_value` (variable x in linear regression). Variable y in our example is the survival time; this is passed from the driver class to MapReduce/Hadoop's `Configuration` object, which will be retrieved by the phase 1 reducer function (for generating the proper input data to be consumed by phase 2's `map()` function). So, we pass `bioset_id(s)` and `survival_time(s)` through MapReduce/Hadoop's `Configuration` object, which will be retrieved by phase 1's reducer function. Let `bio set_ids` be $\{B_1, B_2, ..., B_n\}$ and `survival_times` be $\{T_1, T_2, ..., T_n\}$ (note that the number of `bioset_ids` and `survival_times` must be the same).

Each reducer will receive and handle a key-value pair. The key is the `gene_id` and `reference` and the value is a list of `gene_values`. The `reduce()` function will get the y values from MapReduce/Hadoop's `Configuration` object (in Hadoop this will be done by the setup() method). Once we have x and y variables, then we write them to a text file, which will be saved in HDFS to be consumed by phase 2's map() function. For example, the reducers will generate the following text files:

```
GENE-ID-1; V₁₁, V₁₂, ..., V₁ₙ; T₁₁, T₁₂,..., T₁ₙ
GENE-ID-2; V₂₁, V₂₂, ..., V₂ₙ; T₂₁, T₂₂,..., T₂ₙ
...
GENE-ID-m; Vₘ₁, Vₘ₂, ..., Vₘₙ; Tₘ₁, Tₘ₂,..., Tₘₙ
```

Note that the gene_values represent xs, and we will pass bioset_ids and survival times (represented by the ys). We need to pass bioset_ids using Hadoop's Configuration object because bioset_id[i] corresponds with survival_time[i], and we have to make sure that we are using the proper xs and ys for linear regression.

Let's say that we have 200 mappers and 30 reducers for phase 1. With this configuration, our MapReduce job for phase 1 will create 30 output files (in HDFS):

```
/<hdfs-output-directory>/part-00000
/<hdfs-output-directory>/part-00001
...
/<hdfs-output-directory>/part-00029
```

The input to the map() function of phase 2 will be these HDFS files (generated by the reducers of the phase 1 job), as shown in Example 27-4.

Example 27-4. Linear regression for phase 1: map() function

```
 1 /**
 2  * @param key is generated by Hadoop (ignored here)
 3  * @param value's format: <gene_id_and_ref><;><bioset_id><,><gene_value>
 4  */
 5 map(key, value) {
 6    String line = value.toString().trim();
 7    if ((line == null) || (line.length() == 0)) {
 8       return;
 9    }
10
11    String[] tokens = StringUtils.split(line, ";");
12    String gene_id_and_ref = tokens[0];
13    String bioset_id_and_value = tokens[1];
14    if (tokens.length == 2) {
15       // prepare (key, value) for reducer
16       emit(gene_id_and_ref, bioset_id_and_value);
17    }
18 }
```

The reduce() function is defined in Example 27-5.

Example 27-5. Linear regression for phase 1: reduce() function

```
1 public class LinearModelReducer extends Reducer<Text, Text, NullWritable, Text> {
2       // instance variables
3       private Configuration conf = null;
4       private String type = null;
5       // biosetIDs as Strings : NOTE order of biosets is VERY IMPORTANT
6       public List<String> biosets = null;
7       // NOTE: order of time items is VERY IMPORTANT
8       public List<Double> time = null;
9
10      // will be run only once
11      public void setup(Context context) {
12        this.conf = context.getConfiguration();
13        this.type = conf.get("type");
14        // get parameters from Hadoop's Configuration
15        String biosetsAsString = conf.get("biosets");
16        this.biosets =
17            DataStructuresUtil.splitOnToListOfString(biosetsAsString, ",");
18        String timeAsCommaSeparatedString = conf.get("time");
19        this.time = DataStructuresUtil.toListOfDouble(timeAsCommaSeparatedString);
20      }
21
22      // key = geneid_and_ref
23      // values = { biosetID,value }
24      public void reduce(Text key, Iterable<Text> values, Context context) {
25            //
26            // we will generate the following per key:
27            // (( key=<geneID><r{1,2,3,4}> [example of key: 1234r2] ))
28            // <geneID><;><V1, V2, ..., Vn><;><T1,T2, ..., Tn>
29            // where V's are gene values and T's are time values
30            //
31            // T1 is for V1
32            // T2 is for V2
33            // ...
34            // Tn is for Vn
35            //
36            int numberOfValues = 0;
37            Iterator<Text> iter = values.iterator();
38            // generates geneID; V1, V2, ...
39            StringBuilder valuebuilder = new StringBuilder();
40            // generates T1, T2, ...
41            StringBuilder timebuilder = new StringBuilder();
42
43            valuebuilder.append(key.toString());
44            valuebuilder.append(";");
45
46            while (iter.hasNext()) {
47                Text pairAsText = iter.next();
48                if (pairAsText == null) {
49                    continue;
50                }
```

```
51              String pairAsString = pairAsText.toString();
52              String[] tokens = StringUtils.split(pairAsString, ",");
53              // biosetID = tokens[0]
54              // value    = tokens[1]
55              if (tokens.length != 2) {
56                  // we're done here, all values must be present for
57                  // linear model; no need to write anything to Hadoop
58                  continue;
59              }
60
61              int index = biosets.indexOf(tokens[0]);
62              if (index == -1) {
63                  // biosetID not found
64                  continue;
65              }
66
67              // biosetID found at index
68              // biosets.get(index) = biosetID;
69              double valueAsDouble = Double.parseDouble(tokens[1]);
70
71              // update value
72              valuebuilder.append(valueAsDouble);
73              valuebuilder.append(",");
74
75              // update time
76              timebuilder.append(time.get(index));
77              timebuilder.append(",");
78
79              numberOfValues++;
80          }
81
82          if (numberOfValues > 2) {
83          // prepare reducer for output
84          String geneAndValues = valuebuilder.toString();
85          // chop off the last ","
86          String geneAndValuesFinal =
87              geneAndValues.substring(0, geneAndValues.length()-1);
88          String timesAsString = timebuilder.toString();
89          // chop off the last ","
90          String timeFinal =
91              timesAsString.substring(0, timesAsString.length()-1);
92          // reducerValue = <geneID><;><V1, V2, ..., Vn><;><T1,T2, ..., Tn>
93          Text reducerValue = new Text(geneAndValuesFinal + ";" + timeFinal);
94          context.write(null, reducerValue);
95          }
96      }
97 }
```

Phase 2

Phase 2 has a mapper, but no reducers are required. The map() function will read text files (the output of the phase 1 reduce() function) and then call R's lm() function.

The input for the `map()` function will be the following HDFS files generated by the reducers of phase 1 (if we had 30 reducers in phase 1, then we will have 30 input files for the mappers of phase 2):

```
/<hdfs-output-directory>/part-00000
/<hdfs-output-directory>/part-00001
...
/<hdfs-output-directory>/part-00029
```

The `map()` function of phase 2 will pass each file to a shell script, which will call R's `lm()` function. R processing becomes very efficient when we bundle lots of input in text files (this way, we can launch only one R process and call `lm()` once per record read from the input files). The R script shown in Example 27-6 (we use FreeMarker as a template engine to generate the actual Linux shell script), *linear_model.template.r*, shows how the `lm()` function is invoked.

Example 27-6. R script for MapReduce solution, phase 2

```
1 #!/usr/local/bin/Rscript
2 # template name: linear_model.template.r
3 # input_file is part-nnnnn file in local filesystem
4 input_file = "${input_file}"
5 cat("input_file=", input_file, "\n")
6 output_file = "${output_file}"
7 cat("output_file=", output_file, "\n")
8
9 #
10 # each record for file will have the following format
11 # <geneID><;><V1, V2, ..., Vn><;><T1,T2, ..., Tn>
12 #
13 # > a = "g1;1,2,3; 4,5,6"
14 # > items = unlist(strsplit(a, ";"))
15 # > items
16 # [1] "g1" "1,2,3 " " 4,5,6"
17 # > geneID = items[[1]]
18 # > geneID
19 # [1] "g1"
20 # > value = as.double(unlist(strsplit(items[[2]], ",")))
21 # >value
22 # [1] 1 2 3
23 # > time = as.double(unlist(strsplit(items[[3]], ",")))
24 # >time
25 # [1] 4 5 6
26 #
27 linear_model_fun <- function(line) {
28    items = unlist(strsplit(line, ";"))
29    geneID = items[[1]]
30    value = as.double(unlist(strsplit(items[[2]], ",")))
31    time = as.double(unlist(strsplit(items[[3]], ",")))
32    fit = lm(value ~ time)
```

```
33    intercept = fit$coef[1]
34    slope = fit$coef[2]
35    pValue = anova(fit)$'Pr(>F)'[1]
36    rsquare = summary(fit)$r.squared
37    cat(geneID, intercept, slope, pValue, rsquare, "\n",
38        file=output_file, append=TRUE)
39 }
40
41 # main driver
42 conn <- file(input_file, open="r")
43 while(length(line <- readLines(conn, 1)) > 0) {
44    try.output <- try( linear_model_fun(line) )
45 }
46 close.connection(conn)
```

Hadoop Implementation Using Classes

Our Hadoop implementation using R's linear model is composed of the classes shown in Table 27-3 (note that there are no reducers for phase 2).

Table 27-3. Required classes for Hadoop implementation using R

Class name	Class description
LinearRegressionClientPhase2	Client class to submit job
LinearRegressionDriverPhase2	The driver class, which defines input/output and registers plug-in classes
LinearRegressionMapperPhase2	Defines the map() function
LinearRegressionAnalyzerPhase2	Defines how output data will be read from HDFS

This chapter provided multiple MapReduce solutions to the linear regression problem, which will scale well as data grows. Chapter 28 discusses *monoids* in the context of MapReduce and shows how they can be used to optimize MapReduce programming.

MapReduce and Monoids

Introduction

This chapter is based on Jimmy Lin's paper[15] titled "Monoidify! Monoids as a Design Principle for Efficient MapReduce Algorithms." Lin clearly introduces monoids as a design principle for efficient MapReduce algorithms. But what is a monoid, what properties define it, and how does it aid the MapReduce paradigm? Lin shows that when your MapReduce operations are not monoids, it is very hard to use combiners efficiently.

Also, David Saile[13] states that:

> A monoid is an algebraic structure with a single associative binary operation and an identity element. For example, the natural numbers[3] N form a monoid under addition with identity element zero. In classic MapReduce, the mapper is not constrained, but the reducer is required to be (the iterated application of) an associative operation. Recent research argued that reduction is in fact monoidal in known applications of MapReduce. That is, reduction is indeed the iterated application of an associative operation "•" with a unit u. In the case of the word-occurrence count example, reduction iterates addition "+" with "0" as unit. The parallel execution schedule may be more flexible if commutativity is required in addition to associativity.

A detailed analysis of common MapReduce computations on the basis of monoids can be found in [5]. Next, we will briefly review MapReduce's combiners and abstract algebra's monoids and see how they are related to each other. Converting nonassociative MapReduce operations into associative equivalents is pretty important, because it

---

3 The term *natural numbers* refers either to the set of positive integers {1, 2, 3, ...} or to the set of non-negative integers {0, 1, 2, 3, ...}.

enables us to utilize combiners (and using combiners by treating them as monoids can improve the performance of MapReduce jobs).

In the MapReduce framework, the combiner (as an optional plug-in component) is a "local reduce" process that operates only on data generated by one server. Successful use of combiners reduces the amount of intermediate data generated by the mappers on a given single server (that is why it is called a *local* reducer). Combiners can be used as a MapReduce optimization to reduce network traffic (by decreasing the size of the transient data) between mappers and reducers. Typically, combiners have the same interface as reducers. The combiner must have the following characteristics:

- The combiner receives as input all the data emitted by the mapper instances on a given server (this is called a *local* aggregation).
- The combiner's output is sent to the reducers; some programmers call this a local server reduction.
- The combiner must be side-effect-free; combiners may run an indeterminate number of times.
- The combiner must have the same input and output key types (see Example 28-1).
- The combiner must have the same input and output value types (see Example 28-1).
- The combiner runs in memory after the map phase.

Therefore, a combiner skeleton should be defined as shown in Example 28-1.

Example 28-1. Combiner template

```
 1 public class MyCombiner {
 2    ...
 3    public void combine(KeyType key, Iterable<ValueType> values) {
 4       ...
 5       KeyType key2 = ...;
 6       ValueType value2 = ...;
 7       ...
 8       emit(key2, value2);
 9       ...
10   }
11 }
```

This template indicates that the key-value pairs generated by a combiner have to match the key-value pairs received (as an input) by the reducers. For example, if the mapper outputs (T_1, T_2) pairs (the key is type T_1 and the value is type T_2), then a combiner has to emit (T_1, T_2) pairs as well.

Lin[15] concludes that "one principle for designing efficient MapReduce algorithms can be precisely articulated as follows: create a monoid out of the intermediate value emitted by the mapper. Once we *monoidify* the object, proper use of combiners and the in-mapper combining techniques becomes straightforward."

The MapReduce/Hadoop implementation does not have a `combine()` function; we just use `reduce()` in Hadoop to implement combiners, but we use the plug-in `Job.setCombinerClass()` to define a combiner class.

The Haskell programming language includes direct support for monoids (*http:// bit.ly/monoid_structure*). In Haskell (*http://bit.ly/haskell_monoids*), "a monoid is a type with a rule for how two elements of that type can be combined to make another element of the same type."

Definition of Monoid

A monoid is a triad (S, f, e), where S is a set (i.e., the underlying set of the monoid), f: S × S → S is a mapping (i.e., the binary operation of the monoid), and e ∈ S is the identity element of the monoid. A monoid with binary operation • satisfies the following three properties (note that f(a, b) = a • b):

- Closure: for all a and b in S, the result of the operation a • b is also in S.
- Associativity: for all a, b, and c in S, the following equation holds:

    (a • b) • c = a • (b • c)

- Identity element: there exists an element e in S, such that for all elements a in S, the following two equations hold:

    e • a = a

    a • e = a

In mathematical notation, we can write these as follows:

- Closure: ∀a, b ∈ S : a • b ∈ S
- Associativity: ∀a, b, c ∈ S : (a • b) • c = a • (b • c)
- Identity element: ∃e ∈ S : ∀a ∈ S : e • a = a • e = a

A monoid might have other properties. For example, the monoid operator might (but isn't required to) obey properties like:

- Idempotency: $\forall a \in S : a \bullet a = a$
- Commutativity: $\forall a, b, \in S : a \bullet b = b \bullet a$

How to Form a Monoid

To form a monoid, first we need a type S, which defines a set of values such as integers: {0, −1, +1, −2, +2, ...}. The second component is a binary function:

$\bullet : S \times S \rightarrow S$

Then we need to make sure that for any two values $x \in S$ and $y \in S$ we get a result object, the combination of x and y:

$x \bullet y : S$

For example, if S is a set of integers, then the binary operation • may be addition (+), multiplication (×), or division (÷). Finally, as the third and most important ingredient, we need • to follow a set of laws. If it does, then S together with • is called a monoid. We say (S, •, e) is a monoid, where $e \in S$ is the identity element (such as 0 for addition and 1 for multiplication).

Also note that the binary division operator (÷) over a set of real numbers is not a monoid:

$((12 \div 4) \div 2) \neq (12 \div (4 \div 2))$

$((12 \div 4) \div 2) = (3 \div 2) = 1.5$

$(12 \div (4 \div 2)) = (12 \div 2) = 6.0$

As "Monoids for Programmers" (*http://bit.ly/monoids_4_prgrmmrs*) puts it:

> Monoids capture the notion of combining arbitrarily many things into a single thing together with a notion of an empty thing [the identity]....One example is addition on natural numbers. The addition function + allows us to combine arbitrarily many natural numbers into a single natural number, the sum. The empty sum is zero. Another example is string concatenation. The concatenation operator allows us to combine arbitrarily many strings into a single string. The empty concatenation is...the empty string.

Monoidic and Non-Monoidic Examples

Several examples are listed in the following subsections to help you understand the concept of a monoid.

Maximum over a Set of Integers

The set S = {0, 1, 2, ...} is a commutative monoid for the MAX (maximum) operation, whose identity element is 0:

MAX(a, MAX(b, c)) = MAX(MAX(a, b), c)

MAX(a, 0) = MAX(0, a) = a

MAX(a, b) ∈ S

Subtraction over a Set of Integers

The subtraction operator (–) over a set of integers does not define a monoid; this operation is not associative:

$(1 - 2) - 3 \neq 1 - (2 - 3)$

$(1 - 2) - 3 = -4$

$1 - (2 - 3) = 2$

Addition over a Set of Integers

The addition operator (+) over a set of integers defines a monoid; this operation is commutative and associative, and the identity element is 0:

$(1 + 2) + 3 = 6$

$1 + (2 + 3) = 6$

n + 0 = n

0 + n = n

We can formalize this monoid as follows (where e(+) defines an identity element):

S = {0, –1, +1, –2, +2, –3, +3, ...}

e(+) = 0, identity element is 0

m(a, b) = m(b, a) = a + b

Multiplication over a Set of Integers

The natural numbers, N = {0, 1, 2, 3, ...}, form a commutative monoid under multiplication (the identity element is 1).

Mean over a Set of Integers

On the other hand, the natural numbers, N = {0, 1, 2, 3, ...}, do not form a monoid under the mean (average) function. The following example shows that the mean of means of arbitrary subsets of a set of values is not the same as the mean of the set of values:

$$MEAN(1,2,3,4,5) \neq MEAN(MEAN(1,2,3), MEAN(4,5))$$

$$MEAN(1,2,3,4,5) = \frac{(1+2+3+4+5)}{5} = \frac{15}{5} = 3$$

$$MEAN(MEAN(1,2,3), MEAN(4,5)) = MEAN(2,4.5) = \frac{(2+4.5)}{2} = 3.25$$

Non-Commutative Example

For a noncommutative example, consider the collection of all binary strings: an element is a finite ordered sequence of 0s and 1s. The binary operation is just concatenation (e.g., concat(1011, 001001) = 1011001001). The identity element is the empty string. Therefore, the concatenation of binary strings is a monoid.

Median over a Set of Integers

The natural numbers do not form a monoid under the median function:

$$MEDIAN(1,2,3,5,6,7,8,9) \neq MEDIAN(MEDIAN(1,2,3), MEDIAN(5,6,7,8,9))$$

$$MEDIAN(1,2,3,5,6,7,8,9) = \frac{(5+6)}{2} = 5.5$$

$$MEDIAN(MEDIAN(1,2,3), MEDIAN(5,6,7,8,9)) = MEDIAN(2,7) = \frac{(2+7)}{2} = 4.5$$

Concatenation over Lists

List concatenation (+) with an empty list (represented as []) is a monoid. For any list, we can write:

L +[] = L

[] + L = L

and concatenation is associative. Using + to combine [] with any list gives you back the same list; for example, []+[1,2,3] = [1,2,3] and [1,2,3] + [] = [1,2,3].

You can use + to join together any two lists; for example, [1,2,3] + [7,8] = [1,2,3,7,8].

Union/Intersection over Integers

Sets under union and intersection over a set of integers form a monoid.

Functional Example

This example is from Mike Stay's Monoids blog (*http://bit.ly/stay_monoids*). Functions from a set T to itself under composition form a monoid:

S = { all functions of the form a : T → T }

e(•) = the identity function

f(a, b) = b ○ a, where ○ is the composition of functions:

(b ○ a)(x) = b(a(x))

For example, given the set T = {0, 1}, we have:

- S contains four possible functions from T back to itself: S = {k_0, 1_T, NOT,k_1}
    - The constant function mapping everything to zero:
        ```
        k₀: T → T
        k₀(t) = 0
        ```
    - The identity function:
        ```
        1ₜ: T → T
        1ₜ(t) = t
        ```
    - The function that toggles the input:
        ```
        NOT: T → T
        NOT(t) = 1 - t
        ```
    - The constant function mapping everything to one:
        ```
        k₁: T → T
        k₁(t) = 1
        ```
- e(•) = 1_T (this is the identity function)
- f(a, b) = b ○ a

Note that the identity function is the unit for composition:

$$(a \bigcirc 1_T)(t) = a(1_T(t)) = a(t)$$
$$(1_T \bigcirc a)(t) = 1_T(a(t)) = a(t)$$

Exercise for the reader: verify that composition is associative.

Matrix Example

This matrix example is from John Perry[22]. Let $N = \{1, 2, 3, ...\}$. Let $m, n \in N$. Then the set of $m \times n$ matrices with integer entries, written $Z^{m \times n}$, satisfies properties that make it a monoid under addition:

- Closure is guaranteed by the definition.
- The associative property is guaranteed by the associative property of its elements.
- The additive identity is 0, the zero matrix.

MapReduce Example: Not a Monoid

In this section we follow the example provided by Jimmy Lin[15]. Given a large number of key-value pairs where the keys are strings and the values are integers, our goal is to find the average of all the values by key. In SQL, this is accomplished as follows (assuming that mytable has key and value columns):

1. Select all data:

```
SELECT key, value FROM mytable;
```

key	value
key1	10
key1	20
key1	30
key2	40
key2	60
key3	20
key3	30

2. Select all data and group by key:

```
SELECT key, AVG(value) FROM mytable GROUP BY key;
```

key	value
key1	20
key2	50
key3	25

Example 28-2 and Example 28-3 comprise the first version of the MapReduce algorithm, where the mapper is not generating monoid outputs for the mean/average function.

Example 28-2. Mapper: not generating monoids

```
1 /**
2  * @param key is a string object
3  * @param value is a long associated with key
4  */
5 map(String key, Long value) {
6     emit(key, value);
7 }
```

Example 28-3. Reducer: not receiving monoids

```
 1 /**
 2  * @param key is a string object
 3  * @param values is a list of longs: [i1, i2, ...]
 4  */
 5 reduce(String key, List<Long> list) {
 6     Long sum = 0;
 7     Integer count = 0;
 8     for (Long i : list) {
 9         sum = sum + i;
10         count++;
11     }
12     double average = sum/count;
13     emit(key, average);
14 }
```

We can make two observations from this first version of the MapReduce algorithm:

- The algorithm is not very efficient, since there will be too much work required of the shuffle() and sort() functions of the MapReduce framework.

- We cannot use the reducer as a combiner, since we know that the mean of means of arbitrary subsets of a set of values is not the same as the mean of the set of values (not a monoid).

Note that using combiners makes MapReduce algorithms more efficient by reducing network traffic (you need to ensure that the combiner provides sufficient aggregation) and reducing the load of the `shuffle()` and `sort()` functions of the MapReduce framework. Now the question is, how can we make our reducer work as a combiner? The answer is to make the output of the mapper a monoid; that is, we need to change the output of our mapper. Once our mapper outputs monoids, then combiners and reducers will behave correctly and efficiently.

MapReduce Example: Monoid

In Example 28-4 we revise the mapper to generate key-value pairs where the key is the string and the value is a pair (`sum`, `count`) that is a monoid.

Example 28-4. Mapper: generating monoids

```
1 /**
2  * @param key is a string object
3  * @param value is a Pair(long : sum, int: count) associated with key
4  */
5 map(String key, Long value) {
6    emit(key, Pair(value, 1));
7 }
```

As you can see, the key is the same as before, but the value is a pair of (`sum`, `count`). Now, the output of the mapper is a monoid where the identity element is (`0`, `0`). The element-wise sum operation can be performed as follows:

$$(a, b) \oplus (c, d) = (a + c, b + d)$$

Now the mean function will be calculated correctly since the mapper outputs monoids:

$$MEAN(1, 2, 3, 4, 5) = MEAN(MEAN(1, 2, 3), MEAN(4, 5))$$

$$MEAN(1, 2, 3, 4, 5) = \frac{(1 + 2 + 3 + 4 + 5)}{5} = \frac{15}{5} = 3$$

$$MEAN(MEAN(1, 2, 3), MEAN(4, 5)) =$$

$$MEAN(MEAN(6, 3), MEAN(9, 2)) = MEAN(15, 5) = 3$$

The revised algorithm, where the just-defined mapper's outputs are monoids, is presented in Examples 28-5 and 28-6.

Example 28-5. New combiner: receiving monoid values

```
1 /**
2  * @param key is a string object
3  * @param value is a list = [(v1, c1), (v2, c2), ...]
4  */
5 combine(String key, List<Pair<Long, Integer>> list) {
6     Long sum = 0;
7     Integer count = 0;
8     for (Pair<Long, Integer> pair : list) {
9         sum += pair.v;
10        count += pair.c
11    }
12    emit(key, new Pair(sum, count));
13 }
```

Example 28-6. New reducer: receiving monoid values

```
1 /**
2  * @param key a string object
3  * @param value is a list = [(v1, c1), (v2, c2), ...]
4  */
5 reduce(String key, List<Pair<Long, Integer>> list) {
6     Long sum = 0;
7     Integer count = 0;
8     for (Pair<Long, Integer> pair : list) {
9         sum += pair.v;
10        count += pair.c
11    }
12    Pair<Long, Integer>  partialPair = new Pair<Long, Integer>(sum, count);
13    emit(key, partialPair);
14 }
```

Hadoop Implementation Classes

The Java classes used in the monoidized MapReduce solution are listed in Table 28-1. In our solution, we utilized the PairOfLongInt[3] class as a Hadoop WritableCompara ble representing a pair consisting of a Long and an Int.

---

3 Part of the Cloud9 toolkit (*http://lintool.github.io/Cloud9/*) developed by Jimmy Lin, a collection of Hadoop tools that tries to make working with big data a bit easier.

Table 28-1. Java classes used in our monoidized MapReduce/Hadoop solution

Class name	Description
`MeanDriver`	A driver program to submit Hadoop jobs
`MeanMonoidizedMapper`	Defines `map()`
`MeanMonoidizedCombiner`	Defines `combiner()`
`MeanMonoidizedReducer`	Defines `reduce()`
`SequenceFileWriterDemo`	Creates a sample `SequenceFile`
`HadoopUtil`	Defines some utility functions
`edu.umd.cloud9.io.pair.PairOfLongInt`	`WritableComparable` representing a pair consisting of a Long and an Int

Sample Run

The following subsections outline the steps of our monoidized MapReduce/Hadoop sample run.

Create input file (as a SequenceFile)

We used the `SequenceFileWriterDemo` class to generate sample input as a `SequenceFile` (*http://bit.ly/sequencefile*). The advantage of `SequenceFile`(s) over text file(s) is that in the `map()` function, we do not need to parse input to identify the key and `value` fields. `SequenceFile`(s) can also be compressed, either per record or per block. To create a `SequenceFile`, we use the `SequenceFile.createWriter()` method, which returns a `SequenceFile.Writer` instance. We then write key-value pairs using the `SequenceFile.Writer.append(key, value)` method. After we are done, we finally call the `close()` method. Our sample input looks like this:

```
$ java SequenceFileWriterDemo test.seq
key1 1
key1 2
key1 3
key1 4
key1 5
key2 2
key2 4
key2 6
key2 8
key2 10
key3 3
key3 6
key3 9
key3 12
key3 15
key4 4
key4 8
key4 12
```

```
key4 16
key4 20
key5 5
key5 10
key5 15
key5 20
key5 25
```

Create HDFS input and output directories

Next, we create the Hadoop distributed filesystem input and output directories as follows:

```
$ hadoop fs -mkdir /monoid
$ hadoop fs -mkdir /monoid/input
$ hadoop fs -mkdir /monoid/output
```

Copy input file to HDFS and verify

Here we copy the input file to HDFS and then verify its contents:

```
$ hadoop fs -copyFromLoal test.seq /monoid/input/
$ hadoop fs -text /monoid/input/test.seq
key1 1
key1 2
key1 3
key1 4
key1 5
key2 2
key2 4
key2 6
key2 8
key2 10
key3 3
key3 6
key3 9
key3 12
key3 15
key4 4
key4 8
key4 12
key4 16
key4 20
key5 5
key5 10
key5 15
key5 20
key5 25
```

Prepare the script

Here is the shell script to run the MapReduce job:

```
$ cat run_monoids.sh
#/bin/bash
export JAVA_HOME=/usr/java/jdk7
export HADOOP_HOME=/usr/local/hadoop/hadoop-2.5.0
export PATH=$PATH:$HADOOP_HOME/bin:$JAVA_HOME/bin
export BOOK_HOME=/mp/data-algorithms-book
export JAR=$BOOK_HOME/dist/data_algorithms_book.jar
$HADOOP_HOME/bin/hadoop fs -rmr /monoid/output
driver=org.dataalgorithms.chap28.mapreduce.MeanDriver
$HADOOP_HOME/bin/hadoop jar $JAR $driver /monoid/input /monoid/output
```

Run the MapReduce job

And finally, we run the MapReduce job as follows:

```
$ ./run_monoids.sh
...
14/10/24 22:19:09 INFO mapreduce.Job: Running job: job_1412870576870_0036
14/10/24 22:19:18 INFO mapreduce.Job:  map 0% reduce 0%
14/10/24 22:19:34 INFO mapreduce.Job:  map 100% reduce 0%
...
14/10/24 22:19:54 INFO mapreduce.Job:  map 100% reduce 83%
14/10/24 22:19:55 INFO mapreduce.Job:  map 100% reduce 100%
     ...
Map-Reduce Framework
Map input records=25
Map output records=25
Combine input records=25
Combine output records=5
Reduce input groups=5
Reduce input records=5
Reduce output records=5
     ...
```

View Hadoop output

Here is our Hadoop generated output:

```
$ hadoop fs -text /monoid/output/part*
key2    6.0
key3    9.0
key4    12.0
key5    15.0
key1    3.0
```

Spark Example Using Monoids

In Spark, calling reduceByKey() will automatically perform combining locally on each machine before computing the global totals for each key. The programmer does not need to specify a combiner. Since combining is automatic, we need to pay extra attention to reduceByKey() to make sure that using combiners will not alter the semantics of our desired function (in this example, the desired functionality is the mean function). Next, we'll implement a solution to the mean function by providing monoid structures so that the correct semantics of the mean function are preserved. In a nutshell, if your data structure has a monoid form, you can plug the data structure directly into the MapReduce or DAG environments and use combiners and reducers effectively.

Note that the mean of a mean is not a monoid. Therefore, to preserve the semantics of the mean function over a set of Long data type numbers, we have to provide a monoid structure so that the combiners can be used efficiently and correctly. So what is a monoid structure for the mean function? One possible monoid is a pair (V,C) for values where V is the value and C is the count. For example:

- Without monoid (combiners generate wrong result):

```
mean(1, 2, 3, 4, 5)
   = mean ( mean(1,2), mean(3,4,5) )
   = mean ( 3/2, 12/3 )
   = mean (1.5, 4)
   = 2.75 [WRONG ANSWER]
```

- With monoid (combiners generate correct result):

```
mean(1, 2, 3, 4, 5)
   = mean ( (1,1), (2,1), (3,1), (4,1), (5,1) )
   = mean ( mean ((1,1), (2,1), (3,1)), mean((4,1), (5,1)) )
   = mean ( (1+2+3, 1+1+1) ), (4+5, 1+1))
   = mean ( (1+2+3+4+5, 1+1+1+1+1) )
   = 15/5
   = 3 [CORRECT ANSWER]
```

Without a monoid structure, we cannot guarantee the correctness if we use combiners. With our monoid structure, we can write:

```
mean( (V, C) )
   = V / C

mean( (V1, C1), (V2, C2) )
   = mean ( (V1+V2), (C1+C2) )
   = (V1+V2) / (C1+C2)

mean( (V1, C1), (V2, C2), (V3, C3), (V4, C4) )
  = mean( mean((V1, C1),(V2, C2)), mean((V3, C3), (V4, C4)))
  = mean( ((V1+V2), (C1+C2)), ((V3+V4), (C3+C4)) )
  = (V1+V2+V3+V4) / (C1+C2+C3+C4)
```

As you can see, the monoid structure is a combiner enabler. We can use combiner optimizations without losing the desired functionality (in this example, the mean function).

High-Level Steps

The entire Spark solution is presented as a single Java class. Spark's `reduceByKey()` uses combiners by default, so our monoid structure will preserve the semantics of the mean function over a set of values. I present the high-level steps of the Spark solution in Example 28-7, after which we'll walk through each step in detail.

Example 28-7. High-level steps for SparkMeanMonoidized

```
1 package org.dataalgorithms.chap28.spark;
2 // Step 1: import required classes and interfaces
3 /**
4  * Given {(K:String, V:Long)}, our goal is to find the mean of values for
5  * a given K. We will create structures in such a way that if a combiner
6  * is used, then the mean of the means will correctly return the mean
7  * of all values. For this example, we create monoids so that the combiners
8  * can be utilized without losing the semantics of the mean function.
9  */
10 public class SparkMeanMonoidized {
11    public static void main(String[] args) throws Exception {
12        // Step 2: handle input parameters
13        // Step 3: create an RDD from input
14        // Step 4: create a monoid
15        // Step 5: reduce frequent Ks by preserving monoids
16        // Step 6: find mean by mapping values
17        System.exit(0);
18    }
19 }
```

Step 1: import required classes and interfaces

This step, shown in Example 28-8, imports the required classes and interfaces.

Example 28-8. Step 1: import required classes and interfaces

```
1 // Step 1: import required classes and interfaces
2 import scala.Tuple2;
3 import org.apache.spark.api.java.JavaRDD;
4 import org.apache.spark.api.java.JavaPairRDD;
5 import org.apache.spark.api.java.JavaSparkContext;
6 import org.apache.spark.api.java.function.Function;
7 import org.apache.spark.api.java.function.Function2;
8 import org.apache.spark.api.java.function.PairFunction;
```

Step 2: Handle input parameters

This step, shown in Example 28-9, reads the input path for finding the means of a set of numbers. Each record is formatted as follows:

```
<key-as-string><TAB><value-as-long>
```

Example 28-9. Step 2: handle input parameters

```
1       // Step 2: handle input parameters
2       if (args.length != 1) {
3           System.err.println("Usage: SparkMeanMonoidized <input-path>");
4           System.exit(1);
5       }
6       final String inputPath = args[0];
```

Step 3: Create an RDD from input

This step, shown in Example 28-10, creates the first RDD (a `JavaRDD<String>`) by reading the input path. Each element of this RDD is a single record, with the format previously specified.

Example 28-10. Step 3: create an RDD from input

```
1       // Step 3: create an RDD from input
2       //     input record format:
3       //         <string-key><TAB><long-value>
4       JavaSparkContext ctx = new JavaSparkContext();
5       JavaRDD<String> records = ctx.textFile(inputPath, 1);
6       records.saveAsTextFile("/output/2");
```

The RDD is listed here for debugging purposes:

```
$ hadoop fs -cat /output/2/part*
key1 1
key1 2
key1 3
key1 4
key1 5
key2 2
key2 4
key2 6
key2 8
key2 10
key3 3
key3 6
key3 9
key3 12
key3 15
key4 4
key4 8
key4 12
key4 16
key4 20
key5 5
key5 10
key5 15
```

```
key5 20
key5 25
```

Step 4: Create a monoid

This step creates a monoid structure, which will enable us to use combiners and reducers effectively without losing the semantics of our desired functionality. In Example 28-11, finding the mean of numbers is the main function of the combiners and reducers.

Example 28-11. Step 4: create a monoid

```
1     // Step 4: create a monoid
2     // map input(T) into (K,V) pair, which is monoidic
3     // mean( (V1,C1), (V2,C2) ) => ( (V1+V2), (C1+C2) )
4     JavaPairRDD<String,Tuple2<Long,Integer>> monoid =
5         records.mapToPair(new PairFunction<String,
6                                            String,
7                                            Tuple2<Long,Integer>
8                                            >() {
9       public Tuple2<String,Tuple2<Long,Integer>> call(String s) {
10        String[] tokens = s.split("\t"); //  s = <key><TAB><value>
11        String K = tokens[0];
12        Tuple2<Long,Integer> V =
13            new Tuple2<Long,Integer>(Long.parseLong(tokens[1]), 1);
14        return new Tuple2<String,Tuple2<Long,Integer>>(K, V);
15     }
16   });
```

The RDD is listed here for debugging purposes:

```
$ hadoop fs -cat /output/3/part*
(key1,(1,1))
(key1,(2,1))
(key1,(3,1))
(key1,(4,1))
(key1,(5,1))
(key2,(2,1))
(key2,(4,1))
(key2,(6,1))
(key2,(8,1))
(key2,(10,1))
(key3,(3,1))
(key3,(6,1))
(key3,(9,1))
(key3,(12,1))
(key3,(15,1))
(key4,(4,1))
(key4,(8,1))
(key4,(12,1))
(key4,(16,1))
```

```
(key4,(20,1))
(key5,(5,1))
(key5,(10,1))
(key5,(15,1))
(key5,(20,1))
(key5,(25,1))
```

Step 5: Reduce frequent keys by preserving monoids

In Spark, calling reduceByKey() will automatically perform combining locally on
each machine before computing global totals for each key. The programmer does not
need to specify a combiner. Since combining is automatic, we need to pay extra attention to reduceByKey() to make sure that using combiners will not alter the semantics
of our desired function (i.e., the mean function). The monoid structure enables
combiner optimization as well as providing the reducer functionality. See
Example 28-12.

Example 28-12. Step 5: Reduce frequent Ks by preserving monoids

```
1     // Step 5: reduce frequent Ks by preserving monoids
2     // Combiners may be used without losing the semantics of mean.
3     JavaPairRDD<String, Tuple2<Long,Integer>> reduced = monoid.reduceByKey(
4         new Function2<
5                         Tuple2<Long,Integer>,
6                         Tuple2<Long,Integer>,
7                         Tuple2<Long,Integer>
8                       >() {
9         public Tuple2<Long,Integer> call(Tuple2<Long,Integer> v1,
10                                 Tuple2<Long,Integer> v2) {
11            return new Tuple2<Long,Integer>(v1._1+ v2._1, v1._2+ v2._2);
12        }
13     });
14     reduced.saveAsTextFile("/output/4");
15     // now reduced RDD has the desired values for final output
```

The RDD is listed here for debugging purposes (note that the output has a monoid
structure):

```
$ hadoop fs -cat /output/4/part*
(key4,(60,5))
(key5,(75,5))
(key2,(30,5))
(key3,(45,5))
(key1,(15,5))
```

Step 6: Find mean by mapping values

Finding the mean value is deferred to the last step. Example 28-13 converts a monoid
structure into an actual mean value.

Example 28-13. Step 6: find mean by mapping values

```
1     // Step 6: find mean by mapping values
2     // mapValues[U](f: (V) => U): JavaPairRDD[K, U]
3     // Pass each value in the key-value pair RDD through
4     // a map function without changing the keys;
5     // this also retains the original RDD's partitioning.
6     JavaPairRDD<String,Double> mean = reduced.mapValues(
7         new Function<
8                         Tuple2<Long,Integer>,    // input
9                         Double                   // output
10                   >() {
11        public Double call(Tuple2<Long, Integer> s) {
12            return ( (double) s._1 / (double) s._2 );
13        }
14    });
15    mean.saveAsTextFile("/output/5");
```

The final output is presented here:

```
$ hadoop fs -cat /output/5/part*
(key4,12.0)
(key5,15.0)
(key2,6.0)
(key3,9.0)
(key1,3.0)
```

Sample Run

Script to run SparkMeanMonoidized

The following is the script to run our Spark solution:

```
$ cat run_spark_monoidized.sh
#!/bin/bash
export JAVA_HOME=/usr/java/jdk7
export SPARK_HOME=/usr/local/spark-1.1.0
export SPARK_MASTER=spark://myserver100:7077
export BOOK_HOME=/mp/data-algorithms
export APP_JAR=$BOOK_HOME/dist/data_algorithms_book.jar
INPUT=/home/hadoop/testspark/kv.txt
# Run on a Spark standalone cluster
$SPARK_HOME/bin/spark-submit \
--class org.dataalgorithms.chap28.spark.SparkMeanMonoidized \
--master $SPARK_MASTER \
--executor-memory 2G \
--total-executor-cores 20 \
$APP_JAR \
$INPUT
```

Log of sample run

The following is the log output of a sample run on a very small cluster, composed of three nodes (myserver100, myserver200, and myserver300). The output has been edited to fit the page:

```
$ ./run_spark_monoidized.sh
...
INFO : Added broadcast_5_piece0 in memory on myserver100:60093
  (size: 21.2 KB, free: 265.4 MB)
INFO : Updated info of block broadcast_5_piece0
INFO : Submitting 1 missing tasks from Stage 4 (MappedRDD[8]
  at saveAsTextFile
  at SparkMeanMonoidized.java:76)
INFO : Adding task set 4.0 with 1 tasks
INFO : Starting task 0.0 in stage 4.0 (TID 4, myserver200,
  PROCESS_LOCAL, 996 bytes)
INFO : Added broadcast_5_piece0 in memory on myserver300:51784
  (size: 21.2 KB, free: 1060.2 MB)
INFO : Finished task 0.0 in stage 4.0 (TID 4) in 224 ms on myserver200 (1/1)
INFO : Stage 4 (saveAsTextFile at SparkMeanMonoidized.java:76)
  finished in 0.226 s
INFO : Removed TaskSet 4.0, whose tasks have all completed, from pool
INFO : Job finished: saveAsTextFile at SparkMeanMonoidized.java:76,
  took 0.322557953 s
```

Conclusion on Using Monoids

We observed that in MapReduce, if your mapper generates monoids then you can utilize combiners for optimization and efficiency purposes (i.e., using combiners reduces network traffic and makes MapReduce's sort() and shuffle() functions more efficient by processing less data). Also, you learned how to monoidify MapReduce algorithms. This is the challenge. In general, combiners can be used when the function you want to apply is both commutative and associative (properties of a monoid). For example, the classic word count is a monoid over a set of integers with the + operation (here you can use a combiner). But the mean function (which is not associative, as shown in the previous counter example) over a set of integers does not form a monoid. Therefore, if combiners are used properly, it will significantly cut down the amount of data shuffled from the mappers to the reducers.

Monoids have applications and uses in functional programming as well. As computer scientist, software engineer, and blogger MarkCC (*http://bit.ly/monoids_markcc*) puts it:

> Why should we care if data structures like are [sic] monoids? Because we can write very general code in terms of the algebraic construction, and then use it over all of the different operations. Monoids provide the tools you need to build fold operations. Every kind of fold—that is, operations that collapse a sequence of other operations into a single value—can be defined in terms of monoids. So you can write a fold operation

that works on lists, strings, numbers, optional values, maps, and god-only-knows what else. Any data structure which is a monoid is a data structure with a meaningful fold operation: monoids encapsulate the requirements of foldability.

Functors and Monoids

Now that you have learned what monoids are and seen their use in the MapReduce framework, we can even apply higher-order functions (like *functors*) to monoids. A functor is an object that is a function (it is a function and object at the same time). The Java[3] programming language (JDK6 and JDK7) does not include the direct concept of functors, because functions are not first-class objects in Java; this means that you cannot pass a function name as an argument to another function. However, you can simulate functors in Java by defining an interface and a method (this is a very simplistic simulation):

```
public interface FunctorSimulation<T1, T2> {
    T2 apply(T1 input);
}
```

For details on implementation/simulation of functors in Java, refer to Guava's `Func tion` interface (*http://bit.ly/guava-libraries*) and the Apache Commons `Functor` interface (*http://bit.ly/commons_functor*). The Haskell programming language (*http://bit.ly/functors_haskell*) does include direct support for monoids and functors. Bruno P. Kinoshita has a good example of using the Apache Commons `Functor` functional interfaces with Java 8 lambdas (*http://bit.ly/functor_w_java8*) on his website.

First, we present a functor on a monoid through a simple example. Let `MONOID = (t, e, f)` be a monoid, where `t` is a type (set of values), `e` is the identity element, and `f` is the + binary plus function:

```
MONOID = {
    type t
    val e : t
    val plus : t x t -> t
}
```

Then we define a functor, `Prod`, as follows:

```
functor Prod (M : MONOID) (N : MONOID) = {
    type t = M.t * N.t
    val e = (M.e, N.e)
    fun plus((x1,y1), (x2,y2)) = (M.plus(x1,x2), N.plus(y1,y2))
}
```

Then we can define other functors, such as `Square`, as follows:

---

3 JDK8 provides direct support for functors through its Project Lambda (for details, see *http://openjdk.java.net/projects/lambda/*).

```
functor Square (M : MONOID) : MONOID = Prod M M
```

Next, we define a functor between two monoids. Let $(M_1,\ f_1,\ e_1)$ and $(M_2,\ f_2,\ e_2)$ be monoids. A functor:

```
F: (M₁, f₁, e₁) → (M₂, f₂, e₂)
```

is specified by an object map (monoids are categories with a single object) and an arrow map, F: $M_1 \to M_2$, and the following conditions will hold:

```
∀a, b ∈ M₁, F(f₁(a, b)) = f₂(F(a), F(b))
F(e₁) = e₂
```

A functor between two monoids is just a *monoid homomorphism*. For example, for the String data type, a function Length() that counts the number of letters in a word is a monoid homomorphism.

- Length('''') = 0 (the length of an empty string is 0).
- If Length(x) = m and Length(y) = n, then the concatenation of x + y has m + n letters. For example:

```
Length("String" + "ology") = Length("Stringology")
                           = 11
                           = 6 + 5
                           = Length("String") + Length("ology")
```

Next, we formally define *monoid homomorphisms*. Let M and N be monoids as follows:

```
M: (m, ×,eₘ)
N: (n, +,eₙ)
```

Then a homomorphism between two monoids M and N is a function:

$$f: M \to N$$

such that:

```
f(x × y) = f(x)+ f(y) for all x, y ∈ M
f(eₘ) = eₙ
```

The classic *word count* (let's call this f) is a monoid homomorphism:

```
f: String → Map[String,Integer]
```

Let $s \in S$ be a string, with $s_1 + s_2$ representing string concatenation. Let $m \in M$ be a count map, with $m_1 \oplus m_2$ representing key-wise addition. Then the word count (f) function can be defined as follows:

```
f: S → M
```

and the monoid homomorphism property is then given by:

```
f(s₁ + s₂) = f(s₁) ⊕ f(s₂)
```

This chapter discussed a MapReduce optimization technique involving monoids. I showed that using monoids enables us to use combiners (local per cluster node optimizations) and hence improve the performance of intensive computations. Chapter 29 solves the "small files problem" in the Hadoop world, which is another optimization technique for MapReduce programming.

The Small Files Problem

This chapter provides an efficient solution to the "small files" problem. What is a small file in a MapReduce/Hadoop environment? In the Hadoop world, a *small file* is a file whose size is much smaller than the HDFS block size. The default HDFS block size is 64 MB (or 67,108,864 bytes), so, for example, a 2 MB, 5 MB, or 7 MB file is considered a small file. However, the block size is configurable: it is defined by a parameter called `dfs.block.size`. If you have an application that deals with huge files (such as DNA sequencing), then you might even set this to a higher size, like 256 MB.

In general, Hadoop handles big files very well, but when the files are small, it just passes each small file to a `map()` function, which is not very efficient because it will create a large number of mappers. Typically, if you are using and storing small files, you probably have lots of them. For example, the file size to represent a bioset for a gene expression data type can be 2 to 3 MB. So, to process 1,000 biosets, you need 1,000 mappers (i.e., each file will be sent to a mapper, which is very inefficient). Having too many small files can therefore be problematic in Hadoop. To solve this problem, we should merge many of these small files into one and then process them. In the case of biosets, we might merge every 20 to 25 files into one file (where the size will be closer to 64 MB). By merging these files, we might need only 40 to 50 mappers (instead of 1,000). Note that Hadoop is mainly designed for batch-processing a large volume of data rather than processing many small files. The main purpose of solving the small files problem is to speed up the execution of a Hadoop program (for example, from 3 hours to 15 minutes) by combining small files into bigger files. Solving the small files problem will shrink the number of `map()` functions executed and hence will improve the overall performance of a Hadoop job.

This chapter presents two solutions to the small files problem:

- Solution 1: using a custom merge of small files; this solution merges small files into big files on the client side.

- Solution 2: using a custom implementation of CombineFileInputFormat<K,V>.[3]

Solution 1: Merging Small Files Client-Side

Let's assume that we have to process 20,000 small files (assuming that each file's size is much smaller than 64 MB) and we want to process them efficiently in the MapReduce/Hadoop environment. If you just send these files as input via FileInputFormat.addInputPath(Job, Path), then each input file will be sent to a mapper and you will end up with 20,000 mappers, which is very inefficient. Let dfs.block.size be 64 MB. Further assume that the size of these files is between 2 and 3 MB (so we assume that on average each small file's size is 2.5 MB). Further, assume that we have M (such as 100, 200, 300, ...) mappers available to us. The following multithreaded algorithm (which is a POJO and non-MapReduce solution) will solve the small files problem. Since our small files on average occupy 2.5 MB, we can put 25 ($25 \times 2.5 \approx 64$ MB) small files into one HDFS block, which we call a *bucket*. Now we just need 800 (20,000 ÷ 25 = 800) mappers, which will be very efficient compared to 20,000 mappers. Our algorithm puts N files (in our example, 25) into each bucket and then concurrently merges these small files into one file whose size is closer to the dfs.block.size.

Before submitting our small files to MapReduce/Hadoop, we merge them into big ones; we then submit these to the MapReduce driver program. Example 29-1 (taken from the driver program that submits MapReduce/Hadoop jobs) shows how to merge small files into one large file.

Example 29-1. Merging small files into a large file

```
1 // prepare input
2 int NUMBER_OF_MAP_SLOTS_AVAILABLE = <M>;
3 Job job = <define-a-job>;
4 List<Path> smallFiles = <HDFS small input files: file1, file2, ...>;
5 int numberOfSmallFiles = smallFiles.size();
6 if ( NUMBER_OF_MAP_SLOTS_AVAILABLE >= numberOfSmallFiles ) {
7     // we have enough mappers and there is no need
8     // to merge or consolidate small files; each
9     // small file will be sent as a block to a mapper
10    for (Path path : smallFiles) {
11        FileInputFormat.addInputPath(job, path);
12    }
```

---

3 org.apache.hadoop.mapred.lib.CombineFileInputFormat<K,V>

```
13 }
14 else {
15     // the number of mappers is less than the number of small files
16     // create and fill buckets with merged small files
17
18     // Step 1: create empty buckets (each bucket may hold a set of small files)
19     BucketThread[] buckets = SmallFilesConsolidator.createBuckets(
20             smallFiles,
21             NUMBER_OF_MAP_SLOTS_AVAILABLE);
22
23     // Step 2: fill buckets with small files
24     SmallFilesConsolidator.fillBuckets(buckets, smallFiles, job);
25
26     // Step 3: merge small files per bucket
27     // each bucket is a thread (implements Runnable interface)
28     // merging is done concurrently for each bucket
29     SmallFilesConsolidator.mergeEachBucket(buckets, job);
30 }
```

The SmallFilesConsolidator class accepts a set of small Hadoop files and then merges these small files together into larger Hadoop files whose size is less than or equal to dfs.block.size (i.e., the HDFS block size). The optimal solution is to create the smallest possible number of files (recall that there will be one mapper per file), so each file should be as close as possible to the HDFS block size. We generate these large files (as GUIDs) under the */tmp/* directory in HDFS (of course, the directory you use is configurable):

```
// this directory is configurable
private static String MERGED_HDFS_ROOT_DIR = "/tmp/";
...
private static String getParentDir() {
    String guid = UUID.randomUUID().toString();
    return MERGED_HDFS_ROOT_DIR + guid + "/";
}
```

The BucketThread class enables us to concatenate small files into one big file whose size is smaller than the HDFS block size. This way, we will submit fewer mappers with big input files. BucketThread class implements the Runnable interface and provides the copyMerge() method, which merges the small files into a larger file. Since each BucketThread object implements the Runnable interface, it will be able to run in its own thread. This way, all BucketThread objects can merge their small files concurrently. The BucketThread.copyMerge() is the core method; it merges all small files in one bucket into another temporary HDFS file. For example, if a bucket holds the small files {File1, File2, File3, File4}, then the merged file will look like Figure 29-1 (note that the MergedFile is the concatenation of all four files).

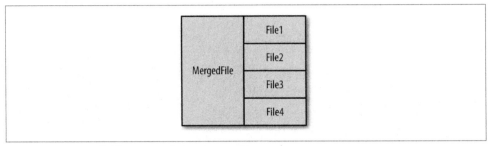

Figure 29-1. Small files merged into larger file

Example 29-2 shows the implementation of the BucketThread.copyMerge() method.

Example 29-2. The copyMerge() method

```
 1 /**
 2  * Copy all files in several directories to one output file (mergedFile).
 3  *
 4  * parentDir will be "/tmp/<guid>/"
 5  * targetDir will be "/tmp/<guid>/id/"
 6  * targetFile will be "/tmp/<guid>/id/id"
 7  *
 8  * merge all paths in bucket and return a new directory
 9  * (targetDir), which holds merged paths
10  */
11 public void copyMerge() throws IOException {
12
13     // if there is only one path/dir in the bucket,
14     // then there is no need to merge it
15     if ( size() < 2 ) {
16         return;
17     }
18
19     // here bucket.size() >= 2
20     Path hdfsTargetFile = new Path(targetFile);
21     OutputStream mergedFile = fs.create(hdfsTargetFile);
22     try {
23         for (int i = 0; i < bucket.size(); i++) {
24             FileStatus contents[] = fs.listStatus(bucket.get(i));
25             for (int k = 0; k < contents.length; k++) {
26                 if (!contents[k].isDir()) {
27                     InputStream smallFile = fs.open(contents[k].getPath());
28                     try {
29                         IOUtils.copyBytes(smallFile, mergedFile, conf, false);
30                     }
31                     finally {
32                         HadoopUtil.close(smallFile);
33                     }
34                 }
```

```
35              } // for k
36           } // for i
37        }
38        finally {
39           HadoopUtil.close(mergedFile);
40        }
41 }
```

The SmallFilesConsolidator class therefore provides three pieces of functionality:

1. Create the required empty buckets. Each bucket will hold a set of small files. This will be done by SmallFilesConsolidator.createBuckets().

2. Fill the buckets. We will place enough small files in a bucket so that the total size of all small files will be about dfs.block.size. This behavior is implemented by SmallFilesConsolidator.fillBuckets().

3. Merge each bucket. Here we will merge all small files in the bucket to create a single large file, whose size will be about dfs.block.size. This is accomplished by SmallFilesConsolidator.mergeEachBucket().

To demonstrate the small files problem, we will run the classic word count program with and without the SmallFilesConsolidator class. For input, for each case we will use 30 small files. We will clearly see that using SmallFilesConsolidator outperforms the original solution; it finishes in 58,235 milliseconds, while the original word count program with small files finishes in 80,435 milliseconds.

Input Data

We use the following input data (30 small files) for both solutions:

```
# hadoop fs -ls /small_input_files/input/
Found 30 items
-rw-r--r-- 1 ... /small_input_files/input/Document-1
-rw-r--r-- 1 ... /small_input_files/input/Document-2
...
-rw-r--r-- 1 ... /small_input_files/input/Document-29
-rw-r--r-- 1 ... /small_input_files/input/Document-30
```

Solution with SmallFilesConsolidator

In this solution we will use the SmallFilesConsolidator class to merge the small files into a larger file.

Hadoop implementation classes

Table 29-1 shows the Java classes we'll require in this solution.

Table 29-1. Required Java classes for solution with SmallFilesConsolidator

Class name	Class description
BucketThread	Used to merge small files into larger files
HadoopUtil	Defines some basic Hadoop utilities
SmallFilesConsolidator	Manages consolidation of small files into a larger file
WordCountDriverWithConsolidator	Word count driver with consolidator
WordCountMapper	Defines map()
WordCountReducer	Defines reduce() and combine()

The SmallFilesConsolidator class is the driver class to consolidate the small files into a larger file whose size is closer to the HDFS block size. The main methods are:

getNumberOfBuckets()
> Determines the number of buckets needed for merging all files into bigger files.

```
public static int getNumberOfBuckets(int totalFiles,
                                     int numberOfMapSlotsAvailable,
                                     int maxFilesPerBucket)
```

createBuckets()
> Creates the required buckets.

```
public static BucketThread[] createBuckets(
                        int totalFiles,
                        int numberOfMapSlotsAvailable,
                        int maxFilesPerBucket)
```

fillBuckets()
> Fills each bucket with small files.

```
public static void fillBuckets(
        BucketThread[] buckets,
        List<String> smallFiles, // list of small files
        Job job,
        int maxFilesPerBucket)
```

mergeEachBucket()
> Merges small files to create a larger file.

```
public static void mergeEachBucket(BucketThread[] buckets,
                                   Job job)
```

Sample run

Here is a sample run for our solution (edited and formatted to fit the page):

```
# ./run_with_consolidator.sh
...
Deleted hdfs://localhost:9000/small_input_files/output
13/11/05 10:54:04 ...: inputDir=/small_input_files/input
13/11/05 10:54:04 ...: outputDir=/small_input_files/output
13/11/05 10:54:05 ...added path: /tmp/906e6c30-c411-4a70-b68f-114ba7511e63/
...
13/11/05 10:54:05 ...added path: /tmp/906e6c30-c411-4a70-b68f-114ba7511e63/
...
13/11/05 10:54:05 INFO input.FileInputFormat: Total input paths to process : 8
...
13/11/05 10:54:05 INFO mapred.JobClient: Running job: job_201311051023_0002
13/11/05 10:54:06 INFO mapred.JobClient: map 0% reduce 0%
...
13/11/05 10:55:01 INFO mapred.JobClient: map 100% reduce 100%
13/11/05 10:55:02 INFO mapred.JobClient: Job complete: job_201311051023_0002
13/11/05 10:55:02 INFO mapred.JobClient: Launched reduce tasks=10
13/11/05 10:55:02 INFO mapred.JobClient: Launched map tasks=8
13/11/05 10:55:02 INFO mapred.JobClient: Data-local map tasks=8
...
13/11/05 10:55:02 INFO mapred.JobClient: Map input records=48
13/11/05 10:55:02 INFO mapred.JobClient: Reduce input records=48
13/11/05 10:55:02 INFO mapred.JobClient: Reduce input groups=7
13/11/05 10:55:02 INFO mapred.JobClient: Reduce output records=7
13/11/05 10:55:02 INFO mapred.JobClient: Map output records=201
13/11/05 10:55:02 INFO WordCountDriverWithConsolidator: returnStatus=0
13/11/05 10:55:02 INFO WordCountDriverWithConsolidator:
    Finished in milliseconds: 58235
```

As you can see from the log of the sample run, we have consolidated 30 HDFS small files into 8 large HDFS files.

Solution Without SmallFilesConsolidator

This solution is just a basic word count application that does not use the SmallFiles Consolidator class. As you can see from the following snippet from the sample run, the total number of input paths to process is 30, which is exactly the number of small files we want to process:

```
...
13/11/05 10:29:13 INFO input.FileInputFormat: Total input paths to process : 30
...
```

This solution is not an optimal solution at all, since every small file will be sent to a mapper. As you know, the ideal case is to send input files whose size is just under or equal to the HDFS block size (because Hadoop is designed for handling large files).

Hadoop implementation classes

Table 29-2 shows the Java classes required for our solution without SmallFilesConsolidator.

Table 29-2. Java classes required for solution without SmallFilesConsolidator

Class name	Class description
HadoopUtil	Defines some basic Hadoop utilities
WordCountDriverWithoutConsolidator	Word count driver without consolidator
WordCountMapper	Defines map()
WordCountReducer	Defines reduce() and combine()

Sample run

Here is the output from a sample run (edited and formatted to fit the page) of our solution without SmallFilesConsolidator:

```
# ./run_without_consolidator.sh
...
Deleted hdfs://localhost:9000/small_input_files/output
13/11/05 10:29:12 ... inputDir=/small_input_files/input
13/11/05 10:29:12 ... outputDir=/small_input_files/output
...
13/11/05 10:29:13 INFO input.FileInputFormat: Total input paths to process : 30
...
13/11/05 10:29:13 INFO mapred.JobClient: Running job: job_201311051023_0001
13/11/05 10:29:14 INFO mapred.JobClient: map 0% reduce 0%
...
13/11/05 10:30:32 INFO mapred.JobClient: map 100% reduce 100%
13/11/05 10:30:33 INFO mapred.JobClient: Job complete: job_201311051023_0001
...
13/11/05 10:30:33 INFO mapred.JobClient: Map-Reduce Framework
13/11/05 10:30:33 INFO mapred.JobClient: Map input records=48
13/11/05 10:30:33 INFO mapred.JobClient: Reduce input records=153
13/11/05 10:30:33 INFO mapred.JobClient: Reduce input groups=7
13/11/05 10:30:33 INFO mapred.JobClient: Combine output records=153
13/11/05 10:30:33 INFO mapred.JobClient: Reduce output records=7
13/11/05 10:30:33 INFO mapred.JobClient: Map output records=201
13/11/05 10:30:33 INFO WordCountDriverWithoutConsolidator:
    run(): status=true
13/11/05 10:30:33 INFO WordCountDriverWithoutConsolidator:
    Finished in milliseconds: 80435
```

Solution 2: Solving the Small Files Problem with CombineFileInputFormat

This section uses the Hadoop API (the abstract class CombineFileInputFormat) to solve the small files problem. This is how CombineFileInputFormat (as an abstract class) is defined in Hadoop 2.5.0 (*http://bit.ly/combinefileinputformat*):

```
package org.apache.hadoop.mapred.lib;
...
@InterfaceAudience.Public
```

```
@InterfaceStability.Stable
public abstract class CombineFileInputFormat<K,V>
    extends CombineFileInputFormat<K,V>
    implements InputFormat<K,V>
```

The idea behind the abstract class CombineFileInputFormat is to enable combining small files into Hadoop's splits (or chunks) by using a custom InputFormat. To use the abstract class CombineFileInputFormat, we have to provide/implement three custom classes:

- CustomCFIF extends CombineFileInputFormat (which is an abstract class with no implementation, so we must create this subclass to support it).

- PairOfStringLong is a Writable class that stores the small filename (as a String) and its offset (as a Long) and overrides the compareTo() method to compare the filename first, then the offset.

- CustomRecordReader is a custom RecordReader:

  ```
  public class CustomRecordReader
      extends RecordReader<PairOfStringLong, Text> {
      ...
  }
  ```

The custom implementation of CombineFileInputFormat is provided in Example 29-3.

Example 29-3. CustomCFIF class

```
 1 import java.io.IOException;
 2 import org.apache.hadoop.fs.Path;
 3 import org.apache.hadoop.io.Text;
 4 import org.apache.hadoop.mapreduce.InputSplit;
 5 import org.apache.hadoop.mapreduce.JobContext;
 6 import org.apache.hadoop.mapreduce.RecordReader;
 7 import org.apache.hadoop.mapreduce.TaskAttemptContext;
 8 import org.apache.hadoop.mapreduce.lib.input.CombineFileSplit;
 9 import org.apache.hadoop.mapreduce.lib.input.CombineFileInputFormat;
10 import org.apache.hadoop.mapreduce.lib.input.CombineFileRecordReader;
11
12 import edu.umd.cloud9.io.pair.PairOfStringLong;
13 // PairOfStringLong = Tuple2<String, Long> = Tuple2<FileName, Offset>
14 // https://github.com/lintool/Cloud9/
15
16 /**
17  *  A custom file input format that combines/merges smaller files
18  *  into big files controlled by MAX_SPLIT_SIZE
19  *
20  *  @author Mahmoud Parsian
21  *
```

```
22  */
23  public class CustomCFIF extends CombineFileInputFormat<PairOfStringLong, Text> {
24      final static long MAX_SPLIT_SIZE = 67108864; // 64 MB
25
26      public CustomCFIF() {
27          super();
28          setMaxSplitSize(MAX_SPLIT_SIZE);
29      }
30
31      public RecordReader<PairOfStringLong, Text> createRecordReader
32          (InputSplit split,
33           TaskAttemptContext context)
34          throws IOException {
35          return new CombineFileRecordReader<PairOfStringLong, Text>(
36          (CombineFileSplit)split,
37          context,
38          CustomRecordReader.class);
39      }
40
41      @Override
42      protected boolean isSplitable(JobContext context, Path file) {
43          return false;
44      }
45  }
```

You should set the MAX_SPLIT_SIZE based on the HDFS block size (default to 64 MB).
If most of your files are bigger than 64 MB, then you may set the HDFS block size to
128 MB or even 256 MB (in some genomic applications, the HDFS block size is set to
512 MB). In Hadoop 2.5.1, the HDFS block size is set to 128 MB (134,217,728 bytes)
by default. You can control the HDFS block size inside the *hdfs-site.xml* file (this is
one of the files to configure a Hadoop cluster) via the dfs.blocksize property. For
example:

```
$ cat $HADOOP_HOME/etc/hadoop/hdfs-site.xml
<?xml version="1.0" encoding="UTF-8"?>

<configuration>

    <property>
        <name>dfs.blocksize</name>
        <value>268435456</value>
        <description>256MB</description>
    </property>

    <property>
    ...
    </property>

    ...

</configuration>
```

Setting the maximum split size (MAX_SPLIT_SIZE) will determine the number of map-pers needed. For example, consider the following HDFS directory:[3]

```
# hadoop fs -ls /small_input_files | wc -l
10004

# hadoop fs -ls /small_input_files | head -3
-rw-r--r-- 3 ... 9184 2014-10-06 15:20 /small_input_files/file1.txt
-rw-r--r-- 3 ... 27552 2014-10-06 15:20 /small_input_files/file2.txt
-rw-r--r-- 3 ... 27552 2014-10-06 15:20 /small_input_files/file3.txt

# hadoop fs -ls /small_input_files | tail -3
-rw-r--r-- 3 ... 27552 2014-10-06 15:28 /small_input_files/file10002.txt
-rw-r--r-- 3 ... 27552 2014-10-06 15:28 /small_input_files/file10003.txt
-rw-r--r-- 3 ... 27552 2014-10-06 15:28 /small_input_files/file10004.txt

# hadoop fs -dus /small_input_files
275584288    /small_input_files
#
```

As you can see, the HDFS directory */small_input_files* has 10,004 small files and requires 275,584,288 bytes. If we do not use the CustomCFIF as our input format, then a basic MapReduce job will queue 10,004 mappers (which takes over *34 minutes* to execute on a three-node cluster). But, using the CustomCFIF, we need only five map-pers (which takes under *2 minutes* to execute on a three-node cluster). Why do we need five mappers? The following calculations answer that question:

```
HDFS-split-size = 64MB = 64*1024*1024 = 67108864
Required Bytes for 10004 small files = 275584288
275584288/67108864 = 4
Therefore we need 5 splits:
    67108864+67108864+67108864+67108864+7148832 = 275584288

Therefore, 5 input splits are required
=> this will launch 5 mappers (one per split)
```

If you set MAX_SPLIT_SIZE to 128 MB (134,217,728 bytes), then the Hadoop job will launch only three mappers, like so:

```
HDFS-split-size = 128MB = 128*1024*1024 = 134217728
Required Bytes for 10004 small files = 275584288
275584288/134217728 = 2
Therefore we need 3 splits:
    134217728+134217728+7148832 = 275584288

Therefore, 3 input splits are required
=> this will launch 3 mappers (one per split)
```

---

3 For testing purposes, you can create a lot of small files using bash; for details, see *http://bit.ly/many_small_files*.

Custom CombineFileInputFormat

The `CustomCFIF` class solves the small files problem by combining small files into splits determined by the `MAX_SPLIT_SIZE` (this is basically the maximum size of the bigger file into which the small files are merged). This custom class (which extends the abstract class `CombineFileInputFormat`) has several functions:

- It sets the maximum split size, invoking `setMaxSplitSize(MAX_SPLIT_SIZE)` in the constructor. The maximum combination of small files will not exceed this size.

- It defines a custom record reader by `createRecordReader()`, and then provides a plug-in class, `CustomRecordReader`, which reads small files into large split sizes (the maximum size is determined by `MAX_SPLIT_SIZE`).

- It defines key-value pairs to be fed to the mappers. We use `PairOfStringLong` as a key and `Text` (a single line of a text file) as a value. `PairOfStringLong` represents two pieces of information: the filename (as a `String`) and offset (as a `Long`).

- It indicates that the combined/merged files should not be split; this is set by the `isSplitable()` method, which returns `false`.

Sample Run Using CustomCFIF

The following subsections provide the script, run log, and output (edited and formatted to fit the page) for our sample run using `CustomCFIF`.

The script

```
# cat run_combine_small_files.sh
#!/bin/bash
BOOK_HOME=/mp/data-algorithms-book
CLASSPATH=.:$BOOK_HOME/dist/data_algorithms_book.jar
APP_JAR=$BOOK_HOME/dist/data_algorithms_book.jar
CLASSPATH=$CLASSPATH:$BOOK_HOME/lib/spark-assembly-1.2.0-hadoop2.6.0.jar
INPUT=/small_input_files
OUTPUT=/output/1
PROG=org.dataalgorithms.chap29.combinesmallfiles.CombineSmallFilesDriver
hadoop jar $APP_JAR $PROG $INPUT $OUTPUT
```

Log of the sample run

```
# ./run_combine_small_files.sh
input path = /small_input_files
output path = /output/1
14/10/06 15:51:39 INFO input.FileInputFormat:
..Total input paths to process : 10003
14/10/06 15:51:40 INFO input.CombineFileInputFormat:
```

```
    DEBUG: Terminated node allocation
    with : CompletedNodes: 3, size left: 7108416
14/10/06 15:51:40 INFO mapreduce.JobSubmitter: number of splits:5
...
14/10/06 15:51:41 INFO impl.YarnClientImpl:
    Submitted application application_1411149084067_0006
14/10/06 15:51:41 INFO mapreduce.Job: The url to track the job:
    http://myserver100:8088/proxy/application_1411149084067_0006/
14/10/06 15:51:41 INFO mapreduce.Job: Running job: job_1411149084067_0006
14/10/06 15:51:49 INFO mapreduce.Job: Job job_1411149084067_0006
    running in uber mode : false
14/10/06 15:51:49 INFO mapreduce.Job:  map 0% reduce 0%
...
14/10/06 15:54:07 INFO mapreduce.Job:  map 100% reduce 100%
14/10/06 15:54:08 INFO mapreduce.Job: Job job_1411149084067_0006
    completed successfully
14/10/06 15:54:08 INFO mapreduce.Job: Counters: 50
...
        Job Counters
                Launched map tasks=5
                Launched reduce tasks=12
...
        Map-Reduce Framework
                Map input records=1650385
                Map output records=41499681
                Reduce input groups=617
                Reduce input records=41499681
                Reduce output records=617
                Shuffled Maps =60
                Merged Map outputs=60
                CPU time spent (ms)=822100
                Total committed heap usage (bytes)=18386780160
```

Output

```
# hadoop fs -ls /output/1
Found 13 items
-rw-r--r--   3 hadoop,hadoop     0 2014-10-06 15:54 /output/1/_SUCCESS
-rw-r--r--   3 hadoop,hadoop   647 2014-10-06 15:53 /output/1/part-r-00000
-rw-r--r--   3 hadoop,hadoop   778 2014-10-06 15:53 /output/1/part-r-00001
...
-rw-r--r--   3 hadoop,hadoop   767 2014-10-06 15:54 /output/1/part-r-00010
-rw-r--r--   3 hadoop,hadoop   534 2014-10-06 15:54 /output/1/part-r-00011

# hadoop fs -cat /output/1/part-r-00000
...
about 30007
against 30007
also 120028
assay 60014
cannot 30007
```

```
carefully 30007
...
```

Output from Hadoop URL

```
Job Output from Hadoop URL:
 http://myserver100:8088/cluster/app/application_1411149084067_0007

User: hadoop
Name: CombineSmallFilesDriver
Application Type: MAPREDUCE
Application Tags:
State: FINISHED
FinalStatus: SUCCEEDED
Started: 6-Oct-2014 16:25:02
Elapsed: 1mins, 54sec
Tracking URL: History
Diagnostics:
```

Alternative Solutions

The filecrush (*http://bit.ly/filecrush*) tool is another possible solution for solving the small files problem. It merges many small files into fewer large ones. Also, it can change files from text to SequenceFile format (binary key-value files) and execute other compression options in one pass.

This chapter provided two concrete and scalable solutions for the "small files" problem. The provided solutions enable proper optimizations for MapReduce jobs using a large number of small files. Chapter 30 discusses another optimization for MapReduce jobs: using "huge caches" for the map() and reduce() functions.

Huge Cache for MapReduce

This chapter will show how to use and read a huge cache (i.e., composed of billions of key-value pairs that cannot fit in a commodity server's memory) in MapReduce algorithms. The algorithms presented in this chapter are generic enough to be used in any MapReduce paradigms (such as MapReduce/Hadoop and Spark).

There are some MapReduce algorithms that might require access to some huge (i.e., containing billions of records) static reference relational tables. Typically, these reference relational tables do not change for a long period of time, but they are needed in either the `map()` or `reduce()` phase of MapReduce programs. One example of such a table is a "position feature" table, which is used for germline[3] data type ingestion and variant classification. The position feature table might have the attributes shown in Table 30-1 (a composite key is (`chromosome_id`, `position`).

Table 30-1. Attributes of a position feature table

Column name	Characteristics
`chromosome_id`	Key-1
`position`	Key-2
`feature_id`	Basic attribute
`mrna_feature_id`	Basic attribute
`sequence_data_type_id`	Basic attribute
`mapping`	Basic attribute

---

3 *Germline* refers to the sequence of cells in the line of direct descent from zygote to gametes, as opposed to somatic cells (all other body cells). Mutations in germline cells are transmitted to offspring; those in somatic cells are not. (Source: *http://bit.ly/germline_def.*)

In expressing your solution in the MapReduce paradigm, either in `map()` or `reduce()`, given a key=(`chromosome_id, position`), you want to return a `List<String>` where each element of the list comprises the remaining attributes {`feature_id, mrna_feature_id, sequence_data_type_id, mapping`}. For the germline data type, a position feature table can have up to *12 billion records* (which might take about 2 TB of disk space in a MySQL or Oracle database system). Now imagine that your mapper or reducer wants to access the position feature table for a given key=(`chromosome_id, position`). Since you will be firing many requests (several million per second) of this type, this will bring your database server to its knees and it will not scale. One possible solution is to cache all static data into a hash table and then use the hash table instead of a relational table. However, as you will see in the next section, this is not a proper solution at all and will not scale—the size of such a hash table will be over 4 TB (a hash table's metadata takes quite a bit of space) and it will not fit in the memory of today's commodity servers.

Implementation Options

So what are the optimal and pragmatic options for caching 12 billion records in a MapReduce environment? In this section, I will present several options and discuss the feasibility of their implementations:

Option #1
Use a relational database (such as MySQL or Oracle). This option is not a viable solution and will not scale at all. A mapper or reducer will constantly hit the database, and the database server will not be able to handle thousands or millions of requests per second. Even if we use a set of replicated relational databases, this option still will not scale out (since the number of database connections is limited for a large set of Hadoop clusters).

Option #2
Use a memcached server. Memcached (*http://memcached.org/*) is an in-memory key-value store for small chunks of arbitrary data (e.g., strings, objects) from the results of database calls, API calls, or page rendering. If for every few slave nodes you have a dedicated memcached cluster (which would be very costly in a large cluster environment), then this is a viable and proper option. This solution will not scale out due to the high cost of having so many expensive memcached servers.

Option #3
Use a Redis server. Redis (*http://redis.io/*) is an open source, BSD licensed, advanced key-value store. It is often referred to as a *data structure server* since keys can contain strings, hashes, lists, sets, and sorted sets. As with memcached, if for every few slave nodes you have a dedicated Redis server (which would be

very costly in a large cluster environment), this is a viable and proper option. But again, this solution will not scale out due to the high cost of having so many Redis servers (for 2 TB of key-value pairs, Redis requires at least 12 TB of RAM).

Option #4

Use a MapReduce join between your input and 12 billion static records. The idea is to flatten the 12 billion records and then use a MapReduce join between this and your input. Perform the join on the key=(chromosome_id, position). This is a viable option if your input is huge too (meaning billions rather than millions). For example, for a germline ingestion process, the VCF[3] file will not have more than 6 million records. It is not appropriate to join a table of 6 million records against 12 billion records (as it wastes lots of time).

Option #5

Partition the 12 billion static records into small chunks (each chunk will be 64 MB, which you can easily load into RAM and evict when it's not needed) and use an LRU-Map (LRU stands for *least recently used*) hash table. This simple but elegant idea works very well: it scales out and does not require dedicated cache servers. This solution is detailed in the following sections. No matter what, in a distributed environment the mapper or reducer does not have access to an unlimited amount of memory/RAM. This solution will work in any MapReduce environment and does not require extra RAM for caching purposes. The LRU map is a local cache on a Linux filesystem, and every cluster worker node will have an identical copy of it (which occupies less than 1 TB of hard disk space). Using solid disk drives (SSDs) improves the cache performance by 8 to 10 times over regular disk drives.

Formalizing the Cache Problem

In a nutshell, given a set of 12 billion records, our goal is to find an associated value for a given composite key, key=(chromosome_id, position). Let's say that you are going to ingest a VCF file (this is our input file, comprising about 5 million records for the germline data type) into your genome system. For every record of a given VCF, you need to find out:

- Mutation class
- List of genes
- List of features

---

3 Variant call format is a text file format. It contains metainformation lines, a header line, and data lines, each containing information about a position in the genome. For more details, see *http://bit.ly/variant_call_format*.

To find this detailed information for each VCF record, you need a set of static tables such as the position feature table outlined at the beginning of this chapter. As we discussed before, a position feature table may contain as many as 12 billion records. The first step of the germline ingestion process is to find records from a position feature table for a given key=(chromosome_id, position) (every VCF record will have chromosome_id and position fields).

An Elegant, Scalable Solution

The solution presented here is a local cache solution. This means that every worker/slave node of a MapReduce/Hadoop or Spark cluster will have its own local cache (on a hard disk, which is cheap enough), and there will not be any network traffic for accessing cache components and data. The local cache will reside in an SSD or HDD and be brought to memory on an as-needed basis via the LRU map caching technique. Assuming that we have a relational table called position_feature (as defined at the start of the chapter) that has over 12 billion records, this is how it works:

1. First, we partition the 12 billion records by chromosome_id (1, 2, 3, ..., 24, 25). This will give us 25 files (let's label these files *chr1.txt*, *chr2.txt*, ..., *chr25.txt*), where each record has the following format (note that key=(chromosome_id, position) returns multiple records from the relational table):

   <position><;><Record1><:><Record2><:>...<:><RecordN>

   and each Record<i> comprises the following:

   <feature_id><,><mrna_fea
   ture_id><,><sequence_data_type_id><,><mapping>

   Therefore, each raw cache data file (*chr1.txt*, *chr2.txt*, ..., *chr25.txt*) corresponds to the following SQL query (you may repeat this script for each chromosome_id; the following query is for chromosome_id=1):

   ```
   select position,
          GROUP_CONCAT(feature_id, ',',
                       mrna_feature_id, ',',
                       seq_datatype_id, ',',
                       mapping SEPARATOR ':')
          INTO OUTFILE '/tmp/chr1.txt'
          FIELDS TERMINATED BY ';'
          LINES TERMINATED BY '\n'
       from position_feature where chromosome_id = 1 group by position;
   ```

2. Next, we sort each of these files (*chr1.txt*, *chr2.txt*, ..., *chr25.txt*) by position and generate *chr1.txt.sorted*, *chr2.txt.sorted*, ..., *chr25.txt.sorted*.

3. Since memory is limited (say, to 4 GB) for each mapper/reducer of a MapReduce job, we partition each sorted file into chunks of 64 MB (without breaking any lines). To do so, we execute the following command:

```
#!/bin/bash
sorted=/data/positionfeature.sorted
output=/data/partitioned/
for i in {1..25} ; do
    echo "i=$i"
    mkdir -p $output/$i
    cd $output/$i/
    split -a 3 -d -C 64m $sorted/$i.txt.sorted $i.
done
exit
```

For example, for `chromosome_id=1` we will have:

```
# ls -l /data/partitioned/1/
-rw-rw-r-- 1 hadoop hadoop 67108634 Feb 2 09:30 1.000
-rw-rw-r-- 1 hadoop hadoop 67108600 Feb 2 09:30 1.001
-rw-rw-r-- 1 hadoop hadoop 67108689 Feb 2 09:30 1.002
...
-rw-rw-r-- 1 hadoop hadoop 11645141 Feb 2 09:33 1.292
```

Note that each of these partitioned files has a range of `position` values (since they are sorted by `position`). We will use these ranges in our cache implementation. Therefore, given a `chromosome_id=1` and a `position`, we know exactly which partition holds the result of a query. Let's look at the content of one of these sorted partitioned files:

```
# head -2 /data/partitioned/1/1.000
6869;35304872,35275845,2,1
6870;35304872,35275845,2,1

# tail -2 /data/partitioned/1/1.000
790279;115457,21895578,12,2:115457,35079912,3,3:...
790280;115457,21895578,12,2:115457,35079912,3,3:...
```

You can see that all positions are sorted within each partition. To support metadata for all partitions using LRU Map, we need an additional data structure to keep track of (begin, end) positions. For each partitioned file we will keep the (partition name, begin, end) information. For example, for `chromosome id=1` and `chromosome id=2` we get:

```
# cat 1/begin_end_position.txt
1.000;6869;790280
1.001;790281;1209371
1.002;1209372;1461090
...
1.292;249146130;249236242
```

```
# cat 2/begin_end_position.txt
2.000;33814;1010683
2.001;1010684;1494487
2.002;1494488;2132388
...
2.279;242617420;243107469
```

The partition data structure is illustrated in Figure 30-1.

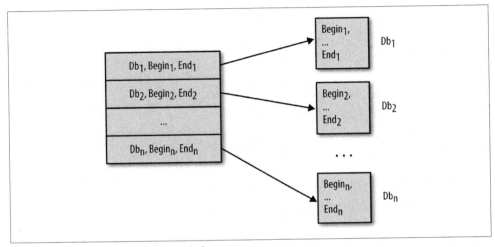

Figure 30-1. Huge cache partition data structure

4. Next, we will convert each partition (of 64 MB) into a hash table, implemented by MapDB (*http://www.mapdb.org*).[3]

   Since memory is limited for each mapper/reducer, we use LRUMap<K,V>(N) to hold at most N MapDB data structures (each MapDB-persistent map corresponds to one sorted partition of 64 MB. The idea of LRUMap<K,V> is to hold at most N partitions such that N × 64 MB will be smaller than the memory available for each mapper/reducer. When you insert the N + 1st entry into LRUMap<K,V>(N), the oldest entry will be evicted (then you can properly close the MapDB object, which releases all memory and closes all file handles). For the LRU Map implementation, we use org.apache.commons.collections4.map.LRUMap<K,V>.

5. The final step is to sort our input (which will use the cache; note that sorting input such as a VCF file can be done in under 3 seconds) by key=(chromo

---

3 MapDB is implemented by Jan Kotek and its source code is hosted at *https://github.com/jankotek/MapDB*. MapDB provides concurrent maps, sets, and queues backed by disk storage or off-heap memory. It is a fast and easy-to-use embedded Java database engine.

some_id, position). This sorting will minimize the eviction of MapDB entries from LRUMap<K,V>(N). The sorting of an input file is a huge design/implementation criterion and will have a big impact on the performance of our MapReduce job (germline ingestion). If we don't sort our input file, the eviction rate might be very high. Conversely, sorting the input file will minimize the eviction rate. Note that sorting the input file is very fast; it should not take more than a few seconds (you can do so through a Linux sort command or by using MapReduce/Hadoop).

Implementing the LRUMap Cache

In this section we'll walk through how to implement our elegant, scalable solution to managing a huge cache size in MapReduce.

Extending the LRUMap Class

To implement the LRU map, I selected LRUMap<K,V>,[3] which is a Map implementation with a fixed maximum size that removes the least recently used (LRU) entry if an entry is added when the map is full. The LRU map algorithm works on the get and put operations only. Iteration of any kind, including setting the value by iteration, does not change the order of entries (for details, you may consult the Apache Commons Collections (*http://bit.ly/commons_collections*)). For our cache implementation, we extend the LRUMap class (the MapDBEntry class is a simple class that represents a sorted partition of 64 MB as a Map data structure implemented in MapDB). See Example 30-1.

Example 30-1. Custom LRUMap

```
1 import org.apache.commons.collections4.map.LRUMap;
2 import org.apache.commons.collections4.map.AbstractLinkedMap.LinkEntry;
3
4 public class CustomLRUMap<K, V> extends LRUMap<K, V> {
5
6     private K key = null;
7     private V value = null;
8     private LinkEntry<K, V> entry = null;
9
10    public CustomLRUMap(final int size) {
11        super(size);
12    }
13
```

---

3 org.apache.commons.collections4.map.LRUMap

```
14    @Override
15    protected boolean removeLRU(final LinkEntry<K, V> entry) {
16        System.out.println("begin remove LRU entry ...");
17        this.entry = entry;
18        this.key = entry.getKey();
19        this.value = entry.getValue();
20
21        if (key instanceof String) {
22            String keyAsString = (String) key;
23            System.out.println("evicting key="+keyAsString);
24        }
25
26        if (value instanceof MapDBEntry) {
27            // release resources held by MapDBEntry
28            MapDBEntry mapdbEntry = (MapDBEntry) value;
29            mapdbEntry.close();
30        }
31
32        return true; // actually delete entry from the LRU map
33    }
34 }
```

Testing the Custom Class

Example 30-2 shows how CustomLRUMap<K,V> works. The CustomLRUMap<K,V> class extends the LRUMap<K,V> class and redefines the eviction policy by the removeLRU() method. In this example, we keep only three map entries at any time. No matter how many entries you add to the LRUMap object, the LRUMap.size() cannot exceed 3 (the maximum size is given at the time of the CustomLRUMap<K,V> object's creation).

Example 30-2. Custom LRUMap test

```
1 # cat CustomLRUMapTest.java
2
3 import org.apache.commons.collections4.map.LRUMap;
4
5 public class CustomLRUMapTest {
6     public static void main(String[] args) throws Exception {
7         CustomLRUMap<String, String> map = new CustomLRUMap<String, String>(3);
8         map.put("k1", "v1");
9         map.put("k2", "v2");
10        map.put("k3", "v3");
11        System.out.println("map="+map);
12        map.put("k4", "v4");
13        String v = map.get("k2");
14        System.out.println("v="+v);
15        System.out.println("map="+map);
16        map.put("k5", "v5");
17        System.out.println("map="+map);
18        map.put("k6", "v6");
```

```
19        System.out.println("map="+map);
20    }
21 }
```

Running this test produces the following output:

```
# javac CustomLRUMapTest.java
# java CustomLRUMapTest
map={k1=v1, k2=v2, k3=v3}
begin removeLRU...
evicting key=k1
v=v2
map={k3=v3, k4=v4, k2=v2}
begin removeLRU...
evicting key=k3
map={k4=v4, k2=v2, k5=v5}
begin removeLRU...
evicting key=k4
map={k2=v2, k5=v5, k6=v6}
```

The MapDBEntry Class

The MapDBEntry class in Example 30-3 defines a single entry of a MapDB object.

Example 30-3. MapDBEntry class

```
1 import java.io.File;
2 import java.util.Map;
3 import org.mapdb.DB;
4 import org.mapdb.DBMaker;
5
6 public class MapDBEntry {
7     private DB db = null;
8     private Map<String, String> map = null;
9
10    public MapDBEntry(DB db, Map<String, String> map) {
11        this.db = db;
12        this.map = map;
13    }
14
15    public String getValue(String key) {
16        if (map == null) {
17            return null;
18        }
19        return map.get(key);
20    }
21
22    // eviction policy
23    public void close() {
24        closeDB();
25        closeMap();
26    }
```

```
27
28      private void closeDB() {
29          if (db != null) {
30              db.close();
31          }
32      }
33
34      private void closeMap() {
35          if (map != null) {
36              map = null;
37          }
38      }
39
40      public static MapDBEntry create(String dbName) {
41          DB db = DBMaker.newFileDB(new File(dbName))
42                      .closeOnJvmShutdown()
43                      .readOnly()
44                      .make();
45          Map<String, String> map = map = db.getTreeMap("collectionName");
46          MapDBEntry entry = new MapDBEntry(db, map);
47          return entry;
48      }
49  }
```

Using MapDB

How do we create a persistent Map<K,V> using MapDB? Example 30-4 shows how to create a MapDB for a sorted partition file using the GenerateMapDB class.

Example 30-4. GenerateMapDB class

```
1 import org.mapdb.DB;
2 import org.mapdb.DBMaker;
3 import java.io.BufferedReader;
4 import java.io.FileReader;
5 import java.io.File;
6 import java.util.concurrent.ConcurrentNavigableMap;
7
8 public class GenerateMapDB {
9
10     public static void main(String[] args) throws Exception {
11         String inputFileName = args[0];
12         String mapdbName = args[1];
13         create(inputFileName, mapdbName);
14     }
15
16     public static void create(String inputFileName, String mapdbName)
17         throws Exception {
18         // Configure and open database using builder pattern.
19         // All options are available with code autocompletion.
20         DB db = DBMaker.newFileDB(new File(mapdbName))
```

```
21                    .closeOnJvmShutdown()
22                    .make();
23
24          // Open a collection. TreeMap has better performance than HashMap.
25          ConcurrentNavigableMap<String,String> map =
26              db.getTreeMap("collectionName");
27
28          //
29          // line = <position><;><v><:><v>:...:<v>
30          // where <v> has the following format:
31          // <feature_id><,><mrna_feature_id><,><sequence_data_type_id><,><mapping>
32          //
32          String line = null;
33          BufferedReader reader = null;
34          try {
35              reader = new BufferedReader(new FileReader(inputFileName));
36              while ((line = reader.readLine()) != null) {
37                  line = line.trim();
38                  String[] tokens = line.split(";");
39                  if (tokens.length == 2) {
40                      map.put(tokens[0], tokens[1]);
41                  }
42                  else {
43                      System.out.println("error line="+line);
44                  }
45              }
46          }
47          finally {
48              reader.close(); // close input file
49              db.commit(); // persist changes to disk
50              db.close(); // close database resources
51          }
52      }
53 }
```

To query the MapDB database, we can write a very simple class, QueryMapDB, as shown in Example 30-5.

Example 30-5. QueryMapDB class

```
1 import java.io.File;
2 import java.util.Map;
3 import org.mapdb.DB;
4 import org.mapdb.DBMaker;
5 import org.apache.log4j.Logger;
6 /**
7  * This class defines a basic query on MapDB.
8  *
9  * @author Mahmoud Parsian
10  *
11  */
```

```
12  public class QueryMapDB {
13
14      public static void main(String[] args) throws Exception {
15          long beginTime = System.currentTimeMillis();
16          String mapdbName = args[0];
17          String position = args[1];
18          THE_LOGGER.info("mapdbName="+mapdbName);
19          THE_LOGGER.info("position="+position);
20          String value = query(mapdbName, position);
21          THE_LOGGER.info("value="+value);
22          long elapsedTime = System.currentTimeMillis() -beginTime;
23          THE_LOGGER.info("elapsedTime (in millis) ="+elapsedTime);
24          System.exit(0);
25      }
26
27      public static String query(String mapdbName, String key) throws Exception {
28          String value = null;
29          DB db = null;
30          try {
31              db = DBMaker.newFileDB(new File(mapdbName))
32                  .closeOnJvmShutdown()
33                  .readOnly()
34                  .make();
35              Map<String, String> map = map = db.getTreeMap("collectionName");
36              value = map.get(key);
37          }
38          finally {
39              if (db != null) {
40                  db.close();
41              }
42          }
43          return value;
44      }
45  }
```

Testing MapDB: put()

The following code segments show how to create MapDB entries:

```
# javac GenerateMapDB.java
# javac QueryMapDB.java

# cat test.txt
19105201;35302633,35292056,2,1:20773813,35399339,2,1
19105202;35302633,35292056,2,1:20773813,35399339,2,1
19105203;35302633,35284930,2,1:35302633,35292056,2,1:20773813,35399339,2,1
19105204;35302633,35284930,2,1:35302633,35292056,2,1:20773813,35399339,2,1

# java GenerateMapDB test.txt mapdbtest
# ls -l mapdbtest*
-rw-r--r--  1 mahmoud  staff  32984 Feb 11 16:40 mapdbtest
-rw-r--r--  1 mahmoud  staff  13776 Feb 11 16:40 mapdbtest.p
```

As you can see from the generated output, MapDB generates two files (*mapdbtest* and *mapdbtest.p*) for each persistent hash table.

Testing MapDB: get()

The following code segments show how to query MapDB entries:

```
# java QueryMapDB mapdbtest 19105201
16:41:16 [QueryMapDB] - mapdbName=mapdbtest
16:41:16 [QueryMapDB] - position=19105201
16:41:16 [QueryMapDB] - value=35302633,35292056,2,1:20773813,35399339,2,1
16:41:16 [QueryMapDB] - elapsedTime (in millis) = 2

# java QueryMapDB mapdbtest 19105202
16:41:21 [QueryMapDB] - mapdbName=mapdbtest
16:41:21 [QueryMapDB] - position=19105202
16:41:21 [QueryMapDB] - value=35302633,35292056,2,1:20773813,35399339,2,1
16:41:21 [QueryMapDB] - elapsedTime (in millis) = 2

# java QueryMapDB mapdbtest 191052023333
16:41:55 [QueryMapDB] - mapdbName=mapdbtest
16:41:55 [QueryMapDB] - position=191052023333
16:41:55 [QueryMapDB] - value=null
16:41:55 [QueryMapDB] - elapsedTime (in millis) = 1
```

MapReduce Using the LRUMap Cache

Now that we have an efficient LRU map cache, we may use it in either the `map()` or `reduce()` function. To use the LRUMap cache in `map()` or the `reduce()`, you need to do the following (this can be applied in the mapper or reducer class):

1. Initialize and set up the LRUMap cache. This step can be accomplished in the `setup()` method. This will be done once.

2. Use the LRUMap cache in `map()` or `reduce()`. This will be done many times.

3. Close the LRUMap cache objects (to release all unnecessary resources). This step can be accomplished in the `cleanup()` method. This will be done once.

To make these steps easier, we define a service class called `CacheManager`, which can be used as shown in Example 30-6.

Example 30-6. CacheManager usage

```
 1 try {
 2    //
 3    // initialize cache
 4    //
 5    CacheManager.init();
 6
 7    //
 8    // use cache
 9    //
10    String chrID = ...;
11    String position = ...;
12    List<String> valueAsList = CacheManager.get(chrID, position);
13 }
14 finally {
15    //
16    // close cache
17    //
18    CacheManager.close();
19 }
```

CacheManager Definition

CacheManager, defined in Example 30-7, is a service class that provides three basic
functionalities: opening the cache, the service (retrieving the desired values), and
closing the cache. Since it is a service class, all methods are defined as static. The
BeginEndPosition object implements the partition data structures such that you can
get the database name (a 64 MB hash table) for a given key of (chrID, position).

Example 30-7. CacheManager definition

```
 1 public class CacheManager {
 2
 3    private static final int DEFAULT_LRU_MAP_SIZE = 128;
 4    private static int theLRUMapSize = DEFAULT_LRU_MAP_SIZE;
 5
 6    private static CustomLRUMap<String, MapDBEntry<String, String>>
 7       theCustomLRUMap = null;
 8    private static BeginEndPosition beginend = null;
 9    private static String mapdbRootDirName =
10       "/cache/mapdb/pf";
11    private static String mapdbBeginEndDirName =
12       "/cache/mapdb/pf/begin_end_position";
13    private static boolean initialized = false;
14
15    public static void setLRUMapSize(int size) {
16       theLRUMapSize = size;
17    }
```

```
18
19    public static int getLRUMapSize() {
20        return theLRUMapSize;
21    }
22
23    // initialize the LRUMap
24    public static void init() throws Exception {...}
25
26    // initialize the LRUMap
27    public static void init(int size) throws Exception {...}
28
29    // close the cache database in the LRUMap
30    public static void close() throws Exception {...}
31
32    // get value from the cache database for a given (chrID, position).
33    public static String get(int chrID, int position) throws Exception {...}
34
35    // get value from the cache database for a given (chrID, position).
36    public static String get(String chrID, String position) throws Exception {...}
37
38    // close the cache database in the LRUMap cache
39    public static void close() throws Exception {...}
40 }
```

Initializing the Cache

Example 30-8 shows how the CacheManager initializes the LRUMap cache.

Example 30-8. CacheManager: initializing the cache

```
1 public static void setLRUMapSize(int size) {
2     theLRUMapSize = size;
3 }
4
5 public static int getLRUMapSize() {
6     return theLRUMapSize;
7 }
8
9 // initialize the LRUMap
10 public static void init() throws Exception {
11    if (initialized) {
12        return;
13    }
14    theCustomLRUMap =
15        new CustomLRUMap<String, MapDBEntry<String, String>>(theLRUMapSize);
16    beginend = new BeginEndPosition(mapdbBeginEndDirName);
17    beginend.build(mapdbRootDirName);
18    initialized = true;
19 }
20
21 // initialize the LRUMap
```

```
22 public static void init(int size) throws Exception {
23     if (initialized) {
24         return;
25     }
26     setLRUMapSize(size);
27     init();
28 }
```

Using the Cache

Example 30-9 shows how the `CacheManager` accesses the `LRUMap` cache to get a desired value.

Example 30-9. CacheManager usage

```
 1 /**
 2 * Get value from the LRUMap cache for a given (chrID, position).
 3 * @param chrID=chrID
 4 * @param position=position
 5 */
 6 public static String get(int chrID, int position) throws Exception {
 7     return get(String.valueOf(chrID), String.valueOf(position));
 8 }
 9
10 /**
11 * Get value from the cache database (value is the snpID)
12 * for a given (chrID, position).
13 * @param chrID=chrID
14 * @param position=position
15 */
16 public static String get(String chrID, String position) throws Exception {
17     String dbName = getDBName(chrID, position);
18     if (dbName == null) {
19         return null;
20     }
21     // now return the cache value
22     MapDBEntry<String, String< entry = theCustomLRUMap.get(dbName);
23     if (entry == null) {
24         entry = MapDBEntryFactory.create(dbName);
25         theCustomLRUMap.put(dbName, entry);
26     }
27     return entry.getValue(position);
28 }
29
30 private static String getDBName(String chrID, String position) {
31     // query parameters are: chrID and position
32     List<Interval> results = beginend.query(chrID, position);
33     if ((results == null) || (results.isEmpty()) || (results.size() == 0)) {
34         return null;
35     }
36     else {
```

```
37          return results.get(0).db();
38      }
39 }
```

Closing the Cache

Example 30-10 shows how the CacheManager closes the LRUMap cache.

Example 30-10. CacheManager: closing the cache

```
1 public static void close() throws Exception {
2      if (theCustomLRUMap != null) {
3          for (Map.Entry<String, MapDBEntry<String, String>>
4              entry : theCustomLRUMap.entrySet()) {
5              entry.getValue().close();
6          }
7      }
8 }
```

This chapter presented a scalable huge cache solution that can be used by the map()
and reduce() functions. Our solution is very simple and can be implemented by just
using commodity servers. Chapter 31 provides a simple introduction to Bloom filters
and shows how they can be utilized in the MapReduce paradigm.

The Bloom Filter

This chapter introduces the concept of a Bloom filter and uses it in a reduce-side join, which engages the Bloom filter in the map phase of a MapReduce job. So what is a Bloom filter? How it can be used in a MapReduce environment? How can it speed up a join operation between two big relations/tables? According to Wikipedia (*http://en.wikipedia.org/wiki/Bloom_filter*):

> A Bloom filter is a space-efficient probabilistic data structure, conceived by Burton Howard Bloom in 1970, that is used to test whether an element is a member of a set. False positive matches are possible, but false negatives are not....In other words, a query returns either "possibly in set" or "definitely not in set." Elements can be added to the set, but not removed (though this can be addressed with a "counting" filter). The more elements that are added to the set, the larger the probability of false positives.

The Bloom filter data structure may return true for elements that are not actually members of the set (this is called a *false-positive error*), but it will never return false for elements that are in the set; for each element in the set, the Bloom filter must return true. There is a very nice tutorial on the Bloom filter (*http://billmill.org/bloomfilter-tutorial/*) by Bill Mill. If you'd like to explore this data structure in more depth, Jacob Honoroff has written a good introduction to the Bloom filter data structure (*http://bit.ly/bloom_filter_intro*).

Bloom Filter Properties

We can summarize Bloom filter properties as follows:

- Given a big set $S = \{x_1, x_2, ..., x_n\}$, the Bloom filter is a probabilistic, fast, and space-efficient cache builder; it basically approximates the set membership operation:

Is $x \in S$?

- The Bloom filter tries to answer the lookup question, does item x exist in a set S?
- The Bloom filter allows *false positive errors*, as they cost us only an extra data set access rather than resulting in a wrong answer. This means that for some x that is not in the set, the Bloom filter might indicate that x is in the set.
- The Bloom filter does not allow *false negative errors*, because they result in wrong answers. This means that if x is in the set, the Bloom filter definitely will indicate that x is in the set.

Two possible errors are:

- False positives: $x \notin S$, but the answer is $x \in S$
- False negatives: $x \in S$, but the answer is $x \notin S$

Let's focus on a simple join example between two relations/tables. Suppose that we want to join $R(a, b)$ and $S(a, c)$ on a common field a. Further assume that:

$size(R) = 1,000,000,000$ (larger data set)

$size(S) = 10,000,000$ (smaller data set)

To do a basic join, we would need to check 10,000,000,000,000,000 records, which would be a huge and time-consuming task. One idea to reduce the time and complexity of the join operation between R and S is to use a Bloom filter on relation S (the smaller data set) and then use the built Bloom filter data structure on relation R. This would eliminate the unneeded records from R (it might reduce the set to 20,000,000) and hence make the join fast and efficient.

Next, we semiformalize the Bloom filter data structure to answer these questions: What is involved in Bloom filter probabilistic data structures? How do we construct one? What is the probability of false positive errors, and how we can decrease their probability? This is how it works, given a big set $S = \{x_1, x_2, ..., x_n\}$:

- Let B be a bit array of size m ($m > 1$), initialized with 0s. B's elements are $B[0]$, $B[1]$, $B[2]$, ..., $B[m-1]$. The memory required for storing array B is only a fraction of that needed for storing the whole set S. By selecting the bigger bit vector (array B), we decrease the probability rate of false positives.

- Let $\{H_1, H_2, ..., H_k\}$ be a set of k hash functions. If $H_i(x_j) = a$, then set $B[a] = 1$. You may use SHA1, MD5, and `Murmur` as hash functions. For example, you may use the following:
    - $H_i(x) = MD5(x + i)$
    - $H_i(x) = MD5(x||i)$
- To check if $x \in S$, check B at $H_i(x)$. All k values must be 1.
- It is possible to have a false positive; all k values are 1, but x is not in S.
- The probability of false positives is:

$$\left(1 - \left[1 - \frac{1}{m}\right]^{kn}\right)^k \approx \left(1 - e^{-kn/m}\right)^k$$

- What are the optimal hash functions? What is the optimal number of hash functions? For a given m (number of bits selected for Bloom filter) and n (size of big data set), the value of k (number of hash functions) that minimizes the probability of false positives is (ln stands for "natural logarithm"[3]):

$$k = \frac{m}{n}ln(2)$$

where:

$$m = -\frac{nln(p)}{(ln(2))^2}$$

Therefore, the probability that a specific bit has been flipped to 1 is:

$$1 - \left(1 - \frac{1}{m}\right)^{kn} \approx 1 - e^{-\frac{kn}{m}}$$

Following Wikipedia (*http://bit.ly/bloom_filter_article*):

Unlike a standard hash table, a Bloom filter of a fixed size can represent a set with an arbitrary large number of elements; adding an element never fails due to the data structure "filling up." However, the false positive rate increases steadily as elements are

---

3 The natural logarithm is the logarithm to the base e of a number, where e is Euler's number: 2.71828183. Let $x = e^y$; then $ln(x) = log_e(x) = y$.

added until all bits in the filter are set to 1, at which point *all* queries yield a positive result.

A Simple Bloom Filter Example

In this example, you'll learn how to insert and query a Bloom filter of size 10 ($m = 10$) with three hash functions, $H = \{H_1, H_2, H_3\}$. Let $H(x)$ denote the result of the three hash functions ($H(x) = \{H_1(x),H_2(x),H_3(x)\}$). We start with a 10-bit-long array B initialized to 0:

```
Array B:
  initialized:
        index  0  1  2  3  4  5  6  7  8  9
        value  0  0  0  0  0  0  0  0  0  0

  insert element a, H(a) = (2, 5, 6)
        index  0  1  2  3  4  5  6  7  8  9
        value  0  0  1  0  0  1  1  0  0  0

  insert element b, H(b) = (1, 5, 8)
        index  0  1  2  3  4  5  6  7  8  9
        value  0  1  1  0  0  1  1  0  1  0

  query element c
  H(c) = (5, 8, 9) => c is not a member (since B[9]=0)

  query element d
  H(d) = (2, 5, 8) => d is a member (False positive)

  query element e
  H(e) = (1, 2, 6) => e is a member (False positive)

  query element f
  H(f) = (2, 5, 6) => f is a member (Positive)
```

Bloom Filters in Guava Library

The Guava (*http://bit.ly/guava-libraries*) library provides an implementation of a Bloom filter. Here's how it works. First, you define your basic type (`Person`, in this case) that will be used in the Bloom filter (this example is from *http://bit.ly/hashingexplained*):

```
class Person {
    final int id;
    final String firstName;
    final String lastName;
    final int birthYear;
    Person(int id, String firstName, String lastName, int birthYear) {
        this.id = id;
        this.firstName = firstName;
```

```
            this.lastName = lastName;
            this.birthYear = birthYear;
        }
    }
```

Then you define a Funnel of the basic type on which you want to use the Bloom filter. A Funnel describes how to decompose a particular object type into primitive field values. Our Funnel might look like:

```
Funnel<Person> personFunnel = new Funnel<Person>() {
    @Override
    public void funnel(Person person, PrimitiveSink into) {
        into
            .putInt(person.id)
            .putString(person.firstName, Charsets.UTF_8)
            .putString(person.lastName, Charsets.UTF_8)
            .putInt(birthYear);
    }
};
```

Once Funnel<T> is defined, then we can define and use a Bloom filter:

```
List<Person> friendsList = {Person1, Person2, ...};
BloomFilter<Person> friends = BloomFilter.create(personFunnel, 500, 0.01);
for(Person friend : friendsList) {
    friends.put(friend);
}

// much later, use the Bloom filter
Person dude = new Person(100, "Alex", "Smith", 1967);
if (friends.mightContain(dude)) {
    // the probability that dude reached this place
    // if he isn't a friend is 1% (0.01); we might,
    // for example, start asynchronously loading things
    // for dude while we do a more expensive exact check
}
```

The Guava library provides the following hash functions for building a Bloom filter data structure:

- md5()

- murmur3_128()

- murmur3_32()

- sha1()

- sha256()

- sha512()

- goodFastHash(int bits)

Using Bloom Filters in MapReduce

The Bloom filter is a small, compact, and fast data structure for determining set membership. As you've learned, it can be used in the join of two relations/tables such as *R(a, b)* and *S(a, c)* where one of the relations has a huge number of records (for example, *R* might have 1,000,000,000 records) and the other relation has a small number of records (for example, *S* might have 10,000,000 records). Doing a join on field *a* between *R* and *S* will take a long time and is inefficient. We can use the Bloom filter data structure as follows: build a Bloom filter out of relation *S(a, c)*, and then test values *R(a, b)* for membership using the built Bloom filter. Note that, for reduce-side join optimization, we use a Bloom filter on the map tasks, which will force an I/O cost reduction for the MapReduce job. Example 31-1 shows one way to implement an optimized reduce-side join with the use of a Bloom filter. This approach comprises two steps:

1. Construction of the Bloom filter. This is a MapReduce job that uses the smaller of the two relations/tables to construct the Bloom filter data structure. For this step, only mappers are needed (more than one Bloom filter will be built—one for each mapper).

2. Use the Bloom filter data structure built in step 1 in the reduce-side join.

Example 31-1. Join R and S

```
1 joinResult = {};
2 for all tuples r in R {
3    for all tuples s in S {
4      if (joinConditionSatisfied(r, s)) {
5        // join condition can be like r.a == s.b
6        add (r;s) to the joinResult;
7      }
8    }
9 }
```

This chapter presented the fundamental concepts of Bloom filter data structures and showed how to use them in a MapReduce environment for optimization purposes. Careful testing is required in deploying Bloom filters to production clusters. This is the last of the optimization techniques we'll be exploring. Appendixes A and B provide supporting material on the concepts of biosets and Spark RDDs.

Bioset

Biosets (also called *gene signatures*[3] or *assays*[4]) encompass data in the form of experimental sample comparisons (for transcriptomic, epigenetic, and copy-number variation data), as well as genotype signatures (for genome-wide association study [GWAS] and mutational data).

A bioset has an associated data type, which can be gene expression, protein expression, methylation, copy-number variation, miRNA, or somatic mutation. Also, each bioset entry/record has an associated reference type, which can be r1=normal, r2=disease, r3=paired, or r4=unknown. Note that a reference type does not apply to the somatic mutation data type.

The number of entries/records per bioset depends on its data type (see Table A-1).

---

3 A gene signature is a group of genes in a cell whose combined expression pattern is uniquely characteristic of a biological phenotype or medical condition. The phenotypes that may theoretically be defined by a gene expression signature range from those that are used to differentiate between different subtypes of a disease, those that predict the survival or prognosis of an individual with a disease, to those that predict activation of a particular pathway. Ideally, gene signatures can be used to select a group of patients for whom a particular treatment will be effective. (Source: *http://en.wikipedia.org/wiki/Gene_signature.*)

4 An assay is an investigative (analytic) procedure in laboratory medicine, pharmacology, environmental biology, continuous delivery, and molecular biology for qualitatively assessing or quantitatively measuring the presence or amount or the functional activity of a target entity (the analyte). The analyte can be a drug or biochemical substance or a cell in an organism or organic sample. (Source: *http://en.wikipedia.org/wiki/Assay.*)

Table A-1. Number of records per bioset data type

Bioset data type	Number of entries/records
Somatic mutation	3,000–20,000
Methylation	30,000
Gene expression	50,000
Copy-number variation	40,000
Germline	4,300,000
Protein expression	30,000
miRNA	30,000

Spark RDDs

Apache Spark (*http://spark.apache.org/*) is a "fast and general-purpose cluster computing system." Its main abstraction is a distributed collection of items (such as log records, FASTQ sequences, or employee records) called a resilient distributed data set (RDD). We can create RDDs from Hadoop InputFormats (such as HDFS files), by transforming other RDDs, or by transforming "collection" data structures (such as Lists and Maps). RDDs can also be created from Java/Scala collection objects as well as other persistent data stores. The main purpose of an RDD is to support higher-level, parallel operations on data through a simple API (such as JavaRDD and Java PairRDD).

This appendix will introduce Spark RDDs through simple Java examples. Its purpose is not to dive into the architectural[35] details of RDDs, but merely to show you how to utilize RDDs in MapReduce or general-purpose programs (as directed acyclic graphs, or DAGs). You can consider an RDD a handle for a collection of items of type T, which are the result of some computation. Type T can be any standard Java data type (such as String, Integer, Map, or List) or any custom objects (such as Employee or Mutation). A Spark RDD performs actions (such as reduce(), collect(), count(), and saveAsTextFile()) and transformations (such as map(), filter(), union(), groupByKey(), and reduceByKey()), which can be used for more complex computations. All the examples provided here are based on Spark-1.1.0.

Typically, Spark programs can run faster than equivalent MapReduce/Hadoop ones if you provide more RAM to the cluster nodes. Spark provides the StorageLevel class, which has flags for controlling the storage of an RDD. Some of these flags are:

- `MEMORY_ONLY` (use only memory for RDDs)
- `DISK_ONLY` (use only hard disk for RDDs)
- `MEMORY_AND_DISK` (use a combination of memory and disk for RDDs)

To learn about Spark and RDDs in detail, refer to the book *Learning Spark*[12].

Spark Operations

Spark jobs perform work (actions and transformations) on RDDs. Note that Spark's main program is executed on the Spark driver, while transformations are executed on the Spark workers. After we create an RDD object in Spark, we can perform a set of operations by calling the Spark API. The two major types of operations in Spark can be thought of as follows:

Transformations
> This type of operation returns a new RDD based on the original. Transformations available through the Spark API include `map()`, `filter()`, `sample()`, and `union()`.

Actions
> This type of operation returns a value based on some computation being performed on an RDD. Actions available through the Spark API include `reduce()`, `count()`, `first()`, and `foreach()`.

Transformations and actions are illustrated in Figure B-1.

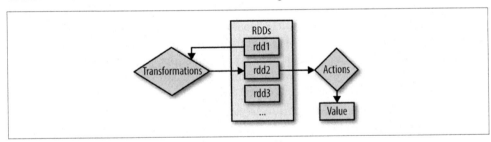

Figure B-1. Spark operations: transformations and actions

Tuple<N>

Spark includes heavy use of tuples, such as `scala.Tuple2` (a tuple of two elements) and `scala.Tuple3` (a tuple of three elements). `scala.Tuple<N>` represents a composite data type of N elements. The Spark API uses the composite data types `scala.Tuple2` (which represents a tuple of two elements; see Example B-1)and `scala.Tuple3` (which represents a tuple of three elements; see Example B-2).

Example B-1. Tuple2

```
 1 import scala.Tuple2;
 2 import java.util.List;
 3 import java.util.Arrays;
 4 ...
 5 Tuple2<String,Integer> t21 = new Tuple2<String,Integer>("abc", 234);
 6 String str21 = t21._1; // str21 holds "abc"
 7 Integer int21 = t21._2; // int21 holds 234
 8
 9 List<Integer> listofint = Arrays.asList(1, 2, 3);
10 Tuple2<String,List<Integer>> t22 =
11    new Tuple2<String,List<Integer>>("z1z2", listofint);
12 String str22 = t22._1;         // str22 holds "z1z2"
13 List<Integer> list22 = t22._2; // int21 points to List(1, 2, 3)
```

Example B-2. Tuple3

```
 1 import scala.Tuple3;
 2 import java.util.List;
 3 import java.util.Arrays;
 4 ...
 5 List<String> listofstrings = Arrays.asList("a1", "a2", "a3");
 6 Tuple3<String,Integer, List<String>> t3 =
 7    new Tuple3<String,Integer, List<String>>("a1a2", 567, listofstrings);
 8 String str3 = t3._1;      // str3 holds "a1a2"
 9 Integer int3 = t3._2;     // int3 holds 567
10 List<String> list3 = t3._3; // list3 points to List("a1", "a2", "a3")
```

Note that scala.Tuple4 through scala.Tuple22 are defined as part of the Java Spark API.

RDDs

As you know, RDD stands for resilient distributed data set, which is the basic data abstraction in Spark. Spark provides many subclasses and wrappers (such as JavaRDD, JavaPairRDD, and JavaHadoopRDD). To perform the mapToPair(), reduceByKey(), or groupByKey() operations (called *transformations*), you use an RDD as input and output. By definition, an RDD represents an immutable,[3] partitioned collection of elements that can be operated on in parallel. This means that if we have a JavaRDD<String> that has 100 million elements, we can partition it into 10, 100, or 1,000 segments, and each segment can be operated on independently. Choosing an appropriate number of partitions is important, and it depends on your cluster size,

---

3 RDDs are read-only and cannot be modified or updated.

the number of cores available per server, and the total amount of RAM available in your cluster. There is no silver bullet for finding the proper number of partitions, but you will be able to properly set it through some trial and error.

JavaRDD and JavaPairRDD are members of the org.apache.spark.api.java package and are defined in Example B-3.

Example B-3. JavaRDD and JavaPairRDD

```
1   public class JavaRDD<T> ...
2   // represents elements of type T
3   // Examples of JavaRDD<T> are:
4   //     JavaRDD<String>
5   //     JavaRDD<Integer>
6   //     JavaRDD<Map<String, Long>>
7   //     JavaRDD<Employee>
8   //     JavaRDD<Tuple2<String, Integer>>
9   //     ...
10
11  public class JavaPairRDD<K,V> ...
12  // represents pairs of (key,value) of type K and V
13  // Examples of JavaPairRDD<K,V> are:
14  //     JavaPairRDD<String,Integer>
15  //     JavaPairRDD<String, Tuple2<Integer,Integer>>
16  //     JavaPairRDD<Integer, Map<String, Long>>
17  //     JavaPairRDD<Tuple2<Integer,Integer>, Tuple2<String,Double>>
18  //     ...
```

How to Create RDDs

For most MapReduce applications, RDDs are created by a JavaSparkContext object or from JavaRDDs, and JavaPairRDDs. The initial RDDs are created by JavaContextOb ject, and subsequent RDDs are created by many other classes (including JavaRDD and JavaPairRDD). For most applications, this is the order to create and manipulate RDDs:

1. Create a JavaSparkContext. You can accomplish this step in many ways: for example, you could create it using the Spark master URL or by using YARN's resource manager hostname. You could also use the SparkUtil (*http://bit.ly/spar kutil*) class. Or you can use the following code:

   ```
   1 import org.apache.spark.SparkConf;
   2 import org.apache.spark.api.java.JavaSparkContext;
   3 ...
   4 // create JavaSparkContext
   5 SparkConf sparkConf = new SparkConf().setAppName("my-app-name");
   6 JavaSparkContext ctx = new JavaSparkContext(sparkConf);
   ```

2. Once you have an instance of `JavaSparkContext`, you can create RDDs. RDDs can be created from many different sources: from Java collection objects, from text files, and from HDFS files (text or binary).

3. Once you have an instance of `JavaRDD` or `JavaPairRDD`, you can create new RDDs easily by using the `map()`, `reduceByKey()`, `filter()`, or `groupByKey()` methods. You may also create RDDs by using Java collection objects or by reading files (text files or text/binary HDFS files).

Creating RDDs Using Collection Objects

As noted in the previous section, you can create RDDs using Java collection objects. Example B-4 creates an RDD (called `rdd1`) from a `java.utl.List` object.

Example B-4. JavaRDD creation

```
 1 import java.util.List;
 2 import com.google.common.collect.Lists;
 3 import org.apache.spark.SparkConf;
 4 import org.apache.spark.api.java.JavaSparkContext;
 5 ...
 6 // create JavaSparkContext
 7 SparkConf sparkConf = new SparkConf().setAppName("myapp");
 8 JavaSparkContext ctx = new JavaSparkContext(sparkConf);
 9
10 // create your desired collection object
11 final List<String> list1 = Lists.newArrayList(
12      "url1,2",
13      "url1,3",
14      "url2,7",
15      "url2,6",
16      "url3,4",
17      "url3,5",
18      "url3,6"
19 );
20
21 // create an RDD from Java collection object
22 JavaRDD<String> rdd1 = ctx.parallelize(list1);
```

Now `rdd1` is a `JavaRDD<String>` containing seven elements (each in the format `<url><,><count>`). Once the RDD is created, you can start applying functions and transformations (such as `map()`, `collect()`, `reduceByKey()`, and many others).

Collecting Elements of an RDD

The generated `rdd1` can be collected as a `List<String>`, as illustrated in Example B-5.

Example B-5. Collecting elements of an RDD

```
1 // create an RDD from Java collection object
2 JavaRDD<String> rdd1 = ctx.parallelize(list1);
3
4 // collect RDD's elements:
5 // java.util.List<T> collect()
6 // Return an array that contains all of the elements in this RDD.
7 java.util.List<String> collected = rdd1.collect();
```

In general, collect() may be used for debugging (to see the content of an RDD) or
saving as a final result. When deploying your Spark programs to the production cluster, make sure that you have removed all instances of collect() that are used for
debugging purposes (the collect() operation takes a considerable amount of time
for collecting RDD elements, which can be a performance hit in production). Note
that calling collect() results in the DAG (directed acyclic graph) up to that point
being scheduled to run, which has performance implications. Calling collect() on a
large RDD can even trigger an OutOfMemoryError. Also note that collect() sends all
the partitions to the single driver (this might be the main reason for an OOM error).
The recommendation is that you should not call collect() on a large RDD.

Transforming an Existing RDD into a New RDD

Let's take rdd1 and transform it into key-value pairs (as a JavaPairRDD object). For
this transformation, we use the JavaRDD.mapToPair() method, as shown in
Example B-6.

Example B-6. JavaPairRDD transformation

```
1 // create an RDD from Java collection object
2 JavaRDD<String> rdd1 = ctx.parallelize(list1);
3
4 // create (K,V) pairs where K is a URL and V is a count
5 JavaPairRDD<String, Integer> kv1 = rdd1.mapToPair(
6      new PairFunction<
7                    String, // T as input
8                    String, // K as output
9                    Integer // V as output
10                   >() {
11    @Override
12    public Tuple2<String, Integer> call(String element) {
13       String[] tokens = element.split(",");
14       // tokens[0] = URL
15       // tokens[1] = count
16       return new Tuple2<String, Integer>(tokens[0], new Integer(tokens[1]));
17    }
18 });
```

Creating RDDs by Reading Files

For most MapReduce applications, you will read data from HDFS and then create RDDs, and possibly save the results in HDFS. Let's assume that we have two HDFS files, as shown here:

```
$ hadoop fs -ls /myinput/logs/
... /myinput/logs/file1.txt
... /myinput/logs/file2.txt

$ hadoop fs -cat /myinput/logs/file1.txt
url5,2
url5,3
url6,7
url6,8
$ hadoop fs -cat /myinput/logs/file2.txt
url7,1
url7,2
url8,5
url8,6
url9,7
url9,8
url5,9
$
```

Next, we create an RDD from these two files as seen in Example B-7.

Example B-7. Creating an RDD from HDFS files

```
 1 // create JavaSparkContext
 2 SparkConf sparkConf = new SparkConf().setAppName("myapp");
 3 JavaSparkContext ctx = new JavaSparkContext(sparkConf);
 4
 5 // read input file from HDFS
 6 // input record format: <string-key><,><integer-value>
 7 String hdfsPath = "/myinput/logs";
 8 // public JavaRDD<String> textFile(String path)
 9 // Read a text file from HDFS, a local filesystem
10 // (available on all nodes), or any Hadoop-supported
11 // filesystem URI, and return it as an RDD of Strings.
12 JavaRDD<String> rdd2 = ctx.textFile(hdfsPath);
```

At this point, rdd2 has 11 String elements (4 from *file1.txt* and 7 from *file2.txt*). Now you can use the techniques from the preceding section to create a Java PairRDD<String,Integer>, where the key is a URL and the value is the URL's associated count.

Grouping by Key

In Example B-8 we will group elements by key for rdd2.

Example B-8. Grouping elements by key for rdd2

```
1 // rdd2 is already created (see previous section)
2 // create (K,V) pairs where K is a URL and V is a count
3 JavaPairRDD<String, Integer> kv2 = rdd2.mapToPair(
4     new PairFunction<
5                     String, // T as input
6                     String, // K as output
7                     Integer // V as output
8                     >() {
9     @Override
10    public Tuple2<String, Integer> call(String element) {
11        String[] tokens = element.split(",");
12        // tokens[0] = URL
13        // tokens[1] = count
14        return new Tuple2<String, Integer>(tokens[0], new Integer(tokens[1]));
15    }
16 });
17
18 // next group RDD's elements by key
19 JavaPairRDD<String, Iterable<Integer>> grouped2 = kv2.groupByKey();
```

The resulting RDD (group2) will have the content shown in Table B-1.

Table B-1. Key-value pairs generated by the groupByKey() method

Key	Value
url5	[2, 3, 9]
url6	[7, 8]
url7	[1, 2]
url8	[5, 6]
url9	[7, 8]

Mapping Values

If you have a JavaPairRDD for which you want to alter values and create a new set of values (without changing the keys), you can use the JavaPairRDD.mapValues() method. In Example B-9, we will take the grouped2 RDD created in the preceding section and return the maximum URL counts.

Example B-9. JavaPairRDD.mapValues()

```
1 // public <U> JavaPairRDD<K,U> mapValues(Function<V,U> f)
2 // Pass each value in the key-value pair RDD through a map
3 // function without changing the keys; this also retains
4 // the original RDD's partitioning.
5 JavaPairRDD<String,Integer> mapped2 = grouped2.mapValues(
6     new Function<
```

```
 7                       Iterable<Integer>, // input
 8                       Integer             // output
 9                       >() {
10       public Integer call(Iterable<Integer> list) {
11           Integer max = null;
12           for (Integer element : list) {
13               if (max == null) {
14                   max = element;
15               }
16               else {
17                   if (element > max) {
18                       max = element;
19                   }
20               }
21           }
22         return max;
23       }
24 });
```

The resulting RDD (mapped2) will have the content shown in Table B-2.

Table B-2. Key-value pairs generated by the mapValues() method

Key	Value
url5	9
url6	8
url7	2
url8	6
url9	8

Reducing by Key

In Example B-10 we will reduce elements by key for rdd2: our goal is to add the counts for the same URL (i.e., create a final count for each URL). We use the Java PairRDD.reduceByKey() method.

Example B-10. JavaPairRDD.mapToPair() and reduceByKey()

```
 1 // rdd2 is already created (see previous section)
 2 // create (K,V) pairs where K is a URL and V is a count
 3 JavaPairRDD<String, Integer> kv2 = rdd2.mapToPair(
 4       new PairFunction<
 5                       String, // T as input
 6                       String, // K as output
 7                       Integer // V as output
 8                       >() {
 9     @Override
10     public Tuple2<String, Integer> call(String element) {
```

```
11        String[] tokens = element.split(",");
12        // tokens[0] = URL
13        // tokens[1] = count
14        return new Tuple2<String, Integer>(tokens[0], new Integer(tokens[1]));
15    }
16 });
17
18 // next reduce JavaPairRDD's elements by key
19 // public JavaPairRDD<K,V> reduceByKey(Function2<V,V,V> func)
20 // Merge the values for each key using an associative reduce
21 // function. This will also perform the merging locally on each
22 // mapper before sending results to a reducer, similarly to a
23 // combiner in MapReduce. Output will be hash-partitioned with
24 // the existing partitioner/parallelism level.
25 JavaPairRDD<String, Integer> counts = kv2.reduceByKey(
26     new Function2<
27                     Integer, // input T1
28                     Integer, // input T2
29                     Integer // output T
30                   >() {
31     @Override
32     public Integer call(Integer count1, Integer count2) {
33       return count1 + count2;
34     }
35 });
```

Note that reduceByKey() operates on two input values of type V and produces output of the same type (i.e., V). If you want to create output of a type other than V, use the combineByKey() transformation. The resulting RDD (counts) will have the content shown in Table B-3.

Table B-3. Key-value pairs generated by the reduceByKey() method

Key	Value
url5	14
url6	15
url7	3
url8	11
url9	15

Combining by Key

Spark provides a generic powerful function to combine the elements for each key using a custom set of aggregation functions. Here we will combine elements by key for a JavaPairRDD (kv2): our goal is to create a unique list of all counts (removing the duplicate counts) for the same URL. To accomplish this, we will use the Java PairRDD.combineByKey() method. The reduceByKey() method cannot be used to solve this problem, because the output type is different from the input type. For this example, we illustrate the following input and output:

> Input: (K: String, V: Integer)
> Output: (K: String, V: Set<Integer>)

The simplest signature of combineByKey() is:

```
public <C> JavaPairRDD<K,C> combineByKey(
                                Function<V,C> createCombiner,
                                Function2<C,V,C> mergeValue,
                                Function2<C,C,C> mergeCombiners
                                )
    // Generic function to combine the elements for each key using a custom
    // set of aggregation functions. Turns a JavaPairRDD[(K, V)] into a result
    // of type JavaPairRDD[(K, C)], for a "combined type" C. Note that V and C
    // can be different -- for example, one might group an RDD of type (Int, Int)
    // into an RDD of type (Int, List[Int]). Users provide three functions:
    // - createCombiner, which turns a V into a C (e.g., creates a one-element list)
    // - mergeValue, to merge a V into a C (e.g., adds it to the end of a list)
    // - mergeCombiners, to combine two Cs into a single one.
```

Therefore, to use combineByKey(), we have to provide/implement three basic functions, as shown in Example B-11.

Example B-11. Aggregate functions for combineByKey()

```
 1 Function<Integer, Set<Integer>> createCombiner =
 2   new Function<Integer, Set<Integer>>() {
 3   @Override
 4   public Set<Integer> call(Integer x) {
 5     Set<Integer> set = new HashSet<Integer>();
 6     set.add(x);
 7     return set;
 8   }
 9 };
10 Function2<Set<Integer>, Integer, Set<Integer>> mergeValue =
11   new Function2<Set<Integer>, Integer, Set<Integer>>() {
12   @Override
13   public Set<Integer> call(Set<Integer> set, Integer x) {
```

```
14      set.add(x);
15      return set;
16    }
17 };
18 Function2<Set<Integer>, Set<Integer>, Set<Integer>> combine =
19    new Function2<Set<Integer>, Set<Integer>, Set<Integer>>() {
20    @Override
21    public Set<Integer> call(Set<Integer> a, Set<Integer> b) {
22       a.addAll(b);
23       return a;
24    }
25 };
```

After implementing these three basic functions, we are ready to use `combineByKey()`:

```
JavaPairRDD<String, Integer> kv2 = ...;
JavaPairRDD<String, Set<Integer>> combined =
    kv2.combineByKey(
                createCombiner,
                mergeValue,
                combine
    );
```

In general it is possible to combine `groupByKey()` and `mapValues()` into a `reduceBy Key()` or `combineByKey()` operation (examples are given in Chapters 4 and 8).

reduceByKey() versus groupByKey()

Which one should you use, `reduceByKey()` or `groupByKey()`? According to their semantics, both will give you the same answer. But `reduceByKey()` is more efficient. In some situations, `groupByKey()` can even cause out-of-disk problems. In general, `aggregateByKey()`, `reduceByKey()`, `foldByKey()`, and `combineByKey()` are preferred over `groupByKey()`. Spark shuffling is more efficient for `reduceByKey()` than `group ByKey()` for this reason: in the shuffle step for `reduceByKey()`, data is combined so each partition outputs at most one value for each key to send over the network, while in the shuffle step for `groupByKey()`, all the data is wastefully sent over the network and collected by the reducers. To help you understand the difference, Figures B-2 and B-3 show how the shuffle is done for `reduceByKey()` and `groupByKey()`

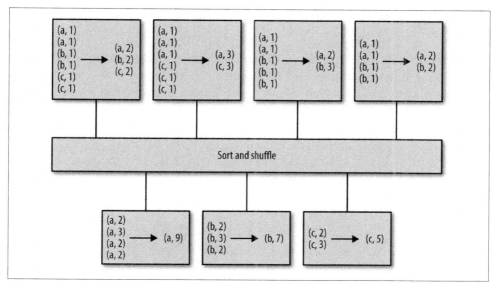

Figure B-2. Sort and shuffle step for reduceByKey()

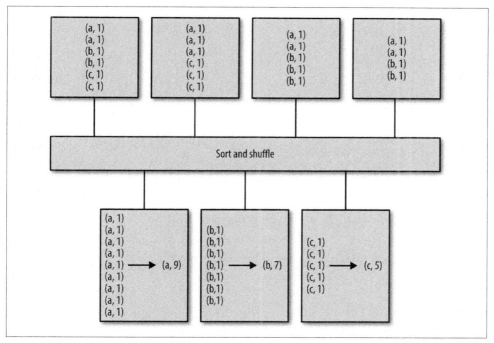

Figure B-3. Sort and shuffle step for groupByKey()

Filtering an RDD

Spark provides a very simple and powerful API for filtering RDDs. To filter RDD elements, you just need to implement a filter() function that returns true for the elements you want to keep, and false for the elements you want to toss out. Consider the RDD labeled logRDD in Example B-12. We write a filter() function that keeps the elements containing the normal keyword and tosses out the rest.

Example B-12. Filtering a JavaRDD

```
1 import java.util.List;
2 import com.google.common.collect.Lists;
3 import org.apache.spark.SparkConf;
4 import org.apache.spark.api.java.JavaSparkContext;
5 ...
6 // create JavaSparkContext
7 SparkConf sparkConf = new SparkConf().setAppName("logs");
8 JavaSparkContext ctx = new JavaSparkContext(sparkConf);
9
10 // create your desired collection object
11 final List<String> logRecords = Lists.newArrayList(
12     "record 1: normal",
13     "record 2: error",
14     "record 3: normal",
15     "record 4: error",
16     "record 5: normal"
17 );
18
19 // create an RDD from Java collection object
20 JavaRDD<String> logRDD = ctx.parallelize(logRecords);
21
22 // To filter elements, we need to implement a filter function:
23 // JavaRDD<T> filter(Function<T,Boolean> f)
24 // Return a new RDD containing only the elements that satisfy a predicate.
25 JavaRDD<String> filteredRDD = logRDD.filter(new Function<String,Boolean>() {
26     public Boolean call(String record) {
27         if (record.contains("normal")) {
28             return true; // do return these records
29         }
30         else {
31             return false; // do not return these records
32         }
33     }
34 });
35
36 // At this point, filteredRDD will have the following 3 elements:
37 //     "record 1: normal"
38 //     "record 3: normal"
39 //     "record 5: normal"
```

Saving an RDD as an HDFS Text File

You may save your RDDs as Hadoop files (text or sequence files). For example, we can save the counts RDD we created in the preceding section in HDFS as a text files:

```
// save RDD as an HDFS text file
// void saveAsTextFile(String path)
// Save this RDD as a text file, using string representations of elements.
// Make sure that your output path -- "/my/output" -- does not exist
counts.saveAsTextFile("/my/output");
```

After it is saved, you may view the saved data as follows:

```
$ hadoop fs -cat /my/output/part*
```

Saving an RDD as an HDFS Sequence File

We can also save the counts RDD we created in the previous section in HDFS as a sequence file (sequence files are binary files in the form of key-value pairs). To save an RDD as a sequence file, you have to convert its elements into Hadoop Writable objects. Since counts is an RDD of type JavaPairRDD<String, Integer>, we cannot directly write it to HDFS as a sequence file; first, we need create a new RDD that has a type of JavaPairRDD<Text, IntWritable>, where we convert String into Text and Integer into IntWritable. Example B-13 shows how we write counts into HDFS as a sequence file.

Example B-13. Creating a sequence file

```
 1 import scala.Tuple2;
 2 import org.apache.hadoop.io.Text;
 3 import org.apache.hadoop.io.IntWritable;
 4 import org.apache.hadoop.mapred.SequenceFileOutputFormat;
 5 ...
 6
 7 // First create a Writable RDD:
 8 JavaPairRDD<Text, IntWritable> countsWritable =
 9     counts.mapToPair(new PairFunction<
10                                 Tuple2<String,Integer>, // T
11                                 Text,                   // K
12                                 IntWritable             // V
13                                 >() {
14     @Override
15     public Tuple2<Text, IntWritable> call(Tuple2<String,Integer> t) {
16         return new Tuple2<Text, IntWritable>(
17                                 new Text(t._1),
18                                 new IntWritable(t._2)
19                                 );
20     }
21 });
22
```

```
23 // Next, write it as a sequence file.
24 // Make sure that your output path -- "/my/output2" -- does not exist.
25 countsWritable.saveAsHadoopFile(
26         "/my/output2",                    // name of path
27         Text.class,                        // key class
28         IntWritable.class,                 // value class
29         SequenceFileOutputFormat.class // output format class
30 );
```

After it is saved, you may view the saved data as follows:

```
$ hadoop fs -text /my/output2/part*
```

Reading an RDD from an HDFS Sequence File

You can create a new RDD by reading a Hadoop sequence file. In Example B-14 the sequence file we created in the preceding section will be read and a new RDD will be created.

Example B-14. Reading a sequence file

```
1 import scala.Tuple2;
2 import org.apache.hadoop.io.Text;
3 import org.apache.hadoop.io.IntWritable;
4 import org.apache.hadoop.mapred.SequenceFileInputFormat;
5 ...
6
7 // JavaPairRDD<K,V> hadoopFile(String path,
8 //                              Class<F> inputFormatClass,
9 //                              Class<K> keyClass,
10 //                              Class<V> valueClass)
11 // Get an RDD for a Hadoop file with an arbitrary InputFormat
12 // '''Note:''' Because Hadoop's RecordReader class reuses the
13 // same Writable object for each record, directly caching the
14 // returned RDD will create many references to the same object.
15 // If you plan to directly cache Hadoop Writable objects, you
16 // should first copy them using a map function.
17 JavaPairRDD<Text, IntWritable> seqRDD = ctx.hadoopFile(
18         "/my/output2",                      // HDFS path
19         SequenceFileInputFormat.class,      // input format class
20         Text.class,                         // key class
21         IntWritable.class                   // value class
22 );
```

Counting RDD Items

The count() method, shown in Example B-15, returns the number of items stored in an RDD.

Example B-15. Counting RDD items

```
1 // count JavaPairRDD
2 JavaPairRDD<Text, IntWritable> pairRDD = ...;
3 int count1 = pairRDD.count();
4
5 // count JavaRDD
6 JavaRDD<String> strRDD = ...;
7 int count2 = strRDD.count();
```

Spark RDD Examples in Scala

If you are interested in the usage of RDDs in Scala, refer to Zhen He's "The RDD API By Example" (*http://bit.ly/rdd_api_examples*).

PySpark Examples

If you are interested in the usage of RDDs in Python, refer to *https://github.com/ mahmoudparsian/pyspark-tutorial*.

How to Package and Run Spark Jobs

This section provides a brief description of how to package and run Spark jobs in a Spark cluster or Hadoop's YARN environment. The details of submitting Spark applications are given in the Spark documentation (*http://bit.ly/submitting_apps*).

The first step is to bundle your application classes in a JAR file (let's call this an *application JAR*). You can generate your application JAR using a build tool (such as Ant or Maven) or manually from a command line by using the *jar* script (*http://bit.ly/ jar_files*):

```
$ export JAVA_HOME=/usr/java/jdk7
$ JAVA_HOME/bin/jar cvf my_app.jar *.class
```

For example, the JAR required to run the examples in this book (called *data_algorithms_book.jar*) can be generated with an Ant build script (described in *http://bit.ly/ da_book*). Once you have your application JAR, you can run your program.

Creating the JAR for Data Algorithms

Here, I show you a sample of how to create the required JAR for running the examples in this book. I assume that you have already cloned the source code for this book from GitHub (*http://bit.ly/da_book*):

```
$ pwd
/home/mp/data-algorithms-book
$ ant clean
Buildfile: build.xml
clean:
```

```
BUILD SUCCESSFUL
Total time: 0 seconds

$ ant
Buildfile: build.xml
init:
    ...
copy_jar:
  [echo] copying spark-assembly-1.1.0-hadoop2.5.0.jar...
build_jar:
[echo] javac
[echo] compiling src...
[javac] Compiling 151 source files to /home/mp/data-algorithms-book/build
...
[jar] Building jar: /home/mp/data-algorithms-book/dist/data_algorithms_book.jar
BUILD SUCCESSFUL
Total time: 3 seconds
```

Running a Job in a Spark Cluster

Example B-16 how to run a Spark program (the Top10 program) in a Spark cluster environment.

Example B-16. Running a job in a Spark cluster

```
 1 $ cat run_top10_spark_cluster.sh
 2 #!/bin/bash
 3 export JAVA_HOME=/usr/java/jdk7
 4 export SPARK_HOME=/usr/local/spark-1.1.0
 5 export SPARK_MASTER=spark://myserver100:7077
 6 export BOOK_HOME=/home/mp/data-algorithms-book
 7 export APP_JAR=$BOOK_HOME/dist/data_algorithms_book.jar
 8 INPUT=$BOOK_HOME/data/top10data.txt
 9 # Run on a Spark standalone cluster
10 $SPARK_HOME/bin/spark-submit \
11    --class org.dataalgorithms.chap03.spark.Top10 \
12    --master $SPARK_MASTER \
13    --executor-memory 2G \
14    --total-executor-cores 20 \
15    $APP_JAR \
16    $INPUT
```

A description of this script is provided in Table B-4.

Table B-4. Description of script to run a job in a Spark cluster

Line number(s)	Description
3	JAVA_HOME is the home directory for JDK7.
4	SPARK_HOME is the home directory for the Spark installation.
5	BOOK_HOME is the installation directory for this book from GitHub.
6	SPARK_MASTER defines the Spark master URL.
7	APP_JAR defines your custom application JAR.
8	INPUT defines the input path for the Spark job.
10	Submits your Spark job to the Spark cluster.

Running a Job in Hadoop's YARN Environment

Example B-17 shows how to run a Spark program (the Top10 program) in a YARN environment.

Example B-17. Running a job in Hadoop's YARN environment

```
 1 $ cat run_top10_yarn.sh
 2 #!/bin/bash
 3 export JAVA_HOME=/usr/java/jdk7
 4 export SPARK_HOME=/usr/local/spark-1.1.0
 5 export BOOK_HOME=/home/mp/data-algorithms-book
 6 export SPARK_JAR=spark-assembly-1.1.0-hadoop2.5.0.jar
 7 export THE_SPARK_JAR=$SPARK_HOME/assembly/target/scala-2.10/$SPARK_JAR
 8 export APP_JAR=$BOOK_HOME/dist/data_algorithms_book.jar
 9 #
10 export HADOOP_HOME=/usr/local/hadoop-2.5.0
11 export HADOOP_CONF_DIR=$HADOOP_HOME/etc/hadoop
12 INPUT=$BOOK_HOME/data/top10data.txt
13 $SPARK_HOME/bin/spark-submit \
14     --class org.dataalgorithms.chap03.spark.Top10 \
15     --master yarn-cluster \
16     --num-executors 12 \
17     --driver-memory 3g \
18     --executor-memory 7g \
19     --executor-cores 12 \
20     --conf "spark.yarn.jar=$THE_SPARK_JAR" \
21     $APP_JAR \
22     $INPUT
```

A description of this script is provided in Table B-5.

Table B-5. Description of script to run a job in YARN

Line number(s)	Description
3	JAVA_HOME is the home directory for JDK7.
4	SPARK_HOME is the home directory for the Spark installation.
5	BOOK_HOME is the installation directory for this book from GitHub.
6	`spark-assembly-1.1.0-hadoop2.5.0.jar` is required for running on YARN.
7	APP_JAR defines your custom application JAR.
9-10	HADOOP_HOME and HADOOP_CONF_DIR are required for running on YARN.
12	Submits your Spark job to the YARN environment.

If you plan to read from and write to HDFS using Spark, there are two Hadoop configuration files you must include on Spark's CLASSPATH:

- *hdfs-site.xml*, which provides default behaviors for the HDFS client
- *core-site.xml*, which sets the default filesystem name

To make these files visible to Spark, set HADOOP_CONF_DIR in *$SPARK_HOME/spark-env.sh* to the location containing the Hadoop configuration files.

Bibliography

[1] Alag, Satnam. *Collective Intelligence in Action*. Greenwich, CT: Manning Publications Co., 2009.

[2] Anderson, Carolyn J. "Exact Tests for 2-Way Tables." Urbana-Champaign: University of Illinois Department of Education Psychology, Spring 2014. *http://bit.ly/2-way_table_exact*.

[3] Batra, Siddharth, and Deepak Rao. "Entity Based Sentiment Analysis on Twitter." Stanford, CA: Stanford University Department of Computer Science, 2010. *http://bit.ly/batra_rao*.

[4] Boslaugh, Sarah. *Statistics in a Nutshell, Second Edition*. Sebastopol, CA: O'Reilly Media, Inc., 2013.

[5] Brandt, Andreas. "Algebraic Analysis of MapReduce Samples." Bachelor's thesis, Institute for Computer Science, 2010.

[6] Chen, Edwin. "Movie Recommendations and More via MapReduce and Scalding." Blog post. February 9, 2012. *http://bit.ly/movie_recs_mapreduce*.

[7] Conway, Drew, and John Myles White. *Machine Learning for Hackers*. Sebastopol, CA: O'Reilly Media, Inc., 2012.

[8] Dean, Jeffrey, and Sanjay Ghemawat. "MapReduce: Simplified Data Processing on Large Clusters." Paper presented at the Sixth Symposium on Operating System Design and Implementation, San Francisco, CA, December 2004.

[9] Garson, G. David. *Cox Regression*. Asheboro, NC: Statistical Associates Publishers, 2012.

[10] Harrington, Peter. *Machine Learning in Action*. Greenwich, CT: Manning Publications Co., 2012.

[11] Jannach, Dietmar, Markus Zanker, Alexander Felfernig, and Gerhard Friedrich. *Recommender Systems: An Introduction*. Cambridge, UK: Cambridge University Press, 2011.

[12] Karau, Holden, Andy Konwinski, Patrick Wendell, and Matei Zaharia. *Learning Spark*. Sebastopol, CA: O'Reilly Media, 2015.

[13] Lämmel, Ralf, and David Saile. "MapReduce with Deltas." Landau in der Pfalz, Germany: University of Koblenz-Landau, Software Languages Team, 2011. *http://bit.ly/lammel_saile*.

[14] Lin, Jimmy. "MapReduce Algorithm Design." Slideshow presented at WWW2013, Rio de Janeiro, Brazil, May 13, 2013. *http://bit.ly/mapreduce_tutorial*.

[15] Lin, Jimmy. "Monoidify! Monoids as a Design Principle for Efficient MapReduce Algorithms." College Park: University of Maryland, 2013. *http://bit.ly/monoidify*.

[16] Lin, Jimmy, and Chris Dyer. *Data-Intensive Text Processing with MapReduce*. College Park: University of Maryland, 2010.

[17] Lin, Jimmy, and Chris Dyer. *Data-Intensive Text Processing with MapReduce*. San Rafael, CA: Morgan & Claypool Publishers, 2013.

[18] Miner, Donald, and Adam Shook. *MapReduce Design Patterns*. Sebastopol, CA: O'Reilly Media, Inc., 2013.

[19] Mitchell, Tom M. *Machine Learning*. New York: McGraw-Hill, 1997.

[20] Netflix. "Netflix Prize." 2009. *http://www.netflixprize.com/*.

[21] Pang, Bo, and Lillian Lee. "A Sentimental Education: Sentiment Analysis Using Subjectivity Summarization Based on Minimum Cuts." Ithaca, NY: Cornell University, 2004. *http://bit.ly/pang_and_lee*.

[22] Perry, John. *Foundations of Nonlinear Algebra*. Hattiesburg: University of Southern Mississippi, 2012. *http://bit.ly/nonlinear_algebra*.

[23] Sarkar, Manish, and Tze-Yun Leong. "Application of K-Nearest Neighbors Algorithm on Breast Cancer Diagnosis Problem." Medical Computing Laboratory, Department of Computer Science, School of Computing, The National University of Singapore, 2000.

[24] Schank, Thomas, and Dorothea Wagner. "Finding, Counting and Listing All Triangles in Large Graphs: An Experimental Study." Karlsruhe, Germany: University of Karlsruhe, 2005. *http://bit.ly/schank_and_wagner*.

[25] Schank, Thomas, and Dorothea Wagner. "Approximating Clustering Coefficient and Transitivity." *Journal of Graph Algorithms and Applications* 9, no. 2 (2005): 265–275.

[26] Segaran, Toby. *Programming Collective Intelligence: Building Smart Web 2.0 Applications*. Sebastopol, CA: O'Reilly Media, Inc., 2007.

[27] Sembiring, Sajadin, M. Zarlis, Dedy Hartama, S. Ramliana, and Elvi Wani. "Prediction of Student Academic Performance by an Application of Data Mining Techniques." Paper presented at the 2011 International Conference on Management and Artificial Intelligence, Bali, Indonesia, April 2011.

[28] Tsourakakis, Charalampos E., Petros Drineas, Eirinaios Michelakis, Ioannis Koutis, and Christos Faloutsos. "Spectral Counting of Triangles in Power-Law Networks via Element-Wise Sparsification." Pittsburgh, PA: Carnegie Mellon School of Computer Science, 2009. *http://bit.ly/tsourakakis_et_al.*

[29] Walker, Michael G. "Survival Analysis." *http://bit.ly/surv_analysis.*

[30] Wellek, Stefan, and Andreas Ziegler. "Cochran-Armitage Test Versus Logistic Regression in the Analysis of Genetic Association Studies." *Human Heredity* 73, no. 1 (2012): 14–17.

[31] White, Tom. *Hadoop: The Definitive Guide, Fourth Edition*. Sebastopol, CA: O'Reilly Media, Inc., 2015.

[32] Wikipedia. "Correlation and Dependence." *http://bit.ly/correlation_article.*

[33] Woo, Jongwook, and Yuhang Xu. "Market Basket Analysis Algorithm with Map/Reduce of Cloud Computing." Los Angeles: Computer Information Systems Department, California State University, 2013. *http://bit.ly/mba_w_mapreduce.*

[34] Yang, Changyu. "Triangle Counting in Large Networks." Master's thesis, University of Minnesota, Duluth, 2012.

[35] Zaharia, Matei. "An Architecture for Fast and General Data Processing on Large Clusters." Berkeley: University of California, 2014. *http://bit.ly/zaharia.*

[36] Zhao, Xi, Einar Andreas Rødland, Therese Sørlie, Bjørn Naume, Anita Langerød, Arnoldo Frigessi, Vessela N Kristensen, Anne-Lise Børresen-Dale, and Ole Christian Lingjærde. "Combining Gene Signatures Improves Prediction of Breast Cancer Survival." Oslo, Norway: Department of Genetics, Institute for Cancer Research, Oslo University Hospital, 2011. *http://bit.ly/zhao_et_al.*

Index

Symbols

+ (addition operator), 641
+ (concatenation operator), 642
- (subtraction operator), 641
[] (square brackets), 642

A

absolute risk, 433
addition operator (+), 641
adenine, 547
adjacency lists, 213
alignByBWA() function, 418
alleles, definition of term, 467
allelic frequency
    basic terminology, 465-471
    chromosomes X and Y, 490
    data sources, 467
    definition of term, 465, 467
    determining monoids, 485
    formal problem statement, 471
    MapReduce solution
        p-values sample plot, 481
        phase 1, 472-479
        phase 2, 482
        phase 3, 486-490
        sample run, 479
Amazon, 227
    (see also content-based recommendations)
Apache
    Common Math, 507
    Commons Math3 , 542
    Mahout, 362
array data structure, 135
ArrayListOfLongsWritable class, 189

B

BAM format, 579
BaseComparator class, 553
Bayes's theorem, 331
BCF (binary call format), 428
binary classification, 300
bioinformatics, 391, 407, 433
    (see also genome analysis)
biosets
    basics of, 467, 699
    data types, 699
    in Cox regression, 437
    in gene aggregation, 585
    number of records in, 699
Bloom filters
    definition of term, 693
    example of, 696
    in Guava library, 696
    in MapReduce, 698
    properties of, 693
    semiformalization, 694
bottom 10 lists, 49
bottom N lists, 61, 79
Broadcast class, 359, 504, 534
buckets, 662
BucketThread class, 663
buildClassificationCount() method, 316
buildOutputValue() method, 462

assays (see biosets)
association rules, 152, 163
associative arrays, 203
associative operations, 637
avg() method, 529

buildPatientsMap() method, 592, 618
buildSortedKey() function, 184
Burrows-Wheeler Aligner (BWA), 411
buy_xaction.rb script, 263

C

cache problem (see huge cache problem)
CacheManager definition, 688-691
calculateCorrelations() helper method, 248
calculateCosineCorrelation() helper method,
    250
calculateDistance() method, 316
calculateJaccardCorrelation() helper method,
    250
calculatePearsonCorrelations() helper method,
    249
calculateTtest() method, 495
callCochranArmitageTest() method, 451
Cartesian product, calculating, 311, 538
cartesian() function, 524
categorical data analysis, 447
censoring, 435
centroids, 289, 291
chaining, xxxii
change() method, 296
checkFilter() method, 596, 607
Chen, Edwin, 227
chromosomes
    definition of term, 466
    special handling for X and Y, 490
        (see also genome analysis)
classifyByMajority() method, 317
cleanup() method, 558
closeAndIgnoreException() method, 598
clustering
    distance-based, 289, 307
    global clustering coefficient, 369
    K-Means clustering algorithm, 289
    k-Nearest Neighbors, 305
    local clustering coefficient, 369
Cochran-Armitage test for trend (CATT)
    algorithm for, 448
    application of, 454
    basics of, 447
    goals of, 449
    MapReduce solution, 456-462
    MapReduce/Hadoop implementation, 463
collaborative filtering, 300
Combination.findSortedCombinations(), 158

combineByKey() function, 196, 222
combineKey() function, 114
combiners, characteristics of, 638
common friends identification
    Hadoop solution
        using ArrayListOfLongsWritable, 189
        using text, 187
    input records, 182
    MapReduce algorithm, 183-187
    overview of, 181
    POJO algorithm, 182
    Spark solution
        sample run, 197-200
        steps for, 190-197
Common Math, 507
Commons Math3, 542
commutative monoids, 485, 641
Comparator class, 286
composite keys, 33-35
compression options, 674
concatenation operator (+), 642
conditional probability, 331
Configuration object, 496
containment tables, 493
content-based recommendations
    accuracy of, 227
    examples of, 227
    input, 228
    MapReduce phases, 229-236
    overview of, 227
    similarity measures, 236, 246
    Spark solution
        helper methods, 248
        high-level solution, 237
        overview of, 236
        sample run, 250
        sample run log, 251
        steps for, 238-248
contingency tables, 447
continuous data, 343
convenient methods, 217
copy-number variation, 699
copyMerge() method, 663
corpus, definition of term, 121
correlation, calculating, 236, 513, 544
Cosine Similarity, 236, 246
counting triangles, importance of, 372
    (see also graph analysis)
covariates, 423, 433

Cox regression
  basic terminology, 435
  basics of, 434
  benefits of, 433
  example of, 433
  MapReduce solution
      input, 439
      phases for, 440-446
  POJO solution, 437
  proportional hazard model, 434
  relative vs. absolute risk, 433
  sample application, 437
  using R, 436
coxph() function, 434
CoxRegressionUsingR class, 445
createDynamicContentAsFile() method, 422
createFrequencyItem() method, 598
Cufflinks, 573, 582
custom comparators, 553
custom partitioners, 5
  based on left key hash, 120
  in DNA base count, 554, 554
  in t-tests, 502
  plug-ins for, 123
custom plug-in classes, 6
custom sorting, 553
CustomCFIF class, 672
customer transactions, generating artificial, 263
Customers Who Bought This Item Also Bought
      (CWBTIAB), 202-206
cytosine, 547

D

d-dimensional space, 294
data mining techniques
  general goal of, 151
  K-Means clustering, 289-304
  k-Nearest Neighbor (kNN), 305-325
  Market Basket Analysis (MBA), 151-180
  Naive Bayes classifier (NBC), 327-362
data structure servers, 677
design patterns, definition of term, 1
dfs.block.size parameter, 661
distance-based clustering, 289, 307
DNA base counting
  applications for, 547
  example, 548
  formats for, 548
  Hadoop solution

FASTA format, 552-556
      FASTQ format, 560
  MapReduce solution
      FASTA format, 550
      FASTQ format, 556
  solutions presented, 547
  Spark solution
      FASTA format, 561-565
      FASTQ format, 566-571
DNA sequencing
  challenges of, 407
  definition of, 407
  goals of, 408
  input, 409
  input data validation, 410
  MapReduce solution
      overview of, 412
      sequencing alignment, 415
      sequencing recalibration, 423
  overview of pipeline, 409
  recent advances in, 407
  sequence alignment, 411
DNASeq.mergeAllChromosomesAndParti-
      tion() method, 420
document classification
  K-Means clustering algorithm, 292
  Naive Bayes classifier (NBC), 327
duplicates, removing, 244

E

edges, 369
email marketing, 257
  (see also Markov model)
email spam filtering, 327
empty lists, 642
Euclidean Distance, 236, 294

F

false-positve errors, 693
FASTA file format
  benefits of, 548
  description of, 548
  DNA base counting
      Hadoop solution, 552-556
      MapReduce solution, 550
      Spark solution, 561-565
  example of, 549
  in RNA sequencing, 574
  reading, 550

FastaCountBaseMapper class, 550
FastaInputFormat class, 550
FASTQ file format
    description of, 549
    DNA base counting
        Hadoop implementation, 560
        MapReduce solution, 556
        Spark solution, 566-571
    drawbacks of, 548
    example of, 549
    in allelic frequency, 467
    in DNA sequencing, 410
    in K-mer counting, 392
    in RNA sequencing, 574
    reading, 557
FastqInputFormat class, 556, 566
FastqRecordReader, 557
file compression, 674
filecrush tool, 674
filter() function, 244, 524
filterType values, 596
findNearestK() method, 316
Fisher's Exact Test, 465, 469
flatMap() function, 95
flatMapToPair() function, 95
foldchange, 436, 467
FreeMarker templating language, 412
frequent patterns, 171
frequent sets, 151
Frequently Bought Together (FBT), 206-211
frequently purchased lists, 201, 206
    (see also recommendation engines)
function classes, in Spark, 51
Function function, 217
functors, 658
Funnels, 697

G

gene aggregation
    computing, 592
    Hadoop implementation, 594
    input, 586
    MapReduce solution, 587-592
    metrics for, 585
    output, 586
    output analysis, 597
    solution overview, 585
    Spark solution
        filter by average, 610-620

filter by individual, 601-609
    overview of, 600
gene expression, 467, 699
gene signatures, 437, 467, 699
GeneAggregationDriverByAverage class, 596
GeneAggregationDriverByIndividual class, 594
GeneAggregatorAnalyzerUsingFrequencyItem
    class, 598
GeneAggregatorUtil class, 592
genome analysis
    allelic frequency, 465-490
    DNA base counting, 547-571
    DNA sequencing, 407-432
    gene aggregation, 585-620
    huge cache problem, 675-691
    K-mer counting, 391-406
    RNA sequencing, 573-583
    t-tests, 491-511
genotype frequency, 454
germline data
    in allelic frequency, 465
    in Cochran-Armitage trend test, 447
    in huge cache problem, 675
    types of, 699
getNumberOfPatientsPassedTheTest() method,
    592, 618
Ghosh, Pranab, 257
global clustering coefficient, 369
Gradient descent optimization primitive, 300
graph analysis
    basic graph concepts, 370
    Hadoop implementation, 377
    importance of counting triangles, 372
    MapReduce solution
        overview of, 372
        steps for, 373-377
    metrics in, 369
    solution overview, 369
    Spark solution
        high-level steps, 380
        sample run, 387-390
        steps for, 381-387
    use in social network analysis, 369
graph theory, 212
GraphX, 211
groupByKey() function, 222, 275, 712
grouping comparators, 6
guanine, 547
Guava library, 696

GWAS (genome-wide association study), 437, 467

H

Hadoop
  benefits of, xxvii
  bottom 100 list solution, 486, 490
  common friends identification
    using ArrayListOfLongsWritable, 189
    using text, 187
  core components of, xxix
  custom comparators in, 553
  custom partitioner plug-in, 123
  default reader in, 557
  DNA base counting solution
    FASTA format, 552-556
    FASTQ format, 560
  gene aggregation implementation, 594
  graph analysis implementation, 377
  grouping control in, 266
  implementation classes
    Cochran-Armitage trend test, 463
    DNA base counting, 560
    left join solution, 93
    linear regression, 628, 635
    market basket solution, 158-160
    monoids, 647
    moving average solution, 140
    order inversion solution, 127
  major applications of, xxx
  Markov model
    state transition model, 272
    time-ordered transactions in, 263
  Pearson correlation solution, 521
  processing time required, xxx
  reducer values in, 119
  secondary sort solution
    implementation, 9-12
    using new API, 37
    using old API, 36-37
  sharing immutable data structures in, xxviii
  small files problem, 661-674
  t-test implementation, 499
  vs. Spark, xxviii
  Writable interface, 347
hash tables, 203
Haskell programming language, 639
helper methods
  calculateCorrelations(), 248

calculateCosinecorrelation(), 250
calculateJaccardCorrelation(), 250
calculatePearsonCorrelations(), 249
for Cochran-Armitage trend test, 461
hidden Markov model (HMM), 259
huge cache problem
  CacheManager definition, 688-691
  formalizing, 677
  local cache solution, 678-687
  MapReduce solution, 687
  overview of, 675
  solution options, 676

I

identity mapper, 92
inner product space, 294
input queries, 308
intensity (of words), 363
item sets, 163
iterative algorithms, 289, 295

J

Jaccard Similarity, 236, 246
Java's TreeMap data structure, 482
java.util.Queue, 134
JavaKMeans class, 300
JavaPairRDD, 217
JavaPairRDD.collect() function, 103, 104, 242
JavaPairRDD.filter() method, 244
JavaPairRDD.flatMapToPair() function, 102
JavaPairRDD.groupByKey() function, 103, 194
JavaPairRDD.leftOuterJoin() method, 107
JavaPairRDD.map() function, 176
JavaPairRDD.mapToPair() function, 246
JavaPairRDD.mapValues() function, 103, 195, 221
JavaRDD, 217
JavaRDD.collect() function, 194
JavaRDD.flatMapToPair() function, 193
JavaRDD.union() function, 95
JavaSpark-Context, 217
JavaSparkContext object, 169
Job.setCombinerClass(), 639
Job.setInputFormatClass() method, 550
join operation, 243, 677
joint events, 121

K

K-Means clustering algorithm
  applications for, 289, 292
  basics of, 290
  distance function, 294
  example of, 289
  formalized, 295
  MapReduce solution for, 295-299
  overview of, 289
  partitioning approach, 293
  Spark solution, 300-304
K-mer counting
  applications for, 391
  definition of K-mer, 391
  HDFS input, 405
  input, 392
  MapReduce/Hadoop solution, 393
  Spark solution
    high-level steps, 396
    overview of, 395
    steps for, 397-405
    YARN script for, 405
  top N final output, 406
k-Nearest Neighbors (kNN)
  applications for, 305
  basics of, 305
  classification method, 306
  distance functions, 307
  example of, 308
  formal algorithm, 309
  informal algorithm, 308
  overview of, 305
  Spark solution
    formalizing kNN, 312
    high-level steps, 313
    input, 313
    overview of, 311
    steps for, 314-324
    YARN shell script for, 325
kNN join (see k-Nearest Neighbors (kNN))

L

least recently used hash table, 677
left outer join
  concept of, 85
  example of, 86
  explanation of, 85
  Hadoop implementation classes, 93
  leftOuterJoin() solution, 107-117
  MapReduce implementation of, 88-92
  running Spark on YARN, 106
  sample run, 93
  solution overview, 85
  Spark implementation, 95-105
  SQL queries related to, 87
  visual expression of, 86
leftOuterJoin() method, 107-117
Lin, Jimmy, 637
linear classification, 327
linear regression
  applications for, 621
  basic facts about, 622
  Cochran-Armitage trend test, 447
  definition of term, 622
  example of, 622
  expected output, 625
  goal of, 622
  Hadoop implementation, 628
  input data, 625
  MapReduce solution
    using R's linear model, 629-635
    using SimpleRegression, 626
  problem statement, 624
  solution overview, 621
  vs. regression, 622
linear relationships, 513
LinkedIn, 211
lists, empty, 642
lm() function, 629
local aggregation, 638
local clustering coefficient, 369
LRU-Maps, 677

M

machine learning-based solutions, 257, 305
Mahout, 362
Manhattan Distance, 236, 294, 307
MapDB, 205, 680
MapReduce
  allelic frequency solution
    p-values sample plot, 481
    phase 1, 472-479
  associative operations in, 637
  benefits of, xxvi, xxx
  Bloom filters, 693-698
  chaining in, xxxii
  Cochran-Armitage test for trend, 456-462
  combiners in, 638, 657

common friends identification solution, 183-187

content-based recommendation phases, 229-236

core components of, xxix

Cox regression solution
  input, 439
  phases for, 440-446

CWBTIAB implementation, 203-206

DNA base counting
  FASTA format, 550
  FASTQ format, 556

DNA sequencing solution
  overview of, 412
  sequencing alignment, 415
  sequencing recalibration, 423

gene aggregation solution, 587-592

graph analysis solution
  overview of, 372
  steps for, 373-377

huge cache solution, 687

incorrect statements about, xxvi

join operation, 677

K-Means clustering algorithm, 295-299

key sorting in, 1, 27
  (see also secondary sort problems)

left outer join implementation, 88-92

major applications of, xxx

market basket analysis solution, 153-157

Markov model using, 261

monoidic vs. non-monoidic examples, 644

moving average problem
  input, 137
  output, 137
  overview of, 137
  sort by MapReduce, 143-149
  sort in memory, 138-142

Naive Bayes classifier (NBC)
  for numeric data, 343
  for symbolic data, 334

order inversion solution, 122-127

overview of process, xxi-xxiv

Pearson correlation solution, 519

pipelining in, xxxii

recommendation engines using, 201-226
  frequently bought together, 208
  recommend connection algorithm, 214

RNA sequencing
  algorithm for, 575

cuffdiff function, 582
  input data validation, 574
  solution overview, 574
  Tophat mapping, 579

sentiment analysis solution, 365

simple explanation of, xxv

t-tests
  problem statement, 495
  solution, 496

time-ordered transactions in, 262

top 10 list with unique keys, 43-46

when not to use, xxv

when to use, xxv

MapReduce/Hadoop
  allelic frequency solution, 479
  Cochran-Armitage trend test, 463
  K-mer counting solution, 393
  left join implementation classes, 93
  market basket analysis
    implementation classes, 158-160
    solution, 151
  monoidized sample run, 648-650
  secondary sort solution, 7-12, 24
  small files problem, 661-674
  top 10 list
    implementation classes, 47
    solution, 81-84

mapToPair() function, 275

mapValues() function, 275

marginal counts, 121

marker frequency (see gene aggregation)

Market Basket Analysis (MBA)
  applications for, 153
  goal of, 151
  MapReduce solution, 153-157
  MapReduce/Hadoop solution, 151
  Spark solution, 163-180

market prediction
  email marketing, 257
  recommendation engines, 201-226

Markov chain (see Markov model)

Markov model
  applications for, 257
  basics of, 258
  chain state names/definitions, 268
  components of, 259
  overview of, 257
  Spark solution
    Comparator class, 286

generate probability model, 284
high-level steps, 276
input, 275
overview of, 275
program structure, 277
sample run, 287
shell script for, 286
steps for, 278-284
toList() method, 284
toStateSequence() method, 285
using MapReduce, 261-275
Markov property, 258
Markov random process, 258
Markov state transition matrix, 271
MAX (maximum) operation, 641
maximum norm, 294
MAX_SPLIT_SIZE parameter, 670
mean (average) function, 642
median function, 642
memcached servers, 676
mergeAllChromosomesAndPartition()
    method, 420
mergeAllChromosomesBamFiles(), 420
metagenomic applications, 392
methylation, 699
migrations, 465
Minkowski Distance, 307
miRNA, 699
MLlib library, 300
monoids
    applications for, 657
    challenges of, 657
    commutative monoids, 485
    definition of term, 637, 639
    forming, 640
    functional example, 643
    functors and, 658
    Hadoop implementation, 647
    Hadoop/MapReduce sample run, 648-650
    in allelic frequency, 485
    MapReduce example
        monoid, 646
        not a monoid, 644
    matrix example, 644
    monoid homomorphism, 659
    monoidic vs. non-monoidic examples,
        640-644
    Spark example, 650-657

movie recommendations (see content-based
    recommendations)
moving average problem
    concept of, 131
    example, 131
    formal definition, 133
    Java object solution, 134
    MapReduce solution
        input, 137
        output, 137
        overview of, 137
        sort by MapReduce, 143-149
        sort in memory, 138-142
    testing, 136
MultipleInputs class, 95
multiplication, 641
multithreaded algorithms, 662
MutableDouble class, 529
mutations, 465
mutual friends, 214
    (see also recommend connection algorithm)

N
Naive Bayes classifier (NBC)
    Apache Mahout, 362
    applications for, 327
    conditional probability, 331
    example of, 327
    in depth exploration of, 331
    MapReduce solution
        for numeric data, 343
        for symbolic data, 334-342
    MLlib library, 361
    overview of, 327
    Spark implementation
        building classifier using training data,
            346-355
        classifying new data, 355-360
        stages of, 345
        training and learning examples, 328
Netflix, 227
    (see also content-based recommendations)
NGS (next-generation sequencing), 429
noncommutative monoids, 642
normalizeAndTokenize() method, 366
normalizing constants, 344
null hypothesis, 467
numeric training data, 328, 343

O

opinion mining (see sentiment analysis)
Oracle, 676
Order Inversion (OI)
    MapReduce solution, 122-127
    sample run, 127-129
    simple example of, 119
    typical application of, 119
org.apache.hadoop.io.Writable, 354
org.apache.spark.api.java, 217, 238, 314
org.apache.spark.api.java.function, 217, 238, 314
org.apache.spark.mllib, 361
org.apache.spark.mllib.classification.Naive-Bayes, 361
org.apache.spark.mllib.classification.Naive-BayesModel, 361

P

p-value (probability value), 467, 481
PairFlatMapFunction, 193, 217
PairFlatMapFunction.call() method, 102
PairOfDoubleInteger class, 592
PairOfLongInt class, 647
partition-SingleChromosomeBam(), 420
Pearson chi-squared test , 447
Pearson product-moment correlation coefficient
    basics of, 513
    data set for, 517
    example, 516
    formula, 514
    Hadoop implementation, 521
    MapReduce solution, 519
    POJO solution, 517
    similarity measures, 246
    Spark solution
        all genes vs. all gene solution, 524
        high-level steps, 525
        input, 523
        output, 523
        overview of, 522
        Pearson class, 542
        steps for, 527-541
        using R, 543
        YARN script for, 544
People You May Know feature, 211
pipelining, xxxii
plug-in classes, 6

POJO (plain old Java object)
    common friends algorithm, 182
    Cox regression solution, 437
    moving average solution, 134
    Pearson correlation solution, 517
position feature tables, 675
probabilistic methods, 327, 331, 693
protein-expression, 699

Q

queue data structure, 134

R

R programming language
    Cox regression, 434, 436
    linear regression with, 629-635
    Pearson correlation with, 543
random samples, 491
RDDs (resilient distributed data sets)
    basics of, 13, 50, 237
    combining by key, 711
    control flags for, 701
    counting items in, 716
    creating, 704
    creating by reading files, 707
    creating using collection objects, 705
    creating with JavaSparkContext class, 169
    examples in Scala, 717
    filtering, 714
    Java packages for manipulating, 98
    partitioning, 76, 502, 703
    purpose of, 701
    reading from HDFS sequence files, 716
    reduceByKey() vs. groupByKey(), 712
    reducing by key, 709
    saving as HDFS sequence files, 715
    saving as HDFS test files, 715
    Spark operations, 702
    tuple<N>, 702
    utilizing, 701
readBiosets() method, 531
readDirectoryIntoFrequencyItem() method, 598
readFileIntoFrequencyItem() method, 598
readInputFiles() method, 607, 617
recalibrationReducer() method, 425
recommend connection algorithm
    applications for, 211
    graphical expression of, 211

input, 213
output, 214
recommendation engines
    applications for, 201
    benefits of, 201
    content-based (see content-based recommendations)
    CWBTIAB, 202-206
    examples of, 201
    frequently bought together, 206-211
    recommend connection algorithm, 211
    Spark implementation
        combining steps, 222
        convenient methods, 217
        program run log, 223
        solution overview, 216
        solution steps, 217-222
RecordReader class, 557
Redis servers, 677
reduceByKey() function
    combining steps with, 114
    in common friend identifications, 196
    in Market Basket Analysis (MBA), 173
    in Markov chain, 275
    in recommendation engines, 222
    vs. groupByKey() function, 712
reference relational tables, 675
regression, 300, 622
Regularized Correlation, 236
relatedness, 392
relational databases, 482, 676
relative frequency
    mapper, 124
    reducer, 126
relative risk, 433
removeOneItem() function, 169
replicated relational databases, 676
RNA sequencing
    data size and format, 574
    MapReduce solution
        algorithm for, 575
        cuffdiff function, 582
        input data validation, 574
        overview of, 574
        Tophat mapping, 579
    overview of, 573
    solutions presented, 573
Rscript, 445

S

SAM format, 579
sampling error, 491
secondary sort problems
    data flow using plug-in classes, 6
    detailed example of, 32-37
    example of, 2
    explanation of, 1
    goal of Secondary Sort pattern, 2
    MapReduce/Hadoop solution, 7-12, 24
    using new Hadoop API, 37-39
    secondary sorting technique, 28-31
    solution implementation details, 3
    solution overview, 3
    sort order in ascending/descending orders, 12
    sort order of intermediate keys, 4
    sorting reducer values, 27
    Spark solution, 12-25
selections, 465
self-join operation, 243
sentiment analysis
    applications for, 364
    challenges of, 363, 367
    definition of sentiment, 363
    definition of term, 365
    MapReduce solution, 365
    scoring positive/negative, 364
    types of sentiment data, 363
sequence alignment, 411
Sequence Alignment/Map (SAM), 411
SequenceFileWriterDemo class, 648
ShellScriptUtil class, 421
shoppers' behavior
    K-Means clustering algorithm, 289
    Market Basket Analysis (MBA), 152-180
    recommendation engines, 201-226
shuffle() function, 645
similarity measures, 236, 246
SimpleRegression class, 621
small files problem
    custom CombineFileInputFormat, 672
    definition of small files, 661
    solution overview, 661
    solution with CombineFileInputFormat, 668
    solution with SmallFilesConsolidator, 665
    solution without SmallFilesConsolidator, 667

soultion with filecrush tool, 674
smaller() method, 528
SmallFilesConsolidator class, 663
smarter email marketing (see Markov model)
SNPs (single nucleotide polymorphisms), 428
social network analysis
    analyzing relationships via triangles,
        369-390
    common friends identification, 181
    recommend connection algorithm, 211
    sentiment analysis, 363-367
somatic mutations, 492, 699
sort order
    controlling ascending/descending, 12
    of intermediate keys, 4
    of reducer values, 27
sort() function, 645
spam filters, 327
Spark
    benefits of, xxvii
    combineByKey() function, 196
    combineKey() function, 114
    common friends identification
        sample run, 197-200
        solution steps, 190-197
    DNA base counting solution
        FASTA format, 561-565
        FASTQ format, 566-571
    function classes in, 51
    gene aggregation solution
        filter by average, 610-620
        filter by individual, 601-609
        overview of, 600
    graph analysis solution
        high-level steps, 380
        sample run, 387-390
        steps for, 381-387
    join operation in, 243
    K-Means implementation, 300-304
    K-mer counting solution
        high-level steps, 396
        overview of, 395
        steps for, 397-405
        YARN script for, 405
    k-Nearest Neighbors
        formalizing kNN, 312
        high-level steps, 313
        input, 313
        overview of, 311

        steps for, 314-324
        YARN shell script for, 325
    leftOuterJoin() method, 107-117
    major applications of, xxx
    market basket analysis solution, 163-180
    Markov model
        Comparator class, 286
        generate probability model, 284
        high-level steps, 276
        input, 275
        overview of, 275
        program structure, 277
        sample run, 287
        shell script for, 286
        steps for, 278-284
        toList() method, 284
        toStateSequence() method, 285
    MLlib library, 300, 361
    modes available, 20
    movie recommendations in
        helper methods, 248
        high-level solutions, 237
        overview of, 236
        sample run, 250
        sample run log, 251
        steps for, 238-248
    Naive Bayes classifier (NBC)
        building classifier using training data,
            346-355
        classifying new data, 355-360
        stages of, 345
    operation types, 702
    parameterizing Top N in, 59
    Pearson correlation solution
        all genes vs. all gene solution, 524
        high-level steps, 525
        input, 523
        output, 523
        overview of, 522
        Pearson class, 542
        steps for, 527-541
        using R, 543
        YARN script for, 544
    processing time required, xxx
    RDD (resilient distributed data sets) in, 13,
        50
    recommendation engine implementation,
        216-226

reduceByKey() function, 114, 173, 196, 222, 275
running in standalone mode, 21
running in YARN cluster mode, 23, 717-720
secondary sort solution, 12-25
sharing immutable data structures in, xxviii
t-test solution
    algorithm for, 507
    final output, 511
    high-level steps, 500
    input, 509
    overview of, 499
    steps for, 503-506
    YARN script for, 510
top 10 list
    with nonunique keys, 62-72
    with takeOrdered(), 73-80
    with unique keys, 50-59
Top N design pattern for, 52
top() function, 80
using monoids, 650-657
vs. Hadoop, xxviii
Spark Summit, 106
Spark/Hadoop
    installing, 50
    modes available, 20
SparkGeneAggregationByAverage class, 600
SparkGeneAggregationByIndividual class, 600
Spearman correlation, 544
speech analysis, 363
splitOnToListOfDouble() method, 315
SQL queries, 482, 676
square brackets ([]), 642
state sequence, generating, 268
statistical hypotheses, testing, 491
Stripes design pattern, 203
subtraction operator (–), 641
support counts, 163
Surv() function, 436
survival analysis (see Cox regression)
survivor function, S(t), 435
symbolic training data, 329, 334-342

T

t-tests
    applications for, 492
    basics of, 491
    expected output, 496
    Hadoop implementation, 499

    implementation of, 493
    input, 496
    MapReduce
        problem statement, 495
        solution, 496
    Spark solution
        algorithm, 507
        final output, 511
        high-level steps, 500
        input, 509
        overview of, 499
        steps for, 503-506
        YARN script for, 510
takeOrdered(), 73-80
TemplateEngine class, 421
TemplateEngine.createDynamicContentAs-File() method , 421
TextInputFormat class, 557, 566
thumbs up/down reviews, 363
thymine, 547
time complexity, 156
time series data, 131
time-ordered transactions, generating, 262
TimeTable data structure, 502
tokenization, 558
toList() function, 169, 284, 607, 616
toListOfString() method, 530
toMap() method, 530
top 10 lists
    MapReduce unique keys solution, 43-46
    MapReduce/Hadoop implementation classes, 47
    MapReduce/Hadoop solution, 81-84
    solution overview, 41
    Spark nonunique keys solution, 62-72
    Spark takeOrdered() solution, 73-80
    Spark unique keys solution, 50-59
    Top N design pattern, 41
    Top N implementation, 42
top 5 lists, 49, 206
Top N design pattern
    example of, 41
        (see also top 10 lists)
    parameterizing in Spark, 59
    for Spark, 52
top() function, 80
Tophat mapper, 573, 579
toStateSequence() method, 285
toWritableList()method, 347

training data, 328
transaction mapper, 90
transaction sequence, converting, 268
transactions, generating time-ordered, 262
transcriptome, 573
transitivity ratio, 369
TreeMap data structure, 482
trends (see Cochran-Armitage test for trend)
triangles, counting, 372
    (see also graph analysis)
Twitter, 365
    (see also sentiment analysis)
two-sample test (see t-test)

U

union() function, 95
unique enough, 392
unsupervised learning, 292
    (see also K-Means clustering algorithm)
user mapper, 90
utility functions, 169, 607

V

value-to-key conversion (see secondary sort
    problems)
variant detection, 428
VCF (variant call format)
    basics of, 467
    in allelic frequency, 465

    in Cochran-Armitage trend test, 447
    in DNA sequencing, 428
vertices, 369

W

word count, 659
word-sense disambiguation, 363
Writable interface, 189, 347

X

X chromosome, 490

Y

Y chromosome, 490
YARN
    gene aggregation solution
        filter by average, 619
        filter by individual, 609
    K-mer counting script, 405
    k-Nearest neighbors script, 325
    Naive Bayes classifier (NBC) script, 355, 360
    Pearson correlation script, 544
    running Spark in cluster mode, 23, 717-720
    running Spark on, 106
    Spark market basket analysis implementa-
        tion, 178
    t-test script, 510

About the Author

Mahmoud Parsian, Ph.D. in Computer Science, is a practicing software professional with 30 years of experience as a developer, designer, architect, and author. For the past 15 years, he has been involved in Java (server-side), databases, MapReduce, and distributed computing. Dr. Parsian currently leads Illumina's Big Data team, which is focused on large-scale genome analytics and distributed computing. He leads the development of scalable regression algorithms; DNA sequencing and RNA sequencing pipelines using Java, MapReduce, Hadoop, HBase, and Spark; and open source tools. He is also the author of *JDBC Recipes* and *JDBC Metadata, MySQL, and Oracle Recipes* (both from Apress).

Colophon

The animal on the cover of *Data Algorithms* is a mantis shrimp, a designation that comprises the entire order *Stomatopoda*. The several hundred species that make up the stomatopod kingdom have so far kept many of their customs and habits secret because they spend much of their lives in holes dug in the seabed or in caves in rock formations. The mantis shrimp appears more abundantly in tropical and subtropical waters, though some species do inhabit more temperate environments.

What is known about the mantis shrimp sets it apart not only from other arthropods, but also other animals. Among its several distinctive traits is the swiftness with which it can maneuver its two raptorial appendages. Capable of striking at a speed 50 times faster than humans can blink, the shape of these claws give the order its common name and is optimized either for clubbing hard-shelled crustaceans to death or for spearing fish and other soft-bodied prey. So fast does each claw move in an attack that it delivers an extra blow to its victim by way of collapsing cavitation bubbles. Mantis shrimp have been known to use the awesome force of this strike to break the glass of aquariums in which they have been confined.

No less singular are the complex eyes of the mantis shrimp. Mounted on stalks, each eye has stereo vision and can make use of up to 16 photoreceptor pigments (compare this to the three visual pigments of the human eye). In the last year, researchers have begun attempting to replicate in cameras the extreme sensitivity of some mantis shrimp eyes to polarized light, which could allow doctors to more easily identify cancerous tissue in humans.

Many of the animals on O'Reilly covers are endangered; all of them are important to the world. To learn more about how you can help, go to *animals.oreilly.com*.

The cover image is from Wood's *Natural History*. The cover fonts are URW Typewriter and Guardian Sans. The text font is Adobe Minion Pro; the heading font is Adobe Myriad Condensed; and the code font is Dalton Maag's Ubuntu Mono.

Get even more for your money.

Join the O'Reilly Community, and register the O'Reilly books you own. It's free, and you'll get:

- $4.99 ebook upgrade offer
- 40% upgrade offer on O'Reilly print books
- Membership discounts on books and events
- Free lifetime updates to ebooks and videos
- Multiple ebook formats, DRM FREE
- Participation in the O'Reilly community
- Newsletters
- Account management
- 100% Satisfaction Guarantee

Signing up is easy:

1. Go to: oreilly.com/go/register
2. Create an O'Reilly login.
3. Provide your address.
4. Register your books.

Note: English-language books only

To order books online:
oreilly.com/store

For questions about products or an order:
orders@oreilly.com

To sign up to get topic-specific email announcements and/or news about upcoming books, conferences, special offers, and new technologies:
elists@oreilly.com

For technical questions about book content:
booktech@oreilly.com

To submit new book proposals to our editors:
proposals@oreilly.com

O'Reilly books are available in multiple DRM-free ebook formats. For more information:
oreilly.com/ebooks

O'REILLY®

CPSIA information can be obtained at www.ICGtesting.com
Printed in the USA
BVOW05s1634080716

454916BV00011B/49/P